Black Scholars on the Line

African American Intellectual Heritage Series

Paul Spickard and Patrick Miller
Series Editors

Black Scholars
on the Line

*Race, Social Science, and American Thought
in the Twentieth Century*

edited by

JONATHAN SCOTT HOLLOWAY

and

BEN KEPPEL

University of Notre Dame Press
Notre Dame, Indiana

Manufactured in the United States of America

Library of Congress Cataloging-in-Publication Data

Black scholars on the line : race, social science, and American thought in
the twentieth century / edited by Jonathan Scott Holloway and Ben Keppel.
 p.   cm. — (The African American intellectual heritage series)
ISBN-13: 978-0-268-03079-7 (cloth : alk. paper)
ISBN-10: 0-268-03079-0 (cloth : alk. paper)
ISBN-13: 978-0-268-03080-3 (pbk. : alk. paper)
ISBN-10: 0-268-03080-4 (pbk. : alk. paper)
 1. African Americans—Social conditions—20th century.   2. African
Americans—Intellectual life—20th century.   3. African American intellectuals—
History—20th century.   4. African American scholars—History—20th century.
5. Social scientists—United States—History—20th century.   6. United States—
Intellectual life—20th century.   7. Social sciences—United States—History—
20th century.   8. United States—Race relations—History—20th century.
9. Racism—United States—History—20th century.   10. United States—Social
conditions—20th century.   I. Holloway, Jonathan Scott.   II. Keppel, Ben.
E185.86.B535   2007
305.5'5208996073—dc22

2007003385

∞ *The paper in this book meets the guidelines for permanence
and durability of the Committee on Production Guidelines for Book Longevity
of the Council on Library Resources.*

CONTENTS

Part 2.   Building a True Social Science

Introduction   102

Part 3.   African Americans in American Cultural Production

Introduction   210

Part 4. The Political Economy of Race

Introduction 270

Part 5. The World and the Color Line Come Home

Introduction 328

Part 6.   A Science of Society

Introduction   406

ACKNOWLEDGMENTS

This project is the result of a shared and continuing interest in how racial segregation has affected the organization and distribution of knowledge in the United States. Our collaboration has been close from the beginning. Over the last decade, our many discussions at every point have created something neither of us could have imagined at the beginning. For this we owe an especially important debt to Barbara Hanrahan and Chuck Van Hof of Notre Dame Press and to Paul Spickard and Patrick Miller, the editors of the series of which this book is a part. They were scrupulous critics and ardent advocates whenever we were in need of either. Their responses, and those of an anonymous reader, were indispensable to the writing of the essay that introduces this project. As this project entered the production process, Matt Dowd brought a fresh set of eyes and vigor to the all-important final phase. We, of course, accept full responsibility for any shortcomings that remain.

The path to publication was made smoother by the help and support of many people at our respective home institutions over the last decade. At the University of California, San Diego, Roderick Ferguson and Natalie Ring (then graduate students, now both professors!) provided invaluable assistance during our first canvass of the social science literature.

From the very start, Robert L. Griswold, chair of the Department of History at the University of Oklahoma, strongly encouraged us even when the bankability of our vision was in serious question. His support made possible the assistance of Kristin Adams. Her skill and attention to detail at implementing the text that made two essays into one was second to none. A grant from the College of Arts and Sciences Committee in Support of Teaching and Research enabled Sarah Eppler-Janda (now also a professor) to launch the permissions process in a thoroughly organized and professional way. That struggle would have been even more intractable without her. Lee Williams, the Vice President for Research at the University of Oklahoma, also provided essential financial support at a crucial moment.

Without the conscientious and thorough assistance of Joshua Guild, Erin Wood, and Brandi Hughes, all graduate students at Yale, we would still be struggling to clear the technical hurdles that too frequently presented themselves as we labored to bring this project to completion. John Johnson's deft use of OCR software (and Ed Kairiss's watchful eye) saved us hours upon hours of difficult and expensive transcribing. The exacting work of reading proof was completed in excellent fashion by Lawrence Mastroni (OU) and Erin Wood (Yale); to the extent that errors remain, the editors take full responsibility. We note, however, that the articles in this volume have been reproduced to appear as they did in their original publication, which means that, occasionally, some mistakes and outdated sylistic choices have also been reproduced. Lloyd Suttle, the Deputy Provost for Undergraduate and Graduate Programs at Yale, offered financial assistance to help meet the cost of permissions. Finally, a senior faculty fellowship from Yale and an external faculty fellowship from the Stanford Humanities Center made it possible to complete this project.

This book is dedicated to our students at the University of California, San Diego; the University of Oklahoma; and Yale University. Their close attention and consistent interest whenever we raised the issues of this book confirmed that we were focused on issues too often overlooked or misunderstood. We hope that our labors have done justice to them.

INTRODUCTION
Segregated Social Science and Its Legacy

Perhaps the most enduring snapshots of American apartheid are of the "colored only" and "whites only" signs that hung outside of public washrooms throughout the segregated South. Beside these photographs place another, this one of Thurgood Marshall and his colleagues standing on the steps in front of the United States Supreme Court after the triumph of *Brown v. Board of Education* in 1954. These images, reprinted in American history textbooks for every grade level, effectively compress and symbolize an extremely complicated historical process. As important as these pictures are, however, they cannot transmit the full texture of the world they seek to represent. *Black Scholars on the Line: Race, Social Science, and American Thought in the Twentieth Century* gives readers the opportunity to develop a more refined understanding of segregation and its legacy. More specifically, *Black Scholars on the Line* asks how segregation has influenced, and continues to influence, the development of American social thought and social science scholarship. Our reference to scholars being "on the line" has a multiple significance. In the most basic and obvious sense, these were intellectuals writing about "the line," the color bar that cleaved American society apart. As black intellectuals whose scholarship traversed an ideological fault line of their society, they were also "on the line." Lastly, as African Americans, no matter what their politics or professions, these individuals were not just students of racism and segregation, they were also constantly "on the line" as their targets.

One of the most important manifestations of our one-dimensional awareness of segregation's comprehensiveness can be seen in the way we represent its impact on the creation and transmission of knowledge in the United States. For most Americans, the segregation of American education is symbolized by the elementary and secondary school, which was the subject of the U.S. Supreme Court's decision in *Brown v. Board of Education*. While we do not seek to overrule this image in the American mind, we do seek to add to it.

The unanimity of attention given to *Brown* in teaching about how legal segregation was overcome has some unintended consequences when it is trimmed to fit into the American curriculum. *Brown* was but one chapter in a larger historical narrative that must be better understood. Between the generation after slavery and the generation after the Second World War, black scholars played important roles in the founding, elaboration, and refinement of American social science. The groundbreaking work that black attorneys and social scientists—many of whom were trained and worked at historically black colleges and universities—pursued in *Brown* was but one part of this larger development. We honor the scholarship that was related to *Brown* by reprinting social psychologists Kenneth and Mamie Clark's most ambitious discussions of their research on racial attitudes. However, as our first obligation in this project is to place this well-known intellectual priority within a larger context, we showcase other black scholars' work on different topics: migration and its effects, the structure of the black family, the disparate impact of race on economic opportunity, the relationship of cultural production and projection to debates over cultural assimilation, and so forth.

Although the black scholars whose work is found in this anthology received their graduate training at some of the nation's leading historically white universities, they lived, worked, and most frequently published from behind the line of segregation. To the extent that they have been seen at all in the curriculum of contemporary higher education it is typically as supporting players, contributing to but not innovating beyond, for instance, the intellectual edifice built by the white sociologists of the "Chicago School." Black social scientists working at Howard University are a case in point. These figures, ranging from Alain Locke to Abram Harris to Emmett Dorsey to E. Franklin Frazier—all of whom were affiliated with that school's Division of Social Science—are seen as constituting an interesting side chapter in the interwar era debates about capitalism and socialism, but they are not fit within a larger and continuing tradition of dissenting social science. The Howard group, however, was not alone in all of this. Many other brilliant analysts of American culture and political economy also struggled to be heard beyond their professional homes on this nation's black campuses. While we cannot linger long on this point, it bears noting that long-ignored institutions within the African American academy played key roles in the development of social scientific thought: Howard, Fisk, Atlanta, Tougaloo, and Wilberforce, to name but a few. In a similar light, it behooves us to mention the central role that Howard's *Journal of Negro Education* played in the dissemination of cutting-edge modern social science scholarship. A safe harbor for scholarship that asked uncomfortable questions about the role of race in American society, the *Journal of Negro Education* deserves attention from any scholar studying social science in the middle third of the twentieth century. A handful of that journal's gems are published here.

Before proceeding further in this historical discussion, we must set forth some of the assumptions that make this textbook different from other anthologies that chronicle the African American intellectual tradition. First and foremost, our intention in this volume has been to query the effects of a particular social, economic, and political system on the creation, structuring, and distribution of specialized knowledge about that society. How does one's location in the racially segregated American social order affect one's ability to obtain material support and visibility for one's social science? How does the intellectual scaffolding of such a society affect how one organizes and expresses one's point of view, especially if it dissents from received wisdom within that society? How does one calibrate the balance between having one's say—"speaking truth to power"—and preserving one's effective right and ability to speak and gain access to that power? All of these questions are crucial to the work at hand because they point to the relation of "social science" to the broader category of "social thought." Social scientists and the work they generate are subject to social and political forces because, like everything else a society produces, they are made from these materials and processes. What is made from these materials and how these processes are expressed by individuals making choices, seeking and seizing opportunities, and responding to the unexpected are what make the social sciences necessary to study. Given the above, we decided that the most efficient and effective way to address this panoply of issues was to train our sights only on those scholars who were African American and either graduated from or had sustained careers at historically black colleges and universities.

We also recognized early on that too close a fidelity to the boundaries of certain disciplines would lead to an intellectual rigidity that could foster an arbitrary absolutism. For example, while a strong case could be made for the poet Langston Hughes as an intellectual who was more important to social analysis and cultural interpretation than many a social scientist, he nonetheless made no claims upon social science expertise or knowledge. The same cannot be said for his contemporaries Zora Neale Hurston, Sterling Brown, and James Weldon Johnson, whose works have been included here.

Finally, fidelity to our intellectual mission required that we set some boundaries about the writings of social scientists themselves. Because we are particularly concerned with the practice of social science, we have stayed away from writings by social scientists that were intended to fulfill a different, if equally worthy goal, such as outright political advocacy. We also chose not to include selections that, in our opinion, were too narrowly bounded by the needs of a particular political crisis or historical moment. To the best of our ability, we strove to include essays that spoke both to the requirements of their particular moment without seeming too remote from our own.

This history is presented in six parts, proceeding in chronological order. In part 1, we introduce the founding parents of African American social science. These were individuals who produced their scholarship outside the boundaries of sustaining institutional support and yet presented cogent arguments about the social, economic, and political problems engendered by racial thinking in America. In part 2, we turn our attention to the first real generation of professionally trained black scholars. These were the academics who often introduced modern social science curricula to their respective home institutions. In part 3, we examine the interactions between cultural production and social scientific knowledge. The issues that are raised in this section prefigure the more elaborate and sustained debates in cultural studies in our current academic world. In part 4, we find the scholarship produced by the leading progressive social scientists of the day on issues of race and class. The conflicting strategic advice offered by these intellectuals underlines the abiding tension between the primacy of race and class in American society. In part 5, we examine social scientific scholarship that put African American struggles in an international context. While the place or role of blacks in the international sphere predates this country's founding, the sustained social science analysis of this vital dimension was a necessity of the Second World War. In part 6, we capture the scholarship that most effectively highlights the terrifically complex state of "raced" social science thought during the age of desegregation in academia. Perhaps the ultimate irony in the history of race and social science is found here: at the moment when black social scientists undeniably came into their own, other intellectual and civil rights activists, black and white, attacked the very value or premise of social science itself.

Before moving to the thirty-one primary sources that comprise this collection it is important to place the entire body of work in context. In the remainder of the introduction we seek to accomplish this by examining the tensions between race and scholarship, the development of the black scholar as a "type," the emergence of modern social science, the challenges posed to "racial thinking" by desegregation, the continuities and discontinuities that the civil rights era brought to the practice of social science, and then the political economy of higher education in our post–civil rights era.

Social Science and Society

In 1899, Fisk- and Harvard-trained scholar W. E. B. Du Bois published *The Philadelphia Negro: A Social Study,* a path-breaking sociological analysis of urban space and race. In what was the first of many painstaking social surveys of African American life that put him at "the frontier of American social science research," Du Bois ruminated over blacks' place in American society, thinking out loud about the phenomenon of a racial group of people being considered a national problem.[1] "Two sorts of answers," Du Bois mused, "are usually returned to the bewildered American who asks seriously: What is the Negro problem?"

> The one is straightforward and clear: it is simply this, or simply that, and one simple remedy long enough applied will in time cause it to disappear. The other answer is hopelessly involved and complex. . . . Both of these sorts of answers have something of truth in them: the Negro problem, looked at in one way is but the old world questions of ignorance, poverty, crime, and the dislike of the stranger. On the other hand it is a mistake to think that attacking each of these questions single-handed without reference to the others will settle the matter: a combination of social problems is far more than a matter of mere addition—the combination is itself a problem. Nevertheless, the Negro problems are not more hopelessly complex than many others have been. Their elements despite their bewildering complication can be kept clearly in view: they are after all the same difficulties over which the world has grown gray: the question as to how far human intelligence can be trusted and trained; as to whether we must always have the poor with us; as to whether it is possible for the mass of men to attain righteousness on earth.[2]

Du Bois's observations here are instrumental for several reasons. First, they capture the highest ideals and aspirations of the founders of social science. Du Bois's thoughts are also valuable because they express an appreciation for the complexity and interdependence of social forces and social problems. Finally, Du Bois's reference to the attainment of "righteousness on earth" points back to the roots of black social science in a preexisting genre of African American protest grounded in the biblical promise of the unitary nature of humanity.[3]

Du Bois was, by far, one of the most accomplished intellectuals of the several generations that constitute his professional career. Nonetheless, the color line constantly delimited his personal and professional life. One can see the effect of racism in his professional life by examining Du Bois's relationship to established social science more than a century ago. Despite the publication of *The Philadelphia Negro* and a critically important series of conferences and sociological studies he organized at Atlanta University when he taught there in the early 1900s, Du Bois is haltingly acknowledged as a founder of social science because, like the other very few African Americans of his class and training, he could only briefly visit the institutions where the formal founding was underway. For example, although he already held a doctorate from Harvard and had published his first book, *The Suppression of the African Slave Trade to the United States of America, 1638–1870* (the inaugural book in the Harvard Historical Studies series, no less), Du Bois had to complete *The Philadelphia Negro* as a "temporary assistant in sociology," invited to the University of Pennsylvania by Professor Samuel McCone Lindsay.[4]

Like other African Americans of his generation (including those who did not share his advantages of class and education), Du Bois worked in a social, political, and cultural context that provided virtually no institutional support for studies dissenting from the segregationist consensus. And, again, like his African American peers, Du Bois had to be especially attentive to how the world that celebrated segregation would receive his contributions to the founding and professionalization of social science. If we broaden the scope of inquiry to include more individuals, we can see that Du Bois's observations and experiences really are illustrative of broader themes and patterns in the evolving relationship between race and social science thought in the twentieth century.

Industrialism, Segregation, and Social Science

All ideas and institutions are the products of the historical contexts into which they are born. The American system of higher education on both sides of the color line was the offspring of a segregated society. On one side of that line, those attending historically white colleges (and in some states this did include a miniscule number of black Americans) learned a version of the "science of society" that endorsed the racial hierarchy of the day. Even if every state in the Union did not enforce separation with the same exactitude, the idea that African Americans were not fit to be participants in the intellectual work of a rapidly industrializing nation (while they were accepted as among the primary providers of physical labor) was a belief that crossed the lines of class, region, and political party.

In the late 1800s, social science was practiced with a strong moralistic and humanistic tone that was rarely far removed from conservative theological and political practices that justified both segregation and imperialism as part of the natural and hierarchical order of things. Early social science primarily ratified deeply held unscientific assumptions about the rise of some people from "savagery" to "civilization."[5] Following the publication of Charles Darwin's *Origin of Species* in 1859 and *The Descent of Man* in 1871, the three stages of human evolution took on a racial cast such that anthropology, sociology, and evolutionary ethnology supported a "racio-cultural hierarchy" that declared that "only large-brained white men, the highest products of organic evolution, were fully civilized."[6]

On the other side of the line, between the last years of the nineteenth century and the middle years of the twentieth, outstanding African American scholars provided virtually the only objective examinations of African American life. Their segregation away from the centers of intellectual, social, and political power had two results: (1) they were only dimly perceived by the white leaders of social science, and (2) their research received paltry outside financial support when it was supported at all. In spite of this material barrier, Du Bois produced his renowned Atlanta University Studies, which historian Michael R. Winston correctly observed, "were among the first of their kind in any American university and obviously superior to the work supported at that time by white universities."[7]

One set of figures highlights the resource deficit faced in these years by historically black institutions. According to historian Dwight O. Holmes, the sum total of all the money spent in 1928 to operate the country's seventeen black land grant institutions—$1,379,484—was roughly equal to the amount given to each of the several white land grant colleges in the same states.[8] This fact makes plain the material underpinning behind the systematic segregation of the creation of knowledge.

In addition to the difficulties rising from the limited resources available at black colleges and universities, African American academics faced other challenges to generating original scholarship. First, teaching, not research, was the mission at even the most prestigious institutions. In 1911, Du Bois described the conditions at his Atlanta University, then the capital of African American social science research, quite directly:

> Our financial resources are unfortunately meager. Atlanta University is primarily a school and most of its funds and energy go to teaching. It is, however, also a seat of learning and as such it has endeavored to advance knowledge, particularly in matters of racial contact and development. . . . In this work [Atlanta University] has received unusual encouragement from the scientific world. . . . On the other hand the financial support given this work has been very small. The cost of the fifteen publications [the Atlanta series] has been about $17,000. . . . Three years ago a small grant from the Carnegie Institution of Washington, D.C., greatly helped us; and for three years our work was saved from suspension by the John F. Slater Fund. . . . May we not hope in the future for such increased financial resources as will enable us to study adequately this greatest group of social problems that ever faced America?[9]

Predictably, these material circumstances had important tangible and intangible consequences for the daily life and work of the black scholar. Decades after Du Bois lamented the tepid financial support for research at Atlanta, sociologist Hylan Lewis outlined the other customary challenges that defined life at historically black colleges:

> With few exceptions, the college for Negroes operates in a setting which is largely alien: if the setting is not actively hostile, it is nearly always potentially so. This is a mental hazard to which adjustment must be made. Most colleges are in the South and many are in small towns or rural areas. In even the most favorable situations, there is but limited access to community resources—meager as they usually are—for classroom and research activities, for leisure time activities, and for the satisfaction of incidental personal interests of students and staff. . . . There is a kind of uneasy self-sufficiency forced upon persons in the campus community. For many, learning and working comes to be a tour of duty and the periodic "return to civilization"—the vacation trip to the metropolis—is a seasonal rite. Many teachers and would-be scholars are wont to moan of their lack of production, their frustration and loneliness.[10]

It ought not come as a surprise that black and white scholars and historically black and white institutions faced qualitatively and quantitatively different hurdles in their respective quests for personal and professional satisfaction and solvency. But, as frustrating and debilitating as the effects of the political economy of racism must have been for individuals and institutions, we cannot afford to be blind to the ways in which the black and white worlds of academe overlapped. Most black and white scholars, for example, mutually embraced some values that we no longer celebrate. What historian Waldo Martin observed about Frederick Douglass applies equally to his immediate successors in "race leadership." Although Douglass denounced the oppression of non-Western people by Europeans and Americans, he "essentially accepted . . . the dominant Anglo-American cultural paradigm . . . though he rejected its racism."[11] In a similar way, Du Bois, despite being a pioneering student of ancient African civilization, an anti-imperialist, and a tireless advocate for African American equality, held a paternalistic attitude toward Africa and the non-Western world generally. Like the other intellectual leaders of his time, Du Bois believed that Africans did not possess among their millions sufficient indigenous leadership for self-rule. Whether one finds it ironic or not, just as leading white scholars felt that they spoke to and for the world's civilized people, Du Bois and his peers were quite convinced that they spoke to the civilized for the uncivilized.[12]

We draw attention to the elitism in the African American scholarly tradition not to engage in some politically facile or morally gratuitous revisionism. For us, these contradictory values must be given some attention because they were also part and parcel of the intellectual world on both sides of the color line. No matter the color of their skin, most individuals who pursued intellectual careers came from environments in which the separation of the intellectual from the masses was cherished if not encouraged. This ideology that separated the "talented tenth" of black America from those they were expected to lead often skewed the analysis that followed in ways that stand out to contemporary eyes.

In addition to this mutual intellectual inheritance of presumptive individual authority and Western superiority, there are also some shared patterns of institutional development in the late nineteenth century that bear noting. For example, where the development of African American institutions is typically seen from a very narrow, restricted, and racial context, the truth is more complicated. For instance, the development of black colleges and land grant schools are seen as creations of segregation and as pawns in a strategic debate between two "race men"—the conservative accommodationist Booker T. Washington and the liberal interracialist Du Bois. Although these interpretations contain important elements of truth, they are never connected to the unifying historical context of industrialization. Higher education in the United States, on both sides of the color line and in all regions of the nation, was created to serve the requirements of the industrial economy.

It is true, for instance, that black colleges and universities operated for many years as the equivalent of high schools before having a majority of students who were enrolled in college-level courses.[13] But, in so doing, these schools were reenacting, to a more extreme degree, a pattern followed by some leading state universities founded in the nineteenth century.[14] The establishment of collegiate institutions to educate newly freed African Americans was part of a larger national effort to professionalize American higher education, and make it at once less exclusive and also more geared to the needs of an expanding industrial order in need of highly trained workers. When we observe the heavy-handedness of Booker T. Washington we should keep in mind the words of historians Merle Curti and Vernon Carstensen. Writing about the particular circumstances of the American state university, they arrive at a conclusion that applies on both sides of the color line, in both public and private contexts. Curti and Carstensen pointed out that "a host of politically pertinent but educationally irrelevant elements," especially the "conflicting and contradictory impulses imposed by individuals and groups who at one time or another have stood in a position of power," have shaped the development of colleges and universities.[15]

What we recognize today as the basic modern university structure—a student body comprised of undergraduates and graduates, and an expressed dual commitment to teaching and research—came later to historically black institutions than to historically white ones. But in the 1930s, an increase in and regularization of federal support for Howard University and the equally heavy investment of philanthropies—especially the Julius Rosenwald Fund and the Rockefeller Foundation—in Howard, Atlanta, and Fisk Universities translated into a new institutional design and structure for these schools.[16] With this largesse, the very best black universities now mirrored their white counterparts, and in short order these institutions attracted the very best black intellectual talent to their respective campuses.

All of the above is not to suggest that black and white scholars shared the same ideological outlook in all aspects of their lives, nor is it to suggest that segregation was an uncomplicated boon to the development of historically black colleges. Rather, this richly contradictory history and intellectual heritage demonstrates two realities of segregated life. First, as much as the color bar worked to separate the black and white worlds of higher education, there were always commonalities that brought them together. Arguably the most important of these, as we have noted earlier, was a deeply entrenched belief in the superiority of Western culture and the corresponding immaturity of African peoples. Second, although the color bar meant that black and white institutions developed at different paces and with different sets of resources, this does not mean that black institutions were structurally incapable of fulfilling any mission beyond the circumscribed one envisioned by some of their philanthropic supporters. As we document the structural barriers faced by black colleges and universities, it is also important that we do not artificially add to the distance created by segregation by holding high the historically white institutions as idealized models of what was meant by the phrase "higher education."

The Development of the Black Scholar

As we have seen, the ideology of white supremacy and the concomitant policy of segregation placed special obstacles in the path of creating an African American intellectual class. The determination of former slaves and their allies to overcome these forces caused a dramatic push to educate blacks. Black schools were built at a stunning rate, black churches extended their work into the educational realm, and a host of normal (teaching) and industrial colleges dotted the landscape. More than any other institution, the church and the school rapidly became the stable center of black community affairs and just as often served similar purposes: the training of good citizens who would then travel forth to save the rest of the race.[17] This practice, commonly referred to as "uplift," was at once simple and complicated. It represented an honest attempt by educated and middle-class blacks to improve the quality of life for those who were less fortunate. But uplift was also burdened with socially conservative class and gender ideologies that denigrated the subjects it sought to cleanse literally and figuratively.[18] Churches and schools were the "discursive spaces" where the ideas for this sort of work took root and then flourished.[19]

Building upon the institutional framework of the black church, the pedagogical training of the black school, and the cultural and moral collaboration of the home, other entities joined this social welfare project. Social service organizations and betterment groups sprang up in the late 1800s and turned their attention to struggling blacks. The National Association of Colored Women, established in 1896, serves as a case in point. Its motto, "Lifting While We Climb," acknowledged both the distance even middle-class blacks had to travel to gain full citizenship rights and the social obligation these blacks had to assist those they identified as beneath them.

It is in this context that we can best understand the genesis of the black scholar. Much as ministers respond to a call to faith in the church, early black thinkers responded to a call to service in their scholarship. As often as not, the church, the school, the home, and the academy were intertwined. Although the institutions of the middle to late 1800s were not literally training the black scholars of the future, they were doing critical work in training a cadre of black teachers, lay and religious, to educate the black masses and improve their life chances. Indeed, these worlds interacted with great frequency and apparent ease. For example, scholarly practices in the black community emerged from critical and, as historian Evelyn Brooks Higginbotham points out, feminist interpretations of the Bible.[20] While this practice did not represent a watershed moment in the history of the Bible as text, it was a dramatic break for a community that less than a generation earlier was denied the opportunity to become literate, much less practice an organized faith. Simply put, the standard educational training for blacks was for an explicit political purpose—uplift—and was often rooted in the traditions of the black church, the black schoolhouse, the home, and the betterment organization.

It is customary to attack segregation for the manifest social and economic inefficiency created by the need for duplicate and alternate institutions. The preceding discussion of the intellectual missionary work done by African American churches and other self-help agencies touches upon something equally important but far harder to capture. Segregation shaped the very texture and substance of the ideas themselves.

The most important move toward an institutional framework for black scholars can be seen in the Reverend Alexander Crummell's brainchild, the American Negro Academy (ANA). Founded in 1897, the ANA represented an attempt by black scholars to improve the community's intellectual life and the quality of its leadership. This new leadership, in turn, would be better equipped to disprove arguments about black social, cultural, and intellectual inferiority.[21] In his capacity as the first president of the ANA, Crummell urged its members to join in his quest to uplift the race. He believed that intellectuals—those who had "secured the vision which penetrates the center of nature"—would provide salvation for blacks: "In all the great revolutions, and in all great reforms which have transpired, scholars have been conspicuous; in the re-construction of society, in formulating laws, in producing great emancipations, in the revival of letters, in the advancement of science, in the renaissance of art, in the destruction of gross superstitions and in the restoration of true and enlightened religion."[22] The backbone of Alexander

Crummell's agenda, then, was a clearly stated and unbending belief in a hierar-chically ordered society where the enlightened intelligentsia guided the masses toward salvation. For Crummell, "The Negro problem in the U.S. [was] a problem of ideas."[23] But Crummell did not expect all blacks to participate in solving this problem. Although he opposed Booker T. Washington's politics and educational policies, he conceded there was an important role to be played by industrial education schools. In this regard, Crummell felt that women had a special, if secondary, role to play.

Crummell epitomized the double-edged nature of uplift when he urged women to do the important work of cleansing the unclean and protecting the unprotected while simultaneously respecting their own second-class status within the black community. Crummell believed, for example, that too many women were receiving "improper" education. He felt that women-only in-dustrial training schools needed to be established in order to support the civi-lizing of the race. After all, he argued, women would be better able to sup-port their male partners' struggles if the women were properly trained in the "practical" and the "home life."[24] The intelligentsia was for men only.

True to form and to Crummell's beliefs, over the course of its thirty-three year existence, the ANA only entertained one female guest speaker: writer and educator Anna Julia Cooper.[25] Cooper, whose 1892 opus *A Voice from the South* embodied both Victorian uplift ideology and a gender analysis of black leadership, was adamantly opposed to Washington's vocational educa-tion schemes. In fact, her anti-Washington opinions in *A Voice from the South* predate Du Bois's similar sentiments in *The Souls of Black Folk* (1903). How-ever, those men who would have been Cooper's colleagues in academia largely ignored her. Cooper perfectly summed up this willful blindness in *A Voice from the South*: "It seems hardly a gracious thing to say, but it strikes me as true, that while our men seem thoroughly abreast of the times on almost every other subject, when they strike the woman question they drop back into six-teenth century logic. . . . I fear the majority of colored men do not yet think it worth while [*sic*] that women aspire to higher education."[26]

The very nature of social science work emerged in a contentious struggle with the daily and professional lives of black scholars. They often accepted the methodological imperatives of their respective disciplines within the orbit of social science, but they did so often by perpetuating destructive stereotypes about group and individual behavior: uncivilized Africans, unworthy poor, and unqualified females. As we consider the intellectual substance of their contributions, it is important to remember the material context in which this generation of black scholars worked.

The Development of Modern Social Science

The pioneers of modern social science self-consciously strove for a more avowedly relativistic tone and scientific method than their moralistic predecessors of the middle to late nineteenth century. William Thomas and Florian Znaniecki's *The Polish Peasant in Europe and America,* which historian Eli Zaretsky notes stood "on the cusp between nineteenth-century social theory and modern empirical social science," is an excellent starting point for examining the founding assumptions of American social science.[27] Thomas and Znaniecki, both sociologists, set out to catalog and understand the forces assisting or preventing immigrant populations from adjusting to life in the United States. Among Thomas and Znaniecki's many methodological innovations was the fact that the scholars let the reader hear the immigrants speak in their own voices—going so far as to convince one of their subjects to write a three hundred page autobiography.[28] Thomas and Znaniecki concluded that Polish immigrants struggled in America because their community's social structures collapsed under the pressure of migration and conflict with a different, dominant culture. Ultimately, the immigrants' best hopes resided within their own social networks. Until these networks learned to assimilate into the dominant cultural norms and mores of American society—and thus created a new Polish American identity—the immigrant community would suffer from its own vice and creeping immorality.[29] Their claims about Polish immigrants aside, here we can see Thomas and Znaniecki's lasting and most problematic conceptual contribution to the social sciences: the concept of "social disorganization."

Robert Park, founder of the "Chicago School" of urban sociology, sought to apply Thomas and Znaniecki's conceptual model to the lives of African Americans who were migrating from the rural South to the urban North in search of greater economic opportunity and personal freedom. Park believed that blacks, though native-born Americans going back generations, were nonetheless "socially disorganized" because they had been stripped of their African culture by slavery. Park argued that this rupture in black American social and cultural structure was a natural phenomenon—as social interaction was cyclical and always tended toward balance, disorganization was simply a step toward reorganization.[30] Park thought balance, which for blacks meant the assimilation into the dominant, white culture, would be achieved as they progressed through the cycle: contact-competition-accommodation-assimilation.[31]

Compared to the ideas that characterized social thought in the first years of the twentieth century, Park's work was an advance, but a relatively modest one. It was no great leap to go from the logic of the anthropologist Robert Bennett Bean to that of the sociologist Park. Writing in 1906, Bean drew conclusions from his measurements of white and black brain capacity. For Bean, whites were "dominant and domineering, and possessed primarily with determination, will power, self control, [and] self-government." In contrast, "the Negro is primarily affectionate, immensely emotional, then sensual, and under stimulation passionate. There is love of ostentation, of outward show, of approbation; there is love of music, and capacity for melodious articulation; there is undeveloped artistic power and taste—Negroes make good artisans, handicraftsmen—and there is instability of character incident to lack of self-control, especially in connection with the sexual relation; and there is lack of *orientation,* or recognition of position and condition of self and environment, evidenced by a peculiar bumptiousness."[32]

Park had similar things to say about blacks in his *Introduction to the Science of Sociology,* a textbook he coauthored in 1924 with fellow Chicago sociologist Ernest Burgess. Park found that blacks' characteristics manifested themselves in a "genial, sunny, and social disposition, in an interest and attachment to external, physical things rather than to subjective states and objects of introspection, in a disposition for expression rather than enterprise and action. . . . He is primarily an artist, loving life for its own sake. His *metier* is expression rather than action. He is, so to speak, the lady among races."[33]

Even though Park became well known for the role he played in training important black sociologists, the fact remains that his viewpoints represented a fundamental challenge for his students. By their very presence at the University of Chicago, his students either were true exceptions to Park's theories about black potential (and, therefore, at some sociological level they could no longer be "black") or they were living embodiments that disproved Park. In addition to finding the intellectual space to incorporate Park's ideas along with their own theories, students such as E. Franklin Frazier had to preserve the sanctity of this space in light of the external realities created by the racial veil. For example, even though Frazier agreed with Park that the ravages and social stresses of the middle passage, slavery, emancipation, and migration erased African culture, Frazier did not subscribe to the view that blacks possessed an inferior culture or that they were "the lady among races." Frazier found comparisons to other cultures "invidious" and, in any event, believed that "black culture" was American culture.[34] Modern social science, because of its critical engagement with the problems of such social processes as cultural contact, migration, assimilation, and struggle, became an area of scholarship particularly germane to the black experience over the course of the twentieth century. Not only did the discipline pay special attention to African Americans, black intellectuals dedicated themselves to the development of the discipline. As the brief Park-Frazier example makes clear, these two streams often flowed in different directions, frequently coming together but creating eddies of dissension where they met. But the story of the black intellectual, social science, and their mutual development did not end with the mid-century emergence of the graduate programs in the social sciences at black universities or the generalized acceptance of modern social science methodologies on college campuses across the country. In fact, quite the opposite occurred.

Desegregated Thinking in a Segregated World

Try as they might, the white leadership of the nation did not have absolute control over the generation of new ideas or the institutions that spawned them. Individual and collective thought and action are too complicated and open-ended to fall easily into line with any particular system of hegemony. For example, the hegemony of segregationist thinking did not prevent the formation of the National Association for the Advancement of Colored People (NAACP), although it did materially impede its effort to make lynching a federal crime. Segregation did not muzzle Du Bois as he systematically wrote against white supremacy and the repression of African Americans. It did, however, powerfully control the distribution of his ideas and those of his colleagues behind the line.

This brings us to two essential episodes immediately preceding the desegregation of American social science: the publication of Gunnar Myrdal's pioneering indictment of segregation, *An American Dilemma: The Negro Problem and Modern Democracy,* and the lesser-known release by the University of North Carolina Press of the important protest anthology *What the Negro Wants,* edited by Howard University historian Rayford Logan. These texts, both published in 1944, tangibly capture the power of the segregationist paradigm even as world events were bringing it down. *An American Dilemma,* a summary of a collaboration between Myrdal and some of the most outstanding social scientists of that time, was six years in the making and was given instant credibility because it had been funded by the Carnegie Corporation. In addition, *An American Dilemma* stood apart because its formal author was a Swedish political economist, someone who had lived outside of American culture and was thus perhaps not so sympathetic to well-worn rationalizations for the dichotomy between American professions of egalitarianism and American practices of discrimination. The intellectual prestige of *An American Dilemma* was so great that the Supreme Court cited it in footnote 11 to its 1954 ruling in the *Brown v. Board of Education* decision.[35]

Myrdal's findings delighted many while infuriating others. Those who advocated a racial status quo were sorely disappointed when Myrdal claimed that the "Negro problem" originated primarily in "what goes on in the minds of white Americans" and that race discrimination was an irrational deviation from the "American Creed" that recognized liberty and justice for all.[36] Although Myrdal was, in a sense, quite brave and revolutionary in assigning responsibility for the unequal treatment of blacks to the psychological delusions of whites, such an approach continued a process of historical evasion by examining black achievement only to the degree that it demonstrated the damage done by whites.[37]

What is most important about *An American Dilemma* for our discussion is that, although published as a single-author study, it was in fact a large-scale recognition of the black scholar as social science expert. Over thirty social science consultants were hired for the project, the majority of whom were African American. Among this group, Howard University political scientist Ralph Bunche was, without doubt, the most important. His prodigious writings covering four book-length volumes provided the factual and analytical foundation for much of Myrdal's writing. Nonetheless, Bunche's and others' work, when accepted by Myrdal, was sequestered to the footnotes.[38] As such, for all its intellectual courage, *An American Dilemma* also reflected the segregation of scholars within the social science of its day.

The decision to mute black scholars' contributions to *An American Dilemma* was symptomatic of publishing practices in academe. In *Social Forces*, the established journal most receptive to publishing work by leading black scholars, African American academics' essays on black life were published in a section at the back on "minorities." Furthermore, much of black social scientists' scholarship was published behind the color line in journals tied to historically black universities, such as *Phylon* at Atlanta University and the *Journal of Negro Education* at Howard. Black social scientists also found publication opportunities in the journals of extra-institutional organizations dedicated to racial matters, such as the *Journal of Negro History,* produced by Carter G. Woodson's Association for the Study of Negro Life and History; *Crisis,* published by the NAACP under Du Bois's editorship; and *Opportunity,* edited by Charles Johnson and published by the National Urban League.

For this reason alone, the publication of *What the Negro Wants* is important for the way that it tested the boundaries of the segregation of intellectuals and ideas. This indispensable collection of African American thought originated in 1942 with W. T. Couch, director of the University of North Carolina Press, and Guy Johnson, a leading sociologist at the university. *What the Negro Wants* was intended as an answer to what Couch and Johnson, both southern white liberals, learned was Myrdal's forthcoming indictment of white America. Couch and Johnson recruited Rayford Logan to edit the volume. Logan's task was, on the surface, simple: have some of the most prominent black leaders in the country across the political spectrum write an essay declaring "what the Negro wants."[39]

The final product angered Couch because it reinforced Myrdal's assertion that segregation was an indefensible conflict with the "American Creed." *What the Negro Wants* was even more effective in scoring this point as it provided what Myrdal did not: direct testimony from African Americans (of all political stripes) that equality was their foremost demand and aspiration. Couch was not to be denied, and wrote an introduction to the text that provided an opportunity to "remove any possible ambiguity" about his own view on the subject of black equality: "the Negro's condition is produced by inferiority, but that this inferiority can be overcome, and the prejudice resulting from it can be cured. The white man can help, *but the main part of the task rests on the Negro.*"[40] Couch also added a peculiar postscript, wrapping his urgings of political quietism on the part of black leaders in a language that clumsily manipulated the rhetoric and logic of egalitarianism to preserve its opposite: "today the Negro's interest requires . . . that he not be so much concerned over the label 'equal,' but that he concentrate all of his energies on being not merely equal to, but better than the white man."[41]

The Civil Rights Movement Challenges Social Science

If the continuing power of segregation as an accepted social norm shaped both the content and distribution of social science through the 1950s, it is natural that the destruction of this consensus by the death of European colonialism and by the rise of the civil rights movement in the United States had important consequences for social science disciplines. This process began with one of the proudest moments for progressive social science: the Supreme Court's verdict in *Brown v. Board of Education.* However, as the implementation of *Brown* moved forward, the role of these scholars got lost in a debate that was made sometimes brutally polarized because it was so long overdue.[42] Intellectual-activists with experience in the civil rights movement rose to ask fundamental questions about the established practice of social science with reference to African Americans: What was the role of social science in society—was it primarily descriptive? On what basis were certain practices privileged as "normative" while others were categorized as "deviant"? What should be the role of the social scientist in the process of social change?

The pivotal moment in the collision between social science and the civil rights movement arrived with the 1965 publication of Daniel Patrick Moynihan's *The Negro Family: The Case for National Action* (more commonly known as "the Moynihan Report"). Moynihan, then an Assistant Secretary of Labor in Lyndon B. Johnson's presidential administration, claimed that black urban poverty was a result of family disorganization, matriarchy, and a pathological culture. In drawing these conclusions Moynihan leaned heavily, but incompletely, on E. Franklin Frazier's pioneering work on the black family. Whereas Frazier saw disorganization as a necessary step in a process of reorganization, Moynihan saw disorganization as the final state of being. Unfortunately for Frazier, the prominence of Moynihan's highly selective citation of his work led to Frazier's indictment, along with Moynihan, as a member of a "pejorative tradition" that attacked black cultural patterns and the urban poor.[43] But perhaps most infuriating to its early critics was that Moynihan dedicated forty-five pages of the report to describing a "tangle of pathology" and a scant few words in its page and a half conclusion to possible solutions beyond advocating, without any further elaboration, a "national effort . . . towards the question of family structure."[44] Given the report's documentation of the history of racism in American life, the subsequent decision to highlight only the depth of the problem struck many as, at best, an act of professional and political negligence of the most serious kind.

For their part, critics of the Moynihan Report within social science and within the civil rights movement treated the text as an official government pronouncement whose thesis had been the basis for an important and well-received presidential address (which it was) and took justified exception to its rhetorical excesses and methodological shortcomings (especially Moynihan's carelessness on the subject of out-of-wedlock births; he neglected to point out the ways in which, for instance, race and class conceal the true rate of out-of-wedlock births among white Americans).[45] The end result, critics charged, was to suggest the intractability of the social dimension of racial segregation at the very moment when American public opinion seemed most supportive of tackling it. For some social scientists whose training included their participation in the civil rights movement, the Moynihan Report symbolized much that was wrong with social science: the unexamined use of language and statistics merely to confirm the widespread stereotypes held by those in power toward those without it.

Young scholars who entered social science in order to continue the work of the civil rights movement were determined to scrutinize the practice of social science disciplines and find ways to include more fully those being studied in the research process. They were, in essence, subjecting the discipline of their elders to a new kind of outside peer review. Although we invoke the phrase "peer review" here as a metaphor, it was also quite literally undertaken. In his contribution to Joyce Ladner's *The Death of White Sociology: Essays on Race and Culture,* the most important revisionist social science anthology of the civil rights years, political scientist Ronald Walters offered the following account of the practices of Boston's Community Research Review Committee:

> The Committee is composed of a primary group of Black social scientists who are accountable to the community through the Black United Front. Its function is to detect the kind of research planned and in progress that relates to the Black Community, to screen actual research proposals and otherwise to evaluate the project and, finally, to provide the results to the community, which decides whether or not it would be advisable for the studies to be carried out there. If the community decides the study is needed—cool. But if it decides that it is either unnecessary or harmful, then, in the age-old manner, it takes care of business. The Black social scientist must participate in a process which says, in effect, we will no longer participate by passiveness [*sic*] in the destruction and dehumanization of our communities through white social science research. But in order to participate, we need to pay much closer attention to the kind of research that is funded, who does the funding, who carries out the research, what the findings are, who is responsible for dissemination of the findings, and how they are used, and be willing to intervene at any stage of the process. This is one type of viable defensive strategy which also has an offensive connotation.[46]

The dangers of such oversight to the conduct of ideologically and politically independent research here are clear. For the moment, however, it is important to focus on what movement social scientists saw as the proper relationship between social science and those groups and individuals being studied. That some blacks were uneasy about social science and its assumptions can be seen as far back as the late 1800s when Du Bois was researching *The Philadelphia Negro*. When Du Bois began his meticulous door-to-door rounds through Philadelphia's Seventh Ward in August 1896, David Levering Lewis tells us that "more than a few times, [Du Bois] was challenged at the front door with the question, 'Are we animals to be dissected and by some unknown Negro at that?'"[47]

As necessary and essential as the questions asked by the civil rights era social science revisionists were, they were no more capable than Moynihan of anticipating the consequences of that debate. Sociologist William Julius Wilson has persuasively argued that the debate over the black family caused by the Moynihan Report squelched further research and caused some scholars to overemphasize strengths at the expense of genuinely worsening conditions.[48] This, Wilson suggested, discouraged liberal social scientists from further investigating the issues spotlighted by Moynihan and created an opening for conservative politicians and their allies in social science to redefine the problems of the African American underclass as originating with that group's alleged pathology.[49]

Black scholars of the civil rights movement came to their work with a different set of values and standards that they believed would better serve objective scholarship and constructive action. In this context, it was not that words such as "deviance" should be banished from the social scientist's descriptive and analytical vocabulary. Rather, such words or concepts needed to be scrutinized and used sparingly. The founding generation had given too little attention to the possibility that the premise of deviant behavior could be, to quote Joyce Ladner, "the invention of a group that uses its own standards as the ideal by which others are to be judged."[50]

Revisionist social scientists who were living through the upending of a social system too long in place proposed a "conflict model" that, in the words of sociologist Edgar G. Epps, "allows us to give full value to the efforts of minority groups to effect change in their own positions relative to other groups."[51] Prior scholarship by the founding generation of African Americans in social science had, like their mentors, interpreted African American life through the prism of the "'order model' [by which] members of ethnic and racial minorities are viewed as 'deviant' groups which must adjust to the institutionalized norms of society."[52]

Even Kenneth and Mamie Phipps Clark, whose "doll studies" remain iconic as examples of research for constructive social action, came in for serious critique.[53] Ladner spoke diplomatically for many of her generation when she argued that, because the Clarks' studies focused so exclusively on the damage caused by white racism, they had missed an important dimension of the black experience. "While it cannot be denied that the system of oppression has taken a heavy toll on the psychological and physical development of the Black child and adult," Ladner acknowledged, "it can be questioned . . . whether or not the impact has been as severe as some scholars maintain."[54] According to social critic Albert Murray, Kenneth Clark's brief for "community action" in Harlem, a monograph titled *Dark Ghetto,* represented "a point of view which is essentially white" because it viewed "all black behavior [as] only a pathetic manifestation of black cowardice, self-hatred, escapism and self destruction." Here, Murray submitted Clark to the same process of distortion that Moynihan and some of his critics had inflicted upon E. Franklin Frazier.[55]

Even though there were real differences separating them, some of the most important scholars who toiled "behind the line" and those blacks who crossed that line during the civil rights movement in the 1960s shared a heightened awareness of the dangers of being too quick to label and theorize about the complex lives of those without power. They insisted that the professional students of human behavior use words like "dysfunctional," "deviant," or "pathological"—and the models of which they are an integral part—sparingly and with exquisite care, understanding that these words are laden with all kinds of unscientific associations and implications about which races, people, and classes are worthy of respect and which are not. Hylan Lewis warned that these words, carelessly deployed, become little more than mere "slogans," a shorthand substitute for doing meticulous fieldwork. Speaking to the conceptual reductionism that the profligate reliance on such terms generated since the 1960s, Lewis asked an especially pertinent question: "If we identify a group of people who live in a certain area by some trait, what do we know about them? We know nothing that we did not *believe* already. And what do we do about their plight? The answer is nothing that we did not already plan to do."[56]

As we look back upon the shifts in ideology and perspective that defined social science's evolution over the twentieth century and place them beside the world in which we live, we must acknowledge the misplaced hope that a socially scientific critical engagement with society would fundamentally change things for the better. Part of the reason for this, of course, lies in the long-term backlash against the mid-century period of reform. Also, social science itself has changed. The range of ideas and approaches represented within the disciplines of social science is far wider and more varied than it was when Gunnar Myrdal acted as a spokesman to the public for an ascending ideology within social science. Today, as historian Dorothy Ross has observed, divisions created during the 1960s have been institutionalized as subfields "rarely communicating with each other or contributing to a common matrix."[57]

The Political Economy of Higher Education in the Postwar Era

The debates over poverty, social structure, and culture ignited by the civil rights generation led to an important reorientation of method and ideology within those disciplines most directly engaged with the issues posed by that movement, especially history, sociology, and psychology. When turning from ideas and intellectual priorities to institutions, however, change is less evident. American higher education, like the society of which it is part, has, in a narrowly legal sense, been desegregated, while the social and economic challenge of access has become a deepening problem as federal and state governmental support for both students and schools decreases. New perspectives on race and poverty from within the academy have not led to a new politics in the communities exterior to them. As historian Charles V. Hamilton suggested in 1971, "the black social scientist has no more certain influence or power with white decision-makers than his forefathers. And, in most cases, he has very little more research funds."[58] Even at their strongest moments, support for sustained attention to the divides of race and class was both fleeting and fragile.

Turning to institutional issues, historically black colleges have, with difficulty, survived the threat to them posed by the desegregation of elite historically white institutions. Black schools have enjoyed a modest growth in federal support, but because they are predominantly small institutions dedicated to teaching rather than research, they never benefited from the vast increase in defense-related federal spending on higher education that began in the 1950s. The most important non-defense source of federal support, and the only one to reach black colleges and universities, was the Higher Education Act of 1965, which established the first student aid awarded entirely on the basis of an individual's economic need and allocated substantial funds for campus buildings.[59] Nonetheless, those historically black colleges and universities that, in the words of Benjamin Mays, long-time president of Morehouse University, had "been kept on 'short grass' for a hundred years" remained there.[60] As late as 1984, only 0.4 percent of National Science Foundation research funds went to an historically black college or university.[61]

The Higher Education Act did earmark $20 million in Title III funds (aimed at assisting "developing institutions") to raise the "academic quality of colleges which have the desire and potential to make a substantial contribution to the higher education resources of our Nation but which for financial or other reasons are struggling for survival and are isolated from the main currents of academic life."[62] This section, according to close students of the legislation, was directed at the needs of small black colleges in the South. It is, perhaps, important evidence of the fragility of the consensus behind the reforms of the 1960s that the allocation to Title III was largely symbolic—and minuscule enough not to trigger debate, much less outright Southern opposition to a bill with otherwise nearly unanimous bipartisan support. As things turned out, according to scholars Hugh Davis Graham and Nancy Diamond, "the most numerous beneficiaries of Title III were historically white, rural, sectarian colleges whose institutional resources were similarly depressed."[63]

It is helpful to raise the question here of the consequences of a road not taken. In view of the historical and structural deficits under which historically black colleges and universities have labored from the beginning, it is worth asking why a larger and more sustained effort was not made to help certain capstone schools among these institutions reach full parity with comparable historically white ones as producers of research as well as graduates. Would this have had the unfortunate unintended consequence of having research on African American life migrate to historically black colleges, at the expense of historically white ones? Such speculation cannot be answered definitively, but given the importance of these issues and their interconnectedness with the challenges facing the general American population, such an outcome should not be assumed as automatic. We can be less speculative, however, about the consequences of the development of other academic models that had and continue to have a direct impact upon the lives and minds of black intellectuals and the scholarship that they produce. We are speaking here about the emergence and development of Black Studies as an institutional space on many college campuses as well as a disciplinary field spanning the globe.

Black Studies—Reinstituting the Line?

This book examines how the social fact of segregation affected the development of a social scientific scholarly discourse in the greater part of the twentieth century. Black academics who were trained or worked behind the veil of segregation at one point in their careers brought to their scholarship a special perspective on the distance between the rhetoric of an equal society and the reality of something quite different. But when the veil began to lift after the Second World War it did not mean that this special perspective—what Du Bois termed a "second sight"—disappeared. Indeed, as black scholars began to teach on historically white campuses (an absolute trickle at first in the early 1940s and then only becoming something approaching a trend in the late 1960s) there was an often explicit understanding that their institutional value was based in the presumptive special knowledge that they brought to bear. More often than not, black scholars were hired at white research universities to placate a rising tide of frustration and disaffection by black undergraduates who saw nothing of their life experiences reflected in the curriculum. These new hires were, in effect, pressure valves. Also, beginning in 1968 (and increasing with a torrid pace in the following five years), black scholars were hired to teach in the new Black Studies programs that were cropping up across the academic landscape.

Concluding our introduction with a discussion of the development of formal Black Studies programs and Black Studies as a recognized discipline is something of a departure from our steady focus on individuals and bodies of knowledge that were fostered behind the color line of higher education. However, a closer examination of much of the founding logic of Black Studies speaks loudly to the persistence of the color line even in an academic world that is desegregated by all obvious legal measures. What we want to suggest is that, for many people, once Black Studies began to appear on historically white college campuses (and that is where it made its presence known at first and then almost exclusively) the color line that defined the life and thought of generations of black scholars merely relocated to these new sites.

We have earlier demonstrated how racist thinking and explicitly segregated social structures provided the scaffolding for American social science for much of the last century. Although our public institutions and culture reject racism and segregation, both continue to shape our institutions and our lives. Think for a moment about how easy it is for us to recognize that Black Studies had political origins. Social conventions in American culture and in the academy remind us of how student-led protests at such schools as San Francisco State, Cornell University, and Yale University led directly to curricular changes and the establishment of Black Studies programs.[64] Too often, these same conventions tell us that such "politically motivated" changes have no place in higher education and have weakened this country's once vibrant and wholesome liberal education. These conventions make it equally difficult to see that one hundred years ago far more powerful social and political interests came together to found institutions that ratified another set of assumptions about social relations and political economy. The obscurity of the founding politics of social scientific fields lies in the fact that sociology or anthropology, to pick but two disciplines, were established in accordance with dominant ideologies that embraced a social and economic hierarchy in which white, middle- and upper-class Americans and their experiences were normative.

The circumstances pertaining to the founding of Black Studies programs reflected the cultural, political, and intellectual debates about what Black Studies actually was from the standpoint of a discipline. Was it sufficiently "intellectual"? Was it merely "recuperative"? Was it "redemptive"? Was it "liberatory"? The only fitting answer to these questions is that Black Studies could be any of these things depending on where it was taught and by whom. Some Black Studies programs were founded or staffed by openly political individuals who were convinced that these new programs had a moral commitment to tell "the truth" to America about its own internal failings. Other programs were organized around a determination to destabilize the Eurocentric approach to education and to present a scholarship and philosophy that adhered to Afrocentric models. And yet others were fiercely traditional in their interdisciplinary approach to studying broad themes that grew out of established modes of inquiry found in fields like history, English, political science, psychology, and sociology.

The debate over what Black Studies should be and how it should be taught traveled beyond the literal space on university campuses and was taken up in print. Several journals began to appear in the late 1960s that were dedicated to scholarship that explored Black Studies as an intellectual project. In no small measure, this was a body of knowledge that constituted the foundation of the emerging discipline. Two of the most important journals in this regard are *Black Scholar* and the *Journal of Black Studies*, established in 1969 and 1970, respectively.[65] Even just a quick glance at these two journals illuminates the extent to which the method, structure, and meaning of Black Studies were contested from its inception.

Black Scholar aimed to provide a forum in which "black ideologies can and will be examined, debated, disputed and evaluated by the black intellectual community."[66] This was not outright racism, reverse discrimination, or intellectual resegregation but an explicit attempt to delineate the terms upon which black scholars' ideas would operate and should matter. Floyd B. McKissick, a founding member of *Black Scholar*'s editorial board, spoke directly to this mission when he offered the following analysis of the black academic's role in contemporary American society:

> It is the task of black intellectuals to provide the cohesive philosophy which will propel the black-led revolution which must happen if justice is

to be achieved in America. But these . . . intellectuals cannot provide that philosophy if they continue to be diverted by the opinions and pressures of the surrounding white society. We need not justify any black demands for "separatism" to anybody white. The real separatists moved to the suburbs long ago. . . . We cannot hope to escape interaction with the dominant whites. We cannot wish them out of existence, nor can we avoid their presence completely. What is important is that we remain aloof to their criticisms and reactions.[67]

Although it relied predominantly on well-established scholars for editorial leadership and publications (including Joyce Ladner and Ronald Walters whose work is found in the pages that follow), *Black Scholar* eschewed establishing a home base at a traditional academic institution and reached out to some of the most important African American politicians, writers, and activists of the day like Alice Walker, Eldridge Cleaver, Bobby Seale, and Shirley Chisholm. This was in tune with the desire of *Black Scholar* to court a new kind of thinker: "the man of thought and action, a whole man who thinks for his people and acts with them, a man who honors the whole community of black experience, a man who sees the Ph.D., the janitor, the businessman, the maid, the clerk, the militant as all sharing the same experience of blackness, with all its complexities and its rewards."[68]

By comparison, the *Journal of Black Studies* emphasized a more traditional sense of intellectual mission and structure. Arthur L. Smith, the director of the UCLA Afro-American Studies Center and the journal's editor, made this much evident in his opening editorial when he stated that "the sustained intellectual development of an area cannot be based upon awakening rhetoric" but instead upon the previous tradition developed by an interracial cadre of scholars including Alain Locke, Carter G. Woodson, and Melville Herskovits "who have labored to tell the truth about people of African descent."[69] Under Smith's editorial hand the *Journal of Black Studies* was unambiguous about the kind of work it sought to publish. The *Journal* welcomed submissions that were "intellectually provocative so long as they indicate scholarly rigor. For these purposes, scholarly rigor cannot be limited to the formal setting down of footnotes and documentation; it is an attitude of authorship."[70] Clearly, the "attitude" that Smith sought was not necessarily the same attitude desired by the editors at *Black Scholar.* Even though it first appeared a year after the genre-breaking *Black Scholar,* the *Journal of Black Studies* more closely resembled the models provided by earlier generations of black-run academic journals like the *Journal of Negro Education, Phylon,* and the *Journal of Negro History.*

Seemingly representing different ends of the intellectual and methodological cal spectrum, seen in the proper light *Black Scholar* and the *Journal of Black Studies* reflect the breadth of the evolving Black Studies scholarly project. We do not minimize legitimate differences about how to create an intellectual community and discipline under the heading of "Black Studies" when we argue that a careful reading of *Black Scholar* and the *Journal of Black Studies* reveals a shared commitment to examine in rich detail the warp and woof of African America.

The struggles over the growth of Black Studies from a disciplinary standpoint were in many ways no different from that of any other emergent discipline. The social sciences, after all, appeared as formal disciplines in the late nineteenth century and then evolved in different ways over the next one hundred years, and their shape and style were consistently dependent upon who was taking a particular approach to addressing a problem and where that approach derived its logic. There is a significant distinction to be made, however, between the disciplinary development of Black Studies (which is typically considered a field within social science) and sociology or anthropology or political science: Black Studies experts have had to face down constant challenges to their basic claim that Black Studies is a discipline in the first place.[71]

This is not to say that Black Studies programs and practitioners operate in a purely defensive mode, nor that Black Studies as a field has been unable to thrive in the nearly four decades since its founding. While the number of Black Studies programs has fallen since its early explosion, the disciplinary contributions of Black Studies scholarship to English, history, political science, sociology, anthropology, economics, psychology, and philosophy are widely recognized; a growing number of Black Studies departments are adding PhD programs to their curricula; and some scholars who are universally recognized as Black Studies specialists have attained unprecedented power and influence in the broader academic/cultural marketplace.[72] Despite the new world in which this scholarship has been produced we cannot afford to forget that it has deep roots that tie it to the previous generations of intellectuals whose work comprises the core of this book.

As an intellectual enterprise, the attention of African Americanists to the interplay of race and economics in demography continues to expand upon, or perhaps outgrow, its origins in the "Chicago School" discussed earlier. The city remains a key laboratory and field of study, joined increasingly by the suburb. To cite but a few examples, we can see how sociologist William Julius Wilson and historians Earl Lewis and Joe William Trotter have built upon Horace Cayton and St. Clair Drake's work as they demonstrate with admirable precision how class and race are mutually embedded in life—impossible to parse out and measure separately.[73] And true to their intellectual ancestors they also examine carefully the variety of cultural practices, traditions, and extended relationships that enabled people to survive. In a similar spirit, sociologist Lawrence Bobo and his colleagues document with impressively conclusive research the ways in which even the post–World War II "Los Angeles growth machine"—part "rustbelt" economy and part "sunbelt" economy—was not strong enough to significantly break down historic racial segregation in the city's economy and neighborhoods.[74]

Scholars studying the lives of the black middle class and black suburbanization bring to their work the same analytical skill, ambition, and attention that Charles Wesley and Abram Harris devoted to the study of African Americans in the industrial workforce at a similarly formative moment seventy years ago. If their counterparts in the industrial economy were relegated to jobs that were both low paying and dangerous, recent research indicates that African Americans in the white-collar executive ranks face a not entirely different fate. According to sociologist Sharon Collins and others, African American executives are often tracked into "racialized jobs" in community relations, personnel, and human relations, positions that are distant from centers of decision making and are therefore more vulnerable to layoffs and downsizing.[75]

Studies of the postwar middle class have also brought the suburbs into clearer focus as a center of middle class African American life, an historical phenomenon that gained special momentum since the 1970s but extends historically back much further to the 1920s.[76] Not surprisingly, the suburbs provide no easy or instant refuge from the problems African Americans encountered in the city. The abiding nature of some of these difficulties is apparent when reading Mary Pattillo-McCoy's observations in *Black Picket Fences,* her important study of black life in a Chicago suburb. In many ways it is dispiriting that one can hear so clearly in Pattillo-McCoy echoes of Du Bois in his *Philadelphia Negro* or Cayton and Drake in their *Black Metropolis:* "Blacks of all socio-economic statuses tend to be confined to a limited geographic space by discriminatory practices of banks, insurance companies and urban planners. . . . Thus, while the size of the black belt has increased, extending beyond the administrative boundaries of cities into adjacent suburbs, it remains effective in strapping in the black community."[77]

Michael Dawson, Adolph Reed Jr., and Cathy Cohen have each in their own way moved the scholarly dialogue in political science well beyond the one-dimensional portrait of African American leaders as flawed giants sliding predictably between the opposing poles of "protest" and "accommodation." Dawson's statistical models and historical narratives about black political behavior, Reed's analyses of black elite brokerage politics and labor activism, and Cohen's discussions of cross-racial political alliances regarding health care crises, poverty, and sexuality are more than a step removed from the 1930s work of Ralph Bunche and Emmett Dorsey, but they share the same commitment to highlighting the diversity of black political expression at the same time that they underscore the alluring power of race-thinking in American society.[78]

Even in the world of cultural studies—a mode of inquiry that has become increasingly influential over the last thirty years—one can see clear linkages between the present and the social science work of past years. Most prominent in this regard would have to be cultural sociologist Paul Gilroy and historian and cultural anthropologist Robin D. G. Kelley. Both scholars pay careful attention to the transnational dimensions of racial formation and the various ways that cultural performance can be employed to subvert the traditional exercise of power. In this way, their work brings together the internationalist commitments that drove much of Rayford Logan's and W. E. B. Du Bois's scholarship and the cultural sensibilities that are at the heart of Zora Neale Hurston's and Sterling Brown's scholarly and creative writing.[79]

The best scholarship of this generation, like that of those past, leaves an essential record to the comprehensive understanding of our society. As historically minded social scientists seek to analyze how race and class continue to shape demography and, hence, destiny in the twenty-first century, these studies—and many others we have not mentioned—will do for them what the work of Du Bois, Frazier, Hurston, and Johnson has done for us: to see reality in all of its contradictory complexity and think in new ways about how the past and the present relate to one another.

There is little doubt that our world is very different from the one in which American social science was founded more than a century ago. Nonetheless, just as we are glad to see signs of a world that has gone, we know that many unwelcome challenges lie ahead. Indeed, the architecture of the present bears a disturbing resemblance to the past. We have no choice but to admit that even as the quality of life for black scholars improved dramatically during the course of the twentieth century our nation remains deeply divided by significant inequalities that run along racial and economic lines. We end this introduction, then, in all too close proximity to where we began, and with less an analytical thunderclap than a frank acknowledgement of a certain enduring reality: the color line continues to be drawn in the lives of millions of Americans. Black scholars, too, live on the line and will continue to move ahead by the best light they can make.

NOTES

1. David Levering Lewis, *W. E. B. Du Bois: Biography of a Race, 1868–1919* (New York: Henry Holt and Company, 1993), 223. See also Lewis, *W. E. B. Du Bois: The Fight for Equality and the American Century, 1919–1963* (New York: Henry Holt and Company, 2000), and Michael Katz and Thomas Sugrue, eds., *W. E. B. Du Bois, Race, and the City: "The Philadelphia Negro" and Its Legacy* (Philadelphia: University of Pennsylvania Press, 1998). Du Bois's historical survey of Reconstruction, *Black Reconstruction in America, 1860–1880* (New York: Harcourt Press, 1935), is equally important to understanding his legacy to American social science.

2. W. E. B. Du Bois, *The Philadelphia Negro: A Social Study* (Philadelphia: University of Pennsylvania Press, 1899; repr., with a new introduction by Elijah Anderson, 1996), 385.

3. Mia Bay, " 'The World Was Thinking Wrong About Race': *The Philadelphia Negro* and Nineteenth Century Social Science," in Katz and Sugrue, *W. E. B. Du Bois, Race, and the City,* 44–47.

4. Lewis, *Biography of a Race,* 179. For a sense of the intellectual milieu in which the social sciences were established, see Dorothy Ross, *The Origins of American Social Science* (Cambridge: Cambridge University Press, 1991).

5. George Stocking Jr. *Race, Culture, and Evolution: Essays in the History of Anthropology* (New York: Free Press, 1968; repr., Chicago: University of Chicago Press, 1982), 114.

6. Ibid., 122.

7. Michael R. Winston, "Through the Back Door: Academic Racism and the Negro Scholar in Historical Perspective," *Daedalus* 100, no. 3 (1971): 691.

8. The seventeen schools include: State Agricultural and Mechanical Institute (Alabama), Agricultural, Mechanical, and Normal College (Arkansas), State College for Colored Students (Delaware), Florida Agricultural and Mechanical College for Negroes, Georgia State Industrial College, Kentucky State Industrial College, Southern University and Agricultural and Mechanical College (Louisiana), Princess Anne Academy (Maryland), Alcorn Agricultural and Mechanical College (Mississippi), Lincoln University (Missouri), The Negro Agricultural and Technical College (North Carolina), Colored Agricultural and Normal University (Oklahoma), State Colored Normal, Industrial, Agricultural, and Mechanical College of South Carolina, Tennessee Agricultural and Industrial State Teachers College, Prairie View State Normal and Industrial College (Texas), Virginia State College for Negroes, and West Virginia State College. Florida, Tennessee, Kentucky, and West Virginia, respectively, appropriated close to or more than the same amount for their single, white land grant school than the amount cumulatively appropriated for the seventeen land grant schools for blacks. Dwight O. Holmes, *The Evolution of the Negro College* (New York: Columbia University Press, 1934; repr., College Park, Md.: McGrath Publishing Company, 1969), 150–156.

9. W. E. B. Du Bois and Augustus Granville Dill, *The College-Bred Negro American* (Atlanta: Atlanta University Press, 1910), 3–4.

10. Hylan Lewis, "Higher Education for Negroes: A 'Tough' Situation," *Phylon* 10, no. 4 (1949): 358–359. For a further discussion of these issues see Richard Bardolph, *The Negro Vanguard* (New York: Holt Rinehart, Winston, 1959; repr., Westport: Negro University Press, 1971), 134–135.

11. Waldo B. Martin, *The Mind of Frederick Douglass* (Chapel Hill: University of North Carolina Press, 1984), 213.

12. Historian Cedric Robinson puts the matter bluntly: "In these early decades of the [twentieth] century . . . the significance of the metropole for colonial Black intelligentsias was their interest in preparing for a role in, and for some share of, the Empire." Robinson, *Black Marxism: The Making of a Black Radical Tradition* (Chapel Hill: University of North Carolina Press, 2000), 261.

13. James M. McPherson, "White Liberals and Black Power in Negro Education, 1865–1915," *American Historical Review* 75, no. 5 (June 1970): 1363–1364.

14. The University of Michigan, established in 1817, spent its first quarter-century establishing "common schools" around the state and did not admit its first students to its college curriculum until 1841. In one of its earliest incarnations, what became the University of California was first known as a "family high school for boys." See, respectively, Howard Peckham, *The Making of the University of Michigan, 1817–1867* (Ann Arbor: University of Michigan Press, 1967), 22, and Verne A. Stadtman, *The University of California, 1868–1968* (New York: McGraw Hill Book Company, 1970), 8.

15. Mel Curti and Vernon Carstensen, *The University of Wisconsin* (Madison: University of Wisconsin Press, 1949), ix.

16. Winston, "Through the Back Door," 695; Jonathan Scott Holloway, *Confronting the Veil: Abram Harris Jr., E. Franklin Frazier, and Ralph Bunche, 1919–1941* (Chapel Hill: University of North Carolina Press, 2002), 48.

17. Michael Winston claims that the black church and school were the two main institutions made by black Americans. Winston, "Through the Back Door," 679.

18. Kevin K. Gaines, *Uplifting the Race: Black Leadership, Politics, and Culture in the Twentieth Century* (Chapel Hill: University of North Carolina Press, 1996), xiv–xv.

19. Evelyn Brooks Higginbotham, *Righteous Discontent: The Women's Movement in the Black Baptist Church, 1880–1920* (Cambridge, Mass.: Harvard University Press, 1993), 2–13.

20. Ibid., 120–149.

21. As defined by its constitution, the American Negro Academy would be an organization of "authors, scholars, artists, and those distinguished in other walks of life, men of African descent, for the Promotion of Letters, Science, and Art." The constitution enumerated the Academy's purposes as follows: "a. To promote the publication of scholarly work; b. To aid youths of genius in the attainment of the higher culture, at home or abroad; c. To gather into its archives valuable data, and the works

of Negro authors; d. To aid, by publication, the dissemination of the truth and the vindication of the Negro race from vicious assaults; e. To publish, if possible, an 'Annual' designed to raise the standard of intellectual endeavor among American Negroes." Alfred A. Moss Jr., *The American Negro Academy: Voice of the Talented Tenth* (Baton Rouge: Louisiana State University Press, 1981), 1.

22. Alexander Crummell, "Civilization, the Primal Need of the Race," Occasional Papers, No. 3 (Washington, D.C.: The American Negro Academy, 1898), 6.

23. Alexander Crummell to F. Miller, 30 June 1898, Crummell Papers, The Schomburg Center for Research in Black Culture.

24. Alexander Crummell, "The Black Woman of the South: Her Neglects and Her Needs," an address before the Freedman's Aid Society in 1883. Published by the Freedman's Aid Society.

25. The invitation may have reflected a friendship. According to Cooper's biographer, Leona C. Gabel, Cooper boarded with the Crummell family when she first arrived in Washington, D.C., in 1887. She also attended St. Luke's Episcopal Church, where Crummell served as rector. Gabel, *From Slavery to the Sorbonne and Beyond: The Life and Writings of Anna J. Cooper* (Northampton, Mass.: Department of History, Smith College, 1982), 33.

26. Anna Julia Cooper, *A Voice from the South* (Xenia, Ohio: Aldine Printing House, 1892; repr., New York: Oxford University Press, 1988), 75.

27. Eli Zaretsky, "Editor's Introduction," in William Thomas and Florian Znaniecki, *The Polish Peasant in Europe and America*, ed. Zaretsky (Urbana: University of Illinois Press, 1984), 2.

28. Ross, *Origins of American Social Science*, 352–355.

29. Ibid., 355–357.

30. Anthony M. Platt, *E. Franklin Frazier Reconsidered* (New Brunswick, N.J.: Rutgers University Press, 1991), 167–168. Frazier frequently reiterated this argument. For example, in the concluding paragraph of *The Negro Family in Chicago*, Frazier wrote, "The widespread disorganization of Negro family life must be regarded as an aspect of the civilizational process in the Negro group. It is not merely a pathological phenomenon." Frazier, *The Negro Family in Chicago* (Chicago: University of Chicago Press, 1932), 252.

31. Robert Bannister, "Sociology," in *The Modern Social Sciences*, ed. Theodore M. Porter and Dorothy Ross, vol. 7 of *The Cambridge History of Science* (Cambridge: Cambridge University Press, 2003), 344.

32. Robert Bennett Bean, "Some Racial Peculiarities of the Negro Brain," *American Journal of Anthropology* 5 (1906): 353–432. As quoted in Stocking, *Race, Culture, and Evolution*, 128.

33. Robert Park and Earnest Burgess, *Introduction to the Science of Sociology* (Chicago: University of Chicago Press, 1924), 138–139. As quoted in Platt, *E. Franklin Frazier Reconsidered*, 83.

34. Holloway, *Confronting the Veil*, 136.

35. The same footnote also referenced the work of E. Franklin Frazier, then a star on the Howard University faculty, and that of social psychologist Kenneth B. Clark, a Howard alumnus. At minimum, their presence here should remind us of the important work done by scholars behind the line in the battle against segregation.

36. Gunnar Myrdal, *An American Dilemma: The Negro Problem and Modern Democracy* (New York: Harper Brothers, 1944), xlvii, xliii.

37. Ralph Ellison confronted the implications of this approach in a famously scathing review of *An American Dilemma*. Ellison was incensed by the Myrdalian idea that blacks' conditions were the result of whites' failure to believe in blacks' ability to be creative or generative. Ellison understood that this logic eliminated black agency and he wondered aloud: "But can a people (its faith in an idealized American Creed notwithstanding) live and develop for over three hundred years simply by reacting? Are American Negroes simply the creation of white men, or have they at least helped to create themselves out of what they found around them? Men have made a way of life in caves and upon cliffs, why cannot Negroes have made a life upon the horns of the white man's dilemma?" Ellison, "An American Dilemma: A Review," in *Shadow and Act* (New York: Vintage, 1972), 315–316.

38. Holloway, *Confronting the Veil*, 182–184; Ben Keppel, *The Work of Democracy: Ralph Bunche, Kenneth B. Clark, Lorraine Hansberry, and the Cultural Politics of Race* (Cambridge, Mass.: Harvard University Press, 1995), 50–58; Ralph Bunche, *A Brief and Tentative Analysis of Negro Leadership*, ed. Jonathan Scott Holloway (New York: New York University Press, 2005), 1–2, 25.

39. The contributors to *What the Negro Wants* include Du Bois, labor leader A. Philip Randolph, educator and political radical Doxey Wilkerson, educator and political moderate Mary McLeod Bethune, writers Langston Hughes and Sterling Brown, and the conservative Frederick D. Patterson, head of the Tuskegee Institute.

40. Rayford Logan, ed., *What the Negro Wants* (Chapel Hill: University of North Carolina Press, 1944). Quoting from the reprinted edition (with a new introduction and bibliography by Kenneth Janken, Notre Dame, Ind.: University of Notre Dame Press, 2001), x–xi, xv. Emphasis added.

41. Ibid., xi.

42. As Dorothy Ross has observed, this debate was part of a larger crisis of confidence in social science in the West; see Ross, "The Changing Contours of the Social Science Disciplines," in Porter and Ross, eds., *The Modern Social Sciences*, 234–237.

43. G. Franklin Edwards, "E. Franklin Frazier," *International Encyclopedia of the Social Sciences* (New York: Macmillan Company, 1965); Charles Valentine, *Culture and Poverty: Critique and Counter-Proposals* (Chicago: University of Chicago Press, 1968). On Moynihan's selective use of Frazier's scholarship, see Platt, *E. Franklin Frazier Reconsidered*.

44. Lee Rainwater and William L. Yancey, *The Moynihan Report and the Politics of Controversy* (Cambridge, Mass.: M. I. T. Press, 1967), 93, 164. This quotation is from page 47 of the full report, reprinted in Rainwater and Yancey.

45. Ibid., 162, 221–232, 451–452, 458–463.

46. Ronald W. Walters, "Toward a Definition of Black Social Science," in *The Death of White Sociology: Essays on Race and Culture,* ed. Joyce A. Ladner (New York: Random House, 1973; repr. Baltimore: Black Classic Press, 1998), 206–207.

47. Lewis, *Biography of a Race,* 190.

48. William Julius Wilson, *When Work Disappears: The World of the New Urban Poor* (New York: Alfred A. Knopf, 1996), 172–174, and *The Truly Disadvantaged: The Inner City Underclass and Public Policy* (Chicago: University of Chicago Press, 1987), 8.

49. Wilson, *The Truly Disadvantaged,* 13–16; Wilson, *When Work Disappears,* 175–178.

50. Joyce A. Ladner, *Tomorrow's Tomorrow: The Black Woman* (New York: Doubleday and Company, 1971), quoting from the revised edition (with a new introduction by the author, Lincoln: University of Nebraska Press, 1995), xx.

51. Edgar G. Epps, "Introduction," in *Race Relations: Current Perspectives,* ed. Edgar G. Epps (Cambridge, Mass.: Winthrop Publishers, 1973), x.

52. Ibid.

53. On Kenneth Clark's public career see Ben Keppel, "Kenneth Clark in the Patterns of American Culture," *American Psychologist* 57, no. 1 (2002): 29–37.

54. Ladner, *Tomorrow's Tomorrow,* 71.

55. Albert Murray, *The Omni-Americans: New Perspectives on Black Experience and American Culture* (New York: Outerbridge and Dienstfrey, 1970), 40.

56. Hylan Lewis, "Pursuing Fieldwork in African-American Communities," in *Against the Odds: Scholars Who Challenged Racism in the Twentieth Century,* ed. Benjamin P. Bowser and Louis Kushnick (Amherst: University of Massachusetts Press, 2002), 137.

57. Ross, "Changing Contours," 235.

58. Charles V. Hamilton, "Black Social Scientists: Contributions and Problems," in Ladner, ed., *The Death of White Sociology,* 473.

59. Lawrence E. Gladieux and Thomas R. Volanin, *Congress and the Colleges: The National Politics of Higher Education* (Lexington, Mass.: D. C. Heath, 1976), 17–18.

60. Benjamin Mays, "'The American Negro College': Four Responses and a Reply," *Harvard Educational Review* 37, no. 3 (1967): 457.

61. Judith B. Roebuck and Kumanduri S. Murty, *Historically Black Colleges and Universities: Their Place in American Higher Education* (Westport, Conn.: Praeger Publishers, 1993), 6.

62. U.S. Congress, House Committee on Education and Labor, *Higher Education Act of 1965: Hearings before the Special Subcommittee on Education,* 89th Congress, 1st Sess., 1965 (Washington, D.C.: United States Government Printing Office, 1965), 10.

63. Hugh Davis Graham and Nancy Diamond, *The Rise of American Research Universities: Elites and Challengers in the Postwar Era* (Baltimore: Johns Hopkins University Press, 1997), 44.

64. Students at San Francisco State, Cornell, and Yale offered three different approaches to calling for significant curricular change. In 1968, San Francisco State created the first Black Studies department. The university administration did not do this without pressure, however, as San Francisco State had to shut its doors in the wake of a student-led campus strike that was a direct outgrowth of a call for major curricular and institutional reform that reflected the need for diverse intellectual and structural approaches to running a university. The following year, students at Cornell armed themselves with shotguns and insisted the university address the needs of its rapidly expanding black undergraduate enrollment. Fairly quickly, the Cornell administration established the Africana Studies and Research Center. At the same time that Cornell officials were sent scurrying in the face of the threat of real violence, Yale administrators were meeting with a small cohort of determined undergraduates who also sought curricular and institutional change at their school. Through a combination of good luck, timing, and the stated recognition that a university was an institution that was in a perpetual state of flux, Yale students, faculty, and staff were able to work together to create a Black Studies program as a result of a series of high-level meetings and a national conference. On San Francisco State, see Nathan Huggins, *Afro-American Studies: A Report to the Ford Foundation* (New York: Ford Foundation, 1985), 22; on Cornell, see Faith Berry, "Introduction," in *A Scholar's Conscience: Selected Writings of J. Saunders Redding, 1942–1977* (Lexington: University Press of Kentucky, 1992), 8; on Yale, see Huggins, *Afro-American Studies,* 26, and Armstead L. Robinson, Craig C. Foster, and Donald H. Ogilvie, eds. *Black Studies in the University: A Symposium* (New Haven, Conn.: Yale University Press, 1969).

65. Nathan Hare and the Black World Foundation established *Black Scholar* in 1969, and the *Journal of Black Studies* had its home at the University of California, Los Angeles's Center for the Study of Afro-American History and Culture beginning in 1970.

66. Untitled editorial statement on the inside front cover of *Black Scholar* 1.1 (November 1969).

67. Floyd B. McKissick, "Toward a Black Ideology," *Black Scholar* 1.2 (December 1969): 16.

68. Ibid.

69. Arthur L. Smith, "Editor's Message," *Journal of Black Studies* 1.1 (September 1970): 3.

70. Ibid., 4.

71. "Black Studies Struggling for Respect," *Journal of Blacks in Higher Education* 3 (Spring 1994): 28; "The Rodney Dangerfield of Academic Pursuits: Black Studies Wins No Respect," *Journal of Blacks in Higher Education* 29 (Autumn 2000): 30–31.

72. Kendra Hamilton, "A New Spectrum," *Black Issues in Higher Education* 17.7 (2000): 24–28.

73. See William Julius Wilson, *The Truly Disadvantaged* and *When Work Disappears*; Earl Lewis, *In Their Own Interests: Race, Class, and Power in Twentieth*

Century Norfolk, Virginia (Berkeley: University of California Press, 1991), and editor with Joe W. Trotter, *African Americans in the Industrial Age: A Documentary History, 1915–1945* (Boston: Northeastern University Press, 1996); and Joe W. Trotter, *African American Workers: An Urban Perspective from the American Revolution to the Present* (New York: Basic Books, 2004) and *Black Milwaukee: The Making of a Black Proletariat* (Urbana: University of Illinois Press, 1988).

74. Lawrence D. Bobo et al., eds., *Prismatic Metropolis: Inequality in Los Angeles* (New York: Russell Sage Foundation, 2000), 55–56. For a close study of the special problems faced by African Americans in an older "rust belt" suburb, see Bruce D. Haynes, *Red Lines, Black Spaces: The Politics of Race and Space in a Middle-Class Suburb* (New Haven, Conn.: Yale University Press, 2000).

75. On blacks in corporate America see Sharon M. Collins, *Black Corporate Executives: The Making and Breaking of a Black Middle-Class* (Philadelphia: Temple University Press, 1997), 141–143; on the economic fragility of the black middle class see Bart Landry, *The Black Middle-Class* (Berkeley: University of California Press, 1986), 74–75, 85–89, 193–196, 221; for a comprehensive survey of African American life between the 1940 and the 1970s, see Dorothy K. Newman et al. *Protest, Politics, and Prosperity: Black Americans and White Institutions, 1940–75* (New York: Pantheon, 1978); extending the debate beyond the 1970s, see Joe R. Feagan and Melvin Sikes, *Living with Racism: The Black Middle-Class Experience* (Boston: Beacon Press, 1994).

76. See Andrew Wiese, *Places of Their Own: African-American Suburbanization in the Twentieth Century* (Chicago: University of Chicago Press, 2004).

77. Mary Pattillo-McCoy, *Black Picket Fences: Privilege and Peril among the Black Middle Class* (Chicago: University of Chicago Press, 2000), 25.

78. For examples of this work see Michael Dawson, *Black Visions: The Roots of African-American Political Ideologies* (Chicago: University of Chicago Press, 2001); Adolph Reed Jr., *Without Justice for All: The New Liberalism and Our Retreat from Racial Equality* (Boulder, Colo.: Westview, 2001); and Cathy Cohen, *The Boundaries of Blackness: AIDS and the Breakdown of Black Politics* (Chicago: University of Chicago Press, 1999).

79. See Paul Gilroy, *The Black Atlantic: Modernity and Double Consciousness* (Cambridge, Mass.: Harvard University Press, 1993) and *Against Race: Imagining Political Culture Beyond the Color Line* (Cambridge, Mass.: Belknap Press, 2000); Robin D. G. Kelley, *Race Rebels: Culture, Politics, and the Black Working Class* (New York: Free Press, 1996); and Sidney J. Lemelle and Robin D. G. Kelley, eds., *Imagining Home: Class, Culture, and Nationalism in the African Diaspora* (New York: Verso, 1994).

PART 1

Founding an Intellectual Tradition

Introduction

One year before he died, Alexander Crummell (1819–1898) founded the American Negro Academy in Washington, D.C. This was the capstone achievement of a long career in the United States and Britain. Crummell took this step to counteract a deliberate and long-standing effort by the white establishment to "becloud and stamp out the intellect of the Negro."[1] According to Crummell, it was not that the leaders of American society honestly believed that African Americans were intellectually inferior; but precisely because the accomplishments of the poet Phillis Wheatley and the mathematician Benjamin Banneker had proven otherwise, these leaders worked systematically to construct an entire social order to thwart its further development.[2] Whites sought to create a society that would, they hoped, produce the African American they wanted: an "unthinking labor machine."[3] As we have argued in our historical introduction, the values of white supremacy became integral to the social science founded to study a rapidly industrializing society. Each of the authors represented in this section is a key figure in the effort to answer slanders disguised as science.

The African American thinkers whose work is sampled here lived in a society significantly shaped by the Civil War. That conflict finally forced the abolition of slavery from the United States Constitution and the formal incorporation of African Americans into that document as citizens and voters. Of the scholars represented here, only one of the five (Woodson) was born after the Civil War; two (Crummell and Williams) were born well before that conflict, and two more (Cooper and Terrell) were born right before or during it.[4] These Americans were continuing, in the worlds of learning and intellect, a conflict that had taken its most violent form in the Civil War itself; these Americans were fighting for the full recognition of African Americans as central participants in the life of the Republic at a time when many of the nation's political and cultural leaders were rushing to reunite the nation by diluting or disavowing the abolitionist implications of that war. [5]

If the intellectual work that occupied these thinkers was an agenda whose history extended back well past even the Civil War, the institutions that trained them and in which they made careers possessed similarly extended roots. Although Alexander Crummell's American Negro Academy provides a key founding location, it also built upon a long preexisting tradition that combined a commitment to abolition with a powerful belief in education. The abolitionist movement, the black church and allied self-help organizations, and (eventually) historically black colleges and universities founded after the Civil War provided institutional support that was elsewhere absent.

Alexander Crummell, the oldest member here, was the son of Boston Crummell, whom Wilson J. Moses identifies as a leader among the free blacks of New York. The younger Crummell had Henry Highland Garnet as a schoolmate at the Canal Street High School and the African Free School. Crummell continued his education in upstate New York before taking a degree in theology from Cambridge University.[6] George Washington Williams (1849–1891), the author of the first "sustained, coherent account of the experiences of the Negro people," received his first education as a 14-year-old volunteer in the Union army, which was followed by a brief stint at Howard University.[7] Williams earned his first collegiate degree in 1874 at the Newton (Massachusetts) Theological Seminary.[8] From there, he embarked on a career in politics and journalism.

Wilberforce University, where Mary Church Terrell (1863–1954) and Anna Julia Cooper (1858–1964) held their first teaching posts, was founded by the Cincinnati Conference of the Methodist Episcopal Church in 1854 as a "literary institution of a high order for the education of Colored People and the preparation of teachers."[9] The connection between abolitionism and the education of African Americans was made clear by the decision to name this institution after the British abolitionist William Wilberforce. The connection between abolitionist institutions and the training and employment of black scholars went beyond Wilberforce. Oberlin College, another Ohio institution with a heritage grounded in abolitionism, was the undergraduate training ground for both Cooper and Terrell. Of her alma mater, Terrell wrote that "there was as much 'social equality' to the square inch in Oberlin College as could be practiced anywhere in the United States."[10]

Despite the social and cultural barriers that so often separated black and white scholars some early black practitioners of social science in the United States followed patterns of professionalization similar to those of their white counterparts. George Washington Williams shared a background with his mentor George Bancroft, the founder of the historical narrative of white America: both came to historical writing not from the seminars of a graduate program but from the rough and tumble world of political advocacy.[11] In contrast, Carter G. Woodson (1875–1950), the first child of slaves to earn a PhD in the field of history, was forced to create a professional trajectory quite different from that of his white counterpart, Frederick Jackson Turner. Woodson, of course, had the additional burden of needing to achieve something Turner could take for granted. Turner may have had to labor mightily to spread his particular interpretation of how the frontier shaped American life and culture, but he did not have to worry that American history itself might not have a secure place in the nation's curriculum. Woodson was concerned with the preservation and institutionalization of the most basic factual resources and interpretive framework for African American history itself, and this led him to found the Association for the Study of Negro Life and History. [12]

Regardless of who their professional models might be, black women scholars faced even more formidable challenges than their male counterparts. As we have observed earlier, the academic branch of the "talented tenth" was designed to be a male preserve. The women who chose to take on the difficult work of building a heritage of consciousness faced, as Anna Julia Cooper noted, "a woman question and a race problem," which further cramped the space for free expression and action.[13] But, though cramped, women's work went on apace. Mary Church Terrell, for example, like many other women of her time and class, created important public lives within the separate sphere of cultural mission assigned to women. She recognized as much herself and made it clear that black women's most compelling duty was found in "educating and elevating their race as though upon themselves alone devolved the accomplishment of this great task."[14]

As historian Mary Jo Deegan writes, women aspiring to lives in the academy toiled behind a "gendered veil."[15] This veil acted in traditional ways by keeping women hidden from view, but it also masked the intense rivalries that could crop up between individuals who were working in a world of extremely limited professional opportunity. The closely proximate careers of Anna Julia Cooper and Mary Church Terrell are a case in point. Not only were both women contemporaries at Oberlin, they also both ended up in the same department at the academically renowned M Street High School (later renamed Dunbar), chaired by Church Terrell's future husband, Robert Terrell. They appear to have shared an equally strong commitment to building up the "talented tenth" and to establishing full equality for African Americans. And yet Terrell makes no mention of Cooper in her autobiography, the only potential primary source for investigating the personal relationship between these two figures. The reasons for this seemingly intentional oversight are unknown, but the fact that Cooper was removed from the M Street faculty and then from the roster of District teachers in a 1905 purge raises at least the possibility of behind-the-scenes chicanery.[16] Cooper turned this unexpected blow to her advantage and went to Paris to pursue a doctorate at the Sorbonne.

The African Americans who worked to found American social science provided a strong and sturdy foundation for the work of later generations.

Today, the best of this work occupies a place of respect in the canons of African American Studies and Cultural Studies. If hindsight provides us with the opportunity to elevate these long neglected scholars, we must, at the same time, acknowledge troubling continuities in thought between them and the larger communities of learning and letters in which they sought membership. In both cases, class inequality and the possession of a certain social standing all too often determined who would receive only a "common education" and who would go beyond that to become an accredited intellectual leader.[17] Membership in this very small world provided unusual opportunities for both influence and intense rivalries that were sometimes as petty and personal as they were intellectual and ideological. As often as exclusivity was intertwined with excellence, it also narrowed the vision and the terms of analysis and debate in important ways. As we shall see in later sections, the form and substance of American social science and social thought would change significantly as access to its citadels broadened.

NOTES

1. Alexander Crummell, "The Attitude of the American Mind toward the Negro Intellect," Occasional Papers, No. 3 (Washington, D.C.: The American Negro Academy, 1898), 10; reprinted in William H. Ferris, *Alexander Crummell: An Apostle of Negro Culture,* Occasional Papers, No. 20 (Washington, D.C.: The American Negro Academy, 1920); collected and reprinted in *Occasional Papers, No. 1–22* (New York: Arno Press and the *New York Times,* 1969).

2. Ibid.

3. Ibid., 15.

4. The birth years are as follows: Crummell, 1819; Williams, 1849; Cooper, 1858; Church Terrell, 1863; Du Bois, 1868; Woodson, 1875.

5. See David W. Blight, *Race and Reunion: The Civil War in American Memory* (Cambridge, Mass.: Belknap Press, 2001).

6. Wilson Jeremiah Moses, *Alexander Crummell: A Study of Civilization and Discontent* (New York: Oxford University Press, 1989), 11–33.

7. John Hope Franklin, *George Washington Williams: A Biography* (Chicago: University of Chicago Press, 1985), 115.

8. Ibid., 10.

9. Resolution quoted in Horace Talbert, *The Sons of Allen* (Exenia, Ohio: The Aldine Press, 1906; published on microfiche by Chadwycke-Healy, 1987), 264.

10. Mary Church Terrell, *A Colored Woman in a White World* (New York: The Arno Press, 1980), 45.

11. John Hope Franklin, *George Washington Williams,* 105.

12. See Jacqueline Goggin, *Carter G. Woodson: A Life in Black History* (Baton Rouge: Louisiana State University Press, 1993). For an inside view of Woodson's work, see the diaries of his colleague, Lorenzo J. Greene, edited by Arvath E. Strickland: *Working with Carter G. Woodson, the Father of Black History: A Diary, 1928–1930* (Baton Rouge: Louisiana State University Press, 1989) and *Selling Black History for Carter G. Woodson: A Diary, 1930–1933* (Columbia: University of Missouri Press, 1996).

13. Anna Julia Cooper, *A Voice From the South* (Xenia, Ohio: Aldine Printing House, 1892; repr., New York: Oxford University Press, 1988), 134.

14. Mary Church Terrrell, *The Progress of Colored Women*, address delivered before the National American Woman's Suffrage Association, Washington, D.C., February 18, 1898 (Washington, D.C.: Smith Brothers Printers, 1898), 9.

15. Mary Jo Deegan, "Transcending a Patriarchal and Racist Past: African-American Women in Sociology, 1890–1920," *Sociological Origins* 2, no. 1 (2000): 42. Francille Rusan Wilson notes that, even in the social service sector of the social sciences, women such as the economist Sadie T. M. Alexander faced a hard road. Despite an Ivy League education that included a doctorate, Alexander "could not find work as an economist in white or black America." Francille Rusan Wilson, "'All the Glory . . . Faded . . . Quickly': Sadie T. Alexander and Black Professional Women, 1920–1950," in *Sister Circle: Black Women and Work*, ed. Sharon Harley et al. (New Brunswick, N.J.: Rutgers University Press, 2002), 167.

16. Cooper's biographer, Leona Gabel, has concluded, "[Terrell's and Cooper's] careers in the Washington school system were so closely interrelated as to raise questions about [Cooper's] experience there." Gabel, *From Slavery to the Sorbonne and Beyond: The Life and Writings of Anna J. Cooper* (Northampton, Mass.: Department of History, Smith College, 1982), 29. For Gable's careful speculation on these matters, see pages 29–30, 46–59.

17. Of particular importance to this discussion are Evelyn Brooks Higginbotham, *Righteous Discontent: The Women's Movement in the Black Baptist Church, 1880–1920* (Cambridge, Mass.: Harvard University Press, 1993); Kevin K. Gaines, *Uplifting the Race: Black Leadership, Politics, and Culture in the Twentieth Century* (Chapel Hill: University of North Carolina Press, 1996); and Adolph Reed Jr., *Stirrings in the Jug: Black Politics in the Post-Segregation Era* (Minneapolis: University of Minnesota Press, 1999).

ALEXANDER CRUMMELL

The Attitude of the American Mind toward the Negro Intellect

For the first time in the history of this nation the colored people of America have undertaken the difficult task, of stimulating and fostering the genius of their race as a distinct and definite purpose. Other and many gatherings have been made, during our own two and a half centuries' residence on this continent, for educational purposes; but ours is the first which endeavors to rise up to the plane of culture.

For my own part I have no misgivings either with respect to the legitimacy, the timeliness, or the prospective success of our venture. The race in the brief period of a generation, has been so fruitful in intellectual product, that the time has come for a coalescence of powers, and for reciprocity alike in effort and appreciation. I congratulate you, therefore, on this your first anniversary. To me it is, I confess, a matter of rejoicing that we have, as a people, reached a point where we have a class of men who will come together for purposes, so pure, so elevating, so beneficent, as the cultivation of mind, with the view of meeting the uses and the needs of our benighted people.

I feel that if this meeting were the end of this Academy; if I could see that it would die this very day, I would nevertheless, cry out—"All hail!"

Alexander Crummell, "The Attitude of the American Mind toward the Negro Intellect," Occasional Papers, No. 3 (Washington, D.C.: The American Negro Academy, 1898); reprinted in William H. Ferris, *Alexander Crummell: An Apostle of Negro Culture,* Occasional Papers, No. 20 (Washington, D.C.: The American Negro Academy, 1920); collected and reprinted in *Occasional Papers, No. 1–22* (New York: Arno Press and the *New York Times,* 1969).

even if I had to join in with the salutation—"farewell forever!" For, first of all, you have done, during the year, that which was never done so completely before,—a work which has already told upon the American mind; and next you have awakened in the Race an ambition which, in some form, is sure to reproduce both mental and artistic organization in the future.

The cultured classes of our country have never interested themselves to stimulate the desires or aspirations of the mind of our race. They have left us terribly alone. Such stimulation, must, therefore, in the very nature of things, come from ourselves.

Let us state here a simple, personal incident, which will well serve to illustrate a history.

I entered, sometime ago, the parlor of a distinguished southern clergyman. A kinsman was standing at his mantel, writing. The clergyman spoke to his relative—"Cousin, let me introduce to you the Rev. C., a clergyman of our Church." His cousin turned and looked down at me; but as soon as he saw my black face, he turned away with disgust, and paid no more attention to me than if I were a dog.

Now, this porcine gentleman, would have been perfectly courteous, if I had gone into his parlor as a cook, or a waiter, or a bootblack. But my profession, as a clergyman, suggested the idea of letters and cultivation; and the contemptible snob at once forgot his manners, and put aside the common decency of his class.

Now, in this, you can see the attitude of the American mind toward the Negro intellect. A reference to this attitude seems necessary, if we would take in, properly, the present condition of Negro culture.

It presents a most singular phenomenon. Here was a people laden with the spoils of the centuries, bringing with them into this new land the culture of great empires; and, withal, claiming the exalted name and grand heritage of Christians. By their own voluntary act they placed right beside them a large population of another race of people, seized as captives, and brought to their plantations from a distant continent. This other race was an unlettered, unenlightened, and a pagan people.

What was the attitude taken by this master race toward their benighted bondsmen? It was not simply that of indifference or neglect. There was nothing negative about it.

They began, at the first, a systematic ignoring of the fact of intellect in this abased people. They undertook the process of darkening their minds.

"Put out the light, and then, put out the light!" was their cry for centuries. Paganizing themselves, they sought a deeper paganizing of their serfs than the original paganism that these had brought from Africa. There was no legal artifice conceivable which was not resorted to, to blindfold their souls from the light of letters; and the church, in not a few cases, was the prime offender.[1]

Then the legislatures of the several states enacted laws and Statutes, closing the pages of every book printed to the eyes of Negroes; barring the doors of every school-room against them! And this was the systematized method of the intellect of the South, to stamp out the brains of the Negro!

It was done, too, with the knowledge that the Negro had brain power. There was *then,* no denial that the Negro had intellect. That denial was an after thought. Besides, legislatures never pass laws forbidding the education of pigs, dogs, and horses. They pass such laws against the intellect of *men.*

However, there was then, at the very beginning of the slave trade, everywhere, in Europe, the glintings forth of talent in great Negro geniuses,—in Spain, and Portugal, in France and Holland and England;[2] and Phillis Wheatley and Banneker and Chavis and Peters, were in evidence on American soil.

It is manifest, therefore, that the objective point in all this legislation was INTELLECT,—the intellect of the Negro! It was an effort to becloud and stamp out the intellect of the Negro!

The *first* phase of this attitude reached over from about 1700 to 1820:— and as the result, almost Egyptian darkness fell upon the mind of the race, throughout the whole land.

Following came a more infamous policy. It was the denial of intellectuality in the Negro; the assertion that he was not a human being, that he did not belong to the human race. This covered the period from 1820 to 1835, when Gliddon and Nott and others, published their so-called physiological work, to prove that the Negro was of a different species from the white man.

A distinguished illustration of this ignoble sentiment can be given. In the year 1833 or 4 the speaker was an errand boy in the Anti-slavery office in New York City.

On a certain occasion he heard a conversation between the Secretary and two eminent lawyers from Boston,—Samuel E. Sewell and David Lee Child. They had been to Washington on some legal business. While at the Capitol they happened to dine in the company of the great John C. Calhoun, then senator from South Carolina. It was a period of great ferment upon the question of Slavery, States' Rights, and Nullification; and consequently the Negro was the topic of conversation at the table. One of the utterances of Mr. Calhoun was to this effect—"That if he could find a Negro who knew the Greek syntax, he would then believe that the Negro was a human being and should be treated as a man."

Just think of the crude asininity of even a great man! Mr. Calhoun went to "Yale" to study the Greek Syntax, and graduated there. His son went to Yale to study the Greek Syntax, and graduated there. His grandson, in recent years, went to Yale, to learn the Greek Syntax, and graduated there. Schools and Colleges were necessary for the Calhouns, and all other white men to learn the Greek syntax.

And yet this great man knew that there was not a school, nor a college in which a black boy could learn his A.B.C's. He knew that the law in all the Southern States forbade Negro instruction under the severest penalties. How then was the Negro to learn the Greek syntax? How then was he to evidence to Mr. Calhoun his human nature? Why, it is manifest that Mr. Calhoun expected the Greek syntax to grow in *Negro brains,* by spontaneous generation!

Mr. Calhoun was then, as much as any other American, an exponent of the nation's mind upon this point. Antagonistic as they were upon *other* subjects, upon the rejection of the Negro intellect they were a unit. And this, measurably, is the attitude of the American mind today:—measurably, I say, for thanks to the Almighty, it is not universally so.

There has always been a school of philanthropists in this land who have always recognized mind in the Negro; and while recognizing the limitations which *individual* capacity demanded, claimed that for the RACE, there was no such thing possible for its elevation save the widest, largest, highest, improvement. Such were our friends and patrons in New England in New York, Pennsylvania, a few among the Scotch Presbyterians and the "Friends" in grand old North Carolina; a great company among the Congregationalists of the East, nobly represented down to the present, by the "American Missionary Society," which tolerates no stint for the Negro intellect in its grand solicitudes. But these were exceptional.

Down to the year 1825, I know of no Academy or College which would open its doors to a Negro.[3] In the South it was a matter of absolute legal disability. In the North, it was the ostracism of universal caste-sentiment. The theological schools of the land, and of all names, shut their doors against the black man. An eminent friend of mine, the noble, fervent, gentlemanly Rev. Theodore S. Wright, then a Presbyterian licentiate, was taking private lessons in theology, at Princeton; and for this offense was kicked out of one of its halls.

In the year 1832 Miss Prudence Crandall opened a private school for the education of colored girls; and it set the whole State of Connecticut in a flame. Miss Crandall was mobbed, and the school was broken up.

The year following, the trustees of Canaan Academy in New Hampshire opened its doors to Negro youths; and this act set the people of that state on fire. The farmers of the region assembled with 90 yoke of oxen, dragged the Academy into a swamp, and a few weeks afterward drove the black youths from the town.

These instances will suffice. They evidence the general statement, *i.e.* that the American mind has refused to foster and to cultivate the Negro intellect. Join to this a kindred fact, of which there is the fullest evidence. Impelled, at times, by pity, a modicum of schooling and training has been given the Negro; but even this, almost universally, with reluctance, with cold criticism, with microscopic scrutiny, with icy reservation, and at times, with ludicrous limitations.

Cheapness characterizes almost all the donations of the American people to the Negro:—Cheapness, in all the past, has been the regimen provided for the Negro in every line of his intellectual, as well as his lower life. And so, cheapness is to be the rule in the future, as well for his higher, as for his lower life:—cheap wages and cheap food, cheap and rotten huts; cheap and dilapidated schools; cheap and stinted weeks of schooling; cheap meeting houses for worship; cheap and ignorant ministers; cheap theological training; and now, cheap learning, culture and civilization!

Noble exceptions are found in the grand literary circles in which Mr. Howells moves—manifest in his generous editing of our own Paul Dunbar's poems. But this generosity is not general, even in the world of American letters.

You can easily see this in the attempt, now-a-days, to side-track the Negro intellect, and to place it under limitations never laid upon any other class.

The elevation of the Negro has been a moot question for a generation past. But even to-day what do we find the general reliance of the American mind in determinating [*sic*] this question? Almost universally the resort is to material agencies! The ordinary, and sometimes the *extraordinary* American is unable to see that the struggle of a degraded people for elevation is, in its very nature, a warfare, and that its main weapon is the cultivated and scientific mind.

Ask the great men of the land how this Negro problem is to be solved, and then listen to the answers that come from divers classes of our white fellow-citizens. The merchants and traders of our great cities tell us—"The Negro must be taught to work;" and they will pour out their moneys by thousands to train him to toil. The clergy in large numbers, cry out—"Industrialism is the only hope of the Negro;" for this is the bed-rock, in their opinion, of Negro evangelization! "Send him to Manual Labor Schools," cries out another set of philanthropists. "Hic haec, hoc," is going to prove the ruin of the Negro" says the Rev. Steele, an erudite Southern Savan. "You must begin at the bottom with the Negro," says another eminent authority—as though the Negro had been living in the clouds, and had never reached the bottom. Says the Honorable George T. Barnes, of Georgia—"The kind of education the Negro should receive should not be very refined nor classical, but adapted to his present condition:" as though there is to be no future for the Negro.

And so you see that even now, late in the 19th century, in this land of learning and science, the creed is—"Thus far and no farther", *i.e.* for the American black man.

One would suppose from the universal demand for the mere industrialism for this race of ours, that the Negro had been going daily to dinner parties, eating terrapin and indulging in champagne; and returning home at night, sleeping on beds of eiderdown; breakfasting in the morning in his bed, and then having his valet to clothe him daily in purple and fine linen—all these 250 years of his sojourn in this land. And then, just now, the American people, tired of all this Negro luxury, was calling him, for the first time, to blister his hands with the hoe, and to learn to supply his needs by sweatful toil in the cotton fields.

Listen a moment, to the wisdom of a great theologian, and withal as great philanthropist, the Rev. Dr. Wayland, of Philadelphia. Speaking, not long since, of the "Higher Education" of the colored people of the South, he said "that this subject concerned about 8,000,000 of our fellow-citizens, among whom are probably 1,500,000 voters. The education suited to these people is that which should be suited to white people under the same circumstances. These people are bearing the impress which was left on them by two centuries of slavery and several centuries of barbarism. This education must begin at the bottom. It must first of all produce the power of self-support to assist them to better their condition. It should teach them good citizenship and should build them up morally. It should be, first, a good English education. They should be imbued with the knowledge of the Bible. They should have an industrial education. An industrial education leads to self-support and to the elevation of their condition. Industry is itself largely an education, intellectually and morally, and, above all, an education of character. Thus we should make these people self-dependent. This education will do away with pupils being taught Latin and Greek, while they do not know the rudiments of English."

Just notice the cautious, restrictive, limiting nature of this advice! Observe the lack of largeness, freedom and generosity in it. Dr. Wayland, I am sure, has never specialized just such a regimen for the poor Italians, Hungarians or Irish, who swarm, in lowly degradation, in immigrant ships to our shores. No! for them he wants, all Americans want, the widest, largest culture of the land; the instant opening, not simply of the common schools; and then an easy passage to the bar, the legislature, and even the judgeships of the nation. And they oft times get there.

But how different the policy with the Negro. *He* must have "an education which begins at the bottom." "He should have an industrial education," &c. His education must, first of all, produce the power of self-support, &c.

Now, all this thought of Dr. Wayland is all true. But, my friends it is all false, too; and for the simple reason that it is only half truth. Dr. Wayland seems unable to rise above the plane of burden-bearing for the Negro. He seems unable to gauge the idea of the Negro becoming a thinker. He seems to forget that a race of thoughtless toilers are destined to be forever a race of senseless *boys;* for only beings who think are men.

How pitiable it is to see a great good man be-fuddled by a half truth. For to allege "Industrialism" to be the grand agency in the elevation of a race of already degraded labourers, is as much a mere platitude as to say, "they must eat and drink and sleep;" for man cannot live without these habits. But they never civilize man; and *civilization* is the objective point in the movement for Negro elevation. Labor, just like eating and drinking, is one of the inevitabilities of life; one of its positive necessities. And the Negro has had it for centuries; but it has never given him manhood. It does not *now,* in wide areas of population, lift him up to moral and social elevation. Hence the need of a new factor in his life. The Negro needs light: light thrown in upon all the circumstances of his life. The light of civilization.

Dr. Wayland fails to see two or three important things in this Negro problem:—

(a) That the Negro has no need to go to a manual labor school.[4] He has been for two hundred years and more, the greatest laborer in the land. He is a laborer *now;* and he must always be a laborer, or he must die. But:

(b) Unfortunately for the Negro, he has been so wretchedly ignorant that he has never known the value of his sweat and toil. He has been forced into being an unthinking labor-machine. And this he is, to a large degree, to-day under freedom.

(c) Now the great need of the Negro, in our day and time, is intelligent impatience at the exploitation of his labor, on the one hand; on the other hand courage to demand a larger share of the wealth which his toil creates for others.

It is not a mere negative proposition that settles this question. It is not that the Negro does not need the hoe, the plane, the plough, and the anvil. It is the positive affirmation that the Negro needs the light of cultivation; needs it to be thrown in upon all his toil, upon his whole life and its environments.

What he needs is CIVILIZATION. He needs the increase of his higher wants, of his mental and spiritual needs. *This,* mere animal labor has never given him, and never can give him. But it will come to him, as an individual, and as a class, just in proportion as the higher culture comes to his leaders and teachers, and so gets into his schools, academies and colleges; and then enters his pulpits; and so filters down into his families and his homes; and the Negro learns that he is no longer to be a serf, but that he is to bare his strong brawny arm as a laborer; *not* to make the white man a Croesus, but to make himself a man. He is always to be a laborer; but now, in these days of freedom and the schools, he is to be a laborer with intelligence, enlightenment and manly ambitions.

But, when his culture fits him for something more than a field hand or a mechanic, he is to have an open door set wide before him! And that culture, according to his capacity, he must claim as his rightful heritage, as a man:— not stinted training, not a caste education, not a Negro curriculum.

The Negro Race in this land must repudiate this absurd notion which is stealing on the American mind. The Race must declare that it is not to be put into a single groove; and for the simple reason (1) that *man* was made by his Maker to traverse the whole circle of existence, above as well as below; and that universality is the kernel of all true civilization, of all race elevation. And (2) that the Negro mind, imprisoned for nigh three hundred years, needs breadth and freedom, largeness, altitude, and elasticity; not stint nor rigidity, nor contractedness.

But the "Gradgrinds" are in evidence on all sides, telling us that the colleges and scholarships given us since emancipation, are all a mistake; and that the whole system must be reversed. The conviction is widespread that the Negro has no business in the higher walks of scholarship; that, for instance, Prof. Scarborough has no right to labor in philology; Professor Kelly Miller in mathematics; Professor DuBois, in history; Dr. Bowen, in theology; Professor Turner, in science; nor Mr. Tanner in art. There is no repugnance to the Negro buffoon, and the Negro scullion; but so soon as the Negro stands forth as an intellectual being, this toad of American prejudice, as at the touch of Ithuriel's spear, starts up a devil!

It is this attitude, this repellant, this forbidding attitude of the American mind, which forces the Negro in this land, to both recognize and to foster the talent and capacity of his own race, and to strive to put that capacity and talent to use for the race. I have detailed the dark and dreadful attempt to stamp that intellect out of existence. It is not only a past, it is also, modified indeed, a present fact; and out of it springs the need of just such an organization as the Negro Academy.

Now, gentlemen and friends, seeing that the American mind in the general, revolts from Negro genius, the Negro himself is duty-bound to see to the cultivation and the fostering of his own race-capacity. This is the chief purpose of this Academy. *Our* special mission is the encouragement of the genius and talent in our own race. Wherever we see great Negro ability it is our office to light upon it not tardily, not hesitatingly; but warmly, ungrudgingly, enthusiastically, for the honor of our race, and for the stimulating self-sacrifice in upbuilding the race. Fortunately for us, as a people, this year has given us more than ordinary opportunity for such recognition. Never before, in American history, has there been such a large discovery of talent and genius among us.

Early in the year there was published by one of our members, a volume of papers and addresses, of more than usual excellence. You know gentlemen, that, not seldom, we have books and pamphlets from the press which, like most of our newspapers, are beneath the dignity of criticism. In language, in style, in grammar and in thought they are often crude and ignorant and vulgar. Not so with *"Talks for the Times"* by Prof. Crogman, of Clark University. It is a book with largess of high and noble common sense; pure and classical in style; with a large fund of devoted racialism; and replete everywhere with elevated thoughts. Almost simultaneously with the publication of Professor Crogman's book, came the thoughtful and spicy narrative of Rev. Matthew Anderson of Philadelphia. The title of this volume is *"Presbyterianism; its relation to the Negro:"* but the title cannot serve as a revelation of the racy and spirited story of events in the career of its author. The book abounds with stirring incidents, strong remonstrance, clear and lucid argument, powerful reasonings, the keenest satire; while, withal, it sets forth the wide needs of the Race, and gives one of the strongest vindications of its character and its capacity.[5]

Soon after this came the first publication of our Academy. And you all know the deep interest excited by the two papers, the first issue of this Society. They have attracted interest and inquiry where the mere declamatory effusions, or, the so-called eloquent harangues of aimless talkers and political wire-pullers would fall like snowflakes upon the waters. The papers of Prof. Kelly Miller and Prof. Du Bois have reached the circles of scholars and thinkers in this country. So consummate was the handling of Hoffman's "Race Traits and Tendencies" by Prof. Miller, that we may say that it was the most scientific defense of the Negro ever made in this country by a man of our own blood: accurate, pointed, painstaking, and I claim conclusive.

The treatise of Prof. Du Bois upon the "Conservation of Race," separated itself, in tone and coloring, from the ordinary effusions of literary work in this land. It rose to the dignity of philosophical insight and deep historical inference. He gave us, in a most lucid and original method, and in a condensed form, the long settled conclusions of Ethnologists and Anthropologists upon the question of Race.

This treatise moreover, furnished but a limited measure of our indebtedness to his pen and brain. Only a brief time before our assembly last year, Prof. Du Bois had given a large contribution to the literature of the nation as well as to the genius of the race. At that time he had published a work which will, without doubt, stand permanently, as authority upon its special theme. *"The Suppression of the Slave Trade"* is, without doubt, the one unique and special authority upon that subject, in print. It is difficult to conceive the possible creation of a similar work, so accurate and painstaking, so full of research, so orderly in historical statement, so rational in its conclusions. It is the simple truth, and at the same time the highest praise, the statement of one Review, that "Prof. Du Bois has exhausted his subject." This work is a step forward in the literature of the Race, and a stimulant to studious and aspiring minds among us.

One further reference, that is, to the realm of Art.

The year '97 will henceforth be worthy of note in our history. As a race, we have, this year, reached a high point in intellectual growth and expression.

In poetry and painting, as well as in letters and thought, the Negro has made, this year, a character.

On my return home in October, I met an eminent scientific gentleman; and one of the first remarks he made to me was—"Well, Dr. Crummell, we Americans have been well taken down in Paris, this year. Why," he said, "the prize in painting was taken by a colored young man, a Mr. Tanner from America. Do you know him?" The reference was to Mr. Tanner's "Raising of Lazarus," a painting purchased by the French Government, for the famous Luxembourg Gallery. This is an expectional [*sic*] honor, rarely bestowed upon any American Artist. Well may we all be proud of this, and with this we may join the idea that Tanner, instead of having a hoe in his hand, or digging in a trench, as the faddists on industrialism would fain persuade us, has found his right place at the easel with artists.

Not less distinguished in the world of letters is the brilliant career of our poet-friend and co-laborer, Mr. Paul Dunbar. It was my great privilege last summer to witness his triumph, on more than one occasion, in that grand metropolis of Letters and Literature, the city of London; as well as to hear of the high value set upon his work, by some of the first scholars and literati of England. Mr. Dunbar has had his poems republished in London by Chapman &

Co.; and now has as high a reputation abroad as he has here in America, where his luminous genius has broken down the bars, and with himself, raised the intellectual character of his race in the world's consideration.

These cheering occurrences, these demonstrations of capacity, give us the greatest encouragement in the large work which is before this Academy. Let us enter upon that work, this year, with high hopes, with large purposes, and with calm and earnest persistence. I trust that we shall bear in remembrance that the work we have undertaken is our special function; that it is a work which calls for cool thought, for laborious and tireless painstaking, and for clear discrimination; that it promises nowhere wide popularity, or, exuberant eclat; that very much of its ardent work is to be carried on in the shade; that none of its desired results will spring from spontaneity; that its most prominent features are the demands of duty to a needy people; and that its noblest rewards will be the satisfaction which will spring from having answered a great responsibility, and having met the higher needs of a benighted and struggling Race.

NOTES

1. *Baptism,* for well nigh a century, was denied Negro slaves in the colonies, for fear it carried emancipation with it. Legislation on Education began at a subsequent date. In 1740 it was enacted in SOUTH CAROLINA: "Whereas, the having slaves taught to write or suffering them to be employed in writing, may be attended with great inconvenience. Be it enacted, That all and every person or persons whatsoever who shall hereafter teach or cause any slave or slaves to be taught to write, or shall use or employ any slave as a Scribe in any manner of writing, hereafter taught to write; every such person or persons shall forever, for every such offense, forfeit the sum of £100 current money."

The next step, in South Carolina, was aimed against mental instruction of *every kind,* in reading and writing.

A similar law was passed in Savannah, Georgia. In 1711, in the Colony of Maryland, a *special enactment* was passed to bar freedom by baptism and in 1715, in South Carolina! See *"Stroud's Slave Laws."*

2. At the time when France was on the eve of plunging deeply into the slave trade and of ruining her colonies by the curse of Slavery, the ABBE GREGOIRE stept forth in vindication of the Negro, and published his celebrated work—"The Literature of Negroes." In this work he gives the names and narrates the achievements of the distinguished Negroes, writers, scholars, painters, philosophers, priests and Roman prelates, in Spain, Portugal, France, England, Holland, Italy and Turkey who had risen to eminence in the 15th century.

Not long after BLUMENBACH declared that "entire and large provinces of Europe might be named, in which it would be difficult to meet with such good writers, poets, philosophers, and correspondents of the French Academy; and that moreover there is no savage people, who have distinguished themselves by such examples of perfectibility and capacity for scientific cultivation: and consequently that none can approach more nearly to the polished nations of the globe than the Negro."

3. "Oberlin College" in Ohio was the first opening its doors to the Negro in 1836.

4. "I am not so old as some of my young friends may suspect, but I am too old to go into the business of 'carrying coals to Newcastle.' * * * * The colored citizen of the U.S. has already graduated with respectable standing from a course of 250 years in the University of the old-time type of Manual labor. The South of to-day is what we see it largely because the colored men and women at least during the past 250 years, have not been lazy 'cumberers of the ground,' but the grand army of laborers that has wrestled with nature and led these 16 States out of the woods thus far on the high road to material prosperity. It is not especially necessary that the 2,000,000 of our colored children and youth in the southern common schools should be warned against laziness, and what has always and everywhere come of that since the foundations of the world."

The Rev. A. D. Mayo, M.A., LL.D.

Address before State Teacher's Association (Colored)
Birmingham, Ala.

5. I owe Mr. Anderson an apology for omitting this references to his book on the delivery of this address. It was prepared while its author was in a foreign land; but had passed entirely from his memory in the preparation of this address.

GEORGE WASHINGTON WILLIAMS

The Negro in Light of Philology, Ethnology, and Egyptology

Cushim and Ethiopia.—Ethiopians, White and Black.—
Negro Characteristics.—The Dark Continent.—The Antiquity
of the Negro.—Indisputable Evidence.—The Military and Social
Condition of Negroes.—Case of Color.—The Term Ethiopian.

There seems to be a great deal of ignorance and confusion in the use of the word "Negro;"[1] and about as much trouble attends the proper classification of the inhabitants of Africa. In the preceding chapter we endeavored to prove, not that Ham and Canaan were the progenitors of the Negro races,—for that is admitted by the most consistent enemies of the blacks,—but that the human race is *one,* and that Noah's curse was not a divine prophecy.

The term "Negro" seems to be applied chiefly to the dark and woolly-haired people who inhabit Western Africa. But the Negro is to be found also in Eastern Africa.[2] Zonaras says, "Chus is the person from whom the Cuseans are derived. They are the same people as the Ethiopians." This view is corroborated by Josephus,[3] Apuleius, and Eusebius. The Hebrew term "Cush" is translated Ethiopia by the Septuagint, Vulgate, and by almost all other versions, ancient and modern, as well as by the English version. "It is not, therefore, to be doubted that the term 'Cushim' has by the interpretation of all ages been translated by 'Ethiopians,' because they were also known by their

George Washington Williams, "The Negro in Light of Philology, Ethnology, and Egyptology," chap. 2 of *History of the Negro Race in America,* 2 vols. (New York: G. P. Putnam's Sons, 1883), 1:12–21.

black color, and their transmigrations, which were easy and frequent."⁴ But while it is a fact, supported by both sacred and profane history, that the terms "Cush" and "Ethiopian" were used interchangeably, there seems to be no lack of proof that the same terms were applied frequently to a people who were not Negroes. It should be remembered, moreover, that there were nations who were black, and yet were not Negroes. And the only distinction amongst all these people, who are branches of the Hamitic family, is the texture of the hair. "But it is *equally* certain, as we have seen, that the term 'Cushite' is applied in Scripture to other branches of the same family; as, for instance, to the Midianites, from whom Moses selected his wife, and who could not have been Negroes. The term 'Cushite,' therefore, is used in Scripture as denoting nations who were not black, or in any respect Negroes; and also countries south of Egypt, whose inhabitants were Negroes; and yet both races are declared to be the descendants of Cush, the son of Ham. Even in Ezekiel's day the interior African nations were not of one race; for he represents Cush, Phut, Lud, and Chub, as either themselves constituting, or as being amalgamated with, 'a mingled people' (Ezek. xxx. 5); 'that is to say,' says Faber, 'it was a nation of Negroes who are represented as very numerous,—*all* the mingled people.'"⁵

The term "Ethiopia" was anciently given to all those whose color was darkened by the sun. Herodotus, therefore, distinguishes the Eastern Ethiopians who had straight hair, from the Western Ethiopians who had curly or woolly hair.⁶ "They are a twofold people, lying extended in a long tract from the rising to the setting sun."⁷

The conclusion is patent. The words "Ethiopia" and "Cush" were used always to describe a black people, or the country where such a people lived. The term "Negro," from the Latin "*niger*" and the French "*noir,*" means black; and consequently is a modern term, with all the original meaning of Cush and Ethiopia, with a single exception. We called attention above to the fact that all Ethiopians were not of the pure Negro type, but were nevertheless a branch of the original Hamitic family from whence sprang all the dark races. The term "Negro" is now used to designate the people, who, in addition to their dark complexion, have curly or woolly hair. It is in this connection that we shall use the term in this work.⁸

Africa, the home of the indigenous dark races, in a geographic and ethnographic sense, is the most wonderful country in the world. It is thoroughly tropical. It has an area in English square miles of 11,556,600, with a population of 192,520,000 souls. It lies between the latitudes of 38° north and 35° south; and is, strictly speaking, an enormous peninsula, attached to Asia by the Isthmus of Suez. The most northern point is the cape, situated a little to the west of Cabo Blanco, and opposite Sicily, which lies in latitude 37° 20' 40" north, longitude 9° 41' east. Its southernmost point is Cabo d'Agulhas, in 34° 49' 15" south; the distance between these two points being 4,330 geographical, or about 5,000 English miles. The westernmost point is Cabo Verde, in longitude 17° 33' west; its easternmost, Cape Jerdaffun, in longitude 51° 21' east, latitude 10° 25' north, the distance between the two points being about the same as its length. The western coasts are washed by the Atlantic, the northern by the Mediterranean, and the eastern by the Indian Ocean. The shape of this "dark continent" is likened to a triangle or to an oval. It is rich in oils, ivory, gold, and precious timber. It has beautiful lakes and mighty rivers, that are the insoluble problems of the present times.

Of the antiquity of the Negro there can be no doubt. He is known as thoroughly to history as any of the other families of men. He appears at the first dawn of history, and has continued down to the present time. The scholarly Gliddon says, that "the hieroglyphical designation of 'KeSH,' exclusively applied to *African* races as distinct from the Egyptian, has been found by Lepsius as far back as the monuments of the sixth dynasty, 3000 B.C. But the great influx of Negro and Mulatto races into Egypt as captives dated from the twelfth dynasty; when, about the twenty-second century, B.C., Pharaoh SESOURTASEN extended his conquests up the Nile far into Nigritia. After the eighteenth dynasty the monuments come down to the third century, A.D., without one single instance in the Pharaonic or Ptolemaic periods that Negro labor was ever directed to any agricultural or utilitarian objects."[9] The Negro was found in great numbers with the Sukim, Thut, Lubin, and other African nations, who formed the strength of the army of the king of Egypt, Shishak, when he came against Rehoboam in the year 971 B.C.; and in his tomb, opened in 1849, there were found among his depicted army the exact representation of the genuine Negro race, both in color, hair, and physiognomy. Negroes are also represented in Egyptian paintings as connected with the military campaigns of the eighteenth dynasty. They formed a part of the army of Ibrahim Pacha, and were prized as gallant soldiers at Moncha and in South Arabia.[10] And Herodotus assures us that Negroes were found in the armies of Sesostris and Xerxes; and, at the present time, they are no inconsiderable part of the standing army of Egypt.[11] Herodotus states that eighteen of the Egyptian kings were Ethiopians.[12]

It is quite remarkable to hear a writer like John P. Jeffries, who evidently is not very friendly in his criticisms of the Negro, make such a positive declaration as the following:—

"Every rational mind must, therefore, readily conclude that the African race has been in existence, as a distinct people, over four thousand two hundred years; and how long before that period is a matter of conjecture only, there being no reliable data upon which to predicate any reliable opinion."[13]

It is difficult to find a writer on ethnology, ethnography, or Egyptology, who doubts the antiquity of the Negroes as a distinct people. Dr. John C. Nott of Mobile, Ala., a Southern man in the widest meaning, in his "Types of Mankind," while he tries to make his book acceptable to Southern slaveholders, strongly maintains the antiquity of the Negro.

"Ethnological science, then, possesses not only the authoritative testimonies of Lepsius and Birch in proof of the existence of Negro races during the twenty-fourth century, B.C., but, the same fact being conceded by all living Egyptologists, we may hence infer that these Nigritian types were contemporary with the earliest Egyptians."[14]

In 1829 there was a remarkable Theban tomb opened by Mr. Wilkinson, and in 1840 it was carefully examined by Harris and Gliddon. There is a most wonderful collection of Negro scenes in it. Of one of these scenes even Dr. Nott says,—

"A Negress, apparently a princess, arrives at Thebes, drawn in a plaustrum by a pair of humped oxen, the driver and groom being red-colored Egyptians, and, one might almost infer, eunuchs. Following her are multitudes of Negroes and Nubians, bringing tribute from the upper country, as well as black slaves of both sexes and all ages, among which are some *red* children, whose *fathers* were Egyptians. The cause of her advent seems to have been to make offerings in this tomb of a 'royal son of KeS*h*—Amunoph,' who may have been her husband."[15]

It is rather strange that the feelings of Dr. Nott toward the Negro were so far mollified as to allow him to make a statement that destroys his heretofore specious reasoning about the political and social status of the Negro. He admits the antiquity of the Negro; but makes a special effort to place him in a servile state at all times, and to present him as a vanquished vassal before Ramses III and other Egyptian kings. He sees no change in the Negro's condition, except that in slavery he is better fed and clothed than in his native home. But, nevertheless, the Negress of whom he makes mention, and the entire picture in the Theban tomb, put down the learned doctor's argument. Here is a Negro princess with Egyptian driver and groom, with a large army of attendants, going on a long journey to the tomb of her royal husband!

There is little room here to question the political and social conditions of the Negroes.[16] They either had enjoyed a long and peaceful rule, or by their valor in offensive warfare had won honorable place by conquest. And the fact that black slaves are mentioned does not in any sense invalidate the historical trustworthiness of the pictures found in this Theban tomb; for Wilkinson says, in reference to the condition of society at this period,—

"It is evident that both white and black slaves were employed as servants; they attended on the guests when invited to the house of their master: and from their being in the family of priests as well as of the military chiefs, we may infer that they were purchased with money and that the right of possessing slaves was not confined to those who had taken them in war. The traffic in slaves was tolerated by the Egyptians; and it is reasonable to suppose that many persons were engaged . . . in bringing them to Egypt for public sale, independent of those who were sent as part of the tribute, and who were probably, at first, the property of the monarch; nor did any difficulty occur to the Ishmaelites in the purchase of Joseph from his brethren, nor in his subsequent sale to Potiphar on arriving in Egypt."

So we find that slavery was not, at this time, confined to any particular race of people. This Negro princess was as liable to purchase white as black slaves; and doubtless some were taken in successful wars with other nations, while others were purchased as servants.

But we have further evidence to offer in favor of the antiquity of the Negro. In Japan, and in many other parts of the East, there are to be found stupendous and magnificent temples, that are hoary with age. It is almost impossible to determine the antiquity of some of them, in which the idols are exact representations of woolly-haired Negroes, although the inhabitants of those countries to-day have straight hair. Among the Japanese, black is considered a color of good omen. In the temples of Siam we find the idols fashioned like unto Negroes.[17] Osiris, one of the principal deities of the Egyptians, is frequently represented as black.[18] Bubastis, also, the Diana of Greece, and a member of the great Egyptian Triad, is now on exhibition in the British Museum, sculptured in black basalt sitting figure.[19] Among the Hindus, Kali, the consort of Siva, one of their great Triad; Crishna, the eighth incarnation of Vishnu; and Vishnu also himself, the second of the Trimerti or Hindu Triad, are represented of a black color.[20] Dr. Morton says,—

"The Sphinx may have been the shrine of the Negro population of Egypt, who, as a people, were unquestionably under our average size. Three million Buddhists in Asia represent their chief deity, Buddha, with Negro features and hair. There are two other images of Buddha, one at Ceylon and the other at Calanee, of which Lieut. Mahoney says, 'Both these statues agree in having crisped hair and long, pendent ear-rings.'"[21]

And the learned and indefatigable Hamilton Smith says,—

"In the plains of India are Nagpoor, and a ruined city without name at the gates of Benares (perhaps the real Kasi of tradition), once adorned with statues of a woolly-haired race."[22]

Now, these substantial and indisputable traces of the march of the Negro races through Japan and Asia lead us to conclude that the Negro race antedates all profane history. And while the great body of the Negro races have been located geographically in Africa, they have been, in no small sense, a cosmopolitan people. Their wanderings may be traced from the rising to the setting sun.

"The remains of architecture and sculpture in India seem to prove an early connection between that country and Africa. . . . The Pyramids of Egypt, the colossal statues described by Pausanias and others, the Sphinx, and the Hermes Canis, which last bears a strong resemblance to the Varaha Avatar, indicate the style of the same indefatigable workmen who formed the vast excavations of Canarah, the various temples and images of Buddha, and the idols which are continually dug up at Gaya or in its vicinity. These and other indubitable facts may induce no ill-grounded opinion, that Ethiopia and Hindustan were peopled or colonized by the same extraordinary race; in confirmation of which it may be added, that the mountaineers of Bengal and Benhar can hardly be distinguished in some of their features, particularly in their lips and noses, from the modern Abyssinians."[23]

There is little room for speculation here to the candid searcher after truth. The evidence accumulates as we pursue our investigations. Monuments and temples, sepulchred stones and pyramids, rise up to declare the antiquity of the Negro races. Hamilton Smith, after careful and critical investigation, reaches the conclusion, that the Negro type of man was the most ancient, and the indigenous race of Asia, as far north as the lower range of the Himalaya Mountains, and presents at length many curious facts which cannot, he believes, be otherwise explained.

> "In this view, the first migrations of the Negro stock, coasting westward by catamarans, or in wretched canoes, and skirting South-western Asia, may synchronize with the earliest appearance of the Negro tribes of Eastern Africa, and just precede the more mixed races, which, like the Ethiopians of Asia, passed the Red Sea at the Straits of Bab-el-Mandeb, ascended the Nile, or crossed that river to the west."[24]

Taking the whole southern portion of Asia westward to Arabia, this conjecture—which likewise was a conclusion drawn, after patient research, by the late Sir T. Stanford Raffles—accounts, more satisfactorily than any other, for the Oriental habits, ideas, traditions, and words which can be traced among several of the present African tribes and in the South-Sea Islands. Traces of this black race are still found along the Himalaya range from the Indus to Indo-China, and the Malay peninsula, and in a mixed form all through the southern states to Ceylon.[25]

But it is unnecessary to multiply evidence in proof of the antiquity of the Negro. His presence in this world was coetaneous with the other families of mankind: here he has toiled with a varied fortune; and here under God— *his* God—he will, in the process of time, work out all the sublime problems connected with his future as a man and a brother.

There are various opinions rife as to the cause of color and texture of hair in the Negro. The generally accepted theory years ago was, that the curse of Cain rested upon this race; while others saw in the dark skin of the Negro the curse of Noah pronounced against Canaan. These two explanations were comforting to that class who claimed that they had a right to buy and sell the Negro; and of whom the Saviour said, "For they bind heavy burdens and grievous to be borne, and lay them on men's shoulders; but they themselves will not move them with one of their fingers."[26] But science has, of later years, attempted a solution of this problem. Peter Barrere, in his treatise on the subject, takes the ground that the bile in the human system has much to do with the color of the skin.[27] This theory, however, has drawn the fire of a number of European scholars, who have combated it with more zeal than skill. It is said that the spinal and brain matter are of a dark, ashy color; and by careful examination it is proven that the blood of Ethiopians is black. These facts would seem to clothe this theory with at least a shadow of plausibility. But the opinion of Aristotle, Strabo, Alexander, and Blumenbach is, that the climate, temperature, and mode of life, have more to do with giving color than any thing else. This is certainly true among animals and plants. There are many instances on record where dogs and wolves, etc., have turned white in winter, and then assumed a different color in the spring. If you start at the north and move south, you will find, at first, that the flowers are very white and delicate; but, as you move toward the tropics, they begin to take on deeper and richer hues until they run into almost endless varieties. Guyot argues on the other side of the question to account for the intellectual diversity of the races of mankind.

"While all the types of animals and of plants go on decreasing in perfection, from the equatorial to the polar regions, in proportion to the temperatures, man presents to our view his purest, his most perfect type, at the very centre of the temperate continents,—at the centre of Asia, Europe, in the regions of Iran, of Armenia, and of the Caucasus; and, departing from this geographical centre in the three grand directions of the lands, the types gradually lose the beauty of their forms, in proportion to their distance, even to the extreme points of the southern continents, where we find the most deformed and degenerate races, and the lowest in the scale of humanity."[28]

The learned professor seeks to carry out his famous geographical argument, and, with great skill and labor, weaves his theory of the influence of climate upon the brain and character of man. But while no scholar would presume to combat the theory that plants take on the most gorgeous hues as one nears the equator, and that the races of mankind take on a darker color in their march toward the equator, certainly no student of Oriental history will assent to the unsupported doctrine, that the intensity of the climate of tropical countries affects the intellectual status of races. If any one be so prejudiced as to doubt this, let him turn to "Asiatic Researches," and learn that the dark races have made some of the most invaluable contributions to science, literature, civil-engineering, art, and architecture that the world has yet known. Here we find the cradle of civilization, ancient and remote.

Even changes and differences in color are to be noted in almost every community.

"As we go westward we observe the light color predominating over the dark; and then, again, when we come within the influence of damp from the sea-air, we find the shade deepened into the general blackness of the coast population."

The artisan and farm-laborer may become exceedingly dark from exposure, and the sailor is frequently so affected by the weather that it is next to impossible to tell his nationality.

"It is well known that the Biscayan women are a shining white, the inhabitants of Granada on the contrary dark, to such an extent, that, in this region, the pictures of the blessed Virgin and other saints are painted of the same color."[29]

The same writer calls attention to the fact, that the people on the Cordilleras, who live under the mountains towards the west, and are, therefore, exposed to the Pacific Ocean, are quite, or nearly, as fair in complexion as the Europeans; whereas, on the contrary, the inhabitants of the opposite side, exposed to the burning sun and scorching winds, are copper-colored. Of this theory of climateric influence we shall say more farther on.

It is held by some eminent physicians in Europe and America, that the color of the skin depends upon substances external to the *cutis vera*. Outside of the *cutis* are certain layers of a substance various in consistence, and scarcely perceptible: here is the home and seat of color; and these may be regarded as secretions from the vessels of the *cutis*. The dark color of the Negro principally depends on the substance interposed between the true skin and the scarf-skin. This substance presents different appearances: and it is described sometimes as a sort of organized network or reticular tissue; at others, as a mere mucous or slimy layer; and it is odd that these somewhat incompatible ideas are both conveyed by the term *reticulum mucosum* given to the intermediate portion of the skin by its original discoverer, Malpighi. There is, no doubt, something plausible in all the theories advanced as to the color and hair of the Negro; but it is verily all speculation. One theory is about as valuable as another.

Nine hundred years before Christ the poet Homer, speaking of the death of Memnon, killed at the siege of Troy, says, "He was received by his Ethiopians." This is the first use of the word Ethiopia in the Greek; and it is derived from the roots αιθω, "to burn," and ωψ, "face." It is safe to assume, that, when God dispersed the sons of Noah, he fixed the "bounds of their habitation," and, that, from the earth and sky the various races have secured their civilization. He sent the different nations into separate parts of the earth. He gave to each its racial peculiarities, and adaptability for the climate into which it went. He gave color, language, and civilization; and, when by wisdom we fail to interpret his inscrutable ways, it is pleasant to know that "he worketh all things after the counsel of his own mind."

NOTES

[The following notes are reproduced to match those in the original publication. Expanded references were not available in that text, and have not been provided here.]

1. Edward W. Blyden, L. L. D., of Liberia, says, "Supposing that this term was originally used as a phrase of contempt, it is not with us to elevate it? How often has it not happened that names originally given in reproach have been afterwards adopted as a title of honor by those against whom it was used?—Methodists, Quakers, etc. But as a proof that no unfavorable signification attached to the word when first employed, I may mention, that, long before the slavetrade began, travellers found the black on the coast of Africa to be called Negroes" (see Purchas' Pilgrimage . . .). And in all the pre-slavetrade literature the word was spelled with a capital *N*. It was the slavery of the blacks which afterwards degraded the term. To say that the name was invented to degrade the race, some of whose members were reduced to slavery, is to be guilty of what in grammar is called a *hysteron proteron*. The disgrace became attached to the name in consequence of slavery; and what we propose to do is, now that slavery is abolished, to restore it to its original place and legitimate use, and therefore to restore the capital *N*."

2. Prichard, vol. II. p. 44.

3. Josephus, Antiq., lib. I, chap. 6.

4. Poole.

5. Smyth's Unity Human Races, chap. II, p. 41.

6. Herodotus, vii., 69, 70. Ancient Univ. Hist., vol. xviii. pp. 254, 255.

7. Strabo, vol. i. p. 60.

8. It is not wise, to say the least, for intelligent Negroes in America to seek to drop the word "Negro." It is a good, strong, and healthy word, and ought to live. It should be covered with glory: let Negroes do it.

9. Journal of Ethnology, No. 7, p. 310.

10. Pickering's Races of Men, pp. 185–89.

11. Burckhardt's Travels, p. 341.

12. Euterpe, lib. 6.

13. Jeffries's Nat. Hist. of Human Race, p. 315.

14. Types of Mankind, p. 259.

15. Types of Mankind, p. 262.

16. Even in Africa it is found that Negroes possess great culture. Speaking of Sego, the capital of Bambara, Mr. Park says: "The view of this extensive city, the numerous canoes upon the river, the crowded population, and the cultivated state of the surrounding country, formed altogether a prospect of civilization and magnificence which I little expected to find in the bosom of Africa." See Park's Travels, chap. ii.

Mr. Park also adds, that the population of this city, Sego, is about thirty thousand. It had mosques, and even ferries were busy conveying men and horses over the Niger.

17. See Ambassades Mémorables de la Companie des Indes orientales des Provinces Unies vers les Empereurs du Japon, Amst., 1680; and Kaempfer.

18. Wilkinson's Egypt, vol. iii. p. 340.

19. Coleman's Mythology of the Hindus, p. 91. Dr. William Jones, vol. iii., p. 377.

20. Asiatic Researches, vol. vi. pp. 436–448.

21. Herber's Narrative, vol. i. p. 254.

22. Nat. Hist. of the Human Species, pp. 209, 214, 217.

23. Asiatic Researches, vol. i. p. 427. Also Sir William Jones, vol. iii. 3d. disc.

24. Nat. Hist. Human Species, p. 126.

25. Prichard, pp. 188–219.

26. Matt. xxiii. 4.

27. Discours sur la cause physicale de la couleur des nègres.

28. Earth and Man. Lecture x. pp. 254, 255.

29. Blumenbach, p. 107.

ANNA JULIA COOPER

The Status of Woman in America

Just four hundred years ago an obscure dreamer and castle builder, prosaically poor and ridiculously insistent on the reality of his dreams, was enabled through the devotion of a noble woman to give to civilization a magnificent continent.

What the lofty purpose of Spain's pure-minded queen had brought to the birth, the untiring devotion of pioneer women nourished and developed. The dangers of wild beasts and of wilder men, the mysteries of unknown wastes and unexplored forests, the horrors of pestilence and famine, of exposure and loneliness, during all those years of discovery and settlement, were braved without a murmur by women who had been most delicately constituted and most tenderly nurtured.

And when the times of physical hardship and danger were past, when the work of clearing and opening up was over and the struggle for accumulation began, again woman's inspiration and help were needed and still was she loyally at hand. A Mary Lyon, demanding and making possible equal advantages of education for women as for men, and, in the face of discouragement and incredulity, bequeathing to women the opportunities of Holyoke.

A Dorothea Dix, insisting on the humane and rational treatment of the insane and bringing about a reform in the lunatic asylums of the country, making a great step forward in the tender regard for the weak by the strong throughout the world.

A Helen Hunt Jackson, convicting the nation of a century of dishonor in regard to the Indian.

Anna Julia Cooper, "The Status of Woman in America," in *A Voice from the South* (Xenia, Ohio: Aldine Printing House, 1892), 127–145.

A Lucretia Mott, gentle Quaker spirit, with sweet insistence, preaching the abolition of slavery and the institution, in its stead, of the brotherhood of man; her life and words breathing out in tender melody the injunction

"Have love. Not love alone for one
But man as man thy brother call;
And scatter, like the circling sun,
Thy charities *on all.*"

And at the most trying time of what we have called the Accumulative Period, when internecine war, originated through man's love of gain and his determination to subordinate national interests and black men's rights alike to considerations of personal profit and loss, was drenching our country with its own best blood, who shall recount the name and fame of the women on both sides the senseless strife,—those uncomplaining souls with a great heart ache of their own, rigid features and pallid cheek their ever effective flag of truce, on the battle field, in the camp, in the hospital, binding up wounds, recording dying whispers for absent loved ones, with tearful eyes pointing to man's last refuge, giving the last earthly hand clasp and performing the last friendly office for strangers whom a great common sorrow had made kin, while they knew that somewhere—somewhere a husband, a brother, a father, a son, was being tended by stranger hands—or mayhap those familiar eyes were even then being closed forever by just such another ministering angel of mercy and love.

But why mention names? Time would fail to tell of the noble army of women who shine like beacon lights in the otherwise sordid wilderness of this accumulative period—prison reformers and tenement cleansers, quiet unnoted workers in hospitals and homes, among imbeciles, among outcasts—the sweetening, purifying antidotes for the poisons of man's acquisitiveness,—mollifying and soothing with the tenderness of compassion and love the wounds and bruises caused by his overreaching and avarice.

The desire for quick returns and large profits tempts capital ofttimes into unsanitary, well nigh inhuman investments,—tenement tinder boxes, stifling, stunting, sickening alleys and pestiferous slums; regular rents, no waiting, large percentages,—rich coffers coined out of the life-blood of human bodies and souls. Men and women herded together like cattle, breathing in malaria and typhus from an atmosphere seething with moral as well as physical impurity, revelling in vice as their native habitat and then, to drown the whisperings of their higher consciousness and effectually to hush the yearnings and accusations within, flying to narcotics and opiates—rum, tobacco, opium, binding hand and foot, body and soul, till the proper image of God is transformed into a fit associate for demons,—a besotted, enervated, idiotic wreck, or else a monster of wickedness terrible and destructive.

These are some of the legitimate products of the unmitigated tendencies of the wealth-producing period. But, thank Heaven, side by side with the cold, mathematical, selfishly calculating, so-called practical and unsentimental instinct of the business man, there comes the sympathetic warmth and sunshine of good women, like the sweet and sweetening breezes of spring, cleansing, purifying, soothing, inspiring, lifting the drunkard from the gutter, the outcast from the pit. Who can estimate the influence of these "daughters of the king," these lend-a-hand forces, in counteracting the selfishness of an acquisitive age?

To-day America counts her millionaires by the thousand; questions of tariff and questions of currency are the most vital ones agitating the public mind. In this period, when material prosperity and well earned ease and luxury are assured facts from a national standpoint, woman's work and woman's influence are needed as never before; needed to bring a heart power into this money getting, dollar-worshipping civilization; needed to bring a moral force into the utilitarian motives and interests of the time; needed to stand for God and Home and Native Land *versus gain and greed and grasping selfishness.*

There can be no doubt that this fourth centenary of America's discovery which we celebrate at Chicago, strikes the keynote of another important transition in the history of this nation; and the prominence of woman in the management of its celebration is a fitting tribute to the part she is destined to play among the forces of the future. This is the first congressional recognition of woman in this country, and this Board of Lady Managers constitute the first women legally appointed by any government to act in a national capacity. This of itself marks the dawn of a new day.

Now the periods of discovery, of settlement, of developing resources and accumulating wealth have passed in rapid succession. Wealth in the nation as in the individual brings leisure, repose, reflection. The struggle with nature is over, the struggle with ideas begins. We stand then, it seems to me, in this last decade of the nineteenth century, just in the portals of a new and untried movement on a higher plain and in a grander strain than any the past has called forth. It does not require a prophet's eye to divine its trend and image its possibilities from the forces we see already at work around us; nor is it hard to guess what must be the status of woman's work under the new regime.

In the pioneer days her role was that of a camp-follower, an additional something to fight for and be burdened with, only repaying the anxiety and labor she called forth by her own incomparable gifts of sympathy and appreciative love; unable herself ordinarily to contend with the bear and the Indian, or to take active part in clearing the wilderness and constructing the home.

In the second or wealth producing period her work is abreast of man's, complementing and supplementing, counteracting excessive tendencies, and mollifying over rigorous proclivities.

In the era now about to dawn, her sentiments must strike the keynote and give the dominant tone. And this because of the nature of her contribution to the world.

Her kingdom is not over physical forces. Not by might, nor by power can she prevail. Her position must ever be inferior where strength of muscle creates leadership. If she follows the instincts of her nature, however, she must always stand for the conservation of those deeper moral forces which make for the happiness of homes and the righteousness of the country. In a reign of moral ideas she is easily queen.

There is to my mind no grander and surer prophecy of the new era and of woman's place in it, than the work already begun in the waning years of the nineteenth century by the W. C. T. U. in America, an organization which has even now reached not only national but international importance, and seems destined to permeate and purify the whole civilized world. It is the living embodiment of woman's activities and woman's ideas, and its extent and strength rightly prefigure her increasing power as a moral factor.

The colored woman of to-day occupies, one may say, a unique position in this country. In a period of itself transitional and unsettled, her status seems one of the least ascertainable and definitive of all the forces which make for our civilization. She is confronted by both a woman question and a race problem, and is as yet an unknown or an unacknowledged factor in both. While the women of the white race can with calm assurance enter upon the work they feel by nature appointed to do, while their men give loyal support and appreciative countenance to their efforts, recognizing in most avenues of usefulness the propriety and the need of woman's distinctive co-operation, the colored woman too often finds herself hampered and shamed by a less liberal sentiment and a more conservative attitude on the part of those for whose opinion she cares most. That this is not universally true I am glad to admit. There are to be found both intensely conservative white men and exceedingly liberal colored men. But as far as my experience goes the average man of our race is less frequently ready to admit the actual need among the sturdier forces of the world for woman's help or influence. That great social and economic questions await her interference, that she could throw any light on problems of national import, that her intermeddling could improve the management of school systems, or elevate the tone of public institutions, or humanize and sanctify the far reaching influence of prisons and reformatories and improve the treatment of lunatics and imbeciles,—that she has a word worth hearing on mooted questions in political economy, that she could contribute a suggestion on the relations of labor and capital, or offer a thought on honest money and honorable trade, I fear the majority of "Americans of the colored variety" are not yet prepared to concede. It may be that they do not yet see these questions in their right perspective, being absorbed in the immediate needs of their own political complications. A good deal depends on where we put the emphasis in this world; and our men are not perhaps to blame if they see everything colored by the light of those agitations in the midst of which they live and move and have their being. The part they have had to play in American history during the last twenty-five or thirty years has tended rather to exaggerate the importance of mere political advantage, as well as to set a fictitious valuation on those able to secure such advantage. It is the astute politician, the manager who can gain preferment for himself and his favorites, the demagogue known to stand in with the powers at the White House and consulted on the bestowal of government plums, whom we set in high places and denominate great. It is they who receive the hosannas of the multitude and are regarded as leaders of the people. The thinker and the doer, the man who solves the problem by enriching his country with an invention worth thousands or by a thought inestimable and precious is given neither bread nor a stone. He is too often left to die in obscurity and neglect even if spared in his life the bitterness of fanatical jealousies and detraction.

And yet politics, and surely American politics, is hardly a school for great minds. Sharpening rather than deepening, it develops the faculty of taking advantage of present emergencies rather than the insight to distinguish between the true and the false, the lasting and the ephemeral advantage. Highly cultivated selfishness rather than consecrated benevolence is its passport to success. Its votaries are never seers. At best they are but manipulators—often only jugglers. It is conducive neither to profound statesmanship nor to the higher type of manhood. Altruism is its *mauvais succes* and naturally enough it is indifferent to any factor which cannot be worked into its own immediate aims and purposes. As woman's influence as a political element is as yet nil in most of the commonwealths of our republic, it is not surprising that with those who place the emphasis on mere political capital she may yet seem almost a nonentity so far as it concerns the solution of great national or even racial perplexities.

There are those, however, who value the calm elevation of the thoughtful spectator who stands aloof from the heated scramble; and, above the turmoil and din of corruption and selfishness, can listen to the teachings of eternal truth and righteousness. There are even those who feel that the black man's unjust and unlawful exclusion temporarily from participation in the elective franchise in certain states is after all but a lesson "in the desert" fitted to develop in him insight and discrimination against the day of his own appointed time. One needs occasionally to stand aside from the hum and rush of human interests and passions to hear the voices of God. And it not unfrequently happens that the All-loving gives a great push to certain souls to thrust them out, as it were, from the distracting current for awhile to promote their discipline and growth, or to enrich them by communion and reflection. And similarly it may be woman's privilege from her peculiar coigne of vantage as a quiet observer, to whisper just the needed suggestion or the almost forgotten truth. The colored woman, then, should not be ignored because her bark is resting in the silent waters of the sheltered cove. She is watching the movements of the contestants none the less and is all the better qualified, perhaps, to weigh and judge and advise because not herself in the excitement of the race. Her voice, too, has always been heard in clear, unfaltering tones, ringing the changes on those deeper interests which make for permanent good. She is always sound and orthodox on questions affecting the well-being of her race. You do not find the colored woman selling her birthright for a mess of pottage. Nay, even after reason has retired from the contest, she has been known to cling blindly with the instinct of a turtle dove to those principles and policies which to her mind promise hope and safety for children yet unborn. It is notorious that ignorant black women in the South have actually left their husbands' homes and repudiated their support for what was understood by the wife to be race disloyalty, or "voting away," as she expresses it, the privileges of herself and little ones.

It is largely our women in the South to-day who keep the black men solid in the Republican party. The latter as they increase in intelligence and power of discrimination would be more apt to divide on local issues at any rate. They begin to see that the Grand Old Party regards the Negro's cause as an outgrown issue, and on Southern soil at least finds a too intimate acquaintanceship with him a somewhat unsavory recommendation. Then, too, their political wits have been sharpened to appreciate the fact that it is good policy to cultivate one's neighbors and not depend too much on a distant friend to fight one's home battles. But the black woman can never forget—however lukewarm the party may to-day appear—that it was a Republican president who struck the manacles from her own wrists and gave—the possibilities of manhood to her helpless little ones; and to her mind a Democratic Negro is a traitor and a time-server. Talk as much as you like of venality and manipulation in the South, there are not many men, I can tell you, who would dare face a wife quivering in every fiber with the consciousness that her husband is a coward who could be paid to desert her deepest and dearest interests.

Not unfelt, then, if unproclaimed has been the work and influence of the colored women of America. Our list of chieftains in the service, though not long, is not inferior in strength and excellence, I dare believe, to any similar list which this country can produce.

Among the pioneers, Frances Watkins Harper could sing with prophetic exaltation in the darkest days, when as yet there was not a rift in the clouds overhanging her people:

> "Yes, Ethiopia shall stretch
> Her bleeding hands abroad;
> Her cry of agony shall reach the burning throne of God.
>   Redeemed from dust and freed from chains
>   Her sons shall lift their eyes,
>   From cloud-capt hills and verdant plains
>   Shall shouts of triumph rise."

Among preachers of righteousness, an unanswerable silencer of cavilers and objectors, was Sojourner Truth, that unique and rugged genius who seemed carved out without hand or chisel from the solid mountain mass; and in pleasing contrast, Amanda Smith, sweetest of natural singers and pleaders in dulcet tones for the things of God and of His Christ.

Sarah Woodson Early and Martha Briggs, planting and watering in the school room, and giving off from their matchless and irresistible personality an impetus and inspiration which can never die so long as there lives and breathes a remote descendant of their disciples and friends.

Charlotte Fortin Grimke, the gentle spirit whose verses and life link her so beautifully with America's great Quaker poet and loving reformer.

Hallie Quinn Brown, charming reader, earnest, effective lecturer and devoted worker of unflagging zeal and unquestioned power.

Fannie Jackson Coppin, the teacher and organizer, pre-eminent among women of whatever country or race in constructive and executive force.

These women represent all shades of belief and as many departments of activity; but they have one thing in common—their sympathy with the oppressed race in America and the consecration of their several talents in whatever line to the work of its deliverance and development.

Fifty years ago woman's activity according to orthodox definitions was on a pretty clearly cut "sphere," including primarily the kitchen and the nursery, and rescued from the barrenness of prison bars by the womanly mania for adorning every discoverable bit of china or canvass with forlorn looking cranes balanced idiotically on one foot. The woman of to-day finds herself in the presence of responsibilities which ramify through the profoundest and most varied interests of her country and race. Not one of the issues of this plodding, toiling, sinning, repenting, falling, aspiring humanity can afford to shut her out, or can deny the reality of her influence. No plan for renovating society, no scheme for purifying politics, no reform in church or in state, no moral, social, or economic question, no movement upward or downward in the human plane is lost on her. A man once said when told his house was afire: "Go tell my wife; I never meddle with household affairs." But no woman can possibly put herself or her sex outside any of the interests that affect humanity. All departments in the new era are to be hers, in the sense that her interests are in all and through all; and it is incumbent on her to keep intelligently and sympathetically *en rapport* with all the great movements of her time, that she may know on which side to throw the weight of her influence. She stands now at the gateway of this new era of American civilization. In her hands must be moulded the strength, the wit, the statesmanship, the morality, all the psychic force, the social and economic intercourse of that era. To be alive at such an epoch is a privilege, to be a woman then is sublime.

In this last decade of our century, changes of such moment are in progress, such new and alluring vistas are opening out before us, such original and radical suggestions for the adjustment of labor and capital, of government and the governed, of the family, the church and the state, that to be a possible factor though an infinitesimal in such a movement is pregnant with hope and weighty with responsibility. To be a woman in such an age carries with it a privilege and an opportunity never implied before. But to be a woman of the Negro race in America, and to be able to grasp the deep significance of the possibilities of the crisis, is to have a heritage, it seems to me, unique in the ages. In the first place, the race is young and full of the elasticity and hopefulness of youth. All its achievements are before it. It does not look on the masterly triumphs of nineteenth century civilization with that *blasé* world-weary look which characterizes the old washed out and worn out races which have already, so to speak, seen their best days.

Said a European writer recently: "Except the Sclavonic, the Negro is the only original and distinctive genius which has yet to come to growth—and the feeling is to cherish and develop it."

Everything to this race is new and strange and inspiring. There is a quickening of its pulses and a glowing of its self-consciousness. Aha, I can rival that! I can aspire to that! I can honor my name and vindicate my race! Something like this, it strikes me, is the enthusiasm which stirs the genius of young Africa in America; and the memory of past oppression and the fact of present attempted repression only serve to gather momentum for its irrepressible powers. Then again, a race in such a stage of growth is peculiarly sensitive to impressions. Not the photographer's sensitized plate is more delicately impressionable to outer influences than is this high strung people here on the threshold of a career.

What a responsibility then to have the sole management of the primal lights and shadows! Such is the colored woman's office. She must stamp weal or woe on the coming history of this people. May she see her opportunity and vindicate her high prerogative.

MARY CHURCH TERRELL

The Progress of Colored Women

Comments

Forty years ago, when the question of suffrage for American mothers, wives, and sisters, was in its 'teens, Sojourner Truth, sometimes called the American Sibyl, was the sole representative of the negro women of the United States, in the movement which has just celebrated its fiftieth birthday so auspiciously.

During the intervening years, since I first saw and heard that wonderfully gifted black woman, in the old Melodeon, Boston, the Woman's Suffrage platform I believe, has never lacked some representative of the race once oppressed, and now partially free.

Many of them were women of peculiar gifts, some of especial achievement, but more selected, through the calm determination of Susan B. Anthony, Anna Shaw, Elizabeth Cady Stanton and the esoteric circle, to have at all times their sister of a darker hue, duly represented on their broad platform.

The distance from Sojourner Truth to Mary Church Terrell is really more than the forty or fifty years of fight for political recognition for women. It is an infinitely greater distance, almost limitless space, between the centuries of debasement and degradation of a sex, and the meteor's flight of education, purity, *a plomb*, rare scholarly training and literary culture.

The cold type cannot give to those who simply read the following earnest words, full of suggestive thought, of pathos and deepest reflection, that warmth

Mary Church Terrell, *The Progress of Colored Women*, address delivered before the National American Women's Suffrage Association, Washington, D.C., February 18, 1898 (Washington, D.C.: Smith Brothers Printers, 1898).

and color which the occasion itself furnished—the brilliant setting, the *entourage* of intellectuality which made this the finest meeting of a most notable assembly.

Nor can the ordinary reader perceive the severity of the test, which set this champion of her sex, in juxtaposition in forensic art, with such warworn and battle-scarred veterans, as Miss Anthony, Mrs. Blake, Mrs. Shaw, Mrs. Foster, and with the able and eloquent representatives of Norway and Sweden.

Never have I seen a more profound impression nor felt myself more stirred at the romance of the American negro as exemplified in the deeper tragedy of the negro woman, who stands today not merely the forlorn hope of the race; but in her achievements and her attainments, in her sorrows, travailing, and aspirations, the highest type of the race—the portion, psychologically and physiologically, upon which its future mainly depends.

That the opportunity was afforded Mary Church Terrell, to sound the note, and sing so strong, beautifully and pathetically the refrain of her struggling sex, is a source of extreme gratification to those of us, who well know her advantages of training, travel and culture; but even we were surprised most agreeably, and delighted at the able treatment and the signal success of her womanly exposition, judged by its cordial reception and its evident effect upon the audience.

Such occasions rarely occur in a race's history and it is no small privilege to be permitted, as I am here, to call attention to one for the history of the race, whose annals unfortunately are only too brief and at best most imperfectly kept.

RICHARD T. GREENER
Washington, D.C., February 19, '98.

On Friday night last a scene was witnessed at the Columbia Theatre, the meeting place of the Women's Suffrage Convention, in this city, that to a majority of the audience, composed as it was, of the upper crust of white society, was a revelation. There were four addresses by eminent women of different nationalities viz., Sweden, Norwegian, American white and American negro. The latter, Mrs. Mary Church Terrell, spoke on the "Progress of Colored Women." She spoke, as she always does, without notes, and for a half hour, in one unbroken chain of eloquence, and with power and fascination of manner such as few women possess, she held her vast audience spell bound with amazement, and the woman suffragists on the platform were so proud of their new discovery that they fell upon her neck upon the conclusion of her great speech and kissed her. She was almost covered with floral offerings.

Mrs. Terrell opened the eyes of her hearers, both white and colored, to many facts of interest occurring among our women throughout the country, especially in the South, showing the surprising progress made along all lines since emancipation. She very pointedly answered a southern white delegate who had spoken earlier in the week, giving her to understand that indiscriminate mixing with the whites was no more desired by the colored than by the whites; that what they wanted was only an equal chance in the race of life. Social questions would regulate themselves.

She made a most magnificent and womanly appeal for the encouragement and assistance of the white women of the country in the work of breaking up some of the obnoxious systems in the South that tend to degrade colored women—the "jim crow" car, convict lease system, and other unsavory institutions corrupting to good morals. The opportunity offered Mrs. Terrell by Miss Susan B. Anthony to address the National Woman's Right Association, composed of the most progressive and brainiest women of our country, was no small compliment viewed from whatever standpoint. That Mrs. Terrell came up to the full measure of her opportunity, none who were present will gainsay she went beyond and over it. She covered almost all the ground of our grievances in the small space of the half hour allotted to her, and to do this she had to speak rapidly, but not a word or syllable was lost to her hearers. Her appeal for the women of her race was a soul-stirring effort; and the long continued applause that followed at the close of her remarks attested that she had won her hearers to her.

CHARLES R. DOUGLASS.
Colored American, February 26, '98

The Progress of Colored Women[1]

Fifty years ago a meeting such as this, planned, conducted and addressed by women would have been an impossibility. Less than forty years ago, few sane men, would have predicted that either a slave or one of his descendants would in this century at least, address such an audience in the Nation's Capital at the invitation of women representing the highest, broadest, best type of womanhood, that can be found anywhere in the world. Thus to me this semi-centennial of the National American Woman Suffrage Association is a double jubilee, rejoicing as I do, not only in the prospective enfranchisement of my sex but in the emancipation of my race. When Ernestine Rose, Lucretia Mott, Elizabeth Cady Stanton, Lucy Stone and Susan B. Anthony began that agitation by which colleges were opened to women and the numerous reforms inaugurated for the amelioration of their condition along all lines, their sisters who groaned in bondage had little reason to hope that these blessings would ever brighten their crushed and blighted lives, for during those days of oppression and despair, colored women were not only refused admittance to institutions of learning, but the law of the States in which the majority lived made it a crime to teach them to read. Not only could they possess no property, but even their bodies were not their own. Nothing, in short, that could degrade or brutalize the womanhood of the race was lacking in that system from which colored women then had little hope of escape. So gloomy were their prospects, so fatal the laws, so pernicious the customs, only fifty years ago. But, from the day their fetters were broken and their minds released from the darkness of ignorance to which for more than two hundred years they had been doomed, from the day they could stand erect in the dignity of womanhood, no longer bond but free, till tonight, colored women have forged steadily ahead in the acquisition of knowledge and in the cultivation of those virtues which make for good. To use a thought of the illustrious Frederick Douglass, if judged by the depths from which they have come, rather than by the heights to which those blessed with centuries of opportunities have attained, colored women need not hang their head in shame. Consider if you will, the almost insurmountable obstacles which have confronted colored women in their efforts to educate and cultivate themselves since their emancipation, and I dare assert, not boastfully, but with pardonable pride, I hope, that the progress they have made and the work they have accomplished, will bear a favorable comparison at least with that of their more fortunate sisters, from whom the opportunity of acquiring knowledge and the means of self-culture have never been entirely withheld. For, not only are colored women with ambition and aspiration handicapped on account of their sex, but they are everywhere baffled and mocked on account of their race. Desperately and continuously they are forced to fight that opposition, born of a cruel, unreasonable prejudice which neither their merit nor their necessity seems able to subdue. Not only because they are women, but because they are colored women, are discouragement and disappointment meeting them at every turn. Avocations opened and opportunities offered to their more favored sisters have been and are tonight closed and barred against them. While those of the dominant race have a variety of trades and pursuits from which they may choose, the woman through whose veins one drop of African blood is known to flow is limited to a pitiful few. So overcrowded are the avocation's in which colored women may engage and so poor is the pay in consequence, that only the barest livelihood can be eked out by the rank and file. And yet, in spite of the opposition encountered, and the obstacles opposed to their acquisition of knowledge and their accumulation of property, the progress made by colored women along these lines has never surpassed by that of any people in the history of the world. (Though the slaves were liberated less than forty years ago, penniless, and ignorant, with neither shelter, nor food, so great was their thirst for knowledge and so herculean were their efforts to secure it, that there are today hundreds of negroes, many of them women, who are graduates, some of them having taken degrees from the best institutions of the land. From Oberlin, that friend of the oppressed, Oberlin, my dear alma mater, whose name will always be loved and whose praise will ever be sung as the first college in the country which was just, broad and benevolent enough to open its doors to negroes and to women on an equal footing with men; from Wellesley and Vassar, from Cornell and Ann Arbor, from the best high schools throughout the North, East and West, colored girls have been graduated with honors, and have thus forever settled the question of their capacity and worth. But a few years ago in an examination in which a large number of young women and men competed for a scholarship, entitling the successful competitor to an entire course through the Chicago University, the only colored girl among them stood first and captured this great prize. And so, wherever colored girls have studied, their instructors bear testimony to their intelligence, diligence and success.

With this increase of wisdom there has sprung up in the hearts of colored women an ardent desire to do good in the world. No sooner had the favored few availed themselves of such advantages as they could secure than they hastened to dispense these blessings to the less fortunate of their race. With tireless energy and eager zeal, colored women have, since their emancipation, been continuously prosecuting the work of educating and elevating their race, as though upon themselves alone devolved the accomplishment of this great task. Of the teachers engaged in instructing colored youth, it is perhaps no exaggeration to say that fully ninety per cent are women. In the back-woods, remote from the civilization and comforts of the city and town, on the plantations, reeking with ignorance and vice, our colored women may be found battling with evils which such conditions always entail. Many a heroine, of whom the world will never hear, has thus sacrificed her life to her race, amid surroundings and in the face of privations which only martyrs can tolerate and bear. Shirking responsibility has never been a fault with which colored women might be truthfully charged. Indefatigably and conscientiously, in public work of all kinds they engage, that they may benefit and elevate their race. The result of this labor has been prodigious indeed. By banding themselves together in the interest of education and morality, by adopting the most practical and useful means to this end, colored women have in thirty short years become a great power for good. Through the National Association of Colored Women, which was formed by the union of two large organizations in July, 1896, and which is now the only national body among colored women, much good has been done in the past, and more will be accomplished in the future, we hope. Believing that it is only through the home that a people can become really good and truly great, the National Association of Colored Women has entered that sacred domain. Homes, more homes, better homes, purer homes is the text upon which our sermons have been and will be preached. Through mothers' meetings, which are a special feature of the work planned by the Association, much useful information in everything pertaining to the home will be disseminated. We would have heart-to-heart talks with our women, that we may strike at the root of evils, many of which lie, alas, at the fireside. If the women of the dominant race with all the centuries of education, culture and refinement back of them with all their wealth of opportunity ever present with them—if these women feel the need of a Mothers' Congress that they may be enlightened as to the best methods of rearing children and conducting their homes, how much more do our women, from whom shackles have but yesterday fallen, need information on the same vital subjects? And so throughout the country we are working vigorously and conscientiously to establish Mothers' Congresses in every community in which our women may be found.

Under the direction of the Tuskegee, Alabama branch of the National Association, the work of bringing the light of knowledge and the gospel of cleanliness to their benighted sisters on the plantations has been conducted with signal success. Their efforts have thus far been confined to four estates, comprising thousands of acres of land, on which live hundreds of colored people, yet in the darkness of ignorance and the grip of sin, miles away from churches and schools. Under the evil influences of plantation owners, and through no fault of their own, the condition of the colored people is, in some sections to-day no better than it was at the close of the war. Feeling the great responsibility resting upon them, therefore, colored women, both in organizations under the National Association, and as individuals are working with might and main to afford their unfortunate sisters opportunities of civilization and education, which without them, they would be unable to secure.

By the Tuskegee club and many others all over the country, object lessons are given in the best way to sweep, dust, cook, wash and iron, together with other information concerning household affairs. Talks on social purity and the proper method of rearing children are made for the benefit of those mothers, who in many instances fall short of their duty, not because they are vicious and depraved but because they are ignorant and poor. Against the one-room cabin so common in the rural settlements in the South, we have inaugurated a vigorous crusade. When families of eight or ten, consisting of men, women and children, are all huddled together in a single apartment, a condition of things found not only in the South, but among our poor all over the land, there is little hope of inculcating morality or modesty. And yet, in spite of these environments which are so destructive of virtue, and though the safeguards usually thrown around maidenly youth and innocence are in some sections withheld from colored girls, statistics compiled by men, not inclined to falsify in favor of my race, show that immorality among *colored women* is *not* so great as among women in countries like Austria, Italy, Germany, Sweden and France.

In New York City a mission has been established and is entirely supported by colored women under supervision of the New York City Board. It has in operation a kindergarten, classes in cooking and sewing, mothers' meetings, mens' meetings, a reading circle and a manual training school for boys. Much the same kind of work is done by the Colored Woman's League and the Ladies Auxiliary of this city, the Kansas City League of Missouri, the Woman's Era Club of Boston, the Woman's Loyal Union of New York, and other organizations representing almost every State in the Union. The Phyllis Wheatley Club of New Orleans, another daughter of the National Association, has in two short years succeeded in establishing a Sanatorium and a Training School for nurses. The conditions which caused the colored women of New Orleans to choose this special field in which to operate are such as exist in many other sections of our land. From the city hospitals colored doctors are excluded altogether, not even being allowed to practice in the colored wards, and colored patients—no matter how wealthy they are—are not received at all, unless they are willing to go into the charity wards. Thus the establishment of a Sanatorium answers a variety of purposes. It affords colored medical students an opportunity of gaining a practical knowledge of their profession, and it furnishes a well-equipped establishment for colored patients who do not care to go into the charity wards of the public hospitals.

The daily clinics have been a great blessing to the colored poor. In the operating department, supplied with all the modern appliances, two hundred operations have been performed, all of which have resulted successfully under the colored surgeon-in-chief. Of the eight nurses who have registered, one has already passed an examination before the State Medical Board of Louisiana, and is now practicing her profession. During the yellow fever epidemic in New Orleans last summer, there was a constant demand for Phyllis Wheatley nurses. By indefatigable energy and heroic sacrifice of both money and time, these noble women raised nearly one thousand dollars, with which to defray the expenses of the Sanatorium for the first eight months of its existence. They have recently succeeded in securing from the city of New Orleans an annual appropriation of two hundred and forty dollars, which they hope will soon be increased. Dotted all over the country are charitable organizations for the aged, orphaned and poor, which have been established by colored women; just how many, it is difficult to state. Since there is such an imperative need of statistics, bearing on the progress, possessions, and prowess of colored women, the National Association has undertaken to secure this data of such value and importance to the race. Among the charitable institutions, either founded, conducted or supported by colored women, may be mentioned the Hale Infirmary of Montgomery, Alabama; the Carrie Steel Orphanage of Atlanta; the Reed Orphan Home of Covington; the Haines Industrial School of Augusta in the State of Georgia; a Home for the Aged of both races at New Bedford and St. Monica's Home of Boston in Massachusetts; Old Folks' Home of Memphis, Tenn.; Colored Orphan's Home, Lexington, Ky., together with others of which time forbids me to speak.

Mt. Meigs Institute is an excellent example of a work originated and carried into successful execution by a colored woman. The school was established for the benefit of colored people on the plantations in the black belt of Alabama, because of the 700,000 negroes living in that State, probably 90 per cent are outside of the cities; and Waugh was selected because in the township of Mt. Meigs, the population is practically all colored. Instruction given in this school is of the kind best suited to the needs of those people for whom it was established. Along with their scholastic training, girls are taught everything pertaining to the management of a home, while boys learn practical farming, carpentering, wheel-wrighting, blacksmithing, and have some military training. Having started with almost nothing, only eight years ago, the trustees of the school now own nine acres of land, and five buildings, in which two thousand pupils have received instruction—all through the courage, the industry and sacrifice of one good woman. The Chicago clubs and several others engage in rescue work among fallen women and tempted girls.

Questions affecting our legal status as a race are also constantly agitated by our women. In Louisiana and Tennessee, colored women have several times petitioned the legislatures of their respective States to repeal the obnoxious "Jim Crow Car" laws, nor will any stone be left unturned until this iniquitous and unjust enactment against respectable American citizens be forever wiped from the statutes of the South. Against the barbarous Convict Lease System of Georgia, of which negroes, especially the female prisoners, are the principal victims, colored women are waging a ceaseless war. By two lecturers, each of whom, under the Woman's Christian Temperance Union has been National Superintendent of work among colored people, the cause of temperance has for many years been eloquently espoused.

In business, colored women have had signal success. There is in Alabama a large milling and cotton business belonging to and controlled entirely by a colored woman who has sometimes as many as seventy-five men in her employ. In Halifax, Nova Scotia, the principal ice plant of the city is owned and managed by one of our women. In the professions we have dentists and doctors, whose practice is lucrative and large. Ever since the publication in 1773, of a book entitled "Poems on Various Subjects, Religious and Moral," by Phyllis Wheatley, negro servant of Mr. John Wheatley of Boston, colored women have from time to time given abundant evidence of literary ability. In sculpture we are represented by a woman upon whose chisel Italy has set her seal of approval; in painting, by Bougerean's pupil, whose work was exhibited in the last Paris Salon, and in Music by young women holding diplomas from the first conservatories in the land.

And, finally, as an organization of women nothing lies nearer the heart of the National Association than the children, many of whose lives, so sad and dark, we might brighten and bless. It is the kindergarten we need. Free kindergartens in every city and hamlet of this broad land we must have, if the children are to receive from us what it is our duty to give. Already during the past year kindergartens have been established and successfully maintained by several organizations, from which most encouraging reports have come. May their worthy, example be emulated, till in no branch of the Association shall the children of the poor, at least, be deprived of the blessings which flow from the kindergarten alone. The more unfavorable the environments of children, the more necessary is it that steps be taken to counteract baleful influences on innocent victims. How imperative is it then that as colored women, we inculcate correct principles and set good examples for our own youth, whose little feet will have so many thorny paths of prejudice, temptation, and injustice to tread. The colored youth is vicious we are told, and statistics showing the multitudes of our boys and girls who crowd the penitentiaries and fill the jails appall and dishearten us. But side by side with these facts and figures of crime I would have presented and pictured the miserable hovels from which these youthful criminals come. Make a tour of the settlements of colored people, who in many cities are relegated to the most noisome sections permitted by the municipal government, and behold the mites of humanity who infest them. Here are our little ones, the future representatives of the race, fairly drinking in the pernicious example of their elders, coming in contact with nothing but ignorance and vice, till at the age of six, evil habits are formed which no amount of civilizing or Christianizing can ever completely break. Listen to the cry of our children. In imitation of the example set by the Great Teacher of men, who could not offer himself as a sacrifice, until he had made an eternal plea for the innocence and helplessness of childhood, colored women are everywhere reaching out after the waifs and strays, who without their aid may be doomed to lives of evil and shame. As an organization, the National Association of Colored Women feels that the establishment of kindergartens is the special mission which we are called to fulfill. So keenly alive are we to the necessity of rescuing our little ones, whose noble qualities are deadened and dwarfed by the very atmosphere which they breathe, that the officers of the Association are now trying to secure means by which to send out a kindergarten organizer, whose duty it shall be both to arouse the conscience of our women, and to establish kindergartens, wherever the means therefor can be secured.

And so, lifting as we climb, onward and upward we go, struggling and striving, and hoping that the buds and blossoms of our desires will burst into glorious fruition ere long. With courage, born of success achieved in the past, with a keen sense of the responsibility which we shall continue to assume, we look forward to a future large with promise and hope. Seeking no favors because of our color, nor patronage because of our needs, we knock at the bar of justice, asking an equal chance.

NOTE

1. Among the speakers of the Convention were Susan B. Anthony, Isabella Beecher Hooker, Rev. Anna H. Shaw, Lillie Deverux, Mary Wright Sewell, and Carrie Chapman Catt.

CARTER G. WOODSON

The Exodus during the World War

Within the last two years there has been a steady stream of Negroes into the North in such large numbers as to overshadow in its results all other movements of the kind in the United States. These Negroes have come largely from Alabama, Tennessee, Florida, Georgia, Virginia, North Carolina, Kentucky, South Carolina, Arkansas and Mississippi. The given causes of this migration are numerous and complicated. Some untruths centering around this exodus have not been unlike those of other migrations. Again we hear that the Negroes are being brought North to fight organized labor,[1] and to carry doubtful States for the Republicans.[2] These numerous explanations themselves, however, give rise to doubt as to the fundamental cause.

Why then should the Negroes leave the South? It has often been spoken of as the best place for them. There, it is said, they have made unusual strides forward. The progress of the Negroes in the South, however, has in no sense been general, although the land owned by Negroes in the country and the property of thrifty persons of their race in urban communities may be extensive. In most parts of the South the Negroes are still unable to become landowners or successful business men. Conditions and customs have reserved these spheres for the whites. Generally speaking, the Negroes are still dependent on the white people for food and shelter. Although not exactly slaves, they are yet attached to the white people as tenants, servants or dependents. Accepting this as their lot, they have been content to wear their lord's cast-off

Carter G. Woodson, "The Exodus during the World War," chap. 9 of *A Century of Negro Migration* (Washington, D.C.: The Association for the Study of Negro Life and History, 1918), 167–192.

clothing, and live in his ramshackled barn or cellar. In this unhappy state so many have settled down, losing all ambition to attain a higher station. The world has gone on but in their sequestered sphere progress has passed them by.

What then is the cause? There have been *bulldozing*, terrorism, maltreatment and what not of persecution; but the Negroes have not in large numbers wandered away from the land of their birth. What the migrants themselves think about it, goes to the very heart of the trouble. Some say that they left the South on account of injustice in the courts, unrest, lack of privileges, denial of the right to vote, bad treatment, oppression, segregation or lynching. Others say that they left to find employment, to secure better wages, better school facilities, and better opportunities to toil upward.[3] Southern white newspapers unaccustomed to give the Negroes any mention but that of criminals have said that the Negroes are going North because they have not had a fair chance in the South and that if they are to be retained there, the attitude of the whites toward them must be changed. Professor William O. Scroggs, of Louisiana State University, considers as causes of this exodus "the relatively low wages paid farm labor, an unsatisfactory tenant or crop-sharing system, the boll weevil, the crop failure of 1916, lynching, disfranchisement, segregation, poor schools, and the monotony, isolation and drudgery of farm life." Professor Scroggs, however, is wrong in thinking that the persecution of the blacks has little to do with the migration for the reason that during these years when the treatment of the Negroes is decidedly better they are leaving the South. This does not mean that they would not have left before, if they had had economic opportunities in the North. It is highly probable that the Negroes would not be leaving the South today, if they were treated as men, although there might be numerous opportunities for economic improvement in the North.[4]

The immediate cause of this movement was the suffering due to the floods aggravated by the depredations of the boll weevil. Although generally mindful of our welfare, the United States Government has not been as ready to build levees against a natural enemy to property as it has been to provide fortifications for warfare. It has been necessary for local communities and State governments to tax themselves to maintain them. The national government, however, has appropriated to the purpose of facilitating inland navigation certain sums which have been used in doing this work, especially in the Mississippi Valley. There are now 1,538 miles of levees on both sides of the Mississippi from Cape Girardeau to the passes. These levees, of course, are still inadequate to the security of the planters against these inundations. Carrying 406 million tons of mud a year, the river becomes a dangerous stream subject to change, abandoning its old bed to cut for itself a new channel, transferring property from one State to another, isolating cities and leaving once useful levees marooned in the landscape like old Indian mounds or overgrown entrenchments.[5]

This valley has, therefore, been frequently visited with disasters which have often set the population in motion. The first disastrous floods came in 1858 and 1859, breaking many of the levees, the destruction of which was practically completed by the floods of 1865 and 1869. There is an annual rise in the stream, but since 1874 this river system has fourteen times devastated large areas of this section with destructive floods. The property in this district depreciated in value to the extent of about 400 millions in ten years. Farmers from this section, therefore, have at times moved west with foreigners to take up public lands.

The other disturbing factor in this situation was the boll weevil, an interloper from Mexico in 1892. The boll weevil is an insect about one fourth of an inch in length, varying from one eighth to one third of an inch with a breadth of about one third of the length. When it first emerges it is yellowish, then becomes grayish brown and finally assumes a black shade. It breeds on no other plant than cotton and feeds on the boll. This little animal, at first attacked the cotton crop in Texas. It was not thought that it would extend its work into the heart of the South so as to become of national consequence, but it has, at the rate of forty to one hundred sixty miles annually, invaded all of the cotton district except that of the Carolinas and Virginia. The damage it does, varies according to the rainfall and the harshness of the winter, increasing with the former and decreasing with the latter. At times the damage has been to the extent of a loss of 50 per cent of the crop, estimated at 400,000 bales of cotton annually, about 4,500,000 bales since the invasion or $250,000,000 worth of cotton.[6] The output of the South being thus cut off, the planter has less income to provide supplies for his black tenants and, the prospects for future production being dark, merchants accustomed to give them credit have to refuse. This, of course, means financial depression, for the South is a borrowing section and any limitation to credit there blocks the wheels of industry. It was fortunate for the Negro laborers in this district that there was then a demand for labor in the North when this condition began to obtain.

This demand was made possible by the cutting off of European immigration by the World War, which thereby rendered this hitherto uncongenial section an inviting field for the Negro. The Negroes have made some progress in the North during the last fifty years, but despite their achievements they have been so handicapped by race prejudice and proscribed by trades unions that the uplift of the race by economic methods has been impossible. The European immigrants have hitherto excluded the Negroes even from the menial positions. In the midst of the drudgery left for them, the blacks have often heretofore been debased to the status of dependents and paupers. Scattered through the North too in such small numbers, they have been unable to unite for social betterment and mutual improvement and naturally too weak to force the community to respect their wishes as could be done by a large group with some political or economic power. At present, however, Negro laborers, who once went from city to city, seeking such employment as trades unions left to them, can work even as skilled laborers throughout the North.[7] Women of color formerly excluded from domestic service by foreign maids are now in demand. Many mills and factories which Negroes were prohibited from entering a few years ago are now bidding for their labor. Railroads cannot find help to keep their property in repair, contractors fall short of their plans for failure to hold mechanics drawn into the industrial boom and the United States Government has had to advertise for men to hasten the preparation for war.

Men from afar went south to tell the Negroes of a way of escape to a more congenial place. Blacks long since unaccustomed to venture a few miles from home, at once had visions of a promised land just a few hundred miles away. Some were told of the chance to amass fabulous riches, some of the opportunities for education and some of the hospitality of the places of amusement and recreation in the North. The migrants then were soon on the way. Railway stations became conspicuous with the presence of Negro tourists, the trains were crowded to full capacity and the streets of northern cities were soon congested with black laborers seeking to realize their dreams in the land of unusual opportunity.

Employment agencies, recently multiplied to meet the demand for labor, find themselves unable to cope with the situation and agents sent into the South to induce the blacks by offers of free transportation and high wages to go north, have found it impossible to supply the demand in centers where once toiled the Poles, Italians and the Greeks formerly preferred to the Negroes.[8] In other words, the present migration differs from others in that the Negro has opportunity awaiting him in the North whereas formerly it was necessary for him to make a place for himself upon arriving among enemies. The proportion of those returning to the South, therefore, will be inconsiderable.

Becoming alarmed at the immensity of this movement the South has undertaken to check it. To frighten Negroes from the North southern newspapers are carefully circulating reports that many of them are returning to their native land because of unexpected hardships.[9] But having failed in this, southerners have compelled employment agents to cease operations there, arrested suspected employers and, to prevent the departure of the Negroes, imprisoned on false charges those who appear at stations to leave for the North. This procedure could not long be effective, for by the more legal and clandestine methods of railway passenger agents the work has gone forward. Some southern communities have, therefore, advocated drastic legislation against labor agents, as was suggested in Louisiana in 1914, when by operation of the Underwood Tariff Law the Negroes thrown out of employment in the sugar district migrated to the cotton plantations.[10]

One should not, however, get the impression that the majority of the Negroes are leaving the South. Eager as these Negroes seem to go, there is no unanimity of opinion as to whether migration is the best policy. The sycophant, toady class of Negroes naturally advise the blacks to remain in the South to serve their white neighbors. The radical protagonists of the equal-rights-for-all element urge them to come North by all means. Then there are the thinking Negroes, who are still further divided. Both divisions of this element have the interests of the race at heart, but they are unable to agree as to exactly what the blacks should now do. Thinking that the present war will soon be over and that consequently the immigration of foreigners into this country will again set in and force out of employment thousands of Negroes who have migrated to the North, some of the most representative Negroes are advising their fellows to remain where they are. The most serious objection to this transplantation is that it means for the Negroes a loss of land, the rapid acquisition of which has long been pointed to as the best evidence of the ability of the blacks to rise in the economic world. So many Negroes who have by dint of energy purchased small farms yielding an increasing income from year to year, are now disposing of them at nominal prices to come north to work for wages. Looking beyond the war, however, and thinking too that the depopulation of Europe during this upheaval will render immigration from that quarter for some years an impossibility, other thinkers urge the Negroes to continue the migration to the North, where the race may be found in sufficiently large numbers to wield economic and political power.

Great as is the dearth of labor in the South, moreover, the Negro exodus has not as yet caused such a depression as to unite the whites in inducing the blacks to remain in that section. In the first place, the South has not yet felt the worst effects of this economic upheaval as that part of the country has been unusually aided by the millions which the United States Government is daily spending there. Furthermore, the poor whites are anxious to see the exodus of their competitors in the field of labor. This leaves the capitalists at their mercy, and in keeping with their domineering attitude, they will be able to handle the labor situation as they desire. As an evidence of this fact we need but note the continuation of mob rule and lynching in the South despite the preachings against it of the organs of thought which heretofore winked at it. This terrorism has gone to an unexpected extent. Negro farmers have been threatened with bodily injury, unless they leave certain parts.

The southerner of aristocratic bearing will say that only the shiftless poor whites terrorize the Negroes. This may be so, but the truth offers little consolation when we observe that most white people in the South are of this class; and the tendency of this element to put their children to work before they secure much education does not indicate that the South will soon experience that general enlightenment necessary to exterminate these survivals of barbarism. Unless the upper classes of the whites can bring the mob around to their way of thinking that the persecution of the Negro is prejudicial to the interests of all, it is not likely that mob rule will soon cease and the migration to this extent will be promoted rather than retarded.

It is unfortunate for the South that the growing consciousness of the Negroes has culminated at the very time they are most needed. Finally heeding the advice of agricultural experts to re-construct its agricultural system, the South has learned in the school of bitter experience to depart from the plan of producing the single cotton crop. It is now raising food-stuffs to make that section self-supporting without reducing the usual output of cotton. With the increasing production in the South, therefore, more labor is needed just at the very time it is being drawn to centers in the North. The North being an industrial and commercial section has usually attracted the immigrants, who will never fit into the economic situation in the South because they will not accept the treatment given Negroes. The South, therefore, is now losing the only labor which it can ever use under present conditions.

Where these Negroes are going is still more interesting. The exodus to the west was mainly directed to Kansas and neighboring States, the migration to the Southwest centered in Oklahoma and Texas, pioneering Negro laborers drifted into the industrial district of the Appalachian highland during the eighties and nineties and the infiltration of the discontented talented tenth affected largely the cities of the North. But now we are told that at the very time the mining districts of the North and West are being filled with blacks the western planters are supplying their farms with them and that into some cities have gone sufficient skilled and unskilled Negro workers to increase the black population more than one hundred per cent. Places in the North, where the black population has not only not increased but even decreased in recent years, are now receiving a steady influx of Negroes. In fact, this is a nation-wide migration; affecting all parts and all conditions.

Students of social problems are now wondering whether the Negro can be adjusted in the North. Many perplexing problems must arise. This movement will produce results not unlike those already mentioned in the discussion of other migrations, some of which we have evidence of today. There will be an increase in race prejudice leading in some communities to actual outbreaks as in Chester and Youngstown and probably to massacres like that of East St. Louis, in which participated not only well-known citizens but the local officers and the State militia. The Negroes in the North are in competition with white men who consider them not only strike breakers but a sort of inferior individuals unworthy of the consideration which white men deserve. And this condition obtains even where Negroes have been admitted to the trades unions.

Negroes in seeking new homes in the North, moreover, invade residential districts hitherto exclusively white. There they encounter prejudice and persecution until most whites thus disturbed move out determined to do whatever they can to prevent their race from suffering from further depreciation of property and the disturbance of their community life. Lawlessness has followed, showing that violence may under certain conditions develop among some classes anywhere rather than reserve itself for vigilance committees of primitive communities. It has brought out too another aspect of lawlessness in that it breaks out in the North where the numbers of Negroes are still too small to serve as an excuse for the terrorism and lynching considered necessary in the South to keep the Negroes down.

The maltreatment of the Negroes will be nationalized by this exodus. The poor whites of both sections will strike at this race long stigmatized by servitude but now demanding economic equality. Race prejudice, the fatal weakness of the Americans, will not so soon abate although there will be advocates of fraternity, equality and liberty required to reconstruct our government and rebuild our civilization in conformity with the demands of modern efficiency by placing every man regardless of his color wherever he may do the greatest good for the greatest number.

The Negroes, however, are doubtless going to the North in sufficiently large numbers to make themselves felt. If this migration falls short of establishing in that section Negro colonies large enough to wield economic and political power, their state in the end will not be any better than that of the Negroes already there. It is to these large numbers alone that we must look for an agent to counteract the development of race feeling into riots. In large numbers the blacks will be able to strike for better wages or concessions due a rising laboring class and they will have enough votes to defeat for reelection those officers who wink at mob violence or treat Negroes as persons beyond the pale of the law.

The Negroes in the North, however, will get little out of the harvest if, like the blacks of Reconstruction days, they unwisely concentrate their efforts on solving all of their problems by electing men of their race as local officers or by sending a few members even to Congress as is likely in New York, Philadelphia and Chicago within the next generation. The Negroes have had representatives in Congress before but they were put out because their constituency was uneconomic and politically impossible. There was nothing but the mere letter of the law behind the Reconstruction Negro officeholder and the thus forced political recognition against public opinion could not last any longer than natural forces for some time thrown out of gear by unnatural causes could resume the usual line of procedure.

It would be of no advantage to the Negro race today to send to Congress forty Negro Representatives on the pro rata basis of numbers, especially if they happened not to be exceptionally well qualified. They would remain in Congress only so long as the American white people could devise some plan for eliminating them as they did during the Reconstruction period. Near as the world has approached real democracy, history gives no record of a permanent government conducted on this basis. Interests have always been stronger than numbers. The Negroes in the North, therefore, should not on the eve of the economic revolution follow the advice of their misguided and misleading race leaders who are diverting their attention from their actual welfare to a specialization in politics. To concentrate their efforts on electing a few Negroes to office wherever the blacks are found in the majority, would exhibit the narrowness of their oppressors. It would be as unwise as the policy of the Republican party of setting aside a few insignificant positions like that of Recorder of Deeds, Register of the Treasury and Auditor of the Navy as segregated jobs for Negroes. Such positions have furnished a nucleus for the large, worthless, office-seeking class of Negroes in Washington, who have established the going of the people of the city toward pretence and sham.

The Negroes should support representative men of any color or party, if they stand for a square deal and equal rights for all. The new Negroes in the North, therefore, will, as so many of their race in New York, Philadelphia and Chicago are now doing, ally themselves with those men who are fairminded and considerate of the man far down, and seek to embrace their many opportunities for economic progress, a foundation for political recognition, upon which the race must learn to build. Every race in the universe must aspire to becoming a factor in politics; but history shows that there is no short route to such success. Like other despised races beset with the prejudice and militant opposition of self-styled superiors, the Negroes must increase their industrial efficiency, improve their opportunities to make a living, develop the home, church and school, and contribute to art, literature, science and philosophy to clear the way to that political freedom of which they cannot be deprived.

The entire country will be benefited by this upheaval. It will be helpful even to the South. The decrease in the black population in those communities where the Negroes outnumber the whites will remove the fear of *Negro domination,* one of the causes of the backwardness of the South and its peculiar civilization. Many of the expensive precautions which the southern people have taken to keep the Negroes down, much of the terrorism incited to restrain the blacks from self-assertion will no longer be considered necessary; for, having the excess in numbers on their side, the whites will finally rest assured that the Negroes may be encouraged without any apprehension that they may develop enough power to subjugate or embarrass their former masters.

The Negroes too are very much in demand in the South and the intelligent whites will gladly give them larger opportunities to attach them to that section, knowing that the blacks, once conscious of their power to move freely throughout the country wherever they may improve their condition, will never endure hardships like those formerly inflicted upon the race. The South is already learning that the Negro is the most desirable laborer for that section, that the persecution of Negroes not only drives them out but makes the employment of labor such a problem that the South will not be an attractive section for capital. It will, therefore, be considered the duty of business men to secure protection to the Negroes lest their ill-treatment force them to migrate to the extent of bringing about a stagnation of their business.

The exodus has driven home the truth that the prosperity of the South is at the mercy of the Negro. Dependent on cheap labor, which the bulldozing whites will not readily furnish, the wealthy southerners must finally reach the position of regarding themselves and the Negroes as having a community of interests which each must promote. "Nature itself in those States," Douglass said, "came to the rescue of the Negro. He had labor, the South wanted it, and must have it or perish. Since he was free he could then give it, or withhold it; use it where he was, or take it elsewhere, as he pleased. His labor made him a slave and his labor could, if he would, make him free, comfortable and independent. It is more to him than fire, sword, ballot boxes or bayonets. It touches the heart of the South through its pocket."[11] Knowing that the Negro has this silent weapon to be used against his employer or the community, the

South is already giving the race better educational facilities, better railway accommodations, and will eventually, if the advocacy of certain southern newspapers be heeded, grant them political privileges. Wages in the South, therefore, have risen even in the extreme southwestern States, where there is an opportunity to import Mexican labor. Reduced to this extremity, the southern aristocrats have begun to lose some of their race prejudice, which has not hitherto yielded to reason or philanthropy.

Southern men are telling their neighbors that their section must abandon the policy of treating the Negroes as a problem and construct a program for recognition rather than for repression. Meetings are, therefore, being held to find out what the Negro wants and what may be done to keep them contented. They are told that the Negro must be elevated not exploited, that to make the South what it must needs be, the cooperation of all is needed to train and equip the men of all races for efficiency. The aim of all then must be to reform or get rid of the unfair proprietors who do not give their tenants a fair division of the returns from their labor. To this end the best whites and blacks are urged to come together to find a working basis for a systematic effort in the interest of all.

To say that either the North or the South can easily become adjusted to this change is entirely too sanguine. The North will have a problem. The Negroes in the northern city will have much more to contend with than when settled in the rural districts or small urban centers. Forced by restrictions of real estate men into congested districts, there has appeared the tendency toward further segregation. They are denied social contact, are sagaciously separated from the whites in public places of amusement and are clandestinely segregated in public schools in spite of the law to the contrary. As a consequence the Negro migrant often finds himself with less friends than he formerly had. The northern man who once denounced the South on account of its maltreatment of the blacks gradually grows silent when a Negro is brought next door. There comes with the movement, therefore, the difficult problem of housing.

Where then must the migrants go. They are not wanted by the whites and are treated with contempt by the native blacks of the northern cities, who consider their brethren from the South too criminal and too vicious to be tolerated. In the average progressive city there has heretofore been a certain increase in the number of houses through natural growth, but owing to the high cost of materials, high wages, increasing taxation and the inclination to invest money in enterprises growing out of the war, fewer houses are now being built, although Negroes are pouring into these centers as a steady stream. The usual Negro quarters in northern centers of this sort have been filled up and the overflow of the black population scattered throughout the city among white people. Old warehouses, store rooms, churches, railroad cars and tents have been used to meet these demands.

A large per cent of these Negroes are located in rooming houses or tenements for several families. The majority of them cannot find individual rooms. Many are crowded into the same room, therefore, and too many into the same bed. Sometimes as many as four and five sleep in one bed, and that may be placed in the basement, dining-room or kitchen where there is neither adequate light nor air. In some cases men who work during the night sleep by day in beds used by others during the night. Some of their houses have no water inside and have toilets on the outside without sewerage connections. The cooking is often done by coal or wood stoves or kerosene lamps. Yet the rent runs high although the houses are generally out of repair and in some cases have been condemned by the municipality. The unsanitary conditions in which many of the blacks are compelled to live are in violation of municipal ordinances.

Furthermore, because of the indiscriminate employment by labor agents and the dearth of labor requiring the acceptance of almost all sorts of men, some disorderly and worthless Negroes have been brought into the North. On the whole, however, these migrants are not lazy, shiftless and desperate as some predicted that they would be. They generally attend church, save their money and send a part of their savings regularly to their families. They do not belong to the class going North in quest of whiskey. Mr. Abraham Epstein, who has written a valuable pamphlet setting forth his researches in Pittsburgh, states that the migrants of that city do not generally imbibe and most of those who do, take beer only.[12] Out of four hundred and seventy persons to whom he propounded this question, two hundred and ten or forty-four per cent of them were total abstainers. Seventy per cent of those having families do not drink at all.

With this congestion, however, have come serious difficulties. Crowded conditions give rise to vice, crime and disease. The prevalence of vice has not been the rule but tendencies, which better conditions in the South restrained from developing, have under these undesirable conditions been given an opportunity to grow. There is, therefore, a tendency toward the crowding of dives, assembling on the corners of streets and the commission of petty offences which crowd them into the police courts. One finds also sometimes a congestion in houses of dissipation and the carrying of concealed weapons. Law abiding on the whole, however, they have not experienced a wave of crime. The chief offences are those resulting from the saloons and denizens of vice, which are furnished by the community itself.

Disease has been one of their worst enemies, but reports on their health have been exaggerated. On account of this sudden change of the Negroes from one climate to another and the hardships of more unrelenting toil, many of them have been unable to resist pneumonia, bronchitis and tuberculosis. Churches, rescue missions and the National League on Urban Conditions Among Negroes have offered relief in some of these cases. The last-named organization is serving in large cities as a sort of clearing house for such activities and as means of interpreting one race to the other. It has now eighteen branches in cities to which this migration has been directed. Through a local worker these migrants are approached, properly placed and supervised until they can adjust themselves to the community without apparent embarrassment to either race. The League has been able to handle the migrants arriving by extending the work so as to know their movements beforehand.

The occupations in which these people engage will throw further light on their situation. About ninety per cent of them do unskilled labor. Only ten per cent of them do semi-skilled or skilled labor. They serve as common laborers, puddlers, mold-setters, painters, carpenters, bricklayers, cement workers and machinists. What the Negroes need then is that sort of freedom which carries with it industrial opportunity and social justice. This they cannot attain until they be permitted to enter the higher pursuits of labor. Two reasons are given for failure to enter these: first, that Negro labor is unstable and inefficient; and second, that white men will protest. Organized labor, however, has done nothing to help the blacks. Yet it is a fact that accustomed to the easy-going toil of the plantation, the blacks have not shown the same efficiency as that of the whites. Some employers report, however, that they are glad to have them because they are more individualistic and do not like to group. But it is not true that colored labor cannot be organized. The blacks have merely been neglected by organized labor. Wherever they have had the opportunity to do so, they have organized and stood for their rights like men. The trouble is that the trades unions are generally antagonistic to Negroes although they are now accepting the blacks in self-defense. The policy of excluding Negroes from these bodies is made effective by an evasive procedure, despite the fact that the constitutions of many of them specifically provide that there shall be no discrimination on account of race or color.

Because of this tendency some of the representatives of trades unions have asked why Negroes do not organize unions of their own. This the Negroes have generally failed to do, thinking that they would not be recognized by the American Federation of Labor, and knowing too that what their union would have to contend with in the economic world would be diametrically opposed to the wishes of the men from whom they would have to seek recognition. Organized labor, moreover, is opposed to the powerful capitalists, the only real friends the Negroes have in the North to furnish them food and shelter while their lives are often being sought by union members. Steps toward organizing Negro labor have been made in various Northern cities during 1917 and 1918.[13] The objective of this movement for the present, however, is largely that of employment.

Eventually the Negro migrants will, no doubt, without much difficulty establish themselves among law-abiding and industrious people of the North where they will receive assistance. Many persons now see in this shifting of the Negro population the dawn of a new day, not in making the Negro numerically dominant anywhere to obtain political power, but to secure for him freedom of movement from section to section as a competitor in the industrial world. They also observe that while there may be an increase of race prejudice in the North the same will in that proportion decrease in the South, thus balancing the equation while giving the Negro his best chance in the economic world out of which he must emerge a real man with power to secure his rights as an American citizen.

NOTES

[In the original document, the note numbers appeared out of order. We have corrected the ordering of the numbers so that the reader can find the proper references more easily.]

1. *New York Times,* Sept. 5, 9, 28, 1916.
2. *Ibid.,* Oct. 18, 28; Nov. 5, 7, 12, 15; Dec. 4, 9, 1916.
3. *The Crisis,* July, 1917.
4. *American Journal of Political Economy,* XXX, p. 1040.
5. *The World's Work,* XX, p. 271.
6. *The World's Work,* XX, p. 272.
7. *New York Times,* March 29, April 7, 9, May 30 and 31, 1917.
8. Survey, XXXVII, pp. 569–571, and XXXVIII, pp. 27, 226, 331, 428; *Forum,* LVII, p. 181; *The World's Work,* XXXIV, pp. 135, 314–319; *Outlook,* CXVI, pp. 520–521; *Independent,* XCI, pp. 53–54.
9. *The Crisis,* 1917.
10. *The New Orleans Times Picayune,* March 26, 1914.
11. *American Journal of Social Science,* XI, p. 4.
12. Epstein, *The Negro Migrant in Pittsburgh.*
13. Epstein, *The Negro Migrant in Pittsburgh.*

PART 2

Building a True Social Science

Introduction

The first African American practitioners of social science worked from an institutional base and perspective that were decidedly distinct from succeeding generations. While the role of the church, the home, and the betterment organization remained pertinent, they were no longer the fundamentally dominant forces driving the production of knowledge. The scholars featured in this section certainly understood and even practiced the kind of uplift politics that represented a mix of scholarship, political activism, and condescending high culture and class bias. But they were different from the black social scientists of the late nineteenth and early twentieth centuries in several important ways. Although black social scientists of this new age did not universally enjoy the benefits of a professional affiliation with a college or university, there was a notable trend that demonstrated black practitioners of social science were grabbing a foothold within the halls of academe.

The historian Charles H. Wesley (1891–1987) represents well this new move toward the professionalization in the social sciences. Wesley was one of the first African Americans to receive a PhD from Harvard University (1925). Before earning that degree he attained a BA from Fisk (1911) and an MA from Yale (1913). He held a range of positions at Howard University over the course of nearly four decades, rising from lecturer to the dean of the college and then the dean of the graduate school. He left Howard in 1942 to become the president of Wilberforce University and then the president of Central State University in Ohio five years later. After retiring from Central State in 1965, Wesley became the director and then director emeritus of the Association for the Study of Negro Life and History.[1] Although working in a field that is frequently considered a humanistic discipline, Wesley crafted pioneering work in the study of how black societies formed and operated in a variety of circumstances. The example that follows is an excerpt from *Negro Labor in the United States*, the first sustained analysis of the role of black labor in the United States. In "Slavery and Industrialism," Wesley pays careful attention to how social and cultural practices obscured the real structural impediments to broad scale industrialism in the slave South. In this history, then, we find a nuanced understanding of psychosocial behavior.[2]

Wesley's study appeared eight years before W. E. B. Du Bois's *Black Reconstruction*, the monumentally important and intellectually radical reinterpretation of the African American experience in the postbellum United States. In more ways than this, however, Du Bois shared intellectual space with Wesley even if they were separated by twenty-three years. Du Bois (1868–1963) took bachelor's degrees from Fisk (1888) and Harvard (1890) universities and then pursued graduate work at the University of Berlin before receiving his doctorate from Harvard in 1895. Du Bois's contribution to American letters is broad and deep, but he played a specific role in moving the study of social science to a more professional orientation. His book *The Philadelphia Negro*, which is excerpted in this section, is often considered the first articulation of urban sociology.[3] Its reliance upon fieldwork, a certain level of participant observation, and census sampling was a marked departure methodologically from the kind of church- and home-based uplift practiced and written about by previous scholars. There is little doubt that uplift always remained part of Du Bois's agenda, but the methodological tools with which he pursued this agenda unmistakably belonged to the world of social science. Du Bois also played a founding role in modern social science through his establishment of the Department of Sociology at Atlanta University and then through the conferences he organized and proceedings he published (familiarly known as the Atlanta University Studies). These studies were essentially a long-range sociological examination of black America and the challenges that this community faced.[4]

E. Franklin Frazier, Charles Johnson, Horace Mann Bond, and Allison Davis were much closer in age to Charles Wesley even though their respective worlds often intersected—and in some cases, collided—with Du Bois's over the course of the elder's extended life. Perhaps more than any other scholars featured in this collection, Frazier and Johnson are linked by historians of social science: both men pursued graduate studies in sociology at the University of Chicago, both were protégés of famed sociologist Robert Park, and both became major figures in the sociological tradition.[5] Though often mentioned in the same phrase, Frazier and Johnson were distinct for their scholarly focus and for their preferred mode of political engagement. Frazier was a specialist on the black family and maintained a very public role in the academic and political debates about the role and place of blacks in American life. Johnson, on the other hand, played a significant role behind the scenes as far as the development of social science studies were concerned. He was a favorite of the philanthropies that funded social science scholarship (in part due to his political quietism relative to Frazier) and built self-sustaining organizations that bridged the gap between academe and "the real world."[6]

Frazier (1896–1962) studied at Howard University for his BA (1916). After graduation, he held a variety of teaching and fellowship positions before serving as the director of the Atlanta School of Social Work from 1922 to 1927. He received his doctorate in sociology from Chicago in 1931, while he taught at Fisk (where Charles Johnson was his boss). Frazier moved to Howard in 1934 as the head of the department of sociology and remained there until his retirement in 1959.[7] In recognition of his role in advancing the discipline of sociology, Frazier was named the president of the American Sociological Association in 1948. While Frazier is best known for his work on the black family, he also produced sometimes highly controversial scholarship on black youth, the black middle class, and black culture. By far his most famous work in this regard is his scathing critique *Black Bourgeoisie,* published in 1957. In the mid-1960s, Frazier's scholarship became the focus of black nationalist critics after Daniel Moynihan misappropriated it for his study of the black family ("The Moynihan Report"). Even though Moynihan fundamentally misread Frazier's work—Frazier felt that the black family's dysfunction was a step in the process to full acculturation to the distinctive rigors of urban life, while Moynihan merely claimed that the black family was mired in a generalized pathology—the attacks against Frazier did not abate.[8] Ironically, in the early years of his career Frazier was well known for a similar relentlessness in his acid criticisms of those he deemed moderate establishment black leaders. And it so happened that Du Bois and Johnson were two of his favorite targets in this regard.

Where Frazier was an aggressive interpreter of the African American condition, Johnson relied more heavily on his skills as an observer. In the excerpt featured here, taken from Johnson's *Shadow of the Plantation,* we find a portrait of black communal life in the plantation South that falls just short of being anthropologically descriptive. This different interpretive mode, however, does not dim Johnson's importance to social science. Indeed, Johnson played a broader role than Frazier in the development of the social sciences in a variety of institutional spaces. Johnson (1893–1956) graduated from Virginia Union in 1916 and he received a bachelor of philosophy in sociology from the University of Chicago the following year. In 1918, Johnson began working as a researcher for the Chicago branch of the National Urban League.[9] His skills as an independent consultant—a precursor to the social science experts of the mid-twentieth century—can be inferred from the fact that he was tapped to join the Illinois governor's special task force investigating the 1919 Chicago race riots. In 1921, Johnson became the director of research and investigation for the National Urban League and founded and edited that group's magazine, *Opportunity.* From 1928 to 1946, Johnson taught at Fisk where he chaired the social science division and organized the Fisk Institute of Race Relations.[10] The Institute conducted research, trained social workers, and produced annual reports that pertained to the social and economic challenges blacks faced in the Tennessee region. In this task Johnson was doing work similar in mission to Du Bois's Atlanta University Studies. He was president of the Southern Sociological Society from 1945 to 1946 and served as the president of Fisk from 1946 until his death in 1956. Through this digest of Johnson's accomplishments, we can see that he embodied the social scientist as intellectual, consultant, and institution builder.[11]

Horace Mann Bond was similar to Johnson in this last regard. A specialist in the field of education, Bond spent the majority of his life and career in the South. A native of Tennessee, Bond (1904–1972) received his BA and LLD (1923 and 1941, respectively) from Lincoln University. In between those degrees Bond took an MA and PhD from the University of Chicago. Bond taught at a range of schools: Lincoln, Langston University, Alabama State Teachers College, Fisk, and Dillard University.[12] Early in his career Bond moved decisively to the world of academic administration. He was only thirty-five years old when he assumed the presidency of Fort Valley State College, and forty-one when he took on the same role at Lincoln. His last administrative position was as the dean of the school of education at Atlanta University (1957–1966). Before he moved into administration, Bond was blazing a trail in academia. His dissertation on southern education won the Susan Colver Rosenberger Prize Essay Award from the University of Chicago in 1937. Two years later, Bond published the revision of his dissertation, *Negro Education in Alabama: A Study in Cotton and Steel.* In "Cotton Plus Steel Equals Schools, 1900–1930" (the eleventh chapter of *Negro Education in Alabama*), we find a damning indictment of education policy enacted along race lines via Bond's use of census data, statistics, and maps. Bond's work here is also impressive for the scope of his investigation. He examines the entire educational "society" in Alabama, from teachers' salaries to school expenditures to test scores to taxation practices and beyond. Taken with Wesley's and Johnson's work on black labor in the agrarian South and Frazier's work on the black family in the urban North, a broad view of black life in the United States began to emerge that was separate from the religious and moral visions of previous generations.[13]

Allison Davis (1902–1983) received his BA from Williams College in 1924, his MA from Howard the following year, and his PhD in anthropology from Chicago in 1942. He was a trailblazer in his field like his other African American professional peers in the world of social science, but he was an anomaly as well because he taught at Chicago for virtually his entire career.[14] Individuals like W. E. B. Du Bois, Charles Johnson, and E. Franklin Frazier did critical work in establishing social science departments at the undergraduate and graduate level when they began teaching at their respective schools—all of which were historically black institutions. These accomplishments do not allow us to ignore the fact that whether they built new programs or not, black scholars were not welcome on the faculty at the very same schools that trained them. In 1941, the dilemma that was common knowledge to the African

American professoriate became known to representatives from the Rosenwald Fund. It was at this moment that these representatives discovered that
no blacks held teaching positions at historically white campuses (two individuals were employed as researchers at white schools). Determined to rectify
this problem, the Fund approached the University of Chicago and offered to
pay the salary of a black scholar the institution felt worthy of a position. With
this deal brokered, Allison Davis, freshly minted with the PhD but already
with two books to his name, began to teach at Chicago and thus began the
slow process of integrating this country's professoriate.[15] But Davis was no
mere poster child for a movement. He was a highly productive and respected
scholar whose work in social anthropology was influential in its day and beyond. As we can also see in "Caste, Economy, and Violence," Davis did not
apply a gentle gloss to his analysis of how race structured United States society. Instead, Davis brought the full weight of his social scientific training to
bear upon what he argued was a social system geared toward the construction
of a caste mentality that overwhelmed any economic logic that might suggest
a different means to organizing society.

Collectively, the scholars featured in this section marked a break from the
past. They were part of a small but growing body of African American scholars who pursued their graduate studies at some of the finest research universities in the world and who, save Allison Davis, moved back across the racial
line (some willingly, some happily, surely some reluctantly) to produce new
scholarship in the modern social sciences. They used methodologies that as-
pired to objective reasoning while focusing their work on some of the most
pressing problems facing the black community: economic oppression or instability, rural poverty and urban squalor, systemic racism, and the attendant
social maladies that accompanied them. They developed new programs in the
social sciences at their home institutions and, by leadership, scholarship, and
mere example, paved the way for future generation of black social scientists.

NOTES

1. W. Augustus Low and Virgil A. Clift, eds., *Encyclopedia of Black America*
(New York: McGraw-Hill, 1981), 850.

2. Francille Rusan Wilson, "Racial Consciousness and Black Scholarship:
Charles H. Wesley and the Construction of Negro Labor in the United States," *Journal of Negro History* 81, no. 1 (1996): 72–88.

3. David Levering Lewis, *W. E. B. Du Bois: Biography of a Race, 1868–1919*
(New York: Henry Holt, 1993), 202–210. For more on *The Philadelphia Negro* and

its impact upon the evolving social sciences see Michael J. Katz and Thomas Sugrue, eds., *W. E. B. Du Bois, Race, and the City: "The Philadelphia Negro" and Its Legacy* (Philadelphia: University of Pennsylvania Press, 1998).

4. Lewis, *Biography of a Race*, 217–225; on Du Bois's experiences at Atlanta University in general, 211–387.

5. Stow Persons, *Ethnic Studies at Chicago, 1905–1945* (Urbana: University of Illinois Press, 1987), 111.

6. Jonathan Scott Holloway, *Confronting the Veil: Abram Harris Jr., E. Franklin Frazier, and Ralph Bunche, 1919–1941* (Chapel Hill: University of North Carolina Press, 2002), 124–127. On Johnson's politics see James O. Young, *Black Writers of the Thirties* (Baton Rouge: Louisiana State University Press, 1973), 83, 104.

7. Low and Clift, eds., *Encyclopedia of Black America*, 398. Also see Holloway, *Confronting the Veil*, 123–156.

8. In the essay we feature and elsewhere in his scholarship, Frazier makes clear that black family pathology is a transitory phenomenon. In writing about southern black migrants' struggles upon reaching northern urban environments Frazier argued the following: "The peasant in the new environment seeks fulfillment of his awakened ambitions and hopes for a new status. The consequent social disorganization is not merely a pathological phenomenon for the care of social agencies but also represents a step towards a reorganization of life on a more intelligent basis." Frazier, "The Changing Status of the Negro Family," *Social Forces* 9 (March 1931): 389–390. For a more detailed examination of the Frazier-Moynihan connection see Anthony M. Platt, *E. Franklin Frazier Reconsidered* (New Brunswick: Rutgers University Press, 1991). Also see Frazier, *The Negro Family in the United States* (Chicago: University of Chicago Press, 1939).

9. Low and Clift, eds., *Encyclopedia of Black America*, 471–472.

10. Patrick J. Gilpin and Marybeth Gasman, *Charles S. Johnson: Leadership Beyond the Veil in the Age of Jim Crow* (Albany: The State University of New York Press, 2003), 93–107.

11. On Johnson as institutional builder and quiet intellectual activist, see Richard Robbins, *Sidelines Activist: Charles S. Johnson and the Struggle for Civil Rights* (Jackson: University Press of Mississippi, 1996).

12. Low and Clift, eds., *Encyclopedia of Black America*, 185; Harry Washington Greene, *Holders of Doctorates Among American Negroes* (Boston: Meador Press, 1946), 86–87.

13. On Bond, see Wayne J. Urban, *Black Scholar: Horace Mann Bond, 1904–1972* (Athens: University of Georgia Press, 1992), and Roger M. Williams, *The Bonds: An American Family* (New York: Atheneum, 1971).

14. Low and Clift, eds., *Encyclopedia of Black America*, 302.

15. Before completing his doctorate Davis had already co-authored two critical monographs: *Children of Bondage: The Personality Development of Negro Youth in the Urban South* (with John Dollard) and *Deep South: A Social Anthropological Study of Caste and Class* (with Burleigh B. Gardner and Mary R. Gardner).

CHARLES H. WESLEY

Slavery and Industrialism

The period during which the Compromise of 1850 was operative was one of the most critical periods in the development of American Sectionalism. Plantation economics and the domestic system were firmly established in the South while the industrial system had taken deep roots in the North and East. The North had found the free labor system profitable and supported it. In like manner the South was more determined than ever before to uphold a system of labor in which slavery was the fundamental condition. The leaders of the South through conventions and newspapers were determined to encourage the introduction of industrialism, and they were equally determined that slavery should be made tributary to it, and if the North insisted upon the abolition of slavery, then separation was the only solution.[1] In all of their discussions, slave labor was regarded as a necessary condition of the economic system of the South. Controversies were raised frequently between northern and southern interests regarding the merits of the systems of labor which were carried on in these sections.[2]

The major agricultural products of the South in 1850 were cotton, tobacco, sugar and rice. These products were raised largely by slave labor. The number of plantations engaged in raising these commodities shows the relative interest in each of them.

Cotton was still the ruling product of the South in 1850 and slaves were the necessary labor units for its production. Therefore, a relatively large num-

Charles H. Wesley, "Slavery and Industrialism," chap. 1 of *Negro Labor in the United States, 1850–1925: A Study in American Economic History* (New York: Vanguard Press, 1927), 1–28.

Number of Cotton, Sugar, Rice, Tobacco and Hemp Plantations in 1850

States	Number of Cotton Plantations Raising Five Bales and Over	Number of Sugar Plantations	Number of Rice Plantations Raising 20,000 Lbs. and Over	Number of Tobacco Plantations Raising 30,000 Lbs. and Over	Number of Hemp Plantations
Alabama	16,100	....	....	....	....
Arkansas	2,175	....	....	....	....
Florida	990	958	....	....	....
Georgia	14,578	....	80	....	....
Kentucky	21	....	....	5,987	3,520
Louisiana	4,205	1,558	....	....	....
Maryland	....	....	....	1,726	....
Mississippi	15,110	....	....	....	....
Missouri	....	....	....	....	4,807
North Carolina	2,827	....	25	....	....
South Carolina	11,522	....	446	....	....
Tennessee	4,043	....	....	2,215	....
Texas	2,262	165	....	....	....
Virginia	198	....	....	5,817	....
Total	74,031	2,681	551	15,745	8,327

(Compendium of the Census of 1850, p. 178.)

ber of the people of the South were interested directly in slavery. It is estimated that the total number of families holding slaves in 1850 was 347,725.
This comprised about one-third of the whole white population of the slave
states and about one-half of the whole population in the states of South Carolina, Alabama, Mississippi and Louisiana.[3] The total slave population was
3,204,313, and its increase since 1840 was 28.8 per cent as against 37.7 per cent
for the white population. The free Negro population of the United States in
1850 was 434,495.[4] This part of the population had increased 12.5 per cent
since 1840. The total Negro population in 1850 was 3,638,808.[5] The presence
of this large population and the demands for labor in agriculture and industry

made possible its participation in the American labor movement before and after the Civil War.

The labor of Negroes, slave and free, has been one of the most important factors in the economic development of the southern part of the United States. The brawn and muscle of the Negro population created the basis for Southern wealth which was derived in the main from the cultivation of the soil. The greater part of the Negroes, therefore, found employment in agriculture. As far as it may be stated with any degree of certainty, the Negro agricultural workers were distributed in 1850 among the great staples of the South in the following proportions:[6]

Hemp	60,000	2.4	per cent
Rice	125,000	5.0	" "
Sugar	150,000	6.0	" "
Tobacco	350,000	14.0	" "
Cotton, etc.	1,815,000	72.6	" "

These workers were employed by the gang and task systems. The latter system was used mainly upon the rice plantations. The cultivation of all of these products demanded the use of large bodies of Negro slaves. These field hands were directed usually by an overseer, and their successful employment depended not only upon their own labor but upon efficient overseers, who, it has been asserted, were hard to find.[7]

Observers found serious fault with the slave's labor. Olmsted stated that the slaves "seemed to go through the motions of labor without putting strength into them," and that they moved "very slowly and awkwardly." He found also that four Virginia slaves could not accomplish in agriculture what one ordinary free farm-laborer could do in New Jersey, and that the excessive weight and clumsiness of the tools made plantation work ten per cent greater.[8] Robinson, a visitor upon a rice plantation, observed that the slaves worked their hoes so slowly that "the motion would have given a quick-working Yankee convulsions."[9] There were also sick, aged and infirm slaves upon many plantations. These persons were unable to work and were often great burdens to their owners. However, in spite of these classes of individual Negroes who, to the Northern observer, seemed to be obstacles to successful labor enterprise, the South held on to its Negro slave labor system. Its advantages in the production of wealth seemed to outweigh its disadvantages. It was estimated that Negro labor contributed annually to the wealth of the South about $30,000,000, and one writer waxed eloquent with the statement that the Negro workers of the cotton states were "the most regular, uniform and efficient body of laborers to be found in the world."[10]

Great effort has been made to show how unprofitable labor with slaves was for the South because of racial inferiority. This has been stated so repeatedly by voice and pen that it has become a very old American tradition; that is, that Negroes have been inefficient workers, not because they were slaves, but because they were Negroes. Says A. H. Stone, "In truth, it was not slave labor but Negro labor which was, at bottom, responsible. The contrast between North and South was not the contrast between free and slave labor, but that between white and Negro labor."[11] The fact is, however, that slave laborers of every race have been unsatisfactory workers, and slave labor as compared with free labor has always been less efficient, whether it was the slavery of Europeans or Africans. War, trade, crime and gambling were the sources of slavery in Europe and the East; and no race group which has been once free and then enslaved has worked as efficiently for others as they have worked for themselves. The slave helpers of the ancient Greek and the Italian cities gave competition to the free workers, but the latter continued to have the advantage in workmanship. Medieval serfdom and English apprenticeship in the eighteenth and nineteenth centuries showed the same decreasing returns in skill and versatility as did Slave Labor in the United States.[12]

In addition, slaves and groups which are depressed by a master class, have always engaged in petty vices—in thievery from their masters, in discontent and rioting, in runaway efforts and indifferent work. The results have been the same whether among Greeks, Romans, Germans, Anglo-Saxons or Africans.[13] It is the economic and social depression which produces the bad effect. The history of slavery and oppression reveals the same results in all groups. Moreover, when it was difficult for slaves to be free, or to hope to be free, or for the early apprentices to become journeymen and masters, the permanent subordination became irksome and the worker soon lost the efficiency which his group may have once possessed and degenerated into a machine operating at the master's command. The results were especially characteristic of the slave system of agricultural labor in the South. It is well to note that this condition among the Negroes was aggravated by their contact with a portion of the population which secured its existence by practicing these vices. This group included those who obtained their "precarious support—by agricultural labor in competition with the slaves—by corrupting the slaves and seducing them to plunder for their benefit."[14] This relation with the slaves was regarded by some as "the most serious burden upon slave labor."

The Negroes of America contributed not only to the planting, growing and harvesting of the great staples of the South as slave field-workers, but also to the skilled and semi-skilled labor which the economic life of the South demanded. The mechanical pursuits of the plantations and of the towns were followed by the slave and free Negro population. Among this group of skilled laborers there were the blacksmith, the carpenter, the wheelwright, the mason, the bricklayer, the plasterer, the painter, the tanner, the miller, the weaver, the shoemaker, the harness-maker, and the cooper.[15] Their presence is shown by the advertisements for the sale of slaves, the purchase of slaves, and by the notices of the rewards for the return of fugitive slaves, of which the following are selected examples:

"Negroes wanted—some good carpenters, blacksmiths, coopers and bricklayers."—Wilmington, (Va.) Journal, September 3, 1847. Slaves for sale—on hand, house servants, field hands and mechanics."—New Orleans Picayune, October 18, 1846. "Fifty Dollars Reward—Runaway from the subscriber, Josey, a carpenter by trade."—Charleston Mercury, October 15, 1853. "... Robert ... a carpenter by trade, who has managed rice and sawmills—Jackey, a good shoe and boot-maker."—Charleston Mercury, December 26, 1853. "... a finished house carpenter, a perfect workman."—New York Tribune, August 29, 1854, quoting the Charleston Mercury. "One Hundred and Fifty Negroes for sale—consisting of field hands, house-servants, bricklayers, carpenters, plasterers, blacksmiths, painters, seamstresses, shirt-makers,—a superior blacksmith accustomed to do all manner of plantation work, and has also worked in repairing machinery."—New Orleans Picayune, January 29, 1853.[16]

In many cases the plantation manufactories were said to be conducted like small commercial industries.[17] These mechanics, slave and free, rendered good service to their communities. In the towns, especially in Georgia and in adjoining states, freedom for the Negro was an evidence of skill in some trade or industry.[18] Some of these mechanics became so successful that they purchased slaves. Their assistants and helpers were often held as slaves by them. In nearly all the states there were Negro plantation owners who were Negro slave owners, and there were many who were known to be prosperous and wealthy.[19]

Proposals were made in 1850 to use slave labor more generally in the quarrying and working of granite and the mining of coal;[20] and a few years later it was proposed to use them on the public works in Virginia. They had been employed in various parts of the state with marked success.[21] They were used at the mills and furnaces where they became "expert workers in iron," and it was hoped that they would be used more widely.[22] The purpose of these proposals was the extension of the use of slaves so that larger numbers of southern people would be more dependent upon slave labor and accordingly more willing to join in its defense. The intention of the pro-slavery group during the antebellum period was not only to urge the extension of slavery in the territories of the United States but to extend it intensively and make larger numbers of the people of the South look to slave labor for their support. The owners of slaves found it profitable to hire their slave mechanics by contract to others who needed their services. This was found to be a very profitable business and the extensive employment of hired slave artisans shows the value of the Negro mechanic to the South. The average annual sum which was paid to owners of hired slaves in Virginia was around one hundred and twenty dollars with board and lodging.[23] Some of these workers enjoyed a virtual monopoly in their industries, as they had processes, unknown to other workmen, by which the tasks assigned to them were done.[24]

The movement for the introduction of machinery and the new industry into the South was at its height during the decade, 1850–1860. William Gregg, a leading manufacturer of South Carolina, writes that the South in industry was at this time where New England was in 1820 or 1822, and that without the foreign obstacles with which New England had to contend, larger success for the Southern states was possible.[25] Leaders in political thought were convinced that efforts must be advanced in the interests of a new movement and that "whatever divisions exist in Southern politics, there can be none upon this of Southern Industrial Independence."[26] The South, it was said, was too dependent upon the North; it must secure a more combined system of railroads, it must build up a manufacturing interest in order to develop its resources, and thus there would be fewer distractions to endanger its peace.[27]. Moreover, the slave population seemed to be increasing in so much greater ratio than the white population that some plan must be undertaken, it was felt, which would encourage immigration of larger numbers of whites. Only by this plan could it be hoped "to keep up the equilibrium of the two races."[28] The burden of the speeches and the debates of the Southern Commercial Conventions, to which attention is called later, was the importance of manufacturing to the future of the South. While there were those in these conventions who could see the incompatibility of manufacturing and slavery, there were others who believed that both could be maintained.[29] A study of the table on page [115] will show the relationship which existed between the slave population of the individual Southern States and manufactures in 1850. This table will permit several conclusions concerning groups of the Southern States.

Looking at this table and comparing the slave percentage of the total population in each state with its manufacturing wealth per capita, one sees that the states with higher slave percentages have less per capita manufacturing wealth. For example, South Carolina ranks first in the proportion of its slave population and eighth in the per capita manufacturing wealth. Mississippi ranks second in the proportion of its slave population to the total population and fifteenth in the per capita manufacturing wealth. Louisiana ranks third in the proportion of its slave population to the total population and seventh in per capita manufacturing wealth. Florida ranks fourth in the percentage of slave population and twelfth in per capita wealth. Thus the states with the largest proportion of slave population have the lowest manufacturing interests and the lowest per capita manufacturing wealth. This conclusion is obvious. But there are variations from this conclusion.

Virginia, which ranks first among the slave states in slave population and seventh in the slave percentage of its total population, was also first in the number of manufacturing establishments, second in the list of those expending large sums upon labor for manufacturing, second in the value of its product, and sixth in the per capita wealth. The presence of the slaves in such large numbers appears to have had little effect upon the relative cost of labor, the value of the product or upon the number of establishments. In this state industry and initiative accompanied a high rate of Negro slave population. A further study of the counties of the state shows that the maintenance of this equilibrium is due largely to the economic interests of the western counties. Thus Virginia may be classed as an exception to the conclusion noted above, since it does not show any perceptible change except in the manufacturing wealth per capita. It was seventh in slave percentage to the total population and sixth in per capita wealth.

Maryland stands out as an exception of the opposite type to Virginia. The state of Maryland ranks tenth in slave population, thirteenth in the slave percentage to the total population, but also first in the amount spent upon labor, second in the number of establishments and first in per capita manufacturing wealth. Both Maryland and Virginia show tendencies toward industry and wealth production in spite of the size of the slave populations. The character of the soil and its rich produce influenced this result without doubt. On the contrary, Georgia and Alabama show the divergence between manufacturing and the number of slaves in the reverse manner to Maryland. They rank high in slaves and low in manufacturing interests.

The Relation of Slavery and Manufacturers in the South

1850 (1)
(2)

Rank	Slave Population in the Southern States in 1850	Rank	Percentage Slave of Total Population	Rank	Number of Manufacturing Establishments	Rank	Cost of Labor Per Annum	Rank	Value of the Product	Rank	Total Population of the State	Rank	Manufacturing Wealth Per Capita
1	Va. 472,528	7	33.2	1	4,740	2	5,434,476	2	29,602,507	1	1,421,661	6	20.80
2	S. C. 384,984	1	57.5	8	1,430	9	1,127,712	8	7,045,477	8	668,507	8	12.50
3	Ga. 381,682	6	42.1	7	1,522	8	1,709,664	7	7,082,075	4	906,185	11	7.09
4	Ala. 342,844	5	44.	9	1,026	10	1,105,824	11	4,528,876	6	771,623	13	5.08
5	Miss. 309,878	2	51.	11	947	12	771,528	12	2,912,068	9	606,526	15	4.08
6	N. C. 288,548	8	33.2	6	2,663	5	2,383,456	6	9,111,950	5	869,039	9	10.04
7	La. 244,809	3	47.2	10	1,008	7	2,033,928	9	6,779,417	11	517,762	7	13.00
8	Tenn. 239,459	10	23.8	5	2,887	6	2,247,492	5	9,725,608	2	1,002,717	10	9.07
9	Ky. 210,981	12	21.4	3	3,609	3	5,106,048	4	21,710,212	3	982,405	5	22.00
10	Md. 90,368	13	15.5	2	3,725	1	7,403,832	1	33,043,892	10	583,034	1	56.00
11	Mo. 87,422	14	12.8	4	2,923	4	4,692,648	3	24,324,418	7	682,044	4	31.00
12	Texas 58,161	9	27.3	14	309	14	323,268	14	1,168,538	12	212,592	14	5.04
13	Ark. 47,100	11	22.4	15	261	16	159,876	16	537,908	13	209,897	16	2.05
14	Fla. 39,310	4	44.9	16	103	15	199,452	15	668,335	15	87,445	12	7.06
15	D. C. 3,687	15	7.1	13	403	13	757,584	13	2,690,258	16	51,687	2	52.00
16	Del. 2,290	16	2.5	12	531	11	936,924	10	4,649,296	14	91,532	3	50.00

(1) Compendium of the Census of 1850, pp. 63, 82, 85, 86
(2) Abstract of the Statistics of Manufacturers, Seventh Census, p. 143.

Carrying the observation to other states, it is found that in North Carolina and Tennessee the positions of the states are fairly equal as regards slave population, slave percentage, the number of establishments, the cost of labor, the value of the product, and per capita wealth. No direct relation between manufacturing and slavery can be discovered in these states. Kentucky and Missouri ranked low in the slave percentage of their population and high in the value of their product, the cost of labor, and per capita wealth. Texas and Arkansas ranked low in the slave percentage of their population and also low in manufacturing interests. Delaware also ranked low in all respects save in its per capita wealth which was high.

This table demonstrates that manufacturing interests in some states varied with the number of the slaves and also with the slave percentage to the total population. But manufacturing progress did not correspond in all the states with the slave population, so that the definite rule may not be developed that manufacturing could not be introduced because of slavery. Slavery was one of the causes for the backwardness of Southern industrial progress but there were other contributing factors. These factors varied with the geographic, the economic and the social conditions of each state and section. A close study of the table reveals this variation. As a rule students of this subject have been content with the statement that it was owing to slavery that manufacturing was not carried on in the South, thus placing the burden directly upon slavery, and by inference upon the slaves.[30]

It is assumed that manufacturing in the South was impossible not only because there were slaves, but more particularly because there were Negroes slaves.[31] On the contrary, the serious student will look beyond the surface differences of color and he will examine the entire system of economic society in the South. It will be seen that there are two factors in the equation, the Negro and the white Southerner. Slavery affected both, the enslaved as well as the enslaver. Not only must the Negro slave be considered, but the life of ease which was made possible among the planter class. This existence did not encourage industry or initiative in business or in agriculture as did the life of the North.[32] The enterprising spirit of the North and East has been the dominating circumstance of American Industrialism. The ideal life in the South was the life of ease and comfort which was guaranteed by freedom from labor and oftentimes from even the direction of labor. This condition was brought about by slavery, but the element of personal aptitudes, personal tastes, individual and group thought, as they were expressed in Southern life, should be given consideration. For these in themselves occasioned slavery. In a rural society, where wealth was reckoned by the extent of land and slave-property owned, where there was a fixed gulf between the land-owning aristocrat and the man who had stained his hands by servile labor, where towns were small and industry was largely domestic, where transportation and commerce were weak—in such a society, manufacturing was impossible. The only way to introduce manufacturing on a large scale was to change the society. The Southern social system was based upon cheap human labor, while the rest of the world was seeking cheap mechanical labor. As long as groups of men were cheaper than machines, industrialism must wait. But by 1850, even in the South, human labor was becoming dearer and mechanical labor cheaper. Modern civilization was being built upon cheap mechanical power while Southern civilization was built upon the degrading of humanity. So long as the basis of a social system remains unchanged, the superstructure—its civilization—remains alike unchanged. But with the basis of the Southern social system shaken by the Civil War, slowly and painfully the entire system has been crumbling.

It had been proposed prior to 1850 that the slaves should be employed in manufacturing in the South. As early as 1827, the proposal was made in Virginia and other Southern states for the employment of slave labor in the manufacturing of coarse cotton and other goods. It was said that this project would diffuse prosperity wherever it would be adopted.[33] In 1845, Governor Hammond of South Carolina wrote to Thomas Clarkson that "We are beginning to manufacture with slaves."[34] The slave population had about doubled since 1820, and it appeared in 1850, that at the end of the next thirty years the slave population would be six millions and a half. The only solution for this increasing population was to employ it "in cotton and woolen factories . . . in iron furnaces . . . in our factories and work shops . . . and in the manufacture of such articles as are now made almost exclusively in the Northern states."[35] It was declared that the United States had become the second commercial nation of the world by the agency of slave labor, and that it could become the first when a portion of this labor should be directed to manufacturing enterprises.[36] The spindles and factories, to be located near the fields, would save not only through cheaper labor costs but also because it would obviate the necessity for transportation.[37] The subject of the use of slaves in industry became so prominent that the Southern and Western Convention at Charleston, April 10–15, 1854, passed a resolution toward the end of the session proposing that a committee should report upon the number of manufacturing plants in the states and the number of operatives, slave and free, in each.[38] There is no evidence in later conventions that this task was ever completed. Another resolution was presented stating that "experiments have fully proven that slave labor can be profitably employed in manufacturing establishments," and that, in the opinion of the convention, "an extensive application of such labor to manufacture would greatly benefit the South."[39]

Throughout the period 1850–1860, arguments were waged in favor of and against the use of Negroes in manufacturing. An appeal was made to the owners of slaves "to bring to the aid of this available and efficient corps of regular laborers in the field, the steam engine and the iron muscle of spindle and loom."[40] Negro labor, properly directed, it was said, would be found as effective as "the ignorant and miserable operatives of Britain."[41] There were differences and also similarities between English apprenticeship and American slavery. The apprentices of England, especially the pauper apprentices, grew up debased and demoralized. They were often driven to work at the point of the lash. Horses were kept saddled to bring back the fugitives who fled from their tasks, and blacksmiths made fetters for them. The English factory workers of the early nineteenth century were ignorant and subjugated men, women and children, until the reform movement gave birth to the factory legislation which improved their condition.[42] While there were writers who thought that the Negroes would be efficient factory operatives and as effective as the English operatives, there were other writers who opposed the use of slaves in manufacturing. It was argued that they should be used in the fields where they were particularly fitted and the mechanical pursuits should furnish employment for the white population.[43] Still others opposed the introduction of the white mechanics, for they would become "hot abolitionists," they would have the vote and they would imagine that, in fighting against the planters, they were fighting against aristocracy."[44]

Meanwhile progress was being made in various localities by the introduction of slaves into small scale manufacturing such as the South afforded. Profitable manufacturing plants for cotton-bagging were established in Kentucky and in South Carolina; and in parts of the Western states manufactories were conducted.[45] Slaves were employed in cotton factories in South Carolina, and there were cotton factories in Tennessee where all the labor was done by slaves and where there was not a single white man except the superintendent.[46] Manufactories were known to be successful with the labor of Negroes in other sections of the South.[47]

Several thousand men were employed in the mining of iron and in conducting the iron furnaces in Tennessee, near the Cumberland River, and without a single exception the employees were slaves. One company which was capitalized at $700,000, owned seven hundred slaves who were engaged in this industry.[48] They were employed in the tobacco factories of Richmond and Petersburg where some of them earned from one hundred and fifty to two hundred dollars a year. Those who were free, in this group in Virginia, were paid according to their tasks. One man had earned nine hundred dollars but it was said that he had saved none of it.[49]

There were other instances of the employment of slaves in manufacturing establishments in the South, particularly in South Carolina, Florida, Alabama, Mississippi and Georgia. Typical instances will be noted. The work of the Saluda factory near Columbia, South Carolina, attracted considerable attention. All the operatives of this plant were Negroes except the overseers and the superintendent, who had come from the Northern manufacturing sections. The company which controlled the factory had a capital of $100,000. It employed 98 operatives and, including children, there were 128 workers. The mill consisted of 5,000 spindles and 120 looms. Heavy brown shirting and Southern stripe, which was a coarse kind of colored goods, were the fabrics which were made. The superintendent found that the labor of slaves was cheaper than free labor and that slaves could endure the work of the cotton mills better than the whites. The Negroes were used first in the spinning department and were transferred gradually to the weaving room. The head weaver stated that there was as much work done by the Negroes and that they were more attentive to the condition of the looms. After two years of experiment, the results were found to be in favor of slave operatives in the mills, as the work was efficiently done and a saving of thirty per cent in the cost of labor was secured. This factory was operated by the labor of slaves until the close of the War, when slave labor was replaced by white labor.[50]

A cotton manufactory was situated also at Arcadia, which was about seventeen miles from Pensacola, Florida. The machinery of this factory was operated by Negroes. Five thousand yards of domestic were turned out weekly. The operatives were "young, intelligent and cheerful." The mill was in operation a little over a year, and the results more than answered the expectations of its originators.[51] At Scottville, Bibb County, Alabama, there was "a manufacturing village" where slaves were employed. The first profits, $2,200, which were realized in 1841, were spent for a family of Negroes who were to work in the factory. After that time the company made other purchases, and in 1858, a value of $25,000 was placed upon its Negroes. This mill was located in a large brick building of three stories. It contained the best machinery, and employed one hundred operatives, three-fourths of whom were females. There were about 25,000 spindles and 50 looms at work. Every year since 1841 a dividend of ten per cent had been declared and the capital stock increased to $117,000. The company owned three thousand acres of land and several buildings, which consisted, beside the factory, of a large hotel, a store, the smithery, the carpenter's shop, the wheelwright's place, and the boot and shoe shops. In addition, there were the saw-mill, the grist mill, a large flouring mill, a church and cottages.[52]

In Mississippi, ten miles south of Greenville, there was a cotton factory in which there were Negro workmen. There were 800 spindles, 10 cards and 12 looms, and the necessary machinery for spinning and weaving. A large Semple engine was used, which was made by Thurston, Green & Company of Providence, Rhode Island. This engine was operated by a Negro who was said to have had no acquaintance with engines before he began to operate this one.[53]

In South Carolina, there was a plantation where machinery was seen which was more extensive and better for threshing and storing rice than any used for grain upon any farm which had been seen in Europe or America.[54] There were shops also where mechanics were at work, all of whom were slaves. The owner stated that these workers exercised "as much ingenuity and skill as the ordinary mechanics that he was used to employing in New England." One particular piece of carpentry was noticed, a part of which had been started by a New England mechanic and a part by one of the plantation workers. Olmsted makes mention of his gratification at this discovery, because he had been told by others in Virginia, that the Negro mechanic was "incapable of working carefully." He had been told this so persistently that he had begun to believe it. One of the workers in this mill was a Negro who acted as a kind of overseer, and who was able to repair all the machinery, including the steam engine. In the same state, in 1856, there was a saw-mill, driven by steam, which was attended by two Negroes;[55] and in Georgia, slaves had been employed with decided success in cotton factories.[56] Negro slave operatives were used in several other cotton factories in South Carolina; at the Vaucluse Factory, the De Kalb Factory, and the Williams Factory.[57] They were employed also in small factories of various kinds in Virginia, North Carolina, and Florida.[58]

Industrialism was making such advances in American life, and the employment of Negro slaves in Southern industry appeared to be so successful that the supporters of the movement were encouraged to greater effort. They insisted that Negroes had learned blacksmithing, carpentry, boot and shoe-making and all the handicraft trades as easily as white men, and that if young slaves were put into the factories so that they might grow up in that employment, "they would make the most efficient and reliable operatives that could be found in any country."[59] The cotton growers and overseers who had experience with Negroes knew that they could be made into efficient operatives, and that this opportunity would give a wider scope "to all the mechanical talent among the slaves."[60] Since the slaves had made shoes and built houses, they could make plows, harrows, etc., and in all mechanical pursuits they could become fine laborers.[61] One writer calculated the time when Negro slaves would become trained engineers, weavers, spinners, smiths, and carpenters.[62] Another, who viewed the matter in the light of experience, was certain that there could be no doubt any longer in the mind of "any intelligent individual who is well acquainted with the mental and physical character of the black population of the United States that slave labor can be made as efficient as any other in this important branch of industry.[63] Slave labor was also termed "the best and cheapest factory labor in the world."[64] At the Macon Convention of Cotton Planters in 1851, and at the Montgomery Convention of 1852, a resolution was introduced recommending the erection of cotton mills in every county of the cotton states, and stating that the slaves were able to attend to the looms.[65]

The goods which were manufactured by slaves were not all of them coarse and heavy materials, but there were fine fabrics as well. While the work of most of the antebellum plants was on crude, common, production, there was some work which was of a high order. The products of one factory had drilling which resembled the best French linen at a short distance. It was of superior quality, and was so regarded by "the most intelligent dry-goods merchants."[66] It was not uncommon to find female slaves who were gifted as milliners and dressmakers. Some had acquired superior skill and were hired to fashionable dressmakers. *The Boston Daily Republican*, August 30, 1840, quotes *The Norfolk Herald*—"For Sale—a colored girl, of very superior qualifications . . . I venture to say that there is not a better seamstress, cutter and fitter of ladies' and children's dresses in Norfolk or elsewhere, or a more fanciful netter of bead-bags, money purses, etc."

However, as a rule, the work of the Southern antebellum plant was of the rudest kind. It did not require a large amount of skill and the use of Negro slaves was not an impossible procedure in 1850. But the skill of some slaves is particularly interesting and indicates the special attainment which some of them had reached. In Montgomery, there was a carpenter who had an unusual ability for calculations. This had been obtained without any instruction. He could give quick estimates of all descriptions of lumber to be used in building. He was an excellent workman and received as wages two dollars per day with overtime work. His efficiency had reached such a degree that he needed to receive little direction from his owner.[67] At Mount Vernon, there was a Negro carpenter who was skilled in the manufacture of cedar canes.[68] In the same state, there was a slave blacksmith who repaired the reaper when it refused to operate.[69] Daniel Williams of Newberne, North Carolina, was an experienced engineer, having attended to steam engines for nine years. He was regarded as a valuable man in this work, and in addition he was a practical tanner.[70]

Since Negro slaves were not granted patents for protection of inventions, there is no accurate record of slave inventions. In 1858, the Commissioner of Patents having refused to grant a patent to a slave inventor, an appeal was taken to the Attorney-General of the United States, Jeremiah S. Black, who confirmed the refusal stating that he could not legally give the patent to either the master or the slave, because a slave, not being a citizen, could not be a party to a contract with either the government, or his master.[71] This opinion followed closely the sentiment of the Dred Scott Decision. The master, without doubt, would be permitted to obtain a patent for himself but not to secure his slave in his right to an invention. An important invention in sugar-making by a slave could not be rewarded by a patent for the same reason.[72] Booker T. Washington is the authority for the statement concerning an invention by a slave of the "Hemp-Brake," which was a machine by which the fiber could be separated from the hemp stalk.[73] A number of mechanical appliances which came out of the ordinary problems of daily employment were attributed to the plantation workers.[74] On account of the denial of a patent to Benjamin T. Montgomery, who was a slave of Jefferson Davis, the Confederate Congress passed an act on May 17, 1861, providing that when the inventor was a slave, the master might take an oath that the slave was the original inventor and on complying with the law, he should receive all rights of a patentee.[75]

It did not escape the view of some thoughtful persons in the South that training the Negro slave as an artisan and a mechanic was utterly unfitting him for slavery. It was said that "wherever slavery has decayed, the first step in the progress of emancipation has been the elevation of the slave to the rank of artisans and soldiers. This is the process through which slavery has receded, as mechanic arts have advanced."[76] In the development of modern European civilization, serfdom was doomed in those places where men began to work in the mechanic arts, and where men abandoned the rough work of the domestic system for the factory system, new conditions of life and liberty came to millions of men. As the craftsmen grew in number and as the craft guilds grew in power, the serfs slowly disappeared: and where serfdom did not give way to the New Day, the violence of revolution resulted. This change marks the beginning of the division between the civilization of the past and the civilization of the present.

This process was fundamentally true in the life of individual Negroes who lived in the medievalism of the South, and it may be noticed in the Free-Negro group in the decade prior to the Civil War. The leaders of insurrections throughout the eighteenth century were Negro mechanics, nearly all of them former slaves. Richard Allen teamster and laborer, was the leader of the peaceful revolution within the Methodist Episcopal Church. Denmark Vesey, the industrious builder and carpenter, planned the insurrection of 1822, and Nat Turner, experimenter in paper, gun powder and pottery, led the Southampton Insurrection in 1831. In the John Brown Raid on Harper's Ferry in 1859, there were five Negroes who took active part—Osborne Perry Anderson, a printer by trade; Lewis Sheridan Leary, saddle-and harness-maker; Shields Green, sailor; John Anthony Copeland, one time student at Oberlin, and Dangerfield Newby, occupation unknown. In urban and rural communities where slavery existed, the slave mechanics were the leaders in Negro life. These persons often purchased their freedom. They fled from slavery to freedom and they either hired themselves or they were hired by their masters on advantageous terms to other persons.[77] Training in the mechanic arts taught them to think and to depend upon their own resources. Such persons were manifestly soon unfitted for slavery.

In spite of the approaching industrial spirit and its evident influence upon Negro life, the extensive use of slave labor was urged by Southern statesmen, and this served to intensify the demand for slaves. The prices of slaves had been rising during the years prior to 1860, and the demand for slaves was unprecedentedly great during the same period. In spite of a growing free labor sentiment, agitation was begun for the reopening of the slave trade.[78] Political considerations as well as economic demands were involved in this movement. The trade was expected to give a large labor supply and this would make it possible for all persons to have farm workers and mechanics.[79] For with slaves more widely owned, a larger number of persons would be interested in the continuance and preservation of the institution. In 1858, a bill which authorized the importation of 2,500 Africans as indentured servants for a term of not less than fifteen years, was passed by the Lower House of the Georgia Legislature.[80] This measure was indefinitely postponed in the Senate by a majority of two.[81] The smuggling of slaves had already begun along the Mississippi River,[82] and a few months later, contrary to the law, coolies were introduced.[83] An effort was made in Mississippi to reopen the trade. Such a bill was introduced into the Lower House. Its purpose was to bring in "a supply of African laborers." The Lower House passed the measure with an overwhelming majority but it was defeated in the Senate.[84] In South Carolina, similar action was reported.[85]

The Southern Commercial Conventions, which met during the fifties, discussed the reopening of the Slave Trade and resolutions were frequently passed which favored this measure.[86] Northern observers regarded these suggestions with suspicion, and attention was called to their influence upon the country's labor situation.[87] By 1850, the agitation was "in full blast" to repeal the Congressional Acts forbidding slave importations and an African Labor Supply Association was formed in Mississippi with J. B. D. De Bow as President.[88] The Southern Commercial Convention which met in Vicksburg, Mississippi, May 9, 1859, passed a resolution stating that it was the opinion of the Convention that all laws prohibiting the African Slave Trade should be repealed. Delegates from Alabama, Arkansas, Louisiana, Georgia, Mississippi and Texas voted for the resolution. Tennessee and Florida voted against it, and the vote of South Carolina was divided.[89] In spite of these efforts, slave labor had about run its course in American history and the movement for free labor and industrialism was steadily winning its way.

Upon the plantation, in skilled and unskilled labor, Negro workers were found. In various parts of the South they were used with measures of success in such manufacturing plants as the economic development of the South permitted. A talented number emerged from the larger group, demonstrated the possession of the special skill which the town and the plantation demanded and made themselves a necessity to a class of individuals who knew neither the value nor the process of labor. If slavery and industrialism had joined hands on an extensive plan, it is reasonable to assume that this cooperation could not have lasted many years. It was not, however, because the slaves—being Negroes—were incapable of attaining the necessary skill, which is demonstrated by the foregoing facts. The causes for this incompatibility between slavery and industrialism were inherent in the entire ante-bellum economic system to which a large part of both races in the South was in bondage.

NOTES

[The original publication includes a bibliography. Where it is available, we have added, in square brackets, material from the bibliography as an aid to the reader of this anthology who wishes to follow Wesley's citations. In a few cases, details in the notes and in the bibliography differ; we have not attempted to correct these instances.]

1. In 1849, Judge Tucker of Williamsburg, Virginia, sent to J. H. Hammond of South Carolina a plan for the establishment of a Southern Confederacy. B. Tucker to J. H. Hammond, January 30, 1849, J. H. Hammond Papers. See also Soule's Speech at Opelousas, Louisiana, September 6, 1851; DeBow, Industrial Resources [of the Southern and Western States, New Orleans, 1852–1853], Vol. II, p. 127; Addresses and Resolutions by the Southern Convention held at Nashville, Tennessee, June 3–12, 1850, to

the People of the South, pp. 14–17; A glance at the Resources of the South in the Event of Separation, A Series of Articles originally published in the Columbia (S.C.) Telegraph.

2. New York Daily Tribune, March 14, 1853, replying to Wilmington (N.C.) Commercial; Speech of J. H. Hammond, U.S. Senator from South Carolina, Congressional Globe, Vol. XIV, 35th Congress, 1st Session, pp. 961–962; Olmsted, [A Journey in the] Seaboard Slave States [with Remarks on Their Economy, New York, 1851], pp. 334–335, quoting the Richmond Examiner; D. R. Goodloe, The South and the North, being a reply to a lecture on the North and the South by Ellwood Fisher; The North and the South, A Review, J. H. Hammond.

3. Compendium of the Seventh Census, p. 94. Negro Population, 1790–1915 [published by the Bureau of the Census, 1918], p.56.

4. Ibid., pp. 62, 63, 82; pp. 25, 83, 85, 86. Cf. Future Wealth of America—Francis Bonynge, p. 189.

5. Negro Population, 1790–1915, p. 53.

6. Compendium of the Seventh Census, p. 94. One Pro-Slavery writer estimated the annual indebtedness of America for articles of slave labor origin, including the value of foreign and domestic cotton, and the cost of groceries, at $162,185,240— Cotton is King, Elliott, pp. 65–66.

7. See The Southern Plantation Overseer as Revealed in His Letters [Smith College Publications, 1925], John Spencer Bassett. Typical plantations are described in Olmsted, Seaboard Slave States, [A] Journey in the Back Country [London, 1860], [Journeys and Explorations in] The Cotton Kingdom [London, 1861]. U. B. Phillips, American Negro Slavery [New York, 1918], Chapter XIII, Types of Large Plantations; H. T. Cooke, The Life and Legacy of David Rogerson Williams, New York, 1916. See also, [Edward] Channing, [A] History of the United States [New York, 1921, 1923], Vol. V, Chap. V, "The Plantation System and Abolition"; F. P. Gaines, Southern Plantation [Columbia University Press, 1925].

8. Olmsted, Seaboard Slave States, pp. 91, 10, 19, 204, 46.

9. American Agriculturist, Vol. IX, p. 93.

10. Western Journal, Vol. III, p. 104. Annals of the American Academy of Political and Social Science, Vol. XXXV, p. 127; [Philip A.] Bruce, The Plantation Negro as a Freeman [New York, 1889], p. 175. Francis Bonynge, Future Wealth of the United States, p. 197.

11. The Negro in the South, Publications of the University of Virginia, Phelps-Stokes Fellowship Papers, Charlottesville, Virginia, 1915.

12. Niebor, Slavery as an Industrial System [The Hague, 1900], p. 299, 436–437. Ingram, A History of Slavery and Serfdom, p. 9–11; Adam Smith, Wealth of Nations, Book III, Chap. II; Walton, Histoire de l'esclavage dans l'antiquité, Vol. I, Chaps. VI, XI. J. E. Cairnes, Slave Power, Chap. II.

13. Adam Gurowski, Slavery in History; A. M. Wergeland, Slavery In Germanic Society during the Middle Ages. In the introduction to this study, Dr. Jameson has

well said that "We cannot hope to attain a true understanding of American Slavery in some of its most essential aspects unless we are somehow made mindful of the history of slavery as a whole."

14. Speech of J. H. Hammond before the South Carolina Mechanical Institute, J. H. Hammond Papers, 1849.

15. The occupations of the slaves have not been recorded by the Census Office, and it is difficult to approximate the number of mechanics or other workers. If there were 2,500,000 slaves engaged in large-scale agriculture and the total slave population was 3,204,313, the remaining number 703,315 would give the number who were engaged in activities aside from large-scale agriculture. If 400,000 of this number were urban slaves, then it would be possible to assume that there were 300,000 slaves who were occupied in the rural sections with activities which were not directly concerned with large-scale agriculture. An allowance should be made for those who were engaged in the raising of quantities of bread-stuffs, and for children, superannuates and domestic workers. Compendium of the Census of 1850, p. 94.

16. New York Tribune, August 16, 1853; January 9, 1855; Columbia South Carolinian, January 2, 1855; New Orleans Commercial Bulletin, January 30, 1855; African Repository, Vol. XXXIX, p. 18, January, 1853.

17. African Repository, Vol. XXIX, September 1853, p. 279.

18. [Victor S.] Clark, History of Manufactures in the United States [Washington, 1916], p. 440.

19. New York Tribune, September 5, 1857; Manuscript Returns of the Census of 1850; Woodson, Free Negro Heads of Families, 1830.

20. DeBow's Review, July–December, 1850, Vol. IX, p 435.

21. Charles Lyell, Second Visit to the United States, Vol. I, pp. 216–217. DeBow's Review, Vol. XVII, July–December, 1854, pp. 76–82. Approximately 400,000 slaves were urban in 1850 and 2,804,313 were rural—Compendium of the Census of 1850, p. 94.

22. The Charleston Mercury, November 19, 1853.

23. DeBow's Review, July–December, 1854, p. 77. Olmsted, pp. 186, 190, 83. At Catt's Tavern in Virginia, the men who were hired brought $100 to $125, and the women who were hired brought $40 to $50—New York Tribune, January 20, 1854. In 1854, the Norfolk Argus reported that the current wages for common labor were $150 and for the best labor $225. This price was said to be too high for employers to pay—The Southern Banner. In Louisiana in 1860, prime field hands brought from $300 to $360, and a blacksmith brought $430—DeBow's Review, Vol. XXIX, p. 374.

24. The North Carolina Historical Society—Historical Publications, Vol. XVII, No. 1. Annals of the American Academy of Political and Social Science, Vol. XXXV, p. 125.

25. Gregg to Hammond, May 30, 1849—J. H. Hammond Papers.

26. DeBow, Industrial Resources of the Southern and Western States, Vol. II, p. 483.

27. Ibid., Vol. II, p. 154.

28. Ibid. Vol. II, p. 127; Vol. III, p. 35. [William] Gregg, Essays on Domestic Industry [Charleston, 1845]; Alvord to Hammond, April 25, 1849. J. H. Hammond Manuscripts.

29. The newspapers of the southern cities gave accounts of these conventions. See also, Ante-Bellum Southern Conventions in Alabama Historical Society Transactions, Vol. V, pp. 153–202; Journal of Proceedings of the Commercial Convention of the Southern and Western States, at Charleston, April 10–15, 1854; The Charleston Mercury, April 14, 1854; New York Tribune, January 20, 1855, gives an account of a convention at New Orleans; Southern Quarterly Review, 2nd Series, Vol. XVIII, pt. 2, pp. 191–232; [Hinton R.] Helper's Impending Crisis [of the South, How to Meet It, New York, 1860].

30. It was with this idea of the antagonism of slavery and manufacture that the opponents of slavery urged the introduction of manufacture in the South. The Annual Report of the American and Foreign Anti-Slavery Society for 1849, quoted the State Banner of Columbia, S.C. in regarding manufacturing as not only a "fatal blow" at free trade but a "covert blow" at the institution of slavery; Annual Report, 1849, p. 49. Cf. C. S. Boucher, The Ante-Bellum Attitude of South Carolina toward Manufacture and Agriculture; Broadus Mitchell, Rise of Cotton Mills in the South, pp. 24–25, 209; D. A. Tompkins, The South in the Building of the Nation, Vol. II, p. 58; Henry George, Progress and Poverty, p. 523; W. H. Garmon, The Landowners of the South and the Industrial Classes of the North, p. 9; Helper, Impending Crisis, p. 25; Clark, History of Manufactures in the United States, pp. 553–554.

31. American Historical Review, Vol. 13, p. 791—Problems of Southern Economic History by A. H. Stone.

32. Olmsted noticed this "in the habits and manners of the free white mechanics and trades people . . . a man forced to labor under this system is morally driven to indolence, carelessness, indifference to the results of skill, inconstancy of purpose, improvidence and extravagance."—Seaboard Slave States, pp. 146–148.

33. Hamilton, Slave Labour In Manufactures, p. 1.

34. DeBow, Industrial Resources, Vol. II, p. 254; Nordhoff, America [for Free Workingmen, New York, 1865], p. 10.

35. DeBow, Industrial Resources, Vol. II, p. 313; New York Semi-Weekly Tribune, June 13, 1854, quoting the Richmond Enquirer.

36. DeBow, Industrial Resources, Vol. II, p. 111.

37. The Western Journal of Agriculture, Manufactures, Mechanics, etc., Vol. III, p. 96.

38. The Charleston Mercury, April 14, 1854; DeBow's Review, Vol. XVI.

39. The Journal of Proceedings of the Commercial Convention of the Southern and Western States held in Charleston, April 10–15, 1854, p. 33.

40. Western Journal of Agriculture, etc., Vol. III, p. 102.

41. DeBow, Industrial Resources, Vol. III, p. 80. Gregg, the proprietor of the Graniteville factory, wrote that experienced overseers gave a decided preference to Negroes as operatives for two reasons: (1) that they give uninterrupted service from

the age of eight years, and (2) that frequent changes of employment, as with the whites, do not affect them—Essays in Industry, p. 21. A Mississippian wrote that in the South it was well known that the slaves were "fine laborers" in mechanical pursuits and in the manufacture of cotton and woolen goods, New York Tribune, February 5, 1856.

42. Reports of the Royal Commissions of Enquiry and of the Factory Commissions of 1838, 1842. See also Gilbert Slater, The Making of Modern England, pp. 52–53. Gaskell, Manufacturing Population of England (1833). Hammond, J. L. and B., The Village Labourer, 1760–1832.

43. DeBow's Review, Vol. VIII, p. 25; Vol. XI, pp. 318–319.

44. Memminger to Hammond, April 28, 1849, J. H. Hammond Manuscripts.

45. Hamilton, Slave Labour in Manufactures (1827).

46. Olmsted, Seaboard Slave States, p. 104; A Journey Through Texas [New York, 1857], p. 18. New York Tribune, February 5, 1856.

47. Nordhoff, America for the Free Workingman, p. 10; DeBow, Industrial Resources, Vol. II, p. 339; Mitchell, Rise of Cotton Mills [in the South, (Submitted to Johns Hopkins University for the degree of Doctor of Philosophy), Boston, 1921], p. 209; DeBow, Industrial Resources, Vol. II, p. 112; Buckingham, The Slave States of America [London, 1842], Vol. II, p. 41.

48. Nordhoff, America for the Free Workingman, p. 7; New York Tribune, January 1, 1857; This paper gives an account of the insurrection of the Negro laborers at the forges in Kentucky; African Repository, Vol. XXVI, p. 302.

49. Olmsted, Seaboard Slave States, p. 127; Lynchburg Republican, Petersburg Democrat, quoted by Atlanta Intelligencer, January 7, 1860.

50. DeBow, Industrial Resources, Vol. I, pp. 232–233; DeBow's Review, Vol. IX, July–December, 1850, pp. 432–433; Vol. XI, July–December, 1851, pp. 319–320; Nordhoff, America for the Free Workingman, p. 10; See also Hunt's Merchant's Magazine, Vol. 23, July–December, 1850, pp. 575–576. Philipps in American [Negro] Slavery [New York, 1918] quotes the Augusta Chronicle, January 5, 1853, and states that the Saluda factory was closed in 1853; the opposite opinion, that this factory continued its slave labor until the close of the war, is stated by Kohn, Cotton Mills of South Carolina [Charleston, 1907], p. 16; Mitchell in the Rise of Cotton Mills in the South states that this factory was burned by Federal troops, p. 212 (note); Annual Report of President and Treasurer of the Graniteville Manufacturing Company for the year 1854, pp. 12–13.

51. The Pensacola Live Oak, quoted by the Western Journal, Vol. I, pp. 154–155.

52. DeBow's Review, January–December, 1858, Vol. XXV, p. 717.

53. Ibid., Vol. LIX, July–December, 1850, p. 433; in Eighty Years of Progress (1862) by Eminent Literary Men, there is an engraving of Negroes running a cotton gin invented by C. V. Mapes; Vol. I, p. 112.

54. Olmsted, Seaboard Slave States, pp. 425–426; Olmsted had been told that the Negros judgment could not be trained, that he would not use his mind and that he depended upon machinery to do its own work. This was the nature of the African, he

was told, and although the disinclination to labor was present in all men, it was said to be stronger in the African race. Ibid., pp. 104–105.

55. New York Tribune, March 22, 1856.

56. DeBow, Industrial Resources, Vol. II, p. 112.

57. Kohn, Cotton Mills of South Carolina, pp. 16, 24–25; The Western Journal, Vol. I, p. 158; Mitchell, Rise of Cotton Mills in the South, pp. 211–213; Clark, History of Manufactures, p. 619, Appendix XI.

58. Hunt's Merchant's Magazine, Vol. XV, p. 548; XVII, p. 323; XXIII, p. 575; XXV, p. 517; DeBow's Review, Vol. XI, pp. 319–320; Mitchell, Rise of Cotton Mills, p. 19 (note); The Rocky Mount Mill in Edgecombe County, North Carolina, had employed Negroes from 1820 to 1851, when whites were then employed. The Manager wrote that "the owners of the slaves objected to the slaves working in the mill and I substituted whites as soon as I could."—[Holland] Thompson, From Cotton Field to Cotton Mill [New York, 1906], p. 251.

59. DeBow. Industrial Resources, Vol. II, pp. 112, 116; Nordhoff, America for the Free Workingman, p. 11.

60. DeBow, Industrial Resources, Vol. I, p. 231; William Gregg, in an address before the South Carolina Institute, stated that experience gave "decided preference to blacks as operatives."—New York Tribune, February 5, 1856.

61. The Mississippian, quoted by New York Tribune, February 5, 1856; DeBow's Review, Vol. II, p. 319.

62. The Western Journal and Civilian, Vol. III, p. 105.

63. Ibid., Vol. I, p. 158.

64. DeBow's Review, Vol. IX, July–December, 1850, p. 435.

65. DeBow, Industrial Resources, Vol. I, p. 139.

66. Hunt's Merchant's Magazine, Vol. XXV, July–December, 1851, p. 517.

67. Olmsted, Seaboard Slave States, pp. 553–554.

68. New York Tribune, March 4, 1859.

69. Nordhoff, America for the Free Workingman, p. 7.

70. African Repository, Vol. XXVI, pp. 304–306, October, 1850. Other slave engineers are mentioned in Olmsted, Seaboard Slave States, pp. 427–428.

71. Official Opinions of the Attorney-General of the United States, 1858, pp. 171–172. It reads in part—"I fully concur with the Commissioner of Patents in the opinion he has given on the application of Mr. O. T. E. Steward of Mississippi. For the reasons given by the Commissioner, I think, as he does, that a machine invented by a slave, though it be new and useful, cannot, in the present state of the law be patented. I may add that if such a patent were issued to the master, it would not protect him in the courts against persons who might infringe it."—J. S. Black to Jacob Thompson, Secretary of the Interior, June 10, 1858.

72. New York Semi-Weekly Tribune, July 7, 1858.

73. Annals of the American Academy of Political and Social Science, Vol. XXXV, p. 126.

74. Henry E. Baker (Assistant Examiner in the Patent Office), The Colored Inventor, p. 6.

75. Journal of the Congress of the Confederate States of America, 1861–1865, Vol. 1, p. 241.

76. DeBow, Industrial Resources, Vol. III, p. 34.

77. Austin Steward, a fugitive himself, writes that as far north as New York, he saw in 1848 many fugitive slaves who were intelligent mechanics. He states that they were engaged in erecting different buildings there—Austin Steward, Twenty-two years a Slave and Forty Years a Freeman [Rochester, 1859], p. 301.

78. Hunt's Merchant's Magazine, Vol. XI, p. 774.

79. DeBow's Review, Vol. XXV, July–December, 1858, pp. 491–506; Twenty-fourth Annual Report of the American Anti-Slavery Society, p. 54.

80. Savannah Republican, March 13, 1858.

81. Ibid., March 22, 1858.

82. Ibid., March 4, 1858, quoting the New Orleans Delta and the Augusta Chronicle and Sentinel.

83. Savannah Republican, May 14, 1858.

84. DeBow's Review, Vol. XXV, p. 627.

85. Olmsted, Seaboard Slave States, p. 521. Report of the Special Committee of the House of Representatives of South Carolina Legislature, 1857, p. 24.

86. DeBow's Review, Vols. XXII, XXIII, XXIV, XXV, XXVII.

87. New York Tribune, May 15, 1858.

88. Vicksburg True Southron, May 13; June 7, 1859. DeBow's Review, Vol. XXVI, pp. 231–235; Twenty-sixth and twenty-seventh Annual Reports of the American Anti-Slavery Society.

89. DeBow's Review, June 1859, p. 713.

W. E. B. DU BOIS

The Size, Age and Sex of the Negro Population

13. The City for a Century. The population of the county[1] of Philadelphia increased about twenty-fold from 1790 to 1890; starting with 50,000 whites and 2500 Negroes at the first census, it had at the time of the eleventh census, a million whites and 40,000 Negroes. Comparing the rate of increase of these two elements of the population we have:

Rates of Increase of Negroes and Whites

Decade from	Negroes	Whites	Decades from	Negroes	Whites
1790–1800	176.42%	42.92%	1840–1850*	.36%	63.30%
1800–1810	52.93	35.55	1850–1860	12.26	39.67
1810–1820	13.00	22.80	1860–1870*	.17	19.96
1820–1830	31.39	39.94	1870–1880	43.13	25.08
1830–1840	27.07	37.54	1880–1890	24.20	23.42

* Decrease for Negroes.

W. E. B. Du Bois, "The Size, Age and Sex of the Negro Population," chap. 5 of *The Philadelphia Negro: A Social Study* (Philadelphia: University of Pennsylvania Press, 1899), 46–65.

The first two decades were years of rapid increase for the Negroes, their number rising from 2489 in 1790 to 10,552 in 1810. This was due to the incoming of the new freedmen and of servants with masters, all to some extent attracted by the social and industrial opportunities of the city. The white population during this period also increased largely, though not so rapidly as the Negroes, rising from 51,902 in 1790 to 100,688 in 1810. During the next decade the war had its influence on both races although it naturally had its greatest effect on the lower which increased only 13 per cent against an increase of 28.6 per cent among the Negroes of the country at large. This brought the Negro population of the county to 11,891, while the white population stood at 123,746. During the next two decades, 1820 to 1840, the Negro population rose to 19,833, by natural increase and immigration, while the white population, feeling the first effects of foreign immigration, increased to 238,204. For the next thirty years the continued foreign arrivals, added to natural growth, caused the white population to increase nearly three-fold, while the same cause combined with others allowed an increase of little more than 2000 persons among the Negroes, bringing the black population up to 22,147. In the last two decades the rush to cities on the part of both white and black has increased the former to 1,006,590 souls and the latter to 39,371. The following table gives the exact figures for each decade:

Population of Philadelphia, 1790–1890

Date	Whites		Negroes		Total	
	City	County	City	County	City	County
1790	...	51,902	...	2,489	28,552	54,391
1800	...	74,129	...	6,880	41,220	81,009
1810	...	100,688	...	10,552	53,722	111,240
1820	56,220	123,746	7,582	11,891	63,802	135,637
1830	...	173,173	...	15,624	80,462	188,797
1838	...	...	...	17,500	...	...
1840	83,158	238,204	10,507	19,833	93,665	258,037
1847	...	...	11,000?	20,240	...	...
1850	110,640	389,001	10,736	19,761	121,376	408,762
1856	...	...	...	...	...	...
1860	543,344		22,185		565,529	
1870	651,854		22,147		674,022*	
1880	815,362		31,699		847,170*	
1890	1,006,590		39,371		1,046,964*	

*These totals include Chinese, Indian, etc.

Increase of the Negro Population in Philadelphia for a Century

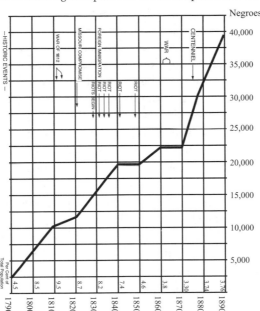

[NOTE— Each horizontal line represents an increment of 2500 persons in population; the upright lines represent the decades. The broken diagonal shows the course of Negro population, and the arrows above recall historic events previously referred to as influencing the increase of the Negroes. At the base of the upright lines is a figure giving the percentage which the Negro population formed of the total population.]

The Negro has never formed a very large percent of the population of the city, as this diagram shows:

Proportion of Negroes in Total Population of Philadelphia

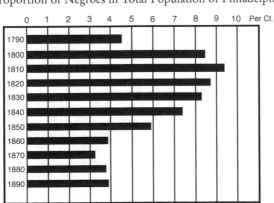

A glance at these tables shows how much more sensitive the lower classes of a population are to great social changes than the rest of the group; prosperity brings abnormal increase, adversity, abnormal decrease in mere numbers, not to speak of other less easily measurable changes. Doubtless if we could divide the white population into social strata, we would find some classes whose characteristics corresponded in many respects to those of the Negro. Or to view the matter from the opposite standpoint we have here an opportunity of tracing the history and condition of a social class which peculiar circumstances have kept segregated and apart from the mass.

If we glance beyond Philadelphia and compare conditions as to increase of Negro population with the situation in the country at large we can make two interesting comparisons: the rate of increase in a large city compared with that in the country at large; and the changes in the proportion of Negro inhabitants in the city and the United States.

A glance at the proportion of Negroes in Philadelphia and in the United States shows how largely the Negro problems are still problems of the country. (See diagram of the proportion of Negroes in the total population of Philadelphia and of the United States on opposite page.)

Increase of Negroes in the United States and in the City of Philadelphia Compared

Decade	Increase in		Census Year	Percentage of Negroes in Total Population in	
	Philadelphia %	United States %		Philadelphia %	United States %
1790–1800	176.42	32.33	1790	4.57	19.27
1800–1810	52.93	37.50	1800	8.49	18.88
1810–1820	13.00	28.59	1810	9.45	19.03
1820–1830	31.39	31.44	1820	8.76	18.39
1830–1840	27.07	23.40	1830	8.27	18.10
1840–1850	.36*	26.63	1840	7.39	16.84
1850–1860	12.26	22.07	1850	4.83	15.69
1860–1870	.17*	9.86	1860	3.92	14.13
1870–1880	43.13	34.85	1870	3.28	12.66
1880–1890	24.20	13.51	1880	3.74	13.12
			1890	3.76	11.93

*Decrease.

Proportion of Negroes in the Total Population of Philadelphia and of the United States

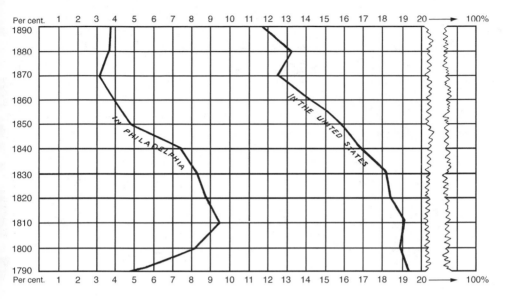

This is even more striking if we remember that Philadelphia ranks high in the absolute and relative number of its Negro inhabitants. For the ten largest cities in the United States we have:

Ten Largest Cities in the United States Arranged According
to Negro Population

Cities	Negro Population	Cities	Proportion of Negroes to Total Population
1. Baltimore	67,104	1. Baltimore	15.49%
2. Philadelphia	39,371	2. St. Louis	5.94
3. St. Louis	26,865	3. Philadelphia	3.76
4. New York	23,601	4. Cincinnati	3.72
5. Chicago	14,271	5. Boston	1.76
6. Cincinnati	11,655	6. New York	1.55
7. Brooklyn	10,287	7. Chicago	1.29
8. Boston	8,125	8. Brooklyn	1.27
9. Cleveland	2,989	9. Cleveland	1.14
10. San Francisco	1,847	10. San Francisco	.61

Negroes of *Philadelphia,* 1890, **39,371.**	Total Population of *Philadelphia,* 1800, **41,220.**	*New York,* Total Population, 1790, **33,131.**	Total Population of *Boston,* 1820, **43,298.**
Washington, Total Population, 1850, **40,001.**	*Chicago,* Total Population, 1850, **29,963.**	*Harrisburg, Pa.,* Total Population, 1890, **39,385.**	*Norfolk, Va.,* Total Population, 1890, **34,871.**

Of all the large cities in the United States, only three have a larger absolute Negro population than Philadelphia: Washington, New Orleans and Baltimore. We seldom realize that none of the great Southern cities, except the three mentioned, have a colored population approaching that of Philadelphia:

Colored* Population of Large Southern Cities

Cities	Colored Inhabitants	Cities	Colored Inhabitants
Washington, D.C.	75,697	Nashville, Tenn.	29,395
New Orleans, La.	64,663	Memphis, Tenn.	28,729
Philadelphia, Pa.	40,374*	Louisville, Ky.	28,672
Richmond, Va.	32,354	Atlanta, Ga.	28,117
Charleston, S.C.	31,036	Savannah, Ga.	22,978

*Includes Chinese, Japanese and civilized Indians, an insignificant number in these cases.

Taken by itself, the Negro population of Philadelphia is no insignificant group of men, as the foregoing diagrams show. (See [above].)

In other words, we are studying a group of people the size of the capital of Pennsylvania in 1890, and as large as Philadelphia itself in 1800.

Scanning this population more carefully, the first thing that strikes one is the unusual excess of females. This fact, which is true of all Negro urban populations, has not often been noticed, and has not been given its true weight as a social phenomenon.[2] If we take the ten cities having the greatest Negro populations, we have this table:[3]

Colored* Population of Ten Cities by Sex

Cities.	Males.	Females.
Washington	33,831	41,866
New Orleans	28,936	35,727
Baltimore	29,165	38,131
Philadelphia	18,960	21,414
Richmond, Va.	14,216	18,138
Nashville	13,334	16,061
Memphis	13,333	15,396
Charleston, S.C.	14,187	16,849
St. Louis	13,247	13,819
Louisville, Ky.	13,348	15,324
Total	192,557	232,725
Proportion	1,000	1208.5

*Includes Chinese, Japanese and civilized Indians—an element that can be ignored, being small.

This is a very marked excess and has far-reaching effects. In Philadelphia this excess can be traced back some years:

Philadelphia Negroes By Sex[4]

County of Philadelphia.				City of Philadelphia.			
Year.	Males.	Females.	Number Females to 1000 Males.	Year.	Males.	Females.	Number Females to 1000 Males.
1820	5,220	6,671	1,091	1820	3,156	4,426	1,383
1838	6,896	9,146	1,326	1838	3,772	5,304	1,395
1840	8,316	11,515	1,387	1840	3,986	6,521	1,630
1850				1850	8,435	11,326	1,348
1890				1890	18,960	21,414	1,127

The cause of this excess is easy to explain. From the beginning the industrial opportunities of Negro women in cities have been far greater than those of men, through their large employment in domestic service. At the same time the restriction of employments open to Negroes, which perhaps reached a climax in 1830–1840, and which still plays a great part, has served to limit the number of men. The proportion, therefore, of men to women is a rough index of the industrial opportunities of the Negro. At first there was a large amount of work for all, and the Negro servants and laborers and artisans poured into the city. This lasted up until about 1820, and at that time we find the number of the sexes approaching equality in the county, although naturally more unequal in the city proper. In the next two decades the opportunities for work were greatly restricted for the men, while at the same time, through the growth of the city, the demand for female servants increased, so that in 1840 we have about seven women to every five men in the county, and sixteen to every five in the city. Industrial opportunities for men then gradually increased largely through the growth of the city, the development of new callings for Negroes and the increased demand for male servants in public and private. Nevertheless the disproportion still indicates an unhealthy condition, and its effects are seen in a large percent of illegitimate births, and an unhealthy tone in much of the social intercourse among the middle class of the Negro population.[5]

Looking now at the age structure of the Negroes, we notice the disproportionate number of young persons, that is, women between eighteen and thirty and men between twenty and thirty-five. The colored population of Philadelphia contains an abnormal number of young untrained persons at the most impressionable age; at the age when, as statistics of the world show, the most crime is committed, when sexual excess is more frequent, and when there has not been developed fully the feeling of responsibility and personal worth. This excess is more striking in recent years than formerly, although full statistics are not available:

Proportion of Population.	1848.	1880.	1890.*
Under 5 years	14.7	9.8	7.8
Under 15 years	33.6	. . . . .	22.5
15 to 50 years	41.8	. . . . .	63.6†
Over 50 years	9.9	. . . . .	6.1‡

*Including Chinese, Japanese and Indians. †15 to 55. ‡Over 55.

This table is too meagre to be conclusive, but it is probable that while the age structure of the Negro urban population in 1848 was about normal, it has greatly changed in recent years. Detailed statistics for 1890 make this plainer:

Negroes* of Philadelphia by Sex and Age, 1890

Ages.	Males.	Per Cent.	Females.	Per Cent.	Total.
Under 1	400	2.1	369	1.7	769
1 to 4	1,121	5.9	1,264	5.9	2,385
5 to 9	1,458	7.7	1,515	7.1	2,973
10 to 14	1,409	7.5	1,567	7.4	2,976
15 to 19	2,455	7.7	2,123	9.9	3,578
20 to 24	2,408	12.9	3,133	14.8	5,541
25 to 29	1,521	13.5	2,774	13.1	5,295
30 to 34	2,034	10.9	2,046	9.6	4,080
35 to 44	3,375	18.0	3,139	14.8	6,514
45 to 54	1,645	8.7	1,783	8.4	3,428
55 to 64	581	3.1	799	3.9	1,380
65 and over	376	2.0	726	3.4	1,102
Unknown	177	..	176	..	353
Total	18,960	100.0	21,414	100.0	40,374

*Including 1003 Chinese, Japanese and Indians.

Comparing this with the age structure of other groups we have this table:[6]

Age.	Negroes of Philad'a.	Negroes U.S.	England.	France.	Germany	United States.
Under 10	15.31	28.22	23.9	17.5	24.2	24.29
10 to 20	16.37	25.19	21.3	17.4	20.7	21.70
20 to 30	27.08	17.40	17.02	16.3	16.2	18.24
30 and over	41.24	29.19	37.6	48.8	38.9	35.77

In few large cities does the age structure approach the abnormal condition here presented; the most obvious comparison would be with the age structure of the whites of Philadelphia, for 1890, which may be thus represented:

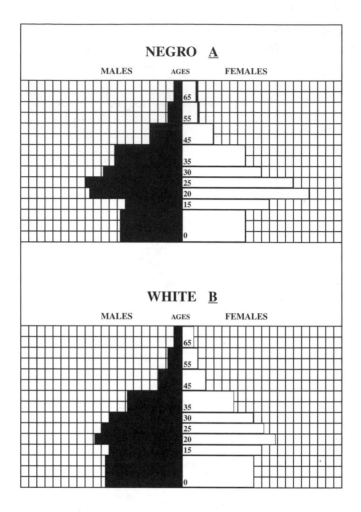

We find then in Philadelphia a steadily and, in recent years, rapidly grow-ing Negro population, in itself as large as a good-sized city, and characterized by an excessive number of females and of young persons.

14. The Seventh Ward, 1896. We shall now make a more intensive study of the Negro population, confining ourselves to one typical ward for the year 1896. Of the nearly forty thousand Negroes in Philadelphia in 1890, a little less than a fourth lived in the Seventh Ward, and over half in this and the ad-joining Fourth, Fifth and Eighth Wards:

Ward.	Negroes.	Whites.
Seventh	8,861	21,177
Eighth	3,011	13,940
Fourth	2,573	17,792
Fifth	2,335	14,619

The distribution of Negroes in the other wards may be seen by the accompanying map. (See [below].)

The Seventh Ward starts from the historic centre of Negro settlement in the city, South Seventh street and Lombard, and includes the long narrow strip, beginning at South Seventh and extending west, with South and Spruce streets as boundaries, as far as the Schuylkill River. The colored population of this ward numbered 3621 in 1860, 4616 in 1870, and 8861 in 1890. It is a thickly populated district of varying character; north of it is the residence and business section of the city; south of it a middle class and workingmen's residence section; at the east end it joins Negro, Italian and Jewish slums; at the west end, the wharves of the river and an industrial section separating it from the grounds of the University of Pennsylvania and the residence section of West Philadelphia.

Wards of Philadelphia, with Negro Population, 1890

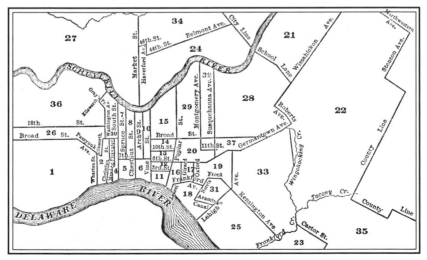

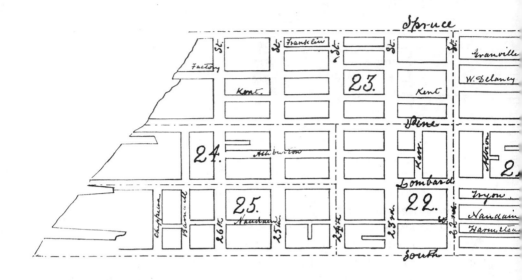

SEVENTH
WARD.

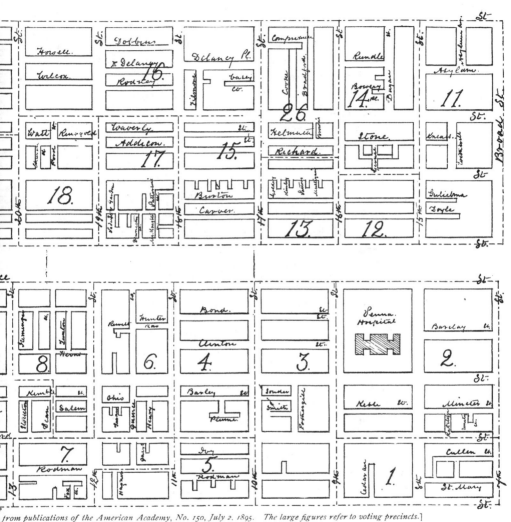

from publications of the American Academy, No. 150, July 2, 1895.   The large figures refer to voting precincts.]

Starting at Seventh street and walking along Lombard, let us glance at the general character of the ward. Pausing a moment at the corner of Seventh and Lombard, we can at a glance view the worst Negro slums of the city. The houses are mostly brick, some wood, not very old, and in general uncared for rather than dilapidated. The blocks between Eighth, Pine, Sixth and South have for many decades been the centre of Negro population. Here the riots of the thirties took place, and here once was a depth of poverty and degradation almost unbelievable. Even to-day there are many evidences of degradation, although the signs of idleness, shiftlessness, dissoluteness and crime are more conspicuous than those of poverty. The alleys[7] near, as Ratcliffe street, Middle alley, Brown's court, Barclay street, etc., are haunts of noted criminals, male and female, of gamblers and prostitutes, and at the same time of many poverty-stricken people, decent but not energetic. There is an abundance of political clubs, and nearly all the houses are practically lodging houses, with a miscellaneous and shifting population. The corners, night and day, are filled with Negro loafers—able-bodied young men and women, all cheerful, some with good-natured, open faces, some with traces of crime and excess, a few pinched with poverty. They are mostly gamblers, thieves and prostitutes, and few have fixed and steady occupation of any kind. Some are stevedores, porters, laborers and laundresses. On its face this slum is noisy and dissipated, but not brutal, although now and then highway robberies and murderous assaults in other parts of the city are traced to its denizens. Nevertheless the stranger can usually walk about here day and night with little fear of being molested, if he be not too inquisitive.[8]

Passing up Lombard, beyond Eighth, the atmosphere suddenly changes, because these next two blocks have few alleys and the residences are good-sized and pleasant. Here some of the best Negro families of the ward live. Some are wealthy in a small way, nearly all are Philadelphia born, and they represent an early wave of emigration from the old slum section.[9] To the south, on Rodman street, are families of the same character. North of Pine and below Eleventh there are practically no Negro residences. Beyond Tenth street, and as far as Broad street, the Negro population is large and varied in character. On small streets like Barclay and its extension below Tenth—Souder, on Ivy, Rodman, Salem, Heins, Iseminger, Ralston, etc., is a curious mingling of respectable working people and some of a better class, with recent immigrations of the semi-criminal class from the slums. On the larger streets, like Lombard and Juniper, there live many respectable colored families—native Philadelphians, Virginians and other Southerners, with a fringe of more questionable families. Beyond Broad, as far as Sixteenth, the good character of the Negro population is maintained except in one or two back streets.[10] From Sixteenth to

Eighteenth, intermingled with some estimable families, is a dangerous criminal class. They are not the low, open idlers of Seventh and Lombard, but rather the graduates of that school: shrewd and sleek politicians, gamblers and confidence men, with a class of well-dressed and partially undetected prostitutes. This class is not easily differentiated and located, but it seems to centre at Seventeenth and Lombard. Several large gambling houses are near here, although more recently one has moved below Broad, indicating a reshifting of the criminal centre. The whole community was an earlier immigration from Seventh and Lombard. North of Lombard, above Seventeenth, including Lombard street itself, above Eighteenth, is one of the best Negro residence sections of the city, centring about Addison street. Some undesirable elements have crept in even here, especially since the Christian League attempted to clear out the Fifth Ward slums,[11] but still it remains a centre of quiet, respectable families, who own their own homes and live well. The Negro population practically stops at Twenty-second street, although a few Negroes live beyond.

We can thus see that the Seventh Ward presents an epitome of nearly all the Negro problems; that every class is represented, and varying conditions of life. Nevertheless one must naturally be careful not to draw too broad conclusions from a single ward in one city. There is no proof that the proportion between the good and the bad here is normal, even for the race in Philadelphia; that the social problems affecting Negroes in large Northern cities are presented here in most of their aspects seems credible, but that certain of those aspects are distorted and exaggerated by local peculiarities is also not to be doubted.

In the fall of 1896 a house-to-house visitation was made to all the Negro families of this ward. The visitor went in person to each residence and called for the head of the family. The housewife usually responded, the husband now and then, and sometimes an older daughter or other member of the family. The fact that the University was making an investigation of this character was known and discussed in the ward, but its exact scope and character was not known. The mere announcement of the purpose secured, in all but about twelve cases,[12] immediate admission. Seated then in the parlor, kitchen, or living room, the visitor began the questioning, using his discretion as to the order in which they were put, and omitting or adding questions as the circumstances suggested. Now and then the purpose of a particular query was explained, and usually the object of the whole inquiry indicated. General discussions often arose as to the condition of the Negroes, which were instructive. From ten minutes to an hour was spent in each home, the average time being fifteen to twenty-five minutes.

Usually the answers were prompt and candid, and gave no suspicion of previous preparation. In some cases there was evident falsification or evasion.

In such cases the visitor made free use of his best judgment and either inserted no answer at all, or one which seemed approximately true. In some cases the families visited were not at home, and a second or third visit was paid. In other cases, and especially in the case of the large class of lodgers, the testimony of landlords and neighbors often had to be taken.

No one can make an inquiry of this sort and not be painfully conscious of a large margin of error from omissions, errors of judgment and deliberate deception. Of such errors this study has, without doubt, its full share. Only one fact was peculiarly favorable and that is the proverbial good nature and candor of the Negro. With a more cautious and suspicious people much less success could have been obtained. Naturally some questions were answered better than others; the chief difficulty arising in regard to the questions of age and income. The ages given for people forty and over have a large margin of error, owing to ignorance of the real birthday. The question of income was naturally a delicate one, and often had to be gotten at indirectly. The yearly income, as a round sum, was seldom asked for; rather the daily or weekly wages taken and the time employed during the year.

On December 1, 1896, there were in the Seventh Ward of Philadelphia 9675 Negroes; 4501 males and 5174 females. This total includes all persons of Negro descent and, thirty-three intermarried whites.[13] It does not include residents of the ward then in prisons or in almshouses. There were a considerable number of omissions among the loafers and criminals without homes, the class of lodgers and the club-house habitués. These were mostly males, and their inclusion would somewhat affect the division by sexes, although probably not to a great extent.[14] The increase of the Negro population in this ward for six and a half years is 814, or at the rate of 14.13 per cent per decade. This is perhaps somewhat smaller than that for the population of the city at large, for the Seventh Ward is crowded and overflowing into other wards. Possibly the present Negro population of the city is between 43,000 and 45,000. At all events it is probable that the crest of the tide of immigration is passed, and that the increase for the decade 1890–1900 will not be nearly as large as the 24 per cent of the decade 1880–1890.

The division by sex indicates still a very large and, it would seem, growing excess of women. The return shows 1150 females to every 1000 males. Possibly through the omission of men and the unavoidable duplication of some servants lodging away from their place of service, the disproportion of the sexes is exaggerated. At any rate it is great, and if growing, may be an indication of increased restriction in the employments open to Negro men since 1880 or even since 1890.

Negro Population of Seventh Ward

Age.	Male.	Female.
Under 10	570	641
10 to 19	483	675
20 to 29	1,276	1,444
30 to 39	1,046	1,084
40 to 49	533	632
50 to 59	298	331
60 to 69	114	155
70 and over	41	96
Age unknown	120	116
Total	4,501	5,174
Grand total		9,675

The age structure also presents abnormal features.[15] Comparing the age structure with that of the large cities of Germany, we have:

Age.	Negroes of Philadelphia.	Large Cities of Germany.
Under 20	25.1	39.3
20 to 40	51.3	37.2
Over 40	23.6	23.5

Comparing it with the Whites and Negroes in the city in 1890, we have:

Age.	Negroes of Philadelphia, 1896, Seventh Ward.	Negroes* of Philadelphia, 1890.	Native Whites of Philadelphia, 1890.
Under 10	12.8%	15.31%	24.6%
10 to 20	12.3	16.37	19.5
20 to 30	28.7	27.08	18.5
30 and over	46.2	41.24	37.4

*Includes 1003 Chinese, Japanese and Indians.

As was noticed in the whole city in 1890, so here is even more striking evidence of the preponderance of young people at an age when sudden introduction to city life is apt to be dangerous, and of an abnormal excess of females.

NOTES

1. The unit for study throughout this essay has been made the *county* of Philadelphia, and not the city, except where the city is especially mentioned. Since 1854, the city and county have been coterminous. Even before that the population of the "districts" was for our purposes an urban population, and a part of the group life of Philadelphia.

2. My attention was first called to this fact by Professor Kelly Miller, of Howard University; cf. "Publications of American Negro Academy," No. I. There is probably, in taking censuses, a larger percentage of omissions among males than among females; such omissions would, however, go but a small way toward explaining this excess of females.

3. In a good many of the Eleventh Census tables, "Chinese, Japanese and civilized Indians," were very unwisely included in the total of the Colored, making an error to be allowed for when one studies the Negro. In most cases the discrepancy can be ignored. In this case this fact but serves to decrease the excess of females, as these other groups have an excess of males. The city of Philadelphia has 1003 Chinese, Japanese and Indians. The figures for the Whole United States show that this excess of females is probably confined to cities:

Negroes According to Sex.

Section.	Males.	Females.
United States	3,725,561	3,744,479
North Atlantic	133,277	136,629
South Atlantic	1,613,769	1,648,921
North Central	222,384	208,728
South Central	1,739,565	1,739,686
Western	16,566	10,515

4. Figures for other years have not been found.

5. In social gatherings, in the churches, etc., men are always at a premium, and this very often leads to lowering the standard of admission to certain circles, and often gives one the impression that the social level of the women is higher than the level of the men.

6. The age groupings in these tables are necessarily unsatisfactory on account of the vagaries of the census.

7. "In the Fifth Ward only there are 171 small streets and courts; Fourth Ward, 88. Between Fifth and Sixth, South and Lombard streets, 15 courts and alleys." "First Annual Report College Settlement Kitchen." p. 6.

8. In a residence of eleven months in the centre of the slums, I never was once accosted or insulted. The ladies of the College Settlement report similar experience. I have seen, however, some strangers here roughly handled.

9. It is often asked why do so many Negroes persist in living in the slums. The answer is, they do not; the slum is continually scaling off emigrants for other sections, and receiving new accretions from without. Thus the efforts for social betterment put forth here have often their best results elsewhere, since the beneficiaries move away and others fill their places. There is, of course, a permanent nucleus of inhabitants, and these, in some cases, are really respectable and decent people. The forces that keep such a class in the slums are discussed further on.

10. Gulielma street, for instance, is a notorious nest for bad characters, with only one or two respectable families.

11. The almost universal and unsolicited testimony of better class Negroes was that the attempted clearing out of the slums of the Fifth Ward acted disastrously upon them; the prostitutes and gamblers emigrated to respectable Negro residence districts, and real estate agents, on the theory that all Negroes belong to the same general class, rented them houses. Streets like Rodman and Juniper were nearly ruined, and property which the thrifty Negroes had bought here greatly depreciated. It is not well to clean a cess-pool until one knows where the refuse can be disposed of without general harm.

12. The majority of these were brothels. A few, however, were homes of respectable people who resented the investigation as unwarranted and unnecessary.

13. Twenty-nine women and four men. The question of race intermarriage is discussed in Chapter XIV.

14. There may have been some duplication in the counting of servant girls who do not lodge where they work. Special pains was taken to count them only where they lodge, but there must have been some errors. Again, the Seventh Ward has a very large number of lodgers; some of these form a sort of floating population, and here were omissions; some were forgotten by landladies and others purposely omitted.

15. There is a wide margin of error in the matter of Negroes' ages, especially of those above fifty; even of those from thirty-five to fifty, the age is often unrecorded and is a matter of memory, and poor memory at that. Much pains was taken during the canvass to correct errors and to throw out obviously incorrect answers. The error in the ages under forty is probably not large enough to invalidate the general conclusions; those under thirty are as correct as is general in such statistics, although the ages of children under ten is liable to err a year or so from the truth. Many women have probably understated their ages and somewhat swelled the period of the thirties as against the forties. The ages over fifty have a large element of error.

E. FRANKLIN FRAZIER

The Changing Status of the Negro Family

Introduction

Attempts to explain the character and problems of the Negro family by seeking their origins in African traditions and customs have ended in barren speculations.[1] These speculations have been based upon two assumptions: first, that pre-marital sex experience among African Negroes indicated the absence of social control; and secondly, that there was an unbroken tradition from Africa to America. Concerning the first assumption it is only necessary to remark that this misconception is only a part of the general body of false opinion concerning 'primitive' peoples.[2] Although a survival of African family life was once reported in Alabama,[3] our present knowledge of the conditions under which slavery was established in America leads us to believe that the Negro was completely stripped of his social heritage in the process.[4] The complete effacement of tribal life in America left the lingering memories of Africa to be borne only by isolated individuals in a world where these memories ceased to have any meaning.

Therefore, for the roots of the Negro family one must go to the slave family as it developed on the plantation and under the system of domestic slavery; and to the free Negro family which developed outside of the slave system. Our information concerning the character of the slave family has been furnished chiefly by apologists for slavery, who have given us a picture of idyllic happiness under benevolent patriarchs; and by abolitionists whose literature abounded in stereotyped scenes of slave families being torn asunder

E. Franklin Frazier, "The Changing Status of the Negro Family," *Social Forces* 9 (March, 1931): 386–393. Reprinted with permission of *Social Forces*.

by soulless masters. The absence of legal marriage, legal family, and legal control over children which DuBois[5] regards as the essential features of the slave family characterize the family negatively. The real social relations between the masters and slaves and between the slaves themselves can neither be deduced from legal definitions nor inferred from the romantic tradition in which antebellum life in the South has been enshrined.[6] While to some extent the Negro slave family was subject to the individual judgment and caprice of the masters, it represented on the whole an accommodation to the slave system as it varied from section to section.[7]

The chief question of sociological interests is, to what extent did the slave family constitute a real social group capable of exercising control and of passing on a tradition? It is impossible to answer this question statistically. One limitation upon the functioning of the slave family as an autonomous group was the control of the master which began often with the choice of a mate. This control varied from friendly, patriarchal oversight under domestic slavery to pure animal breeding where the slave was regarded as a utility for trade. Within the family group itself the status of the father was always subject to limitations which could be imposed by the masters. The mother who represented the more stable element in the slave family probably occupied a more important position than in a free family. Under the most favorable conditions of slavery, especially among the house slaves and skilled artisans who were allowed to hire their time, the father's position was dominant and family discipline was good. The extent to which family consciousness was developed in some slave families is shown in the life of J. W. C. Pennington. When Pennington's father was given a whipping, he said, "This act created an open rupture with our family—each member felt the deep insult that had been inflicted upon our head; the spirit of the whole family was roused; we talked of it in our nightly gatherings, and showed it in our daily melancholy aspect."[8]

The organization and solidarity of the slave family was not only affected by the character of the institution of slavery in different sections but also by the varying fortunes of masters which caused the disruption of families under the most favorable conditions. On the other hand, where families of slaves were retained in the same family for generations we can note the beginnings of traditions as, for example, in the case of those slaves who succeeded their fathers as preachers and in positions of trust under slavery.

However much the slave family served as an accommodation of the personal wishes and family interests of the slaves to the institution of slavery, a crisis was precipitated by emancipation. During this crisis the social bonds of the slaves were dissolved in the general breakup of the social organization that had sustained them. In order to realize his new status the slave began to move about and in many cases changed his identity by acquiring a new name.[9] Thus the Negro family became subject to all the fluctuations of vagrant impulses and individual wishes. The subsequent history of the Negro family in the South has been the establishment of new accommodations to the rural South. Increase in farm ownership up to 1910 has been an index to the stabilization of Negro life. Descendants of slaves have acquired farms which have been parcelled out from the larger plantations. In the towns of the South a few families have achieved some degree of economic independence and culture that has set them apart from the mass of laborers and domestic servants. In many cases these families are descended from slaves having the advantage of contacts with the master class as house slaves. In the larger cities, especially the educational centers, there has grown up a class of educated Negroes with middle class standards and outlook on life. Within this group family traditions have been built up and from this class many of the leaders in the northern cities have come.

Of great significance for the family life of the Negro have been the free Negroes who were scattered for the most part in the cities along the Atlantic seaboard. The usual picture of the free Negro has represented them as a group of social outcasts living in ignorance and poverty.[10] Yet in Charleston, South Carolina, after the abortive attempt at insurrection by Denmark Vesey, it was argued in a memorial to the Senate and House of Representatives that the free Negroes through their monopoly of the mechanical arts were preventing the settlement of immigrants in that city.[11] In New Orleans the property owned by free Negroes amounted to fifteen million dollars in 1860.[12] It was through the guilds of caterers that the more energetic Negroes in Philadelphia were able to meet the competition of foreign labor before the Civil War.[13] There were settlements of free Negroes in Baltimore, New York, Washington, D.C., in the Northwest Territory, and in the Tidewater Region of Virginia in which families were founded with a tradition of achievement coming down to the present. Consciousness of the distinction which free birth gave caused even the poorer elements of the free Negroes to look down on the new "ishy"— recently emancipated from slavery.[14] The free Negro class furnished many of the leaders of the emancipated slaves, and their descendants are still playing an important rôle in the Negro group.

I

The northward migration of Negroes during and since the World War tended to dramatize the process of urbanization of the Negro population. Between

1900 and 1910 the urban Negro population increased 34.1 per cent for the entire country. During this period southern cities showed a larger percentage increase than northern cities. This aspect of the urbanization of the Negro has often been overlooked. Although during the decade from 1910 to 1920 the increase in Negro urban population was 32.6 per cent for the whole country, the increase in southern cities was 21.4 per cent and nearly 60 per cent for northern cities. The migrating Negro population has gone chiefly to northern cities of 100,000 and over, which showed an increase in the Negro population of 98.4 per cent.[15]

Table I. Birthplace of 496 Atlanta Negroes*

Birthplace	Number	Per cent
Cities of 50,000 or more:		
Atlanta	70 ⎫	
Macon	4 ⎬ 75	15.1
Savannah	1 ⎭	
Cities of 25,000 or more: Columbus	3	0.6
Five Cities of 10,000–25,000	21	4.2
Cities of 2,500–10,000	48	9.6
Rural Communities	281	56.6
Fifteen other states	66	13.3
Foreign Countries	2	0.4
Total	496	99.8

*This information was given on questionnaires used in a study of the Negro family. These families were selected from both the better class and the poorer neighborhoods and included professional people as well as common laborers.

The movement of the Negro to northern industrial centers has been regarded as the second emancipation of the race. The effects of the migrations on the social life of the Negro have been similar to those resulting from the Civil War. The old accommodations to life in the South were destroyed and the disorganization of Negro life in northern cities has been registered in social agencies and courts. In Chicago, for example, the Negro cases constituted a fifth of the major service cases handled by the United Charities in 1928. The extent of family disorganization among Negroes is indicated by the large number of cases of family desertion and non-support, illegitimacy, and juvenile delinquency. The disorganizing effect of urban life on the Negro has caused forebodings concerning his ability to withstand the rigorous competition of the North.[16]

Table II. Birthplace and Place of Residence of 314 Persons Listed in Who's Who in Colored America

Place of Birth	Place of Residence				Total
	North	Border	South	West	
North	40	4	2	0	46
Border	24	21	3	1	49
South	98	23	83	6	210
West	4	1	1	3	9
Total	166	49	89	10	314

Table III. Birthplace and Place of Residence of 125 Graduates of a Negro College

Place of Birth	Place of Residence				Total
	North	Border	South	West	
North	11	2	3	1	17
Border	8	12	2	0	22
South	32	10	40	3	85
West	0	0	0	1	1
Total	51	24	45	5	125

An important but often neglected aspect of the migration of the Negro has been the movement of the more intelligent and energetic members of the race. The rise of large Negro communities in northern cities has opened a field for enterprise and service.[17] A study of the birthplace and residence of 314 persons listed in Who's Who in Colored America and 125 graduates of a Negro college indicates the northward movement of educated Negroes.

In the *Who's Who in Colored America* group we find that only about 40 per cent of those born in the South have remained there. The college group in Table III shows a slightly smaller migration northward. This group was composed to a large extent of teachers who were compelled to find employment chiefly in the South.

These two groups give some indication of the changing status of the Negro family when we study the occupations of the fathers of those engaged in business and the professions. In both groups about 25 per cent of the professional men and women have come from families whose heads were in the professions. This group represents the second generation of the Negroes in fields where their fathers were pioneers. On the other hand, the rise in occupational status for the majority of the group represents a tremendous change in social status in the Negro group. This change in status carries with it new conceptions of life which affect the stability and the organization of the Negro family.

Between the Negro peasant from the South with his fatalistic resignation to the place given him by the white man and the educated Negro, sometimes representing several generations of culture, both seeking their fortunes in the northern city, there is a disparity in cultural development that only the nascent race consciousness, engendered in part by race conflict, tends to bridge. The peasant in the new environment seeks fulfillment of his awakened ambitions and hopes for a new status.[18] The consequent social disorganization is not merely a pathological phenomenon for the care of social agencies but also represents a step towards a reorganization of life on a more intelligent basis. In the next section there will be exhibited some of the results of an attempt to measure the processes of disorganization and reorganization of Negro life in a northern city.

II

The city of Chicago has offered a laboratory in which to study the changes taking place in Negro life. The expansion of the Negro community in this city has followed the growth of the city. Studies of city growth have shown that the process of expansion can be measured in rates of change in home ownership, poverty, and other variable conditions for unit areas along the main thoroughfares radiating from the center of the city.[19] The growing Negro community was an opportunity to study statistically the social selection and segregation of different elements of the Negro population.

Table IV. Occupations of the Fathers of Selected Groups of Negroes in
the Professions and Business

	Occupation of Father								
Occupation of Person	Agriculture	Common labor	Domestic and per social service	Skilled occupations	Clerical	Business	Professional service	Public office	Total
Who's Who in Colored America									
Professional	62	36	23	46	12	20	70	3	272
Business	10	4	3	5	1	4	6	0	33
Total	72	40	26	51	13	24	76	3	305
Graduates of a Negro college									
Professional	21	16	7	24	6	13	30	0	117
Business	2	1	0	1	1	0	1	0	6
Total	23	17	7	25	7	13	31	0	123

The majority of the 110,000 Negroes in Chicago in 1920 constituted the Negro community which extended from the outer boundary of the business center or the Loop—twelfth Street—southward along one of the main arteries, State Street, for a distance of over seven miles. The area occupied by this community of Negroes, who comprised as much as about ninety per cent of the total population in some sections in it, was about a mile and a quarter wide except where it was bounded by Lake Michigan. By dividing this whole area into seven unit areas bounded by streets running east and west at intervals of about one mile each, it has been possible to study small enough units of the Negro population in order that the changes taking place in the social life of the Negro could be measured.[20] The differences in the character of the Negro population in these zones together with the varying rates of home ownership, poverty, and family disorganization become indices of the social processes which we seek to measure.

The process of selection and segregation of economic classes in the Negro community is reflected in the distribution of occupational classes in these seven unit areas.[21] In the first area near the Loop where marked deterioration, high land values, and low rental presage the expansion of the business center, Negro laborers and servants, most of whom were born in the South, are able to get a foothold in the city. The second area showed the same characteristics as the first but gave some indication of the character of the third area where the higher occupational classes were more largely represented. The proportion of the higher occupational classes in the Negro population increased for the succeeding three areas. It was especially in the seventh area that the higher classes were concentrated. The steady decline in the proportion of females employed was also an index to higher culture in the succeeding areas. The rate of home ownership among Negro families in these areas was an indication of family stability. Among the poorer migrant families of the first area, there was no homeownership and the 1.2 per cent for the second area was due to the presence of a small group of Negroes of a higher cultural status. The gradual increase for the succeeding areas followed the increase in the proportion of the higher occupational classes in the population. In the seventh area where a third of the men and women employed were in professional services, about thirty per cent of the families owned their homes. The variation in proportion of the different occupational groups living in these areas and in the rate of homeownership indicated the differences in cultural levels and organization of the Negro community.

Table V. Rate per Hundred Population 10 Years of Age and Over

	Zone I	Zone II	Zone III	Zone IV	Zone V	Zone VI	Zone VII
Professional and Public Service, Trades and Clerical:							
Male	5.8	5.5	10.7	11.2	12.5	13.4	34.2
Female	3.0	6.5	13.3	13.3	14.8	15.2	33.3
Skilled:							
Male	6.2	10.8	12.3	13.6	11.1	14.4	13.0
Female	3.9	3.9	7.5	7.7	7.8	7.4	16.6
Railroad Porters	1.4	3.9	6.7	6.5	7.5	7.7	10.7
Semi-skilled, Domestic Service, and Laborers:							
Male	86.1	78.8	68.9	67.9	68.6	63.6	41.6
Female	92.9	88.3	78.4	78.1	76.1	76.8	46.9
Women Employed	46.1	48.1	42.3	45.2	39.7	36.6	34.5
Home Ownership	0	1.2	6.2	7.2	8.3	11.4	29.8

Table VI. Rate per Hundred

	Zone I	Zone II	Zone III	Zone IV	Zone V	Zone VI	Zone VII
Charity Cases:							
1927	8.0	8.2	5.3	2.8	1.9	1.0	1.1
Family desertions:							
January 1, 1926, to June 30, 1928	2.5	2.6	2.1	1.5	1.1	0.4	0.2
Delinquent boys:							
1926	42.8	31.4	30.0	28.8	15.7	9.6	1.4

When the statistics on the breakdown of Negro family life were related to the culture and organization of the Negro community instead of being taken as a description of average conditions in the entire population, the significance of these statistics as indices to the processes of disorganization and reorganization becomes apparent. In the first and second areas in which, as we have seen, were located the propertyless migrants of the lower occupational classes, the rate of dependency measured by charity cases was about eight per cent. The rates of family desertion were also high for these areas. The high rates of juvenile delinquency—42.8 per cent and 31.4 per cent— were also indicative of the breakdown of family discipline and social organization in a large northern city. The extent of family disorganization reflected in these three indexes declined gradually from the third to the seventh area. The decline in the rate of dependency, desertion, and juvenile delinquency followed the rise in the rate of home ownership and the increase in the proportion of the higher occupational classes in the population.

The significance of these changes in the rates of family disorganization is due to the fact that they reflect the processes of selection and segregation in the Negro community. In Chicago, as in most northern cities, there was a small group of families, many of them mulattoes with free ancestry, who had achieved an economic and cultural status that separated them from the masses. Some of these families which had acquired a place in the community represented the successful struggles of earlier migrants. These people regarded the migration of the ignorant black masses from the South as a menace to their own position. Before the flood of ignorance, crudeness and poverty from the South, they moved to areas where they could maintain their own standards of behavior. The migrant families who possessed some wealth and culture acquired in the South sought a congenial environment in these same areas.

In the keen competition to serve the newly created desires and wants of the Negro community a new leadership has come to the top with a new conception of life. Among high and low alike, life has come to have a different meaning from that in the South or that of a small Negro community accommodated to a large city. These changes mean disorganization and reorganization of life on another basis. The family is the social group which bears the burden of these cultural changes. In the third area where social disorganization is greatest in the Negro community, family life tends to disappear. In the area near the "Loop" the poorer migrant families struggle against the anonymity and mobility of urban life, while at the other end of the community both those who have been successful in the struggle and those who had the advantage of family traditions and cultural contacts seek to secure these advantages for coming generations.

Summary

In this brief account of the changing status of the Negro family it has been necessary to give some account of the two-fold background from which it had developed. On the one hand, the Negro family developed under the institution of slavery as an accommodation of the sex and family interests of the slaves to the various forms of slavery. On the other hand, there grew up alongside of slavery a class of free Negroes, among whom some achieved wealth and culture which became the basis of a tradition extending down to the present day. The slave family failed to withstand the crisis produced by the Civil War which swept away the only social organization sustaining the slave family. Since the Civil War the Negro family has been making new accommodations to the South. Increase in farm and home ownership has been an indication of the growing stabilization. The general urbanization, which has been signalized by the northern migrations during and since the World War, has produced another crisis in the Negro family. The disorganization and reorganization of Negro life in the northern city offers a laboratory for the study of these changes. Some of the results of a quantitative study of these changes in the city of Chicago, where the indices of family disorganization could be related to cultural differences and the processes of community growth, indicate the civilizational process in Negro life.

NOTES

1. Joseph Alexander Tillinghast. *The Negro in Africa and America*. Publications of the American Economic Association. New York, May, 1902, p. 160. Corinne Sherman. "Racial Factors in Desertion." *Family*, III. Oct.–Jan., 1922–23. W. D. Weatherford. *The Negro From Africa To America*. New York, 1924. p. 42.

2. Charles W. Margold. *Sex Freedom and Social Control*. Chicago, 1926. p. 36. Bronislaw Malinowski. *Sex and Repression in Savage Society*. New York, 1927. p. 195.

3. W. E. B. DuBois. *The Negro American Family*. Atlanta, 1908. p. 21.

4. Robert E. Park. The Conflict and Fusion of Cultures. *Journal of Negro History*, IV, 117.

5. W. E. B. DuBois. *Op. cit.*, p. 21.

6. Francis P. Gaines. *The Southern Plantation*. New York, 1925. Ch. VII.

7. E. Franklin Frazier. The Negro Slave Family. *The Journal of Negro History*, XV, 198–259.

8. J. W. C. Pennington. *The Fugitive Blacksmith; or Events in the History of James C. Pennington*. London, 1850. p. 7.

9. Booker T. Washington. *Up From Slavery*. New York, 1902.

10. H. B. Schoolcraft. By a Southern Lady. *Letters on the Condition of the African Race in the United States*. Philadelphia, 1852.

11. Documentary History of American Industrial Society. *Plantation and Frontier*, II, 108.

12. Charles H. Wesley. *Negro Labor in the United States: 1850–1925*. New York, 1927.

13. W. E. B. DuBois. *The Philadelphia Negro*. Philadelphia, 1899. pp. 32–39.

14. David Dodge. "The Free Negroes of North Carolina." *Atlantic Monthly*, 57, pp. 20–30.

15. T. J. Woofter. *Negro Problems in Cities*. New York, *n. d.* p. 31.

16. The Negro Migration—A Debate. *The Forum*, 72, pp. 593–607.

17. Louise V. Kennedy. *The Negro Peasant Turns Cityward*. New York, 1930. p. 85.

18. Charles S. Johnson. "The New Negro in a New World" in *The New Negro*, edited by Alain Locke. New York, 1927. pp. 285–288.

19. Ernest W. Burgess. "The Determination of Gradients in the Growth of the City." *Publication of the American Sociological Society*, XXVI (1927), pp. 178–184.

20. Statistics on the Negro population in these unit areas were secured from the data given in census tracts used as units for the 1920 enumeration. This information was furnished by the Social Research Laboratory of the University of Chicago.

21. E. Franklin Frazier. "Occupational Classes Among Negroes in Cities." *American Journal of Sociology*, XXXV, 718–738.

CHARLES S. JOHNSON

The Background
(from *Shadow of the Plantation*)

The Pattern of the Plantation

The plantation as represented in tradition and popular fancy is so far removed from the existing institution as to be but slightly related to the character of the folk that it bred. In the romantic fiction, which has so largely supported the concept, it is a far-flung, comfortably self-contained agricultural unit, crested by a spacious white mansion with imposing colonnades supporting cool and spacious verandas, and surrounded in ample and flower-laden grounds. In the background are the cotton fields stretching far and white into the distance. There are long rows of white-washed Negro cabins; sleek, contented slaves, laughing and singing as they work; little pickaninnies capering with the abandonment of irresponsible fledglings in the clearings of the cabins or on the smoothly clipped lawns. As further evidence of opulence and self-sufficiency there are the smokehouse, the sawmill, the blacksmith and carpenter shops, and the commissary.

.   .   .

The actual plantation devoted to cotton was based on a rigorous and dull routine, with strict diversification of labor: house servants, field hands, cooks,

Charles S. Johnson, selections from "The Background," chap. 1 of *Shadow of the Plantation* (Chicago: University of Chicago Press, 1934), 1, 2–3, 6–7, 11–12, 16–22, 25, 27–28. Reprinted by permission of the University of Chicago Press.

blacksmiths, carpenters, the midwife "for white and black of the neighbor-hood, as well as a doctress of the plantation," overseers, and, when they could be afforded, drivers to maintain discipline and order on the place, and be responsible for the quiet of the Negro houses and for the proper performance of tasks. In January there was ginning, sorting, and moting of cotton; in February more ginning and moting, ground-cleaning, fence-mending, and ditching. In March there was bedding of cotton ground; in April planting, fencing, ditching, picking joint grass, working cotton—the eternal hoe industry. In May, June, July, and August more hoeing and working and some picking; in September, October, and November more picking, clearing new ground; in December moting and ginning. There were tasks and punishments for falling short. Every detail of life was regulated not by any internal compulsions but by a system of physical punishments and rewards. Once established, custom and routine gave permanence to the structure of relations. Life, on the whole, was a grim business. Such were the imperatives of the economic system.

The Negro of the plantation came into the picture with a completely broken cultural heritage. He came directly from Africa or indirectly from Africa through the West Indies. There had been for him no preparation for, and no organized exposure to, the dominant and approved patterns of American culture. What he knew of life was what he could learn from other slaves or from the examples set by the white planters themselves. In the towns where this contact was close there was some effect, such as has many times been noted in the cultural differences between the early Negro house servants and the plantation hands. On the plantation, however, their contact was a distant one, regulated by the strict "etiquette" of slavery and the code of the plantation.

.   .   .

Of the possibilities and consequences of isolation in our own culture the American Negroes present an excellent example—an example all the more interesting because Negroes now represent virtually every stage of the acculturation process in America, and have found a place somewhere in every occupation from the most backward to the most forward.

Actually, distance from the centers of larger activity plays only a minor rôle in an isolation which is for them fundamentally cultural. According to accepted social theory, there is no American "folk" because there is no American peasantry. But everyone knows that this is less a fact than an ideal. There are persistent social blocs which for one reason or the other defy prompt incorporation into the approved general pattern.

The Negroes in areas of the South, notably in the cotton and cane belts, represent an American type which can most nearly be described as "folk," and so far as their lives are rooted in the soil, they are, perhaps, the closest approach to an American peasantry. "To be shaped in mind and social reaction, to some extent in character and finally in expression," says Mary Austin, "is to be folk." The marks of such an encircled life may be observed in their fixed accommodation, to the prevailing economic system, an accommodation so complete as to be commonplace. It may be observed in the characteristic folk ways associated with this life; in the characteristic forms of its thought and expression; in the illiteracy which shields them from the contacts and influences by which social changes are introduced, and which limits the range of their interests; restricts the development of thought and speculation beyond the requirements of their simple routine of life. It may be observed in the survival, with but small modifications, of the tradition of slavery; in the survival of the tradition of the plantation, which in turn embodies an economic system affecting the proprietors as well as the tenants. If these folk groups have a social life, it is unique and is due in large measure to the fact that they are cut off from the most direct channel of communication with the outside world and its interests through the economic system itself, which restricts economic negotiations virtually to their immediate white landlords.

Given the setting of a high degree of Negro tenantry in the familiar cotton economy, and similar measure of isolation, differences between these Negro folk groups are not great. In the area studied in Macon County, Alabama, the group was a fairly homogeneous one, and was adjusted, both physically and mentally, to the tradition of cotton cultivation inherited from the period in which it reached its nadir as a system, before the Civil War.

The Tradition of the Plantation

The state of Alabama is a country of extremes, from the rich Black Belt area, superbly adapted to cotton cultivation, to the wretched pine barrens where impoverished whites were driven before the Civil War by the richer and stronger slave-owning proprietors. Three belts of the Appalachian Mountains terminate in the state, merging with one another and with the gulf coastal plains. The northern portion of the state, transected by the Tennessee River, is a part of the Allegheny-Cumberland Plateau. It is fertile land, but not so richly fertile as other sections. To the south is the convulsive irregularity of the Appalachians, which became at a late period in the development of the state the

center of the mining industry around Birmingham. These were sparsely populated as late as 1850.[6] Across the center of the state, extending from Randolph
County on the Georgia border to Fayette County near the Mississippi line,
is another area of barely fertile territory but with occasional patches of rich
fertility.

The Black Belt begins along the line marked by Montgomery and includes
eleven counties, among which is Macon, the focal point of these observations.
This section has been historically the home of the planters. South of the Black
Belt is the sandy stretch which has resisted cultivation and was little known
throughout the early history of the state except to be dismissed with the designation of "Piney Woods."

·   ·   ·

Throughout the area are scattered the homes of Negroes which date back,
for the most part, to a period of forty years and more. The small unpainted
or whitewashed cabins, surrounded by a disordered array of outhouses, are
spaced at distances convenient for plantation development. Most of the buildings have the worn and sagging aspect of age, with their invariable "dog run"
providing a cooling shade; vagrant and inclosed patches of garden, growing
close to the house, their newspaper wall covering, and, piled in some spare
corner, a dirty heap of cotton seed.

In the early summer there are wide areas of cotton, except for patches
of undeveloped woods, sandy areas, where nothing will grow, and the essential stretches of corn and sorghum. Here and there is a house of different
design, with weatherboarding. These are the homes of white residents, and
occasionally of Negro owners. The villages are small concentrations around
a general store or commissary, gin, post-office, a church, and the homes of
the proprietorial white landowners and residents. Roughly, the present arrangement is a survival of the earlier plantation system under the old parish
division.

The old blacksmith shop and stable of the early days of the county have
given place to an automobile repair shop. The inn is a grocery store. The
houses are the same, only generations older. The white of the mansion house
has gone, symbolizing, it would almost seem, the inevitable abandonment by
the lords of the manor to the Negroes who still hang on, trying to nurse a living out of the earth. Foxtail and broomsedge, harbingers of senility, and the
ubiquitous boll weevil, a new pestilence, keep this black labor alive, vainly
fighting against the approaching final desolation. Everywhere there are the
sad evidences of an artless and exhausting culture of cotton.

The hard white highways of Alabama have drawn a ring as distinct as the color line around these decaying plantations—each with its little settlement of black peasantry. Here they live almost within sight of the passing world, dully alive, in an intricate alliance with a tradition which has survived the plantation itself. The plantation of olden times has gone, leaving them a twin partner of the earth, and upon these two—black man and the earth—the proprietor himself, growing ever poorer, depends for the mutual preservation of all. The machine has not entered here yet, for the routine of cotton cultivation, and especially weeding and picking, demands a discrimination which can be taught the dullest peasant, but which no machine as yet has mastered. As a consequence, the system has continued to breed its own labor support in the thousands of Negroes whose lives and only hopes are bound up with its fate.

.   .   .

Survivals

The essential observation of this study is that the Negro population of this section of Macon County has its own social heritage which, in a relatively complete isolation, has had little chance for modification from without or within. Patterns of life, social codes, as well as social attitudes, were set in the economy of slavery. The political and economic revolution through which they have passed has affected only slightly the social relationships of the community or the mores upon which these relations have been based. The strength and apparent permanence of this early cultural set have made it virtually impossible for newer generations to escape the influence of the patterns of work and general social behavior transmitted by their elders.

Macon County has a Negro population with a tradition much older than that of a Negro population in any city of either the North or the South. It offers little encouragement to new blood. The strength of tradition thus is magnified because of the low level of literacy and consequent imperviousness of the area to the modifying influence of news and the experiences of other communities. Together these factors tend, naturally, to give unwonted prestige and authority to the older families, who have at least the factual argument of survival to bolster their claims to importance.

A useful clue to the character of the present population is to be found in the character of the elders themselves, and their active memories of the past. Much of this study will be concerned with the social tradition of this group and how it is being modified, even though slowly, by various new outside influences. One of the first circumstances encountered in dealing with this older population is the confusion about ages. Only with their presumed independent status have they found it necessary to reckon their own ages. It is only natural, thus, that ages are calculated from the coming of freedom, but even with such a point of reference there is a wide range of speculation. Georgiana Jackson explained: "I don't know how old I am. I was born in slavery. I remember when the Yankees first come and say dere want no more slavery." Liza Cloud, now blind, decrepit, and extremely dirty in her neglect, said: "Slavery I know all about, looks like. I was sixteen years old when the Yankees come through. I can't tell about the year I was born but I know the month. I was born the first of May. You know back there colored folks didn't know nothing about the years." Still another, a male family head reckoned his age, with no qualms of uncertainty, from the fact that he was "a half-hour old when freedom come." Even this type of record lends itself more satisfactorily to calculation than some other speculations based, for example, upon the type of clothing worn, or the amount of work one was able to do, or the condition of the plank road running through the county at the time of their first age consciousness.

The most common method of keeping reasonably accurate ages is through their "white folks," who made and kept this record for the Negroes. Those who lacked the continuing relationship with a single white family would have them set down the most likely age or date of birth in a Bible. If the white folks died, or the Bible was lost, their ages were also lost and this was counted as irrevocable, not to be troubled about further. After all, ages are only needed at rare intervals, when a census is being taken or for the even less exacting requirement of an obituary and death certificate. With the utmost casualness the matter of ages could thus be dismissed: "I had all our ages in the Bible and one of my boys what got married tuk it and when I got it back so many of the leaves was tore out I didn't know it was a Bible and all the ages was gone." Or: "I don't know my age. My Bible got burnt up and hit was in it."

The importance attached by the younger people to the keeping of one's own age was one of the faint but important symbols of independent status. A young woman who had been reared by her grandmother from an infant said with some feeling: "The only thing I hate about my grandma is she wouldn't tell me my age." The old folks would observe that "people didn't tell ages in dem days lak dey do now," and make no effort to alter the easier arrangement of relying upon their white folks to supply this information when necessary. This continued reliance was only one of the numerous points of their dependent relationship. Occasionally there would be exhibited courage sufficient to doubt the estimate, even though made by their white folks, as in the case of Jennie Smith who gave this account of her age: "I am about seventy-seven years old this last gone February. I am satisfied I'm older'n this but that's what the white folks gied me when I was freed, but if I don't disremember that is my sister's age. When the war was declared, and freedom come, I was nursing and working at the white folks' home. They just got us niggers mixed up. I remember well when the people was drilling to free the slaves. That's why I know I'm older'n dat."

Memories of Slavery

The former slaves have not only retained memories of their earlier status, but have maintained a certain dignity and prestige for themselves by contrasting these memories with the pretensions to freedom of the younger generation. For these older ones it has been a part of the technique of survival to rationalize the social adjustments made. There are, at the same time, former slaves who, with a certain defiance, refer to slavery as an ill which they were fortunate and grateful to escape. This they do with vigor and eloquence, but also with a becoming caution. There is enough spirit in their recital of slave conditions, however, to set them apart from some of their brethren who, like many of their masters, find these memories glowing with increasing charm and romance as time separates them from the period.

The older Negro families are, indeed, divided rather sharply in their memories of slavery, and both groups have in turn passed them along in both practice and philosophy to their own offspring. Zack Ivey, for example, is one of the older heads and strong spirits of the community. He was more frank than is the custom of Negroes to be in contrasting his present condition with that of slavery. He complained: "I done had a harder time since I been free than when I was a slave. I never had such a hard time in my life as I'm having now." Then, with awareness of the implied treason of this remark, he added, compromising: "I'm saying this for myself. I ain't saying hit for nobody else. I wish I had stayed a slave." There was to him nothing offensive in his attachment to his master, particularly since his was a good master; besides, he drew distinction from the very power and wealth of his owner. "In slavery my master and mistress tuk care of me. I lived down in the quarters but I was always up at the house. Them quarters was 'ranged just like a garden. Here was a row and there was a row, and up there was the white folks' house. My mother had to see atta all the chillun in the quarters 'cause they kept so much fuss. I was small and light and done 'bout most as I pleased."

One does not have to look far to see the lively survivals of the early social attitudes in the present population which figure so largely in the memory of Zack Ivey. For a most significant feature of the culture of this group is the slow pace of its transformation. Life was regimented for Zack Ivey but not unpleasantly. The rations were especially memorable in the face of the dull monotony of their present daily fare. "In slavery days," he reminisced, "we et peas, onions, hog head, liver, cow's milk, butter, Irish potatoes, and everything what grows in gardens. That's why I'm here now. I'm just living on the strenk of that. Hit's the strenk of that done kept me alive." For Zack Ivey life was a simple, elemental process of love-making, child-breeding, frolics, and religion, very much as it is now in the community. "I had three chillun by my first wife and fifteen by my second wife. We had frolics. We had them in the white folks' yard. The white folks made you play and run and jump. Your feet an' things had ter be washed and you had ter be all clean and white ter set at table. We had guitars and blowing quills. We had the best kinda time. The only thing I didn't like they kept me in my shirt tail so long. I thought I was too big fer ter be in my shirt tail and ever' time they come round and tell me ter jump my shirt tail would fly up, and I'd say, 'You gotta put some pants on me.' I was keeping company wid my lady frien', going cross the creek, and I looked and there my shirt tail was a floating."

The difference in opinion as well as in memories on the question of slavery found frequent enough expression. So close was the group in the ordinary routine of life, and so well known the opinions, that they would frequently take the form of debate through the investigator.

Riny Biggers, a character of equal strength in the community, without being informed of the views of Zack Ivey, began her own reminiscences with a warning: "Don't you believe no nigger when he says he ruther be no slave. Things happen then too awful to talk about. If they catch you with a pencil in your hand it would be too bad. When de white folks' chillun would come through wid books from school by the quarters and dropped a piece of they school paper and if dey seed you pick hit up dey would clare you tryn' to learn to read and write, and over Sunday for a month you'd be put in a strait-jacket."

The immediate difference between these two types could be observed in the children of these old family heads. Riny Biggers made her own children learn their letters under the threat and free employment of a handy stick. When they had grown up and she was no longer capable of having children of her own, she adopted others and sent them to school in the same manner. Of Zack Ivey's eighteen children, five were dead; four had left the county for Montgomery; two remained with him; of the whereabouts of the others he had no knowledge. None of them had had more than a few months of schooling, and the two who remained still lived with him, one of them an unmarried daughter with four children.

Riny Biggers, taking advantage of the extended privilege of her sex, was more aggressive about her freedom and made a fetish of education, although she herself was illiterate. The high value of literacy had been implanted in her in slavery as firmly as Zack Ivey's memory of the care-free days of frolics and food and courting. She was what one might call "race conscious." She told her children often the story of a figure who seemed to stand out in her memory as the heroic one of slavery. "Red Ann," as she was commonly known, knew the secret of letters when she was bought by Riny's mistress. It was a trade-off as unethical as selling a blind horse without confessing his defect. Red Ann's literacy in this case was her defect. Riny's mistress bought Red Ann from a speculator but she did not know that she could read. She was called "Red Ann" in contempt for nature's presumption to endow a slave with a swarthy Caucasian complexion and quite straight soft hair, sometimes referred to as Titian. When in the presence of her mistress, or any white person for that matter, Ann carried a blank, uncomprehending stare. She would handle papers on which there was writing without showing the slightest curiosity. Once securely out of sight, she would read them and keep her intelligence to herself. Later she began to read letters coming to the house and, becoming still bolder, would show them to other slaves whom she took into her confidence. They watched as she read, then one day a slave, secretly jealous, whispered to her mistress Red Ann's secret. There was consternation confounded by unbelief. In a culture which denied the ability of Negroes to read, it was easier to believe as well as to wish that they could not. Suspicion grew and she was questioned. Red Ann persisted that she could not read. The mistress left notes around to trap her, but Red Ann was too clever. Finally, she wrote her mistress' name to a pass and disappeared.

This secret power was a lasting lesson for Riny, and she ground it into her own children from the day they were large enough to understand. For that reason she was accounted the equivalent of a radical in her society, and the variant fate of her children testified to the conflict between her own determination and the pressure of environment. Of Riny's first set there was one living and two dead. The living child, now in his fifties, eventually shook off the county, the state, and left the South forever. She knew only that he had a family in Detroit and children in school somewhere. Another son died at the age of ten. A daughter grew to womanhood, married, and died in childbirth. Of the second set, one daughter, Aggie, was living with her mother; a son, Arch, was killed in a fight with a white man; and still another, Jerry, had been away from home about fifteen years and had finally worked his way through a school in South Carolina. Two other children had died at early ages and there had been three miscarriages. With her now was the second of the adopted children which she had begun to rear. Her memories of slavery were fresh, no doubt from frequent rehearsing:

> My master's people? Some of them masters would take they slaves and lock 'em in the house all day and you couldn't stick your head out of the door. We could lay on our porch and hear 'em hollering and working all night tel day. I seed 'em walk in sand tel they fell dead. Had been me I would been fightin' now. I come from the fightin' class, but I'm too old ter fight now. My master's brother's wife was so mean tel the Lord sent a peal of lightenin' and put her to death. She was too mean ter let you go ter the well and git a drink of water, and God come long and "squshed" her head open. One of the other masters was so mean he made his slaves crow. Whenever he got ready ter go ter Prattville he had him a chariot fixed up wid eight horses. Lak we settin' here done been two packs of hounds done passed chasing atta slaves and he had more slaves runned away.

.   .   .

Stability

Year after year these families continue to live and move about within the county, but rarely leaving it. The tenant turnover is high. Their one outstanding means of asserting freedom is this mobility, although within an extremely narrow range. Planters can never tell which of their tenants will be with them the following year, but of one thing they can be fairly certain—that they will not leave the county, and in time, will rotate, of their own choice, back to the point of beginning. The past is thus kept ever alive, since it is never seriously broken. This restlessness is expressed in such statements as:

> We moved here in 1925. Getting time to move now, ain't it? We been here too long now.

> I just been here two months. . . . I'll just be here 'til the last of the month and everything gets settlement.

.   .   .

The Tradition of Dependence

For those still living in the county there is, it would appear, one unfailing rule of life. If they would get along with least difficulty, they should get for themselves a protecting white family. "We have mighty good white folks friends, and ef you have white folks for your friends, dey can't do you no harm."

How this practical policy, so clearly a carry-over from the past, can extend to controlling advice on the most intimate matters is apparent in the domestic experience of Josh Walker, who sought the judgment of his white folks on the merits of his last wife.

> This last wife I had, she was a blizzard, 'cause she was no count no way. Hers was her way and my way was my way, and she quit me and carried off all the money I had. I had done saved $80. She carried hit all off. That was six years ago. She was too old ter draw water and ter cook, but she had the devil in her. Hit tuk four men to carry her away. She went off. Said I'd be wid my chillen an' she gwine ter hers. *White folks tole me that I better let that hussy go and atta she left I jes shouted.*

The sense of dependence has crystallized into a sort of practical philosophy: "You know when you get where you can't behave yourself you better move. You got to be loyal, 'cause you know this is a white man's country." And again: "You can't do nothing with white folks agin you." Nor should it be supposed that all of this dependence upon the whites is based upon fear. There is a solid and sympathetic paternalism among some of the white planters toward their Negro dependents which is felt by them. Max Wheeler, for example, was a stolid, illiterate, but hard-working head of a large family who experienced the perennial difficulty of breaking even. Year after year he went to his white planter friend. Times were hard in 1931. Max explained sympathetically: "He said he had so many folks on his place to feed, it was hard, but he wanted to try to give all of us a little feed." It worried Mandy Williams that she was "so sympathetic with white people." Sarah Owens, now sixty-eight, achieved her own freedom from the sense of dependence by claiming her white folks as her own. "Honey, them's my own good white folks. Done had me [in the family] since I been three weeks old and had my mother before me." Booker T. Washington, in a memorial address at Hampton Institute in 1893 on General Samuel Chapman Armstrong, was, no doubt, thinking of his neighbors back of Tuskegee when he asserted with vigor: "The greatest injury that slavery did my people was to deprive them of that sense of self-dependence, habits of economy, and executive power which are the glory and distinction of the Anglo-Saxon race."

The older members of the community who find ample satisfaction in the old culture are aware of some queer difference manifesting themselves in the attitude of younger members who have been away from the section. Caleb Humphries went to Montgomery to try to adjust a matter of compensation due on the death of one of his sons in France. He tells the story now of how he was sitting in the Red Cross Office in Montgomery when a white man, whom he promptly assumed to be the governor of Alabama, came in. "He was tall as a tree, and I said 'Good-morning, Master'—so uster slavery I still say hit. They [other Negroes] stopped me from hit 'cause dey say you don't hafta treat white folks like dat dese days."

The community is being affected at present by at least four factors: migration of a portion of the younger generation away to other states and to the North; return of a small number of younger members who have been sent away to school in Tuskegee and Montgomery; the gradually increasing literacy of the group, beginning with the children; and the introduction of certain programs of welfare from the outside. The interplay of these new influences with the old habits of the community may be observed in some measure against the background of the present structure and functioning of the Negro family in this area.

NOTES

[Because of selective reproduction of the text, only a single note has been reproduced. The original text does not contain fuller bibliographical information.]

6. Boyd, *Alabama in the Fifties.*

HORACE MANN BOND

Cotton Plus Steel Equals Schools, 1900–1930

In a prior chapter[1] it was shown that up to the first decade of the twentieth century Negroes found a place in Alabama industrial development only as laborers furnishing unskilled work. Skilled occupations were regarded as the natural province of white workers. When great national accumulations of capital entered the Alabama area the larger industrial concerns, especially in coal and iron, changed their policy to allow Negroes to reach slightly higher occupational levels.

Objectives in the Education of Negroes for the New Industry

The educational implications of this changed policy are illustrated by the self-conscious planning for industrial development in Alabama instituted by the Tennessee Coal and Iron Company in its history since 1906 as a subsidiary of United States Steel. The principal labor in the mines was formerly furnished by Negro convicts, farmed out to private companies by the State of Alabama.[2] With no "decent houses, no decent schools," the situation was described as "terrible" for George Crawford, installed as managing president, "who had a complicated metallurgical and developing problem thrust upon him and who

Horace Mann Bond, "Cotton Plus Steel Equals Schools, 1900–1930," chap. 16 of *Negro Education in Alabama: A Study in Cotton and Steel* (Washington, D.C.: The Associated Publishers, Inc., 1939), 240–261.

needed steady, trustworthy labor if he was to succeed."[3] The large industrial corporations were also faced with the problem of labor trouble; and the elevation of the Negro in the industrial scale seemed to promise, in the Birmingham area, a respite from a continuation of such difficulties in Northern centers.

The Tennessee Company began at once to build up complete industrial and housing units, fitted with hospitals, welfare centers, and schools, by which means it was frankly hoped to regularize the uncertain Negro labor.[4] It was officially stated that this was not a philanthropic movement: "The Steel Corporation is not an eleemosynary institution," and its first object was "to make money for its stockholders."[5]

The peculiar racial situation of the Alabama workers permitted the development of a paternalism unmatched elsewhere in the country. While a semblance of self-control was permitted the inhabitants of company towns in Minnesota, Ohio, and Pennsylvania, it was "necessary for the Tennessee Coal and Iron Company to manage directly the affairs of the settlements of its workers."[6] In those localities "where municipal, county or state educational facilities are poor," in the words of a less hard-headed eulogist, "it has gladly assumed the burden."[7] The paramount difficulty which the Tennessee Company found, after its acquisition by United States Steel, was the ignorance, and poor educational facilities of Negro workers.[8] Especial attention was given to "dilapidated buildings" in Jefferson County, and to the "inadequate pay offered teachers (which) failed to attract men and women competent to train the youthful mind."[9]

The Tennessee company made an agreement with the authorities of Jefferson county by which the company was to build and equip a sufficient number of school houses in the neighborhood of its plants and mines. The county authorities agreed to turn over to the company the annual appropriations received from the State for teachers' salaries.[10] The result was that the Tennessee Coal and Iron Company was able to operate an educational system for its workers, using State funds, but supplementing them, free of any regulation from local school officials.[11] A self-appraisal of results is not exaggerated: "the instructors in charge are of a high average type and the schools are recognized as having no equals in the South."[12] The 1919 Survey of Alabama Schools described the T. C. I. system as follows:

> One of the most interesting educational experiments in the bituminous coal region of the Appalachian system is conducted by the Tennessee Coal, Iron and Railroad Company. The work is done in complete cooperation with the county school board, which apportions funds to

the mining town school on the same basis as to other schools. The superintendent of the schools in the mining towns is an assistant county superintendent, but is paid entirely by the company.

Social work is required by the company, and special stress is placed on personality and fitness for this additional service. The classroom work is of splendid quality. The teaching staff shows good organization, enthusiasm, loyalty, and a high degree of professional spirit.

As a whole it is an object lesson in efficiency which may well be studied by other mining communities. It shows conclusively what can be done by the expenditure of reasonable funds, business encouragement, and professional service. . . . What can be accomplished here can be accomplished elsewhere, with similar management and expenditure.[13]

The educational system of the T. C. I. interests was joined to an extensive program of community service and welfare work. The Company generally preferred to establish towns for workers entirely owned by it. One of the "model" examples of such company-owned communities was Westfield, Alabama, where houses equipped with modern conveniences, a community house, athletic fields, and school houses have been constructed by the Company within a kind of general compound which has no equal in the South for the comfort of living provided for industrial workers.[14] A general hospital for T. C. I. employees is maintained at Fairfield, and through this institution, according to Ida Tarbell:

> . . . . Judge Gary himself has given the highest endorsement possible to the Employee's Hospital of the T. C. and I., by going there himself for treatment and rest. Under the same roof with him, *though out of his hearing,*[15] Negro and white mothers bear their babies, Negro and white workers are treated for burns and broken bones, Negro and white children are nursed through measles and mumps.[16]

The policies of the United States Steel Corporation in Alabama with reference to employer's welfare have admittedly been taken in self-interest, and have not escaped severe criticism. Confessedly not "an eleeymosynary" institution, it is probably true that "in building 'model' company towns, the companies have one leading motive, namely, to cut down labor turnover while at the same time continuing to pay low wages."[17] It is further alleged that the policies of the Corporation in giving decent living and educational quarters to Negroes were in line with a careful, long-range policy to keep Negro and white workers apart, and labor subordinated, by exalting the Negroes as competitors of the whites. From this view, the welfare work for Negroes was "a deliberate policy of flattering the Negro workers," by building Negro schools from the same plans as the white schools, and admitting Negroes to "the pretentious base hospital at Fairfield on payment of the usual fee, and of course strictly on a Jim-Crow basis."[18] In contrast to the glowing accounts of magnanimity in the descriptions of Tarbell and Cotter, Davis says the company "achieved its aim, cut down turn-over, and wages of laborers in the Alabama steel industry remained at a level of about 60 per cent of that of the steel industry in Chicago, and Pittsburgh."[19]

The Tennessee Company issues no specific reports by which the sources of its income for this work, and the exact distribution of funds, can be traced.[20] It is, therefore, impossible to see to what degree the welfare services contributed by the Company are paid for out of the "cuts" usually deducted from the workers' weekly pay checks.

Yet the superiority of the T. C. I. schools was undeniable. In 1930 the writer, in conjunction with Clark Foreman,[21] had occasion to visit all of the Negro schools in Jefferson County, Alabama. Tests were administered to all of the children enrolled in the third and sixth grades. Comparative scores indicated a considerable superiority for the children of the T. C. I. system by comparison with the Negro children enrolled generally both in the other county and city schools and in the South at large. The average educational score made by the third grades in the T. C. I. schools was the normal score for that grade.

One interesting reflection of the status of the Negro as indicated by educational opportunities provided in the T. C. I. schools is the fact that the system provided education only up to the high school level.[22] Apparently it was believed that this moiety of education sufficed for the industrial purposes to which the Company intended to set its Negro labor.

President Harding on Socio-Economic Status of Negro and Education

An excellent example of the social and educational philosophy derivative from the industrial setting of Negro labor in the Birmingham area was furnished by the speech made in that city in 1921 by the late President Warren G. Harding. President Harding, it may be agreed, represented the industrial North. To some extent his speech was a document resembling that of Booker T. Washington at the Atlanta Exposition in 1895.

The Negro, said President Harding, should be allowed to vote "when he is fit to vote. I would," he continued, "insist upon equal educational opportunity" both for white and for black. Both should "stand uncompromisingly against every suggestion of social equality." This was because of a "fundamental, eternal, inescapable difference." By bringing Negro labor to the North the World War had made people of that section cognizant of the problems which the South had always faced. The proper course of race development would emphasize equal opportunity of a cultural and economic nature, while recognizing "physical difference" and paving the way for the "natural segregations" noticeable in the South.[23]

There should be equal educational opportunity; but "this does not mean that both would become equally educated within a generation or two generations or ten generations." Negroes should not, by implication, necessarily receive the same education that white people receive.

> I would accept that (sic) a black man cannot be a white man, and that he does not need and should not aspire to be as much like a white man as possible in order to accomplish the best that is possible for him. He should seek to be, the best possible black man, and not the best possible imitation of a white man.[24]

Every consideration led back to the question of education. There was skillful double *entendre* in this section of the President's speech.

> When I speak of education as a part of this race question, I do not want the States or the nation to attempt to educate people, whether black or white, into something they are not fitted to be. I have no sympathy with the half-baked altruism that would overstock us with doctors and lawyers, of whatever color, *and leave us in need of people fit and willing to do the manual work of a workaday world.*[25]

Mr. Harding envisioned a continued ban on foreign immigration, and of a draft upon the South of black labor for Northern industry. To keep its labor present in the South, that section would be obliged, he thought, to offer greater educational opportunities.

> If the South wishes to keep its fields producing and its industry still expanding it will have to compete for the services of the colored man. If it will realize its need for him and deal quite fairly with him, the South will be able to keep him in such numbers as your activities make desirable.[26]

The speech is more than the skillful phrasing of a politician; to no small degree it was the philosophy behind the establishment and maintenance of the T. C. I. system. It was "enlightened" industrialism speaking to a section in the process of industrialization.

Objectives for the Education of Negroes as Determined by Agriculture

Our survey has shown little change occurring in the status of the Negro in the agricultural system. One might therefore expect that no change in the education of Negroes took place in agricultural areas. Yet change took place, not as a result of fundamental influences incident to the culture itself, but proceeding from external philanthropy. These influences will be traced in another chapter. We have seen that the migration of Negroes, threatening the basis of agriculture in the State, was used by the Negro leaders to obtain more money for Negro schools. This strategy may have been successful; the transference of large numbers of Negroes to urban communities is explanation enough for the increases in educational expenditures within the State in the last three decades covered by this study.

There are even occasional indications of a survival of the oldest conceptions regarding the role of the Negro in rural society, and the type of education befitting him. In a curious pamphlet published in 1933,[27] there occurs the following statement:

> The taxing of poor white people to furnish "HIGHER EDUCATION" for negro wenches and sassy bucks, is an OUTRAGE upon the WHITE and an injury to the negroes. The schools and colleges are turning loose on the country thousands of negro men and women who have been taught the smattering of the higher branches and who, in consequence, consider it beneath their dignity to work with their hands. There is absolutely no place in this land for the arrogant, aggressive, school-spoilt Afro-American, who wants to live without manual labor.[28]

The author was opposed not only to the support of higher education for Negroes but also to "taxing the white man to educate negro children."

> You can go on with your foolery, Mr. Politician and Mr. Philanthropist, insisting upon a high grade of education for the negro, whether he is fit or not. We people of the South are perfectly willing for our brethren who

do not agree with us to take care of the so-called Afro-American, and we of the South will be glad to have those who only have sense enough to fear God and obey the laws of the land.[29]

It would, of course, be a mistake to assume that these sentiments are too widely shared by Southern whites in view of the development in recent years of county training schools offering high school work.

A sober student of the plantation economy believes that the situation in plantation areas today is not far different from that of ante-bellum days when "Literacy was not an asset in the plantation economy, and it was not only discouraged but usually forbidden."[30] In Macon County expenditures for Negro teachers' salaries have tripled since 1915, amounting to $27,813 for 7,145 children in 1930, as compared to 9,545 expended for 7,853 children in the former year. The result has not been a widespread enlightenment of the population; on the contrary, the school has to some degree served as a disruptive social agency. Those who receive what education the community has to offer become migrants from the community to the small towns and cities. The illiterate are left behind. The Black Belt setting is described as one "that bred few land-owners, tolerated few innovations, and placed a penalty upon too much book-learning."[31] The most successful individuals in the plantation economy are those "neither too illiterate to take advantage of their surroundings, nor (those who) have more schooling than is demanded by their dependent economic situation." The present ineffectiveness of the Negro schools is a reflection of the type of educational preparation which the social and economic setting appears to demand.

An Analysis of the Financial Basis of Public School Education in Alabama, 1900–1930

In addition to social and economic factors influencing the education of Negroes at public expense in Alabama is the important consideration that the Negro schools are a portion of a dual educational system maintained for a minority group which is without political power but must receive what educational funds are expended upon its children from the same general tax sources as those open to white children. The Negro schools, accordingly, become competitors with the white schools for educational money; and no survey of factors influencing public provisions for Negro children could at all be adequate without understanding the conditions surrounding the demands of white children upon the State for tax-supported schools.

The Alabama State Tax System

The Alabama Constitutions of 1819, 1861, and 1865 are described by a Brookings Institution Survey as "open," so far as taxation was concerned; "the exercise of the taxing power was discretionary with the legislature except for the provision that 'all lands liable to taxation in this State, shall be taxed in proportion to their value'."[32] The Constitution of 1868 marked the first step toward restricting, through the Constitution, the taxing power of the legislative branch.[33] This fact is paradoxical in view of the common belief that the 1868 Constitutional Convention in no wise protected the interests of those persons with large property interests. In truth, the Constitution of 1868 was dictated by persons who had a wider concept of governmental services to the people than their agrarian predecessors, but who had an even more keenly developed sense of the necessity for protection of business and commercial interests.

The Constitution of 1875, according to Governor O'Neal, was designed: ". . . . to place constitutional inhibitions on legislative power, to reduce expenditures and make impossible the renewal of that saturnalia of misgovernment and extravagance, which during the Reconstruction had brought the State to the verge of bankruptcy and governmental chaos . . . ."[34]

The result was the limitation of state taxes by the Constitution of 1875 to 7½ mills. The Constitution of 1901 was enacted at a time when the State had enjoyed a surplus for five preceding years; accordingly, a reduction was made in the Constitutional tax limit from 7½ to 6½ mills.[35] It has been shown above that the permission accorded counties by the Constitution of 1901, to levy a one-mill tax for schools, was in the nature of a compromise to afford the fiction of lower taxes and greater provision for education.[36]

The thorough-going rate limitations of the 1901 Constitution are described by the Brookings Institution as "crude and inadequate."[37] The result in Alabama has been the "haphazard development of privilege or license taxes, special assessments, etc."[38] The Constitutional limitations on taxation in Alabama are held to have "distorted and warped" the development of the entire revenue system of the State.[39]

A survey of the taxing machinery of the State shows that the license and corporation taxes adopted in the intervening years have been a makeshift, while "the framework of the revenue system has been congealed by constitutional restrictions."[40] The Brookings Survey characterizes the paradox as accentuated by a change in the State from an agricultural to an industrial economy.[41]

The Convict Department was vital in the financial structure of the State until recent years, yielding, of all state revenues, 4.5 per cent in 1900, 19.9 per cent in 1910, and 20.7 per cent in 1920. The abolition of the convict lease system, beginning in 1927, by 1930 had made this source of income insignificant.

Taxation and Education

Educational financing in Alabama rests, according to the Brookings Survey, on (a) constitutional and (b) statutory taxes. In both classes are to be found some taxes which are state applied, and others with only local application. The constitutional state tax comprises principally a three-mill tax levied *ad valorem* on property. Poll taxes collected and retained within counties are another constitutional tax. By Amendment III, adopted in 1916, a three-mill district tax was permitted in districts.[42]

For the State at large the result of the taxing system of Alabama was to place "a disproportionate share of the burden of educational support on the owners of property."[43] In addition to constitutional levies for taxes, the statutory provisions for providing educational money have in recent years been enlarged to include specific and general allotments of funds. State funds furnished 28.7 per cent of all educational funds in 1927, and 37.0 per cent in 1930.[44]

In 1931 property taxes amounted to 76.5 per cent of all county revenue from taxation; and, in turn, school taxes within the counties accounted for 44.7 per cent of all county tax revenue.

To make this matter more germane to Negro schools, it is only necessary to point out that the burden of a property tax would rest more heavily on the residents of the almost entirely agricultural, black belt counties where Negroes lived in large numbers, than in industrial areas where there are smaller percentages of Negroes. With Negroes owning little or no land, and possessing, at the polls, no power, it is easy to understand how effective the slogan "Don't pay taxes to educate Negro children" might be among white farm owners.

An analysis of tax revenues for schools in three differing counties— Jefferson, highly industrialized; Jackson, a "white" rural county; and Wilcox, a rural "black belt" county—shows significant changes since 1920 in the source of educational moneys, as well as the great reliance of rural counties upon State funds for educational expenditures. Thirty-seven and sixty-six hundredths per cent of all tax revenues in Jackson County in 1930 was derived from local tax funds; 23.50 per cent in Wilcox County; while 77.44 per cent of tax revenue for schools in Jefferson County was derived from local taxes. State funds accounted for the high total of 59.76 per cent of all tax revenue for schools in Wilcox County, and for 44.37 per cent of the tax revenue

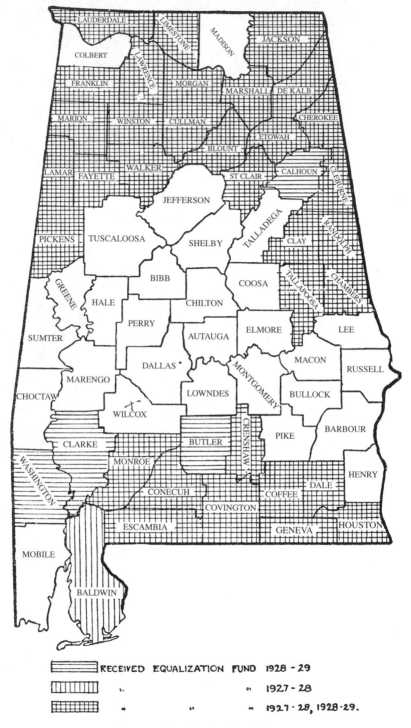

Figure 7. Equalization in Alabama

for schools in Jackson County, while only 16.61 per cent of this revenue in Jefferson County was derived from State funds.

In 1920 the percentage of aid received from the State, of total school monies, was remarkably similar in all counties; 64.18 per cent for Jackson, 64.14 per cent for Jefferson, and 65.70 per cent for Wilcox. In the ten-year period since 1920 legislation regarding education shifted the support of schools for Jefferson County—and, likewise, for other industrial communities—almost entirely to the community, while maintaining the high percentage of total cost borne by the rural counties.

This significant trend may be explained by the Alabama Equalization Law of 1927 which provided for help to "poor" counties determined by a variety of indices of ability to support schools.[45] Figure 7 indicates the distribution of this supplementary aid in the school year 1928–1930.

There are two classes of counties that do not participate in benefits of the Equalization Fund. The first includes those counties, like Jefferson and Mobile, with industrial and urban centers which might be presumed to yield sufficient taxes to support schools without any equalizing aid. The second class, however, presents a highly paradoxical situation; for it includes the black belt counties where Negroes occur in heavy percentages in the population, while, at the same time, possessing some of the lowest per capitas of assessed valuation in the State. The paradox consists in the fact that the counties which do not receive equalization aid in Alabama are, first, the richest, and, second, the poorest counties in the State.

The explanation of this paradox lies in the *Requirements for Participation in the Equalization Fund*; and in the simple fact that the black belt counties use the general state appropriation received per capita for Negro educables as an equalization fund; a device by which they save themselves from levying local taxes. In other words, even though among the poorest in the State, the black belt counties in general would find it more expensive to qualify for participation in the Equalization Fund through maintaining the minimum standards for Negro schools, than to receive such aid.

To participate in the Equalization Fund in Alabama in 1930, a county must have (a) levied both the one-mill and three-mill county-wide taxes; and, for maximum participation, have also levied the three-mill district tax in all districts in the county. (b) The participating county was required to have maintained, "as nearly as practicable," the same length of term in all schools within the county. (c) A minimum term length of 140 days for elementary and 180 days for high schools was required. (d) The county was required to have expended funds equivalent to a minimum program adopted by the State Board of Education.

The relative valuations of white and Negro teacher units may be gauged from the 1928–1929 program which proposed values of $708 and $354, respectively, for the two racial systems. A teacher unit is defined by the Alabama regulations as including thirty pupils in average daily attendance during the preceding year "in other than one-teacher schools; with one-teacher rural schools, where consolidation is impracticable, being counted as units even though the attendance does not meet the stipulated figures."[46] (e) The participating county was required to have expended an amount for teachers' salaries "at least 75 per cent of the current expenses."[47] (f) It was finally stipulated that counties must meet such other regulations as might be set up by the State Board of Education.

Typical Budgets

The source of funds for Negro schools, theoretically, is the same as that for all other children enrolled in the public schools. An examination of typical budgets indicates the precise nature of the problem of financing Negro schools. Lowndes County, a "black" county, Jackson County, a "white" county, and the cities of Birmingham and Montgomery reflect fairly typical situations.

The assessed valuation of Lowndes County in 1930 was $6,485,309, giving, with its total of 11,014 black and white children between the ages of 6 and 20, a per capita valuation of $588. Jackson County had in the same year an assessed valuation of almost twice as much, $11,826,064, giving a valuation per capita for the 12,474 Negro and white children in the county of $948. In any scientific system of equalization, the expert would be inclined to regard Lowndes as the "poor" county and Jackson, by comparison, as a relatively "rich" county.

However, we find that the white children of Jackson county enrolled in school in 1929–1930 had total expenditures per capita of only $24.72, while the white children of Lowndes County had total per capita expenditures of $95.93. The per capitas for Negro children in the two counties show a reversed standing, with Jackson County paying $7.79 for each of the Negro children enrolled while Lowndes County paid only $4.76 for each Negro child enrolled.

This apparently paradoxical situation is not difficult to explain. Wealth as shown by assessed valuation is illusory so far as reflecting the true capacity of the two counties to support schools for their *white* children. The Negro children of Lowndes County furnish the explanation for the tremendous total payment made for white children in the county. There were enumerated in 1930 at the time of the biennial school census, 975 white and 10,059 Negro children between the ages of 6 and 20. The State apportionment in that year amounted to $4.86 per child of school age from the state distributive school fund, and, for the 11,014 children of both races, amounted to $53,525 for Lowndes County—$4,739 on account of the 975 white children, and $48,786 on account of the 10,039 Negro scholastics.

The solution of Lowndes County's educational problem is clear. By spending a total of $22,049 of the amount derived from the state apportionment on all schools for Negro children, a residue of $26,737 is left which can be devoted to the education of white children of the county. The expenditure budget of $80,103 for the white children of the county may count this sum as an initial income item. To this may be added the $4,739 received as a state apportionment for white children. A state "bonus" fund for high school attendance adds $3,000, a state illiteracy fund, $164 more. A state erection, repair and equipment fund gives an additional $355. A state county-high-school grant of $4,500 made uniformly to each of the sixty-seven counties of the state is an additional item. An elementary-school attendance fund of $5,466, contributed to in some degree by the attendance of Negro children; an attendance fund based on high-school enrollment and attendance, amounting to $5,205; and state funds for vocational education amounting to $780, with Federal funds in the sum of $480, give a total of $51,246, which in itself would provide a per capita payment for the white children of the county, without the levy of a single local tax, twice as large as the total payments made in Jackson County for white children. Lowndes County levies local taxes in the ratio of only one dollar for school purposes to every $258.00 of assessed valuation, while Jackson County, with a per capita payment for white children almost four times smaller than Lowndes, is forced to raise locally one dollar to every $160.36 of assessed valuation.

In connection with the statement frequently made that Negro schools are not deserving more aid because Negroes pay no taxes, it is interesting to note that in 1930 Lowndes County paid, altogether, $58,730.32 into the State Treasury of Alabama, and received back from the state for pensions and schools alone $60,664.68. Of the property assessed in the county, $1,674,082 represented public utility corporation valuations of property which, comprised principally of holdings of such corporations as the Louisville and Nashville Railroad, the Western Railway of Alabama, and the Alabama Power Company, was probably owned by "foreign" stock and bond holders not even resident in the State. Assuming that all other property in the county was owned by white people resident there, we have a "native tax" of $43,572, in return for which, as pointed out above, $60,664 was returned to the county for schools and pensions alone, without including such additional services financed by the state treasury as highways and courts. Logically, the white school children of Lowndes County might be regarded as having been educated at the expense of outside interests, as it might be claimed that Negro children are educated at the expense of the white people of Lowndes County.

An analysis of these expenditures indicates how new services render almost impossible the prospect of obtaining any equalization of educational expenditures for Negroes in such a black belt county as Lowndes. A per capita of $24.19 was paid in 1930 for the transportation, alone, of white children, compared to a per capita payment of $4.76 for all expenses for the Negro schools; and, in fact, Lowndes County in 1929–1930 spent only slightly less per capita for the transportation of each white child than Jackson County spent for all expenses for the education of its white children. The per capita expenditures for fuel, light, and water for the white high school child was $3.36, 70 per cent of the total per capita expenditures for Negro children.

The situation in Jackson County has been noted by implication. The only fund which it shares to the exclusion of Lowndes County is the Equalization fund, which adds $9,831 to the resources of the county. It is of the greatest significance, historically considered, to note here that each of the state funds, with the exception of the attendance and equalization funds, gave approximately equal payments to the counties, irrespective of burden. In this we may see the power of the politically dominant "black belt" counties until very recent years in placing all state apportionments on a blanket county basis. The equalization fund, enacted in 1927, marks (a) the decline of the black belt as a political factor; and (b) a specifically devised instrument to meet the requirements of white children in the "white" counties by setting up a fund to offset the great advantage of the black counties derived from racial discrimination in the use of other state funds.

The net result of this peculiar system, unique in the respect that it could occur only in Southern states, is that a "poor" county like Lowndes has a per capita payment for white children four times as high as that in Jackson County, which has assessed wealth twice as great. Another peculiar feature is that the equalization law, by an ironic twist, is obliged to "equalize" education in the state by giving money to a county with an assessed valuation of $948 for each educable while the county with an assessed valuation of $588 is levying very low local taxes and refuses the offer of "equalization" because it would cost too much to put it into effect.

Sample budgets for the cities of Birmingham and Montgomery indicate the wide variations in payments for services rendered to Negro and white children in urban centers. In Jackson County, and in Birmingham and Montgomery, more money is spent on Negro children than is received by the unit in state apportionments.

Development of Public Schools for Negroes — 1900–1930

In the face of a grossly inadequate provision for financing public schools for Negroes in the period surveyed it would be a mistake to conclude that no progress has been made. A brief summary of salient facts with reference to the condition of the schools from 1900 to 1930 indicates that the Negro schools have enjoyed steady improvement, although by comparison this progress has been exceeded by what has been done in the development of public schools for white children. The percentage of educables enrolled has increased, during the period, from 55.9 to 76.9 per cent for whites, and from 43.4 to 61 per cent for Negroes.

A further analysis by areas within the State shows that much of the improvement in the enrollment in Negro schools is due to progress made in the urban and industrial centers. The industrial "Mineral Area" showed in 1930 a high percentage of 89.14 Negro educables enrolled, as compared to a low of 53.06 per cent in the Black Belt.

A study of grade distribution shows steady improvement for the schools in this significant index of general efficiency. Here appears the same picture shown by the percentage of educables enrolled, with the industrial and urban centers beginning to approximate a normal distribution, but with the rural, black belt centers showing an abnormally high percentage of children enrolled in the beginning school grades, and little or no high-school enrollment.

In some instances the development of a small sprinkling of the total enrollment in the high-school grades has been accompanied by an even greater accumulation in the lower grades than existed before. In excess of 75 per cent of the total enrollment in the Black Belt (Area VII) is to be found in the first three grades, compared to slightly more than 53 per cent in the Mineral Area (Area III). The only areas showing a normal distribution of the pupils over the grades, consistent with the increased enrollment, were Areas III and X. On the whole, the increased enrollment in the Negro public schools of Alabama from 1920 to 1930 has not been accompanied by a corresponding development of efficiency which might be expected to redistribute, more normally, grade placement throughout the system.

Term Length

It is difficult to get an adequate picture of the extension of the school term length in the State. In 1920 an average length of term for rural Negro schools was reported of 87 days, as compared to 113 days reported in 1930; while urban schools reported a term length of 155 in 1920 and 175 in 1930. Individual counties reveal a highly varied picture. Dallas County reported a school term of 100 days in 1900, 76 in 1910, and 95 in 1930. Lowndes had a term of 94 days in 1900, but one of only 89 in 1930.

In general, the length of term in schools provided for Negro rural children in Alabama has been extended from 1900 to 1930 from approximately four and one-half to nearly six months. Urban schools have developed a term almost nine months long. The typical rural school term in the Black Belt, however, was in 1930 less than five full school months, and little progress is noticeable here as compared to thirty years before.

Illiteracy

For the State at large, the illiteracy of Negroes over ten years of age has been reduced spectacularly during the past forty years. In 1900, 69.1 per cent of Negroes in Alabama were reported illiterate.[48] By successive decades, this percentage has dropped steadily to 57.4 per cent in 1900, 40.1 per cent in 1910, 31.3 per cent in 1920, and to 26.2 per cent in 1930.[49]

An analysis of the state illiteracy figures by areas shows the decisive character of the social and economic factors basic to this index of educational efficiency.

Table X. Percentage of Negro Illiteracy—1910–1930—by Areas

Area	1910	1930
I	40.09	25.07
II	42.18	28.65
III	25.74	16.75
IV	35.74	24.66
V	34.67	19.91
VI	53.36	26.61
VII	45.65	31.53
VIII	42.90	27.85
IX	41.75	31.75
X	29.67	21.32

A close correlation exists, both between the incidence of illiteracy and various indices of economic and social disorganization, and between the relative rate of reduction of illiteracy and social and economic factors. The Black Belt reports the highest rate of Negro illiteracy with the exception of a contiguous rural area. The industrialized Area III reports the lowest index of illiteracy.

It is clear that the high rates of illiteracy observable here are directly traceable to the effects of a poor educational system, and the social and economic defects characteristic of the milieu which surrounds the Negro population.

Secondary Schools

In 1930, of 109,216 Negro children of high-school age in Alabama, only 5.8 per cent were in high school, as compared to 29.5 per cent of whites. The development of the public Negro high school in Alabama is of such recent growth as to demand but little attention in a historical sense. An extended discussion of the rural Negro high school will be found in the following section having to do with the work of philanthropic bodies in public education; for high-school work for rural Negroes in Alabama to 1930 was almost entirely a matter of stimulation from the Slater Fund and the General Education Board.

The State report for 1911 first reports Negroes as in high-school grades. The lack of specification regarding the type of high school described must lead us to place little reliance on these early figures. In many instances it is probable that figures of public high-school enrollment in the period from 1910–1920 consisted largely of adventitious grades with work of no real consequence which had been superimposed on an elementary school by an ambitious teacher. In 1912 there were reported in high-school grades 724 Negroes. Of this number 201 were reported from Jefferson County, with the next largest number from Barbour County[50] In 1916 the number attending high school was reported as 1,428; and in 1920 as 1,595. In 1926 the number reported was 3,435, and in 1930, 6,365.[51] Of the last-named number, 3,128 were reported from Jefferson County alone.

The low status of high-school education for Negroes in the State may be judged from the fact that Montgomery, the Capital City, with a Negro population in excess of 30,000, maintained no public senior high school for Negroes in 1930. In the same year 50.5 per cent of all Negroes enrolled in the tenth, eleventh, and twelfth grades of public high schools in the State were to be found in one high school in Birmingham, the Industrial High School. In

1930 there were 22 counties where Negroes were in excess of 12.5 per cent of the population, and in which Negroes of high-school age numbered 38,183, that had no four-year high school accessible. Nine counties with a Negro high school population of 22,705 had no four-year high school. These were black belt counties, in each of which Negroes were in excess of 51 per cent of the total population.[52]

The Teacher

On account of diversified reporting practices in the State Reports, it is impossible to obtain, by counties, an exact description of several highly important facts concerning Negro teachers. The change from certification based on examination to certification based on training makes it difficult to make a comparative estimate.

As to adequacy, the period from 1910 to 1930 shows a gradual adjustment of the teaching staff to something approaching reasonable ratios between the teaching staff and the student enrollment per teacher. By areas, enrollment per teacher ranged from 42.6 to 63.7 in 1910, and from 38.6 to 53.7 in 1936. The Black Belt had the highest ratio of students enrolled per teacher in 1910 and in 1930. The smallest ratios for both years appear in the "white" counties, showing that with a sparsely settled Negro population a small ratio is maintained which is not an index of superior teaching conditions. This fact is reflected in higher costs for educational services in "white" counties as compared to the Black Belt counties.

Table XI. Enrollment of Negro Children Per Teacher, 1910, 1930

Area	1910	1930
I	61.3	47.8
II	63.7	44.8
III	57.0	48.1
IV	42.8	28.0
V	64.3	50.5
VI	59.0	42.9
VII	69.0	53.7
VIII	62.5	45.2
IX	56.4	46.7
X	52.2	38.6

Comparative figures for training over a period of years are wanting. As the result of an investigation made in 1930–1931, Caliver reports the following data for Alabama teachers:

Table XII.* Percentages of Negro and White Elementary
Teachers of Various Educational Levels

4 Years of High School or Less		6 Weeks to 2 Years of College	
Negro	White	Negro	White
19.2	2.3	72.1	65.4

3 to 4 Years of College		1 Year or More of Graduate Work	
Negro	White	Negro	White
8.4	30.6	0.2	1.7

*Caliver, *Education of Negro Teachers*, p. 12.

McCuistion found comparable results in a survey conducted in 1930.[53] The vast superiority of the industrial, urban Jefferson County to a Black Belt county like Wilcox is striking. More than half of the Jefferson County teachers have more than two years of normal or college work in advance of high school graduation; almost two-thirds of the Wilcox County teachers have not been graduated from high school.

Table XIII. Expenditures for Teachers' Salaries Per Capita Negro and
White Child Enumerated in Alabama by Areas 1910–1930

Area	1910		1930	
	White	Negro	White	Negro
I	$4.76	$1.06	$14.39	$4.48
II	5.80	1.08	19.65	4.14
III	9.60	2.76	31.79	13.66
IV	3.31	1.13	12.94	6.33
V	4.43	1.01	17.39	4.36
VI	5.03	1.06	17.12	8.38
VII	14.55	.80	31.99	2.73
VIII	6.56	.92	18.53	3.41
IX	5.63	.92	14.90	3.29
X	9.57	1.79	22.19	9.40

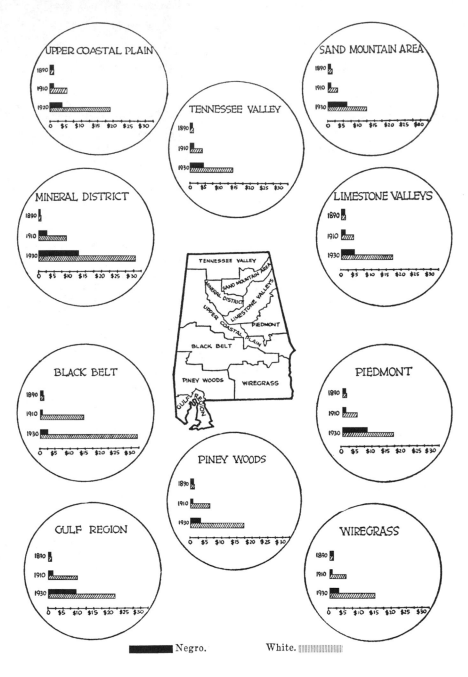

Figure 8. Expenditures per capita school child for salaries of white and negro teachers in Alabama, 1890, 1910, 1930.

Salaries of Negro teachers have enjoyed a gradual advance although they are far from approaching either relatively or absolutely similar advances made in the payment of white teachers. An analysis of per capita expenditures for each child enumerated in the years 1910 and 1930 gives an outline of the picture. A qualification is that in this period the provision of more teachers for Negro children results in individual salaries rising more slowly than the per capita figures might indicate.

NOTES

[The original publication includes an extensive bibliography. Where it is available, we have added, in square brackets, material from the bibliography as an aid to the reader of this anthology who wishes to follow Bond's citations. In some cases, further information was not available, and we have left Bond's notes intact.]

1. Chapter X, above ["Economic and Political Changes as Affecting the Education of Negroes, 1875–1900"].
2. [Ida M.] Tarbell, *The Life of [Judge] Albert H. Gary,* [(New York: D. Appleton & Co., 1925),] p. 310.
3. *Ibid.*
4. *Ibid.*
5. [Horace B.] Davis, *Labor and Steel,* [i.e., *The Condition of Labor in the American Iron and Steel Industry* (New York: International Publishers, 1933),] p. 170.
6. [Arundel] Cotter, *United States Steel: A Corporation with a Soul,* [(Garden City, N.Y.: Doubleday, Page, & Co., 1921),] p. 171.
7. *Ibid.,* p. 176.
8. *Ibid.*
9. *Ibid.*
10. *Ibid.,* p. 177.
11. *Ibid.*
12. Cotter, *op. cit.,* p. 177.
13. Quoted in Tarbell, *op. cit.,* p. 313.
14. Tarbell, *Ibid.,* p. 311; Cotter, *op. cit.,* p. 171.
15. Italics mine.
16. Tarbell, *op. cit.,* p. 313.
17. Davis, *Labor and Steel,* p. 146.
18. *Ibid.,* p. 147.
19. *Ibid.,* pp. 147–48.
20. On application to the office of the Assistant Superintendent, in Birmingham, in 1930, these data were said not to be available.

21. Clark Foreman, *Environmental Factors in Negro Elementary Education* (New York: Published for the Julius Rosenwald Fund, Chicago, by W. W. Norton & Co., 1932.)

22. Cotter, *op. cit.*, p. 177.

23. Cited in the *New York Times,* October 26, 1921.

24. *Ibid.*

25. *Ibid.*

26. *Ibid.*

27. G. Woodford Mabry, *A Reply to Southern Slanderers: In Re the Nigger Question.* (Grove Hill, Alabama: By the Author, 1933.)

28. *Ibid.*

29. *Ibid.*

30. [Charles S. Johnson,] *The Shadow of the Plantation,* [(Chicago: University of Chicago Press, 1934),] p. 129.

31. *Ibid.*, p. 143.

32. *Taxation of the State Government of Alabama,* p. 37. Report on a survey submitted to Governor B. M. Miller, Vol. 4 Part 3, prepared by the Institute for Government Research of the Brookings Institution, Washington, D.C., 1932. (Montgomery: The Wilson Printing Company, 1932.)

33. *Ibid.*, p. 38.

34. *Ibid.*, p. 39.

35. *Ibid.*, pp. 39–40.

36. See Chapter XIII, above ["The Constitutional Convention of 1901: Taxation and Education"].

37. Brookings Institution Survey, *op. cit.*, p. 45.

38. *Ibid.*, p. 47.

39. *Ibid.*

40. *Ibid.*, p. 59.

41. *Ibid.*

42. *Brookings Survey,* Vol. I, Part I, p. 266.

43. *Ibid.*, p. 276.

44. *Ibid.*, p. 264.

45. Department of Education, *Equalization in Alabama* (pamphlet). (Montgomery: State Department of Education, 1929.)

46. [Division of Research and Information,] *Apportionment and Distribution of Alabama's Equalization Fund,* [(State Board of Education, 1930),] p. 4.

47. *Ibid.*, p. 7.

48. *Negro Population in the United Sates, 1790–1915,* p. 415.

49. *Fifteenth Census Reports on Population, Illiteracy,* p. 1231.

50. *Annual Report, 1911,* pp. 35–40.

51. *Annual Reports, passim.* Although Alabama adopted officially the 6–3–3–plan in 1920, figures given here are for enrollment in the last four grades. Few of the Ala-

bama "Junior High Schools" or "High Schools" for Negroes have separated buildings. See Edward E. Redcay, *County Training School and Public Secondary Education for Negroes in the South,* pp. 67–68. (Published for the Slater Fund; Washington, D.C.: The Monumental Printing Co., 1935.)

52. [Ambrose] Caliver, *Secondary Education for Negroes,* [(Washington: Government Printing Office, 1933),] p. 28.

53. Fred McCuistion, *The South's Negro Teaching Force.* (Julius Rosenwald Fund, Southern Office: Nashville, Tennessee, 1931.)

ALLISON DAVIS

Caste, Economy, and Violence

Abstract

Caste in the Deep South integrates into one system all aspects of white-Negro behavior: social, sexual, economic, political, educational, religious, legal, associational, and recreational. The only institution which is not completely organized on caste lines is the economic. Whenever Negroes as a group achieve economic mobility, they meet with severe punishment from the whites. Thus conflict and violence indicate that Negroes are beginning to compete more effectively with whites.

Caste in the Deep South integrates into one system all aspects of white-Negro behavior: social, sexual, economic, political, educational, religious, legal, associational, and recreational. The basic subsystem—caste—is a rigid stratification, maintained by physical, social, and psychological punishments and rewards. Everywhere in the South, caste establishes and maintains an endogamous and socially separate system of white-Negro relationship in which by birth the Negroes are all of lower, and the whites all of higher status. This so-

Allison Davis, "Caste, Economy, and Violence," *The American Journal of Sociology* 61, no. 1 (1945): 7–15. Reprinted by permission of the University of Chicago Press.

cial caste system is more rigid than that described in the classic literature on Hindu castes.

All white or colored institutions of the southern community, including the church, the school, and the courts, systematically organize and defend the caste system. The only institution which is not completely so organized is the economic. The purpose of this paper is to distinguish caste in the area[1] studied from social class and similar types of hierarchical relationships, to define the legal and customary sanctions of caste status, to describe the integration of the basic institutions into the largest system—that of color caste—and to state a theory of violence as a reaction to the breakdown of caste in the economic sphere.

I

Color caste in Old and Rural counties is a system of relationships which prevents intimate social participation between white and Negro persons. It is maintained by *endogamous* sanctions for each color group and by the associated negative sanctions upon *familial* or *clique* participation of whites with Negroes. Since caste in this society denies legal or customary recognition to sexual relationships between white and Negro people, no individual, white or Negro, can change his caste status by marriage.[2]

Nor can any person change his caste in Old and Rural counties by changing his occupation, or his religion, as is true in some other caste societies in the world. Even the absence in a "Negro" of the physical caste marks of pigmentation, conformation of the face, and hair form does not make him a member of the white caste. Caste status is determined by a legal and social definition of "blood" or kinship; it is therefore inherited from one's parents. If both of an individual's parents were not socially defined as "white," he is a "Negro" (lower caste) even if he is indistinguishable—as a physical type—from many of the upper-caste members. In the great majority of cases however, a person's caste status can be defined at once by the inhabitants upon the basis of his skin color and hair form alone.

The basic caste marks of "blood" and physical appearance and the fundamental endogamous rule operate within the economic, occupational, educational, political, and social hierarchies so as to assure the great majority of whites a rank superior to Negroes. Thus the system of regulating marriage is strengthened by controls which subordinate Negroes to whites in all the institutions of the society and, consequently, establish a very strongly defined ranking of the two groups.

Social Class

The form which color-caste stratification has assumed in Old and Rural counties appears unusual to the comparative ethnologist, because it includes a system of social classes *within each caste.* The Negro or white person is born into a social class just as he is born into a color caste. As here conceived, caste and class are both systems for limiting and ranking social participation, but they differ in the degree to which they permit an individual to change from his birth rank. *Caste,* in the area studied, categorically prevents marriage or intimate social participation outside of one's color *birth group.* Within a color group, furthermore, *class* restricts marriage and participation to those individuals identified by symbols and behavior as of a similar kind and rank.

Unlike caste, however, class stratification allows an individual to change his birth rank and his group of intimate participants in his lifetime by changing his class-typed participation, behavior, and symbols. He may also marry outside his class.

As here conceived, therefore, and as defined in another study of this society,[3] a social class is the largest group of people whose members have intimate social access to each other. A class is composed of families and cliques. These units likewise are evaluated by the class members in a hierarchy of rank. The interrelationships between families and intimate cliques in such informal activities as visiting, dancing, receptions, teas, parties, fish-fries, and larger informal affairs constitute the structure of a social class. A person is a member of that social class within which most of his intimate participation occurs.

Not all the members of a color caste in Old and Rural counties, therefore, possess equal rank and similar ranges of participation. Within the Negro and white castes, all individuals are further stratified by their caste members into a social class hierarchy. Whereas there is a chance that they may move out of their class, there is no possibility, as the system now operates, that they may change their color-caste membership or participation. Through physical birthmarks an individual is assigned his caste position; whether he is white or Negro, he also dies in his birth caste.

Legal and Customary Sanctions of Caste

This system of defining white-Negro rank is not termed "caste" by the inhabitants. The white group refers to this complex of sanctions as "the color line," "white supremacy," "controlling the Negroes," "race superiority" and "race inferiority," and "keeping this a white man's country." Negroes use such protective euphemisms when talking to whites as "race relations" or "getting along with the white people"; in their own organizations they speak of "race prejudice," "the oppression of Negroes," and "racial injustice." In these expressions the natives refer to the societal controls which make whites superordinate as a group and Negroes subordinate. When these sanctions of rank are examined by the anthropologist, they are seen to have the essential characteristics of a caste system. They define the behavior of both whites and Negroes in such a way as to make their caste rank and prestige universally clear. They operate upon both groups. In all white-Negro relationships they restrict the behavior of both individuals; that is, a white person, as well as a Negro, has a well-defined caste role which he must accept. For learning and maintaining the appropriate caste behavior, an individual of either the Negro or the white group is rewarded by approval and acceptance from his caste; if he violates the controls, he is punished physically, economically, socially, or legally, depending upon the seriousness of the infraction.

Although both the white and the Negro society support the caste system, these sanctions assure high status and privileges to the white individual, and the opposite to the Negro, in all mixed relationships. The relative prestige of the castes is socially defined by color sanctions with respect to occupation, wages, public gatherings, politics, and education. It is this complex of privileges, socially and biologically evaluated, which establishes the superordinate rank of the white, and the subordinate rank of the Negro, group.

The caste controls range from taboos upon Negro-white marriage and intimacy to those upon the most detailed point of Negro-white etiquette.[4] The basic sanctions in Old and Rural counties will be listed here in decreasing order of inviolability. Infringement by a Negro of any of these, even those concerning deference, is punished by death, whipping, expulsion from the county, or socioeconomic penalties. Whites, though seldom controlled by physical means, are stigmatized and economically punished by their own caste for violating any of these taboos.

Marriage between whites and Negroes is prohibited by a law which is rigidly observed and enforced, thus supporting the cultural rule of endogamy. By law, also, the offspring of Negro-white unions must be defined as Negroes. Any individual with one Negro ancestor is therefore a Negro, no matter what number of white ancestors he may have had. "Blood" is thus defined so as to prevent mobility across caste lines. Associated with the rule of endogamy is the rule of separate group-seating of whites and Negroes in all public carriers and assemblages. This control is also legalized.

In maintaining the separate and endogamous nature of white-Negro relationships, the informal social controls are elaborately systematized, so as to prevent what the whites call "social equality." Not only are family and kinship relations legally and culturally interdicted between Negroes and whites but a white and a Negro may not visit as intimates. Thus clique relationships are likewise prevented between members of different color groups. With the taboo upon visiting are taboos upon eating or drinking together, dancing, playing cards, and upon all other types of intimacy. All these controls operate to support the endogamous restriction, by making intimate social access impossible.

When Negro-white sexual unions occur, they must therefore take place outside of the white, and usually of the Negro, family. Such unions are permitted only in the case of a white man and a Negro woman. In this area of sexual and social relationships, Negro-white unions are not regarded as establishing "social equality"; the same attitude is maintained with regard to association between Negro and white criminals, gamblers, or "low-life" persons. Although the white and Negro societies disapprove of all these types of association, the whites permit them because they are not a threat to the white family or social class system and are, therefore, not a violation of the endogamous ("legal marriage") caste taboo.

The socially separate, endogamous, superordinate-subordinate system of Negro-white relationships is further maintained by well-defined restrictions upon face-to-face participation. These controls establish an etiquette in all Negro-white contacts; they prescribe masterful or condescending behavior for the white and deferential behavior for the Negro. Caste etiquette varies slightly according to the class position of the white and Negro interacting in the face-to-face relationship; except in the case of the Negro-customer-white-salesman relationship, however, these modifications in etiquette never violate the masterful role of whites and the deferential role of Negroes. Even in this commercial relationship, white salesgirls in Old City address all upper-class colored women, except one, by their first names only.

Whites in this area must not shake hands with Negroes or address them as "Mr.," "Miss," or "Mrs." They address all Negroes either as "girl" or "boy" or by their first names. On the other hand, Negroes must address all whites honorifically. Even an upper-class Negro planter or physician will always address a lower-class white as "Mr.," "Mrs.," or "Miss," whereas whites will not address Negroes in this way, although they may address them as "Professor" or "Doctor." The few exceptions to these rules are limited to Negro domestics who may address their white employers by their first names plus the honorific form, such as "Miss Alice" or "Mr. John," and to some upper middle-class whites who occasionally address a Negro as "Mr." or "Mrs."

Deference to whites by Negroes also includes a conciliating and often whining tone in speaking, removal of the hat, and acquiescence to statements or demands by the white.[5] An absolute taboo prevails against any Negro's contradicting, cursing, or shouting angrily at any white. In the more isolated communities of the area, caste deference requires that a Negro shall not wear expensive "dressy" clothes on weekdays, shall not smoke cigars in the presence of whites, and shall drive his automobile to the side of the road at once to allow a white driver to pass.

The roles of deference for Negroes and of dominance for whites are supported by both physical and psychosocial punishments. In preventing what the whites call "social equality," caste etiquette ranks below only endogamy and social separateness in universality and inviolability. In certain contexts the smallest lapse in deference by a Negro may be punished by beating or death.

The whites place all Negroes into two categories: "good Negroes" and "bad Negroes." The former type meticulously observes the rules of deference; the latter type is slow, "sullen," or "sassy" or "smart" toward whites. Negroes, however, use the term "good Negro" to refer to a Negro who is more deferential than the white society requires. Like the whites, they employ the term "bad Negro" to mean a Negro who openly violates caste etiquette, but there is usually an implication of social approval in the Negro usage.

The masterful role of whites and the deferential role of Negroes, learned and maintained as specific behavior patterns and reinforced by powerful sanctions, extend into every type of Negro-white relationship. They underlie the patriarchial "gift" pattern of white behavior toward Negroes in governmental, court, and economic relations and the begging, clowning, flattering, or subservient behavior of the Negroes. Within these caste-typed roles, Negroes and whites have their *modus vivendi.* The caste subordination of Negroes, which is enforced by the complex of legal, political, economic, educational, and social restrictions placed upon them, still allows the deferential Negro to attain certain limited rewards within his lower-caste status. The Negro "leader," minister, or school principal depends upon the patronage of whites to maintain Negro institutions like the school, or the church. The behavior of the effective Negro in this community is directed toward maneuvering the white into accepting more fully a patriarchal relationship to the Negro; both the Negro servant and the Negro leader thus attempt by flattery, cunning, and deference to compel the powerful white individual to act out his patriarchal role.

Caste Dogmas

The sanctions of endogamy, social separateness, and white mastery and Negro deference are likewise supported by dogmas in each color group. The most general dogmas of whites in Old and Rural counties concerning the reasons for the subordination of Negroes are that Negroes are inherently childish, primitively sexual, and, except for a few unusual individuals, incapable of intellectual and emotional maturity (socialization) on the level achieved by whites. These secular teachings are supported by the religious dogma that Negroes are inherently faithful, subservient, humble, and otherworldly. Within the Negro caste, the individual is taught that the whites as a group are superior in skills and power, extremely dangerous, all-powerful, and sinful. Negro ministers and leaders express this dogma as follows: Since whites are all-powerful, Negroes should avoid aggressive behavior toward the individuals and toward the white community as a whole; the successful accommodation of Negroes to whites requires their being deferential to whites and working conscientiously for them; Negroes have many invidious characteristics which account for white domination; and Negroes should develop their own Negro society more fully by "race loyalty" to Negro businesses, professional men, and leaders.[6]

Thus the dogmas of each caste positively sanction the separate, ranked, and endogamous relationship. Since the Christian dogma of the brotherhood of man and the democratic dogma of the inherent equality of all men before the law and state are also a part of Negro culture, however, the complete acceptance of caste dogma by Negroes includes only the inviolability of caste endogamy and social separateness. Although Negroes necessarily accept caste-ranking controls also, there is abundant evidence of psychological conflict over this categorical subordination.

The caste sanctions and teachings vary slightly according to age, sex, class, and rural-urban groups. For example, in Old and Rural counties, social separateness is less strictly enforced among very young children; also caste controls are more elaborate and severe in rural than in urban communities and in towns than in cities. Under all conditions, however, the basic restrictions upon marriage, public gatherings, social intimacy, and etiquette operate to maintain the superordinate-subordinate relationships of whites and Negroes and to make this ranking unchangeable and dependent upon birth.

Caste and Community Structure

All other systems of behavior within the society of Old and Rural counties are adjusted in some degree to the caste system. In formal organization, the caste sanctions are most rigidly applied in the political and governmental systems, the organization and functioning of the courts, the educational system, the church and associations, and in organized recreation. In local government, only whites vote or hold state, county, or municipal offices. Only six Negroes in Old City had been allowed to register as voters in national elections; these registered Negroes admitted they did not vote, because they felt, as a leading Negro professional man said, that government was "the white man's business." In the rural counties, no Negro was registered. No Negroes were registered as voters in state or municipal elections, nor had any been a candidate for any county or municipal office since Reconstruction. The white officers in charge of registration and elections stated to one of the white interviewers that the whites prevented Negroes from registering as voters by intimidation and, if necessary, by violence.

In all law courts all judges, court officers, lawyers, and juries are white persons. Criminal cases involving a white and a Negro are almost invariably decided in favor of the white, even if he has been the attacker. Civil cases between Negroes and whites, involving damage to person or property, may be won by a Negro, especially if the white party to the suit is an insurance company or nonlocal corporation. Negroes very rarely sue local whites, however. Murder of a white by a Negro is always punished by death, whereas the murder of a Negro by a white is seldom punished by the courts. Attacks by Negroes upon Negroes usually are very slightly punished, even in the case of murder.

The educational and associational institutions of the community are all segmented into white and Negro structures. Negro public schools are markedly inferior to white in teaching staff and in equipment; the per capita appropriation by the school board for Negroes is only a fraction of that for whites. The salaries of Negro teachers are lower than those for whites in parallel status. The churches and associations have either all-Negro or all-white membership; the only exceptions anywhere in the surrounding area are in certain labor unions in the building trades and in the Spiritualist and Sanctified churches. All other Protestant and Catholic churches exhibit a quite rigid form of segregation. The highest authority in the Episcopal church, the bishop, stated to a white interviewer the caste policy of his church as follows:

> I think that the only solution of the situation is for Negroes to develop independently of the whites. They must recognize the situation as it is and conform to it. They must work out their own destiny without attempting social equality.

The Catholic bishop likewise stated the acceptance of the caste structure of the community by his church:

Actually we adapt ourselves to local conditions. Not only because the Negroes usually have a separate church but also because we feel it is better for them to have their own. They also prefer to have a separate church and request it.

Negro-white relationships, therefore, conform to a caste structure in the formal organizations of the society, as well as in the family, social clique, and more informal relationships. The only structure which does not exhibit this sharp dichotomy is the economic organization of the society. Although color-caste sanctions operate as occupational taboos to a high degree, the economic structure is not caste-segmented upon an all-or-none color basis, as are the political and religious structures. That is, economic status does not follow color status with the well-nigh perfect correlation formed in regard to political and legal status.

II

In certain fields, notably in storekeeping, contracting, fanning, and professional service to colored persons, the economic system is still sufficiently "free" in competition to prevent the rigid application of caste taboos. Although a large proportion of colored proprietors and contractors, lacking adequate capital, have been unable to compete successfully, the economic system has maintained a small group of colored persons of relatively high status. It has thus prevented the full development of caste—that development in which *all* members of the lower caste are legally, or by virtue of unbreakable custom, below *all* members of the upper caste in wages, occupational status, and the value of property owned.

The evidence establishes the following relationship between the systems of color caste and of economic stratification in the area studied. In general, the economic status of Negroes is inferior to that of whites; nevertheless, economic behavior openly conflicts with caste dogma at times, such as when white landlords accept Negro farm tenants in preference to white. The distribution of economic status is strongly bimodal for color; nevertheless, both Negroes and whites occupy every sort of occupational status—from landlord to day laborer. The same distribution is observed for economic status as measured by landownership, amount of cotton produced, and fertility of soil cultivated.

A study of income, savings, property ownership, and occupations has revealed the marked statistical tendency of economic and occupational status to follow caste lines; together with an actually wide intra-caste spread of economic status. With regard to the first system of behavior, that is, the economic-class stratification *within* each color caste, the chief determinants are considered to be the laws and customs of a "freely competitive" economy, the differential control and fertility of land, the differential availability of credit, and powerful economic-class dogmas and antagonisms.

The second characteristic of economic stratification, namely, the great preponderance in higher economic status of whites over Negroes, is related to the operation of the direct primary caste sanctions, which enable the white landlord to subordinate the Negro tenant even more effectively than the white tenant by law, by custom, and, if necessary, by force. The primary caste controls likewise assure the white landlord a marked competitive advantage over the Negro landlord with regard to the purchase of land, the command of credit, and the securing of tenants. In the urban society, moreover, direct caste sanctions operate to exclude Negroes from practically all preferred occupational status.

The crucial observation remains, however, that some few Negroes enjoy higher economic symbols and rank than many whites. This skew in the relationship between color caste and economic status is observed as a conflict between economic behavior patterns in a competitive system and caste patterns, deriving from a system of social stratification based upon marks of color and "blood." The criteria of status in the two systems are essentially different. A Negro landlord enjoys the economic functions and symbols of a person in the higher positions of the economic hierarchy: he may even have a white tenant working for him. But in social relationships, even with his white tenant, he is lower caste. The existence of these two systems is historically demonstrated by the position of free Negroes in the period of slavery. Most free Negroes actually possessed higher economic status than the chattel slaves and than some "poor whites." Like the slaves, however, they were lower caste, that is, members of a socially separate, endogamous, and subordinated group.

In so far as the present economic system has prevented the full extension of the caste system, it appears to have been operating upon two principles: that of the sanctity of private property and that of free competition. This latter aspect of the national economic and legal structures gives rise to the presence in Old County of nonlocal factories and sawmills. These manufacturing firms hire labor as cheaply as they can get it, with the result that in industries where white workers have not been able to establish caste taboos, colored workers are employed to do much the same type of labor as whites. They may even be preferred to white workers, because they can be hired for a lower wage.

These nonlocal industries not only tend to disrupt caste relations in labor but they put into the hands of colored workers money which the local white storekeepers are extremely anxious to obtain. Since money has the highest value in the economic system, it causes white middle- and lower-class storekeepers to wait upon colored patrons deferentially. Money thereby increases the difficulties of adjusting caste, which seems to be essentially a structure of pastoral and agricultural societies, to a manufacturing and commercial economy. This money economy likewise leads the group of entrepreneurs and middlemen to whom it has given rise—the most powerful group in the production of cotton because they control credit and therefore production—to be unmindful whether they buy cotton from a colored or white farmer, whether they sell food, automobiles, and clothes to one or the other, whether they allow nonlocal industries to subordinate the lower economic group of whites to the lower group of colored workers. They care principally about increasing their money. Even the local white farmowners prefer colored tenants to white, because they can obtain higher profits from the former. From the point of view of the white lower group, such behavior is a violation of caste. It indicates a fundamental conflict between the economic system and the caste dogma.

In the second place, the principle of the sanctity of private property has generally operated to prevent the expropriation of colored owners. Even during the period of slavery, free colored persons were allowed to own property in Old City and in the state generally. This right was not taken from them during the twenty years immediately preceding the Civil War, when the legislature severely restricted their behavior in other respects. At the close of the Civil War, the same reactionary legislature which passed the so-called "Black Code" in Mississippi, providing "apprentice" laws, *granted* to freedmen the right to own property in incorporated towns and cities. Since that time, colored owners have not been expropriated, except in isolated cases of terrorization. To expropriate colored property owners would be to violate the most fundamental principle of the economic system and to establish a precedent for the expropriation of other subordinated groups, such as the lower economic group of white people, Jews, Italians, and "foreign" ethnic groups of all kinds.

It is necessary to point out, however, that the modification of the caste system in the interests of the profits of the upper and middle economic groups of white people by no means amounts to an abrogation of caste in economic relationships. The economic interests of these groups would also demand that cheaper colored labor should be employed in the "white-collar" jobs in business offices, governmental offices, stores, and banks. In this field, however, the interests of the employer group conflict not only with those of the lower economic group of whites but also with those of the more literate and aggressive middle group of whites. A white store which employed colored clerks, for example, would be boycotted by both these groups. The taboo upon the employment of colored workers in such fields is the result of the political power and the purchasing power of the white middle and lower groups. As a result of these taboos in the field of "white-collar" work, the educated colored person occupies a well-nigh hopeless position in Old County.

The superior political power of the middle and lower groups of white people consequent upon the disfranchisement of the colored population, has enabled them to establish a caste barrier to the employment of colored clerical workers in municipal, state, and federal governmental offices. The inability of these white groups to extend caste taboos so as to prevent colored persons from owning real estate and from competing with white skilled and unskilled labor may be attributed to the fact that the rights of private property and of a free labor market for the planter and the manufacturer are still sacred legal rights in Old County.

A more detailed knowledge of the caste system as it exists in economic settings which differ from the old plantation economy of Old County would enable one to define the degree of subordination of the lower caste according to the type of economy. A tentative hypothesis might be advanced that the physical terrorization of colored people is most common in those areas where their general economic status is highest. In the "newer" agricultural, oil-producing, and manufacturing sections of Mississippi and of the South in general, where relatively large groups of colored people are economically superordinate to relatively large groups of white people, open racial conflict and terrorization seem to be at their height. Such conflict results from the fact that in many economic symbols, such as clothes, automobiles, and houses, a relatively large number of colored people are superior to many of the poorer whites. The white society, as a whole, often resorts to terrorization to reassert the dogma of caste and to indicate that in physical and legal power over the life and limb of colored people, at least, the caste sanctions are effective.

In the Mississippi Delta, where white and colored farm tenants are competing at an increasing rate, and in a mill-town society, a sawmill society, or an oil-mining society, where similar competition exists, most of the white men *work* for a living, as contrasted with the white planters in Old County—and work in daily contact with colored men, even though the former may be termed "supervisors." Here, where most white men, dressed in overalls or work clothes, are almost as poor as the colored workers and occupy approximately the same occupational level, it is most difficult to maintain the caste lines with the rigidity and authority which the dogma demands. In such a community, therefore, the white population continually must resort to terrorization in order to impress the colored group with the fact that *economic* equality, or even superiority on the part of the latter, is not *real* equality or superordination; in other words, that caste exists all along the line, as the myth demands, and that actually *any* white man, no matter how poor or illiterate, is superordinate to any colored man, and must be treated with the appropriate deference.

In the old plantation areas in South Carolina, Alabama, and Mississippi, on the other hand, where almost all the colored people are families of poverty-stricken tenants and almost all the white people are families of owners of large landlords, caste is almost "perfect" economically and socially, and therefore relatively little terrorization of the lower caste is needed to support it. In fine, where caste is most fully extended there is little need for violence, because the colored people are thoroughly subordinated economically, occupationally, and socially. When the castes are in economic competition as laborers and tenants, however, violence and conflict seem to be at their height.

UNIVERSITY OF CHICAGO

NOTES

1. The counties specified in this article are those which were reported on in detail in Allison Davis, Burleigh B. Gardner, and Mary R. Gardner, *Deep South* (Chicago: University of Chicago Press, 1941).

2. In the legal and customary rigidity of the endogamous control, the color-caste taboo here described appears to be more inviolable than the endogamous rule of most Hindu castes. See Professor Warner's survey of the evidence on this point in W. Lloyd Warner and Allison Davis, "A Comparative Study of American Caste," *Race Relations and the Race Problem*, ed. Edgar T. Thompson (Durham, N.C.: Duke University Press, 1939), pp. 219–29.

3. Davis, Gardner, and Gardner, *op. cit.,* chaps. iii–xi.

4. Extensive illustration of the evidence gathered on caste sanctions is given in *ibid.,* chap. ii.

5. Scratching the head and shuffling the feet, as if in indecision, are also deferential gestures of most Negroes in this area.

6. A detailed analysis of the operation of color-caste and class controls in the Negro church and associations in Old and Rural counties and in New Orleans has been prepared for the Carnegie Corporation by the writer, under the title, *The Negro Church and Associations in the Lower South: A Research Memorandum.*

PART 3

African Americans in
American Cultural Production

Introduction

Just as scholars like Charles Wesley, E. Franklin Frazier, and Charles Johnson accomplished great things developing and then institutionalizing the social sciences on our nation's historically black college and university campuses, there were other African American intellectuals who were committed to developing a more refined understanding of blacks' place in American society. These scholars also engaged in a pursuit of knowledge that aggressively distanced itself from the ecclesiastical urgings of their intellectual ancestors. To be sure, their work was no less committed to the goal of achieving racial justice and full citizenship, but their chosen means to this end made it clear that they were fully "modern."

The scholars featured in this section—Alain Locke, Zora Neale Hurston, Sterling Brown, and James Weldon Johnson—were of roughly the same generation as the modern social scientists found in the previous section. It is also clear that they interacted with ease, familiarity, and frequency with social scientists (either a result of socializing or working in overlapping environments, typically in New York City or at Howard University). What distinguishes Locke, Hurston, Brown, and Johnson from the likes of Horace Mann Bond or Allison Davis is that the former recognized in African American cultural forms the same kinds of liberatory possibility that social scientists seemed only to find in economics and politics. In fact, the lines between culture and social science that might at first seem so distinct were quite blurred for these scholars. Whether it is through their ardent faith in the scientific value of cultural studies, their personal familiarity with social scientific methods, or their determination to study culture from a reasoned, objective scientific approach, we learn from the intellectuals in this section that we cannot accept a definition of "social science" that is narrowly tailored to fit into the disciplinary boundaries by which it is most frequently delineated: sociology, anthropology, economics, psychology, political science, and occasionally history. The scientific study of social groups can emanate from a variety of perspectives and shed new light in previously darkened corners.

Alain Locke (1886–1954) was the most adamant proponent in thinking across disciplinary boundaries in order to meet the need for an objective study of the African American experience. A recipient of the BA and PhD from Harvard (1907 and 1918, respectively), Locke made an early splash in academe when he won a Rhodes Scholarship in 1907, thus becoming the first African American to garner that honor.[1] Locke taught at Howard for nearly forty years in the department of philosophy but is best known for the important role he played in highlighting the rise of a new mentality among black Americans after World War I. "The New Negro," Locke averred, had arrived and was impatiently pushing the "Sociologist, the Philanthropist, and the Race-leader" aside.[2] While Locke's opening claim overstepped reality by several paces, he did successfully tap into an emerging mentality that was consumed with understanding social forces in new ways. A humanist by disciplinary training in philosophy, Locke preferred to think of himself as a social scientist who saw in his work and advocacy the solutions for African Americans' second-class citizenship status.[3] Locke's 1926 opus *The New Negro* is often considered the manifesto of the New Negro or Harlem Renaissance, a movement most popularly seen as strictly cultural in its orientation. As scholars reexamine the long history of the modern civil rights movement, however, more are beginning to understand that the New Negro Renaissance involved much more than the production and consumption of "authentic" black cultural forms. These scholars were finding alternative sites of resistance and independence that fueled the political move toward progressive and radical politics in the 1930s.[4]

There is little disputing the fact that the figure who most successfully crossed the lines separating disciplines was Zora Neale Hurston (1907–1960). A trained anthropologist as well as a folklorist, Hurston was a pioneer in giving a voice to the very populations social scientists so often analyzed from a critical—some, like Hurston, would claim "sterile"—distance. Hurston had a peripatetic undergraduate career, moving from Morgan State to Howard and then finally to Barnard College where she received her BA studying anthropology with Franz Boas. With the support of Guggenheim and Rosenwald research grants, Hurston traveled to Florida to conduct ethnographies.[5] These studies—based on movies, interviews, participant observation—were the sources for her anthropological novels like *Jonah's Gourd Vine* and books like *Mules and Men* that explored voodoo practices in various black communities. In all of these works and again in her most famous book, *Their Eyes Were Watching God*, Hurston made great use of African American vernacular in her attempt to demonstrate black cultural authenticity and self-sufficiency and to chart the influence of African American culture upon the "mainstream." Indeed, from the opening pages of "Characteristics of Negro Expression," we find Hurston making this claim when she declares: "the American Negro has done wonders to the English language. It has often been stated by etymologists that the Negro has introduced no African words to the language. This is true, but it is equally true that he has made over a great part of the tongue to his liking and has had his revision accepted by the ruling class. No one listening to a Southern white man talk could deny this."[6]

Even though it gave voice to populations typically rendered silent by social science surveys, Hurston's use of dialect was controversial because some prominent blacks felt that revealing black speakers using anything less than proper English undermined efforts to uplift the race.[7] The literary scholar Sterling Brown (1901–1989) was not one of these critics. Just as Hurston crossed lines that separated the socially scientific from the cultural, Brown wrote in two voices. A graduate of Williams College in 1922 and then the master's program at Harvard the following year, Brown produced a respected body of literary criticism as well as a popular body of poetry. The literary criticism employed the voice of the professional academic while much of the poetry relied upon rural African American dialect. The sample we provide in this section is essentially an essay that presents a sociology of literary production—specifically concerned with how American writers wrestled with the abiding social problem that race presented across time and space. Although he was not a trained ethnologist like Hurston or a self-declared non-traditional-disciplinary social scientist like Locke, Brown rubbed shoulders with the era's leading social scientists on a daily basis from his teaching post at Howard (where he taught for four decades) and certainly was familiar with their mode of disciplinary engagement. Lending further credence to the fact that Brown's literary style also spoke to those who admired social scientific interpretations of phenomena is the fact that Brown consulted for many important research projects that were explicitly concerned with the study of black life in America. He headed the Negro Affairs division of the Federal Writers Project during the New Deal and then consulted for Gunnar Myrdal's mammoth research project, *An American Dilemma*.

James Weldon Johnson also felt at ease in several worlds. Closer in age to Du Bois than to Locke, Hurston, or Brown, Johnson (1871–1938) shared in the commitment they all possessed to the improvement of blacks' social, economic, and political position in America. A graduate of Atlanta University in 1894, Johnson pursued graduate work at Columbia. He passed the Florida bar in 1897 and within a decade had co-authored with his brother Rosamond such songs as "Lift Ev'ry Voice and Sing" (otherwise known as the "Negro National Anthem") before assuming a series of consular posts in the diplomatic corps, first to Venezuela in 1906 and then to Nicaragua in 1909. He left the corps in 1913.[8] Johnson maintained his dual interests in culture and politics via his creative writing, like the classic *An Autobiography of an Ex-Coloured Man* (published anonymously in 1912), his critical prose and scholarly collections of poetry and spirituals, and his ten-year career as first a field secretary and then the executive secretary of the NAACP. Of the four authors in this section, Johnson is perhaps the furthest removed from the emergent modern social sciences, but he merits inclusion here at least in part for his perceptive understanding of the way that racial faultlines in American society forced often impossible decisions upon African American scholars and writers, particularly when it came to "solving the race problem," one of the main obsessions of the social sciences in the twentieth century. Johnson's essay, "The Dilemma of the Negro Author," addresses this faultline when it acknowledges that "The Aframerican [*sic*] author faces a special problem which the plain American author knows nothing about—the problem of the double audience; it is a divided audience, an audience made up of two elements with differing and often opposite and antagonistic points of view. His audience is always both white America and black America. The moment a Negro writer takes up his pen or sits down to his typewriter he is immediately called upon to solve, consciously or unconsciously, this problem of the double audience. To whom shall he address himself, to his own black group or to white America?"[9]

Locke's, Hurston's, Brown's, and Johnson's scholarship remind us that the modern social sciences emerged at almost the same moment as black cultural forms and production became popularized. Social scientists' fascination with black bodies and the larger white consuming public's desire for black culture (and black bodies in the cultural sense as well) are both tied to the massive rural-to-urban migration of African American laborers in the early decades of the twentieth century. The mutual fascination also reminds us how closely social science fields are wed to the cultural forms and practices that defined so much of African American life prior to the Second World War.

NOTES

1. Harry Washington Greene, *Holders of Doctorates Among American Negroes* (Boston: Meador, 1946), 201–202, 209.

2. Alain Locke, "The New Negro," in *The New Negro,* ed. Locke (New York: A. and C. Boni, 1925), 3.

3. Jeffrey Stewart, "Introduction," in Alain Locke, *Race Contacts and Interracial Relations,* ed. Jeffrey Stewart (Washington, D.C.: Howard University Press, 1992), xxxii–xxxiii, xliv–xlv.

4. See, for example, William J. Maxwell, *New Negro, Old Left: African American Writing and Communism Between the Wars* (New York: Columbia University

Press, 1999), and James Smethurst, *The New Red Negro: The Literary Left and African American Poetry, 1930–1946* (New York: Oxford University Press, 1999).

5. W. Augustus Low and Virgil Clift, eds. *The Encyclopedia of Black America* (New York: McGraw-Hill, 1981), 457.

6. Zora Neale Hurston, "Characteristics of Negro Expression," from *Negro: Anthology,* ed. Nancy Cunard (New York: Negro Universities Press, 1969 reprint of 1934 original by Wishart & Company), 39–40. For more on this see Mary Katherine Wainwright, "The Aesthetics of Community: The Insular Black Community as Theme and Focus in Hurston's *Their Eyes Were Watching God,*" in *The Harlem Renaissance: Revaluations,* ed. Amritjit Singh et al. (New York: Garland, 1989), 233–247; Smethurst, *The New Red Negro,* 10, 30–31; Maxwell, *New Negro, Old Left,* 153–178.

7. Smethurst, *The New Red Negro,* 10; Arnold Rampersad, "Langston Hughes and Approaches to Modernism," in Singh et al., eds., *The Harlem Renaissance,* 49–71.

8. Low and Clift, eds., *The Encyclopedia of Black America,* 474–475.

9. James Weldon Johnson, "The Dilemma of the Negro Author," *The American Mercury* 15, no. 60 (1928): 477.

ALAIN LOCKE

The New Negro

In the last decade something beyond the watch and guard of statistics has happened in the life of the American Negro and the three norns who have traditionally presided over the Negro problem have a changeling in their laps. The Sociologist, the Philanthropist, the Race-leader are not unaware of the New Negro, but they are at a loss to account for him. He simply cannot be swathed in their formulae. For the younger generation is vibrant with a new psychology; the new spirit is awake in the masses, and under the very eyes of the professional observers is transforming what has been a perennial problem into the progressive phases of contemporary Negro life.

Could such a metamorphosis have taken place as suddenly as it has appeared to? The answer is no; not because the New Negro is not here, but because the Old Negro had long become more of a myth than a man. The Old Negro, we must remember, was a creature of moral debate and historical controversy. His has been a stock figure perpetuated as an historical fiction partly in innocent sentimentalism, partly in deliberate reactionism. The Negro himself has contributed his share to this through a sort of protective social mimicry forced upon him by the adverse circumstances of dependence. So for generations in the mind of America, the Negro has been more of a formula than a human being—a something to be argued about, condemned or defended, to be "kept down," or "in his place," or "helped up," to be worried with or worried over, harassed or patronized, a social bogey or a social burden. The thinking Negro even has been induced to share this same general attitude, to

Alain Locke, "The New Negro," in *The New Negro*, ed. Locke, 3–16 (New York: A and C. Boni, 1925).

focus his attention on controversial issues, to see himself in the distorted perspective of a social problem. His shadow, so to speak, has been more real to him than his personality. Through having had to appeal from the unjust stereotypes of his oppressors and traducers to those of his liberators, friends and benefactors he has had to subscribe to the traditional positions from which his case has been viewed. Little true social or self-understanding has or could come from such a situation.

But while the minds of most of us, black and white, have thus burrowed in the trenches of the Civil War and Reconstruction, the actual march of development has simply flanked these positions, necessitating a sudden reorientation of view. We have not been watching in the right direction; set North and South on a sectional axis, we have not noticed the East till the sun has us blinking.

Recall how suddenly the Negro spirituals revealed themselves; suppressed for generations under the stereotypes of Wesleyan hymn harmony, secretive, half-ashamed, until the courage of being natural brought them out—and behold, there was folk-music. Similarly the mind of the Negro seems suddenly to have slipped from under the tyranny of social intimidation and to be shaking off the psychology of imitation and implied inferiority. By shedding the old chrysalis of the Negro problem we are achieving something like a spiritual emancipation. Until recently, lacking self-understanding, we have been almost as much of a problem to ourselves as we still are to others. But the decade that found us with a problem has left us with only a task. The multitude perhaps feels as yet only a strange relief and a new vague urge, but the thinking few know that in the reaction the vital inner grip of prejudice has been broken.

With this renewed self-respect and self-dependence, the life of the Negro community is bound to enter a new dynamic phase, the buoyancy from within compensating for whatever pressure there may be of conditions from without. The migrant masses, shifting from countryside to city, hurdle several generations of experience at a leap, but more important, the same thing happens spiritually in the life-attitudes and self-expression of the Young Negro, in his poetry, his art, his education and his new outlook, with the additional advantage, of course, of the poise and greater certainty of knowing what it is all about. From this comes the promise and warrant of a new leadership. As one of them has discerningly put it:

> We have tomorrow
> Bright before us
> Like a flame.

Yesterday, a night-gone thing
A sun-down name.

And dawn today
Broad arch above the road we came.
We march!

This is what, even more than any "most creditable record of fifty years of freedom," requires that the Negro of to-day be seen through other than the dusty spectacles of past controversy. The day of "aunties," "uncles" and "mammies" is equally gone. Uncle Tom and Sambo have passed on, and even the "Colonel" and "George" play barnstorm rôles from which they escape with relief when the public spotlight is off. The popular melodrama has about played itself out, and it is time to scrap the fictions, garret the bogeys and settle down to a realistic facing of facts.

First we must observe some of the changes which since the traditional lines of opinion were drawn have rendered these quite obsolete. A main change has been, of course, that shifting of the Negro population which has made the Negro problem no longer exclusively or even predominantly Southern. Why should our minds remain sectionalized, when the problem itself no longer is? Then the trend of migration has not only been toward the North and the Central Midwest, but city-ward and to the great centers of industry— the problems of adjustment are new, practical, local and not peculiarly racial. Rather they are an integral part of the large industrial and social problems of our present-day democracy. And finally, with the Negro rapidly in process of class differentiation, if it ever was warrantable to regard and treat the Negro *en masse* it is becoming with every day less possible, more unjust and more ridiculous.

In the very process of being transplanted, the Negro is becoming transformed.

The tide of Negro migration, northward and city-ward, is not to be fully explained as a blind flood started by the demands of war industry coupled with the shutting off of foreign migration, or by the pressure of poor crops coupled with increased social terrorism in certain sections of the South and Southwest. Neither labor demand, the boll-weevil nor the Ku Klux Klan is a basic factor, however contributory any or all of them may have been. The wash and rush of this human tide on the beach line of the northern city centers is to be explained primarily in terms of a new vision of opportunity, of social and economic freedom, of a spirit to seize, even in the face of an extortionate and heavy toll, a chance for the improvement of conditions. With each successive wave of it, the movement of the Negro becomes more and more a mass movement toward the larger and the more democratic chance—in the Negro's case a deliberate flight not only from countryside to city, but from medieval America to modern.

Take Harlem as an instance of this. Here in Manhattan is not merely the largest Negro community in the world, but the first concentration in history of so many diverse elements of Negro life. It has attracted the African, the West Indian, the Negro American; has brought together the Negro of the North and the Negro of the South; the man from the city and the man from the town and village; the peasant, the student, the business man, the professional man, artist, poet, musician, adventurer and worker, preacher and criminal, exploiter and social outcast. Each group has come with its own separate motives and for its own special ends, but their greatest experience has been the finding of one another. Proscription and prejudice have thrown these dissimilar elements into a common area of contact and interaction. Within this area, race sympathy and unity have determined a further fusing of sentiment and experience. So what began in terms of segregation becomes more and more, as its elements mix and react, the laboratory of a great race-welding. Hitherto, it must be admitted that American Negroes have been a race more in name than in fact, or to be exact, more in sentiment than in experience. The chief bond between them has been that of a common condition rather than a common consciousness; a problem in common rather than a life in common. In Harlem, Negro life is seizing upon its first chances for group expression and self-determination. It is—or promises at least to be—a race capital. That is why our comparison is taken with those nascent centers of folk-expression and self-determination which are playing a creative part in the world to-day. Without pretense to their political significance, Harlem has the same rôle to play for the New Negro as Dublin has had for the New Ireland or Prague for the New Czechoslovakia.

Harlem, I grant you, isn't typical—but it is significant, it is prophetic. No sane observer, however sympathetic to the new trend, would contend that the great masses are articulate as yet, but they stir, they move, they are more than physically restless. The challenge of the new intellectuals among them is clear enough—the "race radicals" and realists who have broken with the old epoch of philanthropic guidance, sentimental appeal and protest. But are we after all only reading into the stirrings of a sleeping giant the dreams of an agitator? The answer is in the migrating peasant. It is the "man farthest down" who is most active in getting up. One of the most characteristic symptoms of this is the professional man, himself migrating to recapture his constituency after a vain effort to maintain in some Southern corner what for years back seemed an established living and clientele. The clergyman following his errant flock, the physician or lawyer trailing his clients, supply the true clues. In a real sense it is the rank and file who are leading, and the leaders who are following. A transformed and transforming psychology permeates the masses.

When the racial leaders of twenty years ago spoke of developing race-pride and stimulating race-consciousness, and of the desirability of race solidarity, they could not in any accurate degree have anticipated the abrupt feeling that has surged up and now pervades the awakened centers. Some of the recognized Negro leaders and a powerful section of white opinion identified with "race work" of the older order have indeed attempted to discount this feeling as a "passing phase," an attack of "race nerves" so to speak, an "aftermath of the war," and the like. It has not abated, however, if we are to gauge by the present tone and temper of the Negro press, or by the shift in popular support from the officially recognized and orthodox spokesmen to those of the independent, popular, and often radical type who are unmistakable symptoms of a new order. It is a social disservice to blunt the fact that the Negro of the Northern centers has reached a stage where tutelage, even of the most interested and well-intentioned sort, must give place to new relationships, where positive self-direction must be reckoned with in ever increasing measure. The American mind must reckon with a fundamentally changed Negro.

The Negro too, for his part, has idols of the tribe to smash. If on the one hand the white man has erred in making the Negro appear to be that which would excuse or extenuate his treatment of him, the Negro, in turn, has too often unnecessarily excused himself because of the way he has been treated. The intelligent Negro of to-day is resolved not to make discrimination an extenuation for his shortcomings in performance, individual or collective; he is trying to hold himself at par, neither inflated by sentimental allowances nor depreciated by current social discounts. For this he must know himself and be known for precisely what he is, and for that reason he welcomes the new scientific rather than the old sentimental interest. Sentimental interest in the Negro has ebbed. We used to lament this as the falling off of our friends; now we rejoice and pray to be delivered both from self-pity and condescension. The mind of each racial group has had a bitter weaning, apathy or hatred on one side matching disillusionment or resentment on the other but they face each other to-day with the possibility at least of entirely new mutual attitudes.

It does not follow that if the Negro were better known, he would be better liked or better treated. But mutual understanding is basic for any subsequent coöperation and adjustment. The effort toward this will at least have the effect of remedying in large part what has been the most unsatisfactory feature of our present stage of race relationships in America, namely the fact that the more intelligent and representative elements of the two race groups have at so many points got quite out of vital touch with one another.

The fiction is that the life of the races is separate, and increasingly so. The fact is that they have touched too closely at the unfavorable and too lightly at the favorable levels.

While inter-racial councils have sprung up in the South, drawing on forward elements of both races, in the Northern cities manual laborers may brush elbows in their everyday work, but the community and business leaders have experienced no such interplay or far too little of it. These segments must achieve contact or the race situation in America becomes desperate. Fortunately this is happening. There is a growing realization that in social effort the co-operative basis must supplant long-distance philanthropy, and that the only safeguard for mass relations in the future must be provided in the carefully maintained contacts of the enlightened minorities of both race groups. In the intellectual realm a renewed and keen curiosity is replacing the recent apathy; the Negro is being carefully studied, not just talked about and discussed. In art and letters, instead of being wholly caricatured, he is being seriously portrayed and painted.

To all of this the New Negro is keenly responsive as an augury of a new democracy in American culture. He is contributing his share to the new social understanding. But the desire to be understood would never in itself have been sufficient to have opened so completely the protectively closed portals of the thinking Negro's mind. There is still too much possibility of being snubbed or patronized for that. It was rather the necessity for fuller, truer self-expression, the realization of the unwisdom of allowing social discrimination to segregate him mentally, and a counter-attitude to cramp and fetter his own living—and so the "spite-wall" that the intellectuals built over the "color-line" has happily been taken down. Much of this reopening of intellectual contacts has centered in New York and has been richly fruitful not merely in the enlarging of personal experience, but in the definite enrichment of American art and letters and in the clarifying of our common vision of the social tasks ahead.

The particular significance in the re-establishment of contact between the more advanced and representative classes is that it promises to offset some of the unfavorable reactions of the past, or at least to re-surface race contacts somewhat for the future. Subtly the conditions that are molding a New Negro are molding a new American attitude.

However, this new phase of things is delicate; it will call for less charity but more justice; less help, but infinitely closer understanding. This is indeed a critical stage of race relationships because of the likelihood, if the new temper is not understood, of engendering sharp group antagonism and a second crop of more calculated prejudice. In some quarters, it has already done so. Having weaned the Negro, public opinion cannot continue to paternalize. The Negro to-day is inevitably moving forward under the control largely of his own objectives. What are these objectives? Those of his outer life are happily already well and finally formulated, for they are none other than the ideals of American institutions and democracy. Those of his inner life are yet in process of formation, for the new psychology at present is more of a consensus of feeling than of opinion, of attitude rather than of program. Still some points seem to have crystallized.

Up to the present one may adequately describe the Negro's "inner objectives" as an attempt to repair a damaged group psychology and reshape a warped social perspective. Their realization has required a new mentality for the American Negro. And as it matures we begin to see its effects; at first, negative, iconoclastic, and then positive and constructive. In this new group psychology we note the lapse of sentimental appeal, then the development of a more positive self-respect and self-reliance; the repudiation of social dependence, and then the gradual recovery from hyper-sensitiveness and "touchy" nerves, the repudiation of the double standard of judgment with its special philanthropic allowances and then the sturdier desire for objective and scientific appraisal; and finally the rise from social disillusionment to race pride, from the sense of social debt to the responsibilities of social contribution, and offsetting the necessary working and commonsense acceptance of restricted conditions, the belief in ultimate esteem and recognition. Therefore the Negro to-day wishes to be known for what he is, even in his faults and shortcomings, and scorns a craven and precarious survival at the price of seeming to be what he is not. He resents being spoken of as a social ward or minor, even by his own, and to being regarded a chronic patient for the sociological clinic, the sick man of American Democracy. For the same reasons, he himself is through with those social nostrums and panaceas, the so-called "solutions" of his "problem," with which he and the country have been so liberally dosed in the past. Religion, freedom, education, money—in turn, he has ardently hoped for and peculiarly trusted these things; he still believes in them, but not in blind trust that they alone will solve his life-problem.

Each generation, however, will have its creed, and that of the present is the belief in the efficacy of collective effort, in race co-operation. This deep feeling of race is at present the mainspring of Negro life. It seems to be the outcome of the reaction to proscription and prejudice; an attempt, fairly successful on the whole, to convert a defensive into an offensive position, a handicap into an incentive. It is radical in tone, but not in purpose and only the most stupid forms of opposition, misunderstanding or persecution could make it otherwise. Of course, the thinking Negro has shifted a little toward the left with the world-trend, and there is an increasing group who affiliate with radical and liberal movements. But fundamentally for the present the Negro is radical on race matters, conservative on others, in other words, a "forced radical," a social protestant rather than a genuine radical. Yet under further pressure and injustice iconoclastic thought and motives will inevitably increase. Harlem's quixotic radicalisms call for their ounce of democracy to-day lest to-morrow they be beyond cure.

The Negro mind reaches out as yet nothing but American wants, American ideas. But this forced attempt to build his Americanism on race values is a unique social experiment, and its ultimate success is impossible except through the fullest sharing of American culture and institutions. There should be no delusion about this. American nerves in sections unstrung with race hysteria are often fed the opiate that the trend of Negro advance is wholly separatist, and that the effect of its operation will be to encyst the Negro as a benign foreign body in the body politic. This cannot be—even if it were desirable. The racialism of the Negro is no limitation or reservation with respect to American life; it is only a constructive effort to build the obstructions in the stream of his progress into an efficient dam of social energy and power. Democracy itself is obstructed and stagnated to the extent that any of its channels are closed. Indeed they cannot be selectively closed. So the choice is not between one way for the Negro and another way for the rest, but between American institutions frustrated on the one hand and American ideals progressively fulfilled and realized on the other.

There is, of course, a warrantably comfortable feeling in being on the right side of the country's professed ideals. We realize that we cannot be undone without America's undoing. It is within the gamut of this attitude that the thinking Negro faces America, but with variations of mood that are if anything more significant than the attitude itself. Sometimes we have it taken with the defiant ironic challenge of McKay:

> Mine is the future grinding down to-day
> Like a great landslip moving to the sea,
> Bearing its freight of débris far away
> Where the green hungry waters restlessly
> Heave mammoth pyramids, and break and roar
> Their eerie challenge to the crumbling shore.

Sometimes, perhaps more frequently as yet, it is taken in the fervent and almost filial appeal and counsel of Weldon Johnson's:

O Southland, dear Southland!
Then why do you still cling
To an idle age and a musty page,
To a dead and useless thing?

But between defiance and appeal, midway almost between cynicism and hope, the prevailing mind stands in the mood of the same author's *To America,* an attitude of sober query and stoical challenge:

How would you have us, as we are?
    Or sinking 'neath the load we bear,
Our eyes fixed forward on a star,
    Or gazing empty at despair?

Rising or falling? Men or things?
    With dragging pace or footsteps fleet?
Strong, willing sinews in your wings,
    Or tightening chains about your feet?

More and more, however, an intelligent realization of the great discrepancy between the American social creed and the American social practice forces upon the Negro the taking of the moral advantage that is his. Only the steadying and sobering effect of a truly characteristic gentleness of spirit prevents the rapid rise of a definite cynicism and counter-hate and a defiant superiority feeling. Human as this reaction would be, the majority still deprecate its advent, and would gladly see it forestalled by the speedy amelioration of its causes. We wish our race pride to be a healthier, more positive achievement than a feeling based upon a realization of the shortcomings of others. But all paths toward the attainment of a sound social attitude have been difficult; only a relatively few enlightened minds have been able as the phrase puts it "to rise above" prejudice. The ordinary man has had until recently only a hard choice between the alternatives of supine and humiliating submission and stimulating but hurtful counter-prejudice. Fortunately from some inner, desperate resourcefulness has recently sprung up the simple expedient of fighting prejudice by mental passive resistance, in other words by trying to ignore it. For the few, this manna may perhaps be effective, but the masses cannot thrive upon it.

Fortunately there are constructive channels opening out into which the balked social feelings of the American Negro can flow freely.

Without them there would be much more pressure and danger than there is. These compensating interests are racial but in a new and enlarged way. One is the consciousness of acting as the advance-guard of the African peoples in their contact with Twentieth Century civilization; the other, the sense of a mission of rehabilitating the race in world esteem from that loss of prestige for which the fate and conditions of slavery have so largely been responsible. Harlem, as we shall see, is the center of both these movements; she is the home of the Negro's "Zionism." The pulse of the Negro world has begun to beat in Harlem. A Negro newspaper carrying news material in English, French and Spanish, gathered from all quarters of America, the West Indies and Africa has maintained itself in Harlem for over five years. Two important magazines, both edited from New York, maintain their news and circulation consistently on a cosmopolitan scale. Under American auspices and backing, three pan-African congresses have been held abroad for the discussion of common interests, colonial questions and the future co-operative development of Africa. In terms of the race question as a world problem, the Negro mind has leapt, so to speak, upon the parapets of prejudice and extended its cramped horizons. In so doing it has linked up with the growing group consciousness of the dark-peoples and is gradually learning their common interests. As one of our writers has recently put it: "It is imperative that we understand the white world in its relations to the non-white world." As with the Jew, persecution is making the Negro international.

As a world phenomenon this wider race consciousness is a different thing from the much asserted rising tide of color. Its inevitable causes are not of our making. The consequences are not necessarily damaging to the best interests of civilization. Whether it actually brings into being new Armadas of conflict or argosies of cultural exchange and enlightenment can only be decided by the attitude of the dominant races in an era of critical change. With the American Negro, his new internationalism is primarily an effort to recapture contact with the scattered peoples of African derivation. Garveyism may be a transient, if spectacular, phenomenon, but the possible rôle of the American Negro in the future development of Africa is one of the most constructive and universally helpful missions that any modern people can lay claim to.

Constructive participation in such causes cannot help giving the Negro valuable group incentives, as well as increased prestigé at home and abroad. Our greatest rehabilitation may possibly come through such channels, but for the present, more immediate hope rests in the revaluation by white and black alike of the Negro in terms of his artistic endowments and cultural contributions, past and prospective. It must be increasingly recognized that the Negro has already made very substantial contributions, not only in his folk-art, music especially, which has always found appreciation, but in larger, though humbler and less acknowledged ways. For generations the Negro has been the peasant matrix of that section of America which has most undervalued him, and here he has contributed not only materially in labor and in social patience, but spiritually as well. The South has unconsciously absorbed the gift of his folk-temperament. In less than half a generation it will be easier to recognize this, but the fact remains that a leaven of humor, sentiment, imagination and tropic nonchalance has gone into the making of the South from a humble, unacknowledged source. A second crop of the Negro's gifts promises still more largely. He now becomes a conscious contributor and lays aside the status of a beneficiary and ward for that of a collaborator and participant in American civilization. The great social gain in this is the releasing of our talented group from the arid fields of controversy and debate to the productive fields of creative expression. The especially cultural recognition they win should in turn prove the key to that revaluation of the Negro which must precede or accompany any considerable further betterment of race relationships. But whatever the general effect, the present generation will have added the motives of self-expression and spiritual development to the old and still unfinished task of making material headway and progress. No one who understandingly faces the situation with its substantial accomplishment or views the new scene with its still more abundant promise can be entirely without hope. And certainly, if in our lifetime the Negro should not be able to celebrate his full initiation into American democracy, he can at least, on the warrant of these things, celebrate the attainment of a significant and satisfying new phase of group development, and with it a spiritual Coming of Age.

ZORA NEALE HURSTON

Characteristics of Negro Expression

Drama

The Negro's universal mimicry is not so much a thing in itself as an evidence of something that permeates his entire self. And that thing is drama.

His very words are action words. His interpretation of the English language is in terms of pictures. One act described in terms of another. Hence the rich metaphor and simile.

The metaphor is of course very primitive. It is easier to illustrate than it is to explain because action came before speech. Let us make a parallel. Language is like money. In primitive communities actual goods, however bulky, are bartered for what one wants. This finally evolves into coin, the coin being not real wealth but a symbol of wealth. Still later even coin is abandoned for legal tender, and still later for cheques in certain usages.

Every phase of Negro life is highly dramatised. No matter how joyful or how sad the case there is sufficient poise for drama. Everything is acted out. Unconsciously for the most part of course. There is an impromptu ceremony always ready for every hour of life. No little moment passes unadorned.

Now the people with highly developed languages have words for detached ideas. That is legal tender. "That-which-we-squat-on" has become "chair." "Groan-causer" has evolved into "spear," and so on. Some individuals even conceive of the equivalent of cheque words, like "ideation" and "pleonastic."

Zora Neale Hurston, "Characteristics of Negro Expression," from *Negro: Anthology*, ed. Nancy Cunard, 39–46 (New York: Negro Universities Press, 1969 reprint of 1934 original by Wishart & Company). Reproduced with permission of the Zora Neale Hurston Trust.

Perhaps we might say that *Paradise Lost* and *Sartor Resartus* are written in cheque words.

The primitive man exchanges descriptive words. His terms are all close fitting. Frequently the Negro, even with detached words in his vocabulary— not evolved in him but transplanted on his tongue by contact—must add action to it to make it do. So we have "chop-axe," "sitting-chair," "cook-pot" and the like because the speaker has in his mind the picture of the object in use. Action. Everything illustrated. So we can say the white man thinks in a written language and the Negro thinks in hieroglyphics.

A bit of Negro drama familiar to all is frequent meeting of two opponents who threaten to do atrocious murder one upon the other.

Who has not observed a robust young Negro chap posing upon a street corner, possessed of nothing but his clothing, his strength and his youth? Does he bear himself like a pauper? No, Louis XIV could be no more insolent in his assurance. His eyes say plainly "Female, halt!" His posture exults "Ah, female, I am the eternal male, the giver of life. Behold in my hot flesh all the delights of this world. Salute me, I am strength." All this with a languid posture, there is no mistaking his meaning.

A Negro girl strolls past the corner lounger. Her whole body panging[1] and posing. A slight shoulder movement that calls attention to her bust, that is all of a dare. A hippy undulation below the waist that is a sheaf of promises tied with conscious power. She is acting out "I'm a darned sweet woman and you know it."

These little plays by strolling players are acted out daily in a dozen streets in a thousand cities, and no ever mistakes the meaning.

Will to Adorn

The will to adorn is the second most notable characteristic in Negro expression. Perhaps his idea of ornament does not attempt to meet conventional standards, but it satisfies the soul of its creator.

In this respect the American Negro has done wonders to the English language. It has often been stated by etymologists that the Negro has introduced no African words to the language. This is true, but it is equally true that he has made over a great part of the tongue to his liking and has had his revision accepted by the ruling class. No one listening to a Southern white man talk could deny this. Not only has he softened and toned down strongly consonanted words like "aren't" to "aint" and the like, he has made new force words out of old feeble elements. Examples of this are "ham-shanked," "battle-hammed," "double-teen," "bodaciously," "muffle-jawed."

But the Negro's greatest contribution to the language is: (1) the use of metaphor and simile; (2) the use of the double descriptive; (3) the use of verbal nouns.

1. METAPHOR AND SIMILE
   One at a time, like lawyers going to heaven.
   You sho is propaganda.
   Sobbing hearted.
   I'll beat you till: (*a*) rope like okra, (*b*) slack like lime, (*c*) smell like onions.
   Fatal for naked.
   Kyting along.
   That's a lynch.
   That's a rope.
   Cloakers—deceivers.
   Regular as pig-tracks.
   Mule blood—black molasses.
   Syndicating—gossiping.
   Flambeaux—cheap café (lighted by flambeaux).
   To put yo'self on de ladder.

2. THE DOUBLE DESCRIPTIVE
   High-tall.
   Little-tee-ninchy (tiny).
   Low-down.
   Top-superior.
   Sham-polish.
   Lady-people.
   Kill-dead.
   Hot-boiling.
   Chop-axe.
   Sitting-chairs.
   De watch wall.
   Speedy-hurry.
   More great and more better.

3. VERBAL NOUNS
   She features somebody I know.
   Funeralize.
   Sense me into it.

Puts the shamery on him.

'Taint everybody you kin confidence.

I wouldn't friend with her.

Jooking—playing piano or guitar as it is done in Jookhouses
(houses of ill-fame).

Uglying away.

I wouldn't scorn my name all up on you.

Bookooing (beaucoup) around—showing off.

NOUNS FROM VERBS

Won't stand a broke.

She won't take a listen.

He won't stand straightening.

That is such a compelment.

That's a lynch.

The stark, trimmed phrases of the Occident seem too bare for the voluptuous child of the sun, hence the adornment. It arises out of the same impulse as the wearing of jewelry and the making of sculpture—the urge to adorn.

On the walls of the homes of the average Negro one always finds a glut of gaudy calendars, wall pockets and advertising lithographs. The sophisticated white man or Negro would tolerate none of these, even if they bore a likeness to the Mona Lisa. No commercial art for decoration. Nor the calendar nor the advertisement spoils the picture for this lowly man. He sees the beauty in spite of the declaration of the Portland Cement Works or the butcher's announcement. I saw in Mobile a room in which there was an overstuffed mohair living-room suite, an imitation mahogany bed and chifferobe, a console victrola. The walls were gaily papered with Sunday supplements of the *Mobile Register.* There were seven calendars and three wall pockets. One of them was decorated with a lace doily. The mantel-shelf was covered with a scarf of deep home-made lace, looped up with a huge bow of pink crêpe paper. Over the door was a huge lithograph showing the Treaty of Versailles being signed with a Waterman fountain pen.

It was grotesque, yes. But it indicated the desire for beauty.

The difference in the two arts is: the white dancer attempts to express fully; the Negro is restrained, but succeeds in gripping the beholder by forcing him to finish the action the performer suggests. Since no art ever can express all the variations conceivable, the Negro must be considered the greater artist, his dancing is realistic suggestion, and that is about all a great artist can do.

Negro Folklore

Negro folklore is not a thing of the past. It is still in the making. Its great variety shows the adaptability of the black man: nothing is too old or too new, domestic or foreign, high or low, for his use. God and the Devil are paired, and are treated no more reverently than Rockefeller and Ford. Both of these men are prominent in folklore, Ford being particularly strong, and they talk and act like good-natured stevedores or mill-hands. Ole Massa is sometimes a smart man and often a fool. The automobile is ranged alongside of the oxcart. The angels and the apostles walk and talk like section hands. And through it all walks Jack, the greatest culture hero of the South; Jack beats them all—even the Devil, who is often smarter than God.

Culture Heroes

The Devil is next after Jack as a culture hero. He can outsmart everyone but Jack. God is absolutely no match for him. He is good-natured and full of humour. The sort of person one may count on to help out in any difficulty.

Peter the Apostle is the third in importance. One need not look far for the explanation. The Negro is not a Christian really. The primitive gods are not deities of too subtle inner reflection; they are hard-working bodies who serve their devotees just as laboriously as the suppliant serves them. Gods of physical violence, stopping at nothing to serve their followers. Now of all the apostles Peter is the most active. When the other ten fell back trembling in the garden, Peter wielded the blade on the posse. Peter first and foremost in all action. The gods of no peoples have been philosophic until the people themselves have approached that state.

The rabbit, the bear, the lion, the buzzard, the fox are culture heroes from the animal world. The rabbit is far in the lead of all the others, and is blood brother to Jack. In short, the trickster-hero of West Africa has been transplanted to America.

John Henry is a culture hero in song, but no more so than Stacker Lee, Smokey Joe or Bad Lazarus. There are many, many Negroes who have never heard of any of the song heroes, but none who do not know John (Jack) and the rabbit.

Examples of Folklore and the Modern Culture Hero:

Why de Porpoise's Tail is on Crosswise.   Now, I want to tell you 'bout de porpoise. God had done made de world and everything. He set de moon and de stars in de sky. He got de fishes of de sea, and de fowls of de air completed.

He made de sun and hung it up. Then He made a nice gold track for it to run on. Then He said, "Now, Sun, I got everything made but Time. That's up to you. I want you to start out and go round de world on dis track just as fast as you kin make it. And de time it takes you to go and come, I'm going to call day and night." De Sun went zoonin' on cross de elements. Now, de porpoise was hanging round there and heard God what he tole de Sun, so he decided he'd take dat trip round de world hisself. He looked up and saw de Sun kytin' along, so he lit out too, him and dat Sun!

So de porpoise beat de Sun round de world by one hour and three minutes. So God said, "Aw naw, this aint gointer do! I didn't mean for nothin' to be faster than de Sun!" So God run dat porpoise for three days before he run him down and caught him, and took his tail off and put it on crossways to slow him up. Still he's de fastest thing in de water.

And dat's why de porpoise got his tail on crossways.

Rockefeller and Ford.   Once John D. Rockefeller and Henry Ford was woofing at each other. Rockefeller told Henry Ford he could build a solid gold road round the world. Henry Ford told him if he would he would look at it and see if he liked it, and if he did he would buy it and put one of his tin lizzies on it.

Originality

It has been said so often that the Negro is lacking in originality that it has almost become a gospel. Outward signs seem to bear this out. But if one looks closely its falsity is immediately evident.

It is obvious that to get back to original sources is much too difficult for any group to claim very much as a certainty. What we really mean by originality is the modification of ideas. The most ardent admirer of the great Shakespeare cannot claim first source even for him. It is his treatment of the borrowed material.

So if we look at it squarely, the Negro is a very original being. While he lives and moves in the midst of a white civilisation, everything that he touches is re-interpreted for his own use. He has modified the language, mode of food preparation, practice of medicine, and most certainly the religion of his new country, just as he adapted to suit himself the Sheik hair-cut made famous by Rudolph Valentino.

Everyone is familiar with the Negro's modification of the whites' musical instruments, so that his interpretation has been adopted by the white man himself and then re-interpreted. In so many words, Paul Whiteman is giving an imitation of a Negro orchestra making use of white-invented musical instruments in a Negro way. Thus has arisen a new art in the civilised world, and thus has our so-called civilisation come. The exchange and re-exchange of ideas between groups.

Imitation

The Negro, the world over, is famous as a mimic. But this in no way damages his standing as an original. Mimicry is an art in itself. If it is not, then all art must fall by the same blow that strikes it down. When sculpture, painting, acting, dancing, literature neither reflect nor suggest anything in nature or human experience we turn away with a dull wonder in our hearts at why the thing was done. Moreover, the contention that the Negro imitates from a feeling of inferiority is incorrect. He mimics for the love of it. The group of Negroes who slavishly imitate is small. The average Negro glories in his ways. The highly educated Negro the same. The self-despisement lies in a middle class who scorns to do or be anything Negro. "That's just like a Nigger" is the most terrible rebuke one can lay upon this kind. He wears drab clothing, sits through a boresome church service, pretends to have no interest in the community, holds beauty contests, and otherwise apes all the mediocrities of the white brother. The truly cultured Negro scorns him, and the Negro "farthest down" is too busy "spreading his junk" in his own way to see or care. He likes his own things best. Even the group who are not Negroes but belong to the "sixth race," buy such records as "Shake dat thing" and "Tight lak dat." They really enjoy hearing a good bible-beater preach, but wild horses could drag no such admission from them. Their ready-made expression is: "We done got away from all that now." Some refuse to countenance Negro music on the grounds that it is niggerism, and for that reason should be done away with. Roland Hayes was thoroughly denounced for singing spirituals until he was accepted by white audiences. Langston Hughes is not considered a poet by this group because he writes of the man in the ditch, who is more numerous and real among us than any other.

But, this group aside, let us say that the art of mimicry is better developed in the Negro than in other racial groups. He does it as the mocking-bird does it, for the love of it, and not because he wishes to be like the one imitated. I saw a group of small Negro boys imitating a cat defecating and the subsequent toilet of the cat. It was very realistic, and they enjoyed it as much as if they had been imitating a coronation ceremony. The dances are full of imitations of various animals. The buzzard lope, walking the dog, the pig's hind legs, holding the mule, elephant squat, pigeon's wing, falling off the log, seabord (imitation of an engine starting), and the like.

Absence of the Concept of Privacy

It is said that Negroes keep nothing secret, that they have no reserve. This ought not to seem strange when one considers that we are an outdoor people accustomed to communal life. Add this to all-permeating drama and you have the explanation.

There is no privacy in an African village. Loves, fights, possessions are, to misquote Woodrow Wilson, "Open disagreements openly arrived at." The community is given the benefit of a good fight as well as a good wedding. An audience is a necessary part of any drama. We merely go with nature rather than against it.

Discord is more natural than accord. If we accept the doctrine of the survival of the fittest there are more fighting honors than there are honors for other achievements. Humanity places premiums on all things necessary to its well-being, and a valiant and good fighter is valuable in any community. So why hide the light under a bushel? Moreover, intimidation is a recognised part of warfare the world over, and threats certainly must be listed under that head. So that a great threatener must certainly be considered an aid to the fighting machine. So then if a man or woman is a facile hurler of threats, why should he or she not show their wares to the community? Hence the holding of all quarrels and fights in the open. One relieves one's pent-up anger and at the same time earns laurels in intimidation. Besides, one does the community a service. There is nothing so exhilarating as watching well-matched opponents go into action. The entire world likes action, for that matter. Hence prize-fighters become millionaires.

Likewise love-making is a biological necessity the world over and an art among Negroes. So that a man or woman who is proficient sees no reason why the fact should not be moot. He swaggers. She struts hippily about. Songs are built on the power to charm beneath the bed-clothes. Here again we have in-dividuals striving to excel in what the community considers an art. Then if all of his world is seeking a great lover, why should he not speak right out loud?

It is all in a view-point. Love-making and fighting in all their branches are high arts, other things are arts among other groups where they brag about their proficiency just as brazenly as we do about these things that others con-sider matters for conversation behind closed doors. At any rate, the white man is despised by Negroes as a very poor fighter individually, and a very poor lover. One Negro, speaking of white men, said, "White folks is alright when dey gits in de bank and on de law bench, but dey sho' kin lie about wim-men folks."

I pressed him to explain. "Well you see, white mens makes out they mar-ries wimmen to look at they eyes, and they know they gits em for just what us gits em for. 'Nother thing, white mens say they goes clear round the world and wins all de wimmen folks way from they men folks. Dat's a lie too. They don't win nothing, they buys em. Now de way I figgers it, if a woman don't want me enough to be wid me, 'thout I got to pay her, she kin rock right on, but these here white men don't know what to do wid a woman when they gits her—dat's how come they gives they wimmen so much. They got to. Us wim-men works jus as hard as us does an come home an sleep wid us every night. They own wouldn't do it and it's de mens fault. Dese white men done fooled theyself bout dese wimmen.

"Now me, I keeps me some wimmens all de time. Dat's whut dey wuz put here for—us mens to use. Dat's right now, Miss. Y'all wuz put here so us mens could have some pleasure. Course I don't run round like heap uh men folks. But if my ole lady go way from me and stay more'n two weeks, I got to git me somebody, aint I?"

The Jook

Jook is the word for a Negro pleasure house. It may mean a bawdy house. It may mean the house set apart on public works where the men and women dance, drink and gamble. Often it is a combination of all these.

In past generations the music was furnished by "boxes," another word for guitars. One guitar was enough for a dance; to have two was considered excellent. Where two were playing one man played the lead and the other sec-onded him. The first player was "picking" and the second was "framming," that is, playing chords while the lead carried the melody by dexterous finger work. Sometimes a third player was added, and he played a tom-tom effect on the low strings. Believe it or not, this is excellent dance music.

Pianos soon came to take the place of the boxes, and now player-pianos and victrolas are in all of the Jooks.

Musically speaking, the Jook is the most important place in America. For in its smelly, shoddy confines has been born the secular music known as blues, and on blues has been founded jazz. The singing and playing in the true Negro style is called "jooking."

The songs grow by incremental repetition as they travel from mouth to mouth and from Jook to Jook for years before they reach outside ears. Hence the great variety of subject-matter in each song.

The Negro dances circulated over the world were also conceived inside the Jooks. They too make the round of Jooks and public works before going into the outside world.

In this respect it is interesting to mention the Black Bottom. I have read several false accounts of its origin and name. One writer claimed that it got its name from the black sticky mud on the bottom of the Mississippi river. Other equally absurd statements gummed the press. Now the dance really originated in the Jook section of Nashville, Tennessee, around Fourth Avenue. This is a tough neighbourhood known as Black Bottom—hence the name.

The Charleston is perhaps forty years old, and was danced up and down the Atlantic seaboard from North Carolina to Key West, Florida.

The Negro social dance is slow and sensuous. The idea in the Jook is to gain sensation, and not so much exercise. So that just enough foot movement is added to keep the dancers on the floor. A tremendous sex stimulation is gained from this. But who is trying to avoid it? The man, the woman, the time and the place have met. Rather, little intimate names are indulged in to heap fire on fire.

These too have spread to all the world.

The Negro theatre, as built up by the Negro, is based on Jook situations, with women, gambling, fighting, drinking. Shows like "Dixie to Broadway" are only Negro in cast, and could just as well have come from pre-Soviet Russia.

Another interesting thing—Negro shows before being tampered with did not specialise in octoroon chorus girls. The girl who could hoist a Jook song from her belly and lam it against the front door of the theatre was the lead, even if she were as black as the hinges of hell. The question was "Can she jook?" She must also have a good belly wobble, and her hips must, to quote a popular work song, "Shake like jelly all over and be so broad, Lawd,

Lawd, and be so broad." So that the bleached chorus is the result of a white demand and not the Negro's.

The woman in the Jooky may be nappy headed and black, but if she is a good lover she gets there just the same. A favorite Jook song of the past has this to say:

> *Singer:*   It aint good looks dat takes you through dis world.
> *Audience:* What is it, good mama?
> *Singer:*   Elgin² movements in your hips
>   Twenty years guarantee.

And it always brought down the house too.

> Oh de white gal rides in a Cadillac,
> De yaller gal rides de same,
> Black gal rides in a rusty Ford
> But she gits dere just de same.

The sort of woman her men idealise is the type that is put forth in the theatre. The art-creating Negro prefers a not too thin woman who can shake like jelly all over as she dances and sings, and that is the type he put forth on the stage. She has been banished by the white producer and the Negro who takes his cue from the white.

Of course a black woman is never the wife of the upper class Negro in the North. This state of affairs does not obtain in the South, however. I have noted numerous cases where the wife was considerably darker than the husband. People of some substance, too.

This scornful attitude towards black women receives mouth sanction by the mud-sills.

Even on the works and in the Jooks the black man sings disparaging of black women. They say that she is evil. That she sleeps with her fists doubled up and ready for action. All over they are making a little drama of waking up a yaller³ wife and a black one.

A man is lying beside his yaller wife and wakes her up. She says to him, "Darling, do you know what I was dreaming when you woke me up?" He says, "No honey, what was you dreaming?" She says, "I dreamt I had done cooked you a big, fine dinner and we was setting down to eat out de same plate and I was setting on yo' lap jus huggin you and kissin you and you was so sweet."

Wake up a black woman, and before you kin git any sense into her she be done up and lammed you over the head four or five times. When you git her quiet she'll say, "Nigger, know whut I was dreamin when you woke me up?"

You say, "No honey, what was you dreamin?" She says, "I dreamt you shook yo' rusty fist under my nose and I split yo' head open wid a axe."

But in spite of disparaging fictitious drama, in real life the black girl is drawing on his account at the commissary. Down in the Cypress Swamp as he swings his axe he chants:

Dat ole black gal, she keep on grumblin,
New pair shoes, new pair shoes,
I'm goint to buy her shoes and stockings
Slippers too, slippers too.

Then adds aside: "Blacker de berry, sweeter de juice."

To be sure the black gal is still in power, men are still cutting and shooting their way to her pillow. To the queen of the Jook!

Speaking of the influence of the Jook, I noted that Mae West in "Sex" had much more flavor of the turpentine quarters than she did of the white bawd. I know that the piece she played on the piano is a very old Jook composition. "Honey let yo' drawers hang low" had been played and sung in every Jook in the South for at least thirty-five years. It has always puzzled me why she thought it likely to be played in a Canadian bawdy house.

Speaking of the use of Negro material by white performers, it is astonishing that so many are trying it, and I have never seen one yet entirely realistic. They often have all the elements of the song, dance, or expression, but they are misplaced or distorted by the accent falling on the wrong element. Every one seems to think that the Negro is easily imitated when nothing is further from the truth. Without exception I wonder why the black-face comedians *are* black-face; it is a puzzle—good comedians, but darn poor niggers. Gershwin and the other "Negro" rhapsodists come under this same axe. Just about as Negro as caviar or Ann Pennington's athletic Black Bottom. When the Negroes who knew the Black Bottom in its cradle saw the Broadway version they asked each other, "Is you learnt dat *new* Black Bottom yet?" Proof that it was not *their* dance.

And God only know what the world has suffered from the white damsels who try to sing Blues.

The Negroes themselves have sinned also in this respect. In spite of the goings up and down on the earth, from the original Fisk Jubilee Singers down to the present, there has been no genuine presentation of Negro songs to white audiences. The spirituals that have been sung around the world are Negroid to be sure, but so full of musicians' tricks that Negro congregations are highly entertained when they hear their old songs so changed. They never use the new style songs, and these are never heard unless perchance some daughter or son has been off to college and returns with one of the old songs with its face lifted, so to speak.

I am of the opinion that this trick style of delivery was originated by the Fisk Singers; Tuskeegee and Hampton followed suit and have helped spread this misconception of Negro spirituals. This Glee Club style has gone on so long and become so fixed among concert singers that it is considered quite authentic. But I say again, that not one concert singer in the world is singing the songs as the Negro song-makers sing them.

If anyone wishes to prove the truth of this let him step into some un-fashionable Negro church and hear for himself.

To those who want to institute the Negro theatre, let me say it is already established. It is lacking in wealth, so it is not seen in the high places. A crea-ture with a white head and Negro feet struts the Metropolitan boards. The real Negro theatre is in the Jooks and the cabarets. Self-conscious individuals may turn away the eye and say, "Let us search elsewhere for our dramatic art." Let 'em search. They certainly won't find it. Butter Beans and Susie, Bo-Jangles and Snake Hips are the only performers of the real Negro school it has ever been my pleasure to behold in New York.

Dialect

If we are to believe the majority of writers of Negro dialect and the burnt-cork artists, Negro speech is a weird thing, full of "ams" and "Ises." Fortu-nately we don't have to believe them. We may go directly to the Negro and let him speak for himself.

I know that I run the risk of being damned as an infidel for declaring that nowhere can be found the Negro who asks "am it?" nor yet his brother who announces "Ise uh gwinter." He exists only for a certain type of writers and performers.

Very few Negroes, educated or not, use a clear clipped "I." It verges more or less upon "Ah." I think the lip form is responsible for this to a great extent. By experiment the reader will find that a sharp "I" is very much easier with a thin taut lip than with a full soft lip. Like tightening violin strings.

If one listens closely one will note too that a word is slurred in one position in the sentence but clearly pronounced in another. This is particularly true of the pronouns. A pronoun as a subject is likely to be clearly enunciated, but slurred as an object. For example: "You better not let me ketch yuh."

There is a tendency in some localities to add the "h" to "it" and pronounce it "hit." Probably a vestige of old English. In some localities "if" is "ef."

In story telling "so" is universally the connective. It is used even as an introductory word, at the very beginning of a story. In religious expression "and" is used. The trend in stories is to state conclusions; in religion, to enumerate.

I am mentioning only the most general rules in dialect because there are so many quirks that belong only to certain localities that nothing less than a volume would be adequate.

NOTES

1. From "pang."
2. Elegant (?).
3. Yaller (yellow), light mulatto.

STERLING A. BROWN

The American Race Problem as Reflected in American Literature

Introduction

In "Calling America," the special number of the *Survey Graphic* which sprang from American concern with the plight of minorities in Europe, William Allan Neilson writes:

> The greatest of the minority problems in the United States concerns *the Negro,* involving as it does some 10 per cent of our population. . . . It would be flagrant hypocrisy to pretend that the position of the Negro in the United States is in harmony with the principles of democracy and equality of opportunity to which we habitually pay lip service.[1]

W. E. B. DuBois considered that the problem of the twentieth century is the problem of the color line. In a blither spirit a historian of Reconstruction assures the readers of *The Road to Reunion* that "The Negro Problem Always Ye Have With You." An alarmist "scientist" titled his book on the Negro *America's Greatest Problem.* American literature seems to second the warnings and the assurance: the problems attendant upon the presence of the Negro in America have engaged the attention of writers from the earliest years of our national literature.

Sterling A. Brown, "The American Race Problem as Reflected in American Literature," *Journal of Negro Education* 8, no. 3 (1939): 275–290. Reprinted by permission of the *Journal of Negro Education.*

It is the purpose of this essay to trace what American writers have said about "the Negro problem." Difficult of precise definition, and therefore not defined here, "the Negro problem" is recognizable enough for such a purpose.

This essay will be confined chiefly to creative literature in which poets, dramatists and fiction writers attempt to reflect the "Negro Problem." The voluminous literature on "the problem" under which library shelves sag has been made use of only to show how influential the ethnologists, psychologists, sociologists, theologians, and historians have been upon the creative artists, who admitted that they were writing fiction.

The essay is divided chronologically into three periods: (1) the antebellum, (2) reconstruction to the turn of the century, and (3) the twentieth century.

Kelly Miller in one of his aphorisms states that "The Negro must get along, get white, or get out." Creative artists have agreed with these as solutions. They see "the problem" or "problems" differently, however. For instance, proslavery authors see the Negro as failing to get along when he was discontented as a slave, or free in the North; antislavery authors when he was treated as a chattel; most Negro authors when he is denied citizenship. The problems then are of two sorts: the problem that the Negro's presence caused those who believed in a white America, *i.e.,* the problem of the Negro to whites; and the problems that the Negro has met with in America, *i.e.,* the problem of America to Negroes.

It is not a purpose of this paper to discuss the question of propaganda in literature, or to evaluate the points of view expressed, although evaluations have not been avoided. This is one of the most controversial subjects in American literature. If one is a good American, it is very difficult to enter this ring where such a rousing battle royal is going on without once raising his arm and letting fly.

The Ante-Bellum Period

American readers had abundant opportunity to learn of the gravity of the problem of slavery from the reports of English travelers such as Charles Dickens, Harriet Martineau, and J. S. Buckingham, and of Northerners such as Frederick Law Olmsted. But such testimony could be dismissed as British or Yankee prejudice. Often too realistic for comfort, the analysis of slavery as an injury to Negroes and a cause of general Southern backwardness, was shunted aside.

Creative artists stated the same conclusions in more emotionally stirring forms. Richard Hildreth, an American historian, was the first to use the novel for antislavery opinions. Published in 1836 as the memoirs of an educated slave, his work was enlarged after the great success of *Uncle Tom's Cabin* and renamed *The White Slave* (1852). Considering the pastoral picture of slavery to be largely mythical, Hildreth, like so many of his followers, stressed the slave's basic humanity, introduced Negro runaways, "maroons," insurrectionists; and described with realistic detail the callousness of the domestic slavetrade, the inevitable miscegenation and the brutalities. In the latter section of the book, Hildreth permits his characters to debate slavery at length. One enlightened slave-owner is a mild colonizationist:

> The late president Jefferson . . . [remarked] that we hold the slaves like a wolf by the ear, whom it is neither safe to hold nor to let go. . . . It seems to me that we whites are the wolf, and the unfortunate negroes the lamb . . . whom, if we only had the will, we might let go without any sort of danger. Why can't we allow freedom to the negroes as well as to the Irish or the Germans? But with the inveterate prejudices of our people . . . [they] would be all up in arms at the very idea of it. The more low, brutal, and degraded a white man is, the more strenuously does he insist on the natural superiority of the white man, and the more he is shocked at the idea of allowing freedom to the "niggers." Our colonization system yields to this invincible feeling.[2]

Hildreth does not disguise his belief that colonization is a visionary solution, that Negroes if set free would prosper, and that the whites more than the Negroes need to be readied for the emancipation of the latter. He tells approvingly of a planter's scheme for freeing his Negroes and setting them up on a plantation in a free state.

The antislavery literary crusade took its start from people whose sense of human dignity was shocked by the idea of men and women being held as property. Transcendentalists like Theodore Parker and Thoreau, Quakers like Whittier and Thomas Garrett, agitators like Garrison and Theodore Weld saw slavery as a curse, in Longfellow's words as "a blind Samson in the temple of our liberties." They wanted the curse removed, the Samson throttled. Attack upon the evil was the pressing task for many of the poets and novelists, and they were not perturbed about what would follow its abolition. Happy endings were fashioned for their heroes and heroines: the octoroon Camilla marries her Northern white rescuer; the white slave Archie Moore at last finds his lost wife and sails for England; broken families are happily united in Canada.

Fugitive slaves, like Frederick Douglass, William Wells Brown, Lewis and Milton Clarke in their autobiographies, and Harriet Tubman, Josiah Henson, and William and Ellen Craft in their dictated narratives told chiefly of the practical, immediate problems of food, clothing and lodging, of avoiding the slave-buyer, of staying out of the ill graces of the driver, the overseer or the slave-breaker, of finding trustworthy mates to dare an escape, of guarding against treacherous slaves, of dodging the patrol, of checkmating the slave-hunters and kidnappers. With such problems solved, it is no wonder that the spirit of much of their writing was that of the fellow who, spirited away by Harriet Tubman to Canada, threw himself upon free soil and shouted his thanks to God that he was free at last. Some of the noted fugitives, especially Douglass, turned their thoughts to the new set of problems, but most of the autobiographies of ex-slaves close with jubilees.

Some of the novelists, however, although deploring slavery, viewed with distrust the presence in America of free Negroes. Some were like Hildreth in fearing race prejudice; others, believing the Negro to have his peculiarities, could not visualize two races living side by side in harmony. This second attitude goes far back: in one of the earliest antislavery pamphlets, *The Selling of Joseph,* Judge Sewall writes:

> Few can endure to hear of a Negro's being made free; and indeed they can seldom use their freedom well; yet their continual aspiring after their forbidden Liberty, renders them Unwilling Servants. And there is such a disparity in their Conditions, Color & Hair, that they can never embody with us, and grow up into orderly Families, to the Peopling of the Land: but still remain in our Body Politick as a kind of extravasat blood.[3]

In *The Spy* Cooper expresses both hope for gradual emancipation and anxiety over the increasing class of free Negroes, vagrants "without principles and attachments."[4] Melville includes antislavery passages in *Mardi* (1849), but convinced that tampering with the peculiar institution will cause secession and revolt, he concludes gloomily that "Time must befriend these thralls!"

At the time of *Uncle Tom's Cabin* (1851) Harriet Beecher Stowe was perplexed about the future of the free Negro. George Harris' reunion with Eliza in Canada is not unadulterated bliss. His future course is a quandary. He decides that "passing for white" would be disloyal to his mother's race and that his individual fight in America for abolition would be ineffectual. In Africa, however, he dreams that a republic, a nation of his people, is rising that will

> roll the tide of civilization and Christianity along its shores, and plant there mighty republics, that growing with the rapidity of tropical vegetation, shall be for all coming ages.

He knows that colonization has been used to retard emancipation, but there is a "God above all man's schemes" who will use it to found a Negro nation. The Negro has rights to be allowed in America, "equal rights . . . as the Irishman, the German, the Swede," and the added claim of "an injured race for reparation." But George does not want those rights.

> I want a country, a nation of my own. I think that the African race has peculiarities yet to be unfolded in the light of civilization and Christianity, which, if not the same with those of the Anglo-Saxon, may prove to be morally, of even a higher type.[5]

In *Dred,* her second antislavery novel, Mrs. Stowe does not dispatch her Negro heroes and heroines to Africa, but leaves them in Canada. Like Harriet Tubman, Mrs. Stowe seems to believe that after the Fugitive Slave Bill fugitives can be safe only near the defending paws of the British lion.

Mrs. Stowe believes that the African race (her militant and intelligent heroes and heroines are almost always nearly white) has its peculiarities (generally of a higher moral caliber than the Anglo-Saxon's). She pleads for humane treatment of Negroes in the North in order to enable them to attain the "moral and intellectual maturity" requisite for missionary service in Africa. Influenced by Mrs. Stowe, H. L. Hosmer's *Adela, The Octoroon* after describing the misery of Mississippi slaves and of Northern free Negroes, shows Liberia to be a happy land of opportunity.

When Frederick Douglass opposed colonization as "an old enemy of the colored people in this country,"[6] he expressed the animus of the outright abolitionists, who, like Garrison, assaulted caste as well as slavery. But Douglass' scornful addition that "almost every respectable man belongs to it by direct membership or by affinity," was true of some antislavery writers. During the Civil War, the *Saturday Review* in England commented upon the strange illusion

> that any respectable party or body of Northerners honestly propose to put the negro on a perfect level with white men . . . neither sober American citizens . . . nor sober Englishmen who have visited . . . The West Indies, will give the slightest adhesion to a principle which makes the negro the social equal of the white man, and encourages the dusky pets of the platform to aspire to a matrimonial alliance with white women.[7]

Besides men like Benjamin Lundy and Joshua Coffin who opposed slavery because of its wrong to Negroes, there were other Southern writers who opposed it as working injury to non-slaveholding whites. J. J. Flournoy, convinced that Negroes were "constitutionally ignorant and uncouth, malicious when in power [written in 1836], and proud without beauty—blasphemous and full of obloquy" and therefore "not fit to associate with the whites" founded a sect called "The Efficient and Instantaneous Expulsion Association of Philosophic and Fearless Patriots."[8] Nearly twenty years later, Hinton Rowan Helper developed Flournoy's ideas. Protesting his dislike for Negroes, he still believed that slavery was a great wrong, and that the system of logic that justified it, merely because "Nature had been pleased to do a trifle more for the Caucasian race than for the African," was "antagonistic to the spirit of democracy." Helper produced "expulsion" as the only stay of the impending ruin.[9]

Many non-slaveholders agreed with Helper, but his book was judged to be as incendiary as *The Liberator*, and the poets and novelists strung along with the master class. They countered Helper's strictures on the waste of slavery with paeans about its blessings to planters and slaves, with the latter chief beneficiaries. They agreed with Helper, however, that Negroes—if free—should be ejected from the paradise.

Proslavery authors found biological warrant for their beliefs in the work of savants whom Helper characterized as "ethnographical oligarchs." The Negro's "different bodily formation" was one of the ways by which Providence assured his political condition. *The Bible Defense of Slavery* established that the Negro was the natural born slave in such ways as citing the great length and width of his foot, "the extraordinary protrusion of the heel backward, placing the leg nearly in the middle of the foot in many instances"; the skin where the "Divine hand" has placed "myriads of little cups of pellucid water mingled with the capillary vessels" to throw off the sun's rays and avert sunstroke.[10]

A later book embodying many of the scientific justifications of slavery was *White Supremacy and Negro Subordination* or *The Negro, A Subordinate Race and (So-Called) Slavery Its Normal Condition*. To its author, C. J. H. Van Evrie, M.D.:

> The beard symbolizes our highest conceptions of manhood—it is the outward evidence . . . of complete growth, mental as well as physical— of strength, wisdom and manly grace.[11]

But the Negro cannot raise a beard, being capable at his best of only "a little tuft on the chin and sometimes on the upper lip, . . . nothing that can be confounded with a beard." He goes on:

> The negro, lowest in the scale, presents an almost absolute resemblance
> to each other [sic]. . . . Except where wide differences of age exist they are
> all alike, and even in size rarely depart from that standard uniformity that
> nature has stamped upon the race. The entire external surface, as well as
> his interior organism, differs radically from the Caucasian. His muscles,
> the form of the limbs, his feet, hands, pelvis, skeleton, all the organs of lo-
> comotion are . . . radically different from the Caucasian.[12]

The Negro's beardlessness, uniformity, and the other biological differences do
more than doom him to subordination. They likewise are reasons why "Music
is to the Negro an impossible art, and therefore such a thing as a Negro singer
is unknown" and why a correctly proportioned brain "could no more be born
of a Negress than an elephant could be!"[13]

Theological warrant for slavery could be quite as fantastic. When Ham
laughed at his father's drunkenness and disarray, he and all of his descendants were doomed to perpetual servitude. "Cursed be Canaan; a servent
of servants shall he be unto his brethren." For the Fugitive Slave Bill divine
sanction could be derived from God's commanding the runaway Hagar to
return to her mistress Sarah (Genesis XVI:9). So ran some of the biblical
arguments.

It was to the biological, psychological, and theological sanctions that the
creative authors turned rather than to the more hard-headed political economy which held that slavery has its *raison d'être* in the need for "sordid, servile, laborious beings" to perform "sordid, servile, laborious offices." J. P. Kennedy's *Swallow Barn* (1832) praised slavery as a beneficent guardianship for an
"essentially parasitical race" noted for "intellectual feebleness." William Grayson in a long poem, *The Hireling and the Slave* (1856), described the life of
the slaves as "unassailed by care," full of "blessings claimed in fabled states
alone." Slavery was the design of Providence to transfer the Negro from bes-
tiality to "celestial light." The hero in Caroline Lee Hentz's *The Planter's
Northern Bride* cribs arguments from *The Bible Defense of Slavery* to prove
the Negro to be divinely ordained to pick his cotton:

> In the first place, his skull has a hardness and thickness greater than our
> own, which defy the arrowy sunbeams of the South. Then his skin . . .
> secretes a far greater quantity of moisture, which like dew, throws back
> the heat absorbed by us. I could mention many more peculiarities which
> prove his adaptedness to the situation he occupies. . . . The mountains
> and the valleys proclaim it.[14]

The fantasies of the scientists and the theologues were dressed up in sentimentality and melodrama by the romancers. They made slavery, according to a Southern critic, into an "unbroken Mardi Gras." But they admitted that a few problems existed. There were serpents in this Eden: abolitionists sneaking about stirring discontent, short-sighted Southerners who would teach Negroes to read and write, and fractious Negroes who resented what was for their best good.

Thus Kennedy regarded the interference of abolitionists as "an unwarrantable and mischievous design to do us injury," sometimes resented "to the point of involving the innocent Negro in the rigor which it provokes."[15] W. J. Smith in *Life at the South* or *Uncle Tom's Cabin As It Is* shows an abolitionist worming his way into the confidence of honest, unspoiled Negroes and changing their happy lives. *A Yankee Slave Dealer* has an abolitionist foolishly trying to decoy satisfied Negroes; Mrs. Hentz's *The Planter's Northern Bride* has a Dickensian villain preaching liberty and causing an abortive revolt.

Vigilance could of course lessen the impact of the abolitionists. Much graver to proslavery authors was the increasing class of free Negroes, some runaways; some manumitted as natural children of white fathers, or as reward for services; some who by hiring themselves out, scraping and hoarding had saved enough money to buy their own bodies. These, not the safely stowed slaves, constituted the Negro problem to slaveowners and their literary men.

W. J. Grayson gave classic form to the Southerners' concept of the free Negro in the North:

There in suburban dens and human sties,
In foul excesses sunk, the Negro lies,
A moral pestilence to taint and stain,
His life a curse, his death a social gain,
. . . with each successive year,
In drunken want his numbers disappear.[16]

William Thompson in a book of burlesque travels in the North, loses his tone of burlesque in writing of the Northern free Negroes. He can only pity the "pore, miserable, sickly looking creaters . . . diseased and bloated up like frogs—[in a condition] to which the philanthropists . . . wants to bring the happy black people of the South." Uncle Tom, in *Life at the South* finds labor for hire in Canada to be harder than slavery in Virginia, and discovers Negroes frozen to death in snowstorms in Buffalo. Crissy in *The Planter's Northern Bride* runs away from unfeeling Northerners to get back to the freedom of the plantation—a sort of Underground Railroad in reverse. The consensus is expressed by Uncle Robin in John W. Page's *Uncle Robin in His Cabin*: "Dis, sir, is no country for free black men: Africa de only place for he, sir."

Proslavery authors sometimes caught up with the spirit of their age and suspected that slavery could not be permanent. W. L. G. Smith writes in the Preface to *Life at the South*:

> The day will yet come when the descendants of Ham will be gathered in the land of their ancestors, and Liberia, in God's own good time, will take its position among the independent states of the world.

W. J. Grayson waxes poetic at the prospect of the Negro (no longer necessary for the development of the South) returning to Africa on missionary duty now instead of agricultural:

> To Africa, their fatherland, they go,
> Law, industry, instruction to bestow:
> To pour, from Western skies, religious light,
> Drive from each hill or vale its pagan rite,
> Teach brutal hordes a nobler life to plan,
> And change, at last, the savage to the man.[17]

This was to take place, however, "In God's own good time."

Reconstruction and After

The Emancipation Proclamation ended one phase of the Negro problem, but only aggravated others. Abraham Lincoln illustrates the indecision that plagued so many humanitarians. In his campaigning for office Lincoln had disclaimed any purpose to introduce political and social equality between the races. "There is a physical difference between the two, which in my judgment, will forever forbid their living together in perfect equality." Lincoln's earlier sponsorship of colonization had resulted in an attempt to settle a cargo of freedmen on the Island of Vache in the West Indies. That ill-fated experiment taught him the futility of colonization, but he was not to live long enough to see the results of his other plans for the freedmen.

Walt Whitman, as contradictory as usual, turned upon the freedmen with surprising invective:

As if we had not strained the voting . . . caliber of American democracy to
the utmost for the last fifty years with the millions of ignorant foreigners, we have now infused a powerful percentage of blacks, with about as
much intellectual caliber (in the mass) as so many baboons.[18]

Whitman described a parade of freedmen in Washington as "very disgusting
and alarming in some respects," the jubilant Negroes looking "like so many
wild brutes let loose."[19]

Lincoln's perplexity and Whitman's disgust were prevalent among Northern writers who had been humanitarians toward the slave. Few retained the
staunchness of such equalitarians as Garrison, Stevens, and Sumner. One honorable exception was David Ross Locke, who, under the pen-name Petro-
leum V. Nasby, attacked copperheads and "dough-faces," laid the bogey of
Negro domination, caricatured Southern chivalry, and ridiculed the superstition that the Negro out of slavery would perish like a fish out of water. But
another humorist, Marietta Holly, after describing the horrors of the Klan in
Aunt Samantha on the Race Problem, could counsel colonization as the only
solution, even as late as 1892. Another Northerner in the South, Constance
Fenimore Woolson, was shocked by the hopelessness of doing anything for
the freedmen, and reserved her pity for the suffering master class.

With reconciliation the watchword of many Northerners, the South seized
the opportunity to glorify its lost cause, and to persuade the North to leave the
Negro problem in Southern hands. This campaign started almost with Appomattox. J. H. Van Evrie re-published his book at the close of the Civil War
with such prefatory remarks:

We will return to the Constitution and the "Union as it was"; and every
man, and woman too in this broad land must accept the simple but stupendous truth of white supremacy and negro subordination, or consent
to have it forced on them by years of social anarchy, horror, and misery![20]

His book was intended to prove that what was called slavery was not slavery at
all, "but a natural relation of the races." Whenever the two races "are in juxtaposition, the normal condition of the Negro . . . is to be guided and controlled
socially and politically by the white race."[21]

Literary artists, with superior skill, sold Van Evie's ideas in a more sophisticated, convincing version to the North which, wearied after the long
war, was ready to forget, forgive and concede. Their contrivance was simple.
Slavery was to be shown as not slavery at all, but a happy state best suited for

an inferior, childish but lovable race. In this normal condition, the Negro was to be shown thriving. Then came his emancipation, which the better class of Negroes did not want, and which few could understand or profit by. Freedom meant anarchy. Only by restoring control (euphemism for tenant farming, sharecroppping [sic], black codes, enforced labor, segregation and all the other ills of the new slavery) could equilibrium in the South, so important to the nation, be achieved.

Thomas Nelson Page is the chief of these glorifiers of the Old South and alarmists about the New. His old relics of slavery, Charley McCarthys in black-face, breathe forth sighs for the vanished days when Negroes were happy: "Dem wuz good old times, marster—de bes' Sam ever see!" Reconstruction showed servants corrupted by scalawags, carpetbaggers, Yankee soldiers and schoolmarms: faithful housedogs injected with hydrophobia. *In Ole Virginia* is a plaintive cry for the lost heaven; *Red Rock* is a turgid description of the new hell. When the "new issue" Negroes, struggling for schooling and for property, do not enrage Page, they succeed in making him laugh as *Pastime Stones* (1899) indicates. An old Negro, approved by Page (he softens his attacks when dealing with decrepit graybeards whose days of menace are over) says:

> You knows de way to de spring and de wood pile, and de mill, an' when you gits a little bigger I's gwine to show you de way to de hoe-handle, an' de cawn furrer an' dats all de geog-aphy a nigger's got to know.

Joel Chandler Harris has his pet, Uncle Remus, likewise scornful of "nigger 'book-larnin'":

> Hits de ruinashun er dis country. . . . Put a spellin' book in a nigger's hans', en right den an' dar' you loozes a plow-hand. I kin take a bar'l stave an' fling mo' sense inter a nigger in one minnit dan all do schoolhouses betwixt dis en de state er Midgigin.

Harris was fundamentally of greater decency than Page, but he still has his mouthpiece Uncle Remus speaking too often the social policy of white Georgians rather than of his own people.

The author who most strongly urged that the Negro be kept "in his place" was Thomas Dixon, whose fiction embodied the creed of the Ku Klux Klan. Dixon makes use of one old trick of the racialist: he equates political equality with sexual license. The argument runs crudely: keep the Negro from the ballot-box, keep him underpaid and uneducated, or else the purity of white womanhood is threatened.

As far back as the Lincoln-Douglas debates, Lincoln was taunted with sponsoring intermarriage when he urged merely that the Negro has "the right to eat the bread which his own hands have earned. . . . Judge Douglas infers that because I do not want a Negro woman for a slave, that I must want her for my wife." In the Reconstruction, intermarriage was dragged out in a more sinister guise. The pat response to assertion of Negro rights became "Would you want your daughter [sister, kinfolks, as the case might warrant] to marry a Negro?" For this, Thomas Dixon and his school are largely responsible. The only Negroes for whom Dixon has any respect are those who dislike Yankees, worship their old masters and mistresses, and prefer slavery. The Negroes engaged in politics are uniformly vicious. The height of their ambition seems to be to make love to a white woman. Negro soldiers abduct white brides; Negro half-wits assault white children. Dixon revels in describing rape. The Ku Klux Klan, the Red Shirts, and other vigilante groups indulge in terroristic activity not for economic or political advantage but to preserve white chastity. A whole school of authors, dreading amalgamation (a bit belatedly) followed Dixon's lead.

Lafcadio Hearn, as fascinated by Negroes as Dixon was repelled, nevertheless expressed one article of the Reconstruction creed. Where Dixon, in company with many others, believed social and political equality would enable a minority to engulf a majority, Hearn foresaw Negro extinction. Freedom would be destruction for "the poor, child-like people":

> Dependent like the ivy, he [the Negro] needs some strong oak-like friend to cling to. His support has been cut from him, and his life must wither in its prostrate helplessness.[22]

Certain Southern writers like George Washington Cable and Mark Twain were sympathetic to the struggles of the freedmen. But Cable's best creative work, where it deals with the tragic injustice of the Negro's lot, is set in the antebellum past and chiefly concerns the abuses of the *Code Noir* and the women of mixed blood. Cable does connect the problems of the old South and the new by pointed asides, and he protests current abuses. At the price of ostracism he condemned the convict lease system and the silence of the South on the general indecency of race relations. But this protest was conveyed in polemical essays, not in fiction. Mark Twain, perfectly aware of America's sorry defaulting of its debt to the Negro, still did not reveal this awareness in creative work.

Albion Tourgee, a Northerner who became part of North Carolina's Reconstruction government, used fiction for propaganda purposes. He showed what his contemporaries refused to touch: the slow but steady progress of the freedmen in education, manliness, social awareness, self-sufficiency; the terrorism of the secret orders; the fraud and violence resorted to in order to reduce freedmen to serfs. He felt that he was waging a futile fight, not because of the unreadiness of the freedman but because of the solidifying South. The titles of his best-known books indicate his doubt; they are *A Fool's Errand* and *Bricks Without Straw.*

Negro writers, however, took up the challenge that Tourgee had spoken. Charles Waddell Chesnutt in his fiction included many of the problems of the color line: the problem of the "half-caste" heroine (overemployed even by this time); of the professional man, hampered by prejudice from performing his best service; of the double standard of morality; of convict labor; of mob violence. Chesnutt handled as well problems within the race which later Negroes have shunted aside: the problem of intraracial color prejudice, of the cleavage between the classes and the masses; of treacherous "hat-in-hand" tactics. Chesnutt wrote melodramatically, but his social understanding should not be underestimated.

Dunbar, Chesnutt's contemporary, was more conciliatory. His dialect poetry was often of the plantation tradition idealizing slavery, or was gently pastoral. His protest was confined to his standard English poems, and those, since they inclined to the romantic school, were inexplicit on the causes for protest. In his fiction, especially *The Sport of the Gods,* Dunbar occasionally confronted problems, but in general he elected to portray the less disturbing aspects of Negro life.

The Twentieth Century

Many of the Negro writers of the early twentieth century preserved their trust in conciliatory tactics, in appeals to the Christianity of white America. Some counselled that no wrong this side of heaven was too great to be forgiven since "Christ washed the feet of Judas," or that "Vengeance is Jehovah's own.... Let us like loving men," or that

> The heart of the world is beating
> With the love that was born of God.

Leslie Pinckney Hill in "Self Determination (The Philosophy of the American Negro)" enumerates "four benedictions which the meek unto the proud are privileged to speak": refusal to hate, philosophic mirth, idealism, and unwavering loyalty. There were others who spoke of the wrongs guardedly, abstractly: "We wear the mask"; "We ask for peace"; "At the Closed Gate of Justice": "To be a Negro in a day like this, demands forgiveness . . . rare patience . . . strange loyalty."

Alas! Lord God, what evil have we done?

This poetry is melancholy with the self-pity of the "talented tenth," but it goes no farther in protest. The dialect poets aimed at farce or sweet bucolics.

But there were some who, disillusioned at the results gained by forbearance, realized that if the struggle for equal rights was to be a long pull, there was even less need to postpone the starting. Novelists, angered at the scorn and hatred of Page and Dixon, retaliated in kind. In their counter-propaganda Negroes were generally faultless victims of white villains, who were generally "poor whites." The heroines were beautiful maidens, the heroes intelligent, militant race-leaders: "As to color he was black, but even those prejudiced as to color forgot that prejudice when they gazed upon this ebony-like Apollo."[23] One novelist had no patience with the school of Booker Washington; "What are houses, land and money to men who are women?"[24]

W. E. B. DuBois recognized the importance of creative writing as a vehicle for propaganda. He made effective use of many types: chants and short stories denouncing prejudice and mob violence, satires of the shams of democracy, essays combining scholarly research with the emotions of an embittered participant. His first novel, *The Quest of the Silver Fleece*, melodramatic and idealized, was crowded with informed discussions of the "problem"; his second novel *The Dark Princess* shares the preoccupation, presenting mordant and convincing realism in the sections dealing with America.

Early poems of James Weldon Johnson presented his deliberation on the "problem"; asserting the Negro's right to be in America because of his service and achievement; expressing faith in God's will; posing the question "To America": "How would you have us. . . . Men or things":

Strong, willing sinews in your wings?
Or tightening chains about your feet?[25]

Johnson's novel *The Autobiography of an Ex-Colored Man* (1912) was the first by a Negro to deal with the dilemmas of the mulatto who, finally beaten by prejudice and lack of opportunity, decides to "pass" for white. Like Chesnutt and DuBois, Johnson reveals many aspects of the problem, subordinating character and action to its exposition.

Most white writers of the early years of the century followed Page and Dixon, urging that the extension of civil rights to Negroes was equivalent to producing a "mongrel race" in America, or else, satisfied that the Negro problem had been safely handled, viewed Negro life jocularly. John McNeill, for instance, in a poem called "Mr. Nigger" comforted his addressee that he should no longer fear expatriation, since minstrel shows, politicians, planters and lynching mobs depended upon him. The poem is intended to be amusing. More honest writers, realists aware of the tragic uneasiness of American life, occasionally wrote of Negroes in a different vein: Upton Sinclair shows Negro strike-breakers in *The Jungle* (1905) and Stephen Crane and Dreiser recorded brutalities. Mary White Ovington continued the abolitionist tradition in *The Shadow* (1920).

After the War to Make the World Safe for Democracy, Negroes began to write more defiant challenges and more ironic appraisals of America. Fenton Johnson might have produced a parallel to *The Spoon River Anthology*, had he continued delineation of what he started in "Tired" and "The Scarlet Woman." Johnson found brooding defeatism instead of gayety and optimism on the other side of the tracks. Claude McKay's poetry protested "the bread of bitterness" America fed him, and described the Harlem streetwalkers, the workers lost in a city of stone and steel, the menials trying to forget their unhappiness in gin and carousing, the lynching mobs. His best known poem "If We Must Die" was a rallying cry in the epidemic of riots during the post-war years.

Although some of McKay's characters talk lengthily of race, McKay's fiction was like so much of the Harlem school. Written during a "boom period" of culture, the Harlem novels generally showed a life free of perplexities graver than boy getting girl. Wallace Thurman's *Blacker the Berry* (1929) approached an intraracial problem generally shied away from: the predicament of the darker woman in upper-class "society." But Thurman showed little depth in characterizing his heroine. He probably shared the flippancy of many of the literati whom he described, not without caricature, in *Infants of the Spring* (1932). These were riding a crest, and Harlem to them—a small, select circle—seemed to be a Mecca of gay abandon. These younger "intellectuals" of the Harlem province, if we are to believe Thurman and their own confessions, sent in repeated orders for the gin of existence and let the bitters go. Others—Rudolph Fisher, George Schuyler, and Countee Cullen—intelligently aware and quite concerned about the Negro's predicament, still wrote good-natured "spoofs" of what they called professional race-men and their organizations.

But the carelessness of the hedonist and the lighter touch of the satirist were not the chief fashions in fiction. Some Negro novelists felt that wonders would be accomplished by revealing to white America that Negroes had a cultivated middle class—that "we aren't all alike." Many saw lynching as the most flagrant wrong to be attacked. Walter White's *Fire in the Flint* is the classic example of the lynching novel: two upstanding ambitious Negroes become victims of mob violence, the first for avenging an insult to his sister, and the second for attending a white patient, which is interpreted as assault. As long as lynching remains the sole American crime protected by filibustering congressmen it is likely that it will be written of by American artists. But many writers isolate lynching as the chief problem of Negroes and, without much knowledge and understanding of the South, handle it in a stereotyped, unconvincing manner.

Another problem unduly emphasized was that of the "passing" heroine, the octoroon of long standing in American literature. Contemporary white writers still celebrate her misery: "It must be unbearable to have to live on that side of the barrier," they say from their side. "I won't be black," says their octoroon, marked with what Artemus Ward jokingly calls the "brand of Kane." Negro novelists insist upon the octoroon's unhappiness when she "passed" from her people, whose gifts are warm humanity and philosophic mirth. Both sets of interpreters made more of her problems than they seem to deserve. Graver problems, even concerning the mulatto, awaited and await interpretation.

For the statements of these, especially in the South (a section not written of by young Negro writers as much as one might expect) one must resort frequently to southern white novelists. The better known, like Julia Peterkin and DuBose Heyward, while writing with sympathy of their characters, deal little with social and economic hardships, showing tragedies caused by fate, or if made by man, springing from the violence of a primitive folk. As Irvin Cobb has said: "Ef you wants to perduse a piece showing a lot of niggers gittin' skinned, let it be another nigger w'ich skins em . . . an' whatever else you does don't mess wid no race problem."[26]

But all Southern writers have not heeded Cobb's injunction. E. C. L. Adam's *Nigger to Nigger* (1928) is one of the sharpest indictments of Southern race relations. A chorus of unfooled folk Negroes speak their minds on the travesty of Southern justice, the fraud and violence with which white "supremacy" is maintained, the daily insults, the high hurdles in the Negro's way to minimum decency of living. The dialogue discussing the Ben Bess Case, where a Negro was jailed for thirteen years on the trumped up charges of a trollop is worth far more than pretentious propaganda. *Nigger to Nigger* is a remarkable book to have been written by a white Southerner. Paul Green's *In Abraham's Bosom* courageously recorded the struggle of a Negro for schools for his people against the fear and hostility of whites and the fear and inertia of Negroes. T. S. Stribling, tracing both the white and Negro branches of a Southern family, is likewise convincing in his portrayal of callous brutality, sanctioned by Southern custom. Erskine Caldwell in his short stories—"Kneel to the Rising Sun" is probably the most effective in this regard—shows the Negro to be an exploited serf, only nominally free, a catspaw for sadistic landlords and their minions. "Niggers will git killt," says his Tobacco Road philosopher. Grace Lumpkin in *A Sign for Cain* (1935), Theodore Strauss in *Night at Hogwallow* (1937) and other left wing writers see the Negro problem now as a challenge to democracy. Like the best of the old abolitionists, they stress the basic humanity of the Negro. They are more interested in his problems as a member of the working class than as a member of a race. Sympathetic in recording his struggles, his aspirations and his tragedies, they have told valuable truths about him, and incidentally have gained stature as artists.

The picture would be false, however, if certain white authors who differ from the liberals and radicals were omitted. There are strange survivals today of the attitudes and proposals of the antebellum and Reconstruction periods. Vachel Lindsay's vision of the "Congo creeping through the black," is coupled with his vision of a Congo paradise with 'sacred capitals, temples clean":

> 'Twas a land transfigured, 'twas a new creation
> Oh, a singing wind swept the Negro nation.[27]

Donald Davidson, distrusting so many things—industrialism, democracy, etc.—warns the Negro, now "perhaps unfortunately . . . no longer a child":

> There is the wall
> Between us, anciently erected. Once
> It might have been crossed, men say. But now I cannot
> Forget that I was master, and you can hardly
> Forget that you were slave. . . .
> Let us not bruise our foreheads on the wall.[28]

NOTES

1. William Allan Neilson, "'Minorities' In Our *Midst,*" *Survey Graphic* (Calling America), 28: 102, 103, F 1939

2. Richard Hildreth, *The White Slave.* Boston: Tappan and Whittemore, 1852, p. 273.

3. Samuel Sewall. *The Selling of Joseph* in Warfel, Gabriel, and Williams, *The American Mind,* p. 64.

4. James Fenimore Cooper, *The Spy.* New York: Charles Scribner's Sons, 1931, p. 44.

5. Harriet Beecher Stowe, *Uncle Tom's Cabin.* New York: The Macmillan Company, 1928, p. 417.

6. Frederick Douglass, "Speech in Faneuil Hall," June 8, 1849, in Woodson, Carter G., *Negro Orators and Their Orations.* Washington: The Associated Publishers 1925, p. 178.

7. Cedric Dover, *Know This of Race.* London: Secker and Warburg, 1939, p. 97.

8. William Sumner Jenkins, *Pro-Slavery Thought in the Old South.* Chapel Hill: University of North Carolina Press, 1935, pp. 92–93.

9. Hinton Rowan Helper, *The Impending Crisis of the South.* New York: A. B. Burdick, 1860. p. 184.

10. Josiah Priest. Bible Defense of Slavery. Glasgow, Ky.: W. S. Brown, 1861, p. 51.

11. C. J. Van Evrie, *White Supremacy and Negro Subordination.* New York: Van Evrie, Horton & Co., 1870. p. 102.

12. *Ibid.,* p. 106.

13. *Ibid.,* p. 130.

14. Caroline Lee Hentz, *The Planter's Northern Bride.* Philadelphia: Perry & McMillan, 1854, II, p. 4.

15. J. P. Kennedy. *Swallow Barn.* New York: G. P. Putnam's Sons. 1895 (reprint) p. 453.

16. W. J. Grayson, *The Hireling and the Slave,* Charleston, S.C.: McCarter & Co., 1856, p. 69.

17. W. J. Grayson, *op. cit.,* p. 73.

18. V. F. Calverton, *The Liberation of American Literature.* New York: Charles Scribner's Sons, 1932, p. 296.

19. Newton Arvin, *Whitman.* New York: The Macmillan Co., 1938, p. 32.

20. J. H. Van Evrie. op. cit. VI.

21. *Ibid.,* VIII.

22. Lafcadio Hearn, *Letters from the Raven.* New York: A. and C. Boni 1930, p. 168.

23. Sutton Griggs, *Unfettered.* Nashville, Tenn.: Orion Publishing Co., 1902, p. 71.

24. J. W. Grant, *Out of the Darkness.* Nashville, Tenn.: National Baptist Publishing Board, 1909, p. 19.

25. James Weldon Johnson, *Fifty Years and Other Poems.* Boston: The Cornhill Publishing Co., 1917, p. 5.

26. Irvin Cobb, *Jeff Poindexter, Colored.* New York; George H. Doran Co., 1922, p. 188.

27. Vachel, Lindsay, "The Congo (A Study of the Negro Race)" in Untermeyer, Louis, *Modern American Poetry.* New York: Harcourt Brace & Co., 1930, p. 317.

28. Donald Davidson, *The Tall Men.* New York: Houghton Mifflin Co., 1927, p. 39.

29. Eleanor Mercein Kelly, "Monkey Notions," in Williams, Blanch Colton, *O. Henry Prize Stories of 1927.* Garden City: Doubleday Doran & Co. 1927. p. 207.

JAMES WELDON JOHNSON

The Dilemma of the Negro Author

The Negro author—the creative author—has arrived. He is here. He appears in the lists of the best publishers. He even breaks into the lists of the best-sellers. To the general American public he is a novelty, a strange phenomenon, a miracle straight out of the skies. Well, he *is* a novelty, but he is by no means a new thing.

The line of American Negro authors runs back for a hundred and fifty years, back to Phillis Wheatley, the poet. Since Phillis Wheatley there have been several hundred Negro authors who have written books of many kinds. But in all these generations down to within the past six years only seven or eight of the hundreds have ever been heard of by the general American public or even by the specialists in American literature. As many Negro writers have gained recognition by both in the past six years as in all the generations gone before. What has happened is that efforts which have been going on for more than a century are being noticed and appreciated at last, and that this appreciation has served as a stimulus to greater effort and output. America is aware today that there are such things as Negro authors. Several converging forces have been at work to produce this state of mind. Had these forces been at work three decades ago, it is possible that we then should have had a condition similar to the one which now exists.

Now that the Negro author has come into the range of vision of the American public eye, it seems to me only fair to point out some of the difficulties he finds in his way. But I wish to state emphatically that I have no intention

James Weldon Johnson, "The Dilemma of the Negro Author," *The American Mercury* 15, no. 60 (1928): 477–481. Reprinted by permission of the Estate of Grace and James Weldon Johnson.

of making an apology or asking any special allowances for him; such a plea would at once disqualify him and void the very recognition he has gained. But the Negro writer does face peculiar difficulties that ought to be taken into account when passing judgment upon him.

It is unnecessary to say that he faces every one of the difficulties common to all that crowd of demon-driven individuals who feel that they must write. But the Aframerican author faces a special problem which the plain American author knows nothing about—the problem of the double audience; it is a divided audience, an audience made up of two elements with differing and often opposite and antagonistic points of view. His audience is always both white America and black America. The moment a Negro writer takes up his pen or sits down to his typewriter he is immediately called upon to solve, consciously or unconsciously, this problem of the double audience. To whom shall he address himself, to his own black group or to white America? Many a Negro writer has fallen down, as it were, between these two stools.

It may be asked why he doesn't just go ahead and write and not bother himself about audiences. That is easier said than done. It is doubtful if anything with meaning can be written unless the writer has some definite audience in mind. His audience may be as far away as the angelic host or the rulers of darkness, but an audience he must have in mind. As soon as he selects his audience he immediately falls, where he wills it or not, under the laws which govern the influence of the audience upon the artist, laws that operate in every branch of art.

Now, it is axiomatic that the artist achieves his best when working at his best with the materials he knows best. And it goes without saying that the material which the Negro as a creative or general writer knows best comes out of the life and experience of the colored people in America. The overwhelming bulk of the best work done by Aframerican writers has some bearing on the Negro and his relations to civilization and society in the United States. Leaving authors, white or black, writing for coteries on special and technical subjects out of the discussion, it is safe to say that the white American author, when he sits down to write, has in mind a white audience—and naturally. The influence of the Negro as a group on his work is infinitesimal if not zero. Even when he talks about the Negro he talks to white people. But with the Aframerican author the case is different. When he attempts to handle his best known material he is thrown upon two, indeed, if it is permissible to say so, upon three horns of a dilemma. He must intentionally or unintentionally choose a black audience or a white audience or a combination of the two; and each of them presents peculiar difficulties.

If the Negro author selects white America as his audience he is bound to run up against many long-standing artistic conceptions about the Negro; against numerous conventions and traditions which through age have become binding; in a word, against a whole row of hard-set stereotypes which are not easily broken up. White America has some firm opinions as to what the Negro is, and consequently some pretty well fixed ideas as to what should be written about him, and how.

What is the Negro in the artistic conception of white America? In the brighter light, he is a simple, indolent, docile, improvident peasant; a singing, dancing, laughing, weeping child; picturesque beside his log cabin and in the snowy fields of cotton; naïvely charming with his banjo and his songs in the moonlight and along the lazy Southern rivers; a faithful, ever-smiling and genuflecting old servitor to the white folks of quality; a pathetic and pitiable figure. In a darker light, he is an impulsive, irrational, passionate savage, reluctantly wearing a thin coat of culture, sullenly hating the white man, but holding an innate and unescapable belief in the white man's superiority; an everlastingly alien and irredeemable element in the nation; a menace to Southern civilization; a threat to Nordic race purity; a figure casting a sinister shadow across the future of the country.

Ninety-nine one-hundredths of all that has been written about the Negro in the United States in three centuries and read with any degree of interest or pleasure by white America has been written in conformity to one or more of these ideas. I am not saying that they do not provide good material for literature; in fact, they make material for poetry and romance and comedy and tragedy of a high order. But I do say they have become stencils, and that the Negro author finds these stencils inadequate for the portrayal and interpretation of Negro life today. Moreover, when he does attempt to make use of them he finds himself impaled upon the second horn of his dilemma.

II

It is known that art—literature in particular, unless it be sheer fantasy—must be based on more or less well established conventions, upon ideas that have some roots in the general consciousness, that are at least somewhat familiar to the public mind. It is this that gives it verisimilitude and finality. Even revolutionary literature, if it is to have any convincing power, must start from a basis of conventions, regardless of how unconventional its objective may be. These conventions are changed by slow and gradual processes—except they be changed in a flash. The conventions held by white America regarding the Negro will be changed. Actually they are being changed, but they have not yet sufficiently changed to lessen to any great extent the dilemma of the Negro author.

It would be straining the credulity of white America beyond the breaking point for a Negro writer to put out a novel dealing with the wealthy class of colored people. The idea of Negroes of wealth living in a luxurious manner is still too unfamiliar. Such a story would have to be written in a burlesque vein to make it at all plausible and acceptable. Before Florence Mills and Josephine Baker implanted a new general idea in the public mind it would have been worse than a waste of time for a Negro author to write for white America the story of a Negro girl who rose in spite of all obstacles, racial and others, to a place of world success and acclaim on the musical revue stage. It would be proof of little less than supreme genius in a Negro poet for him to take one of the tragic characters in American Negro history—say Crispus Attucks or Nat Turner or Denmark Vesey—, put heroic language in his mouth and have white America accept the work as authentic. American Negroes as heroes form no part of white America's concept of the race. Indeed, I question if three out of ten of the white Americans who will read these lines know anything of either Attucks, Turner or Vesey; although each of the three played a rôle in the history of the nation. The Aframerican poet might take an African chief or warrior, set him forth in heroic couplets or blank verse and present him to white America with infinitely greater chance of having his work accepted.

But these limiting conventions held by white America do not constitute the whole difficulty of the Negro author in dealing with a white audience. In addition to these conventions regarding the Negro as a race, white America has certain definite opinions regarding the Negro as an artist, regarding the scope of his efforts. White America has a strong feeling that Negro artists should refrain from making use of white subject matter. I mean by that, subject matter which it feels belongs to the white world. In plain words, white America does not welcome seeing the Negro competing with the white man on what it considers the white man's own ground.

In many white people this feeling is dormant, but brought to the test it flares up, if only faintly. During his first season in this country after his European success a most common criticism of Roland Hayes was provoked by the fact that his programme consisted of groups of English, French, German and Italian songs, closing always with a group of Negro Spirituals. A remark frequently made was, "Why doesn't he confine himself to the Spirituals?"

This in face of the fact that no tenor on the American concert stage could surpass Hayes in singing French and German songs. The truth is that white America was not quite prepared to relish the sight of a black man in a dress suit singing French and German love songs, and singing them exquisitely. The first reaction was that there was something incongruous about it. It gave a jar to the old conventions and something of a shock to the Nordic superiority complex. The years have not been many since Negro players have dared to interpolate a love duet in a musical show to be witnessed by white people. The representation of romantic love-making by Negroes struck the white audience as somewhat ridiculous; Negroes were supposed to mate in a more primeval manner.

White America has for a long time been annexing and appropriating Negro territory, and is prone to think of every part of the domain it now controls as originally—and aboriginally—its own. One sometimes hears the critics in reviewing a Negro musical show lament the fact that it is so much like white musical shows. But a great deal of this similarity it would be hard to avoid because of the plain fact that two out of the four chief ingredients in the present day white musical show, the music and the dancing, are directly derived from the Negro. These ideas and opinions regarding the scope of artistic effort affect the Negro author, the poet in particular. So whenever an Aframerican writer addresses himself to white America and attempts to break away from or break through these conventions and limitations he makes more than an ordinary demand upon his literary skill and power.

At this point it would appear that a most natural thing for the Negro author to do would be to say, "Damn the white audience!" and devote himself to addressing his own race exclusively. But when he turns from the conventions of white America he runs afoul of the taboos of black America. He has no more absolute freedom to speak as he pleases addressing black America than he has in addressing white America. There are certain phases of life that he dare not touch, certain subjects that he dare not critically discuss, certain manners of treatment that he dare not use—except at the risk of rousing bitter resentment. It is quite possible for a Negro author to do a piece of work, good from every literary point of view, and at the same time bring down on his head the wrath of the entire colored pulpit and press, and gain among the literate element of his own people the reputation of being a prostitutor of his talent and a betrayer of his race—not by any means a pleasant position to get into.

This state of mind on the part of the colored people may strike white America as stupid and intolerant, but it is not without some justification and not entirely without precedent; the white South on occasion discloses a similar sensitiveness. The colored people of the United States are anomalously situated. They are a segregated and antagonized minority in a very large nation, a minority unremittingly on the defensive. Their faults and failings are exploited to produce exaggerated effects. Consequently, they have a strong feeling against exhibiting to the world anything but their best points. They feel that other groups may afford to do otherwise but, as yet, the Negro cannot. This is not to say that they refuse to listen to criticism of themselves, for they often listen to Negro speakers excoriating the race for its faults and foibles and vices. But these criticisms are not for the printed page. They are not for the ears or eyes of white America.

A curious illustration of this defensive state of mind is found in the Negro theatres. In those wherein Negro players give Negro performances for Negro audiences all of the Negro weaknesses, real and reputed, are burlesqued and ridiculed in the most hilarious manner, and are laughed at and heartily enjoyed. But the presence of a couple of dozen white people would completely change the psychology of the audience, and the players. If some of the performances so much enjoyed by strictly Negro audiences in Negro theatres were put on, say, in a Broadway theatre, a wave of indignation would sweep Aframerica from the avenues of Harlem to the canebrakes of Louisiana. These taboos of black America are as real and binding as the conventions of white America. Conditions may excuse if not warrant them; nevertheless, it is unfortunate that they exist, for their effect is blighting. In past years they have discouraged in Negro authors the production of everything but *nice* literature; they have operated to hold their work down to literature of the defensive, exculpatory sort. They have a restraining effect at the present time which Negro writers are compelled to reckon with.

This division of audience takes the solid ground from under the feet of the Negro writer and leaves him suspended. Either choice carries hampering and discouraging conditions. The Negro author may please one audience and at the same time rouse the resentment of the other; or he may please the other and totally fail to rouse the interest of the one. The situation, moreover, constantly subjects him to the temptation of posing and posturing for the one audience or the other; and the sincerity and soundness of his work are vitiated whether he poses for white or black.

The dilemma is not made less puzzling by the fact that practically it is an extremely difficult thing for the Negro author in the United States to address himself solely to either of these two audiences. If he analyzes what he writes he will find that on one page black America is his whole or main audience, and on the very next page white America. In fact, psychoanalysis of the Negro authors of the defensive and exculpatory literature, written in strict conformity to the taboos of black America, would reveal that they were unconsciously addressing themselves mainly to white America.

III

I have sometimes thought it would be a way out, that the Negro author would be on surer ground and truer to himself, if he could disregard white America; if he could say to white America, "What I have written, I have written. I hope you'll be interested and like it. If not, I can't help it." But it is impossible for a sane American Negro to write with total disregard for nine-tenths of the people of the United States. Situated as his own race is amidst and amongst them, their influence is irresistible.

I judge there is not a single Negro writer who is not, at least secondarily, impelled by the desire to make his work have some effect on the white world for the good of his race. It may be thought that the work of the Negro writer, on account of this last named condition, gains in pointedness what it loses in breadth. Be that as it may, the situation is for the time one in which he is inextricably placed. Of course, the Negro author can try the experiment of putting black America in the orchestra chairs, so to speak, and keeping white America in the gallery, but he is likely at any moment to find his audience shifting places on him, and sometimes without notice.

And now, instead of black America and white America as separate or alternating audiences, what about the combination of the two into one? That, I believe, is the only way out. However, there needs to be more than a combination, there needs to be a fusion. In time, I cannot say how much time, there will come a gradual and natural rapprochement of these two sections of the Negro author's audience. There will come a breaking up and remodelling of most of white America's traditional stereotypes, forced by the advancement of the Negro in the various phases of our national life. Black America will abolish many of its taboos. A sufficiently large class of colored people will progress enough and become strong enough to render a constantly sensitive and defensive attitude on the part of the race unnecessary and distasteful. In the end, the Negro author will have something close to a common audience, and will be about as free from outside limitations as other writers.

Meanwhile, the making of a common audience out of white and black America presents the Negro author with enough difficulties to constitute a third horn of his dilemma. It is a task that is a very high test for all his skill and abilities, but it can be and has been accomplished. The equipped Negro author working at his best in his best known material can achieve this end; but, standing on his racial foundation, he must fashion something that rises above race, and reaches out to the universal in truth and beauty. And so, when a Negro author does write so as to fuse white and black America into one interested and approving audience he has performed no slight feat, and has most likely done a sound piece of literary work.

PART 4

The Political Economy of Race

Introduction

Although there is a tendency to pay particular attention to the cultural work of the Harlem or New Negro Renaissance when one studies the African American experience between the world wars, it would be a mistake to overlook the very real political and economic circumstances that increasingly framed debates within black America. To be sure, the beginning of a worldwide economic depression, the election of Franklin Delano Roosevelt, and the establishment of the New Deal affected all Americans in significant ways. But concurrent with these dramatic structural shifts in society was an increased willingness by a new generation of African American scholars to examine the foundations of America's social order and to critique the efforts of previous cohorts of black intellectuals who also sought to analyze society. In this regard, perhaps, many black scholars of this generation were no different from many of their white counterparts: both expressed interest in the radical political and economic experiments in the Soviet Union and sympathized (openly or not) with the various strains of radicalism that were taking root in American soil.[1]

Leading the charge in articulating a new call for an understanding of United States racial politics was a cohort of intellectuals—many of them social scientists—who argued that a new biracial labor movement presented the best opportunity to improve blacks' daily condition. Race, for these young radicals, was a subjective phenomenon whose roots lay in economic and social structures. One of the leaders in advancing this new perspective was Abram Harris, an economist teaching at Howard University. He, along with figures like sociologists E. Franklin Frazier and Ira De A. Reid, political scientists Ralph Bunche and Emmett Dorsey, literary scholar Sterling Brown, and legal experts Louis Redding, William Hastie, and Charles Houston (all of whom, save Reid and Redding, were teaching at Howard in the early 1930s), articulated a consistent line during the interwar era that despaired of a romantic racialization among black and white scholars.

Harris (1899–1964) received his BA from Virginia Union in 1922 and almost immediately moved to New York City where he worked for the radical magazine the *Messenger* as well as the relatively moderate National Urban League (where he soon started serving as Charles Johnson's research assistant). In short order he received a masters in economics from the University of Pittsburgh and then became the executive director of the Minneapolis Urban League. The Midwest was not for Harris, however, and he soon returned to

New York City to pursue his doctorate in economics at Columbia. When he graduated in 1931 Harris had already been teaching at Howard for four years.[2] This brief sketch of his résumé is important for at least two reasons: it reminds us of how deeply involved social scientists were with organizations like the Urban League, and it allows us to reflect upon the extent to which Harris was a disciplinary groundbreaker, as he was the first African American to receive a doctorate in economics and then teach in higher education.[3] In this latter regard, Harris's exceptionalism is accompanied by an asterisk: Sadie T. M. Alexander took the PhD in economics a full decade before Harris but was unable to find a teaching position at a university. She became an assistant actuary with North Carolina Mutual Insurance Company before returning to school to get a law degree and pursuing a successful legal career.[4]

Among his African American social science peers, Harris may have been one of the most cosmopolitan at the same time that he was also one of the most mercurial. He was consistently aggressive in crossing the race line that too often kept black and white scholars apart. He befriended leading figures of the 1920s New York left, such as journalist Benjamin Stolberg and *New Masses* editor V. F. Calverton, and he never hesitated to voice to them his intense frustration with racial politics. Although at the start of his career he wrote almost exclusively on the relationship of blacks to labor, by the late 1920s he lamented the impression—a conviction to most—that blacks could only specialize on "black topics." Harris acted upon his lamentation a decade later when he turned his attention to economic philosophy for the remainder of his career.[5] Before he did that, however, Harris offered intellectual leadership to his peers who shared his frustration with the race bar and its many manifestations.

In 1933, the NAACP invited Harris, numerous other Howard faculty, and a sampling of young scholars and educators across the country to a summer conference dedicated to analyzing the organization's mission and direction. Du Bois, still the head of research for the NAACP, had urged the organization to hold this conference, but he could not have anticipated the hostile assessment many of the NAACP's young guests had of the civil rights group. Harris's economic determinism that shunned race conscious civil rights activism was embraced by fellow conferees like Bunche and Frazier. NAACP leaders disagreed with the assessment—Du Bois felt their ideas were an expression of the folly of youth—but a new voice had been heard and recognized.[6] Harris's "The Economic Foundations of American Race Division" is emblematic of the work spawned by the class-based orientation of this new generation of social scientists.

Frazier's "The Du Bois Program in the Present Crisis" is also emblematic of the new mentality embraced by many of these scholars. If one can look past Frazier's acerbic wit and critique of Du Bois's elitism—asserting, for example, that Du Bois would only assent to living in a black nation if he were annointed king—one will notice a commitment to a model of economic determinism as well as an insistence that older race romantics like Du Bois step aside. The final paragraph of Frazier's essay neatly summarizes both the critique and the claim that embody so much of the new social scientists' mentality as intellectual-activists. One sees here the critique that past leaders step aside due to their misguided and ineffective worldview and the claim that the new generation of scholars was prepared to carry the torch. Frazier writes: "The status of the race in America, which has been determined by those economic forces which have shaped the country at large, has remained unaffected by the programs of Negro leaders. [Booker T.] Washington's program of industrial education and scientific farming offered no more salvation than [Frederick] Douglass's naïve faith that the Republican Party was the ship and all else the sea. Nor can Du Bois, either as the intellectual or the romanticist, furnish the kind of social criticism which is needed today in order that the Negro may orient himself in the present state of American capitalism."[7]

But what of Du Bois? Was he really the outlier that Frazier cast him as? Did Frazier's assessment accurately reflect the extent to which Du Bois was a relic of an older race-first mentality? We find answers to some of these questions in Du Bois's "Social Planning for the Negro, Past and Present." Here we have an essay that speaks with many voices: the first voice is that of the revisionist historian who offers a new interpretation of Reconstruction. This section presents Du Bois as Marxist, evincing, like his younger social science peers, an economic model for understanding United States history.[8] The second voice is of the political historian who, with an astonishingly understated subjectivity, is able to parse through the histories of organizations like the Niagara Movement and the NAACP in which Du Bois himself played a founding role. Finally, in the last section of the essay we find the social scientist as political analyst when Du Bois brings the full force of his relatively new Marxist ideology to bear upon the contemporary moment and blacks' place within it.

Du Bois advocates a race-based consumer cooperative movement in "Social Planning" that welcomed segregation if that were the only means of advancing black Americans' cause and then, by example, inspiring a new global vision of humanity. This was a marked step away from the NAACP's faith in liberal democracy and civil rights legalism, and it signaled Du Bois's break with the organization. Regardless of those elements of the essay that appealed to the racial romantic that Harris and Frazier disdained, the fact that Du Bois's call for a new social planning appeared in a special issue of Howard University's *Journal of Negro Education* underscores the heightened attention being paid to the new political economy of race. This particular issue of the journal (January 1936) was comprised of a collection of papers given the previous year at a Howard conference. At that gathering, titled "The Position of the Negro in Our Current Economic Crisis," black and white liberals, progressives, and radicals from around the country came to the District of Columbia campus to participate in an examination of African American life in the midst of the Great Depression.

Aside from the fact that the conference caused an uproar that led to a federal investigation of "communistic activities" at the university, the gathering is noteworthy for the way in which it captured the progressive, politically active mentality articulated by the era's leading social scientists. In fact, a direct result of the conference was a call for a new organization that reflected the desire for a biracial workers' alliance. A year after the conference adjourned, the National Negro Congress (NNC) opened its founding convention in Chicago. The NNC was a quintessential organization of its political era. By endeavoring to create a coalition of moderates, liberals, socialists, and communists to fight a militarily powerful fascist movement, the NNC was true to the strategic thinking of what was known as the "Popular Front." Although he would split from the organization a few years after its establishment due to his conviction that it had been taken over by the Communist Party, Ralph Bunche played a leading role in the formation of the NNC and of the Howard conference that led to its birth.

An Africanist by training, Bunche (1903–1971) presented a paper at the conference that focused on the domestic transgressions of capitalism (as is noted in the next section, Bunche also paid attention to the international transgressions of capitalism). Those who are accustomed to remembering Bunche as an international mediator for the United Nations and the consummate diplomat will be surprised to find the stridency of Bunche's critique. The New Deal, Bunche argued, was "suspended in mid-air, bewildered, and innocuous," the ideology of which was "illogical, inconsistent, vague, and confused."[9]

A close friend of Harris and Frazier, Bunche was one of the leaders of Howard's Social Science Division as well as the founder and chair of its department of political science. For the decade that all three scholars were together at Howard they formed the most important nucleus of social science expertise on the race question. As was the case with Harris and Frazier, the scholarly foundation for Bunche's later social science work was laid at a leading white research university, Harvard, in Bunche's case. When Bunche received his PhD in 1934 he was the first African American to earn the doctorate in political science anywhere in the country. (He received his BA from UCLA in 1927.) Bunche had been teaching at Howard for several years by the time he received his doctorate and he spent much of the 1930s struggling to balance his research needs with his teaching load, service to the university, and a commitment to social, political, and economic justice movements in the United States.[10] Toward the end of the decade Bunche began consulting for organizations as diverse as the Republican Party and the Carnegie Corporation (specifically for its *An American Dilemma* project run by Gunnar Myrdal). By the 1940s, Bunche's teaching career was essentially over as he took extended leaves to work as the senior social science analyst for the Office of Strategic Services (the precursor to the CIA), the State Department, and then the newly formed United Nations. Bunche went through his own evolution in this process, moving from political progressivism to a more sphinxlike public political quietism, but even in this move he embodied the formalization of a critical role for the social scientist: professional consultant. And as the country lurched toward the civil rights battles of the 1950s and beyond, these social science experts began to play an increasingly central role in providing strategy and leveling critiques.

Before that transition, however, Bunche and colleagues like fellow Howard political scientist Emmett Dorsey were quite open about their progressive politics and their insistence upon a class-based understanding of the American social system. Little is known about Dorsey beyond the fact that he taught at Howard for a while and was an eager participant in numerous campus- and community-based protests for desegregation and a federal anti-lynching law. He also attended the 1933 NAACP conference that ushered in a new generation of intellectual-activists that sought to distance itself from the civil libertarianism of the old guard. Dorsey was firmly in the Harris camp on these issues and even concluded his contribution to the Howard conference on the New Deal with a point-by-point delineation of the economic plan that Harris had proposed the NAACP pursue. Although his star did not shine as brightly as that of his Howard colleagues and those at other institutions, Dorsey captured the worldview of his generation of social science progressives when he offered the following assessment of how race should be properly read into American history: "The ills of American capitalism are systemic and organic. Palliatives turn into an infection of reaction. The only correctives feasible are ones which are basic and fundamental. The economic plight of the American Negro is that of the American working class. Our economic problem differs in degree, not in kind. Our special disabilities are organically related to our class exploitation."[11]

NOTES

1. See Robert Cohen, *When the Old Left Was Young: Student Radicals and America's First Mass Student Movement, 1919–1941* (New York: Oxford University Press, 1993); Alan Wald, *Exiles from a Future Time: The Forging of the Mid-Twentieth Century Literary Left* (Chapel Hill: University of North Carolina Press, 2002), and *The New York Intellectuals: The Rise and Decline of the Anti-Stalinist Left from the 1930s to the 1980s* (Chapel Hill: University of North Carolina Press, 1987).

2. Augustus Low and Virgil Clift, eds., *The Encyclopedia of Black America* (New York: McGraw-Hill, 1981), 419; Harry Washington Greene, *Holders of Doctorates Among American Negroes* (Boston: Meador, 1946), 61.

3. A case in point here is the career of George E. Haynes, who received his PhD in 1912 from Columbia University in social economy and who helped establish the National Urban League. Greene, *Holders of Doctorates*, 62.

4. Francille Rusan Wilson, "'All of the Glory . . . Faded . . . Quickly': Sadie T. M. Alexander and Black Professional Women, 1920–1950," in *Sister Circle: Black Women and Work*, ed. Sharon Harley et al. (New Brunswick, N.J.: Rutgers University Press, 2002), 164–167.

5. Harris did publish once more on the African American experience, an article titled "Education and the Economic Status of the Negro in the United States" for a 1964 anthology called *100 Years of Emancipation*. This posthumously published essay was a screed that attacked blacks who were unable to compete in the open marketplace, dismissed concerns about abiding racism, and accepted uncritically arguments about black family pathology. For more on Harris see Jonathan Scott Holloway, *Confronting the Veil: Abram Harris Jr., E. Franklin Frazier, and Ralph Bunche, 1919–1941* (Chapel Hill: University of North Carolina Press, 2002); Abram Harris Jr., *Race, Radicalism, and Reform: Selected Papers*, ed. William Darity Jr. (New Brunswick, N.J.: Transaction Publishers, 1989); and James O. Young, *Black Writers of the Thirties* (Baton Rouge: Louisiana State University Press, 1973).

6. Holloway, *Confronting the Veil*, 4–16.

7. E. Franklin Frazier, "The Du Bois Program in the Present Crisis," *Race* 1 (Winter 1935–1936): 13.

8. Du Bois's *Black Reconstruction* appeared the same year as this essay. His revisioning of Reconstruction in the essay, then, is a distillation of the main themes of his magisterial book.

9. Ralph J. Bunche, "A Critique of New Deal Social Planning as it Affects Negroes," *Journal of Negro Education* 5, no. 1 (1936): 59.

10. Holloway, *Confronting the Veil*, 157–163.

11. Emmett E. Dorsey, "The Negro and Social Planning," *Journal of Negro Education* 5, no. 1 (1936): 108.

ABRAM L. HARRIS

Economic Foundations of American Race Division

The apologetic school of American race relations considers the social distance[1] between white and black Americans as conforming to a natural order of pre-ordained and inescapable physical, mental and moral differences between different branches of the human species. And according to the philosophy of this school, the abridgment of social distance is undertaken only at the penalty of provoking inherent racial antipathy; the price of social peace being the maintenance of mutually exclusive worlds of racial habitation characterized by reciprocal racial tolerance. The fatalism which runs through this viewpoint hinges upon a belief in well established race differences upon which race prejudice is believed to be based, and, the corresponding conviction that the only way to lessen the belliose manifestations of race prejudice is by rendering wholesale contact between members of each race impossible.

Assuming as the above argument does that American Negroes and whites are distinguishable by marked dissimilarities in physiognomy, mentality and social traditions, and that whatever hostility exists between the races arises from an aversion to these differences, the only means by which antipathy can be eradicated is the very association and intimacy which the apologists shun. Social experience substantiates this.

"There must be something," said Livingstone,[2] "in the appearance of white men frightfully repulsive to the unsophisticated natives of Africa, for on entering villages previously unvisited by Europeans, if we met a child com-

Abram L. Harris, "Economic Foundations of American Race Division," *Social Forces* 5 (March, 1927): 468–478. Reprinted with permission of *Social Forces*.

ing quietly and unsuspectingly toward us the moment he raised his eyes and saw the men in 'bags' he would take to his heels in an agony of terror, such as we might feel if we met a live Egyptian mummy at the door of the British Museum. Alarmed by the child's wild outcries, the mother rushes out of the hut but darts back again at first glimpse of the fearful apparition. Dogs turn tails and scurry off in dismay, and hens, abandoning their chickens, fly screaming to the top of the houses." Here we have the elements of race prejudice. On the negative side, the stigmata of race prejudice are the feelings of wonder at the strange, fear of that which is unknown, and repulsion aroused in one individual by another who differs in physical features or cultural traits; and, on the positive side, they are contempt for and hate and hostility toward others who differ in these respects. But if race prejudice is not accompanied with competitive activities or the subjugation of one group by the other it is soon removed through association. And the accommodation of groups and individuals to others of different physiognomy and aesthetic standards takes place with relative ease. According to Livingstone, after one has associated with the blacks for a long period, "one feels ashamed of the white skin. It seems unnatural like blanched celery or white mice."[3] And Stanley's report of his feelings on first meeting white men after crossing Africa coincides with Livingstone's. He said: "As I looked into their faces, I blushed that I was wondering at their paleness. . . . The pale color after so long gazing on rich black and richer bronze, had something of an unaccountable ghastliness. I could not divest myself of the feeling that they must be sick."[4]

Does the foregoing analysis cast much light on the causes of race antipathy in the United States? Not very much, if any. In the first place the association between whites and blacks has been and is today more intimate than either the race-conscious white or black citizenry is willing to admit. Not only have white boys and girls kissed their black mammies but have been suckled by them. It is not infrequent that leading persons in the white race, desiring to impress audiences with their devotion to the Negro race, cite as evidence of fidelity their recognition of some unpaid debt to an "old darkey" friend or to a black mammy who was their wet nurse. Moreover the existence of a large mulatto population is evidence of a very intimate physical contact which could not have taken place had dominant whites, the aggressors, been repelled by the Negro's physical appearance; and conversely, whatever race prejudice arose from the introduction of Negroes in America was soon lost through sex relations and other close association. In the second place the present antipathy cannot be attributed to a difference in social traditions and aesthetic standards, since the life of the Negro in the United States bespeaks knowledge of only those cultural traditions that are American. It is not infrequent that the economic and social subjugation of one race or class by another has led the subordinated group to adopt the culture of the dominant. This has happened to the Negro in the United States. If the first African Negroes who came to America brought with them concepts of social institutions or a culture typically African they could not put them to practice in America. Moreover, we have no evidence of any attempts made by Negroes to establish African culture in the United States. Nor can the American Negro be considered in any logical sense African. The assimilation of the Negro to American culture has been so complete that one observer has remarked: "With most marvelous certainty, when we consider the conditions, the Negro in the South could be trusted to perpetuate our political ideas and institutions if our republic fell, as surely as the Gaul did his adopted institutions."[5] This cultural accommodation and above all the physical contact which preceded and paralleled it, could have but one effect upon the Negro—the annihilation of a Negro national physiognomy—and, in consequence, the Negro's repudiation of African aesthetic standards. The ready market which sellers of bleaching and hair straightening compounds find among Negroes indicates the extent of this repudiation. But a surging race consciousness among Negroes which has expressed itself in art and other forms may seem to belie the repudiation of African aesthetic standards, or it may be mistaken as the Negro's attempt to establish a Negro culture within the United States. Considerable controversy has centered about the question of Negro culture as a product distinct from United States culture.[6] But close examination of the social facts underlying the Negro's position in the United States shows his race consciousness to be merely a device which he has contrived to compensate his thwarted ambition for full participation in American institutions. Thus, neither cultural differences nor the horror of the Negro's external aspect account for present race antipathy in the United States. Racial antipathy in the United States cannot, therefore, be attributed to race prejudice. Some other explanation must be sought.

Slavery was an economic system which involved white freemen as masters and black men as slaves. The Negro was not enslaved because his complexion, and nose and lip formation differed from the white man's.[7] It would be just as reasonable to assign the servitude of white serfs to the color of their skin which conformed in paleness to that of the dominant whites. As a matter of fact both the lower white and black classes were weak. Their impotence coupled with the need for cheap labor meant their subjugation. For a short period white and black bondsmen were on the same indefinite legal footing. And it did not at first seem that the institution of serfdom and, later, slavery could thrive in colonial United States. Several of the colonies actually opposed the purchase of Negroes and the dumping of expatriated Europeans and prisoners upon American soil. Serfdom was mild as compared with slavery into which it developed. In 1661, there seemed to have been the absence of any law or custom which established the institution of slavery. The court records of Virginia, for example, refers to Negroes as servants and not as slaves.[8] Like the white servants the Negro became free at the expiration of their indentures. Many freed Negroes of the colonial period acquired property in slaves and land. But conditions did not long remain rosy. The chains of chattel slavery which were to bind the Negro were already being forged in the South at the anvil of economic necessity. Meanwhile industrial conditions in the New England and Middle States were slowly working the transformation of white serfs into wage-earners.

The supply of Negro labor was more plentiful than white labor. It was also more easily secured, and consequently, cheaper than the latter. Negro labor being cheaper than cheap white labor was more desired. Emmanuel Downing wrote his brother-in-law, John Winthrop: "You know verie well how we shall mayntayne 20 Moores cheaper than one English servant."[9] During the same period Negroes in the South not bound for a term were coming to be appraised as high as thirty pounds while the most valuable white redemptioners were worth not above fifteen pounds.[10] Because of the increasing significance of Negro labor to the germinating agricultural system in the South and the diminishing importance of it to budding domestic capitalism in the North, the thrifty New Englanders found it profitable to capture Indians, exchange them for Negroes, and sell the Negroes to the southern planters.[11] These were the faint murmurs of the régime which the rise of the southern tobacco, *cotton*, rice and sugar plantations would crystallize through successive legal enactments. The invention of the cotton gin by Eli Whitney in 1793 gave impetus to cotton culture. A great cotton kingdom arose extending from the uplands and covering the alluvial plains of the southwest. Before the cotton gin was invented the sale of a Negro rarely brought more than $300 but afterwards the price was twice as high. The average value of a Negro was $800 in 1830, $1200 in 1850 and from $1400 to $2000 in 1860.[12] The invention of the cotton gin made slavery more profitable now than ever; and the anti-slavery agitation which was sprouting in the South was stifled. On the other hand, New England's barrenness made extensive agriculture and slavery futile undertakings. However, its indented coast line enabled it to build a commercial and shipping enterprise which supplied the South with Negro labor; and its favorable position for manufacture developed a domestic capitalism which wrought the metamorphosis of disadvantaged white men from serfs to wage earners. These conditions determined the rise of bourgeois democracy based upon economic competition and individualism in the North and of landed aristocracy based upon slavery and custom in the South.

Slavery was a profitable institution to the landed class who desired to perpetuate it and to extend its geographical limits and the political power based upon it. Like every economic system based upon the exploitation of human labor, the slave régime sought rationalization for its exploitation of Negroes. Slavery was therefore designated by the whites to be God's way of educating ignorant blacks and bringing them into the marvelous light of His gospel. The literature which grew in this period reveals much talk on the Negro's natural unfitness for civilization, his inhumanity and his uneducability. Charles Carroll wrote a book and established from biblical texts that man was created in the image of God, and, since, as everyone knows God not to be a Negro, it follows that the Negro is not a man. John C. Calhoun, at a time when Negro slaves were everywhere by intention deprived of the elements of education, ventured that if he could find a Negro capable of giving the syntax of a Greek verb he would be disposed to call him human. Thomas Jefferson observed that a Negro could scarcely be found who was capable of tracing and comprehending the investigation of Euclid.[13] These and similar dogmas on the Negro's predisposition to crime and his lack of sexual restraint furnished by clergy and learned doctors established the psychological breastworks of the slave empire.

On the other hand, the attitude of the landed aristocracy to the white peasant and artisan was hardly better than that exhibited toward the Negro. Negro slaves were usually much better off materially than the submerged whites. This contrast in material lot undoubtedly inflamed the lower white stratum against the Negro and rendered the Negro contemptuous of it. Yet an ill founded fear of seditious combination between outnumbering Negro slaves and landless whites led the dominant whites to foster and augment race distinctions just as many modern employers maintain a definite proportion of representatives of different races and nationalities as a bulwark against labor organization and as others, more ruthless, exploit race antipathy upon the theory of *divide et impera*. That this fear was something of a plaguing nightmare Thomas Jefferson testified by his references to the landless whites in the South, the growing mass of propertyless wage-earners in the towns, and Negro slavery which he said made him tremble with anxiety when he contemplated the future of his country. Foremost among the distinctions initiated by the dominant whites was the statute against marriages between white and black. Massachusetts prohibited white and black marital unions as early as 1680.[14] The prohibition against intermarriage soon became the rule in all of the colonies although no laws were ever enacted against the cohabitation of white masters with black female slaves. The running away of white servants in company with Negroes must have occurred frequently, else Virginia in 1661 would never have enacted a statute penalizing white servants guilty of this offense.[15] Suggestion and imitation did their share in further promoting hostility between the lower classes. To the master class the landless white was "po' white trash" and the Negro slave "nigger." Each of the disadvantaged classes seized the counter-appellation invented by the aristocrat out of its contempt for it and arrogantly hurled it back at the other. Under this growing race sentiment revolutionary coalition between the Negro slaves and whites serfs need never have been feared; and if not actually feared it was only because submerged blacks and whites in their weakness and arrogance toward each other could be pitted one against the other. Mutual animosity between poor whites and black slaves was strengthened by the competition offered by free Negro artisans in the northern and southern cities and by slave apprentices who upon being let to contractors were used to beat down wages.[16] The degree to which slavery was opposed by white workingmen, especially immigrants, is revealed in the opposition of eighty German newspapers to the opening up of new federal territory to possible slave settlement by the Kansas-Nebraska Act.[17] But the opposition to slavery which emanated from the Northwest and the eastern wage-earners was caused by their recognition of a fundamental antagonism of interest between the slavery system and free labor rather than by their humanitarism. As a matter of fact the northern wage-earners were as hostile to Negro freemen as to the slaves. The mobbing of Negroes was quite a common occurrence in the northern and middlewestern cities during the pre-civil war period.[18]

Upon the slave régime the social relationship of the white man and Negro in the United States was founded. It was the relationship of master and servant. The traditions which were its psychological props did not wholly disappear after the dissolution of the slave régime.[19] The white man's divine right to rule and exploit, and the Negro's divine heritage to hue wood and draw water for the master in the big house are sacrosanct traditions which the régime bequeathed to our not incredulous generation. Yet it should be obvious that the caste psychology which was built around white masters as the "exalted of God" differed very little from that of the ancient theocracy in which Jews were "Jahweh's elect;" or from that of feudalism wherein serfs were bitches and trollopes and, humble handicraftsmen, the lineal ancestors of modern capitalists, might have their ears boxed by offended patricians; or from that of the contemporary plutocracy which has raised up a host of panegyrists to extol the virtues of those who rule by divine right of superior chromosomes. Nor should it not be equally discernible to our generation that a past economic circumstance fashioned a psychology which sets in contemporary society the limits of racial association and determines its mental norms. One observer in noting this psychology points out: "The especially caste nature of the division—as distinguished from those personal differences which democratic tradition recognizes—is seen in the feeling, universal among the whites, that the Negro must be held apart and subordinate not merely as an individual, or any number of individuals, but as a race, a social whole. That is, the fact that many individuals of this race are equal, and some superior, to the majority of whites does not, in the opinion of the latter, make it just or expedient to treat them apart from the mass of their race. To dine with a Negro, to work or play by his side, or to associate in any relation where superiority cannot be asserted is held to be degrading and of evil example, no matter what kind of Negro he may be. It is the practice and policy of the dominant race to impress upon the Negro that he belongs by birth to a distinct order out of which he can in no way depart. There or nowhere must he find his destiny. If he wishes to mingle with whites it must be as an acknowledged inferior."[20] Thus agitation against segregation and jim crowism come to be interpreted by the dominant whites as advocacy of intermarriage or "social equality" as it is more euphemistically called in the South. Social equality is not taboo because of any abhorrence to blackness, as we have already noticed, but because social approval of mixed marriages would mean guaranteeing to members of each race equal protection and rights in their sex relations. To do this would be to recognize Negroes as equals. But society demands that the Negro's social and economic infirmity be maintained. Rather than permit equality between the races, it is thought best to leave the males of the dominant race unfettered by law and custom in their relations with women of the lower race and to lynch Negroes who look with lust in their eyes upon white women. When such suggestion as "Negroes prefer being to themselves" is ineffective in keeping obstreperous Negroes in "their place" the more drastic methods of segregation and jim crowism are invoked. Even though an inviolate and sacred institution, segregation may be temporarily suspended in the case of the Negro servant who accompanies his master or his master's children on public carriers.

In none of the foregoing phenomena does color serve as the basis of racial antipathy as much as it does the means by which a socially submerged class is distinguished from a dominant. The antipathy between white and black bears all of the earmarks of class prejudice which has been rationalized in justification of the exploitation and subjugation of the Negro. As a result of this a whole crop of ideas have been shaped into a Negro stereotype to which the public reacts. For example, the author has been very often told that Negroes make excellent domestics and personal servants because of their affection and slowness to insult but that their mentality is such that one could never trust them with technical processes in industry. Again in matters of health, the Negro is viewed with pitying fatalism. The Negro's high mortality is attributed to the fact that he is a Negro. In other words, the fact that Negro mortality is higher than that of the white is believed to be the resultant of a difference in organic structure which lessens the Negro's chances for survival in rigorous climates. To race and not to environic factors such as inadequate and poor housing, and insufficient income is the high mortality of the Negro attributed.

The extent to which these opinions are prevalent is ascertainable. The author prepared a questionnaire on race relations and submitted it to 144 prominent white persons selected at random. Two questions in the schedule read: "What distinguishing traits of mentality or character do you believe Negroes to possess?" and "On what facts, authorities or sources of information do you base your opinions?" The table that follows is a summary of 37 replies. Column 1 in the table gives "the kind of contact or observations" subjects had. Column 2 gives "the distinguishing traits" which Negroes are believed to possess.

Underlying the whole maze of assumptions on Negro mental and character differences is the opinion actually stated in one of the replies: "*The Negro and white man are physiologically, mentally and morally different.*" It is but one step from this dogma to another belief which was stated by a social service worker: "*The average Negro's capacity for loyalty exceeds the white man's but the average white man excels the average Negro in drive, persistence and punctuality.*" Now capacity implies potentiality which is a factor in heredity. To say that one individual or that one race has greater capacity than another for loyalty as against persistence or punctuality is to say that these traits are hereditary in that individual or race. It is not to be doubted, however, that the social environment in which the Negro has lived and that in which the white man has lived has made for the development of loyalty in the former and for the development of punctuality and drive in the latter. Contrast the traits of temperament fostered by a world of competitive business enterprise with those that are not only encouraged, but actually enforced by a social status which demands submissiveness and which until recently existed apart from modern industry and its cultural accompaniments. If there is racial capacity for punctuality, loyalty and persistence these traits inhere in the chromosomes, are transmissible and, are, therefore, not due to nurture. If, on the other hand, they do not inhere in germplasm they are not transmissible and one race does not have any greater capacity than another for the expression of such traits. The known traits that are hereditary include neither punctuality nor loyalty nor persistence.[21]

From contact with Negro servants and with a limited number of Negro school children *instability of character, superstitiousness, laziness, irresponsibility, moral laxity, mental inferiority, unreliability, naïveté, emotionalism, and incapacity for sustained mental effort* are deduced as *negroid traits by 9 out of a total of 18 persons.* Not only is this association which was restricted to servants inadequate as a logical basis for judging the mentality of Negroes as a race, but the conclusions based upon this limited contact are contradicted by the experience of 7 other persons who had employed Negroes; by that of 1 who knew Negroes intimately; and by that of another who taught Negroes in college and had associated with intellectual Negroes. None of the latter 9 persons had discovered mental differences or could distinguish between Negroes and other people of little training and opportunity.

The second main classification "Scientific Experimentation and Study" comprises 9 persons, mainly college teachers, whose opinions were based almost wholly upon scientific studies, having themselves either administered mental tests to Negroes or studied the literature on racial and individual differences of mentality, and, the general anthropological and statistical theory involved in the subject. This classification may be roughly sub-divided under the three following headings:

1. Those who from scientific study found no distinguishable traits of mentality among Negroes;

2. Those who found distinguishable mental traits and believed them to be racial and inherent; and

3. Those who found mental differences but attributed them to social environment rather than to heredity and race.

In the first class there was only one person; in the second there were five; and in the third there were 3 persons—a wide variety of opinion among college professors and teachers all of whose opinions were based upon almost identical scientific data.

The opinions outlined above pass as legal tender on "Race." They have gained wide currency, first, by the fabrication of fictions on Negro character and mentality; second, by the crystallization of these fictions into dogmas of racial, biological and psychological superiority and inferiority in justification of the *status quo;* third, by the constant exploitation of these dogmas by certain investigators whenever race difference has furnished easy explanation of phenomena, which, while readily lending themselves to an interpretation on the basis of race, have been shown by later less subjective inquiry to be caused

A Tabulation of Observed Opinions on Racial Difference

(1) Kind or Contract or Observation upon which Judgment of Traits of Negroes Was Based	(2) Distinguishing Mental or Character Traits which Negroes Are Believed to Possess
I. Personal Contact 1. With Negro servants	1. Mentality fair; loyal to friends and industrious. 2. No traits of mentality that are distinguishable. 3. Superstitious, lazy, untrustworthy and greedy. 4. Not stable in character. Some Negro characters of the older generation were loyal friends.
2. With Negro servants and students	1. Irresponsibility; not the same moral standards or values as white race. 2. Traits of character rather than of mentality; interested in concrete rather than abstract things. 3. Inability of average to rise above mental or moral level of children. There are of course striking exceptions.
3. Negro School Children and Students and Race Leaders	1. Emotional; follow the course of Students and Race Leaders least resistance; not inclined to be strict observers of the law. 2. No traits of mentality as far as I can tell. Some traits of temperament, not well determined, such as interest in music. When given the same environment possessed by persons of other races the Negro develops the same way and manifests the same traits.
4. Personal observations of Negroes and acquaintance with them as clients and associates in law, medicine, social work and in the ministry	1. All the traits that a white man has. The Negro is free from rancor, naturally, because of lack of training. *As a race* they have not the power of sustained mental effort and concentration or analysis. 2. Some few Negroes show mentality equal to white man. The Negro is simple, imaginative and optimistic. 3. Not certain that there are any traits of mentality or character which are soley the possession of Negroes or whites. The average Negro is more courteous, fonder of the finer graces of life, and, on the whole more kindly and cheerful in adversity than the average white person. The Negro's capacity for loyalty exceeds the white man's; the average white man excels the average Negro in drive, persistence and punctuality.

(*1*) Kind or Contract or Observation upon which Judgment of Traits of Negroes Was Based	(*2*) Distinguishing Mental or Character Traits which Negroes Are Believed to Possess
	4. Emotional and unreliable.
	5. All of the traits that other races possess.
	6. No distinguishable traits.
	7. Cannot distinguish between Negroes and other people of little training and opportunity. They are loyal and improvident.
	8. Physically, mentally and morally the Negro race is quite different from the white race. When these differences are thoroughly understood by both races their relations are amicable. But the intermarriage of any black and white is disastrous to both races.
II. Scientific Experimentation and Study	
1. General reading of anthropological and statistical theory and summaries of Army Mental Tests and treatises by Galton, Pearson, etc., on individual and racial differences	1. Generally supposed to average less in intelligence and mentality than white.
	2. No traits of any absolutely distinguishable character. Am fairly convinced that the Negro is less intelligent than white. I am prepared to believe that emotional and artistic talent may be superior in Negroes.
	3. The average mental power of Negroes I should not consider as high as that of the white race. Their character I believe not to be stable. I am inclined to think that they are impelled to action by emotions and not inhibited by conventions as much as white people.
	4. Opinions are not blanket ones applied to whole group indiscriminately. In one sense the Negro possesses the same mental and character traits as all other races. In a quantitative sense they are on the average of limited "academic intelligence" although individual Negroes are found all along the scale from idiots to near genius. There is no reason to suppose *a priori* that they are any different from other races in capacity to be socialized, hence good citizens with proper training.
	5. None in kind; all in degree. There is probably more feeblemindedness among Negroes; less education and culture; less training in business and in ethics; less experience in adjustment. I do not believe these traits to be *inherited*. They are merely the result of environment and opportunity.

(1) *Kind or Contract or Observation* *upon which Judgment of Traits* *of Negroes Was Based*	*(2)* *Distinguishing Mental or Character* *Traits which Negroes Are* *Believed to Possess*
	6. Inferior mentally. Not all. I recall at least 4 of possibly a hundred who surpassed many of their white fellows.
2. Personal Application of Mental Tests	1. As a class the Negro is of lower mental rank than white. Morality is less well founded than that of white.
	2. It has not been proved that there are qualitative differences; apparently good evidence that in general intellectual ability Negroes as a whole are somewhat inferior to American white people. Of course, there is much over-lapping in the range of mentality, many Negroes excelling whites in intelligence.
	3. All traits that are and would be possessed by individuals in similar environment. They do not vary innately from any other race as far as my knowledge goes. Psychological testing has never established its ability to test innate capacity.
III. General Reading and Observation 1. History, literature, and immigration and related sociological sources	1. Docility, joviality, indolence. Not impressed with mentality of Negro students.
	2. Mentality below that of average.
	3. There are some limitations to mental development believed by psychologists to be racial. But the arrestive power of limited opportunity and economic handicap has not as yet been determined. Supposed to be light hearted, improvident and fond of clothes, kindly and generous.
2. Slight observation and information from others interested in subject	1. Highly emotional.
	2. Joyousness and disposition to conform.
IV. No Contact or Experience of Consequence	1. Do not know of distinguishing mental or character traits (5 replies)

by factors more social than racial; and above all, by the popularization of these things through press, pulpit, school and other media of popular education until racial fictions gain general acceptance and become intrenched social habit which by verbalization is translated into a public opinion on the Negro. This public opinion is not wholly the contemporary mind's creation; it is a part of American heritage on race. It persists although the more flagrant aspects of its economic determinants have been obliterated. Its universality is felt in the arrangements of almost every social institution. Even in the labor movement color-caste feeling has determined the degree and manner of Negro affiliation. And the logic which teaches that the ultimate interests of socially disadvantaged whites and blacks are more coincidental than that of white capitalists and white wage-earners or of black capitalists and black wage-earners has not convinced either American white workers or Negroes of its soundness as the American Federation of Labor's policy relative to the organization of Negro workers exemplifies. Aside from the operation of peculiar economic forces within the Federation to which should be ascribed its oscillating attitude toward the organization of Negroes, is the fact that the proletariat just as the bourgeoisie cuts its social cloth according to tradition-pattern.[22]

Another sidelight on the universality of the popular Negro stereotype is the opinions of the psychologists reflected in main classification II in the foregoing table. The psychologists are probably not entirely immune to its unconscious influence, despite their maturing habit of academic objectivity. An analysis of the mental tests and the judgment of Negro mentality based upon them, seems to reveal a prescience for discovering Negro inferiority. Nevertheless, Negro inferiority is Negro inferiority no matter by whom invented. For all of the labyrinthal technology western civilization has put at our disposal, we have done little more than confirm the pronouncements of Jefferson, Carroll, Calhoun and the rest of the sages of democracy who consigned the Negro to a menial station in American life.

NOTES

1. Social distance is defined by Dr. Emory Bogardus as the grades and degrees of understanding, feeling and intimacy that persons experience regarding each other. It charts the character of their social relations. Vid. "Social Distance and Its Origin," E. S. Bogardus, *Journal of Applied Sociology,* January, 1925.

2. Livingstone, *The Zambesi and its Tributaries,* p. 181.

3. Op. cit., p. 379.

4. Stanley, *Through the Dark Continent,* p. 462.

5. George Burton Adams, *Civilization during the Middle Ages,* p. 30.

6. See the very able article by George Schuyler, "The Negro Art Hokum," in *The Nation,* June 16, 1926, and Langston Hughes' reply in the June 23 issue. In *Opportunity* for August, Charles S. Johnson writes a discriminating editorial on the points of view advanced by Messrs. Hughes and Schuyler. Equally stimulating are the current discussions in the *Crisis* beginning January 1926 on "The Negro in Art—How Should He be Portrayed?" and J. Milton Sampson's brilliant essay "Race Consciousness and Race Relations," *Opportunity,* May, 1923.

7. Blacks assisted in conducting the slave traffic. In 1772, the state of Georgia issued a certificate to a certain Fenda Lawrence reciting that she [was] "a free black woman and heretofore a considerable trader in the river Gamba on the coast of Africa hath voluntarily come to be and remain for some time in this province" and giving her permission to "pass and repass unmolested within the said province on her lawful and necessary occasions." U. B. Phillips, *American Negro Slavery,* p. 20.

8. U. B. Phillips, *op. cit.* p. 73.

9. Ibid.

10. Ibid. p. 76.

11. Ibid., Chapt. VI.

12. Faulkner, *American History,* pp. 224–225.

13. Charles S. Johnson, "Public Opinion and the Negro," *Opportunity,* July, 1923.

14. U. B. Phillips, p. 103.

15. Ibid., p. 76.

16. See Commons and Associates, The Documentary History of American Industrial Society.

17. See A. M. Schlesinger, *New Viewpoints in American History,* p. 12.

18. Vid. *Life and Times of Frederick Douglass,* Part I, Chap. 20, and Part II, Chap. 5. Also *The New York Riots.*

19. As a legal institution slavery disappeared. The plantation system upon which the slave empire was based remained intact and what was slavery often became peonage. During the past decade the South has been experiencing an economic revolution. The penetration of large capital and industry will revolutionize the South's political and social institutions as greatly as it will the Negro's position. Economic and industrial changes continue to pull and push the Negro from the farms to the cities. Already the transformation of the Negro from a peasant into an industrial wage earner is rapidly taking place. The Negro migrations are the means of this accomplishment.

20. C. H. Cooley, *Social Organization,* p. 218.

21. Vid. John Langdon-Davies for list of traits that respond to Mendelian law, *The New Age of Faith,* p. 209.

22. Vid. "A White and Black World in American Labor and Politics" Abram L. Harris, SOCIAL FORCES, December 1925. Also, "Negro Labor's Quarrel with White Workingmen," Abram L. Harris, *Current History,* September 1926.

E. FRANKLIN FRAZIER

The Du Bois Program in the Present Crisis

Since Emancipation, three outstanding Negro leaders have played the role of making articulate the changing phases of the Negro's philosophy of adjustment to American life. Frederick Douglass, who, prior to the Civil War, was a fiery anti-slavery orator, became the uncompromising defender of the Negro's right to full participation in American civilization. Just as Douglass died, Booker T. Washington rose to fame as the author of the formula for resolving the conflict between the whites and blacks in the South and as the hope of the disillusioned masses who had seen the concrete fruits of freedom snatched from them. But scarcely had Washington entered upon the stage with his preachments on thrift and humility, when W. E. Burghardt DuBois, representing the educated Negro elite—or Talented Tenth as he called them—began his bitter attacks. With scathing pen and in brilliant style he tore the rags of hypocrisy from the northern white philanthropists who supported Washington; he castigated the savagery of southern poor whites and the hollow caste pretenses of the Bourbons. When Washington passed from the stage DuBois' philosophy was becoming more and more acceptable to the educated Negro both north and south, but Washington did not live to see his felicitously phrased platitudes falsified by the social and economic forces in American life.

On the other hand, DuBois had been denied the kindness of fate which his predecessors enjoyed. No outstanding successor has arisen to follow him on the stage of racial leadership. In fact, the scene has changed, and when

E. Franklin Frazier, "The Du Bois Program in the Present Crisis," *Race* 1 (Winter 1935–1936): 11–13. Reprinted with the permission of the Moorland-Springarn Research Center.

DuBois attempts to act his former role his words become meaningless. Even when he attempts to say his own lines he often forgets them or gives a new version of his predecessor's or tries to anticipate the successor who should fit into the new scene. It is not difficult to discover why the role, which DuBois played in a masterly way because of his unique gifts and cultural background, cannot be fitted into the new social and economic scene. His role was one that derived its significance and character from that of his predecessor, Douglass, and his contemporary, Washington. All three of these leaders played upon a stage of racial leadership that took as its foundation the American economic and social system.

Marginal Man

However, the unique role which DuBois has played in American life can be understood only through a knowledge of the forces which molded his personality. He was born in New England, where his mulatto characteristics permitted him a large degree of participation in the life of the white world. During his short sojourn in the South as an undergraduate at Fisk University, where he was under New England white teachers, he never was thoroughly assimilated into Negro life. His return to New England afforded him a more congenial environment where he thoroughly absorbed the genteel intellectual tradition of Harvard. Two additional years in European universities made him a finished product of the aristocratic intellectual culture of the last decade of the nineteenth century.

But DuBois, aristocrat in bearing and in sympathies, was in fact a cultural hybrid or what sociologists have termed a "marginal man." Once back in America and in Atlanta, he was just a "nigger." Fine flower of western culture, he had here the same status as the crudest semi-barbarous Negro in the South. In the *Souls of Black Folk* we have a classic statement of the "marginal man" with his double consciousness: on the one hand highly sensitive to every slight concerning the Negro, and feeling on the other hand little kinship or real sympathy for the great mass of crude, uncouth black peasants with whom he was identified. For, in spite of the way in which DuBois has written concerning the masses, he has no real sympathetic understanding of them. *The Souls of Black Folk* is a masterly portrayal of DuBois' soul and not a real picture of the black masses. When he takes his pen to write of the black masses we are sure to get a dazzlingly romantic picture. Some one has remarked aptly that the Negroes in *The Quest of the Silver Fleece* are gypsies. The voice of DuBois is genuine only when he speaks as the representative of the Talented Tenth; for he is typical of the intellectuals who spring from oppressed minorities.

Romantic

DuBois' program may be considered in its economic and social or cultural aspects. Perhaps it should be remarked in passing that there was no difference between the economic program of DuBois and that of Washington. Both envisioned the economic advancement of the Negro through thrift and intelligence. Whenever DuBois wrote of socialism, it was in a romantic vein. According to the recently released, seventh edition of the *Atlanta Creed*, socialism is a far-off, divine event toward which all creation moves. But, for the immediate economic salvation of the race he proposes that Negroes build "a co-operative industrial system in America, which to some extent will furnish employment, direct production and regulate consumption for gradually increasing numbers" of the Negro race. The Negro race is to "avoid the past errors of capitalism." This program, of course, is to be directed by the Talented Tenth who "refuse to remain parasites feeding on white philanthropy" and "welcome the burden of the uplift of our own masses until as a conscious and intelligent proletariat they can themselves assume democratic control of the whole group in the interest of our working class. Only in this way can the American Negro enter the new industrial kingdoms of the world, standing on his own economic feet."

The section of the program involving the encouragement of racialism should not occasion surprise. While it is true that only during recent years has DuBois advocated Negro schools and proposed that Negro colleges foster a racial culture, he has always displayed the typical racial consciousness of the cultural hybrid. While the Negro race is the same as any other, yet it has certain peculiar endowments. A statement by DuBois nearly a quarter of a century ago that the Negro was primarily an artist and that he had a characteristic "sense of beauty, particularly for sound and color" is a striking example of his romantic notions concerning the Negro's racial traits. In his recent program he would avoid "all artificial and hate-engendering deification of race separation as such" but would "just as sternly repudiate an enervating philosophy of Negro escape into an artificially privileged white race."

DuBois' racial program needs not to be taken seriously. Cultural hybrids often have "returned" to the minority race with which they were identified, glorified it and made significant additions to the artistic culture of the group.

But DuBois remains an intellectual who toys with the ideas of the Negro as a separate cultural group. He has only an occasional romantic interest in the Negro as a distinct race. Nothing would be more unendurable for him than to live within a Black Ghetto or within a black nation—unless perhaps he were king, and then probably he would attempt to unite the whites and blacks through marriage of the royal families. When Garvey attempted his genuine racial movement no one was more critical and contemptuous than DuBois of the fantastic glorification of the black race and all things black. Garvey's movement was too close to the black ignorant masses for DuBois. On the other hand, he was more at home with the colored intellectuals who gathered at the Pan-African congresses. If a fascist movement should develop in America, DuBois would play into the hands of its leaders through his program for the development of Negro racialism. As the situation is at present, the dominant social and economic forces in American life are destroying the possibility of the development of Negro nationalism.

Economically Impossible

The economic aspects of DuBois' program merit more serious consideration, since many educated Negroes who are groping for a solution of the race's economic problems may be deceived by the so-called practical nature of his program. Let us consider first this proposal that the Negro build a co-operative industrial system in America. When Garvey proposed a grandiose scheme for building a black commercial empire DuBois ridiculed his naïveté. But what could be more fantastic than his own program for a separate non-profit economy within American capitalism? Even if DuBois were ignorant of the mechanism of credit and the control of basic commodities by corporations, he must realize that consumers' co-operatives presuppose an income on the part of the consumers. With thousands of Negroes being displaced from the farms of the South while many more thousands are depending upon relief in the cities, a co-operative program could only adopt "Share Your Poverty" as a slogan. Even if Negroes, as DuBois implies, have an unusual endowment of altruism and will run businesses for service instead of profit, Negro consumers are going to buy where they can get goods at the cheapest prices. To be effective on a large scale, co-operatives must compete with the modern corporation and there is no evidence that the Negro has the capital and skill to overcome this competition. Thus DuBois' co-operatives, which supposedly are a more practical approach to the solution of the Negro's economic plight than the alignment of black workers with economic radicals who can only offer salvation in the remote future, turn out to be fantastic. More than that, they set up false hopes for the Negro and keep him from getting a realistic conception of capitalist economy and the hopelessness of his position in such a system.

Since DuBois is an intellectual who loves to play with ideas but shuns reality, whether it be in the form of black masses or revolution, he likes to display a familiarity with Marxian ideology. In an article in the *Crisis* he demonstrated, in a few hundred words, the error of applying Marxian conceptions to the economic condition of the Negro in America. Later, in his *Black Reconstruction*, he played with Marxian terminology as a literary device. This is all as it should be, for DuBois has said that there shall be no revolution and that economic justice and the abolition of poverty shall come through reason (the intellectual speaks), sacrifice (the romanticist speaks), and the intelligent use of the ballot (in the end he remains a liberal).

The status of the race in America, which has been determined by those economic forces which have shaped the country at large, has remained unaffected by the programs of Negro leaders. Washington's program of industrial education and scientific farming offered no more salvation than Douglass' naïve faith that the Republican party was the ship and all else the sea. Nor can DuBois, either as the intellectual or the romanticist, furnish the kind of social criticism which is needed today in order that the Negro may orient himself in the present state of American capitalism.

W. E. B. DU BOIS

Social Planning for the Negro, Past and Present

Violence and Rebellion

From the day of the Negro's landing in the United States down to the present, there have been four well-defined plans of emancipation and social uplift. The first plan was naturally that of violence; the individual and organized resistance to slavery. The extent of this is usually misapprehended in the United States because the plan began in Africa and the West Indies and only its last efforts were extended to the mainland. Henry M. Stanley estimates that in the African slave raids for every slave captured, at least four persons were left dead in the villages; and where the cause of Negro slavery was inter-tribal war, the toll of death was even greater. On the middle passage to America there were repeated efforts at mutiny in the 18th and 19th centuries, down to the celebrated cases of the "Amistad" and the "Creole."

The Negroes once landed in the Western world were for many years a cause of turmoil. Ovando solicited that no Negro slaves be sent to Haiti for they "fled among the Indians and taught them bad customs and could never be captured." The story of the fugitive Maroons in South America and Jamaica is one of the sagas of modern history. They fought the English government for a hundred years; they resisted the Spanish and Portuguese and they achieved freedom which continues to our day in Haiti and Guiana.

W. E. B. Du Bois, "Social Planning for the Negro, Past and Present," *Journal of Negro Education* 5, no. 1 (1936): 110–125. Reprinted by permission of the *Journal of Negro Education*.

The fear of slave violence on the American mainland is sufficiently proven by the legislation. The laws of South Carolina in 1712 were defended as necessary "to restrain the disorders, rapiness and inhumanity to which they are naturally prone and inclined." The law of 1740 declared that "many late, horrible and barbarous massacres have actually been committed and many more designed on the white inhabitants of this province by Negro slaves." Harsh and pitiless legislation based on these promises continued during slavery and especially was revived and increased after the attempts of Vesey and Nat Turner.

We must not forget that the last effective act of violence which the slaves used was their mass movement during the Civil War which added 200,000 soldiers and even larger numbers of servants and laborers to the Union Army. It was this actual adherence of slaves to the Union cause and the threat that it would be extended indefinitely that made the Civil War hopeless for the South and led to its sudden cessation.

Fugitive Slaves

The third plan which acted as the safety valve for slavery was that of the fugitive; it was by far the most successful attack on slavery, and began a real social reorganization for the Negro. In a comparatively empty country, the individual slave who could not and would not endure the system would not have to wait until he got the assent and support of a large number of his fellows. He could steal away to the swamps of Florida and Virginia and along the Appalachian Mountains and the Mississippi Valley into the North. This running away of slaves was first an individual enterprise; then it became organized and systematized under Negro leaders and finally gained the cooperation and active help of whites during the era of the Underground Railroad.

The Underground Railroad led to the Civil War. It meant that the capital invested in slaves was continually suffering losses, and the slave owners demanded, more and more peremptorily, the enactment of severe fugitive slave laws. The last one, which they secured on the eve of the Civil War, not only interfered with individual rights, but state rights. It led to retaliatory nullification in the North, intensified the bitterness between the sections, and eventually resulted in Civil War.

It is difficult to say how many slaves escaped, but the black population of the North increased from 130,000 in 1820 to 345,000 in 1860; this is a considerably larger increase than that of the total Negro population, and if we remember that this Northern group was composed of poor emigrants with broken family life and insecure economic basis suddenly transferred from city to town, it seems certain that at least 100,000 of them were fugitives from slavery and represented a loss of at least $25,000,000 in invested capital, and perhaps much more than that. It was this economic loss that spurred secession.

Meantime, there were especial centers of runaway slaves. There were the fugitive slaves at the time of the Revolutionary War who not only took part in the hostilities, but caused infinite difficulties in peace negotiations. There were the 1,000 Negroes, who in 1815 manned a former British port in Georgia and resisted the power of the United States. And finally there were the so-called Seminole wars which were simply slave raids for runaway property.

Mass Migration

Besides these efforts, there were more far-reaching efforts to settle the Negro problem by mass migration. A proposal to leave this country for Africa seemed logical in the 18th century when so many Negroes were newly come to the country. This plan was not simply a plan of white folk. Paul Cuffe was actually the first person who successfully transported emigrants, taking 38 Negroes to Africa, at his own expense. Later, came the American Colonization Society, but their plan for wholesale migration was spoiled by the effort of the radical South to turn this migration into an attempt to bolster slavery by getting rid of free Negroes. Nevertheless, out of that effort, together with the attempt to enforce the slave trade laws, came the settlement at Liberia.

Among the free Negroes of the North, plans for social amelioration began about 1830 when the Nat Turner insurrection in the South and the new foreign immigration to the North, made the economic situation of the free Negroes difficult. Riots and discriminatory laws in Ohio and Pennsylvania led to the Conventions of 1830 and 1831 and to a well thought-out plan of migration. The British government was approached and offered asylum, at first in Canada and later, after the West Indian emancipation, in the West Indies. The Canadian migration was financed by Negroes themselves and large numbers went to Ontario where they built up successful settlements. Their influence on American Negroes has been great. They were headquarters of the Underground Railroad. It was here that John Brown went to perfect his plans for the Harper's Ferry raids; and it was here that Richard B. Harrison was born.

Between 1830 and 1860, the situation of American Negroes became increasingly difficult because of the spread of the abolition controversy and the rise of the cotton kingdom. An increasing number of Negroes in the 50's began to consider that wholesale migration was the only escape. They saw no chance of emancipation in the United States. Even Frederick Douglass placed his whole hope on war and blood, but, nevertheless, steadfastly opposed migration.

In 1854, a remarkable convention met in Cleveland, Ohio. They made three proposals: Martin R. Delaney proposed migration to the Niger Valley of Africa; James M. Whitfield proposed to go to Central America; and Theodore Holly, to Haiti. They not only made these propositions, but they actually made the necessary investigation and at the next colonization convention in Canada in 1856, Holly made a report which resulted, eventually, in 2,000 Negro emigrants going to Haiti. Delaney concluded eight treaties with African kings and brought evidences of land concessions and welcome. Whitfield did not actually get to Central America before the Civil War broke out.

The war stopped migration schemes, until black fugitives began to pour into the Union armies. For a while, Lincoln did not realize the significance of this tremendous secession of power to the North and withdrawal of labor force from the South. The first problem, and an irritating problem it was, was what was going to be done to get rid of the Negroes. If some plan of mass migration could be devised there was the possibility not simply of withdrawing these slaves from work in the South, but of inducing the border states to give up slavery. Lincoln had long been an advocate of colonization. He said frankly that he could not conceive Negroes and white people living together in the United States as equals. He, therefore, secured in 1861 an appropriation of $100,000 from Congress and a further appropriation of $500,000 in 1862. He consulted delegations of Negroes and made contacts with foreign countries, but before he went further, he suddenly saw just what the significance of Negro soldiers and laborers was.

He saw that without their help, the war against the South could not be won, while with their help and the threat of increased accessions from the slaves, the opposition in the South was doomed. Moreover, he became convinced that mass migration of the Negroes could not be carried on with their consent nor at a price which the United States was willing to pay. His one venture with 500 Negro settlers on a little island near Haiti was a disastrous failure and nearly half of the victims died of disease and were cheated outrageously by their white manager.

Then came the era of Reconstruction and with the thrill of political power in the minds of the Negro and his friends, social reconstruction by migration was practically given up, except that Negroes moved in considerable groups from place to place in the South, in order to find free land and better working conditions. When, however, the revolution of 1876 came and the Negro by force and fraud was disfranchised, a great migration movement to the West was conceived by Henry Adams in Louisiana and Benjamin Singleton in Tennessee. Some 50,000 Negroes actually migrated to Kansas and the West and it took conciliation and violence in the South to stop the stream. Its more effectual stoppage, however, was due to poverty and cold welcome in the West. Nevertheless, a Negro population was planted in Kansas and its descendants remain there. Later, Bishop Turner and Congressman Morgan of Alabama tried to revive the project of migration to Africa, but its only result was one shipload of 200 Negroes in 1885.

On the other hand, the migration of Negroes from South to North has gone on continually since the Civil War. Between 1880 and 1900, some 10,000 to 20,000 a year went into the North, while from 1910 to 1930, between 1,000,000 and 1,500,000 moved in one of the great mass movements of the history of migration.

Political Enfranchisement

Meantime, the fourth great plan for the social emancipation of Negroes began with the Reconstruction efforts in the Civil War. From 1867–1876, the Negroes placed their whole hope of full emancipation and economic security upon their vote and this forms one of the most interesting episodes in American history. It was not simply the enfranchisement of black folk, it was the attempt to reconstruct the basis of American democracy and to put the political power in the hands of the lowest working group. The bottom economic rail was put on top. If this group had had leadership and a greater chance for industrial development, there might have ensued in the South a dictatorship of the proletariat which might have led the modern world. But, of course, no such rapid transition from feudal slavery to industrial democracy could be expected. These laborers were themselves under the direction and ideology of a capitalistic form of industry. Their ideas of emancipation was the rise of an exploiting class of black capitalists. Nevertheless, their realistic grasp of the situation led them to preliminary efforts not to exploit labor but to make the situation of the emancipated workers as advantageous as possible. They tried cooperative farming in Louisiana and state division of large plantations in South Carolina. They advocated and made actual free public school education in every Southern state. They gave opportunity for the poor man, not only to vote, but to represent his class in the legislature and the greatest charge against Reconstruction—that the legislature was filled by people who did not pay taxes—was really its greatest glory. The non-taxpaying laborer was the man who for a long time dominated the legislature with both white and black representatives.

There were, however, two unconquerable centers of opposition: one was the white landholder, who despite the fortunes of war, was enabled to continue his monopoly of the land through the determination of Andrew Johnson. It was one of the ironies of fate that the poor white who was the author of the legislation which distributed free land to the peasants of Europe and the North, was also the man who succeeded in keeping the emancipated Negroes of the South as landless serfs.

The second unconquerable center of opposition was the new capitalism of the North which was rising to tremendous and ruthless power. This new capitalism looked upon the South not as a center of new democracy, but as a center of exploitation. So long as the Southern land monopolist threatened the power and career of the Northern industrialists, he was perfectly willing to let black and white labor have its way in the South. But when Southern labor began to increase its demands and power, and on the other hand, the Southern landholder showed himself willing to unite with the Northern capitalists in new exploitation, the bargain of 1876 was made and the laborers, white and black, were disfranchised. What ensued in the South after emancipation was not at all the classical bourgeoise revolution but something far more complicated and reactionary.

However, the plan for Negro emancipation by political means did not end in 1876. The Negro held on to vestiges of his political power, first, by black congressmen, up until the beginning of the 20th century, by a few members of Southern legislatures, and especially by their power inside the Republican Party. This latter power was gradually undermined by the fact that it had back of it less and less of real democratic control and, therefore, could more easily be seduced by bribery and manipulation.

Appointments of Negroes to federal office also became less in number, as Reconstruction receded. Nevertheless, there were certain compensations in the North. Negroes appeared in the legislature of 11 or 12 Northern states and sometimes played a conspicuous part. They were elevated to the judicial bench in the District of Columbia and three other states, and in cities, particularly like Chicago and New York, they occupied from time to time positions of real power.

The result of this political influence can be shown in many ways. Between 1884 and 1897, 25 civil rights laws, in addition to the national civil rights law, were passed in 16 Northern states. Many of them, including the national law, were emasculated by judicial interpretation, but others, like the Massachusetts and New York laws, are effective today. Federal appropriations for Negro education in the case of Howard University and the land grant colleges have been secured. On the other hand, further discriminatory legislation has been held up. Jim-Crow cars have been kept out of Delaware, West Virginia, and Missouri, and partially out of Maryland. A flood of anti-racial intermarriage laws introduced in 1913 in Congress and 12 different states were defeated in every instance but one.

On the other hand, in the South, Jim-Crow legislation and disfranchisement laws between 1881 and 1910 swept through with little opposition.

It became clearer and clearer, as the plan of political power to emancipate the American Negro was followed, that something was lacking; that the poverty and inexperience of the Negro made it impossible for him to exercise his political power in full, and that as a minority, even then, he could not succeed unless he could make some alliance with the majority. There ensued, therefore, two plans which both explain and supplement the plan of political power from 1867–1930.

One of these movements came in 1896–1920 and it sought firmly to integrate the American Negro into American industry as a farmer, laborer, skilled artisan, and capitalist. The other movement, sought by agitation and legal defense, to clear away race discrimination and allow untrammeled advancement of black folk according to ability. These two latter movements fell into bitter controversy. The economic movement ended with the World War and the anti-discrimination movement declined with the depression.

The Washington Plan

The plan of social Reconstruction advocated by Booker T. Washington was not simply a plan for the uplift of labor as is so often assumed, and it can be only understood as we consider its immediate background. The late William H. Baldwin, President of the Long Island Railroad and slated to be President of the Pennsylvania, was a young man trained in Southern industry. He was one of the first to conceive of the training of black laborers who should share work with white laborers and at the same time keep the white labor movement from too strong and insistent demands in its fight with capital.

This idea began in the day when the "one big union" of the Knights of Labor had changed to the craft unionism of the American Federation of Labor. The strength of the labor movement was growing but almost without exception it excluded black skilled labor. However, black skilled labor was valuable and could be trained in the South. It was the idea of Mr. Baldwin and gradually of many others that you would not only do a service to and open opportunity for black folk, but you would in this same way serve capital and hold white labor in check.

About this time, Booker T. Washington took charge of Tuskegee in Alabama. He was an opportunist with high ideals. He believed in political rights for people who could exercise them, but in the case of Southern Negroes, he knew that they could not exercise them without the consent of the white South. He took the position, therefore, that the Negro must gain an economic status before he could use his political rights and in this he was undoubtedly right; but on the other hand, his idea of the economic status which Negroes must gain was based unquestionably on the capitalistic organization of the United States.

Mr. Washington's program included a temporary acquiescence in giving up Negro political rights and agitation for civil rights and insistence upon training young Negroes for farming and industry. Up from a thrifty solid class of black landlords and artisans, Washington expected a class of Negro capitalists to arise and employ Negro workers. The plan was launched by the Atlanta Speech in 1896 and was triumphant from that date until about 1910. It included alliance with white capital and was rewarded by large contributions toward Negro education, especially such schools as conformed to the Hampton-Tuskegee type.

As a first step toward this new Negro capitalism, Mr. Washington especially stressed landholding, widespread peasant proprietorship, and even large farms among Negroes; and then a training of Negro laborers and artisans for use in industry at a wage if necessary less than that demanded by union labor. The result of this compromise was a new understanding between leading elements, North and South, with regard to the Negro. The Negro college, while not entirely discouraged, was looked upon with some suspicion, and positions for Negro college graduates became difficult. To some extent, appointments and opportunities for young Negroes were carefully censored and referred for approval to Tuskegee, over a very wide extent of country. Negro newspapers were brought in line by judicious advertising and other means of control. This was really regarded as a clever and farsighted compromise, which, if it did not solve, would at least peacefully postpone the solutions of a baffling, intricate problem of race contact until more favorable times. Between 1900–1910, Mr. Washington became one of the most popular men in America, in constant demand North and South as a speaker, adviser, and referee.

As the current opinion of the land became unified, Mr. Washington's program began to become increasingly suspicious in the eyes of Negroes. A wave of Jim-Crow legislation and disfranchising bills swept over the South and the border states. Already separation of the races in travel had been made compulsory in eight Southern states before 1891, but had paused. Now, a new wave of legislation began in 1898 and covered South Carolina, North Carolina, Virginia, Maryland and Oklahoma. Determined and repeated efforts were made in Missouri, West Virginia, and Delaware. Disfranchising laws swept over the South and border states, from 1890–1910, at the very time when Negro political power and agitation had been lulled to its lowest by the Washington compromise. This triumph of the radical, anti-Negro South and the continued prevalence of lynching which went on at the rate of one to two a week during most of Mr. Washington's career, greatly embarrassed him. He hated caste and lawlessness as much as any man. He wanted the best for his people, but he implicitly believed that once his economic program could be put through all else would follow. He made the fatal mistake of trying to forestall criticism from Negroes and of acquiescing in the neglect if not the suppression of Negro colleges.

The result was the outburst of wrath and criticism led by the younger college-bred Negro group, an outburst which eventually split the Negro group in twain. But it was not that criticism that doomed the Washington program. It was plain failure of the economic rebuilding which I emphasized. This is shown by the trend of Negro employment. Despite the effort of both Hampton and Tuskegee to train farmers and servants, both of these decreased in number. Farmers, instead of forming 57 per cent of the workers, as in 1890, now formed 37 per cent. Servants have decreased from 31 per cent in 1890 to 22 per cent in 1920. Since then, they have increased to 29 per cent. Manifestly, then, there were forces at work to drive the Negroes off the farm and out of the servant quarters. On the other hand, the number of Negroes in commerce and transportation and in the manufacturing and mechanical industries, increased largely from 10 per cent in 1890 to 29 per cent in 1930, but it was not at all the kind of increase that Mr. Washington had in mind. The newcomers were mainly laborers. They made some headway into the semiskilled industries, but were kept out by the trade unions. The trade unions held against them as an excuse the fact that they had been trained and that the plan had been to train them as strikebreakers and low-cost laborers. The caste system in the South increased the whole ideology of caste throughout the United States until laboring men felt themselves degraded to work with black men. Moreover, the attempt of Negroes to enter the employing class as merchants and landholders was made impossible by severe competition and monopoly.

The attempt to teach Negroes the skill of modern industry was also frustrated by the changing of skill, mass production, and use of machinery. While, therefore, land ownership among Negroes and the accumulation of property increased until 1910, it then began to decrease and the increase in Negro property, while a creditable index of thrift, was dwarfed by the immense piling up of capital in the hands of whites. Without doubt, the Washington program improved the economic status of the Negro, but on the other hand, and just as surely, it did not show a way out because it fastened the chains of exploitation on Negro labor and increased labor antagonism in the laboring classes.

This was particularly shown in the new development in the South where white labor used its political and social influence to replace black labor and eliminate the so-called Negro jobs. At the time of the depression, therefore, the status of Negro labor, both North and South, was precarious, through the opposition of unions and the discrimination of employers in the North and the competition of poor white labor in the South.

Legal Defenses

The next plan for social reorganization was that of agitation of legal defense. It was at first a part of the plan for political power and not a demand for fixing the unconstitutionality of disfranchisement legislation and the enforcing of war amendments. One of the earliest group movements to agitate for this was the National League formed in Boston in 1885. It was local in its membership but had some influence.

In 1887, T. Thomas Fortune, Editor of what is now the *New York Age,* issued an appeal for a national organization, and repeated this in 1889. The so-called Afro-American League, afterward changed to Afro-American Council, met in Chicago with 21 states represented in January, 1890. J. C. Price was president, and Mr. Fortune, secretary. The League held another meeting in Tennessee and then died, until Bishop Walters revived it in 1898. It met that year in September at Rochester and later in November in Washington. The object of the organization was to investigate lynching, to test the constitutionality of discriminatory laws, to secure civil-rights legislation, to promote migration from the South and to encourage organization. It met for several years and practically died with a final meeting in St. Paul, Minnesota, about 1900. Its weakness was that it consisted simply of an annual meeting without a continuous working organization. The result was that it did little more than meet, organize, and pass resolutions. In the year 1905, a new aspect came over the plans for American Negroes for social reconstruction.

The new disfranchisement laws and the wave of discriminatory legislation, coupled with Mr. Washington's concessions, alarmed the colored people. Particularly the young colored college man began to fear the dictatorship of the Tuskegee machine and the difficulty of expressing even legitimate criticism. This opposition was crystalized by the jailing of Monroe Trotter in Boston for trying to heckle Mr. Washington during a speech at the colored church. It seems to me that this was going too far, and that while Trotter was much more bitter and outspoken than was necessary, yet he did have a right to talk even though he criticized Mr. Washington. The result was that a call was issued in June, 1905, signed by 59 men from 17 states. In July, 1905, 29 of these men, representing 14 states, met at Niagara Falls and formed the Niagara Movement. The Movement grew, and in 1906 held a significant meeting at Harper's Ferry. The manifesto which it sent out was plain and bitter.

The Niagara Movement, however, had certain inherent difficulties. First it was a racial movement of men entirely unknown outside their group and with no means of contact by which they could easily reach influential persons in the white group. And secondly, Mr. Trotter, who owned and edited the one organization journal, was not an organization man. He was an extreme individualist. When, therefore, in 1909 there was held a conference in New York with practically the same program that the Niagara Movement had, practically all of the leading members of the Niagara Movement went into the N. A. A. C. P., seven of them going upon its Board of Directors, and thus to a large measure the work of the Niagara Movement became merged with that of the N. A. A. C. P. The N. A. A. C. P. said in its first report:

> The National Association for the Advancement of Colored People seeks to uplift the colored men and women of this country by securing to them the full enjoyment of their rights as citizens, justice in all courts, and equality of opportunity everywhere. It favors and aims to aid, every kind of education among them save that which teaches special privileges or prerogative, class or caste. It recognizes the national character of the Negro problem and no sectionalism. It believes in the holding, of the Constitution of the United States and its amendments, in the spirit of Abraham Lincoln. It upholds the doctrine of "all men up and no man down." It abhors Negro crime, but still more the conditions which breed crime, and most of all the crimes committed by mobs in the mockery of the law, by individuals in the name of the law.

It believes that the scientific truths of the Negro problem must be available before the country can see its way wholly clear to right existing wrongs. It has no other belief than that the best way to uplift the colored man and the best way to aid the white man to peace is social content; it has no other desire than exacting justice, and no other motive than patriotism. (First Annual Report, January 1, 1911. N. A. A. C. P.)

The work of the N. A. A. C. P. is too well-known to call for review here. I need only point out that its greatest triumph was in the matter of legal defense. Practically, it made the Supreme Court for the first time in the history of the country affirm the validity of the 15th Amendment, outlaw the Grandfather Clauses, and curtail the segregation ordinances. It also secured some protection for accused Negroes from mob violence and made the most effective anti-lynching campaign in the history of the country.

The first sign of change that faced the N. A. A. C. P. was falling off of its income and the decrease in the circulation of *The Crisis.* This was not due to the fact that the American Negro did not want to fight discrimination and lynching and was not willing to pursue cases in legal defense which should build up the foundation of the whole caste system in marriage, in travel and education. But it did come from the fact that the colored people, economically, were unable to stand the expense. It had been the proud boast of the N. A. A. C. P. that beginning as a quasi-philanthropic institution, expecting to rely upon funds furnished mainly by rich white friends, it had become during its best years supported in the main by the mass of colored workers and that *The Crisis* had been made financially independent by the same kind of support. The amounts of money which it received, from rich white people were small and their withdrawal would have made no particular difference in its program. The falling off now of this income meant that the colored people were financially unable to sustain this program and especially to back its expansion. We realized this before the depression and the causes lay in a new industrial development, North and South. In the South, the Negro was losing the monopoly of certain jobs which he had had. The machine was displacing semi-skilled and skilled labor among both Negroes and whites. A new monopoly of capital and materials was so changing the face of industry that the Negro was becoming a reservoir of casual labor and the general causes of the collapse of agriculture throughout the world were at work in increased degree among Negro farmers.

The mass migration of Negroes to the North alleviated but did not change the basic trouble. They found themselves in the midst of difficulties connected with housing, difficulties connected with unions, difficulties connected with the casual character of their labor and the low wage for which they were obliged to work. This should have taught the Negroes of the United States that a change of tactic was absolutely necessary. Agitation and legal defense must be kept up so far as possible but that possibility at present has its limitations. Before them, and of more importance and of fundamental influence even to the campaign against race discrimination itself, was a new plan of social security.

The Present Dilemma

I began to advocate, therefore, for the N. A. A. C. P. a new social program as early as 1928. I was by no means clear in my own thinking, but was groping for light and for that reason had visited Russia, had begun the study of Karl Marx and had voted the Socialist ticket since 1912. My efforts brought little reaction; no particular opposition and at the same time no emphasis of agreement until the wave of depression overwhelmed us. Then, suddenly, there came to the force, a peculiar situation made by the fact that the problem of race discrimination always cuts across and hinders the settlement of other problems, and we are repeatedly forced to give up direct attack upon it in order to save our very lives.

It happened in the Civil War. In the midst of a fight for physical freedom, civil and political rights, the Negro was suddenly faced with the problem of fighting when the outcome was by no means clear nor was it altogether certain just where his interest lay. He was compelled for a time to lay aside his racial demands to become Union soldiers and laborers and afterward was rewarded by receiving a greater measure of political power and civil rights than he had dreamed of. The same kind of dilemma came at the time of the World War.

We had no choice between war and peace—the nation was rushing headlong. We had no allies save a small group of thinkers who for the most part were not interested in Negroes. Labor was near unanimous for war and so were most socialists here and abroad. We were in a raging flood and our only real choice was to fight swimming with the current or to be drowned in impotent opposition. I said then and under similar circumstances would say again, close ranks and fight for our own liberty while the world was committing suicide.

The victim of mob violence, lynching and residential segregation for a time had to concentrate his efforts toward securing decent treatment of his segregated regiments, an opportunity for men to become officers even if they were black and permission to fight at the front instead of work blindly in the rear. After the World War, the Negro was able to return to his attack upon prejudice with increased power and efficiency. The years from 1919 to 1929 represent a high water mark of our organized striving for increased political power, the suppression of lynching and legal defense.

The irony of the situation, however, proved to be the fact that the cause for which we were verbally compelled to fight itself failed in its very victory and cast us with all men, workers and owners, in the maelstrom of world depression. Today, then, our original paradox again appears with wider ramification and vaster perils.

We are in the midst of a national and world movement to reconstruct the basis of industry. In order to be efficient coworkers in this reconstruction, we have got to escape the present threat of starvation, to conserve our schools and social organizations and to get regular, decently paid work. With that foundation settled, even in a reasonable degree we can begin again to fight discrimination. But until unemployment among American Negroes is decreased and a decent standard of living reestablished, we have no resources upon which the battle against discrimination can effectively be carried.

Here, then, is the dilemma and how has it been met? Briefly put, there have been three moves: (1) toward invoking the protection of restored capitalism, (2) a movement toward alliance with organized labor, and (3) a movement toward socialism.

In the first category may be placed practically all of the older organizations: the Urban League, the Federation of Churches, the N. A. A. C. P. Nearly all of these organizations have, to be sure, shown signs of uneasiness at their position. The Urban League organized a National Economic Council, which through an executive committee and workers' council was designed to guide the Negro through the crisis. Apparently, this never functioned. The N. A. A. C. P. sought to adopt an economic program but was unable to agree on anything definite. The Federation of Churches had adopted a liberal labor program, but has not applied it to Negroes. Gradually, most of these and many other organizations under the guidance of the Joint Committee on Recovery, fell back upon a drive on the administration to secure justice for the Negro in relief and reorganization; but the difficulty was in determining just what economic justice for the Negro involved and how it could best be secured. The organizations themselves had scant common ground. Ten of them were religious. Four were academic fraternities and sororities, one is a fraternal order, one an organization for agitation and reform, four organizations of professional men, one designed for club work, and three are industrial organizations. The only thing upon which this conglomerate body could wholeheartedly unite was the matter of race discrimination.

Of the fact of discrimination, the Joint Committee has unearthed ample proof, but as to what we are going to do about it, the Joint Committee, quite naturally, has nothing to say and nothing to think.

Indeed, everything that has happened in the NRA and the New Deal might easily have been foretold before the NRA was established.

If the United States government comes in to the depression picture to administer local relief, that relief must be directly carried out by local people and these local people in the places where Negroes are most numerous are going to be prejudiced and narrow.

If the government is going to relieve the farmer by a scarcity program or bonuses, the people who are going to reap the benefit from that program are going to be the white people who own the land. If the government is going to establish a great power organization with towns and industries, in these towns and industries there is going to be repeated the same pattern of discrimination and segregation that is current in the nation. If we are going to have housing projects, subsistence homesteads, farm credit and credit unions, we are going to find in the carrying out of these plans the same American prejudice against color that we find everywhere. What, then, are we to do? Are we to starve to death until we settle color discrimination in America or are we first to secure the power to fight before we enter battle? The one thing that we are bound to do in self-defense is to see that in the midst of all this whirlpool we make sure of such beginnings of economic security that in the future we shall have power to work out our destiny; and to this, everything else is subordinate.

If segregated homesteads and segregated land will give us more secure employment and higher wage, we cannot for a moment hesitate. If segregated schools will give us better education, then we must have segregated schools. If segregated housing will give us decent homes, we have no right to choose for our children and our families slums for the sake of herding with the white unfit. Our first business in the midst of the great economic revolution, which is going on, is to secure a place for ourselves.

To this, the advocates of labor alliance answer: There is only one haven of refuge for the American Negro. He must recognize that his attempt to enter the ranks of capital as an exploiter came too late, if it were ever a worthy ideal for a group of workers. He is now forever excluded by the extraordinary monopoly which white capital and credit have upon the machines and materials of the world. Moreover, that solution after all was possible only for the few. The great mass of Negroes belong to the laboring class. They have the same interests that white laborers have. They must join the white labor movement.

This, however, is not nearly as easy as it might seem. Not only has the attempt of American Negroes to join the ranks of the white labor movement been discouraging for more than a century, but even today, the welcome which they are accorded is questionable. In the first place, the farmers and servants who compose the mass of workers among colored people are not organized. If we take the 30,000,000 of organizable laborers, less than 7,000,000 are organized, even if we include the company unions. If we take the less than 5,000,000 who are organized, the overwhelming majority of them will not allow the Negroes to join their ranks under any circumstances, and most of the rest have only allowed Negroes to intrude when the power of Negro labor was such that they did not dare to oppose its competition. There are undoubtedly today a number of unions which are disposed to welcome Negro members and who recognize something of the real solidarity of labor interests; but their total number must be less than half a million. With such workers, Negro labor ought by all means to unite; but to say that the union of American Negro labor with a half million out of 5,000,000 organized laborers is a labor alliance, is seriously to overstate the case.

Suppose, now, that the Negro turns to the promise of socialism whither I have long looked for salvation. I was once a member of the celebrated Local No. 1 in New York. I am convinced of the essential truth of the Marxian philosophy and believe that eventually land, machines and materials must belong to the state; that private profit must be abolished; that the system of exploiting labor must disappear; that people who work must have essentially equal income; and that in their hands the political rulership of the state must eventually rest.

Notwithstanding the fact that I believe this is the truth and that this truth is being gradually exemplified by the Russian experiment, I must, nevertheless, ask myself seriously; how far can American Negroes forward this eventual end? What part can they expect to have in a socialistic state and what can they do now to bring about this realization? And my answer to this has long been clear. There is no automatic power in socialism to override and suppress race prejudice. This has been proven in America, it was true in Germany before Hitler and the analogy of the Jews in Russia is for our case entirely false and misleading. One of the worst things that Negroes could do today would be to join the American Communist Party or any of its many branches. The Communists of America have become dogmatic exponents of the inspired word of Karl Marx as they read it. They believe, apparently, in immediate, violent and bloody revolution, and they are willing to try any and all means of raising hell anywhere and under any circumstances. This is a silly program even for white men. For American colored men, it is suicide. In the first place, its logical basis is by no means sound. The great and fundamental change in the organization of industry which Karl Marx with his splendid mind and untiring sacrifice visualized must, to be sure, be brought about by revolution, but whether in all times and places and under all circumstances that revolution is going to involve war and bloodshed, is a question which every sincere follower of Marx has a right to doubt.

The most baffling paradox today is the attitude of men toward war. On the one hand, we have the advocates of radical reform in our fundamental, economic and political structure, insisting that the only path to this era of peace and justice is through violent revolution. On the other hand, we have the advocates of the present system insisting that they can only insure peace by worldwide preparation for the same kind of war which recently took the lives of ten million men.

The ordinary man seeking peace, has, then, apparently not a choice between peace and war, but only a choice of the kind of war in which he will fight and the object for which he will fight, and apparently he must strive to make this last great murder of the West, this new War to end War, as peaceful and reasonable as possible.

Leaving for a moment the question as to how inevitable this dilemma is, we American Negroes under the race hate now prevalent, will in any case stand between the two armies as buffer and victim, pawn and peon. And we can only take this attitude: We abhor violence and bloodshed; we will join no movement that advocates a program of violence, except as the last defense against aggression.

We see today as the chief aggressor and threatener of violence, not indeed communism, but greed and reaction, masquerading as patriotism and fascism, armed to the teeth, intolerant and ready to kill and repress not only those who oppose them, but those who dare to express opposing thoughts.

Such discrimination, represented in the United States by various patriotic women's organizations, by war veterans' leagues, by the army and navy and its friends, are the most dangerous advocates of war and murder; and it is foolish for those who believe in world peace and economic justice to be so misled by this reaction as to burst into wild words and futile deeds and thus give greed a chance to kill the innocent.

Granted that the Marxian dialectic is a masterful statement of a great truth, yet the revolution which it sets down as inevitable, may logically, even if not probably, come by votes without violence, by restricted violence, or if with

widespread violence, not with cruelty and unnecessary bloodshed. They are
fools who think that successful and beneficial revolution consists primarily in
raising the devil, and it is very doubtful if such persons will ever lead America to
peace and justice. It may well be that in the awful and fundamental changes to
come, calm, silent and compassionate men may be compelled to lead the world
to peace through irresistible force but never through irresponsible deviltry.

In any real revolution, every step that saves violence is to the glory of
the great end. We may not save all, but we may never forget that revolution is
not, the object of socialism or communism rightly conceived; that their object is justice and if haply the world can find that justice without blood, the
world is the infinite gainer. Persistent and dominant denial of this possibility
may be made and may be true, but wise men will never cease to seek it. We
black men say, therefore, we do not believe in violence. Our object is justice
not violence, and we will fight only when there is no better way.

The proletariat which stands for violence is that proletariat which becomes the tool to carry out capitalistic violence. The first study of workers
is not to fight but to convince themselves that union of workers, class solidarity, is better than force and a substitute for it.

The real problem, then, is this concert of the workers. The real emphasis today is not on revolution but on class consciousness and this is the job of
socialism and the first proof of conversion is the abolition of race prejudice.

It is the duty of socialism to battle the war psychologically and not to
promote it. Early Christianity with its battle hymns and war metaphors made
the same ghastly mistake—"Its blood-red banner streams afar" down to our
own day.

If, now, reaction toward capitalism can no more save Negroes today than
it could in the past; and if the opportunity to ally the Negro with white labor
has been limited in the past and while wider today is still too limited for effective action, and if a program of avowed violence is out of the question, what
can the Negro do? This brings me really to the end of my part of this program,
but I may say for the benefit and attack of my good friend, Mr. Harris, to my
mind, this is our program; so to organize the vast consumers' power of this
group as to secure wide economic independence through the exchange of services and the exchange and manufacture of goods. Through these methods, to
train the American Negroes so that they will realize in their own group and
realize at first, the kind of social reformation which the whole world is bound
to come to some day. And above all to stop this great people from being
ashamed of itself, of its color and history; of living together and working together and to realize that race segregation is the white man's loss and not the
black man's damnation.

RALPH J. BUNCHE

A Critique of New Deal Social Planning As It Affects Negroes

New Deal "Equilibrium"

The New Deal, at its inception, confronting an economy of chaos, proclaimed its major purpose to be the application of planning to our entire social structure. In pursuance of this objective a whole series of complicated and contradictory mechanisms have been invented and set up with the purpose of effecting a regulated orderliness in the economic life of the nation. But after two years of frantic trial and error, the New Deal, and most of its elaborate machinery, remains suspended in mid-air, bewildered, and innocuous. Relief expenditures have continued to rise, and unemployment was greater at the end of the year 1934 than it was in December, 1933. Even the staunchest supporters of the New Deal, though still weakly professing optimism, are often compelled to admit that its ideology is illogical, inconsistent, vague, and confused; that its program is composed of a mass of self-contradictory experimentation, and that, in its unblushing rôle of political coquette, it turns now to the left, now to the right.

The explanations of the New Deal and of its apparent failure are not far to seek. The New Deal merely represents our domestic phase of the almost universal attempt in capitalistic countries to establish a new equilibrium in the social structure; an attempt made necessary by the fact that the collapse

Ralph J. Bunche, "A Critique of New Deal Social Planning As It Affects Negroes," *Journal of Negro Education* 5, no. 1 (1936): 59–65. Reprinted by permission of the *Journal of Negro Education*.

of the economic structures under the world-wide depression brought out, in bold relief, the sharp class antagonisms which the developing capitalistic economies had nurtured. The history of the operation of social forces in the Western world since the World War is sharply outlined in at least two particulars: (1) Capitalists, *i.e.,* Big Owners, have clearly indicated their inability and unwillingness to afford any leadership in the society which would promise even a meager measure of social justice to the masses of population, though the productive and organizational genius of capitalism is unchallenged; (2) on the other hand, the working classes of the countries of Western Europe, Russia excepted, though winning their way to a position of real power in the state, completely failed to take over the controls of the state, either through political channels or by force. The result has been a significant upsurge of the middle classes of the Western world, whose claim to national leadership is predicated on their assumed ability to reconcile these conflicting class interests in the society through the establishment of a new equilibrium;—a new society, in fact, in which conflicting group interests and inequalities will be merged in a higher national purpose.

Unwittingly or not, President Roosevelt was responsive to these social forces when he sounded the key note of the New Deal in his radio address of May 7, 1933.

> It is wholly wrong to call the measures that we have taken government control of farming, control of industry, and control of transportation. It is rather a partnership in profits, for profits would still go to the citizens, but rather a partnership in planning and a partnership to see that the plans are carried out.

The New Deal which was then visited upon us embraced no significant shift of ideas, traditions, or loyalties. In large degree it represented merely an effort to refurbish the old individualistic-capitalistic system and to entrust it again with the economic destinies and welfare of the American people. It recognized, of course, that the American economy had slowed down, and particularly that the forces within it were no longer in equilibrium—a rude awakening for our traditional class-consciousless society. The intellectual pilots of the New Deal would remedy this condition, though certainly not by revolution, nor even by fascist counter revolution, (not immediately, at any rate); but in the words of one author: "abhorring the thought of violence and having no conscious class interests of their own, [they] have refused to agree that the mechanism has run down. They will wind it up again and, having done that, will suspend in balance and for all time the existing class relations in American society."[1]

The Tenets of the New Deal

Certain postulates have been laid down as fundamental in the New Deal program. The private ownership of the means of production is to continue, but on the one hand, capitalism must be stopped from exploiting the producers of its raw materials and, on the other, its labor supply. Agriculture, despite its over-capitalized plant and its reluctant but almost complete restriction to the domestic market, is to be permitted a large enough return to allow for the meeting of fixed charges and the purchase of capital and consumer's goods. Wage-earners, although it is admitted that in a machine economy there are too many of them in the white-collar and laboring categories, are to be assured employment and at least the means of subsistence, with a large hope thrown in for incomes conducive to a decent standard of living.

Our own rather short experience with middle-class planning, not to mention the clearer and even more disastrous experiences of Italy, Germany, and Austria with similar schemes, permits us to raise a serious question concerning the ability of the middle classes to construct a new equilibrium which will afford a proper consideration of the interests of the masses of the population. The weakness of the middle classes is precisely that they are "in the middle," i.e., they hold an intermediate position between the working masses and the finance capitalists. Included in their ranks are many whose economic status is continually precarious, and who are weak, uncourageous, and unskillful. In the U.S. today they are largely petty bourgeois. There are many who would incline sympathetically toward the cause of the proletariat, but there are many others whose aspirations ally them ideologically with big business, thus adding greater confusion to the American scene.

Yet this rather ambiguous middle class,—opportunistic and ambitious, lacking class cohesion and ideology—whose members have been completely captivated by the lure of the American Dream, has but two alternatives in the present situation. The middle class itself must take over and operate industry or it must allow private industry to retain its tenacious grip on the economic structure of the nation. But the middle-class leadership is well aware of the violent nature of the struggle that would be necessary in any attempt to wrest industry out of the hands of big ownership. Consequently, the tendency is to take the easier path and to employ the power of the state to keep the masses in check while handling the industrialists with velvet gloves. That is merely another way of saying that the working masses become ever more dependent upon the intervention of the state in their straggle to obtain social justice from the owners and directors of industry. But coincidentally, the alliance between the middle-class political power and the economic power of big business, becomes more unholy. Italy and Nazi Germany afford classic illustrations of the sort of "balance" the working masses can expect from such a process.

The dilemma of the New Deal, then, merely reflects the basic dilemma of capitalism. Either capitalism must surrender itself to intelligent and scientific social planning, (and this it cannot do, for such planning involves a single ownership of the means of production for use rather than for profit), or else it must blunder on, repeating the errors and perpetuating the rigidities which inevitably lead a poorly planned industrial society into periodic depression.

The measures of intervention employed by the New Deal have really been measures of state capitalism which have already been employed by social democratic and fascist governments in Europe, and which obviously have not restored prosperity there, nor settled any of the fundamental conflicts within the modern capitalistic state.

Class lines are more sharply drawn, but state capitalism attempts to balance these class interests within the limits of middle-class democracy. The NRA, for example, began with sympathetic gestures toward labor, if section 7a can be so considered. But it soon became a means of preventing and settling strikes, usually to the disadvantage of labor, as witnessed by the defeat of labor in the settlements of the automobile, San Francisco, textile and other strikes.

American state capitalism has no choice but this, for it proposes to salvage the old order. It retains formal democracy and may make minor concessions to labor. The government intervenes to aid industry, to limit output. But this is not the planned economy of socialism, where all phases of economic activity are placed under planful regulation and control, because here class interests remain in bitter conflict and big ownership retains its economic power. It is not without great significance to the subject of middle-class planning under capitalism, that Secretary Wallace, in his book *New Frontiers*, readily acknowledges, with amazing frankness for one in his position, the enormous influence wielded over the New Deal administration and legislation by the paid lobbies of powerful industrial interests. He clearly suggests that several of the important features of the New Deal represent, not the mature wishes and policies of the Roosevelt administration, but the demands of self-seeking pressure groups, whose demands were too insistent and vigorous to be withstood. The NRA and its codes, he confesses, were not the brain-children of the brain-trusters, but were the products of a swarm of hard-headed business men intent on group price-fixing, who swooped down on Washington and its New Dealers. In America, then, the New Deal follows the classical pattern of middle-class planning by compromise with Big Business,—a policy fatal to the interests of labor.

The New Deal and the Negro

For the Negro population, the New Deals means the same thing, but more of it. Striking at no fundamental social conditions, the New Deal at best can only fix the disadvantages, the differentials, the discriminations, under which the Negro population has labored all along. The traditional racial stereotypes,— which have been inherited from the master-slave tradition and which have been employed by the ruling class of large land-holders in the South and industrialists in the North to give effective expression to their determination to keep the Negro in a servile condition and as a profitable labor supply,— remain, and are indeed, often heightened by the New Deal.

Intelligent analysis and the dictates of a purely selfish policy of promoting the profit motive should have made clear to the NRA that the competitive exploitation of any significant part of the population, such as the Negro, would frustrate its efforts toward recovery. The poverty of the Negro is an ever-present obstacle to the prosperity of the dominant population. Therefore the first efforts of the NRA should have been directed toward assuring Negro workers that real wage which would make possible for them a decent standard of living.

Negro Wage Earners

To the contrary, however, from the beginning, relatively few Negro workers were even theoretically affected by the labor provisions of NRA. The evils of part-time work, irregular work and occupational and wage differentials, suffered especially by the great mass of Negro workers in the South, were perpetuated under NRA. Through the codes, occupational and geographical differentials were early used as a means of excluding Negro workers from the benefits of minimum wage and hour provisions. Subsequently, the continuation of the inferior economic status of the Negro was assured by NRA through code provisions basing wage rates on the habitual wage differential existing between Negro and white workers. Such measures failing to keep Negro wages at the desired low level, there was still the device of securing a specific exemption from the code of the Negro wage-earners in any given plant. In the power laundry code approved by the President, in an industry employing nearly 30,000 Negro women, a 14 cent per hour minimum wage was established, and even this miserable level was not enforced. Dr. Peck,[2] Executive Director of the Labor Advisory Board, who has maintained staunchly that the NRA has benefited Negro workers, in that the "rates in codes have greatly narrowed the differentials which existed before codes," admits however, that in the service industries in which so many Negroes are employed, "habit, standard of living, cost of living and the level of income of the local population may have a long-time result in a continuance of differential wages." To make still more illusory the theoretical benefits of the NRA to Negro wage-earners, the compliance machinery has been so constructed and operated as virtually to deny any just treatment to the Negro workman, especially in the South.

The FERA relief figures portray graphically enough the effect of NRA upon the Negro. In October, 1933, approximately 2,117,000 Negroes were in families registered on relief rolls, or about 18 per cent of the total Negro population in 1930. In January, 1935, about 3,500,000 Negroes in families on relief were reported, approximating 29 per cent of the 1930 population. Most significantly, too, the proportion of Negroes on relief in relation to total population was greater in rural than in urban centers. In addition, it is reliably estimated that there are now some 1,000,000 male Negroes unemployed, exclusive of agricultural pursuits.

Agriculture

The dilemma of American Agriculture is the dilemma of the American economy. There are too many farmers and too much land in cultivation, just as there are too many industrial workers and too much industrial production. These surpluses exist because American agriculture and industry have developed too much efficiency for our profit-motivated economic system. The welfare of the Negro farmer is bound up in the government's solution to the basic dilemma of capitalism—the necessity of providing a decent standard of living, based on a much higher consumption level, for all of the surplus workers and farmers, while retaining an economic order which is founded on profit and not on use. The New Deal, in its agricultural program expressed through the AAA, grabbed vigorously at one horn of the dilemma, and the Negro farmer and farm worker have been left dangling precariously from the other. It goes without saying that the Negro tenant fanner has borne more than his share of this burden. The AAA bears the responsibility for other methods of fixing the Negro population as a poverty-stricken group. It has winked at wide-spread violations of the rights of tenant farmers under the crop-reduction contracts; though the acreage reductions under the government rental agreements dispensed with the need of a great number of the tenants, the government contract theoretically proscribed the reduction of tenants by the land owner. The AAA has blandly permitted the white owner to employ the traditional methods of intimidation of the Negro to deprive him of his benefits from the crop reduction program in payment of parity checks.

The apparent failure of the government's pay-as-you-*not*-grow agricultural program, the growing conviction that the European market for our agricultural products is gone for good, together with the ever-present worry of too many farmers and too much land—we could probably get along with about one-half the number of farmers we now have and could remove from cultivation one-third to one-half of the land now used through the application of efficiency and technical advances to the industry. It is these conditions which have compelled the administration in desperation to flirt with the essentially fantastic "planning" scheme of subsistence homesteads. This scheme proposes to move the inefficient farmers, who thereby are doomed, out of their present economic graveyards and transplant them to semi-rural villages, where they will establish "model" communities. Living on plots ranging from five to forty acres, they will continue to till the soil, but only for family consumption, and are supposed to undergo a sort of economic atavism by reviving the fine old peasant pastimes of pottery making, woodwork, spinning, weaving, etc. To keep life from becoming too monotonous, as it most certainly would under such positive economic security, the government will provide some "factory" seeds for them to plant in the early spring. After the transplanted farmers get through fiddling around in their garden plots, and have indulged in a bit of handicraft, they will thus have the chance to pick up a bit of pin money for automobiles, radios and electric refrigerators, by working in the factories. In this way the submarginal farmer is to be kept on the land and so prevented from swelling the steadily mounting ranks of the industrial unemployed, and likewise kept out of competitive production. In other words the subsistence homesteader will be lifted out of the mainstream of our economic life and laid up on an economic shelf to dry (rot).

The real catch to the scheme is of course in the fact that the bill for the construction, the equipment, repair, taxation, and provision of social services for these communities of "official" peasants, will be footed chiefly by the employed industrial wage earners and the producing commercial farmers; not to mention the serious consequences for a capitalism which thrives on markets and profits, resulting from the consequential contraction of its domestic market for both consumer's and capital goods. This policy Mr. Webster Powell and Mr. Harold M. Ware aptly call "planning for permanent poverty."

Insofar as the program has applied to Negroes it has followed the traditional patterns of racial discrimination and segregation, two Jim Crow projects for Negroes having been recently established.

Primarily, the New Deal is a great relief program which guarantees at level best only a precarious livelihood of the most meager essentials for the millions of distressed workers and farmers who are on the outside of our economic life looking in. Middle-class New Deal planning has adequately demonstrated an utter inability to attain its necessary objectives of lower prices, greater output, and elimination of unemployment in industry. The New Deal policy of planning by separate private industries inevitably tends to raise prices and restrict output,—that is to say, it tends to perpetuate an economy of scarcity. Whether consciously or not, it has placed agricultural scarcity in competition with industrial scarcity, and the resultant increases in the prices of both agricultural and manufactured products have deepened the economic depression in which both agriculture and industry had sunk. It has shown only confusion when faced with the problem of administering prices and production in the interest of the whole population.

In the nature of the case it could at best do but little for the Negro within the existing social structure. The Negro does not even boast a significant middle class which, at least, might share some of the gains made for that class by the New Deal. For the Negro middle class exists, in the main, only psychologically, and can be briefly defined as "a hope, a wish and caricature." In fact, the New Deal planning only serves to crystallize those abuses and oppressions which the exploited Negro citizenry of America have long suffered under laissez-faire capitalism, and for the same reasons as in the past.

NOTES

1. Hacker, *Short History on the New Deal.* p. 26.
2. "The Negro Worker and the NRA," *Crisis,* S 1934.

EMMETT E. DORSEY

The Negro and Social Planning

The Negro in the United States has had imposed on him a caste status. In this most highly developed of all capitalistic countries, the Negro's relation to the community has been heavily characterized by pre-capitalistic and semi-feudal aspects. The Negro's bourgeois revolution, the Civil War and Reconstruction, was abortive. It failed to emancipate the Negro from his feudal state, his caste status. The war was fought to release industrial capitalism from the restraints imposed by the political power of the slavocratic agrarian community. Emancipation and the Reconstruction legislation were dictated by the need of Northern capital to disfranchise the white South until it had made permanent the economic freedom that it had won during the war. Indeed, Reconstruction was the continuation of the Civil War in another form. When industrial capitalism had established its economic hegemony in our national economy it no longer needed the Negro as a political ally. The North collaborated with the Southern section in acquiescing in the nullification of the Negro's civil rights and political privileges.

The *sine qua non* of full bourgeois status for the Negro was the destruction of every vestige of the master-slave relation and its economic basis. This would have meant the breaking up of the large plantations and the introduction of small farming. But the only agent capable of bringing this to pass was the industrial North. The industrial and political leaders of the North, however, were prevented from fulfilling the Civil War's revolutionary meaning to the Negroes because of their need to conciliate the South in order to capture

Emmett E. Dorsey, "The Negro and Social Planning," *Journal of Negro Education* 5, no. 1 (1936): 105–109. Reprinted by permission of the *Journal of Negro Education*.

its markets. The interest of the North in the South was that of economic penetration. This would be most quickly and easily accomplished by allowing the white South to retain its economy and institutions with only a minimum of reform. Thus, the democratic status of the Negro, got by the Civil War, was a caricature of its reality.

The Negro played no significant part in the great movement of settling the West. He was too preoccupied with the illusory politics of Reconstruction. Thus, his future was largely suspended in the activity of Reconstruction.

The post-Reconstruction prospects of the Negro were indeed dismal. The South was given almost a free hand in carrying out its program of disfranchisement and economic and social subjugation of the Negro.

The ideology of acquiescence to this condition was enunciated by Booker T. Washington. It met with the enthusiastic approbation of North and South alike. Northern philanthropy poured millions into the Tuskegees and the Hamptons. Washington taught skills that industrial technology was obliterating or that trade unions monopolized. He would have Negroes become deft servants with the appropriate attitude. Pseudo-scientific farming was taught to youths who, if they became farmers, which most of them didn't, would be agricultural helots. He castigated the labor movement. He thus, by leading Negroes up economic blind alleys, effectively kept them out of the labor struggles. For this yeoman service and the additional one of persuading the Negro to accept the South's political and social proscriptions, the wealthy were willing to pay well.

Washington's encouragement of Negro business enterprise was not resisted by the big capitalists of the country. A Negro middle class sustained by the slender pickings that the colored community afforded was a valuable reservoir of conservatism that would dilute the disaffection of the Negro masses.

The more sensitive and educated leadership rebelled against this crude distortion and through capitulation. W. E. B. Du Bois insisted that the economic opportunities of a capitalist society are open to those who are politically and socially emancipated. He began a militant fight against the Washington school. This fight was basically a struggle for civil liberties. It involved the creation of a Negro intelligentsia. The Talented Tenth was to embody the best in American culture. For a time this educated fringe did struggle valiantly to emancipate the group, from its political and civil bondage. Unfortunately, in the twenties it began to think of itself as a sort of priestly caste in the Negro group. It became the "New" Negro.

The DuBois group advocated business enterprise as vigorously as did the followers of Washington. The logic of their drive to create a Negro middle class demanded an economic basis. Negro business activity was to absorb much of the black working population. As to the feasibility of this scheme Spero and Harris have the following to say:

> The ideal of an independent black economy within the confines of the white is a living force in every black community in the land. Yet how such an independent economy is to rise and function when the white world outside controls credit, basic industry and the state is something which the sponsors of the movement prefer to ignore. If such an economy is to rise it must do so with the aid of white philanthropy, and will have to live upon white suffrance. If the great white banks and insurance companies decide that they want Negro business it is hard to see how the little black institutions can compete successfully against them. The same holds for the chain stores and various retail establishments. They will be able to undersell their Negro competitors if they want to, and the Negro world will not continue indefinitely to pay higher prices for its goods merely out of pride of race. Basic industry will continue to remain in the hands of the white world for even the most ardent supporters of an independent black economy will admit that there is no prospect of the Negro capitalists amassing enough wealth to establish steel mills, build railroads and pipe lines, and gain control of essential raw materials.

Nearly every Negro organization lent rigorous support to this economic will-o-the-wisp. The N. A. A. C. P., the Garvey Movement, the churches, the lodges, and the Urban League agreed upon this type of economic emphasis. To the degree to which this ideology permeated Negro life there was necessarily an augmentation of racial separation. It made more difficult a labor orientation of the black working masses. The Negro businesses employed only an insignificant percentage of the black working men and women. The masses dependent upon industry, personal service, and agriculture, were left without leadership or direction.

The great depression is seemingly disillusioning the masses of the Negroes. They have lost their faith in the N. A. A. C. P. They are beginning to see that, to a considerable degree, American capitalism has been built on the political disfranchisement and the social debasement of the Negro. The wage differentials so beneficial to Southern industry and the system of agricultural labor are dependent upon the retention of this caste status of the Negro. A civil-libertarian struggle is essentially an appeal to the consciousness of the ruling class. It is becoming more and more apparent that the conscience of the economic and political masters is becoming less tender. The wave of reaction that the depression has occasioned makes apparent the need of a more basic attack. In the face of the steady crystallization of reaction, the N. A. A. C. P.'s one-time militancy is rapidly evaporating and its ideology is become increasingly tenuous. It has not and cannot develop an economic program because such a program must necessarily stress labor solidarity and fundamental social reforms. Such a program is incompatible with the Association's middle class and thoroughly racial philosophy.

The depression has made heavy depredations on Negro business. In its crippled condition its grandiose claims have become ridiculous. The middle-class Negro finds it necessary to find other means of employment. In many great cities he has organized movements designed to get Negroes employment in those concerns that cater largely to Negro patronage. The slogan of these campaigns is "Don't buy where you can't work." By boycott and picketing he has forced these white concerns to employ Negro clerks. By this means they have got no more than 1,000 jobs in all of the cities in which this program has been tried. In Washington after one such organization had been carrying on very vocally for over a year 43 jobs had been got. It thus seems highly improbable that this movement will have any economic significance. The sort of agitation surrounding such movements intensifies the consciousness of the job competition relationship between white and black workers. It further deepens the chasm between white and black labor, and the Negroes are led up one more economic blind alley.

Moreover, this bitterness against the white shopkeeper expresses itself in very vituperative anti-semitism. The exploitation of Jewish storekeepers, landlords, etc., is explained on racial grounds. The racial antipathy that is thus engendered obfuscates the real issues and the forces behind the Negro's dilemma. The middle-class Negro, interested in preempting the Jew's position in order the more effectively to monopolize this market raises the bogle of anti-semitism either openly or in concealed fashion. The hope of establishing an economic basis to sustain bourgeois ideals is so tenaciously clung to by the middle-class Negro that in attempting to achieve his ends he is forced to appeal to the very racial chauvinism from which he suffers so much. Even at Howard University the job-conscious members of the Negro middle class have begun to carry grist to the anti-semitic mill. They are making capital of the fact that there are some five or six Jews on a faculty of some 200.

The fantastic idea of organizing the Negro's consumptive powers is now being dangled before the black masses as a means of solving our economic problem—the consumptive power of dispossessed tenant farmers and relief clients! The Negro is to boycott the white retailers and pay more to a coop-erative for an inferior product. One shudders to think of what the chambers of commerce and the state legislatures would do about the relief grants if such a movement threatened white business on a large scale. Dr. Du Bois' plan calls for the production of consumptive commodities by these Negro cooperatives. We are to do what we have never been able to do in the past as valiantly busi-ness community has tried. We are to compete with increasingly integrated in-dustry which in the nature of the case makes small business enterprise more and more difficult. This is another variation of the attempt to make the Negro community an independent oasis in the desert of American capitalism. For-tunately, the advocates of this program have no following. Although their proposals have aroused sporadic academic discussion, they have not touched the masses and it is unlikely that the masses will be moved if and when these ideas finally percolate down to them.

The ills of American capitalism are systemic and organic. Palliatives turn into an infection of reaction. The only correctives feasible are ones which are basic and fundamental. The economic plight of the American Negro is that of the American working class. Our economic problem differs in degree, not in kind. Our special disabilities are organically related to our class exploitation.

The only tenable economic program for Negroes at this moment is one that is pointed in the direction of a transformation of our economic system and the de-segregation of the Negro population. Such a program involves united action by white and black workers. The drive must be toward basic so-cial legislation and ultimately political power. The sharecroppers of the South and Southwest are pointing the way.

The following program, worked out by Abram L. Harris for the N. A. A. C. P., is the program of economic planning for the Negro which I am submitting to you.

Instead of continuing to oppose racial discrimination on the job and in pay and various manifestations of anti-Negro feeling among the workers, we should attempt to get Negroes to view their special grievances as a natural part of the larger issues of American labor as a whole. We should show the Negro that his special disadvantages are but the more extreme manifestations of the exploitation of labor and, on the other hand, it would show white labor that the disadvantages suffered by the Negro workmen and frequently sup-ported by white labor not only perpetuate the hostility between white and black labor, but also place a reserve of cheap labor at the disposal of the em-ployers, serving as a dead weight upon the effective unity and organization of labor. It would show that the world which labor would gain is not a white world, nor a black one, and that this world can only be gained through the solidarity of white and black labor.

To this end the following program is proposed:

A. There should be set up in strategic industrial and agricultural centers workers' and farmers' councils. The function of these councils would be as follows:

1. To conduct classes in workers' education designed to create among Negro working men a knowledge of their historic and present role in modern industry and a realization of their identity of interests with labor.

2. To foster the building of a labor movement, industrial rather than craft in character, which will unite all labor, white and black, skilled and unskilled, agricultural and industrial.

3. To lay the intellectual basis for united action between white and black workers in local, state and national politics for securing passage of adequate legislation on immediate problems, such as (a) old age pensions, (b) child and female labor, (c) lynching, (d) public discrimination and Jim Crowism;

4. To serve as an opposition force to every manifestation and form of racial chauvinism in the labor movement and among workers everywhere, and to attempt to break down discrimination on the job and in pay, and Jim Crowism in the local and national trade union bodies, by showing the mutually disastrous effects of these conditions upon the interests of white and black labor.

5. To serve as centers of education in the use of the ballot, state and national politics.

B. These workers' and farmers' councils are not to be established in a separatist or racial spirit. Wherever possible white workingmen should be persuaded to join. In communities where similar work is being carried on by other agencies, the local branches should assist in making it function more effectively. They are not to be mere discussion groups but through actual participation in strikes, lockouts and labor demonstrations will seek to protect the interests of Negro workingmen and to promote their organization and unity with white labor.

PART 5

The World and the Color Line
Come Home

Introduction

Forty years after W. E. B. Du Bois first identified the existence of an international color line in his classic, *Souls of Black Folk,* his early projection of American segregation and racial injustice against an international backdrop became part of American conventional wisdom.[1] The political and military necessities of the Second World War and of the Cold War that followed required greater sensitivity on the part of the nation's leaders to how racial injustice and unrest might appear to the world at large, especially the peoples emerging from European colonial rule.[2]

Two of the five scholars presented here—Ralph Bunche and Rayford Logan—were born at the turn of the century and were reaching their years of prime intellectual productivity in the 1930s and 1940s.[3] These years of economic depression and world war also provided these black scholars with professional opportunities and limited access to decision makers. Three other figures—Kelly Miller, Du Bois, and Mary McLeod Bethune—entered or were well into middle age during the First World War and (with the exception of Miller, who died in the last days of 1939) met the Second World War as battle-hardened distinguished elders in a long struggle, intellectually armed and ready to reprise and expand upon their arguments of a quarter century before.[4]

As powerful as the internationalist symbolism became in the battle for human rights, its strength was strictly confined by more enduring patterns. For instance, the new salience of civil rights and human rights to the pragmatic conduct of United States foreign policy did not prevent the appointment of Senator James Byrnes of South Carolina, an outspoken segregationist, to be President Harry S. Truman's first Secretary of State. "Negro Americans," Rayford Logan (1897–1982) wrote at war's end, "hardly know what to say about . . . the insistence of Secretary of State Byrnes that there should be free elections in Bulgaria [when] there has been no indication that he has called for free elections in South Carolina."[5] This bold inconsistency is a reminder of Kelly Miller's observation twenty years earlier, in reference to the internal and external reconstructions that *should* have been the aftermath of the First World War: "The only reconstruction worth while [*sic*] is a reconstruction of thought. Permanent reforms grow out of a change in the attitude of mind. The weaker element is always governed by the attitude of the stronger."[6] In measuring the strength of pragmatism versus humanitarian awakening in American attitudes on race, humanitarian concerns were the weaker element, pragmatic calculation the stronger. As Logan put the issue: "This second world war has made [the American people] conscious of the 1,700 miles from Dakar on the West Coast of Africa to Natal in Brazil and of the vital strategic importance of the South Pacific islands. They are therefore desirous of acquiring the outlying posts that will protect them from invasion, but there is no evidence of any greater altruism in 1945 than there was in 1919 or 1920."[7]

Logan, a graduate of M Street High School in Washington, D.C., Williams College, and Harvard University, was well qualified to write on the practical implications of the international color line. He was fortunate to begin his career with both W. E. B. Du Bois and Carter G. Woodson as mentors. As a result, his academic work was not only of high quality, it was fused with a robust commitment to political activism that extended from his local community to the United National, Educational, Scientific and Cultural Organization. In addition, he had experienced the international reach of American segregation as an officer in the American armed forces in World War I.[8]

Ralph J. Bunche's prescient comments from *A World View of Race* introduce an early and leading advocate for interpreting American social and political challenges within the context of an international system still defined primarily by European colonialism. In his Harvard dissertation, Bunche diplomatically found little difference between (and little to praise about) the administration of adjacent "dependent areas" in West Africa, whether by the French colonial administration or the League of Nations. In neither case was the native population being prepared for a future of independence and self-government.[9] Bunche saved a frank discussion of the larger meaning of this conclusion for *A World View of Race*, a strongly Marxian analysis of European colonialism that stood in stark contrast to the text that had earned Bunche a doctorate in political science and had won him the coveted Tappan Prize at Harvard University. Barely concealed behind the imperialist's shallow rhetoric of humanitarian concern for those living in "retarded" or "backward areas" was "the directing motive . . . human greed."[10]

If the language and political orientation of *A World View of Race* was a sharp departure from Bunche's previous writings, the internationalism extends back at least as far as his undergraduate days at UCLA in the mid-1920s. Bunche's earliest public writings were as an early and vocal advocate of greater American involvement in world affairs generally and United States membership in the League of Nations specifically (the League was the predecessor to the United Nations).[11] The selection reprinted here, "Race and Imperialism," sounds some ideological themes that will be very familiar to those who have read his writing in section 4 of this volume.

Ralph Bunche's *A World View of Race* is an excellent overture to the writings of Mary McLeod Bethune, Rayford Logan, and W. E. B. Du Bois. Taken as a group, these essays afford the reader entry into a political culture whose center of gravity was well to the left of American conventional thinking during much of the century. Rayford Logan and W. E. B. Du Bois challenge quite directly the capacity of even liberal intellectuals to meet the challenges of a postcolonial world in which class inequalities on a global scale, if uncorrected, could reestablish imperial and colonial relationships without the benefit of its formerly defining institutions. Du Bois cuts to the quick with his observation that although the "treatment of the Jews in Germany" is historically unique in the dimensions of its cruelty, the ideology of white supremacy at its foundation "has dominated both Great Britain and the United States in relation to colored people."[12] In Du Bois's opinion, the first test of what kind of world and what kind of peace would emerge from the war was whether those in the West who pledged to create "one world"—especially the New Dealers in power in the United States and the democratic socialists about to take power in Britain—could look beyond their own racial blinders. Du Bois criticized those who failed to appreciate the shortcomings of their own worldview: "When we think of unemployment, we mean unemployment in the developed countries of Western Europe and America. We do not have in mind any fundamental change insofar as the darker labor of the world is concerned. We do not think of full employment and a living wage for the East Indian, the Chinese coolie, and the Negro of South Africa, or even the Negro of our own South."[13]

Placed beside the writings of Logan, Du Bois, and Bunche, Mary McLeod Bethune's (1875–1955) essay, "Certain Unalienable Rights," may seem unexceptionally reformist. She does not argue for deep systemic change but for the program that was before the political establishment of the 1940s and 1950s: full citizenship rights (with the understanding, quite prevalent among social democrats in Western Europe and the United States, that citizenship has a socio-economic as well as a political dimension). Bethune, though not a social scientist, was an educator and institution builder. She was, for example, the founder of Bethune-Cookman College in Daytona Beach, Florida; the Southwestern Federation of Colored Women; and the National Council of Colored Women. One consequence of this work was that Bethune became a key advisor to Eleanor Roosevelt as head of the Negro Division of the New Deal's National Youth Administration between 1936 and 1943. As World War II drew to a close, she was also, along with Du Bois and NAACP Executive Secretary Walter White, an observer-consultant to the United States delegation to the United Nations at the founding San Francisco conference in the spring of 1945.

Bethune's essay suggests a keen sense of the razor-thin line between that which is just within reach and that which is just beyond it. If her program is unremarkable to the eyes of the present, her presentation demonstrates how deeply the internationalization of American racial issues had become absorbed by those whose closeness to the center of power commanded a countervailing caution. In her brief for reform, Bethune obliterates the traditional American distinctions between "over here and over there," civilian and soldier, African Americans and all others everywhere "stirred by the clarion call of the Four Freedoms" with an eloquent resolution.[14]

African Americans, no less than others across the world, are "swelling to the breaking point against the walls of ghettos."[15] African Americans rioting against denials of rights and liberty in Los Angeles, Detroit, and Harlem are, according to Bethune, fighting in the same war and in the same spiritual army as the African American troops fighting abroad. The damage done in these domestic conflicts should "recall cities laid in ruins by war." The rioters "are part of a people's war. The little people want 'out.' Just as the Colonists at the Boston Tea Party wanted 'out' from under tyranny and oppression . . . the Chinese want 'out,' the Indians want 'out,' and colored Americans want 'out.'"[16]

Bethune's words serve as a reminder of a special challenge that confronted her and individuals like Ralph Bunche, Walter White, and the economist Robert Clifton Weaver:[17] their influence was informal and advisory—difficult to measure or evaluate. In each case, these figures were diplomats in the emerging symbolic politics of the wartime and Cold War years. As such, each had to wrestle with the fact that their historic proximity to power was a pragmatic response to a world in which the combined forces of demography and technology had finally rendered questions of racism and human rights to be urgently international rather than more easily contained and concealed domestic ones. But did proximity and visibility translate into real power and influence? Far more often than not, the answer was no.

Judged by traditional criteria, the essays in this section are not, in the generally accepted sense, social science scholarship that is the product of formal and properly controlled research. Only one of the five essays was published in a major refereed journal. In addition, they are each, in content, broadsides in a public debate rather than a specialized discussion. And yet it is essential that they all appear here. The focus of the wartime debate on racism and the need for self-determination created a vast new and historically unique public space for discussing the questions that had been so central to these specialists. If they did not wield the influence they had hoped, they were nonetheless making bold efforts as citizen-scholars to set forward the outlines of the postwar world. Working without the institutional support that was on the other side of the color line, these perceptive students of society were nonetheless seeking entry into the same national discussion by every means at their disposal. That they were forced to do so is a reminder that, as Du Bois observed in 1944, "The social sciences from the beginning were deliberately used as instruments to prove the inferiority of the majority of the people of the world."[18]

NOTES

1. On the history of African American thinking on world affairs, see Brenda Gayle Plummer, *Rising Wind: Black Americans and U.S. Foreign Affairs, 1935–1960* (Chapel Hill: University of North Carolina Press, 1996).

2. Although the foci of her research and writing are generally beyond the scope of this anthology, no consideration of writing about international affairs by scholars working and living behind the line can overlook political scientist Merze Tate (1905–1996), who taught during a long career at several historically black colleges, including Morgan State University and Howard. Tate, who earned advanced degrees at Oxford and Harvard, is best known for her ambitious studies of arms control, a process about which she was profoundly skeptical. On this subject see her *The Disarmament Illusion: The Movement to Limit Arms to 1907* (New York: The MacMillan Company, 1942), and *The United States and Armaments* (Cambridge, Mass.: Harvard University Press, 1948). In later years, she studied the politics of annexation, colonialism, and self-government by native peoples in Hawaii and the South Pacific. On the annexation of Hawaii, see her *The United States and the Hawaiian Kingdom: A Political History* (New Haven, Conn.: Yale University Press, 1965). The following articles should be of special interest to readers of this volume: Merze Tate, "Slavery and Racism as Deterrents to the Annexation of Hawaii, 1854–1855," *Journal of Negro History* 47, no. 1 (1962): 1–18; and Merze Tate and Fidel Foy, "Slavery and Racism in South Pacific Annexations," *Journal of Negro History* 50, no. 1 (1965): 1–21. On Tate's career, we are indebted to Joseph E. Harris, "Professor Merze Tate (1905–1996): A Profile," *Negro History Bulletin* 61, nos. 3–4 (1998): 77–93.

3. Bunche was born in 1903 and Logan in 1897.

4. Miller was born in 1863; Du Bois in 1868; Bethune in 1875.

5. Rayford Whittingham Logan, *The Negro in the Post War World: A Primer* (Washington, D.C.: The Minorities Publishers, 1945), 62.

6. Kelly Miller, *The Everlasting Stain* (Washington, D.C.: The Associated Publishers, 1924; reprinted together with Miller's *Race Adjustment*: New York: Arno Press and the *New York Times*, 1968), 70.

7. Rayford W. Logan, *The Senate and the Versailles Mandate System* (Washington, D.C.: The Minorities Publishers, 1945), 102.

8. On Logan see Kenneth Janken's biography, *Rayford W. Logan and the Dilemma of the African-American Intellectual* (Amherst: University of Massachusetts Press, 1992).

9. Ben Keppel, *The Work of Democracy* (Cambridge, Mass.: Harvard University Press, 1995), 38–39.

10. Ralph J. Bunche, *A World View of Race* (Washington, D.C.: The Association in Negro Folk Education, 1936), 39. For a detailed analysis of this work, see Charles P. Henry, "*A World View of Race* Revisited," *The Journal of Negro Education* 73, no. 2, (2004): 137–146.

11. See Ben Keppel, "Thinking Through A Life: Reconsidering the Origins of Ralph J. Bunche," *The Journal of Negro Education* 73, no. 2 (2004): 120–122.

12. W. E. B. Du Bois, "Prospects of a World Without Race Conflict," *The American Journal of Sociology* 49, no. 5 (1944): 450.

13. Du Bois, "Prospects," 453–454. Rayford Logan argued for the United States as a colonial power in Latin America and the West Indies and observed a similar American blindness toward social justice there when compared to American attitudes toward humanitarian needs and social reform in Europe. See Logan's *The Negro and the Postwar World,* 41.

14. Mary McLeod Bethune, "These Unalienable Rights," in *What the Negro Wants,* ed. Rayford W. Logan, ed. (Chapel Hill: University of North Carolina Press, 1944; quoting form the reprinted edition with a new introduction and bibliography by Kenneth Robert Janken, Notre Dame, Ind.: Notre Dame University Press, 2001), 249.

15. Ibid.

16. Ibid., 249–250.

17. Robert Clifton Weaver was another member of the New Deal "Black Cabinet" and became the first African American to serve as an actual member of a president's cabinet when Lyndon Johnson appointed him the first Secretary of Housing and Urban Development.

18. Du Bois, "Prospects," 455.

KELLY MILLER

The Negro in the New World Order

The inherent rights of man receive emphasis and new assertion at moments of social stress and strain. When society is in travail, liberty is born. During the long eras of leisure, the spirit of liberty languishes. Existing order is transformed, and all things made new amidst the fire and smoke of revolution. In times of quietude and peace, social evils accumulate and crystallize. The acquisition of wealth and the attainment of culture and refinement constitute the goal of endeavor. Discontent is decried and the soul seeks its ease. The voice of the reformer is denounced as tending to disturb social placidity and repose. The troublesome issues of the rights of man are banished from consciousness. Inequalities arise, aristocratic prerogative is asserted, and divine sanction assumed as the ordained scheme of social adjustment. When reform becomes impossible, revolution becomes imperative. It requires periodic upheavals to startle the soul from its complaisant slumber, discredit the dominance of material aims, frustrate the assumption of arrogance and pride, and vindicate the rights of man as the highest attainable human value.

History abounds in convulsive epochs when the acute evils of society are eradicated. We have but to recall the tremendous outburst of moral energy during the Revolutionary Struggle and the Civil War, to bring to mind the operation of this principle within our own national experience. Each of these great upheavals served to curb the arrogant assumption of irresponsible power, and to give impulse to the doctrine of the inherent claims of man as man. The titanic struggle which has just engulfed the whole world in red ruin

Kelly Miller, "The Negro in the New World," chap. 3 of *The Everlasting Stain* (Washington, D.C.: The Associated Publishers, 1924), 44–86.

of revolution is but another act in the drama of human liberation, and the up-lifted curtain shall fall on a world transformed.

Revolutions Never Go Backward

Revolutions never go backward. When a nation puts its hand to the plow of liberty, although it might wistfully reverse its vision, yet the furrow which marks the forward path can never be effaced. Revolutions always lessen the domain of oppression and increase the area of liberty. By the inexorable logic of events, the poor and oppressed receive the chief benefits of these great movements of history. The world convulsions precipitate the showers of liberty whose droppings fall upon the needy and neglected of the children of man. The despised Jew of Europe, the oppressed millions of Asia, the Negro in Africa and America, and the under-man throughout the world will be the beneficiaries of the blessings which flow from the greatest epoch in the history of social evolution.

Power and Principle

The fundamental issue involved in this struggle is but the consummation of the age-long struggle between power and principle. The Central Powers, under the compulsion of Germany, espoused the ancient dogma of the dominance of power and the divine right of the strong. Through their ruthless acts, which spoke louder than their arrogant words, they defiantly declared that the weak has no rights which the strong is bound to respect. When the Belgian border was crossed, the die was cast. The Allies were forced, willingly or otherwise, to accept the challenge. Right and might once more met in open conflict. There is in the human heart a deep-seated conviction of the indomitability of right. The universal and spontaneous response to this appeal confirms the same conviction. Power may seem to triumph for a while; might may be enthroned while right is enchained; but final defeat is never accepted until the verdict is reversed, and right is crowned victor. If it appears that God is on the side of the heaviest battalion, a deeper insight and closer scrutiny reveal the fact that ultimately the heaviest battalion gets itself arrayed on the side of right. Power may put on efficiency and seem to work wonders for a while, but conscienceless efficiency is no match for efficiency quickened by conscience. The victorious outcome of this titanic struggle has given to the cause of right a sanction that can never again be shaken. The inviolability of the rights of man has become a sacred principle for all time to come.

The Overruling Purpose

Shakespeare was not uttering threadbare theological dogma, when he declared that "there is a divinity which shapes our ends." This belief is in harmony with universal human experience. No statesman or philosopher was able to foresee or guide the trend of events during these five foregone fateful years. The wise statesmen have but followed the flow of events. The foolish tried to stem the tide. Men and nations have been moved, as it were, by an unseen hand, as pawns upon the chessboard of the world. Those who were at first impelled by the traditional motives of greed, ambition, animosity, and revenge, have been led to a broader vision as the involved purpose of the great drama was unfolded. If there have been hesitation, indecision, and revised or substituted statements of the objects and aims of the war, it has been only in proportion as a constantly clarifying vision has been vouchsafed to those who were sincerely seeking after the right way, if haply they might find it. The wrath of man has been made to serve the great consummation, and the remainder of wrath has been held in restraint. The offense must needs come, but woe unto that man or nation by whom [i]t cometh. The Serbian assassin of an Austrian Prince fired the shot that shocked the world. But we have already forgotten the name of the prince and assassin, in the momentous results which transcended the part which these unwitting participants were made to play. The little fire kindleth a great matter, when the fuel has already been accumulated for the flame. This tragedy was but the exciting occasion of a deep-seated cause. The idle gust overtopples the giant oak only when the foundation has already been undermined. The fullness of time had come. The world was ripe for a great moral revolution. The rapid scientific and material advancement had outrun ethical restraint. Culture had supplanted conscience. Deeds had become glorified over ideals; the thing counted for more than the thought. Success meant more than righteousness. The rights of the weak were subordinated to the interests of the strong. Religion had become silent in the face of wrong. The church with pious cant continued to repeat archaic phraseology, while the world plunged headlong into sin.

The Failure of Prophecy

It is a sad commentary on the human understanding that the so-called wise men and seers of the time were proclaiming the era of universal peace and the end of war, at the moment when the world was on the edge of a precipice. Their eyes were holden, so that they could not discern the signs of the times nor see the shadow of coming events. They proceeded in the even tenor of their satisfied way. Moral maxims were mouthed without moral meaning. The church preached a lukewarm gospel and a tepid righteousness that had reconciled itself with arrogance of class and prejudice of race. It attempted the forbidden rôle of trying to serve God and Mammon. The moral deluge engulfed the complaisant world with suddenness and shock as completely as the Mosaic flood startled and overwhelmed the convivial devotees in the days of Noah. The fountain was suddenly swept away by that hand which rules over events and brings to naught the purposes of man. The highest human wisdom has little predictive value. We can with no greater assurance foretell what the next five years will bring forth than, in 1914, we could predict the momentous movements of the intervening quinquennium. Czar and Kaiser, King and Mikado, Sultan and President, were made to play their assigned parts. The Kaiser of the Germans may be considered the Pharaoh of modern times, whose heart had been hardened, in order that the dominance of right over might might be vindicated anew. The voice spoke through the mouthpiece of the Allies to the heart-hardened leader of the hosts of oppression, saying, "Let my people go." The horse and rider have been overthrown in the Red Sea of destruction, as a modern reminder to kings and nations of the fate of those who would stand between the people and liberty which is their due.

A Righteous Cause

It is not necessary to invoke the doctrine of perfection in order to justify the part which the Allies are playing in this great issue. A righteous cause may be better than any man or nation involved in it. An evil propaganda may be worse than its most wicked advocate. Christianity, in nineteen hundred years, has not yet produced a single Christian according to the rigid exactions of the cult. Nor has the kingdom of evil produced a single unmitigated devil. The modern crusade of liberty is better than any allied nation which espoused it. The doctrine of oppression is more detestable than its most wicked adherent.

Not one of the allied nations could pose as model of the virtue which is espoused, nor yet claim freedom from the evil practices which were so bitterly denounced in the adversary. A nation without sin cannot be found to cast the first stone. In the readjustment of historical wrongs of nation against nation and race against race, the victorious Allies will be forced by considerations of prudence to choose a comparatively recent date as point of departure, to save themselves from serious embarrassment. In order to make ourselves worthy devotees of a righteous cause it is not necessary that we should be free from sin, but that we acknowledge our sin, and promise to do so no more. Any nation that enlists in the crusade of humanity with vainglorious assumptions of self-righteousness thereby proclaims its own insincerity. They who would prepare themselves for vicarious and sacrificial service, must first submit themselves to serious self-searching with deep humiliation and contrition of soul.

Abraham Lincoln was the one commanding moral genius that has arisen in the Western Hemisphere. He followed the leading of the inner light. He heard and heeded the call, and accepted the commission to lead the unrighteous hosts in behalf of righteousness. But he was all the while deeply conscious of our national unworthiness, and accepted the chastening hand of affliction with a groaning of spirit that was too deep for utterance. In an outburst of moral anguish he exclaims: "Yet if God wills that it (the war) continue until all the wealth piled up by the bondsmen's two hundred and fifty years of unrequited toil shall be sunk, and until every drop of blood drawn with the lash shall be paid by another drawn with the sword, as was said three thousand years ago, so still it must be said, 'The judgments of the Lord are true and righteous altogether.'"

The vital difference between the Central Powers and the Allies, all of whom had fallen far short of the standard of national rectitude, consisted in the fact that the Allies stood ready to acknowledge their faults and prayed forgiveness as moral preparation for the great contest. On the other hand, the Germans valued the discarded methods which the Allies repudiated. They had the foolish hardihood to justify their misdeeds as a part of their code of national morality. Great indeed is the condemnation of that man or nation who breaks the moral law and justifies its transgression. A nation cannot wait until it has become perfect before espousing right ideals. But a declaration of high purpose arouses the conscience and reacts upon the conduct. Nations, like individuals, rise on stepping stones of their dead selves to higher things. But all moral progress is estopped when misdeeds are justified. The American people were not in favor of the emancipation of the slave when they entered upon the Civil War. England was not committed to the doctrine of world democracy when she joined hands with Russia, the most autocratic state in Europe, to protect a violated treaty. But just as the battle-cry of freedom soon became the dominant motive in our Civil War, so the World War had not progressed far before it became imperative that the allied cause be impelled by the dynamic power of a moral watchword. To Woodrow Wilson was vouchsafed the high privilege of uttering this word. All the nations of the world have been made nobler and worthier by reason of the righteous doctrine which they have espoused and extolled. Never again can the weak peoples of the world be ruthlessly overridden by arrogant power. The United States has assumed the world's spokesmanship for the doctrine of human liberty. Never again can the American Negro be dealt with in ruthless disregard of this declared doctrine without discrediting our righteous advocacy and making our high pretensions of non-effect.

The Power of Right Doctrine

Historic epochs enounce dynamic doctrines surcharged with pent-up revolutionary power. These doctrines epitomize and express the oppressive burden under which the people have been laboring and embody their ideals of relief. The doctrine is more than the deed. The thought precedes the thing. The issues of life flow from the fountain-head of thought and belief. The Christian church, not unwisely, emphasizes the supreme importance of orthodox belief, which serves as the standard by which right conduct is regulated and controlled. If the people's ideals are right, their conduct cannot be wrong. If the people's ideals are wrong, their conduct cannot be right. A pure fountain cannot send forth a corrupt stream. The world is ruled by opinion. Revolutions always emphasize the right opinion concerning human liberty and the equality of man. "Liberty, fraternity, equality"; "all men are created equal"; "no distinction on account of race and color," are maxims which epitomize the outcome of the three great social revolutions of modern times. These maxims have become axioms and are appealed to as self-evident principles in all subsequent social progress. Revolutionary fervor heats the thermometer of public sentiment many degrees beyond its normal registry. Great truths are uttered by the entranced prophets of reform which transcend the calculated and cautious judgment of calm and quiet reflection. Like the enraptured apostle on the Mount, they utter words of marvelous wisdom, though they wist not what they say. The moral watchword of the French Revolution was principally intended for Frenchmen who were oppressed beneath the heavy heel of haughty autocracy. The author of the Declaration of Independence was a slaveholder, and must have penned that immortal document with serious reservation of mind or disquietude of conscience. The abolition of race and color in civil and political procedure marks the most daring concrete application of this abstract philosophy of human rights to which this doctrine has yet been subjected. The world is still amazed at the moral audacity of the great apostles of human liberty who made the despised Negro a citizen and clothed him with political and civil prerogative power.

The Inherent Truth of Sound Doctrine

The value of doctrine does not depend upon its interpretation by the one who first uttered it, but rather upon the meaning which it suggests and the response which it evokes in the minds of those who receive it. The telling sermon depends upon the meaning which the minister imputes to his text. Shakespeare, who fathomed the depths of human thoughts and feelings, was incapable of profound intellectual or moral convictions. His maxims of wisdom were called forth to meet the requirements of mimic art. We read into his words a profundity of thought and meaning of which the author never dreamed. A word once uttered can never be recalled. He who sends it forth cannot retract or limit its meaning and interpretation to his narrow interest or intention. The early apostles of Christianity were profoundly impressed with the conviction that the gospel dispensation was limited to the Jewish race. It required a divine revelation to convince its chief spokesman of its higher intent and purpose to embrace all mankind. Universal truth enforces universal application, despite the narrow judgment of men who may not be able to see beyond the circle of their own circumstances. The story runs, that a colored citizen of a southern state became sorely perplexed as to a practical definition of the word "democracy," which had recently become current in the discussion of the issues of the day. The dictionaries at his disposal furnished no satisfactory relief from his dilemma, in view of the proscriptive civil and political policy of which he was made to bear the brunt. In the midst of his bewilderment he decided to write to his senator, who is far-famed for his reactionary attitude towards manhood rights of the Negro race. This distinguished senator, not knowing that the request came from a colored constituent, replied: "Democracy means that you are as good as I am." He was thus beguiled into telling the truth, which no subsequent qualification can affect, though he may expostulate until the day of judgment.

World Democracy

Democracy for the world, and the world for democracy, has become the key-word of the convulsive struggle in which the nations and races of mankind are involved. This instantly appeals to the moral energy of those who labor and are heavy laden in all the ends of the earth. It is needless to speculate as to what reservations of thought or qualifications of judgment lay in the mind of the statesman who first gave utterance to this expression, or to point out inconsistency between word and deed. It is more important to know that those who stand in need of the beneficence of the great truth hear it gladly. All races, colors and creeds have fought under the inspiration of its banner. It has become the battle-cry of those who yearn for freedom, the tidings of great joy for those who sit in the shadow of arrogance and power.

Divine Right

The dominance of power over weakness was the only sanction that primitive man needed for his overlordship among his feebler fellows. As soon as the troublesome qualms of conscience emerged, they were assuaged by assumption of divine right. All of the historical evils of nation against nation, and race against race, and class against class have sought justification on this ground. The overbearing attitude of the Germans toward the other nations of Europe was based primarily upon might backed up by assumed divine sanction. Because this nation had reached certain superior attainments, it asserted the right to impose its imperious will upon others without let or hindrance. The arguments which the German apologists used to justify their conduct towards other European nations are paralleled in every particular by the assertions of the anti-Negro propagandists in the United States, who would hold the Negro in everlasting subordination to the white race. One distinguished German philosopher declared:

"As the German bird, the eagle, hovers high over all the creatures of the earth, so also should the German feel that he is raised high: above all other nations who surround him, and whom he sees in the limitless depths beneath him."

Another tells us:

"One single highly cultured German warrior, of those who are, alas! falling in thousands, represents a higher intellectual and moral life-value than hundreds of the raw children of nature whom England and France, Russia and Italy, oppose to them."

With the proper substitution of terms, these citations might be adopted bodily by those American publicists who believe that God has appointed the Negro an inferior place in his all-wise scheme of things. It was but logical that the German nation should raise the race issue in the world conflict. They first appealed to England on the basis of a common Teutonic blood to refrain from entering the conflict in behalf of the inferior Celts and Slavs. The invited participation of the yellow and black races was reprobated as the crowning act of apostasy against the ordained superiority of the white race. It is interesting to note that a certain type of southern opinion which is welded to the divine theory of race relationship agreed with the German point of view, and denounced the enlistment of the black and yellow races to fight against the lordly white race as a crime against humanity.

Deep-Seated Evils

There are certain evils which get themselves so firmly lodged in the human mind that they can be eliminated only by shot and shell. Men at one time sincerely and honestly believed in the right of the strong to own the weak, as master and slave, especially if the strong man were white and the weak one black. This doctrine was shot to death at Appomattox. The last important public utterance of Senator Benjamin R. Tillman, the oracle of a certain school of opinion, was to the effect that he was glad that the Civil War was resolved in favor of the Union, and that the Negro was made free. The mind of the defeated reactionary gives its tardy assent to the righteous judgment enforced by the sword. The German people sincerely believed in the divine right of kings and the German nation. But this doctrine received its death wound at the battle of the Marne. Enlightened German opinion will soon express gratification that the World War was resolved in favor of the Allies, and that the detested doctrine of divine right of kings and nations has been shot out of the minds of men forever. It is the lost cause that never can be revived. The antislavery advocates used to declare that whenever a practice became too despicable for human responsibility, it sought vindication under the shelter of divine sanction. It is noticeable that those who assume familiarity with divine intendment, exhibit least of the divine spirit in dealing with their fellowmen. To suppose that there could be any traceable connection between an All-wise and All-good Providence and the workings of the minds of those who have been loudest in denying the inalienable rights of man, on both sides of the Atlantic, would reverse all our received notions of the divine attributes.

The Divine Right of Race

But along with the divine right of kings must go every other semblance of the divine right, including divine right of race. There is no more reason to suppose that God has chosen the white race to exercise lordship over the darker races of men than that He has chosen Germans to lord it over the other European nations. There exists in the minds of many the deep-seated opinion that the white race has some God-ordained mission to which the weaker breeds must bow in humble submission. Rudyard Kipling's *White Man's Burden* is but the modern refrain of the exploded conceit that God has given his chosen race the heathen for their possession to be broken to pieces with a rod of iron. The divine right of kings is a more acceptable doctrine than the divine right of race. It is more consoling to be required to submit to one ruler of divine designation than to be compelled to bow in subjection to a whole race of persons so designated. Most of the unjust and unrighteous discriminatory regulations against the Negro are based upon the assumed or implied superior claim of the white race. Wherever and whenever the white man is accorded a single advantage because he is white and the Negro subjected to a single disadvantage because he is black, it represents a discrimination without any reasonable justification, human or divine. A social fabric built upon this basis rests upon the foundation of sand which will surely be shaken down when the wind and rain of democracy blow and beat upon it; and great will be the fall thereof.

Kinship in Iniquity

The advocates of race discrimination are spiritual descendants of the defenders of human slavery, who in turn bear close kinship of spirit with the Germans who believe in the divine right of kings. It is a tragedy to see men of genius prostituting their power on the side of human oppression instead of liberty. The most tragic chapter in history is the collapse of the Germans, the most highly favored of nations. They misjudged their mission and misapplied their powers. It will never again be possible for the black man and the yellow man, who fought side by side with the better element of the white race against the outrageous pretensions of the minor and meaner fraction, to believe that color confers any divine favor. By what possible process of logic can it be claimed that one-third of the human race, because it happens to be white, should exercise lordship forever over two-thirds which happens to be colored?

Noblesse Oblige

Some individuals, some nations and some races have present advantages over other individuals, nations and races. If there is any divine attribute to whose appeal the human conscience responds, it requires that the strong should encourage and strengthen the weak, and not aggrandize their own conceit at the expense of those more helpless and hapless than themselves. Germany might have uplifted the whole human race to a higher level of science and achievement, had she chosen the way of liberty rather than oppression. The strong will fulfill their mission in the world by playing the rôle of the big brother rather than that of the big bully. The divine right of kings, the divine right of race, the divine right of class, the divine right of power must go the way of all wicked and detestable dogmas. The only divine right that will be acceptable to a democratic world is the divine right of each individual to make the most of himself.

Race Prejudice

Human history abounds in deep and bitter political, religious and social animosities. The dawn of history breaks upon a world at war. Society, like nature, has been red in tooth and claw. The ape and tiger have had little time to slumber. But race prejudice, as it is understood in the world today, is the product of comparatively modern times. It has sprung up during the past four hundred years, since the Western European has forced himself upon the weaker breeds of man in all parts of the world. Ancient literature contains little or nothing of this form of race prejudice, under which eligibility is based upon the flesh and blood rather than upon mind and spirit. The Germanic races are more seriously afflicted with this idolatry of blood than those of Latin or Slavonic origin. The Latin races have had as wide and varied contact with weaker peoples as the Teuton or his Anglo-Saxon cousin. But the Latin dispensation, despite its manifest imperfections, has never sown the seeds of race hatred in the portions of the world where its power held sway. In South America and in the West Indian Archipelago where the Latin blood and authority dominated for centuries, the people live and move in racial peace and good will. But in the Teuton cult, color is more than creed, race counts for more than religion. The Negro in France may rise to the level of his talent or genius in the civil, social or military life, but race intolerance among the Germanic races would restrict his aspiration on the mere ground of race and color.

A Negro soldier might rise to superior command in the French army; but should a Negro possess the military genius of Alexander, Caesar and Napoleon combined into one, he could not rise above a designated level in the armies regulated by this restrictive spirit. Someone has written a book entitled *If Christ Came to Congress,* and pointed out the strange contradiction which He would witness among those who profess to follow in His footsteps. But should the Man of Sorrows return to earth under the similitude of a man of color, in many parts of the world, He would be denied communion with the saints in His own church which He died to establish; or at most, restricted to spiritual relationship with those of His own assumed complexion.

An Anomaly

It is one of the curious anomalies or history that in the recent World War the climax of bitterness was reached between German and Anglo-Saxon of kindred blood and spirit. The German nation translates its doctrine of intolerance into logical and unmitigated action. The Anglo-Saxon rose up in his might to defeat the logical conclusion of his own intolerant attitude. His good sense has redeemed his bad logic. The spirit of intolerance based on race and blood has received a shock at the hand of its own adherents from which it can never recover. Italy, Spain, France and Russia and the Balkan States do not show the same aversion of race as the Teuton and the Saxon. The Saxon who is but a Teuton of diluted blood is better than the Teuton. Some Saxons are better than others. Race aversion whose stubbornness and strength override considerations of conscience does not characterize the entire white race, but only a lesser fraction of that race. Of these the Germanic element is the dominating force of the world today. But this tough Teutonic intolerant spirit must yield by attrition with the milder and more human disposition of the great majority of the human race whether European, Asiatic or African. For the first time in the history of the world, all elements of the European peoples have come into council with representatives of other races and colors to deliberate upon the fate of the world. This council will be brought to naught unless it is based upon the underlying principles of the brotherhood of man. The Japanese, the foremost section of the Asiatic peoples, are now speaking with authority for the yellow races. They have already put the world on warning that the intolerant spirit of the more arrogant portion of the white race can never be accepted as the final basis of peace on earth and good will among men. Race prejudice is the greatest evil that afflicts the world today. Animosities growing out of greed, religious schisms, and political ambition may be made amenable to reason of force. Those who foster race hatred are defeating the millennium of world civilization, whatever form of value their contributions to human culture may take. What profit is it to gain the whole world at the expense of the soul? German efficiency dwindles in importance when weighed against her accompanying arrogance and intolerance of spirit. Unless the higher soul values shall be universally recognized as transcending the intolerant exactions of flesh and blood, the moral unity of mankind cannot be attained, the devoutly hoped for brotherhood of man is a delusive dream, and Jesus Christ, as Savior of the world, has lived and died in vain.

Moral Consistency

The Allied Nations will be bound in ethical consistency to live up to the doctrines which they espoused to meet the great moral emergency. All permanent progress depends upon the stability of law. The Savior tells us: "Till heaven and earth pass, one jot or one tittle shall in no wise pass from the law, till all be fulfilled." This is characteristic of all universal law, whether spiritual or scientific. It is independent of time and place. This is true of the multiplication table. It cannot be varied or modified to satisfy human arrogance or pride. Great indeed is the condemnation of that one who violates law and justifies the violation. The business man who would misapply the multiplication table in his dealings and justify his conduct, must be placed under drastic penalty, or else our economic fabric would fall. When the German nation would ruthlessly destroy weaker nations for its own aggrandizement and justify the destruction, it was establishing a new code of morality which must not be allowed, lest civilization be imperiled. There cannot be one law for the weak and another for the strong, or one law for black men and another for white men. The ethical principles have no respect for geographical latitudes nor for the conventional pride of men or nations. What is wrong in Germany, is equally wrong in Georgia. Atrocities in Texas and atrocities in Turkey call for like condemnation. The United States, as sponsor for the moral issue upon which the world struggle is waged, will be bound to treat all of its citizens with the equal justice which it is now proclaiming as the saving doctrine for the world. The nation cannot longer permit its own Constitution to be violated with impunity, while insisting that other nations shall observe the letter and spirit of international law. It must practice and inculcate the principles of justice and equality at home, as preparation to serve as moral monitor of mankind.

Reconstruction of Thought

The only reconstruction worth while is a reconstruction of thought. Permanent reforms grow out of a change in the attitude of mind. The weaker element is always governed by the attitude of the stronger. Programs proceed from principles. As long as man looked upon woman as a plaything and a toy, she was a nullity in the state. But in proportion as his more enlightened view leads him to regard her as a co-equal in the equation of life, she will be accorded a larger and larger measure of privilege and prerogative. The Negro was at first regarded as representing an inferior order of creation, fit only for drudgery and rough toil. Under the dominance of this idea, he was made a slave. So long as this notion prevailed, he could hope for no other status. But when it began to dawn that he was a man, with all the involved potentialities of manhood, his captors began to become unquiet concerning the inhuman treatment heaped upon him.

The anti-slavery struggle resulted in profoundly changing that attitude of the people toward the Negro race, which finally resulted in emancipation. Chief Justice Taney's name has been damned to everlasting fame by a single sentence that failed to synchronize with the sentiment of the nation at the time it was uttered. The institution of slavery rested upon the foundation of the dogma that the Negro had no rights that a white man was bound to respect. The leaven of the Declaration of Independence and the anti-slavery propagandists had wrought a great change in public sentiment concerning the place and function of the Negro. It was in view of this altered attitude of mind that the Negro was set free and clothed with the prerogative of citizenship. As the American mind began to grow cold and indifferent on this issue, a strong sentiment was arising which demanded the annulment or abolition of the reconstruction amendments to the Federal Constitution. But at this juncture the World War was precipitated, which reëmphasized the doctrine of the rights of man. The gallant part which the Negro played in bringing victory to the side of liberty has also served to liberalize the feelings and sentiment in his behalf. The new reconstruction, therefore, in so far as it may affect the Negro, will grow out of this new attitude of mind. According to the present state of sentiment, the Negro has some rights which the white man is bound to respect, but others which he is privileged to ignore. The moral revolution must create a new heart and renew the right spirit. All the rights of every man must be respected by every other man. It is needless to attempt to formulate in detail the particular forms which this reconstruction will take. If the spirit of democracy prevails, the statutes, articles, and clauses will take care of themselves.

The African Colonies

The future government of the African colonies will form a chapter in the new reconstruction of the greatest interest and concern to the American Negro. During the past four hundred years the European has been brought into contact with the African. But the one motive has been exploitation of the weak for the aggrandizement of the strong. The poet Pope has embalmed the deep infamy of motive which has dominated the European in his contact with the weaker breeds of men. Lo, the poor Indian, is described as seeking release from it all in his happy hunting grounds beyond the skies,

"Where slaves once more their native land behold
No thieves torment, no Christians thirst for gold."

But a new note has been uttered. The beneficence of democracy is extending even to the man farthest down. The enlightened statesmen have united in declaring that, hereafter colonies must be governed in the interest of the people themselves, and not for the aggrandizement of their exploiters. The haughty Germans, relying on the ancient dogma of divine right, have ruthlessly ruled the African colonies with iron efficiency, with sole reference to gain. It is agreed on all sides that these colonies must be taken over by the Allies in the interest of humanity. They are to be governed, as far as practicable, on the basis of self-determination. The United States is under heavy moral obligation to the African continent and its people. Under the spell of the old dogma, America reached out her long arm across the sea and captured helpless African victims and subjected them to cruel bondage. The Peace Conference will be confronted with the question of requiting the historic wrong of one nation against the other; the American can never requite the Indian whose land she despoiled and whose race she extinguished; nor yet the African, whose simple-souled sons and daughters were snatched from their native land and made to labor for centuries in unrequited toil. But the adjustment of grievances of French against German, and Italian against Austrian, suggests the deep moral obligation to this helpless and expatriated people. The United States represents the highest type of democracy among the nations. Democracy will never justify itself as a world influence unless it can be becomingly related to the backward and belated peoples of the world in such a way as will lead to their speedy development and reclamation. Indeed the immediate, persistent problem of civilization is the satisfactory adjustment of the advanced sections of the human race to their less fortunate fellowmen.

The infamy which has hitherto characterized this relationship stands in ever-lasting discredit against the claims of Christianity and civilization. While the Constitution of the United States does not bestow authority of government over subject races and peoples, nevertheless, we have taken over Hawaii, Porto Rico [*sic*] and the Philippines on the ground of national necessity and benevolent assimilation. The United States is under both moral and political obligation to assume responsibility for the future welfare of the African colonies taken from Germany for reasons of humanity. It might be well for the United States to assume complete responsibility over a section of the German colonies as an example to the world of how a backward people can be governed without exploitation, and lifted to higher planes of civilization under the guidance of the democratic spirit. This government would naturally enough utilize the talents and attainments of its Afro-American element to help sympathetically in the government and development of their African kinsmen.

Self-Determination

No people, however lowly and backward, can be effectively governed unless an element of self-determination is involved in their government. There are ten million Americans of African descent in the United States. They have naturally a vital interest in the welfare of their motherland. The Afro-American, on the whole, constitutes the most advanced section of the African race to be found anywhere in the world. He is best qualified to utter the voice of two-hundred million black people in the continent of Africa and scattered over the face of the globe.

Race Leadership

All true leadership must be autochthonous. It must spring from the midst of those to be led. The real leader must be of the same blood and sympathies and subjected to the same conditions and linked to the same destiny as his followers. No race can speak for another or give utterance to its striving of soul. Before an individual of one class can assume to be spokesman for another, he must forego his former allegiance and naturalize himself in the class for which he aspires to speak. He must leave the one, and cleave to the other. Should a conflict arise between the two, he must eschew the old and espouse the new.

Napoleon Bonaparte was by blood an Italian. He became not only the mouth-piece but the oracle of the French people; but he must first become a French-man by adoption. The white man is not disposed to become naturalized in the Negro race, nor to forego the privilege and prestige which his class and color confer. The Kaiser is the most detested white man on the face of the earth today. And yet the Anglo-Saxon *amour propre* would revolt against the suggestion of subjecting him to the humiliating conditions which without compunction of conscience it forces upon the Negro.

The Limit of Philanthropy

In the days of slavery when the black man's tongue was tied, noble champions arose to plead his cause. The voices of Phillips, Garrison and Sumner, ringing with righteous indignation, quickened the conscience of the nation. This race can never repay the debt of gratitude for this vicarious service. But the slave has been made a freeman. His sons and daughters have been taught the art of disquisition and persuasive appeal. The black man must now plead with his own voice and give tongue to his own complaints. The white man can yet do much to champion the cause of the Negro, and to arouse the conscience of his own race against injustice and wrong heaped upon the defenseless head of the weak and helpless people. Altruistic advocacy, however genuine, fails to arouse the desired response in public feeling and judgment. The people who fail to produce their own spokesman can hardly convince the world that they feel a deep-seated sense of injustice and wrong. The man who feels the wound must utter the groan. Although the retained advocate may have a genuine interest in the welfare of his clients, the persuasive power of his plea is weakened by the thought that his own destiny is not involved in the verdict. It was neces-sary that Moses should be one in flesh and blood and spirit with the oppressed people of Israel, to qualify him to stand before the court of Pharaoh, and plead their cause with plenary power and unimpeachable moral authority.

The Voice of the Negro

The white man, with amazing assumption of wisdom and goodness, has un-dertaken to set the proper régime for the Negro without consulting his ad-vice or consent. The all-wise physician disdains inquiry of the patient of the nature of his ailment. But experience proves that the civilized man is not en-lightened enough to govern the savage; that the saint is not sanctified enough to govern the sinner; the philosopher is not wise enough to govern the fool, without involving the consent and participation of the one to be governed. John Locke was a keen expert in the workings of human understanding, and yet he was unable to draft a satisfactory constitution for the people of South Carolina. It is now conceded that the European, with all of his assumed power, has woefully failed in establishing efficient and satisfactory government of weaker races and peoples. This failure has been in proportion to his neglect to consult the interest and feelings of those to be governed. There can be no good government where the principle of self-government is not involved and invoked.

The Negro represents one-eighth of the population of the globe. The Peace Conference now sitting at Paris has assumed the function of the Parliament of Man. The common sense of most must hold the fretful world in awe. All classes and races with just grievances to be remedied or wrongs to be righted are seeking a hearing before this tribunal of law, justice and peace. The laboring men throughout the world, the Irish, the Jews, dissatisfied elements of every race and class, are demanding a hearing through voices of their own choosing. Shall not the voice of the Negro be heard and heeded, if the world is to establish an enduring peace or equality and righteousness?

The New Reconstruction

The United States belongs to the victorious nations, and is not subject to technical reconstruction. Our whole fabric, however, economic, political, social and moral, will be transformed by the new democratic spirit. The Negro need not expect to be made the subject of special legislation, but may expect to be included in the program of social justice and human opportunity. Proscriptive and restrictive regulations will be nullified under the mollifying influence of these ideals.

Rights and Fights

The Negro represents a minority in the midst of a more powerful and populous people; but unlike minority races in the Balkan States, he does not hope to win his cause by primary conflict. He must rely upon the essential righteousness of his claim and the aroused moral sense of the nation. He is a coward who will not exert his resistive power to its utmost for the unlimited enjoyment of every right which God or man has conferred upon him. There are certain God-given rights which man may be mean enough to deny but never can be mighty enough to take away. The contest which the Negro must wage incessantly and unceasingly is not a conflict that would result in the destruction of the social fabric of which he forms a part, but would rather lead to the fulfillment of its declared aims and ideals. The Negro's cause is right, and right must finally win. The devils believe this, and tremble.

States' Rights

As a striking result of this new reconstruction, the old doctrine of States' rights, which had its origin in the purpose to subordinate the Negro and perpetuate his inferior status, will be wiped away. This reactionary doctrine has stood athwart every great moral reform which our nation has undergone. It opposed unity of the nation and the freedom of the slave. It sought to defeat prohibition and women's claim for the suffrage. Provincialism has been the bane of our national life. The Civil War created a new nation with dominant powers over the states. The World War will create a new world whose sanction will transcend that of any nation. Great reform movements, now sweeping through the world and the nation, will benefit all of the people, and no race or class can be shunted from the benefits thereof.

The Old Reconstruction and the New

The reconstruction growing out of the Civil War resulted in adding the Thirteenth, Fourteenth and Fifteenth Amendments to the Constitution of the United States. The Thirteenth Amendment, abolishing slavery and giving the Negro his freedom, is universally accepted and uncontested. The Fourteenth and Fifteenth Amendments, which made the Negro a citizen and clothed him with the elective franchise, have never been accepted in all parts of the nation. The refractory states have in a large measure nullified the intended effect of these Amendments. But the new reconstruction through which we are now passing must complete the work of the old, so that in truth and in deed, as well as in word and phrase, "There shall be no discrimination on account of race or color."

The failure of the old reconstruction, in so far as it may be so considered, was due to the fact that it never met with the unanimous acceptance of the American people, but was forced by one section upon the unwilling acquiescence of the other. The new reconstruction, on the other hand, must meet with the unanimous consent of the American people, North and South, East and West. What American dares rise up and say nay to the demands of democracy?

Government Based on Inequality

Alexander Stephens, the vice-president of the Confederacy, stated in his inaugural address, that the Confederate States would attempt to found a government based frankly upon human inequality. For four long years the bloody struggle raged around this issue. Strange to relate, the World War, waged upon the survival of the same issue, lasted for the same duration of time. The Confederate cause was lost. The German cause has been lost. Any cause that openly advocates human inequality is bound to be lost under the assault of democratic ideals. By the irony of history, the political heirs and assigns of the advocates of government based upon inequality were in control of the affairs of this nation during the World War, when it was committed most unequivocally to the doctrine of government based frankly upon human equality. Woodrow Wilson was spokesman for democracy, not merely for this nation but for all nations. It may be said, in homely phrase, that the South was in the saddle, but she was riding a democratic horse which was headed to the goal of human equality. She must ride straight or dismount.

Reaction

Reactionary voices here and there may be expected to rise, but they will be drowned in the triumphant course of democracy. Over-buoyant expectation may meet with disappointment. Negro soldiers, returning from across the seas with laurels of victory, may here and there be made to feel the sting of rebuff and insult by the very people whose liberties they fought to secure. Intense local animosities may be engendered in one place or another. Outbreaks and murder may spasmodically occur. A comprehensive understanding of the far-reaching effect of forward movements must discount all this. Black laws followed the Thirteenth Amendment. The Ku Klux Klan came after reconstruction. There was a recrudescence of race prejudice after the Spanish-American War, in which the Negro had played a glorious part. These are but backwaters in the current of democracy. The tide is now at flood and cannot be stemmed. The most conspicuous opponents of democracy, for fear it might include the Negro, with dying gasp of defiance, were driven from places of public power under the excoriating lash of President Wilson, Southerner. The logic of events overrides the narrow purposes of men. The sign of democracy is written across the sky, in letters so bold and pronounced, that he who runs may read; and those who are too foolish to read will be compelled to run.

Rights and Duties

The Negro must not be allowed to make the same mistake in the new reconstruction that he was permitted to make in the old. All of his energies were focused upon the issue of political rights and privileges with little or no reserved power for economic and industrial advancement. Could Booker T. Washington have come upon the stage a generation earlier, preaching the doctrine of industry, thrift and economy alongside of Frederick Douglass, proclaiming in thunderous tones the gospel of human rights, the advancement of the race would have been built upon a foundation that could not be shaken. The desired product involves both factors. In this new day, the Negro must place equal emphasis upon rights and duties. He must deserve all that he demands, and demand all that he deserves.

Self-Reclamation

The government can give the individual only a fair chance. The race, he himself must run. No trick or contrivance of government can ennoble the Negro beyond the level of his work and worth. When democracy prevails, the upward struggle has just begun. Soil, sunshine, and moisture may abound, but the seed must send its own roots into the soil, and its blades into the air by the push of its own potency.

War energizes the powers, and liberalizes the faculties of man. In the wake of war, reconstruction always builds mightier structures than those that have been torn down. The United States is on the threshold of a mighty economic, educational, and moral awakening. The worker will feel a new zest, the thinker will have a new thought, and the poet will sing a new song. Opportunities will be open to every competent and willing worker for the best development and exercise of his highest powers and attainments. The Negro must contribute his bit and his best to the general welfare, and derive his just share from it. He must enter as a competent and willing participant in the new issues of life, and must not fail to help promote the glory of that new freedom whose beneficiary he devoutly hopes to be.

RALPH J. BUNCHE

Race and Imperialism

Modern imperialism has given added impetus to the tendency to classify human peoples as "superior" and "inferior" for race has been a convenient device for the imperialist. Under imperialism's zone of conquest the population of the earth has been arbitrarily divided into "advanced" and "backward" races or peoples. Imperialist propaganda has taught the world to regard certain peoples as helplessly backward and incapable of keeping step with the modern industrial world. In fact, strenuous efforts are made to make these peoples think of themselves as backward. But this classification is not a mere theoretical one. It is used as the basis for justifying conquest and exploitation and for dividing the world into dominant and subordinate peoples. Thus imperialism has attempted to mask its cruelly selfish motives under high-sounding titles. Powerful industrial nations have raped Africa under the false pretense of shouldering "the white man's burden." It has been held to be the particular mission of the dominant peoples to bring civilization to the backward peoples of the earth; to convert them to the Christian religion and to expose them to the benefits of an advanced European culture. A new "moral" philosophy is invented which holds that some peoples are naturally backward and therefore properly may be kept in a more or less permanent state of subjection to the advanced peoples. But since the backward peoples have often been reluctant to receive these blessings they have been forced to accept them at the point of the bayonet. In this way Italy is bestowing the "blessings of civilization" upon the hapless Ethiopians today. After the

Ralph J. Bunche, "Race and Imperialism," chap. 3 of *A World View of Race* (Washington, D.C.: The Associates in Negro Folk Education, 1936), 38–65.

conquest has been completed, the backward peoples bitterly learn that the "blessings" consist of brutal suppression, greedy economic exploitation of the natural and human resources of a country which is no longer their own, forced labor, the introduction of previously unknown diseases, vice and social degeneration.

The Designs of Imperialism

More than half of the land surface of the world and over a billion human beings comprise the colonies, protectorates and "retarded" or "backward" areas dominated by a few imperialist nations. Thus approximately one-third of the human race is directly subject to imperialist domination. Powerful nations such as England, France, Italy, Japan and the United States, have been guilty of many acts of imperialist aggression. Even small countries like Belgium, Holland and Portugal exploit great colonial areas with large native populations.

The directing motive in this process is human greed. The so-called backward peoples would hold no attraction for the advanced peoples if they possessed no human or material resources which are needed by the industrial nations. The right of property is given a new twist to fit the needs of these nations. Thus the backward races are told that the natural resources of the world can no longer be regarded as the exclusive property of those peoples who happen to control them at the moment. Natural resources are now said to belong to those who demonstrate the best ability to exploit and use them. Since the backward peoples are often less concerned with the exploitation of men and resources for the purpose of creating wealth for the few, they are held to have no right to their domain. They are conquered, control of their territory is wrung from them, and they are put to work making their own resources available to the rest of the world. It also follows that the backward peoples themselves are given little opportunity to share in the new wealth thus made available.

Imperialism is an international expression of capitalism. The rapid growth and expansion resulting from the development of industrialism and capitalism led the peoples of industrial countries to seek raw materials and new markets all over the world. This led to more general group contact, and because of the base motives of imperialism, to more widespread racial conflict. The invasion of a territory by a more powerful race results not only in racial conflict but makes more difficult the struggle for existence of the weaker race. In addition the culture and social structure of the latter race tend to be disorganised.

The intensity of the race conflict as the result of imperialism depends in some measure upon the cultural background and the economic status of the , conquering race. The white invaders who conquered North America were motivated by economic considerations which were supported by a strong sense of racial superiority. Thus the Indians were driven out of the desirable areas of the country and almost completely exterminated. In South America, Spanish plantation owners were equally animated by economic motives. However, they assumed a milder and more humane attitude on the problem of race status. The Indians of South America were allowed to remain on the land, though they had to work for their Spanish masters. Intermarriages between Spanish and Indians often took place. In this way the South American Indians were able to keep their only means of subsistence, the land, and were permitted the opportunity for gradually adapting themselves to the new civilization which the Spanish brought with them.

In Africa, with the exception of South, and more recently, East Africa, large-scale settlement of white populations has not been possible largely because of the climate. Consequently, colonisation in Africa has proven much more difficult for the white races than in either America or Australia. Moreover, the Negro demonstrates a strong power of survival. Some of the "blessings" which the European brought to Africa and the Africans were truly "in disguise." They have taken the form of the slave trade, forced labor, and dangerous diseases such as syphilis, with which the African peoples had had no previous contact. Such factors have led to great decimation of population in many parts of Africa and to the break-down of African civilization and tribal social structure. Africa is imperialism's greatest and most characteristic expression.

African Imperialism

Africa, and particularly West Africa, may be taken as an excellent illustration of how the dominant and "superior" races of Europe have conquered peoples less expert in "civilized" methods of warfare. It also demonstrates how race has been employed as a device not only to justify the conquest to the world, but how in some instances it has proved an effective means of emotional appeal in order to make the exploitation of the conquered peoples more acceptable to them. The technique of governing subject races and minimizing racial conflict in West Africa is both revealing and fairly typical of the methods employed elsewhere in the Far East, Australia and the Caribbean.

In considering the impact of Western imperialism upon the African it must be borne in mind that the partition of the Dark Continent among the nations of Europe is an affair of only the past half-century. The penetration of Africa actually began much earlier, but the imperialism of today is a product of modern capitalism, and the beginning of its application to Africa coincides with the deep penetration into the hinterland and the partition of the continent in the last quarter of the nineteenth century. Back of this partition of Africa were the compelling economic forces of modern industrial capitalism. The need of industrial countries for expanded markets, for raw materials found in the tropics and sub-tropics, the accumulation of "surplus capital" and the resultant demand for overseas investments, all tended to force European imperialist nations to invade completely the African continent. In addition, it should be remembered that until the twentieth century the colonizing nations had little to offer Africa but imperialist exploitation in its crudest form, accompanied by greed, hostility and misunderstanding. It has been this brief but unsavory early history of Europe in Africa which has impelled some writers to indict the general effects of European policy as "almost wholly evil," and to regard the process in its entirety as one of fraud and robbery.[1]

It should not be surprising that a defenseless people, regarded as members of an "inferior," primitive race by invading conquerors, should be as much victimized in their own country in which they are in the great majority as where they are a minority racial group, as is the case of the Negro in this country. Moreover, there is in both instances the same lack of serious effort to work out a just and intelligent policy for the government and control of these peoples.

The representatives of Western civilization in Africa from the beginning set about considering the new country mainly in relation to their own needs and interests. The fertility of the soil, the richness of natural resources, the salubrity of the climate, the industry and health of the primitive population are all important to the European only in terms of potential exploitation. Commonplace as the observation may be, seldom, if ever, has the welfare of the native population been given front rank in these considerations.

The European administrator in Africa is generally quite indifferent to the conditions of native life. Forced to take many precautions to preserve his health in a severe and trying climate, he finds it difficult to exert an interest beyond the immediate demands of his job. For example, the West African administrator quite often forgets that many of the West Africans are culturally in a transitional stage: in reality they are neither primitive nor civilized in their present mode of living. Residing in the coastal towns of West Africa are thousands of natives who have become detribalized, who have picked up many European customs and who have forgotten many of their own. There are many of them who wear fine European clothing, speak polished French or English, construct beautiful homes and send their children to school. Yet they may worship fetishes, marry several wives, eat without cutlery and sleep on the floors in bare bedrooms despite elaborately furnished parlors. They will scorn the authority of chiefs whose education is often inferior to their own. Their conception of property is private, no longer communal.

The bold fact is that quite generally the colonizer has gone into the African territory with only one idea in mind, and that quick riches. He has found the native there, considered him only incidentally, arranged for him a makeshift system of administration without serious study of his needs or wishes, and has then been startled when the native protests, when uprisings occur and when the whole thing seems to work out badly. But the Europeans have pacified Africa. Violent racial conflict, except in sporadic instances, has disappeared, with the lone exception of the recent struggle in Ethiopia, and even this one was soon settled in favor of the European, just as all the others have been in the past. Every tribe on the African continent with the exception of those in Liberia is governed and taxed by some European power. True, an occasional tax-gatherer or other administrative officer gets cuffed about a bit or even killed, but tax-collectors and policemen meet similar fates in more civilized societies. Except for extreme instances, Africa is subdued. Cultural conflict goes on, however, and there is much smouldering resentment among the native masses which may some day break out in violent conflict.

There have been significant changes in the views of peoples of the Western World toward the African since Kipling's lyrical description of him as "half devil and half child," and since the Frenchman, Jules Ferry, first explained the "duty" of the "superior" races, such as the French, to civilize the "inferior" races. Most of the inhabitants of what some modern anthropologists hold to be the cradle of the human race, have now become "official wards" of civilization. No longer an obstacle to European penetration of Africa, they are regarded as a valuable labor-supply. While scholars may debate whether this African Negro, whom "only sun, malaria and sleeping sickness have saved from extermination at the hands of the white man," is or is not an inferior race, colonial policies and colonial officials usually proceed on the assumption that he is. To the European colonizer he is still the "happy beast," the docile primitive, with the mind of a child.

The characterization of the African by the celebrated South African administrator, General Smuts, is that most prevalent among the Europeans who rule him. To Mr. Smuts the native has "largely remained a child type, with a child psychology and outlook. No other race is so easily satisfied, so good-tempered, so care-free." Hardships mean little to him: despite them he remains "the most happy human." A high official in Togoland will relate that the native, though trained in the schools of Togo and Dakar, can rarely be trusted to work without white supervision because he "does not have the brain-power." Another, who can get more roads and official palaces built than two ordinary French administrators, will say that these "child-like" primitives "must be kept in servitude another hundred years." Like the typical white American from the South, these men *know* the African; they have lived and worked with him for many years. They are benevolent toward him, unless he becomes "impudent" and protests against injustice, and they know how to get the most work out of him too. Africa is their laboratory and their blind experience is all the science they need. No further information is needed than that the African is and remains true to their conception of what the African ought to be. When he attempts to become something else he is "dangerous," a menace, and must be "put in his place."

Modern anthropologists, geneticists, and unbiased social scientists take a different viewpoint and attempt to explain the African, to analyse his condition and interpret him in scientific terms. They ask themselves whether the African Negro is intellectually inferior to the other human races. They find it necessary to draw a distinction between lack of intellect and ignorance; they emphasize the significance of environment. They point out that the African Negro is a race which has had to depend almost entirely upon itself for progress, and that the external contacts which Africans have had have been as much a force for retardation as for progress. They often wonder whether their own races would have done any better under similar circumstances.

How the African Is Governed

By what devices is the African governed? In the history of the contact of Europe with the African two extremes of policy have been applied to him. The one, based entirely on greed, regarded him as the essentially inferior, sub-human, without soul, and fit only for slavery. The other, based entirely on sentiment, regarded him as a man and brother, extended to him the equalitarian principles of the French Revolution and attempted to "Europeanize" him overnight. Both desired to get as much from him as possible. Both were unscientific and devoted little attention to the needs and desires of the African.

The basic weakness of the policies which have so often been applied to the African is in the fact that these policies still remain so vague as to the actual objectives aimed at. Where is the African headed? Is he to have eventual independence or is he to remain forever a subject race in "harmonious cooperation" with his administrators? Or is he to be completely absorbed by the conquering people? These questions the French have attempted to answer, on paper, at least, much more clearly than the other colonizing nations. But a colonial policy which aims to do justice to the native must embody much more than platitudes and vague assurances that the "welfare of the natives is paramount." It must exhibit a definite program for native development which will lead the native toward an ultimate specific political and social status. Few, if any, existing colonial policies have gone that far.

It would seem that the only sound objective of African colonial policies should be to prepare the Africans for membership in the community of the civilized world, not as individuals but as communities. Any other policy applied to regions of Africa such as West Africa, for example, where extensive white settlement is definitely proscribed by nature, leads to the inescapable inference that the native is to be kept forever in political bondage, even though of a milder sort, by a handful of his "superiors." Second only to this first principle of colonial policy toward subject peoples should be the premise that the social and political development of the native in the African colony must at least keep pace with the economic exploitation of his country and whatever economic development may be presumed to accompany that exploitation. An analysis of the colonial policies in effect in present-day Africa, however, indicates clearly that they fall far short of meeting either of these desirable ends.

In general, particularly insofar as West Africa is concerned, it may be said that there are two policies of native administration in vogue among the colonial powers. One of these is commonly identified as the "French system," and the other as the "British system." Neither nation employs one or the other system exclusively, however, and there are certain fundamental factors which each has in common with the other. In the first place French and English alike are in Africa primarily for economic exploitation and not from motives of philanthropy. In the second place both powers intend to retain control of their respective possessions and their subject populations indefinitely. England and France are not thinking in terms of native independence or self-government for the West Africans except in its most meager local sense. For the English the objective is what is styled "harmonious cooperation;" for the French what is called "association." Colonial authorities like the noted Englishman, Lord Lugard, doubt that the African race, whether in Africa or America, can develop capability for self-government. Let us examine the native policies of these two nations.

The French Native Policy

In the early period of her colonial activity in Africa, France, like all other colonizing powers at the time, pursued a ruthless policy of subjection and exploitation. The colonies were regarded only as a "privileged" market for French goods and a source of raw materials for French manufacturers. Commercial freedom for the colony was out of the question and the trade regulations were just as stern as the British Navigation Laws. It was thought to be a waste of time to consider the education, health and general welfare of the native; he was more a natural-born beast of burden than a human. Gradually the French policy of assimilation of native subject races developed. This policy gave expression to the words of Napoleon, "wherever the flag is, there is France." Economically and politically the colony and its population was to be absorbed as rapidly as possible in the Greater France. Native customs were to be disregarded and as quickly as possible the native populations were to be steeped in French culture and civilization and drawn to the bosom of France as "citizens."

This policy of assimilation has been called the "policy of the Latin races." It was based upon an extreme egoism in that it accepted nothing in the native civilization as good, and was fired by a desire to spread the French culture over the face of the earth. Its underlying philosophy involved the vaunted ability of the French, as other Latin peoples, to cordially welcome, without prejudice of race, darker peoples, and to win their loyalty by offering brotherhood.

In considering the merits of the former French policy of assimilation in its application to their black colonials, some French writers have attempted to draw on the experience of the United States with her black population. They have seen immediately the paradox of the American system, with its policy of political assimilation set off against social (and often economic) segregation based on an assumption of racial inferiority. But the American analogy is a poor one for French purposes. The American Negro is an exceptional case in that he has been torn away from his origins and dumped into an entirely new milieu in which he finds himself a minority group. The French African peoples are in an exactly opposite position, living as they do (or used to do) on their tribal lands and affected in their customs only by the influence of a slim minority of Europeans.

The French in recent years have found it expedient to abandon their pretensions at the wholesale assimilation of native populations in favor of the less ambitious, utilitarian, and somewhat more liberal policy of "association." From this point of view native customs and native society come to be regarded as something slightly more than a mere obstacle to progress, which should be wiped out in due haste. The new policy recognizes rather timidly that it is dealing with peoples who have some right, at least, to live their own lives. Under this new policy the native is supposed to lose his former role of the black robot and become a "collaborator" in a system of "colonial planning." But the native remains the all important cog in the scheme, for he is the indispensable auxiliary in furnishing the manpower which is necessary to exploit the wealth of the colony. The native is supposed to be led to a material civilization comparable to that of Europe,—(and essentially French)—through the multiplication of public works, the development of cultivation, the creation of industries, and the expansion of commerce, in all of which he is supposed to be an "associate." The policy frankly proposes to exploit the "backward" African and just as candidly believes that he will not only like it but will enthusiastically aid and abet the process.

The "Elite" Native

Many factors may be mentioned as contributing to the operation of this new French policy, but one of the most significant is the seemingly genuine freedom of the French mentality from race prejudice in its more vulgar forms, which facilitates more cordial social contacts between the governing and the governed, and avoids the dangers of rigid caste distinctions. Intimately related with this racial attitude of the French is the formation of a privileged or *elite* class of natives, who become definite allies of the French administration in keeping the native masses in check. Special concessions exist for the members of this elite group under the provisions of which they may acquire citizenship and other civil and political privileges, such as membership in local assemblies and subordinate administrative positions, in proportion as their capacity develops and their numbers increase.

It is upon the assumed loyalty of this elite class of natives that the permanency and success of the French relationship with the colony are to rest. The members of this elite, above all others, are to be bound to the French state, and, through absorption of French culture, they will become assimilated, i.e., "black Frenchmen." In this group are included all notable members of the native community—chiefs, wealthy merchants, government clerks, members of the village councils of elders. This concept of an elite class among subject peoples is not a new one in colonial practice nor is it peculiar to the French practice. Every colonizing power has found it helpful to foster a small class of privileged natives who can be depended upon to defend and aid in the execution of the policies of the nation which has so favored them. It has often been a subtle and very effective form of bribery. The native chief who receives handsome subventions from the government, the clerk or other government employee, the wealthy merchant who has been knighted, are not likely to become overly critical of government policy, whether it is in the interest of the masses of the native population or not. When an African, educated abroad, returns to his homeland and in rare instances refuses to become obligated by the acceptance of such dubious honor or position, and proceeds fearlessly to criticize the administrative policy, he is immediately blacklisted as "dangerous" by the administration. If he persists he will be branded as a radical and sooner or later as a communist, and perhaps exiled from the colony.

Obviously then the employment of this racial elite class as a device for the control of the country is a condition viciously inimical to the best interests of the masses of the natives.

The elite native truly becomes a black Frenchman. The French feel that they have been successful in the inoculation of the black populations in their colonies of the Antilles with the French culture. Why not Africans then? The educated Martiniquian or Guadeloupian, and there are very many, is as cultured and highly polished as any white Frenchman. Representatives of the elite have held many high positions in the French government and military service. They have occupied the position of Under-Secretary of State for the Colonies. They have been generals in the army; others have held high positions in the colonial service, even as high as Governor of a colony; they are judges, lawyers, doctors. But above all they are Frenchmen, regard themselves so, and are so regarded.

Perhaps the most striking feature of the French contact with the Negro peoples has been its success in winning the loyalty of this class of elite natives. There are exceptions, of course, but on the whole it can be said that the colonials of African descent of no other nation, including the British West Indian Negroes, evidence a spirit of loyalty and cordiality toward the peoples of the dominant country equal to that expressed by the French Negro elite. They will criticize, but always as Frenchmen, who have this right against their own government. They are proud of being a part of the French whole.

The French Attitude on Race

What is responsible for this apparent popularity of the French with the native elite? The French will immediately answer that it is due to the fullness of the French heart which will accept the native as a brother with no thought of race or color. In this lack of race and color prejudice the French seem to have a measure of sincerity. There is no real color line in France and none in her colonies, though individual instances of prejudice and discrimination may be encountered in both places. This French attitude is strikingly evident on the boats of the French lines which transport colonial administrators, merchants and other travelers to and from the African colonies. Here there is to be found a genial cordiality among the French and their elite associates of the darker races. On all such boats there are numbers of black-skinned men and women from Martinique, Guadeloupe and Reunion who are employed in the French colonial service, together with native Africans, likewise employed. The genuine warmth of the associations between these groups of upper-class black and white, the apparent lack of any race consciousness on the part of either, is quite startling when contrasted with similar groups on board the English and German vessels engaged in the same service. On the latter most of the practices of segregation and aloofness common to the United States in its attitude toward its Negro population are in evidence.

On a voyage down to West Africa from France a few years ago it happened that the writer was a passenger on the S. S. *Foucauld,* a luxurious liner in the West African service. Among the large number of passengers traveling in first-class, practically all of whom were French subjects, including many high administrators, was the young son of the black Senegalese deputy and Under-Secretary of State for the Colonies, Blaise Diagne. Tall, lithe, self-confident, he is the issue of the union of this native African, who, until his recent death belonged to an "elite of the elite," and a white French mother. The young man had been schooled in France and was but recently graduated from medical school. Along with several other young French officers, some of whose wives were in the party, he was going down to Africa for his first assignment in the French Colonial Service as a lieutenant in the Medical Corps. Promenading the decks arm in arm with his fellow officers and their wives, seated with them at table, dancing with their wives and sweethearts, young Diagne was one of them, and the life of the party. It was an example of a perfectly normal human relationship; no condescension, no solicitousness, no strain. When he debarked at Dakar amid the adieus of his white companions, he was more a Frenchman coming out to foreign service than a child of Africa returning home.

There were many such instances on the same boat and on other boats on the return trip to France. There was the native of the French colony, Dahomey, who held a responsible administrative position in the Treasury Service, who was returning with his family from leave of absence spent in France. Only his color and his place of birth were African; he was French like his many cordial white friends. His son will go to school in France, of course. When one dines with him at his home in Porto Novo, white wine always follows the fish, and champagne tops the dinner. His native servant or "boy," barefoot, but wearing a white jacket, who serves the meal, is called *stupide,* and is the butt of tolerant ridicule, just like the "boy" at the home of the French chief administrator not far distant. In his conversation he draws careful distinctions between "the blacks," "the natives" and "Frenchmen," like himself.

Then there was the Martiniquian, a mulatto with a mulatto wife, who though young, was already a veteran in the French Customs Service of Equatorial Africa. His son had been born in Gabon on his previous assignment. He was seated at table with the ponderous and affable Alsatian whose immediate superior he was in the customs service. It apparently had never occurred to the white Alsatian to resent the superior status of his darker friend and boss.

There was never a question of race or color in these relationships. They were all Frenchmen under the Tricolor, with the same interests and engaged in the same service. France draws them all to her with a single embrace. In the Sunday morning services in the ship bar, they all worshipped to the prayers of a young mulatto priest, who also was going out in service

When the passengers debark from the boats at the stops other than Dakar, in the "paniers" or "mammy-baskets" which deposit them in the waiting native canoes below, there is no thought of race or color either. White women and black men are indiscriminately crowded together, with never a complaint from either. In the great market at Dakar, white and black retailers occupy adjoining stalls, and many of the whites are French women. They peddle their wares to Europeans and natives alike. French women act as waitresses in the restaurants where white and native customers are equally welcome. The same situation prevails in many of the stores, while French laborers, skilled and unskilled, may be seen working side by side with the blacks. Natives may ride in the first-class coaches of the railways if they have the price to pay for the added comfort, and many of them do in Senegal.

The policy of equality of races has an official stamp too. It is no uncommon thing to see a white French subordinate administrator taking orders from his dark-skinned chief. This latter will usually be an evolved native from Martinique, Guadeloupe or Reunion, but his ancestry is African. He may be a judge, a commandant of a district, a colonel of artillery or a governor of a colony. France employs many of her assimilated black subjects from the older colonies in her African service. She seemingly has no fear that her African populations will become restive through seeing such demonstrations of respect for black men, and so come to believe that they too merit such respect. France wants the elite, at least, to believe so and encourages them in that belief by sending outstanding members of this class on tours of the colonies so that they may parade before the natives the possibilities which lay open to them if they will have faith in their masters and benefactors, the French.

In the schools at Conakry, Porto Novo, and at many other places in the French West African possessions it is not unusual to see a handful of white children dispersed throughout a packed roomful of little blacks. On occasion the teacher himself may be black, or perhaps a mulatto. These white children are the sons and daughters of the administrators and occasionally the traders. In Morocco there are "mixed battalions" in which French conscripts and native soldiers are mingled quite indiscriminately. In the civil and military offices whites and blacks work side by side, sleep in the same barracks and eat at the same tables, just as they argue together in the halls of the colonial councils.

The vital significance of this racial attitude of the French cannot be overestimated. The educated African is an extremely touchy person in many respects. He is proud of his exalted position and jealous of his rights. He is keenly sensitive to any suggestion of inferiority. His education, whether French or English, has "Europeanized" him and he has adopted European standards of conduct, culture and achievement as his own. It is slight wonder that he is captivated by a French culture which receives him with open arms. But unfortunately, only a few natives are ever able to attain this privileged status. The French policy of association has an entirely different meaning for the native African masses.

The Native Masses

The native masses are given no such privileged status. Racial equality is not for them; nor is the right to vote, to hold office or to become French citizens. The French know that these native masses cannot be quickly assimilated. Therefore they must be left alone to develop under their own culture, while close guard is kept over them by the French administrators and their able assistants, the native elite. They are given enough education to make them more efficient workers for the French. Their health is the subject of increasing concern and protection because they are a valuable labor-supply. The trained and alert members of the race having been drawn into the privileged class by subtle bribery, by the attraction of attaining superior status and racial equality, the native masses are left without effective leadership through which they can voice their protests against harsh and unjust policies effected by the French. The emotions involved in the concept of race and its implications in respect to social status are thus employed by the French, rather deliberately, it seems, to keep down racial conflict while a whole population is subjected to severe economic exploitation.

The British Policy

Like the French, the British are confident of their colonizing genius as a "superior" race. They are confident that Africa needs their "civilizing" influence just as they are painfully aware of their dependence upon Africa for much of her material wealth. As Lord Lugard, a leading English spokesman on colonial affairs put it: ". . . so in Africa today we are . . . bringing to the dark places of the earth, the abode of barbarism and cruelty, the torch of culture and progress, while ministering to the material needs of our own civilization. . . . We hold these countries because it is the genius of our race to colonize, to trade and to govern."[2]

Where the French have always labored under the influence of the doctrine of ultimate assimilation of their darker colonial populations, the British never have done so. The French ego has led them to believe in the superiority of their culture and it has been their aim wherever possible to inoculate their native subjects with it. The British equally believe in the superiority of their culture, but in a very different way; apparently to such a great extent that they have never supposed that primitive peoples could ever become sufficiently elevated to absorb it. They do not, at any rate, offer it willingly to the West African. This, and the traditional Anglo-Saxon attitude toward darker races, constitute the two main lines of departure between the British and the French colonial philosophies.

The English policy toward the government of their African subjects seems largely subject to the dictates of administrative expediency. The number of British colonial administrators can never be more than a mere handful in proportion to the area and population which they must control. Therefore it is much simpler to administer the territory through the native chiefs and to help these latter maintain the respect of their subjects. Moreover, the maintenance of tribal institutions and social organisation is expedient in order to preserve native law, which greatly simplifies this complex administrative problem. The English seem content to let native customs and institutions follow their own course of development, so long as they do not greatly interfere with British administrative policy. Until very recently, England has done but little officially even with the education of the natives.

The British policy of maintaining hereditary native chiefs in power, even though they may be incompetent and illiterate, has often proved irksome to the educated African commoner. The members of the educated native group of the British colonies thus find themselves frozen out of the select circle. Elevated by education and training above the general level of the masses, they are not eligible to highest positions of authority among their own people because of their blood (or lack of it), nor can they find admission to an English society which has emphatically closed the door to them. Therefore they frequently become professional agitators and trouble-makers, causing great worry for the British administrators.

This spontaneously developing elite of commoners will be an increasing source of difficulty to the English under the existing system. In a large town like Lagos, Nigeria, for instance, the native population is already dividing into very distinct groups and classes. There is an upper stratum of rich traders and of professional men who live in substantial houses, sending their sons and daughters to England to be educated. In addition there is developing a small middle class of clerks, retailers and skilled technicians, together with the typical working class masses of any city with a population of one hundred and fifty thousand. The life of the two upper classes assumes a distinct English cast. There are churches representing some twenty sects, whose crowded congregations are dressed in the best European manner; there are literary, tennis and cricket clubs, and elaborate social functions where formal dress is much in evidence. Some half-dozen newspapers are supported by this African middle-class. Yet these classes exert a minimum of influence in the control of the government and administrative policy. It is only natural, therefore, that they quite generally regard with suspicion a system which seems to proffer them Western civilization with one hand and withdraw its fruits with the other.

Disillusioned and resentful, the educated English Africans, frequently attribute their anomalous position in the colonies to the British attitude on the color question. They regard it as their misfortune that the English have never shown the fraternal sympathy for men of the darker races which they believe is characteristic of the French. The tolerance and cordiality of the French toward the elite members of the African natives seems foreign to the English racial temperament. There is not the same ease and freedom of relations between the races in the English colonies. The native is politely but firmly made aware of an insurmountable barrier between himself and Englishmen. In other words there exists in the English colonies, as distinct from the French, a "race problem" in the narrower sense of the term as it is employed in the United States. It is often declared by Englishmen, however, that there is no color bar in the British colonies. Official pronouncements have decreed equal treatment for persons of every race and religion. The African is allowed to run newspapers, engage in trade, in professional practice and to hold such administrative positions as he may be qualified for. Yet the educated African, who is much more proud and sensitive than his distant American cousin, realizes that race has erected a bar which is much more rigid than any official decree could produce or offset.

There is much in the English racial attitude to remind one of the doctrines advanced in some sections of the United States as "the true way out" of a problem of racial contact. Lord Lugard has expressed views which he notes with pride were quoted by a President of the United States in a speech at Birmingham, Alabama. He writes:

> Here, then, is the true conception of the interrelation of colour: complete uniformity in ideals, absolute equality in the paths of knowledge and culture, equal admiration for those who achieve; in matters social and racial a separate path, each pursuing his own inherited traditions, preserving his own race-purity and race-pride; equality in things spiritual, agreed divergence in the physical and material.

This is the essence of Booker T. Washington's well-known "separate as the fingers of the hand" analogy, and of the familiar American legal fiction of "separate but equal rights."

This characteristic English attitude may be due in part to the cultivated aloofness of the English toward all other peoples of whatever race, to a deep pride in the "innate" superiority of English culture and race, and in part to a physical aversion for peoples of darker skin. But whatever the cause, the effect on the sensitive native is important. The British natives, even the most advanced in education and culture, are far more race-conscious than are the French natives. In this respect the former have much in common with the American Negro. A policy which aims at pigeon-holing a racial group in a different world and keeping it there, while contact between the races must continue, is fraught with many difficulties, as American experience will testify.

Many Africans look upon the English policy of segregation which is so widely practiced in many sections of British Africa as a by-product of the English racial attitude. While this is probably not altogether true, the fact remains that segregation, for whatever motive, involves racial discrimination. The policy of segregation assumes a variety of forms, and may be motivated by European or native interest, or both. It may place the native in reserves or compounds and thus control his manner of living and the extent of his contact with European civilization. Or it may define the trade activities in which he may or may not engage and thus control his economic status. In the rural areas, it is used to determine to what extent he may work the land by restricting him to the reserves, thus rendering him dependent. In any of these forms segregation becomes a strong factor in controlling the evolution of the native. To the extent that it limits his contact with the forces that are at work in the transformation of his country, it is an obstacle to his progress. Moreover it is a policy which stirs up natural resentment on the part of the native populations subjected to it and intensifies group conflicts.

White Settlement

Segregation is particularly acute in areas of white settlement. Many English writers have defended the British practice of encouraging white settlers to establish themselves permanently in Africa, particularly South and East Africa. The South African General Smuts takes the view that any enduring civilization in Africa must be based on intensive permanent white settlement wherever that settlement is possible.[3] Coupled with this doctrine is a rigid policy of separation of white and black populations. That is to say that any civilization in Africa which is desirable and progressive must have a "white backbone."

White settlement does not exist to any great extent in the French African dominions. But in the British South and South Central Africa it is the dominant feature of English influence, and is now making rapid progress in British East Africa. Wherever it has been pursued as an extensive policy it has created problems which seem to defy solution. It has been the cause of much hard feeling between the races and a great deal of injustice to the native populations who have been shoved off their most fertile lands, compelled to work on plantations owned in many instances by absentee landlords, and robbed of valuable mineral lands contrary to treaty agreements.

What Hope for the Native?

Thus the concepts of race and race difference play a significant role in the control of subject African peoples by the French and British. The French have so far been able to use the emotional appeal of race brotherhood as a very helpful device in keeping down unrest in their African dominions. The British find race a sore problem. The Englishman might say with some grace "If I were a cultivated native I would prefer to live under the French system, where the cultivated natives have undoubted equality. But if I were a primitive native of the masses I would prefer the English system." The French might retort with equal cause: "The African can never be more than a *good native* to the Englishman and the best native is never thought by the English to be as good as even a bad Englishman." To all of which many educated Africans will aver that neither French nor English offer very much of fundamental benefit to the native, though both take a great deal from him. Probably the greatest error is the mistake of assuming that the African and his problems are so essentially different from the problems confronting the peoples of the Western World. In truth the African is confronted with the same difficulties encountered by any people in process of social development. There is nothing particularly unique about either the African or his problems. The African native today is comparable with the peasants and workmen of England and France of a century ago and with other workers and peasants today in less advanced countries of the modern world.

The "race-problem" has reared its ugly head in Africa as elsewhere in the modern world, but there as everywhere else, with increasing clarity, it can be identified as one sordid and acute aspect of the class problem. Both France and England will sooner or later have to face a day of reckoning with their Negro populations which are daily becoming more intelligent and articulate. The French may be able to postpone this day longer than will the British, because France finds it possible to mollify the native elite by giving them racial and social equality. But even for the elite native, racial and social equality without economic and political equality on a broad scale, can offer no real solution to the problem of native life.

With the intensified development of monopoly capitalism in the modern world, the outlook for anything but continued and severe exploitation of the subject peoples of the world does not seem bright. It is of no little significance that the Fascist or semi-Fascist states, as Italy, Germany and Japan, are all eagerly in quest of new colonial conquests. The policies of these nations would seem to be nothing less than the logical outcome of industrial capitalism driven by its internal distress to secure a field of expansion lest it confront utter internal disaster. Such nations have but slight opportunity and even less reason than the older colonizing nations to regard the welfare and rights of subject peoples. Their policies will inevitably lead to greater, more bitter and more disastrous racial conflicts.

The plain fact is that the contemporary international order, characterized by its capitalist-imperialist organization, has no possibility of effectively controlling the destiny of such peoples and areas. For the international order cannot override the existing vested capitalistic interests which muster the forces of the state for their protection. As the world is now organized these interests cannot be overcome, for they are intimately tied up with the class-relations of capitalist society. The same forces which protect them are the exact forces which protect and promote the interests of the capitalist within the capitalist state to which he claims allegiance. Just as the capitalist state in its internal affairs maintains a legal and constitutional system designed to protect absentee ownership and safeguard those property rights which make the capitalist supreme, just so, in the realm of external affairs, the state's authority, by the very nature of his relationship to it, must be employed to impose that type of supremacy over other peoples.

It is only when this supremacy and privilege are dissolved and when it is no longer within the power of the privileged property-holding class to determine the institutional life and habits of the modern state, that there can be hope for the development of an international order and community which will promise the subject peoples of the world genuine relief from the heavy colonial burdens of imperialist domination. At the present their outlook is not bright: the international order and their race are both arrayed against them.

NOTES

1. Leonard Woolf. *Empire and Commerce in Africa.* p. 352.
2. Lord Frederick Lugard. *The Dual Mandate in British Tropical Africa.* p. 618.
3. General J. C. Smuts. *Africa and Some World Problems.* p. 50.

MARY MCLEOD BETHUNE

"Certain Unalienable Rights"

It is a quiet night in December, 1773. A British merchant ship rides easily at
anchor in Boston Harbor. Suddenly, some row boats move out from the shore.
Dark stealthy figures in the boats appear to be Indians in buckskin jackets
and with feathers in their hair; but as they reach the ship, clamber abroad,
climb down into the hold and carry out boxes of the cargo, the muffled voices
speak English words. Their voices grow more excited and determined as they
open the boxes and dump the King's tea into the ocean. The Boston Tea Party
is in full swing. Resentment has reached flood tide. "Taxation without representation is tyranny!" The spark of the American Revolution has caught
flame and the principle of the "consent of the governed" has been established
by a gang disguised as Indians who take the law into their own hands. In this
action a small and independent people struck out against restrictions and tyranny and oppression and gave initial expression to the ideal of a nation "that
all men are created equal, that they are endowed by their Creator with certain unalienable Rights."

It is a Sunday night in Harlem in the year of our Lord 1943. Along the
quiet streets dimmed out against the possibility of Axis air attack, colored
Americans move to and fro or sit and talk and laugh. Suddenly electric rumor
travels from mouth to ear: "A black soldier has been shot by a white police-
man and has died in the arms of his mother." No one stops to ask how or why
or if it be true. Crowds begin to gather. There is a rumbling of anger and re-

Mary McLeod Bethune, "Certain Unalienable Rights," in *What the Negro Wants*, ed.
Rayford W. Logan, 248–258 (Chapel Hill: The University of North Carolina Press,
1944). Reprinted by permission of the University of North Carolina Press.

sentment impelled by all the anger and all the resentment of all colored Americans in all the black ghettos in all the cities in America—the resentment against the mistreatment of Negroes in uniform, against restriction and oppression and discrimination breaks loose. Crowds of young people in blind fury strike out against the only symbols of this oppression which are near at hand. Rocks hurtle, windows crash, stores are broken open. Merchants' goods are tumbled into the streets, destroyed or stolen. Police are openly challenged and attacked. There are killings and bodily injury. For hours a veritable reign of terror runs through the streets. All efforts at restraint are of no avail. Finally the blind rage blows itself out.

Some are saying that a band of hoodlums have challenged law and order to burn and pillage and rob. Others look about them to remember riots in Detroit and Los Angeles and Beaumont. They will look further and recall cities laid in ruins by a global war in which the forces of tyranny and oppression and race supremacy attempt to subdue and restrain all the freedom of the world. They are thinking deeply to realize that there is a ferment aloose among the oppressed little people everywhere, a "groping of the long inert masses." They will see depressed and repressed masses all over the world swelling to the breaking point against the walls of ghettos, against economic social and political restrictions; they will find them breaking open the King's boxes and throwing the tea into the ocean and storming the Bastilles stirred by the clarion call of the Four Freedoms. They are striking back against all that the Axis stands for. They are rising to achieve the ideals "that all men are created equal, that they are endowed by their Creator with certain unalienable Rights, that among these are Life, Liberty and pursuit of Happiness." With the crash of the guns and the whir of the planes in their ears, led by the fighting voices of a Churchill and a Franklin Roosevelt, a Chiang Kai-shek and a Stalin, they are realizing that "Governments are instituted among Men" to achieve these aims and that these governments derive "their just power from the consent of the governed." They are a part of a peoples' war. The little people want "out." Just as the Colonists at the Boston Tea Party wanted "out" from under tyranny and oppression and taxation without representation, the Chinese want "out," the Indians want "out," and colored Americans want "out."

Throughout America today many people are alarmed and bewildered by the manifestation of this world ferment among the Negro masses. We say we are living in a period of "racial tension." They seem surprised that the Negro should be a party to this world movement. Really, all true Americans should not be surprised by this logical climax of American education. For several generations colored Americans have been brought up on the Boston Tea Party and the Declaration of Independence; on the principle of equality of opportunity, the possession of inalienable rights, the integrity and sanctity of the human personality. Along with other good Americans the Negro has been prepared to take his part in the fight against an enemy that threatens all these basic American principles. He is fighting now on land and sea and in the air to beat back these forces of oppression and tyranny and discrimination. Why, then, should we be surprised when at home as well as abroad he fights back against these same forces?

One who would really understand this racial tension which has broken out into actual conflict in riots as in Harlem, Detroit, and Los Angeles, must look to the roots and not be confused by the branches and the leaves. The tension rises out of the growing internal pressure of Negro masses to break through the wall of restriction which restrains them from full American citizenship. This mounting power is met by the unwillingness of white America to allow any appreciable breach in this wall.

The hard core of internal pressure among the Negro masses in the United States today is undoubtedly their resentment over the mistreatment of colored men in the armed forces. The Negro faces restrictions in entering certain branches of the service, resistance to being assigned posts according to his ability; and above all there is the failure of the Army and his government to protect him in the uniform of his country from actual assault by civilians.

Letters from the men in Army camps have streamed into the homes of their parents and friends everywhere, telling of this mistreatment by officers, military police and civilians, of their difficulties in getting accommodations on trains and buses, of numerous incidents of long, tiresome journeys without meals and other concrete evidences of the failure of their government to protect and provide for its men, even when they are preparing to fight in defense of the principles of that government.

They need no agitation by newspaper accounts or the stimulation of so-called leaders. These things are the intimate experiences of the masses themselves. They know them and feel them intensely and resent them bitterly.

You must add to these deep-seated feelings a whole series of repercussions of the frustrated effort of Negroes to find a place in war production: the absolute denial of employment in many cases, or employment far below the level of their skills, numerous restrictions in their effort to get training, resistance of labor unions to the improving and utilization of their skills on the job. Pile on to these their inability to get adequate housing even for those employed in war work, and often, where houses are available, restrictions to segregated units in temporary war housing. At the same time they see around them unlimited opportunities offered to other groups to serve their country in the armed forces, to be employed at well-paying jobs, to get good housing financed by private concerns and FHA funds.

Even those observers who have some understanding of the Negro's desire to break through all those restrictions will charge it to superficial causes, such as the agitation of the Negro press and leaders; or they counsel the Negro to "go slow." It is as though they admit that the patient is sick with fever and diagnosis reveals that he needs twelve grains of quinine, but they decide that because he is a Negro they had better give him only six. They admit that he is hungry and needs to be fed, but because he is a Negro they suggest that a half meal will suffice. This approach, of course, is a historical hang-over. It is a product of the half-hearted and timorous manner in which we have traditionally faced the Negro problem in America.

In order to maintain slavery, it was necessary to isolate black men from every possible manifestation of our culture. It was necessary to teach that they were inferior beings who could not profit from that culture. After the slave was freed, every effort has persisted to maintain "white supremacy" and wall the Negro in from every opportunity to challenge this concocted "supremacy." Many Americans said the Negro could not learn and they "proved" it by restricting his educational opportunities. When he surmounted these obstacles and achieved a measure of training, they said he did not know how to use it and proved it by restricting his employment opportunities. When it was necessary to employ him, they saw to it that he was confined to laborious and poorly-paid jobs. After they had made every effort to guarantee that his economic, social and cultural levels were low, they attributed his status to his race. Therefore, as he moved North and West after Reconstruction and during the Industrial Revolution, they saw to it that he was confined to living in veritable ghettos with convenants that were as hard and resistant as the walls of the ghettos of Warsaw.

They met every effort on his part to break through these barriers with stern resistance that would brook no challenge to our concept of white supremacy. Although they guaranteed him full citizenship under the Constitution and its Amendments, they saw to it that he was largely disfranchised and had little part in our hard won ideal of "the consent of the governed." In the midst of this anachronism, they increasingly educated his children in the American way of life—in its ideals of equality of all men before the law, and opportunities for the fullest possible development of the individual.

As this concept took hold among the Negro masses, it has evidenced itself through the years in a slow, growing, relentless pressure against every

restriction which denied them their full citizenship. This pressure, intensified by those of other races who really believed in democracy, began to make
a break through the walls here and there. It was given wide-spread impetus by
the objectives of the New Deal with its emphasis on the rise of the forgotten
man. With the coming of the Second World War, all the Negro's desires were
given voice and support by the world leaders who fought back against Hitler
and all he symbolizes. His efforts to break through have responded to Gandhi
and Chiang Kai-shek, to Churchill and Franklin Roosevelt.

The radios and the press of the world have drummed into his ears the
Four Freedoms, which would lead him to think that the world accepts as legitimate his claims as well as those of oppressed peoples all over the world.
His drive for status has now swept past even most of his leaders, and has become imbedded in mass-consciousness which is pushing out of the way all
the false prophets, be they white or black—or, be they at home or abroad.

The Negro wants to break out into the free realm of democratic citizenship. We can have only one of two responses. Either we must let him out
wholly and completely in keeping with our ideals, or we must mimic Hitler
and shove him back.

What, then does the Negro want? His answer is very simple. He wants
only what all other Americans want. He wants opportunity to make real what
the Declaration of Independence and the Constitution and the Bill of Rights
say; what the Four Freedoms establish. While he knows these ideals are open
to no man completely he wants only his equal chance to attain them. The
Negro today wants specifically:

1. *Government leadership in building favorable public opinion.* Led by the
    President himself, the federal government should initiate a sound pro-
    gram carried out through appropriate federal agencies designed to indi-
    cate the importance of race in the war and post-war period. The cost of
    discrimination and segregation to a nation at war and the implications of
    American racial attitudes for our relationships with the other United
    Nations and their people should be delineated. Racial myths and super-
    stitions should be exploded. The cooperation of the newspapers, the radio
    and the screen should be sought to replace caricature and slander with
    realistic interpretations of sound racial relationships.
2. *The victory of democracy over dictatorship.* Under democracy the Negro
    has the opportunity to work an improvement in his status through the in-
    telligent use of his vote, the creation of a more favorable public opinion,
    and the development of his native abilitites. The ideals of democracy and
    Christianity work for equality. These ideals the dictatorships disavow.

Experience has taught only too well the implications for him and all Americans of a Nazi victory.

3. *Democracy in the armed forces.* He wants a chance to serve his country in all branches of the armed forces to his full capacity. He sees clearly the fallacy of fostering discrimination and segregation in the very forces that are fighting against discrimination and segregation all over the world. He believes that the government should fully protect the persons and the rights of all who wear the uniform of its armed forces.

4. *The protection of his civil rights and an end to lynching.* He wants full protection of the rights guaranteed all Americans by the Constitution; equality before the law, the right to jury trial and service, the eradication of lynching. Demanding these rights for himself, he will not be misled into any anti-foreign, Red-baiting, or anti-Semitic crusade to deny these rights to others. Appalled by the conditions prevailing in Washington, he joins in demanding the ballot for the District of Columbia and the protection of his rights now denied him within the shadow of the Capitol.

5. *The free ballot.* He wants the abolition of the poll tax and of the "white primary"; he wants universal adult suffrage. He means to use it to vote out all the advocates of racism and vote in those whose records show that they actually practise democracy.

6. *Equal access to employment opportunities.* He wants the chance to work and advance in any job for which he has the training and capacity. To this end he wants equal access to training opportunities. In all public programs, federal, state and local, he wants policy-making and administrative posts as well as rank and file jobs without racial discrimination. He wants a fair share of jobs under Civil Service.

7. *Extension of federal programs in public housing, health, social security, education and relief under federal control.* Low income and local prejudice often deprive him of these basic social services. Private enterprise or local government units cannot or will not provide them. For efficiency and equity in administration of these programs, the Negro looks to the federal government until such time as he has gained the full and free use of the ballot in all states.

8. *Elimination of racial barriers in labor unions.* He demands the right of admission on equal terms to the unions having jurisdiction over the crafts or industries in which he is employed. He urges that job control on public works be denied to any union practising discrimination.

9. *Realistic interracial co-operation.* He realizes the complete interdependence of underprivileged white people and Negroes, North and South— laborers and sharecroppers alike. He knows that they stay in the gutter

together or rise to security together; that the hope of democracy lies in their cooperative effort to make their government responsive to their needs; that national unity demands their sharing together more fully in the benefits of freedom—not "one as the hand and separate as the fingers," but one as the clasped hands of friendly cooperation.

Here, then, is a program for racial advancement and national unity. It adds up to the sum of the rights, privileges and responsibilities of full American citizenship. This is all that the Negro asks. He will not willingly accept less. As long as America offers less, she will be that much less a democracy. The whole way is the American way.

What can the Negro do himself to help get what he wants?

1. In the first place, he should accept his responsibility for a full part of the job of seeing to it that whites and Negroes alike understand the current intensity of the Negro's fight for status as a part of a world people's movement. As individuals and as members of organizations, we must continue to use every channel open to affect public opinion, to get over to all Americans the real nature of this struggle. Those of us who accept some measure of responsibility for leadership, most realize that in such people's movements, the real leadership comes up out of the people themselves. All others who would give direction to such a movement must identify themselves with it, become a part of it, and interpret it to others. We must make plain to America that we have reached a critical stage in the assimilation of colored people.

    We have large and growing numbers of young and older Negroes who have achieved by discipline and training a measure of culture which qualifies them for advanced status in our American life. To deny this opportunity creates on the one hand frustration with its attendant disintegration, and, on the other, deprives American civilization of the potential fruits of some thirteen millions of its sons and daughters.

    Through our personal and group contacts with other racial groups, we must increasingly win their understanding and support. Only in this way can the swelling force among minority racial groups be channeled into creative progress rather than exploded into riots and conflicts, or dissipated in hoodlumism. While we seek on the one side to "educate" white America, we must continue relentlessly to make plain to ourselves and our associates the increased responsibility that goes with increased rights and privileges. Our fight for Fair Employment Practices legislation must go hand and hand with "Hold Your Job" campaigns; our fight for anti-poll tax legislation must be supported equally by efforts of Negroes themselves to exercise fully and intelligently the right of franchise where they have it.

2. We must challenge, skillfully but resolutely, every sign of restriction or limitation on our full American citizenship. When I say challenge, I mean we must seek opportunity to place the burden of responsibility upon him who denies it. If we simply accept and acquiesce in the face of discrimination, we accept the responsibility ourselves and allow those responsible to salve their conscience by believing that they have our acceptance and concurrence. We should, therefore, protest openly everything in the newspapers, on the radio, in the movies that smacks of discrimination or slander. We must take the seat that our ticket calls for and place upon the proprietor the responsibility of denying it to us.

We must challenge everywhere the principle and practice of enforced racial segregation. We must make it clear that where groups and individuals are striving for social and economic status, group isolation one from the other allows the rise of misunderstanding and suspicion, providing rich soil for the seeds of antagonism and conflict. Recently in the city of Detroit, there was no rioting in the neighborhoods where whites and Negroes lived as neighbors, and there was no conflict in the plants where they worked side by side on the assembly-lines. Whenever one has the price or can fill the requirements for any privilege which is open to the entire public, that privilege must not be restricted on account of race.

Our appeal must be made to the attributes of which the Anglo-Saxon is so proud—his respect for law and justice, his love of fair-play and true sportsmanship.

3. We must understand that the great masses of our people are farmers and workers, and that their hopes for improvement in a large measure lie in association with organizations whose purpose is to improve their condition. This means membership in and support of labor and farmer unions. Within these organizations it means continuous efforts with our allies of all racial groups to remove all barriers which operate in the end to divide workers and defeat all of their purposes. The voice of organized labor has become on of the most powerful in the land and unless we have a part in that voice our people will not be heard.

4. We must take a full part in the political life of our community, state and nation. We must learn increasingly about political organization and techniques. We must prepare for and fight for places on the local, state, and national committees of our political parties. This is a representative government and the only way that our representatives can reflect our desires

is for us to register and vote. In a large measure the whole of our national life is directed by the legislation and other activities of our governmental units. The only way to affect their action and to guarantee their democratic nature is to have a full hand in electing individuals who represent us. The national election of 1944 represents one of the most crucial in the life of this nation and of the world. The Congressional representatives that are elected to office will have a large hand in the type of peace treaty to be adopted and the entire nature of our post-war domestic economy. All of our organizations and individuals who supply leadership must fully acquaint our people with the requirements of registering and voting, see to it that they are cognizant of the issues involved and get out to register and vote.

Negro women and their organizations have a tremendous responsibility and opportunity to offer leadership and support to this struggle of the racial group to attain improved cultural status in America. We have always done a full part of this job. Now, with large numbers of our men in the armed forces and with considerable numbers of new people who have migrated into our communities to take their part in war production, we have a bigger job and a greater opportunity than ever. Our women know too well the disintegrating effect upon our family life of our low economic status. Discrimination and restriction have too often meant to us broken homes and the delinquency of our children. We have seen our dreams frustrated and our hopes broken. We have risen, however, out of our despair to help our men climb up the next rung of the ladder. We see now more than a glimmer of light on the horizon of a new hope. We feel behind us the surge of all women of China and India and of Africa who see the same light and look to us to march with them. We will reach out our hands to all women who struggle forward—white, black, brown, yellow—all. If we have the courage and tenacity of our forebears, who stood firmly like a rock against the lashings of slavery and the disruption of Reconstruction, we shall find a way to do for our day what they did for theirs. Above all we Negro women of all levels and classes must realize that this forward movement is a march of the masses and that all of us must go forward with it or be pushed aside by it. We will do our part. In order for us to have peace and justice and democracy for all, may I urge that we follow the example of the great humanitarian—Jesus Christ—in exemplifying in our lives both by word and action the fatherhood of God and the brotherhood of man?

W. E. B. DU BOIS

Prospect of a World without Race Conflict

Abstract

The philosophy of biological race differences which divide the world into superior and inferior people will persist after this war. This is shown in the persecution of Jews, the refusal to emancipate India, the relations between Asia and Europe, and the attitude toward South America and the Caribbean. To leave out discussions of race in postwar planning enables Europe and America to fight for democracy and the abolition of poverty while ignoring the fact that race prejudice makes this fight consistent with compulsory poverty, disease, and repression of most of the workers of the world.

It is with great regret that I do not see after this war, or within any reasonable time, the possibility of a world without race conflict; and this is true despite the fact that race conflict is playing a fatal role in the modern world. The supertragedy of this war is the treatment of the Jews in Germany. There has been nothing comparable to this in modern history. Yet its technique and its reasoning have been based upon a race philosophy similar to that which has dominated both Great Britain and the United States in relation to colored people.

W. E. Burghardt Du Bois, "Prospect of a World without Race Conflict," *The American Journal of Sociology* 49, no. 5 (1944): 450–456. Reprinted by permission of the University of Chicago Press.

This philosophy postulates a fundamental difference among the greater groups of people in the world, which makes it necessary that the superior peoples hold the inferior in check and rule them in accordance with the best interest of these superiors. Of course, many of the usual characteristics were missing in this outbreak of race hate in Germany. There was in reality little of physical difference between German and Jew. No one has been able to accuse the Jews of inferiority; rather it was the superiority of the Jews in certain respects which was the real cause of conflict. Nevertheless, the ideological basis of this attack was that of fundamental biological difference showing itself in spiritual and cultural incompatibility. Another difference distinguishes this race war. Usually the cure for race persecution and subordination has been thought to be segregation, but in this case the chance to segregate the Jews, at least partially, in Palestine, has practically been vetoed by the British government.

In other parts of the world the results of race conflict are clear. The representative of Prime Minister Churchill presiding over the British war cabinet has been the prime minister of the Union of South Africa. Yet South Africa has without doubt the worst race problem of the modern world. The natives have been systematically deprived of their land, reduced to the status of a laboring class with the lowest of wages, disfranchised, living and working under caste conditions with only a modicum of education, and exposed to systematic public and private insult. There is a large population of mixed-bloods, and the poverty, disease, and crime throughout the Union of South Africa are appalling. Here in a land which furnishes gold and diamonds and copper, the insignia of the luxury and technique of modern civilization, this race hate has flourished and is flourishing. Smuts himself, as political leader of the Union of South Africa, has carried out much of the legislation upon which this race conflict is based; and, although from time to time he has expressed liberal ideas, he has not tried or succeeded in basically ameliorating the fundamental race war in that part of the world.

The situation in India is another case of racial conflict. The mass of people there are in the bondage of poverty, disfranchisement, and social caste. Despite eminent and widely known leadership, there has not come on the part of the British any effective attempt fundamentally to change the attitude of the governing country toward the subject peoples. The basic reason for this, openly or by inference, is the physical difference of race which makes it, according to British thought, impossible that these peoples should within any reasonable space of time become autonomous or self-governing. There have been promises, to be sure, from time to time, and promises are pending;

but no one can doubt that if these people were white and of English descent, a way out of the present impasse would have long since been found.

There is no doubt but that India is a congeries of ignorant, poverty-stricken, antagonistic groups who are destined to go through all the hell of internal strife before they emancipate themselves. But it is just as true that Europe of the sixteenth century was no more ready for freedom and autonomy than India. But Europe was not faced and coerced by a powerful overlord who did not believe Europeans were men and was determined to treat them as serfs to minister to his own comfort and luxury.

In India we have the first thoroughgoing case of modern colonial imperialism. With the capitalism built on the African slave trade and on the sugar, tobacco, and cotton crops of America, investment in India grew and spread for three hundred years, until there exists the greatest modern case of the exploitation of one people by another. This exploitation has been modified in various ways: some education has been furnished the Indians, a great system of railroads has been installed, and industrialism has been begun. But nothing has been done to loosen to any appreciable degree the strangle hold of the British Empire on the destinies of four hundred million human beings. The prestige and profit of the control of India have made it impossible for the British to conceive of India as an autonomous land.

The greatest and most dangerous race problem today is the problem of relations between Asia and Europe: the question as to how far "East is East and West is West" and of how long they are going to retain the relation of master and serf. There is in reality no difference between the reaction to this European idea on the parts of Japan and China. It is a question simply of the method of eliminating it. The idea of Japan was to invoke war and force — to drive Europe out of Asia and substitute the domination of a weak Asia by a strong Japan. The answer of China was co-operation and gradual understanding between Great Britain, France, America, and China. Chinese leaders are under no illusions whatever as to the past attitude of Europe toward Chinese. The impudence, browbeating, robbery, rape, and insult is one long trail of blood and tears, from the Opium War to the kowtowing before the emperor in Berlin. Even in this present war and alliance there has occurred little to reassure China: certain courtesies from the British and belated and meager justice on the part of the United States, after the Soong sister had swept in on us with her retinue, jade, and jewels. There has not only been silence concerning Hong Kong, Burma, and Singapore but there is the continued assumption that the subjugation of Japan is in the interest of Europe and America and not of Asia. American military leaders have insisted that we must have in the Pacific after this war American bases for armed force. But why? If Asia is going to develop as a self-governing, autonomous part of the world, equal to other parts, why is policing by foreigners necessary? Why cannot Asia police itself? Only because of the deep-seated belief among Europeans and Americans that yellow people are the biological inferiors to the whites and not fit for self-government.

Not only does Western Europe believe that most of the rest of the world is biologically different but it believes that in this difference lies congenital inferiority; that the black and brown and yellow people are not simply untrained in certain ways of doing and methods of civilization; that they are naturally inferior and inefficient; that they are a danger to civilization as civilization is understood in Europe. This belief is so fundamental that it enters into the very reforms that we have in mind for the post-war world.

In the United States the race problem is peculiarly important just now. We see today a combination of northern investors and southern Bourbons desiring not simply to overthrow the New Deal but to plunge the United States into fatal reaction. The power of the southerners arises from the suppression of the Negro and poor-white vote, which gives the rotten borough of Mississippi four times the political power of Massachusetts and enables the South through the rule of seniority to pack the committees of Congress and to dominate it. Nothing can be done about this situation until we face fairly the question of color discrimination in the South; until the social, political, and economic equality of civilized men is recognized, despite race, color, and poverty.

In the Caribbean area, in Central and South America, there has been for four hundred years wide intermixture of European, African, and Red Indian races. The result in one respect is widely different from that of Europe and North America; the social equality of Negroes, Indians, and mulattoes who were civilized was recognized without question. But the full results of this cultural liberalism were largely nullified by the economic control which Western Europe and North America held over these lands. The exploitation of cheap colored labor through poverty and low prices for materials was connived at as usual in the civilized world and the spoils shared with local white politicians. Economic and social prestige favored the whites and hindered the colored. A legend that the alleged backwardness of the South Americans was due to race mixture was so far stressed in the world that South America feared it and catered to it; it became the habit to send only white Brazilians, Bolivians, and Mexicans abroad to represent their countries; to encourage white immigration at all costs, even to loss of autonomy; to draw color lines in the management of industry dominated by Europe and in society where foreigners were entertained. In short, to pretend that South America hated and distrusted dark blood us much as the rest of the world, often even when the leaders of this policy were known themselves to be of Negro and Indian descent.

Thus the race problem of South and Central America, and especially of the islands of the Caribbean, became closely allied with European and North American practice. Only in the past few decades are there signs of an insurgent native culture, striking across the color line toward economic freedom, political self-rule, and more complete social equality between races.

There still is a residual sense of racial difference among parts of Europe; a certain contemptuous attitude toward Italy has been manifest for a long time, and the Balkans have been a byword for inefficiency and muddle. The pretensions of the Greeks to represent ancient Greek culture and of the Rumanians to be Roman have been laughed at by Western Europe. The remainder of the Balkans and Russia have been looked upon as Asiatic barbarism, aping civilization. As quasi-Asiatic, they have come in for the racial contempt poured upon the yellow peoples. This attitude greeted the Russian revolution and staged almost a race war to uphold tottering capitalism, built on racial contempt. But in Eastern Europe today are a mass of awakening men. They know and see what Russia has done for her debased masses in a single generation, cutting across race lines not only between Jew and Gentile but between White Russians, Ukrainians, Tartars Turks, Kurds, and Kalmuks. As Sidney and Beatrice Webb declared:

All sections of the community—apart from those legally deprived of citizenship on grounds unconnected with either race or nationality—enjoy, throughout the USSR, according to law, equal rights and duties, equal privileges and equal opportunities. Nor is this merely a formal equality under the law and the federal constitution. Nowhere in the world do habit and custom and public opinion approach nearer to a like equality in fact. Over the whole area between the Arctic Ocean and the Black Sea and the Central Asian mountains, containing vastly differing races and nationalities, men and women, irrespective of conformation of skull or pigmentation of skin, even including the occasional African Negro admitted from the United States, may associate freely with whom they please; travel in the same public vehicles and frequent the same restaurants and hotels; sit next to each other in the same colleges and places of amusement; marry wherever there is mutual liking; engage on equal terms in any craft or profession for which they are qualified; join the same churches or other societies; pay the same taxes and be elected or appointed to any office or position without exception.

This, Eastern Europe knows, while Western Europe is still determined to build its culture on race discrimination and expects Russia to help her. But how far can Russia be depended upon to defend, in world war, British and American investments in Asia and Africa?

The attitude of America and Britain toward De Gaulle is puzzling until we remember that, since Gobineau, racial assumptions have entered into the relations between France and the Nordic world. During the first World War the United States was incensed at the social equality attitudes of the "frogs," while Britain as well as Germany resented the open dependence of France on her black colonial soldiers. One present great liberal statesman, Smuts, led a crusade against arming blacks in any future European war. Yet De Gaulle not only uses Senegalese soldiers but recognizes the Negro governor of a strategic French colonial province; while Burman, writing of the history of the Free French, exclaims: "I am witnessing a miracle, the rebirth of France in the jungles of Africa!" Racial caste and profitable investment after the war indicate a halt in our support of De Gaulle. France since the eighteenth century has insisted on recognizing the social equality of civilized men despite race. She has for this reason been regarded as traitor to the white colonial front, in government and in society, despite her investors who have supported British methods. Hitler is not the only modern statesman who has sneered at "mongrel" France.

These are some but by no means all of the race problems which face the world; yet they are not being discussed except indirectly. The Atlantic Charter as well as the agreements in Moscow and Teheran have been practically silent on the subject of race. It is assumed that certain fundamental matters and more immediate issues must be met and settled before this difficult question of race can be faced. Let us now ask ourselves if this is true. What *are* the fundamental questions before the world at war?

If we measure the important matters by current discussion, we may range them somewhat as follows: (1) defense against aggression; (2) full employment after the war; (3) eventual fair distribution of both raw materials and manufactured goods; (4) abolition of poverty; and (5) health.

To anyone giving thought to these problems, it must be clear that each of them, with all of its own peculiar difficulties, tends to break asunder along the lesions of race difference and race hate. Among the primary factors entering into the discussion is the folklore and superstition which lurks in the mind of modern men and makes them thoroughly believe, in accord with inherited prejudice and unconscious cerebration, that the peoples of the world are divided into fundamentally different groups with differences that are eternal and cannot be forgotten and cannot be removed. This philosophy says that the majority of the people of the world are impossible.

Therefore, when we discuss any of the listed problems, we usually see the solution within the frame of race and race difference. When we think of defense against aggression, we are thinking particularly of Europe, and the aggregation which we have in mind is not simply another Hitler but a vaster Japan, if not all Asia and the South Sea Islands. The "Yellow peril" as envisaged by the German Emperor William II has by no means passed from the subconscious reactions of Western Europe. That is the meaning of world police and "our way of life."

When we think of the problem of unemployment, we mean especially unemployment in the developed countries of Western Europe and America. We do not have in mind any fundamental change so far as the labor of the darker world is concerned. We do not think of full employment and a living wage for the East Indian, the Chinese coolie, and the Negro of South Africa or even the Negro of our own South. We want the white laborer in England and in America to receive a living wage and economic security without periodic unemployment. In such case we can depend on the political power of white labor to maintain the present industrial organization. But we have little or no thought of colored labor, because it is disfranchised and kept in serfdom by the power of our present governments.

This means, of course, that the industrial organization of these countries must be standardized; they must not clog their own avenues of trade by tariff restrictions and cartels. But these plans have very seldom gone far enough to envisage any change in the relations of Europe and America to the raw material of Africa and Asia or to accepting any idea of so raising the prices of this raw material and the wages of the laborers who produce it that this mass of labor will begin to approach the level of white labor. In fact, any such prospect the white laborers with votes in their hands would in vast majorities oppose.

In both the United States and the Union of South Africa it has been the organized white laborers who have systematically by vote and mob opposed the training of the black worker and the provision of decent wages for him. In this respect they have ranged themselves with exploiting investors and disseminators of race hatred like Hitler. When recently in the United States the President's Fair Employment Practices Commission sought to secure some steps of elementary justice for black railway workers, the railway unions refused even to attend the hearings. Only the Communists and some of the C. I. O. unions have ignored the color line—a significant fact.

Our attitude toward poverty represents the constant lesion of race thinking. We have with difficulty reached a place in the modern white world where we can contemplate the abolition of poverty; where we can think of an industrial organization with no part of its essential co-operators deprived of income which will give them sufficient food and shelter, along with necessary education and some of the comforts of life. But this conception is confined almost entirely to the white race. Not only do we refuse to think of similar possibilities for the colored races but we are convinced that, even though it were possible, it would be a bad thing for the world. We must keep the Negroes, West Indians, and Indonesions poor. Otherwise they will get ambitious: they will seek strength and organization; they will demand to be treated as men, despite the fact that we know they are not men; and they will ask social equality for civilized human beings the world over.

There is a similar attitude with regard to health; we want white people to be well and strong, to "multiply and replenish the earth"; but we are interested in the health of colored people only in so far as it may threaten the health and wealth of whites. Thus in colonies where white men reside as masters, they segregate themselves in the most healthful parts of the country, provided with modern conveniences, and let the natives fester and die in the swamps and lowlands. It is for this reason that Englishmen and South Africans have seized the high land of Kenya and driven the most splendid of races of East Africa into the worst parts of the lowland, to the parts which are infested by the tsetse fly, where their cattle die and they are forced laborers on white farms.

Perhaps in no area of modern civilized endeavor is the matter of race revealed more startlingly than in the question of education. We have doubts as to the policy of so educating the colored races that they will be able to take part in modern civilization. We are willing to educate them so that they can help in our industrial development, and we want them to become good workmen so long as they are unorganized. But when it comes to a question of real acquaintanceship with what the more advanced part of the world has done and is doing, we try to keep the backward races as ignorant as possible. We limit their schools, their travel, and their knowledge of modern tongues.

There are, of course, notable exceptions: the Negro colleges of the southern United States, the Indian universities, and some advance even in university training in South Africa and in East and West Africa. But this advance is hindered by the fact that popular education is so backward that the number of persons who can qualify for higher training is very small, especially the number who can enter the professions necessary to protect the economic status of the natives and to guide the natives in avoidance of disease. In all these matters race interferes with education.

Beyond this we have only to mention religion. There is no denying that certain missionaries have done fine work in ameliorating the lot of backward people, but at the same time there is not a ghost of a doubt that today the organized Christian church is unfavorable toward race equality. It is split into racial sections and is not disposed to disturb to any great degree the attitude of civilization toward the Chinese, the Indians, and the Negroes. The recent pronouncement of the Federation of Churches of Christ was a fine and forward-looking document, but it has aroused no attention, much less enthusiasm, among the mass of Christians and will not. The Catholic church never champions the political or economic rights of subject peoples.

This insistent clinging to the older patterns of race thought has had extraordinary influence upon modern life. In the first place, it has for years held back the progress of the social sciences. The social sciences from the beginning were deliberately used as instruments to prove the inferiority of the majority of the people of the world, who were being used as slaves for the comfort and culture of the masters. The social sciences long looked upon this as one of their major duties. History declared that the Negro had no history. Biology exaggerated the physical differences among men. Economics even today cannot talk straight on colonial imperialism. Psychology has not yet recovered from the shame of its "intelligence" tests and its record of "conclusions" during the first World War.

Granted, therefore, that this is the basic attitude of the majority of civilized people, despite exceptions and individual differences, what must we expect after this war? In the first place, the British Empire is going to continue, if Mr. Churchill has his way, without "liquidation"; and there is slight chance that the English Labour party or any other democratic elements in England are going to be able to get past the suspensory veto of the House of Lords and the overwhelming social power of the British aristocracy. In America the control of wealth over our democracy is going to be reinforced by the action of the oligarchic South. A war-weary nation is going to ignore reform and going to work to make money. If, of course, the greedy industrial machine breaks down in 1950 as it did in 1929, there will be trouble; but the Negroes will be its chief victims and sufferers. Belgium has held its Congo empire with rare profit during the war, and the home land will recoup its losses in Europe by more systematic rape of Africa. So Holland will batten down again upon the South Seas, unless the Japanese interlude forces some slight change of heart. South America will become an even more closely integrated part of British and American industry, and the West Indies will work cheaply or starve, while tourists throw them pennies.

The only large cause for disquiet on the part of Western Europe and North America is the case of Russia. There they are reassured as to the attitude of Stalin toward the working people of the Western world. Evidently he has decided that the Western European and American workers with votes in their hands are capable of deciding their own destiny; and, if they are not, it is their own fault. But what is going to be the attitude of Russia toward colonial peoples? How far and where and when is Russia going to protect and restore British and American investments and control in Asia and Africa? Certainly her attitude toward the Chinese has shown in the past and still shows that she has the greatest sympathy with coolie labor and no love for Chiang Kai-shek. Will she have a similar attitude toward the other peoples of Asia, of Africa, and of the South Seas? If so, smooth restoration of colonial imperialism is not going to be easy.

What now can be done by intelligent men who are aware of the continuing danger of present racial attitudes in the world? We may appeal to two groups of men: first, to those leaders of white culture who are willing to take action and, second, to the leaders of races which are victims of present conditions. White leaders and thinkers have a duty to perform in making known the conclusions of science on the subject of biological race. It takes science long to percolate to the mass unless definite effort is made. Public health is still handicapped by superstitions long disproved by science; and race fiction is still taught in schools, in newspapers, and in novels. This careless ignorance of the facts of race is precisely the refuge where antisocial economic reaction flourishes.

We must then, first, have wide dissemination of truth. But this is not all: we need deliberate and organized action on the front where race fiction is being used to prolong economic inequality and injustice in the world. Here is a chance for a modern missionary movement, not in the interest of religious dogma, but to dissipate the economic illiteracy which clouds modern thought. Organized industry has today made the teaching of the elementary principles of economic thought almost impossible in our schools and rare in our colleges; by outlawing "Communistic" propaganda, it has effectually in press and on platform almost stopped efforts at clear thinking on economic reform. Protest and revelation fall on deaf ears, because the public does not know the basic facts. We need a concerted and determined effort to make common knowledge of the facts of the distribution of property and income today among individuals; accurate details of the sources of income and conditions of production and distribution of goods and use of human services, in order that we may know who profits by investment in Asia and Africa as well as in America and Europe, and why and how they profit.

Next we need organized effort to release the colored laborer from the domination of the investor. This can best be accomplished by the organization of the labor of the world as consumers, replacing the producer attitude by knowledge of consumer needs. Here the victims of race prejudice can play their great role. They need no longer be confined to two paths: appeal to a white world ruled by investors in colored degradation or war and revolt. There is a third path: the extrication of the poverty-stricken, ignorant laborer and consumer from his bondage by his own efforts as a worker and consumer, united to increase the price of his toil and reduce the cost of the necessities of life. This is being done here and there, but the news of it is suppressed, the difficulties of united action deliberately increased, and law and government united in colonial areas to prevent organization, manipulate prices, and stifle thought by force. Here colored leaders must act; but, before they act, they must know. Today, naturally, they are for the most part as economically illiterate as their masters. Thus Indian moneylenders are the willing instruments of European economic oppression in India; and many American and West Indian Negroes regard as economic progress the chance to share in the exploitation of their race by whites.

A union of economic liberals across the race line, with the object of driving exploiting investors from their hideout behind race discrimination, by freeing thought and action in colonial areas is the only realistic path to permanent peace today.

A great step toward this would be an international mandates commission with native representation, with power to investigate and report, and with jurisdiction over all areas where the natives have no effective voice in government.

ATLANTA UNIVERSITY

RAYFORD LOGAN

Plans for World Peace

For more than six hundred years statesmen and dreamers have made plans for world peace. These plans have all failed for the simple reason that they tried to do two conflicting things at the same time. They tried to make sure that the victors would keep what they had won and they tried to build a decent world on the continuing domination of the victors. Now, during the past five hundred years—the period of the degradation of the black man—the victors have usually been the slave-holding and colonial nations. At one time Spain, at another Portugal, at still another France, and then England had what historians like to call preponderance. They were at various times the most powerful nation in the world. All of them have been slaveholding and colonial nations.

This second world war has shifted the balance of power in world affairs. During the next generation at least, this preponderance will rest with the United States and the Soviet Union. Both of them are imperialist powers even though many friends of the Soviet Union would deny that it is. There are, truly, differences between the imperialism of the United States and that of the Soviet Union. The United States actually has colonies regardless of the name given to them, namely Puerto Rico and the Virgin Islands. We have other territories the people of which have no real voice in their own government, namely, Hawaii and Alaska. And we shall probably get a number of islands in the Pacific where the inhabitants will not have even a delegate who can speak but not vote in the congress of the United States. All of these possessions are detached from the mainland of the United States.

Rayford Logan, "Plans for World Peace," chap. 7 of *The Negro and the Post-War World: A Primer* (Washington, D.C.: The Minorities Publishers, 1945) 76–88.

The Soviet Union has no such possessions. But it seems, on the basis of acceptable information, that many neighboring peoples have not been permitted to choose their form of government. One does not have to be an enemy of the Soviet Union simply because he believes that the inhabitants of Esthonia, Latvia, Lithuania have not been allowed to vote for control by the Soviet Union. In the eastern Balkans the Soviet Union has also imposed its domination rather than sought the desires of the masses of the people. It is open to question whether the Communist regime at Yenan in China represents the wishes of a large number of the Chinese people in western China.

The United States is also an imperialist nation in the sense that she exercises a great deal of influence over small and weak nations. In Cuba, Haiti, some of the other Latin American nations, in Liberia, the United States either politically or economically or culturally exercises influence over the governments and peoples.

There is wide difference of opinion as to the aims of the United States and of the Soviet Union in the regions that they control or dominate. Since the supremacy of the white race is part of the pattern of life in the United States, it is only natural that this aim should be pursued outside the United States. Since the capitalistic organization of economic life is the pattern in the United States, it is only natural that this organization of the economic life of areas outside the United States should be followed.

In the Soviet Union, on the other hand, there is an almost complete absence of race prejudice. It is natural that this same policy should be followed outside the Soviet Union. Since, moreover, the Soviet Union has established in large measure the supremacy of workers over the capitalists, it is to be expected that a similar policy will be followed in those areas controlled by the Soviet Union.

Advocates of a just and lasting peace for all mankind must prefer the racial attitude and policy of the Soviet Union to that of the United States. But many advocates of this just and lasting peace sincerely doubt that the economic policies of the Soviet Union are the best for all peoples everywhere. Many persons believe that the political forms of democracy—freedom of speech, of the press, of the suffrage—are better than the denial of these which usually goes along with the political organization of states in which the supremacy of workers over capitalists is the goal. Of course, true democracy exists in no state or dependent area inhabited by Negroes. Consequently, many persons insist that equality for Negroes, most of whom are workers rather than capitalists, can not be established under a capitalist society. Even those who believe this equality possible under a capitalist society must admit that its establishment will require a long time.

Even more important from a practical point of view is the possibility of establishing the superiority of workers over capitalists in all parts of the world. Belief in the ideals of democracy even when they are violated is so strong in many areas that it will be difficult to win enough converts to communism to overthrow or change the so-called democratic form of government. The forces of capitalism are so strong in many areas that it will be extremely difficult to destroy them. Regardless, then, as to whether the professed democracy of the United States or the communism of the Soviet Union is more likely to gain equality for Negroes, we must base our considerations for the future upon the continuation in many areas of white supremacy attitudes and the capitalistic structure of society. What has been said about the United States is true in only slightly less degree of the areas controlled by the other imperialist powers, namely, England, France, Belgium, the Netherlands, Portugal, Spain, Australia, New Zealand. Conditions are, of course, even worse in the Union of South Africa and South-West Africa.

To some extent, the San Francisco Conference, which resulted in the signing of the United Nations Charter, was a contest between the attitudes and policies of the colonial powers on the one hand and of Russia on the other. But the contest was not a clear-cut one. For example, the Charter begins with the words, "We the peoples of the United Nations." No one can argue that the peoples of the United States Empire, of the British Empire, the French Empire, the Belgian Empire, the Dutch Empire, the subject peoples of Australia, New Zealand, the Union of South Africa were represented at San Francisco. The American delegates spoke for a government that permits the disfranchisement of most Negroes living in the South. The inhabitants of the dependent areas of the other nations named just above had absolutely no voice in the election of the governments that appointed their delegates. Furthermore, it may be doubted that any of the Latin American states truly spoke for the masses of the peoples of those countries. The Indian delegation was chosen by the British government that had not held an election for ten years. Few persons still believe that the government of Chiang Kai-shek speaks for the masses of China. In fact, practically none of the European delegates spoke for the great masses of their peoples.

The Communist Party in the Soviet Union, the only party permitted there, numbers about four millions out of some one hundred sixty or more millions. Perhaps these four millions speak for the others. But the simple fact is that these four millions and the government of the Soviet Union do not permit the others to speak for themselves.

In brief, "We the peoples" is at best a half-truth. The peoples represented at San Francisco were in overwhelming numbers the white people of the world and the ruling classes of China and of Russia. Negroes were represented only by Haiti, Liberia, Abyssinia and to a limited degree by some Latin American delegates. But in the case of the three Negro nations, Haiti, Liberia, and Abyssinia, the delegates spoke for the so-called elite or upper classes of their countries. And in the words of Jan Smuts, the voice of Africa, by which he probably meant all the Negro peoples, was not very important because they do not count for much in world affairs.

As a consequence, we should not be surprised that the Charter represents primarily the wishes of the white nations of the world. It is true that they wrote into the Charter a high ideal that was not placed in the Covenant of the League of Nations at the end of World War I. The Charter states as one of its purposes "promoting and encouraging respect for human rights and for the fundamental freedoms for all, without distinction as to race, sex, language or religion." But at the same time the Charter left it to each nation to enforce or not enforce this ideal as it sees fit. For the Charter specifically provides that the United Nations Organization shall not interfere in any way in matters that are "essentially within the domestic jurisdiction of any state." In other words, the United States, like all other nations, is perfectly free to continue any and all of its discriminatory practices—poll tax laws, the white primary in those states where it continues to exist, lynching, segregation in all its forms, and all the other inequalities inflicted upon Negroes.

In the same way, the Charter contains high-sounding words about the well-being, independence or self-government of peoples living in dependent areas. As already pointed out, more than one hundred fifty million Negroes live in these dependent areas. The Charter provides for a trusteeship council that is supposed to guide these dependent areas to independence or self-government. In order to understand why many of us have little faith in these pronouncements or in the machinery, the reader should review what has been said about the mandate system established at the end of World War I. Although article 22 of the Covenant which established the mandate system did not specify independence or self-government for the African and Pacific mandated areas, Woodrow Wilson who deserves more than does Smuts credit for setting it up definitely stated that this was the goal. In the second place, article 73 of the Charter uses the same language as does the Covenant in speaking of the "sacred trust" which the colonial powers assume toward these non-self-governing areas (article 22). Although the trusteeship provisions spell out in more detail the goals of the trusteeship system than did the mandate system, there is not much reason for believing that the colonial powers in 1945 are any more sincere than they were in 1919. Indeed, one may be inclined more to doubt their sincerity in 1945 than in 1919. For in 1919 article 22 specified the areas that were to be placed under mandate. But the Charter of 1945 provides no assurance that a single inch of territory will be placed under trusteeship. *Each nation is permitted to determine for itself what territory, if any, is to be placed under trusteeship.* The action of the Union in South Africa in proclaiming its intention at San Francisco of incorporating its mandated area of South West Africa into the Union suggests that this voluntary aspect of the trusteeship system may be used by the other mandatories also to get rid of the mandate system and place their mandates under their own colonial office instead of under some form of international supervision. Recent reports indicate that Belgium is planning likewise to incorporate the mandated area of Ruanda-Urundi into the colony of Belgian Congo.

Nor is there much likelihood that many of the areas captured from the enemy or the existing colonies will be placed under trusteeship. Many authoritative spokesmen for the United States have already insisted that the islands captured in the Pacific shall be administered by the United States without interference by any trusteeship system. No one seriously believes that Puerto Rico, for example, will be placed under the trusteeship system. If the leading "democratic" nation fails to place territories under the trusteeship system, what reason is there for believing that any more frankly imperialistic nations will do so? As one expert on colonial affairs told me in San Francisco, "The trusteeship council probably will not be swamped." Recent efforts to restore the former Italian colonies to Italy confirm this conclusion.[1]

Not only will the trusteeship council probably not be swamped with areas to supervise, but its power over any trust areas that it may have will be woefully weak. It has already been pointed out that the Permanent Mandates Commission could do very little to compel or even induce the mandatories to improve conditions in the mandated areas. The new Trusteeship Council is just about as weak as was the old P. M. C. It has been granted one definite power that the P. M. C. did not have, namely, the right to draw up a questionnaire as the basis for the annual reports. Consequently, if there are any trust areas, the annual reports should be more complete about conditions in the trust areas.

On the other hand, I doubt that the Charter provides for oral petitions by the Native peoples. This doubt is increased by the history of the drafting of article 87. The American draft of May 4 provided that the Trusteeship Council "shall be empowered to accept petitions." Some of us in San Francisco strongly urged Commander Stassen and the other American delegates to specify oral petitions. Not only was this not done but the final language of the Charter states that the Trusteeship Council "may . . . accept petitions and examine them in consultation with the administering authority." Note, first of all, that the Council "may" but not is empowered to as in the American draft of May 4. Note, moreover, the addition of the words "and examine them in consultation with the administering authority." One excuse for not adding "oral petitions" was that it was impossible to "spell out everything." But while it was not found possible to add two words, "oral petitions," it was possible to add nine words. Moreover, these nine words seems to make even clearer than the language of May 4 that only written petitions may be accepted. For it is a simple rule of law that the enumeration of one thing indicates the exclusion of others. The specific reference "in consultation with the administering authority" excludes the petitioners. I have been told that in the minutes of the trusteeship council it is recorded that this language includes oral petitions. But the very fact that it was deemed necessary to record the interpretation in the minutes shows clearly that there was doubt as to the meaning. Since there was doubt, why not remove the doubt in the language of the Charter instead of recording the interpretation in the minutes which the public may not see for the next twenty-five years? Moreover, I seriously question whether an interpretation recorded in the minutes of a committee is binding upon a plenary session that ratifies the action of the committee unless the interpretation is made a part of the act of ratification by the plenary session. And I doubt even more strongly that the interpretation recorded by the Trusteeship Committee is binding upon the nations that ratify the Charter unless that interpretation is made a part of the act of ratification. There is no evidence that the United States did this, nor that any other nation has done so.

The history of the drafting of the provision dealing with inspections by the Trusteeship Council similarly makes us doubt the sincerity of the colonial powers. The American draft of May 4 stated that the Trusteeship Council "shall be empowered to institute investigations." Many of us considered this a great improvement over the mandate system which did not provide for such inspection. But we wanted the inspection to result in reports that would be given to the public. Again, we were told that the "charter can't spell out everything." But the final wording of the Charter did spell things out sufficiently to weaken the American draft. For the final wording says that the Trusteeship Council "may," again not is "empowered to," "make periodic visits to the respective trust territories at times agreed upon with the administering authority." If we were not dealing with the fate of several tens of millions of people, we should say that this language is a huge joke. For it permits the administering authority to specify the time when the "visit" will be made. Any butcher can get his scales in order if he sets the time when the inspector from the Bureau of Weights and Measures comes to look at his scales. In many years of studying international documents, I have rarely seen a statement which so clearly reveals, under the disguise of a lot of words, the determination to make an apparent grant of power worthless.

Once more, while it was found possible to add a lot of words that made the visit of little value in discovering real conditions, it was found not possible to add a few words specifying that the reports would be made public. I have not been told that it was recorded in the minutes that the publication of the reports was understood. Even if it was, the interpretation would have no more value than that with respect to oral petitions.

Our attempt to gain effective representation on the Trusteeship Council for the Native Peoples got absolutely nowhere. Not only is there no reference to representation of the Native peoples, but the personnel of the Trusteeship Council is more weighted against fairness to the Native peoples than was the personnel of the P. M. C. The latter had a majority of members from non-mandatory states. But the Trusteeship Council has an equal number from those nations that administer trust areas and those that do not. Moreover, those nations that do not administer trust areas and that, consequently, should be more likely to support the cause of the Native peoples, are to appoint members who serve for only a three-year term. The members appointed by the nations administering trust areas may serve indefinitely. It is, of course, apparent that the experience acquired over a long period of years should give a distinct advantage to these latter.

The Charter is worse than the Covenant in one other respect. At Paris in 1919 Lloyd George finally yielded to Clemenceau's desire to use troops from the French mandates in a European war. This concession was in recognition of France's declining birthrate in the presence of an increasing birthrate in Germany and the far-flung obligations of the British Empire which would make it impossible for Britain to come to France's aid in overwhelming strength promptly. But Native troops were not to be raised in the other mandated areas for use outside the mandated areas. In the Charter, however, it is specified that volunteer troops may be raised in the trust areas for the purpose of aiding in enforcing the provisions of the Charter. Thus, one of the consequences of the second world war may be the use of a larger number of so-called savages in preserving "white civilization."

At the close of this discussion of the provisions in the Charter for dependent peoples, most of whom are Negroes, let it be repeated that, however weak the Trusteeship Council is, there is no assurance that it will have any areas placed under its trusteeship. The colonial powers are giving wide publicity to the "advances" their colonies are making under their national control. This publicity can only be interpreted as a justification for not placing dependent areas under the Trusteeship Council. Why, then, one may ask, were nineteen articles of the Charter devoted to non-self-governing areas? The answer would seem to be that the colonial powers were making a concession in words to those persons and organizations that since the first World War have been demanding some form of international supervision of the dependent areas. If the colonial powers under the inspiration of these demands will lead their dependent areas to economic well-being and some form of self-government or full citizenship, we shall hail this emancipation of almost a hundred and a fifty millions of Negroes. But we shall have to continue to marvel at the apparent necessity for providing in the Charter some form of international supervision.

The same doubts created by the trusteeship provisions exist with respect to the proposed international educational and cultural organization. Certainly, few peoples in the world are in more need of an expanded educational and cultural program. But neither the draft proposal for this organization nor the attitude of most American educators holds out a great deal of hope.

It so happens that I have represented the Association of Colleges and Secondary Schools at the meetings of American and foreign educators that for more than two years have been actively interested in suggesting plans for this organization. At the Harpers Ferry Meeting of this International Education Assembly I succeeded in having incorporated in the recommendations the following statement: "Provision should be made for appropriate representation of all countries irrespective of their political status, including such non-self-governing areas as may exist at the end of the war."

There is no such provision included in the draft proposal released by the State Department on July 31, 1945. Only those who were present in London where the proposal was drafted can tell whether any attempt was made to include this provision and if so what nations were responsible for its noninclusion.

The draft proposal calls for the appointment of as many as five representatives from each nation that becomes a member of the international educational and cultural organization. I proposed that in the case of nations holding dependent areas at least one of these appointees should be a person of wide experience in education in dependent areas and that he should be preferably a Native. While the Chairman of the meeting was personally sympathetic to the suggestion, the vast majority of the other American educators were not. Although prolonged discussion had followed practically every other statement made by those present, the Chairman almost had to beg for expressions of opinion on this subject. There was no final agreement on it.

The proposals also call for an executive board of fifteen. I proposed that at least one of the fifteen should be a person of wide experience in education in dependent areas. Perhaps some persons other than the Chairman were sympathetic to the idea, but if so they expressed their support by their silence.

The proposals also state that "Subject to the requirements of efficient and technical competence, the staff shall be recruited on as wide a geographical basis as possible." I suggested that this language be strengthened by changing it to the language of the Charter which reads: "The United Nations shall place no restrictions on the eligibility of men and women to participate in any capacity and under conditions of equality in the principal and subsidiary organs." There were one or two nods of approval, but no general agreement.

This negative attitude does not necessarily mean that the proposals will not be given consideration. A memorandum has been submitted to the State Department expressing these views. The State Department may support them and urge them upon the conference that is to meet in November, 1945, to approve the proposals. But the main point is that not enough prominent educators in this country are actively interested in education in dependent areas. Only the representative of the American Association of University Women on her own initiative had already seen the possibility of linking the activities of the international educational and cultural organization with those of the trusteeship council.[2]

Because of the inadequacies of the Trusteeship Council and of the international educational and cultural organization, those who seek a fuller life for Negroes in dependent areas must look elsewhere. Perhaps this search will end with the World Trade Union Congress which is scheduled to meet in Paris on September 25, 1945. Organized labor feels that it is not adequately represented in the Conference of the International Labor Organization because each nation has two representatives of government and one of management to one of labor. There is thus always the *possibility* that labor will be out-voted three to one. Consequently, labor wants its own international labor organization that will speak for labor only.

The World Trade Union Congress holds out all the more hope because American Labor is represented by the CIO and not by the AF of L which alone has spoken for American labor in the Conferences of the I. L. O. Moreover, Russia, who has not in recent years been represented in the conferences of the I. L. O. is participating in the meetings of the World Trade Union Congress.

It should be remembered, however, that no actions of the W. T. U.C. are binding upon any nation any more than are the conventions or recommendations of the I. L. O. But just as the conventions and recommendations of the I. L. O. have sometimes influenced labor legislation in the members of the I. L. O., just so the decisions of the W. T. U.C. may result in beneficial labor legislation in the various countries. This may be more difficult than in the case of the conventions and recommendations of the I. L. O. since the latter have been voted in the presence of representatives of government and of management while those of the W. T. U.C. will have been voted only by representatives of labor.

On the other hand, it may be expected that labor in the dependent areas will have fuller representation and a more sympathetic hearing at the meetings of the W. T. U.C. than in those of the I. L. O.

In brief and in conclusion, I see in the growing power of labor in international affairs the best hope for a fuller life for Negroes in independent nations and in dependent areas. The extent of this influence will depend therefore upon the growing power of labor in each nation. The recent victory of the Labour Party in England may foreshadow a new era. For this reason it is necessary to watch the program of that party. This is the first time that labor has had a clear majority in an English government. Its accomplishments or its failures will therefore have world-wide significance. This statement is especially true with respect to dependent areas. Unless the Labour Government of England puts into operation a program that will, as quickly as possible, lead the dependent peoples of the British Empire to a fuller life, to independence or self-government, those peoples may well despair that there is any hope from their overlords. Since the atomic bomb has rendered futile the right of revolution proclaimed in the Declaration of Independence, in the documents and history of most of the other United Nations, these despairing and desperate dependent peoples in all parts of the world may look to Russia as their only salvation. The mere statement of this proposition might suffice to cause the nations that have held Negroes in subjection for the last five hundred years to wonder whether applying their democratic principles to all peoples, "without distinction as to race, sex, language or religion" might not be better for themselves than a third and more deadly world war.

Envoi

Is it too utterly fantastic to conceive that black men will one day perfect an atomic bomb? No, it is not. I can picture an international conference, not more

than twenty-five years from now, in which a black delegate will rise and declare: "Gentlemen: five hundred years is long enough for any people to be
held in bondage, degraded, spit upon, exploited, disfranchised, segregated,
lynched. Here is the formula for a home-manufactured atomic bomb. Give us
liberty, or we will give you death."

NOTES

1. As this book goes to press, the London Conference of the Big Five has been
unable to agree as to the future of the former Italian colonies.

2. At a meeting of some fifty representatives of educational organizations and
learned societies called by the American Council on Education in Washington on September 21 and 22, 1945, it was unanimously voted, on my recommendation, that the
State Department be urged to give serious consideration to adequate representation
of non-self-governing areas.

PART 6

A Science of Society

Introduction

This section brings together the work of seven scholars from two different generations.[1] Whether they were members of the generation whose politics and aspirations were importantly defined by of the Crash of '29 or that somewhat larger cohort for whom *Brown v. Board of Education* and "massive resistance" were politically and socially formative, both stood, in the words of Richard Bardolph, "on a wavering color-line" and understood themselves to be "poised on precarious social frontiers and keenly aware of the fateful role they were playing as symbols of the race."[2]

The progress of this generation of black scholars was both quite real and, like the color line they strove to overcome, wavering. According to W. E. B. Du Bois, between 1823 and 1908 the annual number of Negro college graduates increased from 2 to 228.[3] In 1960, little more than fifty years later, at the demographic peak of a youth culture in which attending college had become far more widespread, the number of black college students had risen to between 100,000 and 125,000 out of a national total of three million.[4] By the early 1970s, as this cohort was entering the academic job market, African American college attendance, though growing rapidly, still lagged well behind the white population. Even though African Americans were 13% of the American college-age population by the early 1970s, persistent socio-economic barriers kept the proportion of African Americans in higher education very low in comparison to their share of the college-age population, a trend that continues today.[5]

Unlike members of the founding and professionalizing generations, those who began their careers after the Crash could, if they survived the challenges of depression and war, look forward to an expanding vista of opportunities for professional development, recognition, and even influence.[6] Perhaps the most prominent example of social scientists and their scholarship participating in this expanding vista of professional opportunity and influence is embodied in Kenneth and Mamie Phipps Clark and their "doll studies" work.[7]

The Clarks were both students at Howard University during its "golden age," when Ralph Bunche, Abram Harris, Alain Locke, and E. Franklin Frazier (among others) were on the faculty. Both Clarks continued their graduate studies in psychology at Columbia and built careers at the center of New York City's liberal left political community, Kenneth as a professor at City College and Mamie as director of the Northside Center for Child Development.[8] Kenneth Clark's reputation as an activist-scholar and his location in

New York made him a visible and much honored commentator on the continually unfolding legacy of *Brown v. Board of Education.*

The Clarks' studies showed that by the time African American children passed through the door of a segregated American public school, they understood, whether or not they lived in a formally segregated region of the country, a fundamental message of American culture: that to be "black" or "Negro" was to be the member of a group subject to unequal treatment and outright discrimination. This argument was first cited by the Supreme Court in *Brown v. Board of Education* and then broadcast by Kenneth Clark (as the sole author) of a book for parents, *Prejudice and Your Child,* published in 1955.[9]

In developing their approach, the Clarks emphasized the damage done to African American children rather than their resiliency. As we try to reconstruct historically the reasons for the Clarks' choice, it is important to remember that they were writing during a period of unusual insistence on ideological conformity. The Clarks, then, were seeking the attention of a political culture that was often unusually self-congratulatory and conformist.[10] So, even though their approach has garnered its critics in the intervening years,[11] we would do well to recognize that the Clarks were arguing something quite ideologically dangerous: the American mainstream was polluted, and needed not only to be cleaned but perhaps entirely reconstituted.

Another member of the student generation of the 1930s and one who also advocated for a more socially challenging and responsive social science is Hylan Lewis. As a graduate student at the University of Chicago, Lewis took the "community study" technique that had been the hallmark of the Chicago School of sociology into the rural South. Although transferring a method designed to study urban communities in the North into the black community of a southern mill town was certainly innovative, perhaps the more important way in which Lewis challenged convention was in the realm of the values and intellectual transparency he sought to bring to the participant-observer process. Working as a self-consciously "inside observer" of a world rendered remote to white social science not by geography or distance but by the rules of racial segregation in their own society, Lewis worried aloud in his classic *Blackways of Kent* about a challenge that also absorbed those publishing revisionist studies ten and twenty years later: the relationship between means and ends in the process of collecting data about fellow humans. Might the research and publication process somehow, against the author's fondest hopes and wishes, "devitalize and caricature" the lives of his friends/subjects?[12] On one point Lewis was especially emphatic: "The Negro people of Kent and people like them need make no apology nor do they need one made for them;

it is rather the 'tough' culture that shapes their behavior and the social science techniques that but approximate the truth and meaning of their lives that need examination and correction."[13] Published in 1955, these words convey—far more directly—reservations expressed more elliptically by Charles S. Johnson and E. Franklin Frazier in the 1930s and 1940s.[14] Lewis's self-conscious and challenging words are, in fact, an early sign of the revisionist spirit that would blow through the social sciences ten years later as the civil rights movement reached its climactic phase. We see some of this spirit in the Lewis essay (written in the 1960s while he was on the faculty at Howard, his alma mater), "The Culture of Poverty Approach to Social Problems."

The renewed scrutiny of American society during the civil rights years caused a younger generation of scholars to ask how social science supported rather than challenged mainstream cultural practices and to call for a new science of society, one in which those who had formerly been "subject" to the analysis of white social science could expose racist politics masquerading as objective inquiry. Thus, as Ronald Walters argued, the black scholar must first seek models and approaches that were grounded in the distinctive, separate, and unique attributes of African American life. At the same time, he or she must recognize how politics necessarily permeates all research and "develop an offensive strategy around the collection, analysis, packaging, dissemination and use of knowledge about Black People in order to properly defend himself against the lead that white social science has established in all of these areas."[15]

Walters sought to fuse the roles of scholar and activist by entering the political realm as a participant observer. During the 1980s, while on the faculty of Howard, Walters served as a high-ranking advisor on policy and politics to presidential candidate Jesse Jackson.[16] Since the Jackson campaigns of 1984 and 1988, Walters has moved to the University of Maryland and continued to be both a careful student of African American political participation and an articulate advocate of its mobilization to change the direction of American social policy.

Part of creating a social science with the capacity to challenge rather than merely observe society required that black social scientists test the traditional models at the center of their formal training against their own "field experience" as black people in American society.[17] This process is eloquently described by Joyce Ladner, who confided the following to readers of *Tomorrow's Tomorrow*, a pioneering revisionist study of African American girlhood: "I *am* sure that the twenty years I spent being socialized by my family and the larger Black Community [in Mississippi] prior to entering graduate school shaped my perception of life, defined my motive responses to the world and enhanced my ability to survive in a society that has not made survival for Blacks easy."[18] In ways that bring to mind Hylan Lewis's dilemmas as an "inside observer" of black life in Kent, Ladner became troubled as her life experience as a black woman simultaneously enabled her to richly and subtly understand the lives of her young subjects while it also placed her in conflict with traditional definitions of her role as an "objective" social scientist.[19]

Ladner followed up *Tomorrow's Tomorrow* with an equally groundbreaking study of cross-racial adoption. Because this research required that she study white parents and families, Ladner revisited familiar methodological ground from a new vantage point. Recalling with a refreshing directness her earlier concerns about the ability of white social scientists to understand black Americans, Ladner asked, "Can a black social scientist effectively conduct research among white subjects?"[20] The answer drawn from her experience was generally yes, in part because she developed the same kinds of relationships of mutual trust that had been the hallmark of her first book. In keeping with the spirit of her question, however, Ladner also provided some noteworthy examples of resistance and asked her readers to judge for themselves.

Like Ronald Walters, Ladner has built an important career combining scholarship and public service, culminating, in her case, in service as president of Howard University. In recent years, Ladner has studied African American political leadership at the community level and contributed to challenging widely held racial stereotypes about black "welfare mothers."[21] In doing this latter work, Ladner was in growing company.

If culture had been an underdeveloped concept for academic analysis through the 1950s, the same was even more dramatically true of gender as a category of cultural and political analysis. This began to change radically in the early 1970s. Political scientist Mae C. King's "Oppression and Power: The Unique Status of the Black Woman in the American Political System," provides a formative and compelling reading of how gender stereotypes have interacted with class formation to prevent the building of alliances across race and gender lines. The first step in the repression of black women was the use of the language and logic of ideal womanhood to define them out of that category. "Black women," King argues, are pictured in American culture as "tough, hard-working domestics who assume the role of matriarch in the home but always somehow manage to know their place and remain appropriately submissive in the white world."[22]

By associating masculine traits with the labor of black women, they are denied the social protection implicit in the stereotype of feminine vulnerability applied to middle-class white women. Decoding the different ways in which black and white women are represented in gender stereotypes leads us back to the underlying class dynamics: inequalities in income between black and white women translate, according to King, into the probability that "a redefinition of sex roles . . . can probably occur for white women without fundamentally restructuring the political system. However, this is not the case for black women. An operational redefinition of their sex status, accompanied by commensurate rewards cannot be realized apart from a redefinition of the status of blacks generally in the American political system."[23]

We conclude this discussion with sociologist William Julius Wilson's consideration of how changes in economics, politics, and cultural conduct converged after World War II to bring positive reform. Wilson, a 1958 graduate of Wilberforce University, has taught at two citadels of American higher education: the University of Chicago and Harvard. Since the publication of his monograph *The Declining Significance of Race* in 1978, Wilson has been a persistent advocate for government intervention to correct the interlocking inequalities of race and class in American society. A man whose intellectual forte is best described by the phrase "political economy," Wilson has been a perceptive analyst of the ways in which institutional racism continues to structure life in a society that has thrown off legally sanctioned segregation.

In the essay reprinted here, "Competitive Race Relations and the Proliferation of Racial Protest, 1940–1970," Wilson lays the foundation for the analysis presented in his 1978 classic. The economy of the postwar years—and of the 1960s in particular—was robust, creating opportunities in the unionized industrial labor force and in the public and private white collar bureaucracy into which African Americans could move without being in competition with whites.[24] Progress, however, was tightly contingent upon continued economic growth; should it slow or stop, so would greater white tolerance. If the years since Wilson wrote "Competitive Race Relations and the Proliferation of Racial Protests" have not been characterized by a renewal of the "violent confrontations between blacks and whites" of the 1950s and 1960s, the conflict and its consequences have nonetheless been very real. Technological change—especially "deindustrialization"—has locked a significant number of black Americans out of the possibility of upward mobility.[25] In addition, the racially coded political combat of the last thirty years has taken Wilson exactly to where Harris and Bunche stood forty years prior to that: advocacy of universalistic social programs aimed at economic and social reconstruction as the best path away from a society divided by race and class.[26]

Engaging the public through social science is a risky but worthwhile venture. Those who braved the social science wars of the 1960s, in their effort to clarify and change the disciplines, sometimes caught worthy work within their net of indictment. Thirty years later, the conventional wisdom of American political culture reports that the social science of the Great Society years overly contextualized—and thus rationalized—social misconduct in the service of a misguided political agenda. We hope that *Black Scholars on the Line* redeems the good names of those in each generation who persistently and relentlessly pressed for the best possible answers under difficult circumstances. The century of scholarship contained in this book should be a reminder that the mission of social science in each generation is not to provide falsely final or deceptively definitive answers to enduring problems, but to speak honestly, *in* and *to* their times in the service of improving the present and securing the future.

NOTES

1. Sociologist Hylan Lewis and psychologists Kenneth and Mamie Clark earned their undergraduate degrees from Howard in 1932, 1935, and 1938, respectively, during the Great Depression. Sociologists Joyce A. Ladner and William Julius Wilson and political scientists Ronald Walters and Mae King all earned their degrees during the civil rights years: Ladner earned her BA at Tougaloo College in 1964, Wilson obtained his BA from Wilberforce University in 1958, Walters received his BA from Fisk University in 1963, and King earned her BA from Bishop College in 1960.

2. Richard Bardolph, *The Negro Vanguard* (New York: Holt, Rinehart and Winston, 1959; repr. Westport: Negro University Press, 1971), 215.

3. W. E. B. Du Bois and Augustus Granville, eds., *The College-Bred Negro American* (Atlanta: Atlanta University Press, 1910; repr., The Arno Press and the *New York Times*, 1968), 45.

4. Daniel C. Thompson, *Private Black Colleges at the Crossroads* (Westport: Greenwood Press, 1973), 41.

5. The demographic figures cited are from *Small Change: A Report on Federal Support for Black Colleges, 1972* (a report of the Southern Education Foundation (SEF) of Atlanta, Georgia), 2. The report also notes that blacks were 4% of the enrollment at historically white schools. On the continuation of these trends, see the SEF's 1998 report, *Miles to Go: Black Students and Post-Secondary Education in the South*, 18–20. For a sense of how racism was institutionalized in federal policy to make the attainment of a college education more difficult for African Americans, see Lizabeth Cohen, *A Consumer's Republic: The Politics of Mass Consumption in Postwar America* (New York: Vintage Books, 2004), 167–170.

6. The research of Harry Washington Greene demonstrates that the Great Depression drove a large number of talented black scholars to graduate school. According

to Greene, 316 of the 381 doctorates awarded to African Americans up to 1943 were awarded between 1930 and 1943 and were clustered heavily in sociology and its allied disciplines. Greene's statistics also confirm the primacy of the University of Chicago as a capital of American social science: 234 of the 381 doctorates were from the University of Chicago. See Harry Washington Greene, *Holders of Doctorates among Negroes* (Boston: Meador Publishing, 1946), 22–24; on Greene's findings relative to the University of Chicago, see Diane Slaughter and Gerald McWorter, "Social Origins and Early Features of the Scientific Study of Black American Children and Families" (Afro Scholar Working Papers, University of Illinois at Urbana–Champaign, March 1981), 9.

7. For a more detailed discussion of Kenneth Clark's career in these years see Ben Keppel, *The Work of Democracy: Ralph Bunche, Kenneth B. Clark, Lorraine Hansberry, and the Cultural Politics of Race* (Cambridge, Mass.: Harvard University Press, 1995), 97–131. On the early career of Mamie Phipps Clark, see Shafali Lal, "Giving the Children Security: Mamie Phipps Clark and the Racialization of Child Psychology," *American Psychologist* 57, no. 1 (2002): 20–28.

8. On Northside, see the important community study by Gerald Markowitz and David Rosner, *Children, Race, and Power: Kenneth and Mamie Clark's Northside Center* (New York: Routledge, 2000).

9. For a sense of how the Clark studies were part of a larger effort to reexamine the foundations of culture, see the work of Howard University classicist Frank Snowden Jr., who argues that in the ancient world the words "black" and "white" in public discourse did not reflect any "special theory as to inferior dark or black peoples and attached no stigma to color." Snowden continues, "There is nothing in the evidence . . . to suggest that the ancient Greek or Roman established color as an obstacle to integration into society. . . . The Greeks and Romans counted black people in." Frank Snowden Jr., *Blacks in Antiquity: Blacks in the Greco-Roman Experience* (Cambridge, Mass.: Harvard University Press, 1970), 216–218. Snowden discusses his career and its connection to postwar social changes in "A Lifetime of Inquiry," in *Against the Odds: Scholars Who Challenged Racism in the Twentieth Century*, ed. Benjamin P. Bowser and Louis Kushnick (Amherst: University of Massachusetts Press, 2002), 41–62.

10. See Ben Keppel, "Kenneth Clark in the Patterns of American Culture," *American Psychology* 57, no. 1 (2002): 31–32. On Kenneth Clark's growing skepticism about the ability of social science to be either a voice in the wilderness or a servant of passing conventional wisdom, see his collection of essays titled *Pathos of Power* (New York: Harper and Row, 1974).

11. Taking the full benefit of hindsight, recent scholars have both honored the motivations behind the "doll studies" while questioning some of their conclusions. Important revisionist discussions of the "doll studies" are provided by William E. Cross, *Shades of Blackness: Diversity in African-American Identity* (Philadelphia: Temple University Press, 1991), 3–38, and Daryl Michael Scott, *Contempt and Pity: Social Policy and the Image of the Damaged Psyche, 1880–1996* (Chapel Hill: University of North Carolina Press, 1997), 19–40. On the Clark legacy to contemporary

psychology see Gina Philogene, ed., *Racial Identity in Context: The Legacy of Kenneth B. Clark* (Washington, D.C.: American Psychological Association, 2004).

12. Hylan Lewis, *Blackways of Kent* (Chapel Hill: University of North Carolina Press, 1955), ix–x.

13. Ibid., xi. Lewis discusses the events leading up to and surrounding this book in his essay, "Pursuing Field Work in African-American Communities: Some Personal Reflections of Hylan Lewis," in Bowser and Kushnick, eds., *Against the Odds,* 126–127.

14. See our discussion in part 2.

15. Ronald W. Walters, "Toward a Definition of Black Social Science," in *The Death of White Sociology: Essays on Race and Culture,* ed. Joyce A. Ladner (New York: Random House, 1973; repr. Baltimore: Black Scholar Press, 1998), 205. For a clear sense of how Walters's vision of a black social science has developed over the years, see his *White Nationalism and Black Interests: Conservative Public Policy and the Black Community* (Detroit: Wayne State University Press, 2003); on the continuing challenges facing the funding and production of social science on black life from within the black community, see 266–271.

16. On this facet of his political/scholarly work, see Walters's *Black Presidential Politics in America: A Strategic Approach* (Albany: State University of New York Press, 1988).

17. Walters, "Toward a Definition," 202, 205.

18. Joyce A. Ladner, "Tomorrow's Tomorrow: The Black Woman," in Ladner, ed. *The Death of White Sociology,* 414–415.

19. Ibid., 414–417.

20. Joyce A Ladner, *Mixed Families: Adopting Across Racial Boundaries* (New York: Anchor/Doubleday, 1977), xi.

21. Joyce A. Ladner, *The New Urban Leaders* (Washington, D.C.: Brookings Institution, 2001); Jane C. Quint and Judith S. Musick with Joyce Ladner, *Lives of Promise and Lives of Pain: Young Mothers after New Chance* (New York: Manpower Demonstration Research Corporation, 1994).

22. Mae C. King, "The Politics of Sexual Stereotypes," *Black Scholar* 4 (March–April 1973), 17.

23. Mae C. King, "Oppression and Power: The Unique Status of the Black Woman in the American Political System," *Social Science Quarterly* 56, no. 1 (1975): 124.

24. William Julius Wilson, "Competitive Race Relations and the Proliferation of Racial Protest, 1940–1970," in *Power, Racism, and Privilege: Race Relations in Theoretical and Sociological Perspectives* (New York: The Free Press, 1973), 127–132. Wilson notes that between 1950 and 1970 the percentage of black males in "middle-class" jobs more than doubled, from 16.4 to 35.3 percent. Conversely, the percentage of blacks in "lower class" jobs dropped dramatically from 62.1 percent in 1950 to 36.4 percent in 1970. See also William Julius Wilson, *The Declining Significance of Race: Blacks and Changing American Institutions* (Chicago: University of Chicago Press, 1978), 129.

25. See especially William Julius Wilson, *Declining Significance of Race*, 19, 91–93; *When Work Disappears: The World of the New Urban Poor* (New York: Alfred A. Knopf, 1996); and also his earlier *The Truly Disadvantaged: The Inner City, the Underclass and Public Policy* (Chicago: University of Chicago, 1987).

26. Wilson, *When Work Disappears*, 140–164; see also Wilson's *The Bridge over the Racial Divide: Rising Inequality and Coalition Politics* (Berkeley: University of California, 1999).

KENNETH B. CLARK AND MAMIE P. CLARK

Racial Identification and Preference in Negro Children

*Condensed by the authors from an unpublished study made possible
by a fellowship grant from the Julius Rosenwald Fund, 1940–1941.*

Problem

The specific problem of this study is an analysis of the genesis and development of racial identification as a function of ego development and self-awareness in Negro children.

Race awareness, in a primary sense, is defined as a consciousness of the self as belonging to a specific group which is differentiated from other observable groups by obvious physical characteristics which are generally accepted as being racial characteristics.

Because the problem of racial identification is so definitely related to the problem of the genesis of racial attitudes in children, it was thought practicable to attempt to determine the racial attitudes or preferences of these Negro

Kenneth B. Clark and Mamie P. Clark, "Racial Identification and Preference in Negro Children," in *Readings in Social Psychology*, ed. Theodore M. Newcomb, Eugene Hartley, et al., 169–178 (New York: Henry Holt and Company, 1947).

children—and to define more precisely, as far as possible, the developmental pattern of this relationship.

Procedure

This paper presents results from only one of several techniques devised and used by the authors to investigate the development of racial identification and preferences in Negro children.[1] Results presented here are from the Dolls Test.

Dolls Test.   The subjects were presented with four dolls, identical in every respect save skin color. Two of these dolls were brown with black hair and two were white with yellow hair. In the experimental situation these dolls were unclothed except for white diapers. The position of the head, hands, and legs on all the dolls was the same. For half of the subjects the dolls were presented in the order: white, colored, white, colored. For the other half the order of presentation was reversed. In the experimental situation the subjects were asked to respond to the following requests by choosing *one* of the dolls and giving it to the experimenter:

1.   Give me the doll that you like to play with—(a) like best.
2.   Give me the doll that is a nice doll.
3.   Give me the doll that looks bad.
4.   Give me the doll that is a nice color.
5.   Give me the doll that looks like a white child.
6.   Give me the doll that looks like a colored child.
7.   Give me the doll that looks like a Negro child.
8.   Give me the doll that looks like you.

Requests 1 through 4 were designed to reveal preferences; requests 5 through 7 to indicate a knowledge of "racial differences"; and request 8 to show self-identification.

It was found necessary to present the preference requests first in the experimental situation because in a preliminary investigation it was clear that the children who had already identified themselves with the colored doll had a marked tendency to indicate a preference for this doll and this was not necessarily a genuine expression of actual preference, but a reflection of ego involvement. This potential distortion of the data was controlled by merely asking the children to indicate their preferences first and then to make identifications with one of the dolls.

Subjects

Two hundred fifty-three Negro children formed the subjects of this experiment. One hundred thirty-four of these subjects (southern group) were tested in segregated nursery schools and public schools in Hot Springs, Pine Bluff, and Little Rock, Arkansas. These children had had no experience in racially mixed school situations. One hundred nineteen subjects (northern group) were tested in the racially mixed nursery and public schools of Springfield, Massachusetts.

Age distribution of subjects:

Age, years	North	South	Total
3	13	18	31
4	10	19	29
5	34	12	46
6	33	39	72
7	29	46	75
Total	119	134	253

Sex distribution of subjects:

Sex	North	South	Total
Male	53	63	116
Female	66	71	137

Skin color of subjects:

Skin color	North	South	Total
Light[a]	33	13	46
Medium[b]	58	70	128
Dark[c]	28	51	79

[a]light (practically white)
[b]medium (light brown to dark brown)
[c]dark (dark brown to black)

All subjects were tested individually in a schoolroom or office especially provided for this purpose. Except for a few children who showed generalized negativism from the beginning of the experiment (results for these children are not included here), there was adequate rapport between the experimenter and all subjects tested. In general, the children showed high interest in and enthusiasm for the test materials and testing situation. The children, for the most part, considered the experiment somewhat of a game.

Results

Racial Identification.   Although the questions on knowledge of "racial differences" and self-identification followed those designed to determine racial preference in the actual experimental situation, it appears more meaningful to discuss the results in the following order: knowledge of "racial differences," racial self-identification, and finally racial preferences.

The results of the responses to requests 5, 6, and 7, which were asked to determine the subjects' knowledge of racial differences, may be seen in Table 1. Ninety-four percent of these children chose the white doll when asked to give the experimenter the white doll; 93 percent of them chose the brown doll when asked to give the colored doll; and, 72 percent chose the brown doll when asked to give the Negro doll. These results indicate a clearly established knowledge of a "racial difference" in these subjects—and some awareness of the relation between the physical characteristic of skin color and the racial concepts of "white" and "colored." Knowledge of the concept of "Negro" is not so well developed as the more concrete verbal concepts of "white" and "colored" as applied to racial differences.

Table 1. Choices of All Subjects

	Request 5 (for white)		Request 6 (for colored)		Request 7 (for Negro)		Request 8 (for you)	
Choice	No.	Percent	No.	Percent	No.	Percent	No.	Percent
Colored doll	13	5	235	93	182	72	166	66
White doll	237	94	15	6	50	20	85	33
Don't know or no response	3	1	3	1	21	8	2	1

The question arises as to whether choice of the brown doll or of the white doll, particularly in response to questions 5 and 6, really reveals a knowledge of "racial differences" or simply indicates a learned perceptual reaction to the concepts of "colored" and "white." Our evidence that the responses of these children *do* indicate a knowledge of "racial difference" comes from several sources: the results from other techniques used (i.e., a coloring test and a questionnaire) and from the qualitative data obtained (children's spontaneous remarks) strongly support a knowledge of "racial differences." Moreover, the consistency of results for requests 5 through 8 also tends to support the fact that these children are actually making identifications in a "racial" sense.

The responses to request 8, designed to determine racial self-identification follow the following pattern: 66 percent of the total group of children identified themselves with the colored doll, while 33 percent identified themselves with the white doll. The critical ratio of this difference is 7.6.[2]

Comparing the results of request 8 (racial self-identification) with those of requests 5, 6, and 7 (knowledge of racial difference) it is seen that the awareness of racial differences does not necessarily determine a socially accurate racial self-identification—since approximately nine out of ten of these children are aware of racial differences as indicated by their correct choice of a "white" and "colored" doll on request, and only a little more than six out of ten make socially correct identifications with the colored doll.

Age Differences.   Table 2 shows that, when the responses to requests 5 and 6 are observed together, these subjects at each age level have a well-developed knowledge of the concept of racial difference between "white" and "colored" as this is indicated by the characteristic of skin color. These data definitely indicate that a basic knowledge of "racial differences" exists as a part of the pattern of ideas of Negro children from the age of three through seven years in the northern and southern communities tested in this study—and that this knowledge develops more definitely from year to year to the point of absolute stability at the age of seven.

A comparison of the results of requests 5 and 6 with those of request 7, which required the child to indicate the doll which looks like a "Negro" child, shows that knowledge of a racial difference in terms of the word "Negro" does not exist with the same degree of definiteness as it does in terms of the more basic designations of "white" and "colored." It is significant, however, that knowledge of a difference in terms of the word "Negro" makes a sharp increase from the five- to the six-year level and a less accelerated one between the six- and seven-year levels. The fact that all of the six-year-olds used in this investigation were enrolled in the public schools seems to be related to this spurt. Since it seems clear that the term "Negro" is a more verbalized designation of "racial differences," it is reasonable to assume that attendance at public schools facilitates the development of this verbalization of the race concept held by these children.

Table. 2. Choices of Subjects at Each Age Level*

Choice	3 yr. No.	Percent	4 yr. No.	Percent	5 yr. No.	Percent	6 yr. No.	Percent	7 yr. No.	Percent
Request 5 (for white)										
colored doll	4	13	4	14	3	7	2	3	0	
white doll	24	77	25	86	43	94	70	97	75	100
Request 6 (for colored)										
colored doll	24	77	24	83	43	94	69	96	75	100
white doll	4	13	5	17	3	7	3	4	0	
Request 7 (for Negro)										
colored doll	17	55	17	59	28	61	56	78	64	85
white doll	9	29	10	35	14	30	12	17	5	7
Request 8 (for you)										
colored doll	11	36	19	66	22	48	49	68	65	87
white doll	19	61	9	31	24	52	23	32	10	13

*Individuals failing to make either choice not included, hence some percentages add to less than 100.

In response to request 8 there is a general and marked increase in the percent of subjects who identify with the colored doll with an increase in age—with the exception of the four- to five-year groups.[3] This deviation of the five-year-olds from the general trend is considered in detail in the larger, yet unpublished study.

Identification by Skin Color.   Table 3 shows slight and statistically insignificant differences among the three skin-color groups in their responses which indicate a knowledge of the "racial difference" between the white and colored doll (requests 5 through 7).

It should be noted, however, that the dark group is consistently more accurate in its choice of the appropriate doll than either the light or the medium group on requests 5 through 7. This would seem to indicate that the dark group is slightly more definite in its knowledge of racial differences and that this definiteness extends even to the higher level of verbalization inherent in the use of the term "Negro" as a racial designation. In this regard it is seen that 75 percent of the dark children chose the colored doll when asked for the doll which "looks like a Negro child" while only 70 percent of the light children and 71 percent of the medium children made this response. The trend of results for requests 5 and 6 remains substantially the same.

Table 3. Choices of Subjects In Light, Medium, And Dark Groups*

Choice	Light		Medium		Dark	
	No.	Percent	No.	Percent	No.	Percent
Request 5 (for white)						
colored doll	2	5	8	6	3	4
white doll	43	94	118	92	76	96
Request 6 (for colored)						
colored doll	41	89	118	92	76	96
white doll	4	9	8	6	3	4
Request 7 (for Negro)						
colored doll	32	70	91	71	59	75
white doll	9	20	27	21	14	18
Request 8 (for you)						
colored doll	9	20	93	73	64	81
white doll	37	80	33	26	15	19

* Individuals failing to make either choice not included, hence some percentages add to less than 100.

These results suggest further that correct racial identification of these Negro children at these ages is to a large extent determined by the concrete fact of their own skin color, and further that this racial identification is not necessarily dependent upon the expressed knowledge of a racial difference as indicated by the correct use of the words "white," "colored," or "Negro" when responding to white and colored dolls. This conclusion seems warranted in the light of the fact that those children who differed in skin color from light through medium to dark were practically similar in the pattern of their responses which indicated awareness of racial differences but differed markedly in their racial identification (responses to request 8 for the doll "that looks like you") only 20 percent of the light children, while 73 percent of the medium children, and 81 percent of the dark children identified themselves with the colored doll.

It is seen that there is a consistent increase in choice of the colored doll from the light to the medium group; an increase from the medium group to the dark group; and, a striking increase in the choices of the colored doll by the dark group as compared to the light group.[4] All differences, except between the medium and dark groups, are statistically significant.

Again, as in previous work,[5] it is shown that the percentage of the medium groups' identifications with the white or the colored representation resembles more that of the dark group and differs from the light group. Upon the basis of these results, therefore, one may assume that some of the factors and dynamics involved in racial identification are substantially the same for the dark and medium children, in contrast to dynamics for the light children.

North-South Differences.   The results presented in Table 4 indicate that there are no significant quantitative differences between the northern and southern Negro children tested (children in mixed schools and children in segregated schools) in their knowledge of racial differences.

While none of these differences is statistically reliable, it is significant that northern children know as well as southern children which doll is supposed to represent a white child and which doll is supposed to represent a colored child. However, the northern children make fewer identifications with the colored doll and more identifications with the white doll than do the southern children. One factor accounting for this difference may be the fact that in this sample there are many more light colored children in the North (33) than there are in the South (13). Since this difference in self-identification is not statistically significant, it may be stated that the children in the northern mixed-school situation do not differ from children in the southern segregated schools in either their knowledge of racial differences or their racial identification. A more qualitative analysis will be presented elsewhere.

Table 4. Choices of Subjects In Northern (Mixed Schools)
And Southern (Segregated Schools) Groups*

Choice	North, Percent	South, Percent
Request 5 (for white)		
colored doll	4	6
white doll	94	93
Request 6 (for colored)		
colored doll	92	94
white doll	7	5
Request 7 (for Negro)		
colored doll	74	70
white doll	20	19
Request 8 (for you)		
colored doll	61	69
white doll	39	29

*Individuals failing to make either choice not included, hence some percentages add to less than 100.

Table 5. Choices of All Subjects

Choice	Request 1 (play with)		Request 2 (nice doll)		Request 3 (looks bad)		Request 4 (nice color)	
	No.	Percent	No.	Percent	No.	Percent	No.	Percent
Colored doll	83	32	97	38	149	59	96	38
White doll	169	67	150	59	42	17	151	60
Don't know or no response	1	1	6	3	62	24	6	2

Racial Preferences.   It is clear from Table 5 that the majority of these Negro children prefer the *white* doll and reject the colored doll.

Approximately two thirds of the subjects indicated by their responses to requests 1 and 2 that they like the white doll "best," or that they would like to play with the white doll in preference to the colored doll, and that the white doll is a "nice doll."

Their responses to request 3 show that this preference for the white doll implies a concomitant negative attitude toward the brown doll. Fifty-nine percent of these children indicated that the colored doll "looks bad," while only 17 percent stated that the white doll "looks bad" (critical ratio 10.9). That this preference and negation in some way involve skin color is indicated by the results for request 4. Only 38 percent of the children thought that the brown doll was a "nice color," while 60 percent of them thought that the white doll was a "nice color" (critical ratio 5.0).

The importance of these results for an understanding of the origin and development of racial concepts and attitudes in Negro children cannot be minimized. Of equal significance are their implications, in the light of the results of racial identification already presented, for racial mental hygiene.

Age Differences.   Table 6 shows that at each age from three through seven years the majority of these children prefer the white doll and reject the brown doll. This tendency to prefer the white doll is not as stable (not statistically reliable) in the three-year-olds as it is in the four- and five-year-olds. On the other hand, however, the tendency of the three-year-olds to negate the brown doll ("looks bad") is established as a statistically significant fact (critical ratio 4.5).

Analyzing the results of requests 1 and 2 together, it is seen that there is a marked *increase* in preference for the white doll from the three- to the four-year level; a more gradual *decrease* in this preference from the four- to the five-year level; a further decrease from the five- to the six-year level; and a continued decrease from the six- to the seven-year level. These results suggest that although the majority of Negro children at each age prefer the white doll to the brown doll, this preference decreases gradually from four through seven years.

Skin color preferences of these children follow a somewhat different pattern of development. The results of request 4 show that while the majority of children at each age below 7 years prefer the skin color of the white doll, this preference increases from three through five years and decreases from five through seven years. It is of interest to point out that only at the seven-year level do the same number of children indicate a preference for the skin color of the colored doll as for that of the white doll.

Table 6. Choices Of Subjects At Each Age Level*

Choice	3 yr. No.	3 yr. Percent	4 yr. No.	4 yr. Percent	5 yr. No.	5 yr. Percent	6 yr. No.	6 yr. Percent	7 yr. No.	7 yr. Percent
Request 1 (play with)										
colored doll	13	42	7	24	12	26	21	29	30	40
white doll	17	55	22	76	34	74	51	71	45	60
Request 2 (nice doll)										
colored doll	11	36	7	24	13	28	33	46	33	44
white doll	18	58	22	76	33	72	38	53	39	52
Request 3 (looks bad)										
colored doll	21	68	15	52	36	78	45	63	32	43
white doll	6	19	7	24	5	11	11	15	13	17
Request 4 (nice color)										
colored doll	12	39	8	28	9	20	31	43	36	48
white doll	18	58	21	72	36	78	40	56	36	48

*Individuals failing to make either choice not included, hence some percentages add to less than 100.

Table 7. Choices of Subjects in Light, Medium, and Dark Groups*

Choice	Light No.	Light Percent	Medium No.	Medium Percent	Dark No.	Dark Percent
Request 1 (play with)						
colored doll	11	24	41	32	31	39
white doll	35	76	86	67	48	61
Request 2 (nice doll)						
colored doll	15	33	50	39	32	40
white doll	31	67	72	56	47	60
Request 3 (looks bad)						
colored doll	31	67	73	57	45	57
white doll	6	13	22	17	14	18
Request 4 (nice color)						
colored doll	13	28	56	44	27	34
white doll	32	70	68	53	51	65

*Individuals failing to make either choice not included, hence some percentages add to less than 100.

The majority of these children at each age level indicate that the brown doll, rather than the white doll, "looks bad." This result shows positively the negation of the colored doll which was implicit in the expressed preference for the white doll discussed above.

The evaluative rejection of the brown doll is statistically significant, even at the three-year level, and is pronounced at the five-year level. The indicated preference for the white doll is statistically significant from the four-year level up to the seven-year level.

It seems justifiable to assume from these results that the crucial period in the formation and patterning of racial attitudes begins at around four and five years. At these ages these subjects appear to be reacting more uncritically in a definite structuring of attitudes which conforms with the accepted racial values and mores of the larger environment.

Preferences and Skin Color.   Results presented in Table 7 reveal that there is a tendency for the majority of these children, in spite of their own skin color, to prefer the white doll and to negate the brown doll. This tendency is most pronounced in the children of light skin color and least so in the dark children. A more intensive analysis of these results appears in a larger, yet unpublished study.

Table 8. Choices of Subjects in Northern (Mixed Schools) and Southern (Segregated Schools) Groups (Requests 1 Through 4)*

Choice	North, Percent	South, Percent
Request 1 (play with)		
colored doll	28	37
white doll	72	62
Request 2 (nice doll)		
colored doll	30	46
white doll	68	52
Request 3 (looks bad)		
colored doll	71	49
white doll	17	16
Request 4 (nice color)		
colored doll	37	40
white doll	63	57

*Individuals failing to make either choice not included, hence some percentages add to less than 100.

North-South Differences.   From Table 8 it is clear that the southern children in segregated schools are less pronounced in their preference for the white doll, compared to the northern children's definite preference for this doll. Although still in a minority, a higher percentage of southern children, compared to northern, prefer to play with the colored doll or think that it is a "nice" doll. The critical ratio of this difference is not significant for request 1 but approaches significance for request 2 (2.75).

A significantly higher percentage (71) of the northern children, compared to southern children (49) think that the brown doll looks bad (critical ratio 3.68). Also a slightly higher percent of the southern children think that the brown doll has a "nice color," while more northern children think that the white doll has a "nice color."

In general, it may be stated that northern and southern children in these age groups tend to be similar in the degree of their preference for the white doll—with the northern children tending to be somewhat more favorable to the white doll than are the southern children. The southern children, however, in spite of their equal favorableness toward the white doll, are significantly less likely to reject the brown doll (evaluate it negatively), as compared to the strong tendency for the majority of the northern children to do so. That this difference is not primarily due to the larger number of light children found in the northern sample is indicated by more intensive analysis presented in the complete report.

Some Qualitative Data.   Many of the children entered into the experimental situation with a freedom similar to that of play. They tended to verbalize freely and much of this unsolicited verbalization was relevant to the basic problems of this study.

On the whole, the rejection of the brown doll and the preference for the white doll, when explained at all, were explained in rather simple, concrete terms: for white-doll preference—"'cause he's pretty" or "'cause he's white"; for rejection of the brown doll—"'cause he's ugly" or "'cause it don't look pretty" or "'cause him black" or "got black on him."

On the other hand, some of the children who were free and relaxed in the beginning of the experiment broke down and cried or became somewhat negativistic during the latter part when they were required to make self-identifications. Indeed, two children ran out of the testing room, unconsolable, convulsed in tears. This type of behavior, although not so extreme, was more prevalent in the North than in the South. The southern children who were disturbed by this aspect of the experiment generally indicated their disturbance by smiling or matter of factly attempting to escape their dilemma either by attempted humor or rationalization.

Rationalization of the rejection of the brown doll was found among both northern and southern children, however. A northern medium six-year-old justified his rejection of the brown doll by stating that "he looks bad 'cause he hasn't got a eyelash." A seven-year-old medium northern child justified his choice of the white doll as the doll with a "nice color" because "his feet, hands, ears, elbows, knees, and hair are clean."

A northern five-year-old dark child felt compelled to explain his identification with the brown doll by making the following unsolicited statement: "I burned my face and made it spoil." A seven-year-old northern light child went to great pains to explain that he is actually white but: "I look brown because I got a suntan in the summer."

NOTES

1. Other techniques presented in the larger study include: (1) a coloring test; (2) a questionnaire and (3) a modification of the Horowitz line drawing technique. (R. E. Horowitz, "Racial Aspects of Self-identification in Nursery School Children," *J. Psychol.*, 1939, VII, 91–99.)

2. These results are supported by similar ones from the Horowitz line drawing technique.

3. These results are supported by those from the use of the Horowitz line drawing technique.

4. These results substantiate and clearly focus the trend observed through the use of the Horowitz line drawing technique.

5. K. B. and M. P. Clark, "Skin Color as a Factor in Racial Identification of Negro Preschool Children," *J. Soc. Psychol.*, 1940, XI, 159–169; "Segregation as a Factor in the Racial Identification of Negro Preschool Children: a preliminary report," *J. Exper. Educ.*, 1939, IX, 161–163; "The Development of Consciousness of Self and the Emergence of Racial Identification in Negro Preschool Children," *J. Soc. Psychol.*, 1939, X, 591–599.

HYLAN LEWIS

The Culture of Poverty Approach to Social Problems

The late Louis Wirth, in the preface to his and Edward Shils' translation of Karl Mannheim's influential treatise on the sociology of knowledge, *Ideology and Utopia*, declared: "Every assertion of a 'fact' about the social world touches the interests of some individual or group."

An almost incidental allusion to the sociology of knowledge becomes cogent and haunting when I reflect on the theme of this meeting. And Louis Wirth's words written a generation ago make a strong bid to be sharply appropriate to our discussion today of approaches to contemporary social problems—and especially to the culture of poverty approach.

The allusion to the sociology of knowledge is haunting because of considerations related to the semantics of the phrase "culture of poverty." The allusion is compelling in light of the recent convergence of spotlights from different directions and of feverish activities from varied quarters—lay and professional, non-political and political, quasi-scientific and scientific—on the phenomenon which I prefer to call the poverty syndrome.

This convergence of concerns enhances the popularity, and probably at the same time encourages exaggerations of the scientific and programmatic promise, of terms and approaches like culture of poverty. This statement is not meant to suggest the term is suspect because it is fashionable. There is no necessary relationship between the validity of the culture of poverty idea and

Hylan Lewis, "The Culture of Poverty Approach to Social Problems," in *Culture, Class and Poverty*, 43–49 (Washington, D.C.: Communicating Research on the Urban Poor [CROSS-TELL], 1967). We thank Ione Lewis for readily seeing the merit of our mission and allowing this essay by her father to be reprinted here.

its related propositions or between the usefulness of the culture of poverty approach to social problems and the appeal and popularity of the phrase culture of poverty itself. Distinctions must be made, however, between behavior of scientists, artists, and practitioners that is truly honoring of the demonstrated validity and potential usefulness of the concept, and that behavior that panders to the popularity and pre-emptive force of the phrase. The social and cultural imperatives that help to make for the popularity and vogue of the term culture of poverty, as well as the consequences that flow from these, are crucially important.

The chief dangers lie in the indiscriminate use of certain phrases and in a particular approach achieving near-monopoly status. These contribute to the slowing down or to the stopping of the "democratic dialogue" by which truth and shadings of "facts" about human beings—those who are poor and those who are not poor and those who make social problems and those who do not—are sharpened and updated.

We who are involved with contemporary social problems are at once victims of and contributors to the verbal technology of the times. This has its consequences without regard to how a social problem is perceived, labeled, and defined; and without regard to what people are involved in the problem. The verbal technology of social problems affects students, teachers, researchers, policy makers, practitioners, or "John Q." and "Jane Q. Public" (whoever he or she might be, and whether he and she are profiled by pollster, market researcher, independent or captured student social surveyor, or non-profit specialists in social survey contracts; or conceptualized out of field observations; or imagined from letters to Congressmen from back home).

Part of the problem comes from the fact that the language of social science and social welfare as applied to social problems is a mixture of the legitimately scientific and of the diluted and the distorted scientific. Social science and social welfare vocabularies have been infiltrated by, and research and action goaded by, faddish and transient and popular shorthand, and by the fetching, the fighting, the soothing, and the seductive catch phrase. The seductive catch phrase reflects the initiative of the mass media mainly, and a tendency for limited trade terms to be adopted and adapted to meet the communication criteria and the circulation needs of the press, television and radio rather than those of the social science and social welfare professions.

If the focus is on "getting something done" about a particular social problem like poverty there may be positive values in some fledgling concept becoming a spread-eagle catch phrase. This is true particularly for those for whom getting action—any action—on any facet or symptom of living poor is the most important thing at a particular time. But here we are referring to instrumental and tactical uses and effects of phrases like culture of poverty as seen specifically in educational and political uses and gains—and not necessarily knowledge gains. The fact that something happens or is attempted about poverty may be incidental to the efforts of those who presume to know something about—or to study—poor people and social problems.

The interesting ironies are that it is possible for an approach or technique suggested first by a student of social problems like delinquency and poverty to be used to provide merely the ritualistic sanction of research for a political position or decisions (the reverse is possible also); and that reiteration and wide or strategic circulation of a slightly distorted or over-simplified version of social science proposition or "fact" may provide the leverage to get something moving. Of course, the something that gets moving may be misguided and end in failure, or it might by happenstance alone succeed or have a salutary effect. (And salutary is sometimes translated as soothing or diverting.)

Many students of social problems act as if they are unaware of, or unconcerned about this kind of unplanned or planned tactical research or tactical uses of it and they appear concerned, sometimes not so much about the consequences of what is happening to society and to the discipline, as they are about the fact that they are not or were not heeded or consulted. Many persons who are involved in working on social problems act ostrich-like about the use that is being made or not being made of their technical skills and concepts; and too many who know what is happening or not happening are wont to pout and piddle.

Working on persons of these types may be more important than discourses about which approach to social problems is most valid and useful. And more important questions might be raised about how an approach to a social problem is initially broached, packaged, and launched and how do the asserted "facts" that precede and follow a launching affect what individuals and groups.

I am not suggesting that the serious and necessary business of studying and working on social problems like poverty is endangered by a big conspiracy—there is none. I am pointing to the danger of having too many professionals concerned about social problems who act as if they do not know or do not want to know the score in—*the Realpolitiks* of—the social change game. And there is equal danger in the many who act as if they are afraid of, or incapable of, tangling with some others who are also concerned with doing something about the same social problems but who are able to ignore the researchers of social problems. The researcher and his products are frequently used for tactical rather than substantive scientific or strategic policy-making purposes.

As suggested earlier, we are all in some degree captives of some of the new terms that are being applied to old problems, as well as of some old terms applied in new ways to both old and new problems. (Re-reading Booth and Roundtree, on the characteristics and behavior of the poor, for example, can be instructive.) And as Wirth noted, some individuals and some groups are potential casualties of these terms and related assertions.

The culture of poverty approach is one of the most popular and best documented of the approaches to the network of social problems involving the contemporary poor in the United States. Related to culture of poverty, but not necessarily neatly, logically, or empirically—and in some instances "spinning off" it—are such terms as lower class culture, culturally deprived, target areas and populations, indigenous leaders and people. These are rapidly getting to be stale, invidious, and sloppy terms. And for better or worse the terms tend to come easily from the lips of politicians and news commentators, as from social scientists and welfare practitioners.

In regard to semantic considerations related to the culture of poverty approach, Frederick Breitenfeld, Jr. of Syracuse University, in "Who Says I'm Uncultured," written for a mass circulation magazine, although talking about art, sets forth a position and criticism that has some relevance to our discussion. In 1962, he wrote:

> I am disturbed partly because of a national disease that could be called *Semanticus Americani.* The symptoms are easily recognized: when a word or phrase has come to lose all meaning except a general connotation of "good" or "evil," and when the majority of people have come to react emotionally to that skeletal meaning, it is time to call the doctor and request a prescription for definition.

Before I go further, I shall summarize and make explicit some of the assumptions and ground rules that underlie, if not frame, this discussion of the culture of poverty approach.

The very fact that we are discussing here several approaches to social problems not only makes clear that we are agreed there is no single approach, but also that a consensus about the best approach has to be related to the particular problem, the time, the resources available and to other variables. There are many kinds and levels of social problems. And an unknown but limited number of these problems is amenable to the culture of poverty approach—

no matter how reasonable, proven, or powerful this approach might prove to be. For both historical and acutely topical reasons, the culture of poverty approach is relevant to that loose collection of perceived pathological symptoms I have referred to as the poverty syndrome. (I use poverty syndrome for descriptive purposes and not as a substitute for, or rival to, the culture of poverty.)

I have little or no quarrel with the culture of poverty approach as a means of understanding and explaining the behavior of some poor people, not yet too clearly defined, so long as it remains just that—an approach that is open and subject to checking and rechecking—and not a bowdlerized slogan. One problem stems from the fact that too frequently the original or scholarly statement of the approach becomes distorted and extrapolated into assertions that both damage or distort the picture of the behavior of many urban poor in the United States. And because of this the picture of social scientists and practitioners as responsible persons may be damaged. The approach also tends to divert and to prevent scientists and laymen alike from looking at the real and primary causes and consequences of being poor. It encourages the application of a specious cultural relativism to contemporary populations in the United States; and it overstresses the differences, and the significance of the differences between the poor and the non-poor in the United States. It can easily result in a kind of sloganeering and name-calling approach that covers up the real issues. In talking about the poor we are not talking about a group isolated by religion, language and custom from the United States mainstream—but a category isolated by money, education, lack of jobs, color.

Our evidence supports the assertion that "it is a complex fate and experience to be poor." The disparity between standards expressed and the actual behavior and condition of many of the poor might itself be taken as evidence that there is not a stable integrated culture of poverty. (For example, in the influential theory of opportunity structure, the main rationalizing idea for current major delinquency programs, posits differential responses to the same value base.)

David Riesman points out that in "Veblen's view, hardly any American is so poor and so benighted as to escape participation in the leisure class in his mode of life as well as in his dreams." (In connection with the admixture of poverty and discrimination—and the changing calculus of these all over, I was intrigued by the protest of the French-Canadian poet who said: "We've been Canada's white Negroes for long enough. We want our slice.")

The implicit and expressed assumptions of homogeneity in some distorted versions of Oscar Lewis' statement of the nature of the culture of poverty, for example, are not borne out by the facts. The hierarchy of limited choices and the options open to and exercised by the poor are variables of time and place. Dennis Bloodsworth of the *London Observer* in describing the urban poor of Hong Kong said:

> The very poor of Asia are not only ignorant, but have a perspective unknown to the sanitized West. Poverty is worse than sickness, they say. "The greater evil will eat the lesser." To spend a few more cents each day on health precautions and safer foods is to play into the hands of the bigger menace, penury.

The culture of poverty approach tends to obscure the point that motivations are related not only to what's inside but also to what's outside.

Mordecai Richler, in an essay in the magazine *Encounter,* wrote impressionistically in 1962:

> I think one of the difficulties—certainly the largest responsibility—in writing about the poor is to set it down so that it is truthful and doesn't deny the colour and yet is not merely an entertainment for the rich. . . .

> Well, most of the poor I ever knew, far from hating the middle-class, were bitterly determined to arrive at that station. And to play on the fantasy of workers being hornier, and more sexually able, than the middle-class is only one short cheap cut above the idea of the noble savage. . . .

I am reminded of some experiments in social psychology that came to the conclusion that there are not honest and dishonest individuals but honest and dishonest situations. Could it be that it might be more fruitful to speak of people as being in poor situations, rather than as being poor individuals and products of and carriers of a culture of poverty? The data of the Child Rearing Study in Washington, D.C. point up the similarity of wants and values, if not behavior and conditions, between the poor and the non-poor. The field materials also show the pragmatic, non-class, non-cultural cast of much of the behavior of many of the low income; and the anti-class, anti-cultural behavior of others. The data further suggest the checkerboard or straddling quality of the behavior and expectations of many poor. Some of the poor we have known have gone from slum to middle-class residential area to slum (or to public housing) in two generations.

Camille Jeffers, a member of the Child Rearing Study staff, described low income "straddlers of poverty and affluence" she observed during fifteen months of participant-observation in a public housing project. And she said in some of her afterthoughts about child rearing priorities of the mothers she got to know and observe:

> There were cupboards . . . in the kitchen and closets in every room. However, my delight at having so much storage space for my accumulations over the years was not shared by all the tenants. "What do they expect you to put in all them cupboards?" one mother asked. And as I began to see open cupboards with little food and few dishes, linen closets with no linen, and clothes closets sparsely hung with clothing, I realized that low incomes do not permit much, if any, accumulation. So, clothes closets became broom closets and were sometimes used as a place for drying clothes, a prevalent need.

. . . . . .

> Gradually, I learned that my preconceptions about, and my initial reactions to, the child rearing performances of some of the mothers were quite different from the mothers' opinions of the jobs they were doing. In terms of where they saw themselves, their self-ranking was relatively high, even though . . . they could not always meet the standards they set for themselves. . . . [They] tended to think they had made, or intended to make, an advance over the child rearing behavior of their parents.

> . . . The childhood experiences of some of these mothers . . . reared in poverty, had left a strong, often indelible sense of shame and indignation over . . . having had to live without many of the needed material and nonmaterial things of life. Their efforts to provide something different for their children, whether it was more food, more clothes, or more affection, had a much greater significance than I had first surmised. It stemmed from an insistent, even though unfocused, thrust to do more and better for their children than had been done for themselves.

> . . . I began to see how they ranked various aspects of child rearing and to understand the importance they attached to different child rearing demands and needs. And, if these mothers sometimes seemed to see their children's needs more in physical terms than psychological terms, I had only to ponder the [words] of one young mother who, in trying to reconcile herself to her family's circumstances, said *After all, you have to crawl before you can walk.*

. . . . . .

The culture of poverty approach has valid, but limited, uses in understanding and in tackling contemporary problems of dependency, delinquency, crime, and mental health. However, the fact that the approach is valid—for certain purposes—and for use on certain levels—does not mean necessarily that in its present form it is either an appropriate guide to action or the most useful single tool to place in the hands of those who have to deal directly with U.S. urban people with problems or with U.S. urban people who are problems.

Because so many of the poor want to be middle-class (whatever that is) they are unwitting partners in upholding the system or community that is most invidious with respect to them. The poor themselves—or significant segments of them—are probably themselves the best restraints on, chief victims of, and harshest critics of the minority of poor who may be really anti-culture.

It has been said that one of the chief differences between the poor and the non-poor in the United States is that the poor have fewer options. That they have fewer options is less likely to reflect their own culture of poverty than it is being shut off from the options and rewards of the larger culture—and they are shut off for a wider range of reasons than the culture of poverty can possibly comprehend.

Whether popgun or shotgun or cannon in character—a culture of poverty approach to the urban United States poor can hurt. And if it is intended to be a cannon, let's be sure it's pointed in the right direction.

RONALD W. WALTERS

Toward a Definition of Black Social Science

In the midst of the Black challenge to make the social sciences more meaningful and practical to the Black condition, there has been an attempt by some Black scholars to develop a "Black social science." Ronald Walters, a political scientist whose approach to this subject is multidisciplinary, sets forth in this essay some of the basic premises of this new perspective, a basic methodological focus and an ideological direction.

. . .

Whether or not one believes in the possibility that there is a body of knowledge about Black life which can be disciplined and made useful in the survival and development of Black people depends upon many factors. Among them are a determination that such knowledge can be disciplined and a conviction that, in such a disciplined state, the knowledge will be useful when applied to actual problems the community faces.

For years both Black and white scholars denied that the "stuff" of Black life constituted a respectable enough body of knowledge to bother about recording it for posterity. Recently, however, there has been a recognition of this gross oversight and a grudging admission that perhaps there is such a thing as Black history (after all, a people have only to have existed to have a history). This is an important admission, because it was this small bit of

Ronald W. Walters, "Toward a Definition of Black Social Science," in *The Death of White Sociology: Essays on Race and Culture*, ed. Joyce A. Ladner, 190–212 (New York: Random House, 1973; repr. Baltimore: Black Classic Press, 1998). Reprinted by permission of author.

intellectual awareness which, supported by Black students' protests, was a major factor in persuading university faculties to vote in favor of adopting Black Studies in the last few years. Once having established such programs, it was easy to see, from a perusal of some sample curricula, that the humanities were legitimate because Blacks have produced some of the most original art forms the country has had, and in some areas constitute the most dominant and dynamic forces existent today. But there is definitely no Black science as yet and no Black social science.

Another problem arises when those involved in Black education insist that the application of African history and culture is essential to Black progress. Most whites and Blacks still do not believe this! Standing in the residue of program after program to reconstruct the Black community by using white social science, these doubters know that something is wrong, but they refuse to believe that there is some efficacy in their own Black being, some Black power that, when added to other relevant factors, becomes the necessary ingredient for the solution. It is all the more confusing when solutions are not found because white social science has acquired a reputation for being oriented toward "social change" and for developing "intervention" strategies.

That the sum of white experiences (and therefore theorizing) does not add up to Black "fact" or reality can be seen in the following—I hesitate to call it an analysis—by an American sociologist.

> [The Negroes] were without ancestral pride or family tradition. They had no distinctive language or religion. These, like their folkways and moral customs, were but recently acquired from the whites and furnished no nucleus for a racial unity. The group was without even a tradition of historic unity or of racial achievement. There were no historic names, no great achievements, no body of literature, no artistic productions. The whole record of the race was one of servile or barbarian status apparently without a point about which a sentimental complex could be formed.[1]

This study, published originally in 1927 (and re-issued recently in the wake of the panic publishing on Blacks) gives the impression of some authority, as the author cites thirty-three separate pieces of "consensus" for the "facts" in the chapter from which this quote was taken. Some of the pieces of evidence he cites are from white and Black authors, and no doubt today one could take the same sources and manage a "modern" interpretation of the nature of Black life. This suggests, at least to this writer, that the business of utilizing methods in arriving at a truth which appears to be objective (for Reuter had one of the best reputations of his day for objectivity) often do little more than yield to "vogueism" in the social sciences.

Black Social Science

Those concepts which discipline, or bring order to, the study of the history and culture of Black people constitute a working definition of the term.[2] Writing at the beginning of the development of Black Social Science, one can say only what it might become. This is suggested in the area of sociology in the writings of Robert Staples, Nathan Hare, Andrew Billingsley, and Joyce Ladner; in political sociology, in the work of Gerald McWorter and James Turner; in history, in the work of Harold Cruse, Lerone Bennett, Jr., John Clarke and Vincent Harding; in political economy, in the work of Robert Browne, Earl Ofari and James Boggs; in politics, in the work of Charles Hamilton. This list is not meant to be exhaustive; it is a subjective selection of the work of Black social scientists who have had the courage to criticize wrong-headed approaches whether from whites or Blacks, and the originality to try to create a Black framework for their analyses.

One should not rejoice prematurely, however, in this meager listing. The white scholar is still winning the race to the documents and to the publishing houses and thereby is still in a position to exercise a great deal of influence over what the younger Blacks read and think. Despite the beginning effort, there is very little internal intellectual Black ferment. For example, in Black history, there is very little consensus but no significant debate over periodization or the significance of various social, political and cultural movements; in sociology, no consensus and no debate over the structure and function of the Black social system; in economics, there is only a waning argument over the efficacy of "Black capitalism." There should be a great debate over the "isms" Black people have historically been sold, in order to clarify our choices. In general, Black intellectual energy at the present time seems to be concerned with a consideration of Pan Africanism (which is absolutely necessary), and we are, still to a considerable extent, in the finishing stages of having to react to the challenge to the legitimacy of Black social science by white and Black skeptics. We are also in the midst of developing embryonic organizations and settling their ideology and operations, hoping they will be the base of activities which will consistently feed attempts of Black social scientists to relate their craft to the struggles of Black people. The lack of volume in our activity may be attributed to many causes, but it may be, as a student of mine said recently, that in this period we are like the old mule who lashed out with his heels to kick the wagon and start it rolling, and who is simply rearing back to strike again.

What comes clearest at this point is that in the works that have been produced, the ideology is profoundly different from that of white social science. Perhaps it will suffice to take a few samples from the work of the authors listed above as evidence for this assertion. In discussing Black Nationalism, James Turner states that biased sociological studies have accepted the consensus model.

> But while consensus models accept the core values of the dominant group as functional for society, some of these values may in fact be inimical to particular groups, who are thus increasingly led to question the legitimacy of the social system. Proper study of Black Nationalism employs a conflict perspective.[3]

Harold Cruse performs a valuable service, writing in the same issue of *Black World,* by pushing Black scholars toward social criticism:

> I reiterate this critical assault on black social, political, and cultural thought was premeditated [speaking of his book *Crisis of the Negro Intellectual*]. It was my conviction that black social thought of all varieties was in dire need of some ultra-radical overhauling if it was to meet the comprehensive test imposed by the sixties. Now that the sixties are history, I am still convinced—even more so—that black social thought is in need of ultra-radical overhauling. In fact, the arrival of the seventies revealed to me that I had underestimated the critical reassessing black social thought really needed.[4]

And he goes on to imply that our political theory needs to be seriously grounded in local conditions and perspectives, using the experiences of political events in other countries selectively. In his subsequent article (Part II) in *Black World,*[5] he chides the Black scholar for not having dealt critically with the revered Black historians of the past, and he is, oh so right.

John Henrik Clarke has a partial answer to what the role of the contemporary Black scholar in the struggle for Black liberation should be when he says that he must be a "scholar-activist" and adds (speaking of the formation of the African Heritage Studies Association)

> We interpret African History from a Pan-Africanist perspective that defines all black people as African People. . . . Our program has as its objec-

tive the restoration of the cultural, economic, and political life of African people everywhere.[6]

In the realm of sociology, Andrew Billingsley points to the fact that "white social science" excludes consideration of the complexity and strength of the Black family as factors of prime importance.[7]

The ideas of Earl Ofari and James Boggs in political economy make a powerful argument as they analyze the reasons for the failure of Black economic life. In looking at the failure of Black business, Earl Ofari finds:

> Examples abound throughout the voluminous reports and studies the mythmakers of black business have conducted. The blame for black business failure for a long time was laid on black people themselves. The main argument [citing E. Franklin Frazier's study, *The Negro in the United States*, p. 410] can be easily summarized: black proprietors are inefficient, lazy, lack education, have little business experience, are slow and discourteous. Black businesses fail because the very economic system in which they are trying to succeed is stacked against them.[8]

If this is true, then Boggs seems to point up the solution:

> Any program for the development of the black community must be based on large-scale social ownership rather than on private individual enterprise. In this period of large-scale production and distribution, private individual enterprise [or small business] can only remain marginal and dependent, adding to the sense of hopelessness and powerlessness inside the black community.[9]

Central to this particular problem seems to be the discussion of whether or not racism in America is endemic to capitalism. This point was settled long ago by one of our most brilliant and neglected Black scholars, Oliver Cox, who listed racism as one of the features of capitalism.[10] But the debate over the form and substance of the system that will guarantee equality to Blacks proceeds from the perceived need to have radical change in the distribution of wealth. Thus far the center of this debate has been over the value of "Black capitalism," but as it begins to appear in social science literature there is a recognition of the need for new concepts as S. E. Anderson says:

> Paradoxically, black business education and most of the relatively few black economists have made the tragic mistake of embracing unequivocally

the principles and practices of American Capitalism; the same system that white people manipulate and scheme to deny black people significant participation.[11]

He continues, in a fashion not dissimilar to Boggs, that if Black people are to be liberated under capitalism they must have the power to effect and control significant changes in their current status. The answers to Black economic development have not been found within the concepts of white social science because it assumes the ideology of the capitalist system.

This discussion has been based on the knowledge that there are questions inherent in the Black experience which have been approached incorrectly by the utilization of both the ideology and the methodology of white social science. But Black truth does not necessarily proceed in dialectical fashion because of the intimate juxtaposition of Black people to whites in the history and culture of America.

The black scholar must develop new and appropriate norms and values, new institutional structures, and in order to be effective in this regard, he must also develop and be guided by a new ideology. Out of this new ideology will evolve new methodology. Though in some regards it will subsume and overlap existing norms of scholarly endeavor.[12]

Black life has been distinctive and separate enough to constitute its own uniqueness, and it is on the basis of that uniqueness that the ideology and the methodology of Black social science rests.

Ideology

In the works cited above it is possible to identify certain elements which contribute to an ideology for Black social science; they refer to radicalism and conflict theory as well as an infusion of the substances of Blackness—Africanism, nationalism, history, cultural style, self-determination and consciousness of racism. Elsewhere I have dealt with the problem of using Basil Matthews' term the "Unity and Order of Blackness."[13] I believe this term (which he is in the process of applying to research as the "Black knowledge process") to be comprehensive enough to include all aspects of a Black social-science ideology. Also, concepts of "unity" and "order" may be regarded as tools which, when applied to the data, help to discipline it. Here, it is useful to turn to the seminal works of Gerald McWorter[14] and Preston Wilcox.

Like McWorter, Preston Wilcox performs a transforming function on terms which, to him, are examples of the "rhetoric of oppression," by his use of a Black educational ideology and a taxonomy resulting from the comparison of scientific colonialism and scientific humanism.[15]

Urban Renewal	really means	Negro Removal
Model Cities	''	Model Colonies
Human Relations	''	Colonial Relations
Culturally Deprived	''	Illegally Deprived
Public Welfare	''	Public Starvation
Code Enforcement	''	Tenant Exploitation
School Decentralization	''	School Recentralization

In each case the writer has "translated" from the white into the Black terminology, using his sense of Black consciousness as the cutting edge to redefine reality so that the Black terms which result are congruent with the objective Black situation.

Terms alone, however, do not make an ideology. If, therefore, we can distill the essential experience which these terms collectively represent, we come to the following figure:

A

Urban-Technological

(Institutionalized white racism)

B

Classic-Colonialism

(Economic, political and cultural exploitation)

X

Black Oppression

(Individualized, group)

Without going into the details of either A-to-X or B-to-X relationship (which would be beyond the scope of this paper and volumes in themselves), perhaps a comment on each would suffice to relate to the subject at hand what the reader must most assuredly know to be some of the facts.

Variable A.   Many of the analyses, particularly in the historical, cultural and political realm, do not yet take into account the pervasiveness of technology as a weapon against us and an impediment to the full expression of our Blackness, or even of the ways in which technology can be utilized to enhance those elements of our culture we would like to emphasize, and how we can control such technology as might make this possible. The functioning of such technology in an urban environment has, we know, increased the effectiveness of institutionalized racism by expelling more Black people from institutions which would theoretically make them productive, and by using such institutions to objectively control our lives—one has only to mention the press, among other institutions, in this regard. The distorted picture of Black life presented in the national media will be changed only if Black people participate in the media in significant ways, and until that happens, the media will continue to contribute to the oppression of Black communities. Increasing levels of unemployment and the disparity between white and Black incomes and economic opportunities make the relationship of oppression starkly evident.

Variable B. The explosive work *Black Power* contains within it the colonial paradigm[16] that explains the connection between the white and Black communities with respect to power relationships and, thus, to all the attendant relationships which logically follow. Sociologist Robert Blauner applies this model to an analysis of the Black community in Los Angeles as a rationale for the rebellion of 1965.[17] The use of this model is no accident; the objective conditions of power prevailing between the groups, plus the fact of an easily identifiable Black group as the target, together with the geographical unity of most Black communities, give every evidence of the colonial characteristic. That such relationships deal in exploitation is a necessary corollary to the existence of the colonial condition, as is the fact that such exploitation is traditionally interpreted by the exploited as base oppression.

Both variables A and B interact with each other in the American context to produce circumstances of unique and unequaled social quality. Together they constitute a powerful source of Black oppression, that is, the consistent reality to which the Black scientist must address himself. Beyond the massive studies which document it and the models which explain it, the Black scientist, through the application of his skill to ideology and the willingness to act out the implications of his findings, must deal with his own oppression and the oppression of his people.

Methodological Focus

Liberation-oriented social science must have an explicit focus. Billingsley's suggestion that the existing disciplines need to be revitalized could begin with the construction of Black social science. For example, there is nothing new about the field of political sociology as one can readily see by reference to the studies compiled by McWorter,[18] but in the dichotomy between it and mere sociology is the realization that it is often necessary to include an operative ideology and, at the least, the recognition that it may be impossible to draw a hard, fast boundary between the fields. Perhaps a sociology rooted in Black social science would on balance emphasize the "end-use" as well as an analysis of the structure and function of Black social institutions. The result is that political sociology would be emphasized more than implicitly neutral sociology.

The same argument could, of course, be made for economics. Black social scientists should not only be concerned with the analysis of the economic system or the state of Black economy, but should seek to develop and utilize theories that lead to the production of economic resources. In this case, we could take a page from Chapter Seven of *Dusk of Dawn* by W. E. B. DuBois, where, as he often did, he made an analysis of the state of Black society, concluded that capitalism was antithetical to Black accumulation of wealth, and put forth a plan of action to radically change the situation. Both in the discipline of sociology and in economics, the focus should be the acquisition of influence (or control or power) over choices in each sector of society, and to that extent we should recognize the inherent political activity involved in the development and espousal of such concepts and their employment in real situations. Certainly, in the other disciplines of social science, the same suggestion could be made about focus, which does not in each case involve the use of the term political, but which recognizes what is involved in emphasizing the "end-use" dimension of the discipline.

Technique

Many of the existing methodologies are valid for the analysis of Black life, but I would argue that the Black researcher's "field experience" in being Black gives him a better potential understanding of the techniques of analysis which are relevant in a given situation. In a way, such a position mirrors the older conflict between the traditionalist researcher who has the knowledge of substance, be it geographical or historical, and the technician who is skilled in the technique of his particular discipline at the expense of substance. My position is that a proper marriage, that is, a balance between substance and technique, is preferable, and that the deficiencies in white social science are revealed when, in dealing with Black life, the analyst comes prepared only with methodology. Studies that are produced in this way are in serious need of reinterpretation by Black scholars with a liberation orientation.

The question of achieving a proper balance, though important, can usually be assessed only after the results of the research are in, and therefore caution at the outset is a greater requirement. Nevertheless, it is possible to suggest that either extreme, using the traditional interpretation or overly quantitative approaches, is unsatisfactory for most questions that deal with any human life. And since the current quantitative fad is in full swing in academic life, perhaps a word should be said about it here.

The assumption upon which quantification is based is that there are units of analysis that stand for a given amount of social value, which, when manipulated mathematically, reveal aspects of social reality, either actual or theoretical. The wish of the user is to come as close to the real situation as possible and even perhaps be able to anticipate and plan for human responses to given situations or events. It strikes this writer as highly plausible that one of the fruits of a highly technological society, such as this one, is the notion of "precise value"—that is, there are many things produced and developed in a manner that makes them amenable to the quantitative approach; this is true from material goods to social services. Indeed, many problems in the field of administrating social services revolve around the necessity to monitor value precisely in quantitative terms, not necessarily for the sake of the user, but for the sake of the decision-maker who allocates resources. The writer is not at all sure, in fact is skeptical that either African or Afro-American culture is thus amenable to the quantitative approach. This is the subject of another discourse, but the problem suggests itself here: To what extent is the exercise of "Blackness" compatible with the vagaries of a Western technological situation? We should be aware that the material aspects of such a civilization have a powerful influence on the way in which we are able to perceive and to express our culture. One of the wonders of Black culture is the way in which it has survived and still flourishes, buffeted by strong historical events both quantitative and qualitative. But the question of compatibility is important on another level, because of the increased desire for analysts to learn and utilize the tools of systems analysis in the disposition of Black problems. The cost-benefit type of analysis has been adapted to "software" output only with questionable results.[19] If there are problems at that level of analysis, the utilization of such techniques on Black problems is even less effective. One has to cope with the effectiveness of the instrument itself, as well as with the fact that even now some of the most elementary facts about Black people, such as an accurate population count, are still in a questionable state, and such data are the life of the quantitative approach.

This leads me to challenge the assumptions upon which some developing graduate programs in Black Studies are founded. One basic assumption is that one should get a degree in an established discipline, while the subject of research for the dissertation may be in the area of Black life. Graduate students need substantive as well as methodological training if such work is to be accurate as well as profitable. *Treating the substance of Black life as something secondhand, which can be "picked-up" at will, or as something "we already know" which does not need systematic and constant elucidation, clarification and development is an insult to the quality and complexity of the Black experience and perpetuates the graduate schools' racist attitude toward the value of the study of Black life in general.*

The caution urged here is in the use of extremes of theory and methodology, and in substantive areas. What the Black social scientist should seek is the balance between efficiency and humanism that puts technique in its proper role as servant rather than lord.

Now that we have explored, and I must say at its fringes, the concept of Black social science, it is necessary to point to the possible "end-use" of the discipline in suggesting the need for a Black research strategy.

Black Research Strategy

Chester Pierce, a Black psychiatrist at Harvard University, in a recent article entitled "Offensive Mechanisms" discusses what it means for Black people to think strategically and for the development of what he calls "street therapists" to know and teach "offensive and defensive tactics" to Black people for their own survival.

> In order for black individuals to both analyze and project propaganda (that is, understanding what is in one's own best interest, which would, of course, include domestic tranquility and good international relations), the applied knowledge of how to defense offensive maneuvers is obligatory.[20]

This knowledge also applies to the Black social scientist, who should also be a "street therapist." He must develop an offensive strategy around the collection, analysis, packaging, dissemination and use of knowledge about Black people in order to properly defend himself against the lead that white social science has established in all of these areas.

The Challenge to White Social Science

One of the clearest duties of the Black social scientist is to vigorously challenge the very foundation of white social science and its effects upon the Black community. In this regard, Nathan Hare says,

> The black scholar must look beneath the surface of things and, wherever necessary and appropriate, take a stand against the bias of white scholarship. He must be biased against white bias, must be an iconoclast, rallying to the call to arms of all the black intelligentsia, to destroy obsolete norms and values and create new ones to take their place.[21]

The best mechanism I have yet seen for providing Black people with a defense against the encroachments of white social science is a new Black institution which has been recently established in Boston called the Community Research Review Committee. The Committee is composed of a primary group of Black social scientists who are accountable to the community through the Black United Front. Its function is to detect the kind of research planned and in progress that relates to the Black community, to screen actual research proposals and otherwise to evaluate the project and, finally, to provide the results to the community, which decides whether or not it would be advisable for the study to be carried out there. If the community decides the study is needed—cool. But if it decides that it is either unnecessary or harmful, then, in the age-old manner, it takes care of business. The Black social scientist must participate in a process which says, in effect, we will no longer participate by passiveness in the destruction and dehumanization of our communities through white social science research. But in order to participate, we need to pay much closer attention to the kind of research that is funded, who does the funding, who carries out the research, what the findings are, who is responsible for dissemination of the findings, and how they are used, and be willing to intervene at any stage of the process. This is one type of viable defensive strategy which also has offensive connotations.

The Challenge to Ourselves

One obvious bit of offense is to begin to build the institutions that will redress the imbalance in expertise, and to support those already in existence, such as the Black World Foundation, the Institute of the Black World, or the many research institutes developing on college campuses across the nation so that we can do the work ourselves. The obvious retort is that this takes money, and so it does; it has been interesting to note that, despite the generally widespread interest in Black Studies, massive funding is nowhere yet in sight. Contrast this picture with the funds which became available to universities and independent agencies to do research on Africa in the early 1960's (one such center with which I am familiar at one point had close to $600,000), or to the figures in the press recently which show the magnitude of financial support for Chinese studies.[22] Many would say that funding was available because both of these areas had strategic or security implications of international significance. But it is equally true that the managers of these funds in Chinese and African studies, down through the bureaucracy into the universities, are essentially white (even in African studies!!), while the socio-academic system for Black studies is largely Black, at least at the working level.

This problem of support has been raised before, both publicly and privately, and one astonishing reply from conservative Blacks and whites has been that Black Studies must demonstrate their validity a priori—that is, in advance of the necessary support. This position is a new kind of Tomism and an old brand of racism; Blacks have always had to overprove themselves to get what whites have had only to ask for. How could anything of value be demonstrated in Black Studies or any other kind of studies without adequate support? Could it be because the payoffs we seek for Black social science are in the Black community? In any case, we must support our activities and institutions from our own meager funds, through forced savings if necessary. Perhaps the realization that we must do this is the price we must pay for our own self-determination. I cannot escape the notion that if the words "freedom" or "independence," both here and in the homeland, mean anything, it all finally comes down to the necessity to be self-reliant, in the words of the document, "Education for Self-Reliance," developed by the Tanzanian government.

Research Priorities

The colonization of African history and culture is international in scope; it may not surprise you to learn that at the international Conference of African Historians in 1968, only four of the eighteen papers presented were by Africans, and that there was one paper presented by a non-African on the periodization of African History. Black social scientists cannot afford to spend a lifetime organizing while other people are deciding upon the very nature, the ebb and flow of our historic experience. In this section I would like to give some support to the increasing problem-solving orientation of Black social scientists by examining the rationale of some of the classic studies on Black life.

Martin Kilson, professor of government at Harvard University, said on one occasion that we who are now engaged in an analysis of Black life "stand on the shoulders of our ancestors" in this endeavor. But it may also be true that the theoretical questions with which they dealt are different in this day and age. The central question which seems to have guided, for example, *The Philadelphia Negro, Black Metropolis* and *An American Dilemma* was "What is the nature of Black life?" The Black man had been defined as a problem in American society, and since all of our investigators were trained in the Western tradition of scholarship, one had to pretend to be interested only in the nature of the problem. At the point one had discovered (researched) the nature of the problem to one's satisfaction, ethical neutrality took over, and the solutions or value questions (which were unobjective and which could not, therefore, be defended in the province of scholarship) were left to politicians and administrators.

W. E. B. DuBois says that the impetus for the study *The Philadelphia Negro* was the need for the white decision-makers of the city to have some data on the significant and largely corrupt Seventh Ward in order to plan a campaign of reforms.[23] So that it was in the nature of his study to emphasize the "nature of the problem"—Black people. DuBois himself says of this methodology:

> The best available methods of sociological research are at present so liable to inaccuracies that the careful student discloses the results of individual research with diffidence; he knows that they are liable to error from the seemingly ineradicable faults of the statistical method; to even greater error from the methods of general observation; and, *above all,* he must ever tremble lest some personal bias, some moral conviction or some unconscious trend of thought due to previous training, has to a degree distorted the picture of his view.[24] [Emphasis mine]

In other words, DuBois himself confirms what a reviewer said of the study at the time: "In no respect does DuBois attempt to bend the facts so as to plead for his race."[25] DuBois performed his role well, and his objectivity was admirable, but an action program for dealing with the ills of the Seventh Ward would have not detracted from the value of his work. He could not do so, however, because of the political problem of the end-use of his product.

Another classic socioanthropological study, *Black Metropolis,* by St. Clair Drake and Horace Cayton started out to be an inquiry into the general social conditions which produced juvenile delinquency on Chicago's South Side, and was eventually enlarged to take into account the entire Black Community. Richard Wright and E. C. Hughes say in the Introduction:

> The authors have not submitted a total program of action in this book; rather they have assumed the ultimate aspirations of the Negro, just as Negroes have always assumed them, and just as Whites assume theirs. Negroes feel that they are politically and culturally Americans. The job of the authors was not to quiet and soothe, but to *aid white people* in knowing the facts of urban Negro life.[26] [Emphasis mine]

In a way, Wright and Hughes are saying that this study, too, was not produced as a blueprint for Black survival, but as something which would provide an accurate picture of Black life of most benefit to the decision-makers in their management of resources in behalf of the Black community.

Finally, the massive study by Gunnar Myrdal, *An American Dilemma*, made with the assistance of numerous Black scholars and the funds of the Carnegie Foundation, is another example of the trend we are viewing here. The main objective of the Foundation, to gather data on the Black condition, is clear from its own description of the usual nature of such studies, "the primary purpose of studies of this character is the collection, analysis and interpretation of existing knowledge."[27] In fact, Myrdal himself at one point almost yielded to a temptation to engage in serious prognosis, as he reports after touring the United States preliminary to undertaking the study:

> When I returned to New York I told Mr. [Frederick P.] Keppel of my deep worries. I should confess that I even suggested a retreat to him; that we should give up the purely scientific approach and instead deal with the problem as one of political compromise and expediency.[28]

However, from the author's Preface to the first edition it is clear that he held fast to tradition, making a "comprehensive study of the Negro in the United States, to be undertaken in a wholly objective and dispassionate way as a social phenomenon."[29]

We are, therefore, in a position to observe from the record above that the generation of hypotheses relating to the analysis of Black life which produced these well-known studies was remarkably similar, dealing with the "nature of the problem" which Black people presented to whites. To say this is not to demean the quality of these studies or the necessity for scholars to search for the objective truth at every opportunity, for, as Wright and Hughes said, no program of action could afford to ignore the validity of the work if it was to be viable. *But we need to recognize the difference in the purpose and context of those earlier studies and the needs of the Black community now for a new generation of hypotheses.* Reducing the theoretical question of this generation to the Unity and the Order of Blackness, I would have to ask, How does Black social science contribute to the survival and development of Black people in the United States and in the Diaspora? And more specifically, now that in a few areas we are beginning to accumulate important knowledge, how do we begin to use what we know to create areas of security and well-being which we can eventually establish as a comprehensive fact (nationhood)?

There are no canons that will answer these questions, but, in general, it is a beginning to know that the search for Black Power has started a number of Black scientists groping for the right methods to help institutionalize that ethic. Doubtless, further questions will be developed in each discipline, and especially between disciplines in interaction between the scientist and his community. In general, however, each social scientist must recognize the need to bend his efforts toward the creation of some form of community power, by whatever definition, and toward ensuring that whatever power is created becomes systematized. These two basic considerations underline the difficulty of using Black social science in a world where white social science dominates. This was the burden carried by DuBois, who started his life believing that a scientific approach to the analysis of racism would help to alleviate its poison— as, indeed, it eventually has. But just as important was his realization that he could go only so far with the tools of social science, that at some point he had to act out the moral and ethical implications of what his keen senses told him to be true. This lesson for the Black social scientist is fundamental; his tools are conservative tools, and he cannot use them to define the whole truth, for there is always that something extra that DuBois sensed, which, when added to analysis, reveals the whole Black truth.

NOTES

1. Edward B. Reuter, *The American Race Problem* (New York: Thomas Y. Crowell, 1970), p. 365.

2. It has been a traditional practice to define items not only by genus but also by function and application as the term "Black" fixed to the phenomenon "social science" implies. To wit, one would catch hell if he used a left-handed monkey wrench to turn a right-handed bolt, which would suggest the necessity to obtain the right tool in the first place!

3. "Black Nationalism, the Inevitable Response," *Black World* (January 1971), p. 9.

4. "Black and White: Outlines of the Next Stage," *Black World* (January 1971), p. 9.

5. "Black and White: Outlines of the Next Stage," Part II, *Black World* (March 1971), pp. 9–14.

6. "The Meaning of Black History," *Black World* (February 1971).

7. See Andrew Billingsley, "Black Families and White Social Science," this volume [*The Death of White Sociology,* ed. Joyce A. Ladner (New York: Random House, 1973)].

8. Earl Ofari, *The Myth of Black Capitalism* (New York: Monthly Review Press, 1970), p. 77.

9. James Boggs, *Racism and the Class Struggle* (New York: Monthly Review Press, 1970), p. 141.

10. Oliver Cox, *Capitalism as a System* (New York: Monthly Review Press, 1964), pp. 32, 65–66.

11. *The Black Scholar,* Vol. 2, No. 2 (October 1970), p. 11.

12. See Nathan Hare, "The Challenge of a Black Scholar," this volume [*Death of White Sociology,* Ladner].

13. Ronald W. Walters, "The Discipline of Black Studies," *The Negro Educational Review,* Vol. 21, No. 4 (October 1970), pp. 138–144.

14. See Abd-l Hakimu Alkalimat, "The Ideology of Black Social Science," this volume [*Death of White Sociology,* Ladner].

15. *Negro Digest,* Part III (March 1970), p. 83.

16. Stokely Carmichael and Charles Hamilton, *Black Power: The Politics of Liberation in America,* Chapter 1, "White Power: The Colonial Situation" (New York: Random House, 1967).

17. Robert Blauner, "Internal Colonialism and Ghetto Revolt," *Social Problems,* Vol. 16, No. 4 (Spring 1969).

18. Gerald A. McWorter, "The Political Sociology of the Negro" (New York: Anti-Defamation League of B'nai B'rith, August 1967), p. 31. Pamphlet.

19. President Johnson directed the Bureau of the Budget to install PPBS analysis throughout the government in 1966. In 1968 this writer was conducting interviews in the Department of State pursuant to a doctoral dissertation, and he discovered that many bureaus had written negative appraisals of the extent to which the new system had been successful. Some had, in fact, recommended that it not be further used, which points up the vulnerability of this method of analysis when used on products such as foreign policy which are difficult to quantify. See also "The Politics of the Budgetary Process," James Oliver, Ph.D. dissertation, American University, 1970, unpublished, for some of the difficulties involved.

20. In *The Black Seventies,* edited by Floyd Barbour (Boston: Porter Sargent, 1970), p. 281.

21. Hare, *op. cit.,* p. 61.

22. In discussing the funding of China scholarship since 1959, James Reston, editor for *The New York Times,* says, "Since then, the Ford Foundation has contributed about $22 million to the China language and area studies, other foundations have added a little over $2 million, and the Government has put up about $15 million under the National Defense Education Act. Meanwhile, the Universities of the nation have contributed another $20 million to this effort over the same period of time." *The New York Times,* Wednesday, May 12, 1971, p. 39m.

23. W. E. B. DuBois, *Dusk of Dawn* (New York: Schocken, 1968), p. 59.

24. *Ibid.*

25. *Outlook,* Vol. 63, 1899, pp. 647–8.

26. St. Clair Drake and Horace Clayton, *Black Metropolis* (New York: Harcourt, Brace and World, 1970), p. xxx.

27. Gunnar Myrdal, *An American Dilemma* (New York: Harper and Row, 1969), Vol. 1, p. xlvii.

28. *Ibid.,* p. xxv.

29. *Ibid.,* p. li.

JOYCE A. LADNER

Tomorrow's Tomorrow: The Black Woman

What problems face the sociologist who attempts to transcend the "liberal bourgeois" perspective in his analysis and substitute for it one that emerges from and is shaped by the Black experience? In this chapter, taken from the introduction to . . . *Tomorrow's Tomorrow: The Black Woman,* some basic assumptions regarding the necessity for reconceptualizing this topic are set forth.

· · ·

It is very difficult to determine whether this work had its beginnings when I was growing up in rural Mississippi and experiencing all the tensions, conflicts, joys, sorrows, warmth, compassion and cruelty that was associated with *becoming a Black woman;* or whether it originated with my graduate school career when I became engaged in research for a doctoral dissertation. I *am* sure that the twenty years I spent being socialized by my family and the broader Black community prior to entering graduate school shaped my perception of life, defined my emotive responses to the world and enhanced my ability to survive in a society that has not made survival for Blacks easy. Therefore, when I decided to engage in research on what approaching womanhood meant to poor Black girls in the city, I brought with me these attitudes, values, beliefs and in effect, a Black perspective. Because of this cultural

Joyce A. Ladner, "Tomorrow's Tomorrow: The Black Woman," in *The Death of White Sociology: Essays on Race and Culture,* ed. Joyce A. Ladner, 414–428 (New York: Random House, 1973; repr. Baltimore: Black Classic Press, 1998). Reprinted by permission of author.

sensitivity I had to the life-styles of the over one hundred adolescent, pre-adolescent and adult females I "studied," I had to mediate tensions that existed from day to day between the *reality* and *validity* of their lives *and* the tendency to view it from the *deviant perspective* in accordance with my academic training.

Deviance is the invention of a group that uses its own standards as the *ideal* by which others are to be judged. Howard Becker states that

> Social groups create deviance by making the rules whose infraction constitutes deviance, and by applying those rules to particular people and labeling them as outsiders. From this point of view, deviance is *not* a quality of the act the person commits, but rather a consequence of the application by others of rules and sanctions to an "offender." The deviant is one to whom that label has successfully been applied; deviant behavior is behavior that people so label.[1]

Other students of social problems have adhered to the same position.[2] Placing Black people in the context of the deviant perspective has been possible because Blacks have not had the necessary power to resist the labels. This power could have come only from the ability to provide the *definitions* of one's past, present and future. Since Blacks have always, until recently, been defined by the majority group, that group's characterization was the one that was predominant.

The preoccupation with *deviancy,* as opposed to *normalcy,* encourages the researcher to limit his scope and ignore some of the most vital elements of the lives of the people he is studying. It has been noted by one sociologist that:

> It is probably a fact and one of which some contemporary students of deviance have been cognizant—that the greater portion of the lives of deviant persons or groups is spent in normal, mundane, day-to-day living. In the researcher's focus on deviance and this acquisition of the deviant perspective, not only is he likely to overlook these more conventional phenomena, and thus become insensitive to them, but he may in the process overlook that very data which helps to explain that deviance he studies.[3]

Having been equipped with the *deviant perspective* in my academic training, yet lacking strong commitment to it because it conflicted with my objective knowledge and responses to the Black women I was studying, I went into the field equipped with a set of preconceived ideas and labels that I intended to apply to these women. This, of course, meant that I had gone there only to validate and elaborate on what was *alleged to exist*. If I had continued within this context, I would have concluded the same thing that most social scientists who study Black people conclude: that they are pathology-ridden.

However, this role was difficult, if not impossible, for me to play because all of my life experiences invalidated the deviant perspective. As I became more involved with the subjects of this research, I knew that I would not be able to play the role of the dispassionate scientist, whose major objective was to extract certain data from them that would simply be used to *describe* and *theorize* about their conditions. I began to perceive my role as a Black person, with empathy and attachment, and, to a great extent, their day-to-day lives and future destinies became intricately interwoven with my own. This did not occur without a considerable amount of agonizing self-evaluation and conflict over "whose side I was on." On the one hand, I wanted to conduct a study that would allow me to fulfill certain academic requirements, i.e., a doctoral dissertation. On the other hand, I was highly influenced by my *Blackness*— by the fact that I, on many levels, was one of them and had to deal with their problems on a personal level. I was largely unable to resolve these strands, this "double consciousness," to which W. E. B. DuBois refers.[4] It is important to understand that Blacks are at a juncture in history that has been unprecedented for its necessity to grope with and clarify and *define* the status of our existence in American society. Thus, I was unable to resolve the dilemmas I faced as a Black social scientist because they only symbolized the larger questions, issues and dilemmas of our times.

Many books have been written about the Black community[5] but very few have really dealt with the intricate lives of the people who live there. By and large, they have attempted to analyze and describe the pathology which allegedly characterizes the lives of its inhabitants while at the same time making its residents responsible for its creation. The unhealthy conditions of the community such as drug addiction, poverty, crime, dilapidated housing, unemployment and the multitude of problems which characterize it have caused social analysts to see these conditions as producing millions of "sick" people, many of whom are given few chances ever to overcome the wretchedness which clouds their existence. Few authorities on the Black community have written about the vast amount of strength and adaptability of the people. They have ignored the fact that this community is a force which not only acts upon its residents but which is also acted upon. Black people are involved in a dynamic relationship with their physical and cultural environment in that they both influence and are influenced by it. This reciprocal relationship allows them to exercise a considerable amount of power over their environs. This also means that they are able to exercise control over their futures, whereas writers have tended to view the low-income Black community as an all-pervasive force which is so devastating as to compel its powerless residents to succumb to its pressures. Their power to cope and adapt to a set of unhealthy conditions—not as stereotyped sick people but as normal ones—is a factor which few people seem to accept or even realize. The ways Blacks have adapted to poverty and racism, and yet emerged relatively unscarred, are a peculiar quality which Americans should commend.

The concept of social deviance is quite frequently applied to the values and behavior of Blacks because they represent a departure from the traditional white middle-class norm, along with criminals, homosexuals and prostitutes.

But these middle-class standards should not have been imposed because of the distinctiveness that characterizes the Black life-style, particularly that of the masses.

Most scholars have taken a dim view of any set of distinct life-styles shared by Blacks, and where they were acknowledged to exist, have of course maintained that these forces were negative adaptations to the larger society. There has never been an admission that the Black community is a product of American social policy, *not* the cause of it—the structure of the American social system, through its practices of institutional racism, is designed to create the alleged "pathology" of the community, to perpetuate the "social disorganization" model of Black life. Recently, the Black culture thesis has been granted some legitimization as an explanatory variable for much of the distinctiveness of Black life. As a result of this more positive attitude toward understanding the strengths of life in the Black community, many scholars, policy makers et al. are refocusing their attention and reinterpreting the many aspects of life that comprise the complex existence of American Blacks.

There must be a strong concern with redefining the problem. Instead of future studies being conducted on *problems* of the Black community as represented by the *deviant perspective,* there must be a redefinition of the *problem as being that of institutional racism.* If the social system is viewed as the *source* of the deviant perspective, then future research must begin to analyze the nature of oppression and the mechanisms by which institutionalized forms of subjugation are initiated and act to maintain the system intact. Thus, studies which have as their focal point the alleged deviant *attitudes* and *behavior* of Blacks are grounded within the racist assumptions and principles that only render Blacks open to further exploitation.

The challenge to social scientists for a redefinition of the basic *problem* has been raised in terms of the "colonial analogy." It has been argued that the relationship between the *researcher* and his *subjects,* by definition, resembles that of the oppressor and the oppressed, because it is the oppressor who defines the problem, the nature of the research and, to some extent, the quality of interaction between him and his subjects. This inability to understand and research the fundamental problem—*neo-colonialism*—prevents most social researchers from being able accurately to observe and analyze Black life and culture and the impact racism and oppression have upon Blacks. Their inability to understand the nature and effects of neo-colonialism in the same manner as Black people is rooted in the inherent bias of the social sciences. The basic concepts and tools of white Western society are permeated by this partiality to the conceptual framework of the oppressor. It is simple enough to say that the difference between the two groups—the oppressor and the oppressed—prevents the former from adequately comprehending the essence of Black life and culture because of a fundamental difference in perceptions, based upon separate histories, life-styles and purposes for being. Simply put, the slave and his master do not view and respond to the world in the same way. The historian Lerone Bennett addresses this problem below:

> George Washington and George Washington's slaves lived different realities. And if we extend that insight to all the dimensions of white American history we will realize that blacks lived at a different time and a different reality in this country. And the terrifying implications of all this is that there is another time, another reality, another America. . . .

Bennett states further that:

> It is necessary for us to develop a new frame of reference which transcends the limits of white concepts. It is necessary for us to develop a total intellectual offensive against the false universality of white concepts whether they are expressed by William Styron or Daniel Patrick Moynihan. By and large, reality has been conceptualized in terms of the narrow point of view of the small minority of white men who live in Europe and North America. We must abandon the partial frame of reference of our oppressors and create new concepts which will release our reality, which is also the reality of the overwhelming majority of men and women on this globe. We must say to the white world that there are things in the world that are not dreamt of in your history and your sociology and your philosophy.[6]

Currently there are efforts underway to "de-colonize" social research on the *conceptual* and *methodological* levels.[7]

Although I attempted to maintain some degree of objectivity, I soon began to minimize and, very often, negate the importance of being "value-free," because the very selection of the topic itself reflected a bias, i.e., I studied Black women because of my strong interest in the subject.

I decided whose side I was on and resolved within myself that as a Black social scientist I must take a stand and that there could be no value-free sanctuary for me. The controversy over the question of values in social research is addressed by Gouldner:

> If sociologists ought not express their personal values in the academic setting, how then are students to be safeguarded against the unwitting influence of these values which shape the sociologist's selection of problems, his preferences for certain hypotheses or conceptual schemes, and his neglect of others? For these are unavoidable and, in this sense, there is and can be no value-free sociology. The only choice is between an expression of one's values as open and honest as it can be, this side of the psychoanalytic couch, and a vain ritual of moral neutrality which, because it invites men to ignore the vulnerability of reason to bias, leaves it at the mercy of irrationality.[8]

I accepted this position as a guiding premise and proceeded to conduct my research with the full knowledge that I could not divorce myself from the problems of these women, nor should I become so engrossed in them that I would lose my original purpose for being in the community.

The words of Kenneth Clark, as he describes the tensions and conflicts he experienced while conducting the research for his classic study of Harlem, *Dark Ghetto*, typify the problems I faced:

> I could never be fully detached as a scholar or participant. More than forty years of my life had been lived in Harlem. I started school in Harlem public schools. I first learned about people, about love, about cruelty, about sacrifice, about cowardice, about courage, about bombast in Harlem. For many years before I returned as an "involved observer," Harlem had been my home. My family moved from house to house, and from neighborhood to neighborhood within the walls of the ghetto in a desperate attempt to escape its creeping blight. In a very real sense, therefore, *Dark Ghetto* is a summation of my personal and lifelong experiences and observations as a prisoner within the ghetto long before I was aware that I was really a prisoner.[9]

The inability to be *objective* about analyzing poverty, racism, disease, self-destruction and the gamut of problems which faced these females only mirrored a broader problem in social research. That is, to what extent should any scientist—white or Black—consider it his duty to be a dispassionate observer and not intervene, when possible, to ameliorate many of the destructive conditions he studies. On many occasions I found myself acting as a counselor, big sister, etc. Certainly the question can be raised as to whether researchers can continue to gather data on impoverished Black communities without addressing these findings to the area of social policy.

This raises another important question, to which I will address myself. That is, many people will read this book because they are seeking answers to the dilemmas and problems facing Black people in general and Black women in particular. A great number of young Black women will expect to find forever-sought formulas to give them a new sense of direction as *Black women.* Some Black men will read this work because they are concerned about this new direction and want to become involved in the shaping of this process. Others, of course, will simply be curious to find out what a Black woman has to say about her peers. I expect traditional-type scholars to take great issue with my thesis and many of my formulations because I am consciously attempting to break away from the traditional way in which social science research has analyzed the attitudes and behavior patterns of Blacks. Finally, a small but growing group of scholars will find it refreshing to read a work on Black women which does not indict them for all kinds of alleged social problems, which, if they exist, they did not create.

All of these are problems and questions which I view as inescapable for one who decides to attempt to break that new ground and write about areas of human life in ways in which they are not ordinarily approached.

There are no standard answers for these dilemmas I faced, for they are simply microcosms of the larger Black community. Therefore, this work is not attempting to resolve the problems of Black womanhood but to shed light on them. More than anything else, I feel that it is attempting to depict what the Black woman's life has been like in the past, and what barriers she has had to overcome in order to survive, and how she is coping today under the most strenuous circumstances. Thus, I am simply saying, "This is what the Black woman was, this is how she has been solving her problems, and these are ways in which she is seeking to alter her roles." I am not trying to chart a course of action for her to follow. This will, in large measure, be dictated by, and interwoven with, the trends set in that vast Black American community. My primary concern here is with depicting the strength of the Black family and Black girls within the family structure. I will seek to depict the lives of Black people I knew who were utilizing their scant resources for survival purposes, but who on the whole were quite successful with making the necessary adaptive and creative responses to their oppressed circumstances. I am also dealing with the somewhat abstract white middle-class system of values as it affects Blacks. It is hoped that the problems I encountered with conducting such a study, as well as the positive approach I was eventually able to take toward this work, will enable others to be equally as effective in breaking away from an intellectual tradition which has existed far too long.

One of the primary preoccupations of every American adolescent girl, regardless of race and social class background, is that of eventually becoming a woman. Every girl looks forward to the time when she will discard the status of child and take on the role of adult, wife and possibly mother.

The official entry into womanhood is usually regarded as that time when she reaches the prescribed legal age (eighteen and sometimes twenty-one), when for the first time she is granted certain legal and other rights and privileges. These rights, such as being allowed to vote, to go to certain "for adults only" events, to join certain social clubs and to obtain certain types of employment, are accompanied by a type of informal understanding that very few privileges, either formal or informal, are to be denied her where age is the primary prerequisite for participation. Entry into womanhood is the point at which she is considered by older adults to be ready to join their ranks because she has gone through the necessary apprenticeship program—the period of adolescence. We can observe differences between racial and social class groups regarding, for instance, the time at which the female is considered to be ready to assume the duties and obligations of womanhood. Becoming a woman in the low-income Black community is somewhat different from the routes followed by the white middle-class girl. The poor Black girl reaches her status of womanhood at an earlier age because of the different prescriptions and expectations of her culture. There is no single set of criteria for becoming a woman in the Black community; each girl is conditioned by a diversity of factors depending primarily upon her opportunities, role models, psychological disposition and the influence of the values, customs and traditions of the Black community. It will be demonstrated that the resources which adolescent girls have at their disposal, combined with the cultural heritage of their communities, are crucial factors in determining what kind of women they become. Structural *and* psychological variables are important as focal points because neither alone is sufficient to explain the many factors involved with psychosocial development. Therefore, the concepts of motivation, roles and role model, identity and socialization, as well as family income, education, kin and peer group relations are important to consider in the analysis. These diverse factors have rarely been considered as crucial to an analysis of Black womanhood. This situation exists because previous studies have substituted simplistic notions for rigorous multivariate analysis. Here, however, these multiple factors and influences will be analyzed as a "Black cultural" framework which has its own autonomous system of values, behavior, attitudes, sentiments and beliefs.

Another significant dimension to be considered will be the extent to which Black girls are influenced by the distinct culture of their community. Certain historical as well as contemporary variables are very important when describing the young Black woman. Her cultural heritage, I feel, has played a stronger role than has previously been stated by most writers in shaping her into the entity she has become.

Life in the Black community has been conditioned by poverty, discrimination and institutional subordination. It has also been shaped by African cultural survivals. From slavery until the present, many of the African cultural survivals influenced the way Blacks lived, responded to others and, in general, related to their environment. Even after slavery many of these survivals have remained and act to forge a distinct and viable set of cultural adaptive mechanisms because discrimination acted as an agent to perpetuate instead of to destroy the culture.

I will illustrate, through depicting the lives of Black preadolescent and adolescent girls in a big-city slum, how distinct sociohistorical forces have shaped a very positive and practical way of dealing and coping with the world. The values, attitudes, beliefs and behavior emerge from a long tradition, much of which has characterized the Black community from its earliest beginnings in this country.

What is life like in the urban Black community for the "average" girl? How does she define her roles, behaviors, and from whom does she acquire her models for fulfilling what is expected of her? Is there any significant disparity between the resources she has with which to accomplish her goals in life and the stated aspirations? Is the typical world of the teen-ager in American society shared by the Black girl or does she stand somewhat alone in much of her day-to-day existence?

In an attempt to answer these and other questions, I went to such a community and sought out teen-agers whom I felt could provide me with some insights. I was a research assistant in 1964 on a study of an all-Black low-income housing project of over ten thousand residents in a slum area of St. Louis.

(This study was supported by a grant from the National Institute of Mental Health, Grant No. MH-9189, "Social and Community Problems in Public Housing Areas.") It was geographically located near the downtown section of St. Louis, Missouri, and within one of the oldest slum areas of the city. The majority of the females were drawn from the Pruitt-Igoe housing project, although many resided outside the public housing project in substandard private housing.

At that time my curiosity was centered around the various activities in which the girls engaged that frequently produced harmful consequences. Specifically, I attempted to understand how such social problems as pregnancy, premarital sex, school dropout, etc. affected their life chances for success. I also felt, at the time, that a less destructible adaptation could be made to their impoverished environments. However, I was to understand later that perhaps a very healthy and successful adaptation, given their limited resources, had been made by all of these girls to a set of very unhealthy environmental conditions. Therefore, I soon changed my focus and attempted to apply a different perspective to the data.

I spent almost four years interviewing, testing (Thematic Apperception Test), observing and, in general, "hanging out" with these girls. I attempted to establish a strong rapport with all of them by spending a considerable amount of time in their homes with them and their families, at church, parties, dances, in the homes of their friends, shopping, at my apartment and in a variety of other situations. The sample consisted of several peer groups which over the years changed in number and composition. I always endeavored to interview their parents, and in some cases became close friends of their mothers. The field work carried me into the community at very unregulated hours—weekends, occasional evenings and during school hours (when I usually talked to their mothers). Although a great portion of the data collected is exploratory in nature, the majority of it is based on systematic open-ended interviews that related to (1) life histories and (2) attitudes and behavior that reflected approaching womanhood. During the last year and a half I randomly selected thirty girls between the ages of thirteen and eighteen and conducted a systematic investigation that was designed to test many of my preliminary conclusions drawn from the exploratory research. All of the interviews and observations were taped and transcribed. The great majority of the interviews were taped *live*, and will appear as direct quotations throughout this book. (All of the girls have been given pseudonyms.)

I feel that the data are broad in scope and are applicable to almost any group of low-income Black teen-age girls growing up in any American city.

The economic, political, social and racial factors which have produced neo-colonialism on a national scale operate in Chicago, Roxbury, Detroit, Watts, Atlanta—and everywhere else.

The total misrepresentation of the Black community and the various myths which surround it can be seen in microcosm in the Black female adolescent. Her growing-up years reflect the basic quality and character of life in this environment, as well as anticipations for the future. Because she is in perhaps the most crucial stage of psycho-social development, one can capture these crucial forces—external and internal—which are acting upon her, and which, more than any other impact, will shape her lifelong adult role. Thus, by understanding the nature and processes of her development, we can also comprehend the more intricate elements that characterize the day-to-day lives of the Black masses.

NOTES

1. Howard S. Becker, *The Outsiders,* New York, Free Press, 1963, p. 9.

2. See the works of Edwin Lemert, *Social Pathology,* New York, McGraw-Hill, 1951; John Kituse, "Societal Reaction to Deviance: Problems of Theory and Method," *Social Problems,* Winter 1962, pp. 247–56; and Frank Tannenbaum, *Crime and the Community,* New York, Columbia University Press, 1938.

3. See Ethel Sawyer, "Methodological Problems in Studying Socially Deviant Communities," this volume [*The Death of White Sociology,* ed. Joyce A. Ladner (New York: Random House, 1973)].

4. W. E. B. DuBois, *Souls of Black Folk,* New York, Fawcett World Library, 1961.

5. I am using the term "Black community" to refer to what is traditionally called the "ghetto." I am speaking largely of the low-income and working-class masses, who comprise the majority of the Black population in this country.

6. Lerone Bennett, *The Challenge of Blackness* (Chicago: Johnson Publishing Co., 1972).

7. Refer to Robert Blauner, "Internal Colonialism and Ghetto Revolt," *Social Problems,* Vol. 16, No. 4, Spring 1969, pp. 393–408; and see Robert Blauner and David Wellman, "Toward the Decolonization of Social Research," in this collection [*Death of White Sociology,* Ladner].

8. Alvin W. Gouldner, "Anti-Minotaur: The Myth of a Value-Free Sociology," *Social Problems,* Winter 1962, pp. 199–213.

9. Kenneth Clark, *Dark Ghetto,* New York, Harper & Row, 1965, p. xv.

MAE C. KING

Oppression and Power:
The Unique Status of the Black Woman
in the American Political System

The unique status of the black woman, when compared to other women in the American political system, is rooted in the heritage of slavery based on race. While racism was institutionalized by the slave system, this ideology assumed a value independent of the particular system under which it first flourished. Consequently, when the plantation slave structures were destroyed, the oppression of the black woman and other blacks, which was now justified on a racial basis, continued in other institutional forms. The belief had been established and internalized that black people were inferior to white people and experienced deserved oppression because of their race, not necessarily because of the slave structures that characterized the American system. Thus, the permanency of their color would incur the continuation of subjugation even in the absence of slavery. As a result, the emergence of new economic, social and political structures in the aftermath of slavery perpetuated the fundamental functional power relationship between blacks and whites. A basic and distinctive feature of the American political system became evident, namely, the primacy of the role of race in the acquisition and loss of power and status.

Any adequate analysis of the prospects of a viable alliance between black women, who are an intrinsic part of the black liberation struggle, and white women, who are intimately connected with the white power-holders who

Mae C. King, "Oppression and Power: The Unique Status of the Black Woman in the American Political System," *Social Science Quarterly* 56, no. 1 (1975): 116–128.

oppress, must begin with a recognition of the uniqueness of the black woman's position in the system which generates the injustices protested by these respective groups. The purpose of this paper is to point out some of these unique differences and to examine their implications for black women in their struggle to liberate themselves from the oppressive power of the American State. Attention will be focused on caste and status differences, and power and interest conflicts as these relate to black women's liberation on one hand and the primarily white women's movement on the other. Three fundamental points will be addressed: (1) sex role differences between black and white women in America; (2) the inappropriateness of the application of the definition of the traditional status of the American woman to the black woman's predicament as a guide for action by the latter; and (3) the political implications of the racial dichotomy and caste structure of American society for the emergence of an effective interracial and intercaste alliance capable of generating equal benefits for both black and white components.

The Slave Heritage and Role Differentials of Black and White Women

In the United States the racial variable is a crucial one in the formation of political coalitions or alliances. The historical fact of white dominance and black subjugation exemplified in the racial caste structure that evolved after slavery[1] must be confronted forthrightly in any consideration of an alliance between black and white women. Here, it should be explicitly noted that the American system is organized on a racial caste basis.[2] Black women are members of the lower caste and white women are members of the upper caste. Each female group is discriminated against by the male members of their respective castes, with whites, because of their power position, exercising discriminatory powers over black females as well. Yet, opposition to this sex discrimination by an interracial women's alliance hardly constitutes a rebellion against the inferior status assigned to blacks and the superior status accorded to whites under the current caste arrangements. This point cannot be overemphasized at this juncture in our history, because too many blacks have fought and died for white-defined causes only to find their inferior power and status intact when the battle was over. A massive, aggressive attack on the caste structure is not likely to be carried out by those who benefit from the status quo. The current holders of power cannot be expected to cooperate in bringing about their own demise.

Since the caste concept is important in our analysis of an alliance across racial lines, a further brief comment on it is appropriate. Frazier, Myrdal, Warner and others have long argued that caste was the most accurate way of defining the position of blacks in America.[3] Warner has defined racial caste as "a system of values and behavior which places all people who are thought to be white in a superior position to those who are thought of as black in an inferior status."[4] Since the status of blacks in America, when compared to that of whites, remains basically unchanged, caste is still an appropriate description of black-white relations, and a useful concept for analyzing the potential of a black-white alliance. Black participation, for instance, in such white-dominated alliances as the Populist party, organized labor, the women's suffrage movement and others, has not erased the inferior status assigned to blacks in America.

It should be noted, however, that several scholars have held that a racial caste system has never existed in the United States.[5] They argued that a caste system is based on consent, or voluntary acceptance, by members of both the upper and lower castes of their status as a group status.[6] The American situation is compared with that of historical India, and the former, it is held, always involved conflict and nonacceptance by blacks, whereas the lower castes of India consented to their status. However, this position is untenable. There is no evidence that shows the existence of a caste system, ancient or contemporary, based on religion, race or some other characteristic, which did not have forceful means of punishing caste violators. Furthermore, "Indian history saw a succession of reform movements against caste and of inter-caste struggles for supremacy and prestige."[7]

The caste stigma is still a significant factor to be considered in any attempt by blacks and whites to establish a power base aimed at the obliteration of both racism and sexism. This is not to deny that the rigidity of American racial stratification has varied over time. It is to emphasize, however, that while the techniques for maintaining the caste system have changed, "the essence of the system, which is the collective subordination, in terms of status and power, of one racial group to another, remains intact."[8]

Within the context of this racially stratified order, the sex roles of black women and those of white were defined differently. Even when they performed the same tasks, these tended to have different meanings within the political system. Historically, the American political system made no distinction between the roles of black women and those of black men. The differences that emerged between their roles were dictated primarily by biological imperatives which determined the ways that black women, as opposed to black men, had to function within the oppressive order. A comparative look at the roles of black and white women in America will sustain this point.

It has been asserted that "in every known society, mankind has elaborated the biological division of labor into forms often very remotely related to the original biological differences that provided the original clues."[9] Pointing to the variation of sex roles among societies, it is further averred that "Some people think of women as too weak to work out of doors, others regard women as the bearers of heavy burdens."[10] This last observation suggests ways in which the images and sex roles accorded to white women differ from those of black women in the American situation. The white female, who is referred to as the "American woman," has been characterized as "small, weak, soft, and light," as well as "dull, peaceful, relaxed, cold, rounded, passive and slow."[11] Her primary occupation is that of housewife, a responsibility that is geared largely to work indoors. Lopata, in her study of this subject, defined a housewife as:

> . . . a woman responsible for running her home whether she performs the tasks herself or hires people to do them. This distinguishes her from an employed housekeeper who maintains a dwelling belonging to someone else without having final responsibility for it.[12]

The overwhelming majority of the women in this study considered the most important role of woman to be that of mother, wife, and housewife. There was hardly any mention of "societal, community, religious, neighbor, friend or work obligation when asked to rank the role of women in its importance."[13]

The housewife image and the subsequent sex roles associated with it in America, do not reflect the reality of the black woman's experience. For example, while the American housewife is described as "suburban" and "freed by science and labor-saving appliances from the drudgery, the dangers of childbirth, and the illnesses of her great-grandmother,"[14] such a portrait hardly activates images of black women. For example, in 1972, maternal mortality was almost three times higher for blacks than whites, and the black infant mortality rate is also much higher.[15] Furthermore, the national policy of "opposition to forced integration of the suburbs" suggests the inappropriateness of the suburban label to the black wife, and signifies the national determination to maintain the racial dichotomy of American society and the concomitant power arrangements that characterize this structure. It should be noted that the "American housewife" is apparently supportive of such a stance:

Many lower-class suburbanites explain their movement away from the city as an escape from a race or ethnic group. Middle-class suburban women are not as likely to make such specific comments for two reasons: their culture does not contain open prejudice to the same degree and their previous residence had less chance of bordering on areas of Negro expansion.[16]

This statement indicates that white females, in their attitudes toward blacks, are no different from white males. Yet the political disposition of the American housewife is crucial in any assessment of the feasibility of a viable alliance between black and white women. It is reasonable to predict that one may search in vain for a political commonality in femaleness that supercedes the racial caste boundaries of the American order.

The image of the white female as a housewife surrounded by the amenities of suburbia is based on an economic affluence of white America which rarely exists in black America. For example, the U.S. Census Bureau reported that the median family income for blacks in 1972 was $6,864 compared to $11,549 for whites. It also reported that one-third of all black Americans are poor and 42.7 percent of all black children were living in poverty, compared to a national average of 14.9 percent.[17] Moreover, in May 1974, the median weekly earnings of black males working full time were $160 compared to $209 for whites.[18] Consequently, while the affluent housewife image may be rooted in reality for white women, it is devoid of any substantive reality for the overwhelming majority of black women. This congruence of racial identity and economics will probably militate against the cementing of an effective alliance between black and white females.

The historical exercise of the traditional housewife role by white females was contingent upon the assumption by white males of the traditional role of the "breadwinner." Since American society has systematically denied black men the job opportunities essential for the fulfillment of the "breadwinner" role of the "American man," it was hardly possible for black women to fit the housewife model. In October 1974, the unemployment rate was about twice as high for blacks as whites.[19] Hence, both the black male and female have been forced by circumstances to contribute—often almost equally—to the economic well-being of the family.

The psychological stress that such racist behavior by the larger society inflicted upon black men and women should not be ignored. For even though traditional sex roles are now being challenged they were accepted as norms by the larger society. Ladner notes that the black woman has been forced to accept the images of what the larger society says a woman should be but at the same time accept the fact that in spite of how she strives to approximate these models, she can never reach the pedestal upon which white women have been put.[20]

The recent resurgence of black consciousness accompanied by "the development of an internal set of standards by which black women have begun to judge themselves"[21] has probably eliminated much of the anxiety generated by the refusal of the dominant society to permit black males and females to assume traditional (white) sex roles.

When the American political and economic system denied black males the opportunity to provide for the economic well-being of their families, the implication of this governmental behavior was not only that black males could not achieve the status of "American men," but also black females could not be "American women." The realization of "American femininity" was contingent upon the actualization of "American masculinity." That neither of these concepts was significantly operational in black America suggests that the source of discontent among black and white women is contextually and substantively different. The possible political implications of this should not be overlooked.

Neither the "American housewife" model nor the "delicate female" image was applicable to black women in America. Instead of being viewed as too "weak" to work out of doors, black women were most likely thought of as strong and as "bearers of heavy burdens." In this sense, their role has differed little from that of black men. Oppression is no respector of sexes. The plantation system, for example, "did not differentiate between the sexes in exploiting slave labor."[22] This slave heritage has continued to shape the role of the black woman. Hence, black women are more apt than white to be working mothers, working wives and housekeepers, rather than a housewife "working indoors." The "hard-working woman model" is still, perhaps, the dominant reality for most black women. Ladner argues that the hard-working woman image

has persisted through the centuries because the conditions are fundamentally unchanged. The same factors which produce black male unemployment and subordination continue to cause the black female to assume the responsibility of her family which this society has relegated to men in other social classes.[23]

Pointing to the historical commonality of roles assumed by black women and black men, DuBois declared that "black women toil and toil hard." Illustrating this point, he stated that:

> There were in 1910, two and a half million Negro homes in the United States. Out of these homes walked daily to work, two million women and girls over ten years of age—over half of the colored female population as against a fifth in the case of white women. These then are a group of workers, *fighting for their daily bread like men;* independent and approaching economic freedom. They furnished a million farm laborers, 80,000 farmers, 22,000 teachers, 600,000 servants and washerwomen, and 50,000 in trades and merchandising.[24]

While acknowledging the commonality of roles assumed by black females and males, DuBois also noted the unique position of the black woman in the American system and voiced the conflict between her role and the dominant culture's ideal of woman's role:

> The family group . . . which is the ideal of the culture with which these folk have been born, is not based on the idea of an economically independent working mother. Rather, its ideal harks back to the sheltered harem with the mother emerging at first as nurse and homemaker, while the man remains the sole breadwinner.[25]

Today, black women continue to shoulder responsibilities which traditional sex roles, as defined by white America, would relegate to males. A larger percentage of black women than white women are still in the labor force, are concentrated in low-paying occupations, and suffer higher rates of unemployment. Department of Labor statistics on minority (blacks constitute about 90 percent) workers released in 1974 indicate, for example, that 49.1 percent of the women workers in the labor force were minorities compared to 44.1 percent for white women.[26] The rate of unemployment among minority women workers averaged 10.5 percent compared to 5.3 percent for white women.[27] Also, 48.6 percent of the minority women workers were mothers with children under 6 years old compared to only 32.2 percent of the white women.[28]

Such statistics also indicate that even as white women challenge traditional sex roles and, either by choice or necessity, enter the labor force in large numbers, the racial boundaries separating black and white females are reflected in the same fashion as those between black and white males. In short, black women are generally subordinate to white women in the occupational structure, earn less, and experience more unemployment. Hence, although the members of the upper caste may redefine sex roles, there is no reason to believe that this intra-caste change will obliterate the racial caste structure of the American political and economic system, and result in achievement of power parity for blacks and whites.

Since the roles of black females and males have been characterized by equalitarianism, with systemic conditions forcing the black woman to assume economic support responsibilities along side the black man, it seems reasonable to conclude that race, rather than sex, has been the decisive determinant of the black woman's status in the United States. Her race shaped her role, and America contemptuously withheld from her the gauze of "American femininity." She, like her male companion, was forced to serve the American order in any manner that the white rulers deemed essential for the maintenance of a system which rewarded whites and degraded blacks. Any variation in the tasks performed by male and female was hardly based on consideration of or respect for the "femaleness" of the black woman. In other words, the black woman was "defeminized" by the American system and was routinely forced to assume responsibilities that were otherwise incompatible with "woman's place."

A Misapplication of the "American Woman" Status Analysis

The difference in the status of black and white women in America points to the inappropriateness of using an analysis of the status of the "American woman" as an action guide for black women. The women's movement is largely a rebellion against the traditional sex roles and concept of American femininity. The images and role requirements of the "feminine one" are now being attacked as untenable by a substantial segment of women in America. However, since the social and political system has generally rendered these images and roles inapplicable to black women, a political movement organized around these as the central issues is not likely to address itself to the root causes of the black woman's discontent.

The primarily white women's movement is directed first and foremost against white male sexism. Since white males dominate or control the institutions and structures instrumental in obtaining the changes sought by the movement, such orientation is to be expected. Yet, while white male sexism is also injurious to the black woman, it is the practice of this phenomenon within the context of racism that differentiates the content of the black woman's problems from those of white females. Consequently, for black women, the issue of race is inextricably linked to the issue of sex when the subject is "white male supremacy." It is this linkage which dictated the emergence of the strong, hard-working woman model and the "deppreciated sex object" image for black women, as opposed to the American housewife model, petted and protected from the world outside of the home. The women's movement address itself primarily to the discontent and problems generated by the latter concept of woman's role. In so doing, it refuses to confront the white racism that undergirds white male supremacy; probably because this is an emotion that is deeply shared by the American housewife whose support is deemed essential to the success of the movement. Perhaps herein lies the greatest obstacle to the formation of a black and white woman's alliance with each component benefiting equally from it as an instrument of change.

In focusing its attention on white male powerholders, the women's movement in effect treats the black male as an insignificant bystander. Such behavior would be undesirable and unrealistic for black women. Black men are also guilty of sex discrimination. Although they almost never control the structures and institutions that shape white women's lives, they are an intimate and indispensable part of the lives of black women, who will be the immediate victims of any sex discrimination that they might practice.

At the present time, one should be cognizant of the possibility that the motivating force and content of sex discrimination practiced by the black male may be as different from that practiced by the white male as the content of the black woman's problems differ from that of the white female. The historical and dynamic force of white racism interposes itself in the relationship of black males and females. Thus, it is difficult to ascertain the extent to which black male behavior that appears sexist is a mere mock of the American image of a "ruler" or the expression of a commitment to a belief in female "inferiority" or weakness. Given the reality of his experience with black women and the egalitarian sex role tradition, his *belief* in female inferiority is hardly likely. In any case, the course of action necessary for abolishing a practice generated by a strong belief may differ significantly from the one required to abolish a practice based on mimicry. Black women may ignore at their peril the different tactics that these possibly different situations require.

In making the American housewife's cause or grievances the paradigm that dictates the direction and dimension of change, the women's movement inherently curtailed its ability to deal with the interests and problems of black women. It focuses instead on assuaging the grievances of white women only within the confines of status quo structures and principles. For example, the use of the "quota" concept as a means of rectifying long-standing injustices is likely to be opposed as vigorously by the American housewife as by her white male counterpart. Suggestive of the conservative thrust of the movement is the assertion by Bailyn that:

> ... the problem of the woman in America takes two distinct forms ... it centers on the continuing quest for social legislation to ensure that any woman who *must* work can do so and be fairly compensated for it. . . . On the other hand, the emphasis is on the attempt to redefine social attitudes in such a way that any woman who *wants* to work can do so without an excessive burden of guilt.[29]

The above statement of the problem is narrowly constructed; while the passage of social legislation aimed at alleviating grievances of the female members of the dominant group may activate concomitant enforcement processes, the racial factor may still prohibit black women from benefiting from such action.

The women's movement is geared toward the attainment of role change within existing structures. A redefinition of sex roles providing for diversity of choice, while maintaining positive rewards that flow from traditional roles, can probably occur for white women without fundamentally restructuring the political system. However, this is not the case for black women. An operational redefinition of their sex status, accompanied by commensurate rewards, cannot be realized apart from a redefinition of the status of blacks generally in the American political system. This requires that blacks be in a position to make and implement demands on the political system, even in opposition to and independent of, if necessary, white majority opinion. The achievement of such a position of power demands structural change as well as role change. The change must be sufficiently extensive to erase the racial caste boundary of power. For in America race is the basis of the black woman's oppression and sex is only the intensifier of this First Burden.

The Limited Viability of an Interracial Women's Alliance

The final point to be examined is the political implications of the caste structure of American society for the emergence of a viable interracial women's alliance. Black women and white women both are engaged in a power struggle.

Each group is attempting to change its social, political and economic status in the American system. There are inherent conflicts of interests involved. As the female components of their separate castes, each group is intricately linked with the male element of their caste and subject to its influence. The dimension of the change sought by each group is significantly different. The upper caste American housewife most likely shares all of the racial prejudices possessed by her white male companion and these in turn will shape the content of the social change she supports. Hence, she will most likely oppose any black-white coalition which commits itself to a program of action considerate of vital concerns of black women (i.e., support for low-income housing outside of the inner-city area). Furthermore, since such a housewife already appears anxious about her status, she may feel that it will be further jeopardized through association with members of the lower caste. In this regard, one observer notes that:

> When whites suffer status anxieties, the pain is eased perceptibly by an assertion of superiority over blacks in ways that range from discriminatory epithets to mayhem and assassination, all to clarify the boundaries of the group and the self.[30]

Meanwhile, since the women's movement is concerned with mobilizing the support of the American housewife, her attitude toward blacks is an important indicator of the likelihood of success of an alliance between black and white women.

Studies published in 1967 and 1971 showed that a great majority of whites opposed the persistent efforts of blacks to demolish racial barriers.[31] Especially noteworthy were the racist attitudes voiced by housewives in the mid-60's.[32] In the later study, whites were asked a series of questions designed to ascertain their attitudes toward black protest, and only six percent of the women and five percent of the men gave sympathetic responses to all five questions.[33] These results suggest a consensus between the white woman and the white male on issues that pierce at the heart of racism. Yet, such issues raise precisely the kinds of questions which black women cannot avoid in adequately assessing the possible effectiveness of an alliance with the women's movement. The ability of the movement to confront and resolve such questions in the interest of racial justice should be considered as the field test of the relevancy of the movement for black women and of its capacity to transcend, in a systematic way, traditional American racial caste boundaries.

So far, the women's movement has evinced little evidence of being any more supportive of defining its issues in a manner so as to ensure inclusiveness and involvement of blacks than were previous white-male dominated "liberal" movements, such as organized labor. In this liberal tradition, Friedan declared that:

> Man is not the enemy, but the fellow victim of the present half-equality. As we speak, act, demonstrate, testify and appear on television on matters such as sex discrimination in employment, public accommodation, education, divorce-marriage reform, or abortion repeal, we hear from men who feel that they can be freed to greater self-fulfillment to the degree that women are released from the binds that now constrain them.[34]

Now, although black women, as well as white women, may in theory benefit from a positive resolution of the issues referred to above, the context in which they are raised tends to restrict resulting benefits to the "system preferred" female group. In short, unless parity sharing, by black women, of the "fruits" of the "revolution" is *explicitly* articulated and made an issue at every stage and level of the "battle," the history of U.S. racism indicates that promised implicit rewards in compensation for steeled sacrifice will not, in fact, be honored.

The status quo approach of the women's movement on the racial question is apparently based on an accurate assessment of the nature of the American housewife constituency. One can reasonably conclude that white women, generally, are either non-supportive or apathetic about precisely those issues and concerns that black women deem very important. This point is sustained by findings of Harris, who conducted a comparative survey of attitudes of black and white women. Harris focused on issues relating to the quality of life, some of which had racial overtones. His study revealed, for example, that the overwhelming majority of black women consider as serious such problems as providing low-income housing, helping poverty-stricken people, providing health care for everyone, and aiding the elderly. On the other hand, only a minority of the white women consider these as very serious problems.[35] Such data suggest poor prospects for the development of an effective alliance between black and white women. After all, as long as American society is stratified along racial lines, racial prejudice will be functional in any power struggle.

Summary and Conclusion

The confluence of a slave heritage, racial oppression, and sex discrimination make for the uniqueness of the black woman's position in the American political system. Racial oppression, intensified by sex discrimination, means that black women are subjugated to white women as well as white men. Moreover, white women are an inseparable part of the dominant group and black women are likewise related to the subjugated black group.[36] Within this context, one can extrapolate that white females will favor the same policy orientations toward black people as white men, namely, continued subjugation in its varied forms or extermination.[37] Consequently, even when white females support efforts to change the status of women, they may not view this action as affecting their relationships with black women. In short, a redefinition of their sex roles in relation to white male powerholders does not constitute or require a redefinition of their power relationship with black people in general, or black women in particular.

The commonality of femaleness which black women share with white women has been ignored by the American political system. The system "defeminized" black women and forced them to assume roles that were otherwise designated as male. Since race is the basis of the black woman's oppression, the power that is necessary to break the chains of oppression should not be dependent on a source which is itself an intrinsic part of the structure that oppresses.

The historical differences between the sex roles assumed by black and white women in America is dictated by a different set of concerns and problems. Politically, the women's movement is aimed at influencing power structures populated primarily by white males. In an attempt to achieve its objectives, tactics which accommodate the prejudices of white males will be emphasized. This means that white women will disassociate themselves from issues of racial justice which tend to alienate the controllers of the status quo power arrangements.

The biological, and familial relationship (mothers, daughters, sisters, wives) between white males and females will dilute any opposition that the former may otherwise exert toward efforts of the latter to redefine sex roles. Supporting this point, Firestone has called attention to the power of the sexual bond as a weapon for change:

> That women live with men while on some levels our worst disadvantage . . . is, in another sense, an advantage; a revolutionary in every bedroom cannot help but shake up the status quo. And if it is your wife who is revolting, *you* can't just split to the suburbs.[38]

Yet, one can reasonably predict that while the "shake up" generated by the female force may be sufficient to demolish the sex factor as the determinant of ruling class status in the upper caste; "revolutionized bedrooms" at the top may have no more impact on changing the status of black women than the passage of the Nineteenth Amendment had on obtaining them the right to vote in the South. In other words, before the latter became a reality, the "black question" had to be explicitly considered in the context of the oppressive experience which had been the lot of black female and black male alike.

Finally, the racial structure of power and status in America virtually rules out the realization of an interracial alliance of "equals" in which both partners would contribute and benefit equally from achievements of the alliance. The racial dichotomy of American society dictates the formulation of issues by interracial groups in the context of the dominant white interests, with the humanitarian appellation employed to suggest the *possibility* of black gains from such an arrangement. Apparently the white element considers the indirect *promise* of improvement sufficient to secure black cooperation. Certainly, the women's movement will hardly risk alienating the American housewife by explicitly articulating and taking positive stands on issues that affect the vital interests of black women, such as police brutality, prison reform, the restructuring of the welfare state or the use of the quota technique as one means of rectifying racial inequities; as well as pressing for the abolition of sex discrimination in pay, hiring, promotion, and career opportunities.

Because black and white women have experienced America politically, economically, socially and emotionally in very different ways, a commonality of interests should not be assumed, it must be explicitly stated and demonstrated. The reality of racial oppression requires this approach, and the realization of the power to destroy it demands the same. Hence, black women must insist that any interracial and inter-caste alliances be compatible with their interests and dignity. For historically, whites have demanded that blacks sacrifice their dignity as well as their interests in order to coalesce in "alliances" that were instruments of white power realignments. Such a price ought never to be paid again. It is too high and contributes little to the alleviation of black people's First Burden.

NOTES

1. See, E. Franklin Frazier, *Race and Culture Contacts in the Modern World* (Boston: Beacon Press, 1958), pp. 253–268.

2. For full discussion of this point, see Mae C. King, "The Political Implications of the Stereotyped Images of the Black Woman in American Society," Paper delivered at Annual meeting of American Psychological Association, September 1–8,

1972, pp. 4–8. Also published in revised form as "The Politics of Sexual Stereotypes," *The Black Scholar,* 4 (March–April, 1973), pp. 12–22.

3. See for example, Gunnar Myrdal, *An American Dilemma* (New York: Harper and Brothers, 1944), Vol. 1, p. 667; Frazier, *Race and Culture Contacts*; and W. Lloyd Warner, "American Caste and Class," *American Journal of Sociology,* 42 (Sept., 1936), pp. 234–237, and Warner, *Social Class in America* (New York: Harper & Row, 1960), pp. 20–21. Although Warner's focus is on the South, the power relationship between blacks and whites resulting from the caste system which he describes are also characteristic of black-white relations in other parts of the U.S.

4. Warner, *Social Class in America,* p. 20.

5. See for example, Oliver C. Cox, *Caste, Class and Race* (New York: Doubleday & Co., 1948); and Brewton Berry, *Race Relations* (New York: Houghton Mifflin Co., 1951).

6. See Frazier, *Race and Culture Contacts,* Ch. 4.

7. Pierre L. Van denBerghe, *Race and Racism: A Comparative Perspective* (New York: John Wiley and Sons, 1967), p. 10.

8. King, "Political Implications," p. 7.

9. Margaret Mead, *Male and Female* (New York: William Morrow & Co., 1949), p. 7.

10. *Ibid.,* p. 7.

11. Robert Jay Lifton, ed., *The Woman in America* (Cambridge: Houghton Mifflin Co., 1965), p. 173.

12. Helena Z. Lopata, *Occupation: Housewife* (New York: Oxford University Press, 1971), p. 3.

13. *Ibid.,* p. 47

14. Betty Friedan, *The Feminine Mystique* (New York: W. W. Norton & Co., 1963), p. 18.

15. *Monthly Vital Statistics Report,* U.S. Department of Health, Education and Welfare, Vol. 23, No. 8, Supplement (2), November 6, 1974.

16. Lopata, *Occupation: Housewife,* p. 43.

17. Reported in *The Washington Post,* July 2, 1973.

18. U.S. Department of Labor, Bureau of Statistics, News Release, November 8, 1974.

19. "Black and White Unemployment," *Monthly Labor Review* (Dec., 1974), p. 88.

20. Joyce A. Ladner, *Tomorrow's Tomorrow: The Black Woman* (Garden City, New York: Doubleday & Co., 1971, p. 30.

21. *Ibid.,* p. 30.

22. *Ibid.,* p. 21.

23. *Ibid.,* p. 132.

24. W. E. B. DuBois, *Darkwater: Voices From Within the Veil* (New York: Schocken Books, 1969), pp. 179–180. Italics mine.

25. *Ibid.*, p. 180.

26. See "Facts on Women Workers of Minority Races," *U.S. Department of Labor, Women's Bureau* (May, 1974), p. 2. Hereafter cited as "Facts."

27. *Ibid.*, p. 3.

28. *Ibid.*, p. 5.

29. Lifton, *Woman in America*, p. 236.

30. Robert J. Seckels, *Race, Marriage and the Law* (Albuquerque: University of New Mexico Press, 1972), p. 13.

31. See William Brink and Louis Harris, *Black and White: A Study of U.S. Racial Attitudes Today* (New York: Simon and Schuster, 1967), p. 12; and Angus Campbell's *White Attitudes Toward Black People* (Ann Arbor: University of Michigan, Institute for Social Research, 1971), p. 4.

32. See Brink and Harris, *Black and White*, pp. 120–124.

33. Campbell, *White Attitudes*, p. 18.

34. In Mary Lou Thompson, ed., *Voices of the New Feminism* (Boston: Beacon Press, 1970), p. 33.

35. Louis Harris and Associates, *The 1972 Virginia Slims, American Women's Opinion Poll: A Survey of the Attitudes of Women in Their Roles in Politics and the Economy* (New York: Louis Harris and Associates, Inc., 1972), pp. 72–73.

36. See Mack H. Jones, "A Frame of Reference for Black Politics," in Lenneal Henderson, ed., *Black Political Life in the U.S.* (San Francisco: Chandler Publishing Co., 1972) for a penetrating analysis and application of these concepts to the black-white struggle in the United States.

37. *Ibid.*, p. 15.

38. Shulamith Firestone, *The Dialectic of Sex* (New York: William Morrow & Co., 1970), p. 43.

WILLIAM JULIUS WILSON

Competitive Race Relations and the Proliferation of Racial Protests: 1940–1970

History will record the mid-twentieth century as one of the most dynamic periods of black-white contact. It was a period that witnessed the proliferation of black protests, ranging from the essentially nonviolent to the violent. It was a period when competitive race relations reached their most fluid pattern and when biological racism declined and cultural racism was revived primarily in institutional form. Fundamentally, however, it was a period when blacks experienced their most significant growth of power resources. Because of black migration to cities, increased urbanization, expanded industrialization, basic shifts in the national economy, and changes ushered in by World War II and the Cold War, new resources became available to black Americans that placed them in greater competition with whites. . . .

.   .   .

White Reaction to Increased Black Competitive Resources

The growth of black competitive resources after World War II was not immediately accompanied by severe white hostility. Except for the South's attempt

William Julius Wilson, selections from "Competitive Race Relations and the Proliferation of Racial Protests: 1940–1970," chap. 7 of *Power, Racism, and Privilege: Race Relations in Theoretical and Sociohistorical Perspectives* (New York: The Free Press, 1973), 121, 127–148, 149–150, 150–151, 153–159, 160.

to resist desegregation in the late 1950s, black advancement prior to 1960 occurred with relatively little white resistance. Black encroachment in the economic sphere did not generate the kind of racial violence that disrupted the country in the early twentieth century. In order to fully understand why the immediate postwar period was spared the intense racial tension that sometimes accompanies changes in competitive race relations, attention must be directed to the fundamental shifts that took place in the national economy and in the structural relations that determined black-white contact. Specifically, whereas the total employed labor force increased 37 per cent between 1941 and 1960, the total number of employed white-collar workers expanded by 81 per cent (by almost twelve million).[1] Even though blacks were virtually excluded from the highest-status positions (e.g., managers, officials, and proprietors), they were able to fill the intermediate-level jobs vacated by hundreds of thousands of upwardly mobile whites who were moving into upper-level positions.[2] Broom and Glenn conclude that

> Because Negro gains could occur without loss to whites, white resistance to Negro advancement was less than it otherwise would have been. Expansion of jobs at the upper levels is not a new trend; it goes back to the start of industrialization, but until recently the upward movement of workers generated by this change did not greatly benefit Negroes. As long as large numbers of European immigrants were entering the country, they, rather than Negroes, replaced most of the native-born whites who moved up. World War I slowed European immigration and the Immigrant Act of 1924 reduced it to a mere trickle, so that by the 1940's there was no longer a large pool of immigrants at the lowest occupational levels to replace the upward-moving native workers. The opportunity for the first great occupational advancement of Negro Americans was at hand.[3]

However, the moment the dominant group perceives particular minority gains as constituting a *distinct* threat to its sense of superior position, racial tensions intensify. Nowhere is this more clearly demonstrated than in the resistance to desegregation exhibited by Southern whites following the 1954 Supreme Court decision. Efforts to implement this decision were viewed by Southern whites as the most serious challenge to their way of life and proprietary claims to rights and privileges since Reconstruction, and they reacted accordingly. To mention a few of the incidents: White Citizens Councils sprang up all over the South, imposing drastic sanctions on blacks who signed integration petitions; the Ku Klux Klan made its reappearance in Alabama,

Florida, Georgia, and South Carolina; Southern politicians attempted to outdo each other in racist militant statements; a black woman, Autherine Lucy, was confronted with a rioting mob when she attempted to enroll in the University of Alabama in 1956; the Alabama Chapter of the NAACP was fined a hundred thousand dollars and slapped with a court injunction that prohibited its operating in the state (for the next two years the NAACP was inactive in Alabama); and national guardsmen joined white mobs to prevent integration of a high school in Little Rock, Arkansas, in 1957.[4] It was clear by the late 1950s that Southern whites were quite optimistic about their ability to defeat desegregation. The Supreme Court decision had been passed, the NAACP had taken steps to implement it with hundreds of suits in courts, but segregation remained well entrenched. Southern whites had little reason to believe that they would soon face the most serious threat in the twentieth century to their group position—the proliferation of black protest movements during the 1960s.

Power and the Changing Character of Black Protest

Throughout our discussion of black social thought and protest in the United States, one pattern of behavior seems to emerge: *the changing goals of black advancement tend to be associated with the changing definition of black despair, and both the defined problem and the conceived goal are ultimately associated with the choice of possible pressure or constraint resources that blacks can mobilize in pressing for the desired solution.* However, it should be noted that despite the definition of the problem and the conception of the goal, the choice of pressure resources is influenced or determined by the extent to which blacks find themselves in competitive relations with whites. The now more conservative black protest movements, such as the NAACP and the National Urban League, developed and gained momentum when racial accommodations were undergoing change but when the dominant-group controls were so strong that the pressure tactics of the mid-twentieth century activist movements would not have been tolerated.[5]

Before the emergence of the activist black protest movements, the drive for civil rights was therefore in the hands of a few professionals competent to work through controlling legal and educational channels.[6] The NAACP achieved great success through these agencies, and its definition of the problem facing black people signified its planned strategy. Specifically, prior to 1960 the NAACP tended to define the racial problem as legal segregation in the South, and its major goal, popularized by the slogan "free by 1963," was the elimination of all state-enforced segregation. Although the officials of the NAACP have lacked a power orientation, the mobilization of their legal machinery has represented a display of power—the power of litigation—in this instance, a power resource of high liquidity. Working through prevailing institutional channels, the NAACP was able to win an overwhelming number of cases in the Supreme Court and thus helped to produce laws designed to improve racial conditions in America, although white Southerners ingeniously circumvented the new laws and thus usually prevented their implementation. Lewis M. Killian has discussed this matter:

> It is ironic that the white South was extremely successful in minimizing the impact of the desegregation decision of the federal court without arousing the indignation of the rest of the nation. As much as the White Citizens Council and the Ku Klux Klan are invoked as symbols of the southern resistance, they and their extra-legal tactics did not make this possible. Far more effective were the legal strategems, evasions, and delays that led Negroes to realize that although they had won a new statement of principle they had not won the power to cause this principle to be implemented.[7]

White procrastination made it apparent to many black leaders that both the goal and the problem had been too narrowly defined. A new definition of the problem thus emerged—token compliance to the newly created laws— and a corresponding new goal—the elimination of both de facto and de jure segregation. Litigation, no longer an effective pressure resource in the face of white procrastination, was replaced by passive or nonviolent resistance. The fact that the power balance between blacks and whites had undergone some alteration also helped bring about the shift to nonviolent direct-action protest. As blacks increased their political and economic resources, as the Supreme Court rendered decisions in favor of desegregation, and as the United States government became increasingly sensitive to world opinion of its racial situation, black expectations were heightened, continued white resistance became more frustrating, and consequently support for direct-action (albeit nonviolent) protests quickly mushroomed. Although some writers have identified the successful Montgomery bus boycott of 1955–1956 as the beginning of the black revolt,[8] Meier and Rudwick have maintained that "the really decisive break with the pre-eminence of legalistic techniques came with the college student sit-ins that swept the South in the spring of 1960."[9] These demonstrations set a chain of nonviolent resistance movements to desegregation into motion that subsequently swept the country from 1960 to 1965. Even though the initial emphasis was on persuasion resources rather than constraint resources, the technique of nonviolence was in reality an aggressive manifestation of pressure. Its twofold goal was to create and to implement civil rights laws. Even though many of the nonviolent protests were not specifically directed at the federal government, they were in many cases intended to apply indirect pressure on it. Black leaders recognized that because of their political and pressure resources and because of the United States' concern for world opinion, the government was not in a position to ignore their stepped-up drive for civil rights.

For a brief period of time, the nonviolent resistance strategy proved to be highly effective. In addition to forcing local governments and private agencies to integrate facilities in numerous Southern cities and towns, the nonviolent demonstrations pressed the federal government into passage of civil rights legislation in 1964 and voting rights legislation in 1965—acts that satisfied many of the black demands of the early 1960s. There are several reasons why the federal government responded favorably to many of the demands emanating from the nonviolent protest movement: (1) the demands that accompanied the protests tended to be fairly specific, e.g., "end discrimination in voting," and hence the government was able to provide "remedies" that clearly approximated the specifications in the demands; (2) the attempt to satisfy these demands did not call for major sacrifices on the part of whites, and hence there was little likelihood that a significant political backlash against the government would occur in sections of the country other than the South; (3) the demands were consistent with prevailing ideals of democracy and freedom of choice, and hence they could not be easily labeled "extreme" either by the white citizens or by governmental authorities; (4) the more blacks pressed their demands and carried out their protests, the more violent was the Southern response, and because these developments were receiving international attention, the government became increasingly concerned; (5) the government was sensitive to the political resources blacks had developed and became cognizant of the growing army of Northern whites sympathetic to the black cause; (6) blacks' political strength seemed to be magnified by the united front they presented, as groups ranging from the relatively conservative NAACP to the radical Student Nonviolent Coordinating Committee all joined in nonviolent protests to effect change.

To understand why many blacks shifted away from nonviolence both as a philosophy of life and as a technique to achieve racial equality, it is necessary to recall our earlier theoretical discussion of minority protest: if an extended period of increased expectations and gratification is followed by a brief period in which the gap between expectations and gratifications suddenly widens and becomes intolerable, the possibility of violent protests is greatly increased. Davies applies this analysis to the black rebellion of the 1960s:

> In short—starting in the mid-1950's and increasing more or less steadily into the early 1960's—white violence grew against the now lawful and protected efforts of Negroes to gain integration. And so did direct action and later violence undertaken by blacks, in a reciprocal process that moved into the substantial violence of 1965–67. That 3 year period may be considered a peak, possibly the peak of the violence that constituted the black rebellion. It merits reemphasis that during this era of increased hostility progress intensified both the white reaction to it and the black counteraction to the reaction, because everytime a reaction impeded the progress, the apparent gap widened between expectations and gratification.[10]

Even though there was no sudden or sharp increase in black unemployment and no sudden reversal in the material gains blacks had accumulated during the prosperous 1960s,[11] "there was, starting notably in 1963, not the first instance of violence against blacks but a sudden increase in it. This resurgence of violence came after, and interrupted, the slow but steady progress since 1940. It quickly frustrated rising expectations."[12] For the first time, there was a real sense of apprehension among blacks that, not only would conditions stop improving, but gains already achieved could very well be lost unless steps were taken to counteract mounting white violence.

Birmingham, Alabama, in 1963 was the scene of this initial wave of white violence and black counterreaction. In April, Birmingham police used high-pressure water hoses and dogs to attack civil rights marchers, and blacks retaliated by throwing rocks and bottles at the police; in May, segregationists bombed the homes of black leaders, and blacks retaliated by rioting, setting two white-owned stores on fire and stoning police and firemen; on September 15, whites enraged by school desegregation bombed a black church, killing four small girls and injuring twenty-three other adults and children, and blacks angrily responded by stoning police.[13]

However, racial violence was not restricted to Birmingham, Alabama, in 1963. Medger Evers, an NAACP official in Jackson, Mississippi, was shot to death in front of his home on May 28, 1963. Whites and blacks in Cambridge, Maryland, engaged in a gun battle after blacks had stormed a restaurant to rescue sit-in demonstrators beaten by whites; the black quarter in Lexington, North Carolina, was attacked by a white mob after blacks had attempted to obtain service at white restaurants, and in the ensuing gun battle a white man was killed; mounted police at Plaquemine, Louisiana, galloped into a group of civil rights demonstrators and dispersed them with electric cattle prods—fifteen demonstrators were injured; police used tear gas, shotguns, and high-pressure water hoses in Savannah, Georgia, to break up a protest demonstration that turned into a riot—at least ten whites and thirteen blacks were injured; and mass arrests of civil rights activists took place in Athena, Georgia; Selma, Alabama; Greensboro, North Carolina; Orangeburg, South Carolina, and several other Southern towns.[14]

The gap between expectations and emotional gratifications[15] increased black support for violent protest and was reflected, not only in the way blacks responded to white attacks beginning with the Birmingham incident in 1963, but also in the changing philosophy of younger civil rights activists. In the early months of 1964, members of the Student Nonviolent Coordinating Committee (SNCC) and the Congress of Racial Equality (CORE) openly challenged the philosophy of nonviolence and called for more belligerent forms of protest.[16] It was during this same period that Malcolm X, shortly after he resigned from the Nation of Islam, called for blacks to arm themselves and abandon nonviolence and that the Brooklyn chapter of CORE attempted to tie up New York traffic (on April 22, the opening of the World's Fair) by emptying the fuel tanks of 2000 automobiles and abandoning them on the freeways leading to the fairgrounds (lacking support, the strategy failed).[17] Continued white violent acts such as the murder of civil rights workers by white terrorists in Mississippi in 1964, Ku Klux Klan terrorism in Mississippi and Alabama in 1965, attacks against CORE organizers in Bogalusa, Louisiana, in 1965, the beating and murder of civil rights activists in Selma, Alabama, in 1965, and police brutality that precipitated rioting in Northern ghettoes in 1964 deepened the militant mood in the black community and widened the gap between expectations and emotional gratification.

In the face of these developments, the call by some black leaders for greater militancy was based on the optimistic belief that the larger society was more likely to respond properly to black demands backed by belligerent and violent protests than to those reinforced by nonviolent resistance. Our earlier theoretical analysis suggests either that blacks believed they possessed sufficient resources not only to disrupt the larger society but also to prevent an all-out repressive reaction by whites, or that they felt that by the mid-1960s the system had developed a high tolerance for minority protests.[18] However, it was lower-class urban blacks who dramatically demonstrated that a more belligerent mood had gripped the black community when they rocked the nation with a proliferation of ghetto revolts from 1964 to 1968. In the early 1960s, nonviolent protests were heavily populated by middle-class or higher-educated blacks, who were far more likely at this period to participate in a drive for social justice that was disciplined and sustained.[19] Ghetto blacks for the most part were not directly involved in the nonviolent resistance movement of the early 1960s, and many of the gains achieved did not materially benefit them (the civil rights movement up to 1965 produced laws primarily relevant to privileged blacks with competitive resources such as special talents or steady income)[20]; nevertheless, the victories of the nonviolent movement increased expectations among all segments of the black population.[21] In the age of mass communication, Northern ghetto blacks, like blacks throughout the country, were very much aware of and identified with the efforts of Martin Luther King, Jr., and other civil rights activists. By the same token, they were also cognizant of the white violence that threatened to halt the gradual but steady progress toward racial equality.

Accordingly, ghetto rebellions cannot be fully explained in isolation or independently of the increasingly militant mood of the black community. However, what made the situation of ghetto blacks unique was the fact that the gap between expectations and emotional gratification was combined with concrete grievances over police brutality, inferior education, unemployment, underemployment, and inadequate housing. It is true that these conditions have always existed in ghetto life and did not suddenly emerge during the 1960s, but the important point is that increased expectations and greater awareness of racial oppression made these conditions all the more intolerable.[22] Charles Silberman was essentially correct when he stated that "it is only when men sense the possibility of improvement, in fact, that they become dissatisfied with their situation and rebel against it. And 'with rebelling' as Albert Camus put it 'awareness is born,' and with awareness, an impatience 'which can extend to everything that [men] had previously accepted, and which is almost always retroactive.'"[23] Likewise, as the number and intensity of ghetto revolts increased, black complaints about human suffering became more explicit and focused.

The Harlem revolt in 1964 actually marked the beginning of ghetto uprisings of the 1960s (where groups of blacks looted stores, burned buildings, and attacked firemen and police in the black community), but the most serious revolts occurred in 1965 in Watts (resulting in 34 deaths, 900 injuries, 4000 arrests, and an estimated property damage of $100,000,000), in 1967 in

Detroit (43 deaths, 1500 injuries, 5000 arrests, and $200,000,000 in property damage), and Newark (26 deaths, 1200 injuries, 1600 arrests, and $47,000,000 in property damage). The assassination of Dr. Martin Luther King, Jr., precipitated the final series of ghetto rebellions in the spring of 1968. During that four-year period (1964–1968) of intense racial violence, thousands of persons, mostly black, were killed or injured, and the property damage was estimated in the billions of dollars.

In addition to these manifestations of greater black militancy, the emergence of the Black Power Movement in 1966, with its shift in emphasis to racial solidarity and its explicit repudiation of nonviolence as a strategy of protest and way of life, can also be associated with the sudden gap between rising expectations and emotional gratification. In a fundamental sense, however, the Black Power Movement represented a return to the self-help philosophy and emphasis on black solidarity that usually occurs "when the Negroes' status has declined or when they experienced intense disillusionment following a period of heightened but unfulfilled expectations."[24]

Unlike the self-help nationalistic philosophies that developed in the 1850s following increased repression in the free states, in the Booker T. Washington era as a response to the growth of biological racism and resurgence of white supremacy, and in the post World War I period as a reaction to white violence perpetrated against black urban immigrants in the North, the Black Power Movement developed during a period when blacks had achieved a real sense of power.

Killian has commented on this new feeling of power:

The nonviolent demonstrations of SCLC, CORE, and SNCC . . . had not solved the bitter problems of the Negro masses, but they had shown that the Negro minority could strike terror into the hearts of the white majority. They had produced concessions from white people, even though the triumph of winning these concessions had soon turned to despair because they were never enough. Watts and other riots reflected no clearly formulated demand for new concessions. They did reflect the basic truth that Negroes, mobilized in ghettoes to an extent never before experienced and made confident by earlier victories, were no longer afraid of white power. Within a few months after Watts, they would begin to proclaim their faith in Black Power.[25]

This new sense of power was reflected not so much in the programs actually introduced under the banner of Black Power as in the revolutionary rhetoric used to articulate Black Power philosophy. That certain black radicals dared, through national media, to call openly for the use of violence to overthrow racial oppression was a clear indication that blacks felt secure enough to threaten the very stability of the larger society. In actual fact, however, although Black Power advocates often disagreed about the aims and purposes of the movement, their various demands and programs were more reformist in nature than revolutionary[26] (e.g., programs emphasizing black capitalism, the running of black candidates for political office, self-help in the area of jobs and housing, black studies in high schools and colleges, and black culture and identity). Some of the programs introduced by Black Power spokesmen were an extension of the conservative separatism advocated by the Nation of Islam (Black Muslims) under the leadership of Elijah Muhammad. From the 1950s to the first half of the 1960s, when black social thought continued to be overwhelmingly supportive of integration,[27] the Nation of Islam served as the major medium for a black nationalist philosophy.[28] Commenting on Muslim philosophy, Cruse wrote that the

> Nation of Islam was nothing but a form of Booker T. Washington economic self-help, black unity, bourgeois hard work, law abiding, vocational training, stay-out-of-the-civil-rights-struggle agitation, separate-from-the-white-man, etc., etc. morality. The only difference was that Elijah Muhammad added the potent factor of the Muslim religion to race, economic, and social philosophy of which the first prophet was none other than Booker T. Washington. Elijah Muhammad also added an element of "hate Whitey" ideology which Washington, of course, would never have accepted.[29]

The most significant influence on the radical flank of the Black Power Movement was ex-Muslim minister Malcolm X. Because of differences with Elijah Muhammad, Malcolm X resigned from the Muslim organization and moved beyond its program of territorial separation and bourgeois economic nationalism. Shortly before he was assassinated in 1965, he had begun to formulate a philosophy of revolutionary nationalism (that "views the overthrow of existing political and economic institutions as a prerequisite for the liberation of black Americans, and does not exclude the use of violence"[30]) subsequently adopted by militant Black Power leaders such as Stokely Carmichael and H. Rap Brown and incorporated into the philosophy of the newly emerging Black Panther Party in the late 1960s.

Yet, of all the philosophies of nationalism or racial solidarity that emerged under the banner of Black Power, none has received as much support from black citizens as has cultural nationalism.[31] Cultural nationalism is concerned

mainly with positive race identity, including the development and/or elaboration of black culture and history. One of the most illustrative statements of
this theme has come from Blauner:

> In their communities across the nation, Afro-Americans are discussing
> "black culture." The mystique of "soul" is only the most focused ex-
> ample of this trend in consciousness. What is and what should be the
> black man's attitude toward American society and American culture has
> become a central division in the Negro protest movement. The spokes-
> men for black power celebrate black culture and Negro distinctiveness;
> the integrationists base their strategy and their appeal on the fundamental
> "American-ness" of the black man. There are nationalist leaders who see
> culture building today as equal or more important than political organi-
> zation. From Harlem to Watts there has been a proliferation of black the-
> ater, art, and literary groups; the recent ghetto riots (or revolts, as they are
> viewed from the nationalistic perspective) are the favored materials of
> these cultural endeavors.[32]

But certainly we must not lose sight of the fact that cultural nationalism,
like other forms of nationalism, has become popular during certain periods in
history—periods when black disillusionment follows a brief interval of black
optimism and commitment to integration. It is not so important that structural
assimilation,[33] especially for middle-class blacks, is occurring at a greater rate
than ever before (a point we will explore more fully in the following section);
what is important is the black perception of the racial changes that are occurring. Black awareness has been heightened by the efforts of both the civil rights
and the Black Power activists, and impatience and frustration with the pace of
racial equality have become more intense. Whereas the cultural nationalism of
the 1850s and of the Harlem Renaissance period was largely confined to segments of the black intelligentsia,[34] the cultural nationalism of the late 1960s and
early 1970s has transcended class lines. Awareness of the evils of racial oppression and of white resistance to racial equality is characteristic of all segments of
the black population; support for racial solidarity with emphasis on black culture and racial identity has reached unprecedented heights.

We shall have occasion to return to a consideration of cultural nationalism's role in the development of black political awareness. For the moment,
however, it is important to examine the extent to which the ideology of racism
has withstood both the onslaught of black protest and the drift toward more
fluid competitive race relations.

From Biological Racism to Cultural Racism

The ideology of biological racism, which received its greatest support in the late nineteenth and early twentieth centuries, has steadily declined as a rationale for black subordination. Although the manifestation of black skills and abilities in a more fluid competitive system has helped to destroy many racist stereotypes, probably the most significant factor in the demise of biological racism has been the unwillingness of most elite leaders and public spokesmen to openly utter racist statements reinforcing public opinion in support of black oppression. Ever since blacks developed political resources and the federal government became increasingly sensitive to world opinion of United States race relations, public remarks by influential political leaders have been designed more to promote racial harmony than to create greater racial cleavages. Moreover, since 1940 thousands of scholarly studies and a significant number of novels sympathetic to black citizens have "disseminated information about the Negro problem and helped to make criticism of the caste system respectable."[35] Current scientific opinion overwhelmingly rejects the validity of arguments equating race with innate intelligence. Even the widely heralded Jensen report,[36] which questioned the native intelligence of blacks, has come under rather devastating criticism from social and biological scientists.[37] Finally, individual attitudes as measured by public opinion polls indicate a decline of white beliefs in the biological inferiority of blacks. By the late 1960s, a majority of whites supported the view that blacks and whites are equal in innate mental ability.[38] Accompanying the decline of such beliefs has been a reduction in support of social norms favoring racial exclusion. By 1970, a large majority of whites verbally supported racial integration in public transportation, public facilities, and schools, and although responses toward neighborhood integration and mixed marriages continue to divide the white population, the trend is unmistakably in the direction of more tolerant attitudes in these two areas.[39]

Taken together, the reduction of support for beliefs in the biological inferiority of blacks and the decreasing support for norms of subordination indicate, it seems safe to conclude, that the ideology of biological racism is on the decline. However, attitudes, like overt behavior, are often a function of existing structural arrangements in society. Glenn has argued that

> White resistance to Negro advancement is almost certainly reduced in periods of rapid economic growth and rapid upward shifts in the occupational structure, when Negroes can advance without whites incurring any

absolute losses in income or occupational status. Even at such times, closing the Negro-white gap entails loss of a white competitive advantage, but
whites who nevertheless are moving up are likely to be less aware of and
less concerned about this loss.[40]

Indeed, research on white public opinion indicates that liberal and tolerant attitudes toward blacks exist among those who occupy upper-status positions and are thus furthest removed from direct competition with blacks
heavily concentrated in lower-status positions. Thus despite the overall reduction of white racist attitudes and increasing support for racial equality, any sudden shift in the nation's economy that would throw whites into greater competition with blacks for, say, housing and jobs could create and intensify racial
tension and, at least for the whites who feel threatened by black advancement,
reverse the trend toward increasing racial tolerance. In analyzing the situation
in the United States, Jan Dizard is insightful when he suggests that

> What we are confronted with, then, is a society whose stability rests on
> its ability to maintain inequality while at the same time acknowledging as
> legitimate subordinate groups' demands for more. The answer to this
> dilemma has been economic growth. When growth does not obtain, sta-
> bility is threatened from two directions. Those at or near the bottom find
> their demands for more implicitly requiring a redistribution, thus chal-
> lenging extant arrangements of power and privilege. At the same time,
> groups enjoying even a modicum of comfort respond to the squeeze in a
> typically defensive fashion, thus becoming available for the demagogic
> mobilization of nativism and racism.[41]

Probably the most effective way that the society of the United States is
able "to maintain inequality while at the same time acknowledging as legitimate subordinate groups' demand for more" is through the pervasive and persistent practice of institutional discrimination. Even though racist norms that
directed the systematic exclusion of blacks from full participation in stable,
patterned, and organized procedures are no longer fervently supported, the
fact that many procedures originally based on these norms continue to persist
is testimony to the lasting influence of institutional racism. For example, black
children continue to be crippled by inferior education, with schooling in the
large urban ghettoes being conducted mostly in dilapidated and overcrowded
buildings. As Kenneth Clark, Charles Silberman, and others have pointed out,
IQ and achievement scores typically drop as black youngsters "progress"

through school.[42] A study of ghetto schools in Harlem in the early 1960s revealed that a majority of black youngsters never finish high school.[43] Also, there continues to exist a very high degree of residential segregation of blacks and whites in urban areas. As Karl and Alma Taeuber have said, "Negroes are by far the most residentially segregated urban minority in recent American history. This is evident in the virtually complete exclusion of Negro residents from most new suburban developments of the past fifty years as well as in the block-by-block expansion of Negro residential areas in the central portions of many large cities."[44] It is true that the black suburban population has increased slightly during the past decade (by roughly 1.1 million persons); however, this population shift was heavily concentrated in black suburbs ("Negroes comprised only about 5 percent of the suburban population in 1970.").[45] What seems to be clear from an analysis of indexes of residential segregation around the nation is that economic factors play a relatively minor role in the physical separation of whites and blacks.

> Regardless of their economic status, Negroes rarely live in "white" residential areas, while whites, no matter how poor, rarely live in "Negro" residential areas. In recent decades, Negroes have been much more successful in securing improvements in economic status than in obtaining housing on a less segregated basis. Continued economic gains by Negroes are not likely to alter substantially the prevalent patterns of residential segregation.[46]

Although such forms of discrimination persist, a fundamental change has occurred in racist norms. Specifically, in the last several decades racist institutional norms that were based on belief in the biological inferiority of blacks are now more heavily dependent on the postulation of black cultural inferiority. For instance, arguments that black children cannot learn because of "deficiencies in cultural and social background" have not only been used as an alibi for educational neglect but have also been invoked by many white parents and school officials opposed to busing and other efforts to desegregate schools.[47] As Clark has noted, earlier explanations that attempted to account for black children's poor average performance in terms of inherent racial inferiority have recently been replaced by arguments focusing on general environmental disabilities.[48] Such explanations tend to stress the point that the deleterious environment of black children renders them incapable of successfully performing in the school system. The contemporary version of the environmentalist approach falls under the general category of "cultural deprivation." As an answer to the biological racist's theories of the early twentieth century, the cultural deprivation approach is viewed by many social scientists as a quite reasonable explanation of black retardation in the school system.[49] Although it would most certainly be unreasonable to assert that social scientists who rely on such theories are themselves cultural racists, it is true that their explanations have been used by others to support institutional discrimination. Clark was one of the first social scientists to question whether cultural deprivation theories were reinforcing institutional racism and discrimination:

> To what extent are the contemporary social deprivation theories merely substituting notions of environmental immutability and fatalism for earlier notions of biologically determined educational unmodifiability? To what extent do these theories obscure more basic reasons for the educational retardation of lower-status children? To what extent do they offer acceptable and desired alibis for the educational default: the fact that these children, by and large, do not learn because they are not being taught effectively and they are not being taught because those who are charged with the responsibility of teaching them do not believe that they can learn, do not expect that they can learn, and do not act toward them in ways which help them to learn.[50]

Arguments that blacks should be excluded from certain labor unions and apprentice programs, from white residential areas, from institutions of higher learning, and from social clubs and gatherings have also become more cultural racist than biological racist in nature. This is not to say that forms of institutional racism and discrimination have been impenetrable to the proliferation of black protests. Although many discriminatory practices continue to exist, others have undergone significant alteration to allow some modicum of black participation. It goes without saying that blacks have accumulated more competitive resources than they had at the turn of the century, thus facilitating greater participation in the institutional processes. But it is necessary to fully understand the nature of the improved competitive position of blacks vis-à-vis whites, because the changing structural relations between the two groups have not been evenly distributed. Specifically, although most segments of the black population find themselves in a more fluid competitive position with whites, others have either experienced no change in position or have actually fallen further behind in recent years. The net effect is that by 1970 there were very definite signs of a deepening economic schism in the black community.[51] A brief description of recent census data will serve to highlight this problem.

The fact that competitive relations between some blacks and whites are becoming more fluid is reflected in the data presented in Table 1. Whereas the number of whites employed in the white-collar, craftsmen, and operatives occupations—the higher-paying positions—increased by 24 per cent to (57.0 million) between 1960 and 1970, "Negro and other races"[52] recorded an increase of 72 per cent (from 2.9 million to 5.1 million). Equally as significant is the fact that the heavily disproportionate representation of blacks in the lower-paying positions (private-household and other service workers, laborers, and farm workers) has declined by 15 per cent (from 4 million to 3.4 million) since 1960, whereas the number of whites in these same occupations has increased by 3.2 per cent (from 12.8 million to 13.2 million).[53]

Table 1. Employment by Broad Occupational Groups:
1960, and 1966 to 1970 (numbers in millions, annual averages)

Year	Total		White-collar workers, craftsmen, and operatives		All other workers *	
	Black and other races	White	Black and other races	White	Black and other races	White
1960	6.9	58.9	2.9	46.1	4.0	12.8
1966	7.9	65.0	4.0	52.5	3.9	12.6
1967	8.0	66.4	4.3	53.6	3.7	12.7
1968	8.2	67.8	4.6	54.9	3.6	12.8
1969	8.4	69.5	4.9	56.4	3.5	13.1
1970	8.4	70.2	5.1	57.0	3.4	13.2
Change, 1960 to 1970 (percent)	+22	+19	+72	+24	−15	+3.2

*Includes private-household and other service workers, laborers and farm workers. Median usual weekly earnings were $50–$100 a week for these workers, compared with $100–$170 a week for white-collar workers, craftsmen, and operatives in March 1970.
Source: U.S. Department of Labor, Bureau of Labor Statistics.

Black penetration into institutions of higher learning has also been impressive. Table 2 includes data on black college enrollment between 1964 and 1970. It is significant to note that the total black college enrollment has increased by 127 per cent (from 234,000 in 1964 to 522,000 in 1970), with 133 of this growth occurring in institutions other than predominantly black colleges.[54] The fact that the percentage of black college students enrolled in institutions other than predominantly black colleges has increased from 48.7 per cent in 1964 to 72.4 per cent in 1970 is indicative of the efforts of white institutions to overcome many of the traditional barriers imposed by institutional racism.[55] Finally, the overall ratio of black to white family income has risen from about 53 per cent in 1961–1963 to roughly 64 per cent in 1970.[56]

Table 2. Black Students Enrolled in Colleges by Type of Institution: 1964 to 1968, and 1970 (numbers in thousands)

Subject	1964	1965	1966	1967	1968	1970
Enrollment in predominantly black colleges*	120	125	134	144	156	144
Percent of total	51.3	45.6	47.5	38.9	35.9	27.6
Enrollment in colleges (not predominantly black)*	114	149	148	226	278	378
Percent of total	48.7	54.4	52.5	61.1	64.1	72.4
Total, black college enrollment	234	274	282	370	434	522

* Data on colleges are for four- and two-year institutions and professional schools, both private and public (including community colleges). Statistics for 1966 to 1970 include enrollment figures for nondegree-credit students. Prior to 1966, only degree-credit students are included. Source: U.S. Department of Commerce, Bureau of the Census, and U.S. Department of Health, Education and Welfare.

Nevertheless, as already indicated, not all segments of the black population have experienced a relative increase in competitive resources vis-à-vis whites. Despite the fact that "Negro and other races" have moved out of such low-paying occupations as private-household workers, laborers, and farm workers more rapidly than whites during the last decade, in 1970 they still held one fifth (about 1.5 million) of the service occupations other than those in private households (jobs that require little skill), about the same proportion as in 1960. Moreover, in the semiskilled operative jobs (primarily in factories) the number of "Negro and other races" expanded by 42 per cent (to slightly over 2 million) compared with an increase of only 13 per cent (to 11.9 million) for whites. By 1970, these two categories of low-skill jobs comprised 42 per cent of the total employment of "Negro and other races," whereas in 1960 their share was only 38 per cent.[57] Furthermore, although the unemployment rate for "Negro and other races" declined from a high of 12.4 in 1961 (during the recession period) to a low of 6.5 in 1969 (but then increased to 8.2 in 1970 and 8.6 in 1971), throughout the 1960s their unemployment rates were about double those for whites, including a disproportionate representation in the long-term unemployment category.[58]

Moreover, blacks have not escaped the category of poverty as rapidly as whites.[59] Whereas "Negro and other races" constituted 29 per cent of all officially poor family members in 1959, by 1969 their percentage had increased to 35 per cent. Even more important, "Negro and other races" accounted for 41 per cent of all the children (under 18 years) in poor families in 1964, whereas in 1959 they accounted for 34 per cent. In poor families headed by women, the number of "Negro and other races" children increased by 756,000 from 1959 to 1969. "Children of Negro and other races accounted for 52 per cent of all children in these families."[60] In 1959, they constituted 42 per cent of the total number of children in households below the poverty level headed by females.

It is clear therefore that although most blacks have improved their socio-economic position relative to whites, a significant minority have experienced no gain or have fallen behind. In fact, as Andrew Brimmer has observed, by the late 1960s the income distribution among black families was considerably more unequal than the distribution among white families (the lowest two fifths among families of "Negro and other races" contributed only 15.3 per cent of the total black income in 1969, whereas the lowest two fifths of white families contributed 18.7 per cent of the total white income; conversely, the upper two fifths among white families contributed 63.7 per cent, whereas the upper two fifths among families of "Negro and other races" contributed 68.2 per cent). And, unlike for whites, the income schism in the black community does not seem to be narrowing.[61]

·   ·   ·

From Protests to Politics

·   ·   ·

Although black protest as a pressure resource had all but subsided in early 1970, there developed increasing reliance on black political activity. However, unlike the civil rights politics of the 1960s, in the early 1970s black politics had begun to integrate various facets of nationalistic philosophy. Drawing on the widespread cultural nationalism in the black community, the new breed of black politicians has increasingly relied on symbols of black pride and black solidarity in their public utterances.[62] It may not be coincidental that black pride and identity are flourishing at the same time that we are witnessing an unprecedented degree of cooperation between black middle-class politicians and ghetto blacks.[63] In addition, as an outgrowth of the Black Power Movement there exists a growing thrust to increase black control of the social, economic, and political institutions in black communities. If the conditions associated with the ebb and flow of black nationalist development in the past are any indication,[64] its continued growth may very well depend on the extent to which black competitive resources expand over the next several years.

.   .   .

Furthermore, as I have indicated, racial intolerance tends to be greater in periods of economic decline, particularly for whites unable to advance themselves and forced by economic strains to compete more heavily with minority groups. Accordingly, not only is it possible that the gains experienced by middle- and upper-income blacks could decline, but it is also possible that the deteriorating circumstances of many lower-class blacks could worsen, further widening the economic schism.

In the short run, if declining expectations and fears of racial oppression are combined with major economic setbacks, black nationalist themes of racial solidarity will intensify. In the long run, there is every reason to believe that violent confrontations between blacks and whites will flare up again and again. We have seen throughout this volume that race relations are extremely variable, shifting back and forth from periods of accommodation (or peace in feud) to periods of overt conflict. Until factors that produce racial conflict are eliminated (such as differential power, racism, strong sense of group position, and intergroup competition for scarce resources), this pattern will continue to persist.

NOTES

[In selecting portions of this chapter to include in this anthology, some notes became superfluous and thus were not included. The numbering here reflects the order of notes on the text that remains, not the original. Hence, the note numbers here do not match those in the original source.]

1. [Leonard] Broom and [Noval D.] Glenn, op. cit., ["The Occupations and Income of Black Americans," in *Blacks in the United States,* ed. by Norval D. Glenn and Charles M. Bonjean (San Francisco: Chandler, 1969),] p. 24.

2. Ibid. "For instance, of white males 25 through 34 years old in 1950 who were employed as clerical and kindred workers, 61,000—or 9 percent—had moved out of these occupations or died by 1960 and had not been replaced by other white males of the same cohort . . . some of these white males were replaced by younger whites, but many were replaced by Negroes." Ibid.

3. Ibid.

4. Peter M. Bergman, *The Chronological History of the Negro in America* (New York: Harper, 1969), pp. 535–554.

5. See Clarence E. Glick, "Collective Behavior in Race Relations," *American Sociological Review,* 13:287–293 (June 1947).

6. James H. Laue, "The Changing Character of Negro Protest," *Annals of the American Academy of Political and Social Science,* 357:120 (Jan. 1965).

7. Lewis M. Killian, *The Impossible Revolution?: Black Power and the American Dream* (New York: Random House, 1968), p. 70.

8. See, for example, Louis Lomax, *The Negro Revolt* (New York: Signet, 1962).

9. [August] Meier and [Elliot] Rudwick, op. cit., [*From Plantation to Ghetto: The Interpretive History of American Negroes,* rev. ed. (New York: Hill and Wang, 1970),] p. 227.

10. [James C.] Davies, op. cit., ["The J-Curve of Rising and Declining Satisfactions as a Cause of Some Great Revolutions and a Contained Rebellion," in *Violence in America: Historical and Comparative Perspectives,* ed. Hugh Davis Graham and Ted Robert Gurr (New York: Bantam Books, 1969),] p. 721.

11. These points will be discussed in the following section.

12. Davies, op. cit., p. 723.

13. Keesing's Research Report, *Race Relations in the USA, 1954–68* (New York: Scribner's, 1970), pp. 152–153.

14. Ibid., pp. 154–155.

15. A number of writers have not made full use of Davies' "J-curve" theory because they have restricted the notion of "gratification" to material gains or physical gratification and have ignored the factor of "emotional gratification." See, for example, James A. Geschwender, "Social Structure and the Negro Revolt: An Examination of Some Hypotheses," *Social Forces,* 43:248–256 (Dec. 1964), and Thomas F. Pettigrew, *Racially Separate or Together?* (New York: McGraw-Hill, 1971), chap. 7.

16. Keesing's Research Report, op. cit., pp. 164–165.

17. Ibid., p. 164.

18. For a discussion of this latter point, see L. H. Massotti and D. R. Bowden, eds., *Riots and Rebellion: Racial Violence in the Urban Community* (Beverly Hills, Calif.: Sage, 1968), and Pettigrew, op. cit., chap. 7.

19. As M. Elaine Burgess observed in 1965, "Neither the lower class nor the upper class could have mounted the resistance movement we are now witnessing throughout the South. The former does not possess the resources, either internal or external, essential for such a movement, and the latter is much too small and, very frequently, too far removed from the masses to do so. Such activity had to wait the development of an ample middle class that was motivated to push for validation of hard-won position, thus far denied by the white power structure. The question of unequal distribution of status and power between Negroes and whites would consequently appear as a special case of the more basic problems of order and change. By no means are we saying that all challenges to established social structures or power distributions are class oriented, or directly concerned with relative social position. Nevertheless, it is true that one of the major sources of tension and therefore of change and potential change in the South, as in the broader society, stems from the new middle-class Negro's disbelief in past rationales for inequality and the desire for substitution of new rationales." M. Elaine Burgess, "Race Relations and Social Change," in *The South in Continuity and Change,* ed. by John C. McKinney and Edgar T. Thompson (Durham, N.C.: Duke U.P., 1965), p. 352.

20. As Martin Luther King, Jr., once observed, "What good is it to be allowed to eat in a restaurant if you can't afford a hamburger?"

21. See, for example, William Brink and Louis Harris, *Black and White: A Study of U.S. Racial Attitudes Today* (New York: Simon & Schuster, 1966), p. 42; H. Cantrell, *The Pattern of Human Concerns* (New Brunswick, N.J.: Rutgers U.P., 1965), p. 43; and Pettigrew, op. cit., chap. 7.

22. See *Report of the National Advisory Commission on Civil Disorders* (New York: Bantam, 1968), and Nathan S. Caplan and Jeffrey Paige, "A Study of Ghetto Rioters," *Scientific American,* 219:15–21 (Aug. 1968).

23. Charles Silberman, *Crisis in the Classroom* (New York: Random House, 1970), pp. 19–20.

24. John H. Bracey, August Meier, and Elliot Rudwick, eds., *Black Nationalism in America* (Indianapolis: Bobbs-Merrill, 1970), p. xxvi. It is true, as John Bracey has argued, that black nationalist philosophy has always existed among some segments of the black population (see "John Bracey Sketches His Interpretation of Black Nationalism," Ibid., pp. lvi–lix), but what available research there is clearly establishes the fact that support for this philosophy increases and declines during certain periods in history.

25. Killian, op. cit., pp. 105–106.

26. Harold Cruse, *Rebellion or Revolution* (New York: Apollo, 1968), chap. 13, and *The Crisis of the Negro Intellectual* (New York: Morrow, 1967), pp. 554–565.

27. According to Bracey et al., "The proliferation of nationalist ideologies and organizations that reached a climax during the 1920's was followed by a thirty year period in which nationalism as a significant theme in black thought was virtually nonexistent. From the thirties until the sixties, with few exceptions, leading Negro organizations stressed interracial cooperation, civil rights, and racial integration. Among

the chief reasons for the temporary demise of nationalism were the effects of the Depression and the consequent necessity of relying on the New Deal for survival, and the influx of trade Unionists and Communists into the black community preaching and practicing racial equality and brotherhood. The principal ideological concerns of articulate blacks during the Depression decade focused on very practical aspects of the Negro's relationship to New Deal agencies and the Roosevelt Administration, on the role of industrial unions in the advancement of the race, and on the relevance of Marxist doctrines of the Negro's problem." Bracey et al., op. cit., p. xiv.

28. Founded in the early 1930s, the Nation of Islam became a viable institution around 1950. It achieved its greater popularity after the late Malcolm X became a convert to the Muslim sect and one of its most influential ministers until he resigned in 1964.

29. Cruse, *Rebellion or Revolution,* op. cit., p. 211.

30. Bracey et al., op. cit., p. xxviii. Also see *The Autobiography of Malcolm X* (New York: Grove, 1964).

31. For example, the Opinion Research Corporation survey in 1968 revealed that 86 per cent of the blacks in their sample felt that black people should be taught subjects in school that added to their feeling of pride in being black. In their study of black attitudes in fifteen American cities, Angus Campbell and Howard Schuman have found that "There is a strong trend in the data that is related to, but different from and much stronger than 'separation.' It concerns the positive cultural identity and achievements of Negroes, rather than their political separation from whites. The finding appears most strikingly in the endorsement by 42 percent of the Negro sample of the statement 'Negro school children should study an African Language.' Two out of five Negroes thus subscribe to an emphasis on 'black consciousness' that was almost unthought of a few years ago." Angus Campbell and Howard Schuman, "Racial Attitudes in Fifteen American Cities," in *The National Advisory Commission on Civil Disorders, Supplemental Studies* (Washington, D.C.: G. P. O., 1968), p. 6.

Despite the strong sentiment for cultural nationalism in the black community, institutional nationalism—i.e., the efforts of black citizens to gain control of the political, economic, and social institutions in their community and/or to establish separate institutions free of control by the dominant white society—although increasing in popularity, still receive support from only a minority of blacks. See, for example, Brink and Harris, op. cit.; *Report of the National Advisory Commission on Civil Disorders,* op. cit.; Campbell and Schuman, op. cit.; Caplan and Paige, op. cit.; and Gary T. Marx, *Protest and Prejudice: A Study of Belief in the Black Community,* rev. ed. (New York: Harper, 1970).

32. Robert Blauner, "Black Culture: Myth or Reality?" in *Americans from Africa: Old Memories, New Moods,* ed. by Peter I. Rose (New York: Atherton, 1970), pp. 417–418.

33. Following Milton M. Gordon, "structural assimilation" is defined as "large scale entrance into cliques, clubs, and institutions of host society on primary group level." Milton M. Gordon, *Assimilation in American Life* (New York: Oxford U. P., 1964), p. 71.

34. As Rober A. Bone has noted, "Even at the peak of Renaissance nationalism the middle-class writers could never muster more than token enthusiasm for a distinctive Negro culture." Robert A. Bone, "The Negro Novel in America" in *Americas' Black Past,* ed. by Eric Foner (New York: Harper, 1970), p. 385

35. Arnold M. Rose, "Race and Ethnic Relations," in *Contemporary Social Problems,* ed. by Robert K. Merton and Robert A. Nisbet (New York: Harcourt, 1966), p. 452.

36. Arthur R. Jensen, "How Much Can We Boost IQ and Scholastic Achievement?" *Harvard Educational Review,* 39:1–123 (Winter 1969).

37. For three of the many excellent critiques of Jensen's thesis, see Martin Deutsch, "Happenings on the Way Back to the Forum: Social Science, IQ, and Race Differences Revisited," *Harvard Educational Review,* 39: 523–557 (Summer 1969); Arthur L. Stincombe, "Environment; The Cumulation of Effects Is Yet to Be Understood," *Harvard Educational Review,* 39: 511–522 (Summer 1969); and Richard A. Goldsby, *Race and Races* (New York: Macmillan, 1971), chap. 7. For a less direct but, nonetheless, important critique of the importance given to genetic factors in accounting for black IQ scores, see Sandra Scarr-Salapatek, "Race, Social Class and IQ," *Science,* 174:1285–1295 (Dec. 24, 1971). It is of course possible that arguments raised by Jensen (and other scientists such as William Schockley and Richard Herrnstein who draw a connection between race and innate intelligence) could become widely accepted in the long run; especially if, as indicated later, demagogic racism becomes widespread.

38. See, for example, Opinion Research Corporation, *White and Negro Attitudes Towards Race Related Issues and Activities* (Research Park, Princeton, N.J., 1968), and Richard T. Morris and Vincent Jeffries, *The White Reaction Study* (University of California, Los Angeles: Institute of Government and Public Affiars, 1967).

39. Andrew M. Greeley and Paul B. Sheatsely, "Attitudes Toward Racial Integration," *Scientific American,* 225:13–19 (Dec. 1971). Also see Frank R. Westie, "Race and Ethnic Relations," in *Handbook of Modern Sociology,* ed. by Robert E. L. Faris (Chicago: Rand McNally, 1963), pp. 576–618.

Some readers may question the extent to which public opinion polls reflect true feelings. However, the important point to remember is that there has in fact been a change in the degree to which people are openly willing to express intolerant views toward blacks.

40. Norval D. Glenn, "White Gains from Negro Subordination," in *Blacks in the United States,* ed. by Norval D. Glenn and Charles M. Bonjean (San Francisco: Chandler, 1969), p. 291.

41. Jan E. Dizard, "Response to Aggression and the American Experience," paper read at the Annual Meeting of the American Sociological Association, Denver, Colo. (Sept. 1971), pp. 9–10.

42. Kenneth B. Clark, *Dark Ghetto: Dilemmas of Power* (New York: Harper, 1965), chap. 6, and Charles Silberman, *Crisis in Black and White* (New York: Random House, 1964), chap. 9. Also see James S. Coleman, *Equality of Educational Opportunity* (Washington, D.C.: G. P. O., 1966).

43. Clark, op. cit., p. 124. In 1970, 44 per cent of black males aged 19 were high school dropouts. See U.S. Bureau of the Census, "The Social and Economic Status of Negroes," *Current Population Reports,* ser. P-23, No. 38 (Washington D.C.: G. P. O., 1970), p. 77.

44. Karl E. and Alma T. Taeuber, *Negroes in the Cities* (Chicago: Aldine, 1965), p. 2.

45. U.S. Bureau of the Census, "Social and Economic Characteristics of the Population in Metropolitan and Nonmentropolitan Areas: 1970 and 1960," *Current Population Reports,* ser. P-23, No. 37 (Washington, D.C.: G. P. O., 1971). Also see Reynolds Farley, "The Changing Distribution of Negroes Within Metropolitan Areas: The Emergence of Black Suburbs," *American Journal of Sociology,* 75: 512–529 (Jan. 1970), and Karl E. and Alma F. Taeuber, "The Negro Population in the United States," in *The American Negro Reference Book,* ed. by John P. Davis (Englewood Cliffs, N.J.: Prentice-Hall, 1966), pp. 96–160.

What seems apparent is that the nation's central cities are becoming increasingly black. The white urban population actually decreased by 2.6 million and the black population increased by 3.1 million during the past decade. In a study by David Birch, evidence is advanced that the rate of the black population's increase in the central cities had actually begun to decline from 400,000 a year in the early 1960s to 262,000 a year in the late 1960s, whereas the black suburban population's yearly increase of 52,000 in the early 1960s had risen to 85,000 by the end of the decade. Birch uses these data to suggest that the pattern of increasing racial imbalance in the central cities may be ultimately reversed (David L. Birch, *The Economic Future of City and Suburbs* [Committee for Economic Development, New York, 1970]). However, it should be noted that Birch does not address the problem of residential segregation in suburbs. Furthermore, definitive statements concerning the future racial makeup of the nation's central cities will have to await analyses of data gathered from subsequent censuses.

46. Taeuber and Taeuber, *Negroes in the Cities,* op. cit., pp. 2–3. Nor can the argument be advanced that blacks prefer to live in all-black neighborhoods. Recent studies reveal that blacks, despite their widespread acceptance of cultural nationalism, overwhelmingly prefer to live in racially integrated communities. See, for example, Campbell and Schumann, op. cit.

47. This is not to say that all opponents of school desegregation rely on cultural racist arguments but rather to indicate that belief in the cultural inferiority of blacks is one of the major arguments used against school desegregation.

48. Clark, op. cit., chap 6.

49. Even so perceptive a social analyst as Charles Silberman accepted this approach uncritically when he published his insightful book *Crisis in Black and White,* op. cit., see chap. 9, only to later repudiate the position in his latest book *Crisis in the Classroom,* op. cit., p. 81.

50. Clark, op. cit., p. 131.

51. Andrew Brimmer, "Economic Progress of Negroes in the United States: The Deepening Schism," paper read at the Founders' Day Convocation, Tuskegee Institute,

Tuskegee, Ala. (Mar. 22, 1970), and "The Black Revolution and the Economic Future of Negroes in the United States," *The American Scholar,* 629–643 (Autumn 1969).

52. "Negro and other races" is a United States Census Bureau designation, and is used in those cases where data are not available solely for blacks. However, because about 90 per cent of the population "Negro and other races," is black, statistics reported for this category generally reflect the condition of the black population.

53. It is interesting to note racial changes in the technical and professional positions and in the managers, officials, and proprietors occupations. Whereas the number of whites in technical and professional positions increased by 45 per cent (to 10,374,000) from 1960 to 1970, "Negro and other races," on the other hand, netted an increase of 131 per cent (to 766,000). Whereas the number of white managers, officials, and proprietors (the second highest paying category) increased by only 16 per cent (to 7,991,000), "Negro and other races" expanded by 67 per cent (to 296,000). See U.S. Bureau of the Census, "The Social and Economic Status of Negroes in the United States, 1970," *Current Population Reports,* ser. P-23, No. 39 (Washington, D.C.: G. P. O., 1971).

54. In order to contrast black gains in higher education with white gains, I have analyzed the census data on the college enrollment of persons 18 to 24 years of age between 1965 and 1970. This analysis shows that blacks have increased their percentage of the total college enrollment in this category from 4.7 per cent in 1965 to 7.3 per cent in 1970.

55. See William J. Wilson, "The Quest for a Meaningful Black Experience on White Campuses," *The Massachusetts Review,* 10: 737–746 (Autumn 1969).

56. U.S. Bureau of the Census, "The Social and Economic Status of Negroes in the United States, 1970," *Current Population Reports,* ser. P-23, No. 38 (Washington, D.C.: G. P. O., 1971), p. 1. However, as Brimmer has pointed out, such data failed to take into account the fact that black families tend to be substantially larger than white families. An analysis of 1967 family income adjusted to a per capita basis reveals that "the median income data unadjusted for differences in family size may have overstated the relative economic status of nonwhite families by something on the order of 11 per cent" (Brimmer, "Economic Progress of Negroes in the United States," op. cit., p. 11). Accordingly, the gap between white and black per capita income, although slowly closing, is probably still very wide indeed. In this connection, it was also reported by the Bureau of the Census that young black and white husband-wife families (35 years and younger) in the North had reached parity in income by 1970. Nevertheless, when the analysis included work experience of the wife it was found that "young Negro families in which only the husband worked were making only about three-fourths as much as many or comparable white families in both 1959 and 1970" (U.S. Bureau of the Census, "Differences Between Incomes of White and Negro Families by Work Experience and Region," *Current Population Reports,* ser. P.-23, No. 39 [Washington, D.C.: G. P. O., 1971], p. 1).

57. U.S. Bureau of the Census, "The Social and Economic Status of Negroes in the United States, 1970," op. cit., p. 59. For a similar analysis of 1960 to 1969 data, see Brimmer, "Economic Progress of Negroes in the United States," op. cit.

58. In 1970, 1.3 per cent of the "Negro and other races" labor force and 0.7 per cent of the white labor force had been unemployed for 15 weeks or more. See U.S. Bureau of the Census, "The Social and Economic Status of Negroes in the United States, 1970," op. cit., p. 56.

59. "The Poverty concept developed by the Social Security Administration classifies a family as poor if its income is not roughly three times as great as the cost of an economy food plan for a family of that particular size and farm or nonfarm residence." Brimmer, "Economic Progress of Negroes in the United States," op. cit., p. 14

60. U.S. Bureau of the Census, "24 Million Americans—Poverty in the United States: 1969," *Current Population Reports,* ser. P-60, No. 76 (Washington, D.C.: G.P.O., 1970), p. 4.

61. Brimmer states that "in the last few years, the distribution of income within the nonwhite community has apparently run counter to the trend among white families. In both the 1961–65 period and the 1965–68 period, the income distribution for white families became more equal. For nonwhite families, the same trend toward greater equality was evident in the first half of the decade. However, it remained roughly constant in the 1965–68 years." Brimmer, "Economic Progress of Negroes in the United States," op. cit., p. 13.

62. This was most clearly revealed at the National Black Political Convention held at Gary, Indiana, in the spring of 1972, where several nationally recognized black politicians were openly endorsing black nationalist themes.

63. Martin Kilson, "Black Politicians: A New Power," *Dissent,* 333–345 (Aug. 1971). The new breed of black politicians such as Richard Hatcher of Gary, Thomas Atkins of Boston, Shirley Chisholm of New York, Kenneth Gibson of Newark, and Julian Bond of Atlanta are rather intimately associated with problems and needs of the black urban community. By 1971, there were "1,500 elected Negro politicians or officials, 62 per cent of them outside the South, representing overwhelmingly city constituencies. They are located in 41 of the 50 states and include, among others, 12 congressmen, 168 state legislators, 48 mayors, 575 other city officials, 362 school board members, and 144 judges and magistrates." Ibid., p. 340.

64. Bracey et al., op. cit.